MOTIVATION

Fourth Edition

MOTIVATION
Theories and Principles

ROBERT C. BECK
Wake Forest University

Prentice Hall, Upper Saddle River, New Jersey 07458

Library of Congress Cataloging-in-Publication Data

Beck, Robert C. (Robert Clarence)
    Motivation : theories and principles / by Robert C. Beck.—4th
ed.
      p.   cm.
    Includes bibliographical references and index.
    ISBN 0-13-011292-5
    1. Motivation (Psychology)   I. Title.
BF503.B38   2000
153.8—dc21   99–12289
                                                       CIP

Editor-in-chief: Nancy Roberts
Acquisitions editor: Jennifer Gilliland
Assistant editor: Anita Castro
Senior managing editor: Bonnie Biller
Production liaison: Fran Russello
Editorial/production supervision: Bruce Hobart (Pine Tree Composition)
Cover director: Jane Conte
Cover photo: Rob Colvin/Stock Illustration Source
Prepress and manufacturing buyer: Tricia Kenny

This book was set in 10/12 Baskerville by Pine Tree
Composition, Inc., and was printed and bound by Courier
Companies, Inc. The cover was printed by Phoenix Color Corp.

Printed in the United States of America
10   9   8   7   6   5   4   3   2

ISBN 0-13-011292-5

Prentice-Hall International (UK) Limited, *London*
Prentice-Hall of Australia Pty. Limited, *Sydney*
Prentice-Hall Canada Inc., *Toronto*
Prentice-Hall Hispanoamericana, S.A., *Mexico*
Prentice-Hall of India Private Limited, *New Delhi*
Prentice-Hall of Japan, Inc., *Tokyo*
Pearson Education Asia Pte. Ltd., *Singapore*
Editora Prentice-Hall do Brasil, Ltda., *Rio de Janeiro*

*This edition is dedicated to Spencer Cash Beck,
Emma Caton Beck, Rebecca Lillian Rominger,
Jessica Lauren Beck, and one player yet to be named.*

Contents

PART II   THE REGULATION OF INTERNAL STATES

Preface

This fourth edition of *Motivation: Theories and Principles* expresses the same orientation toward motivation as that found in earlier editions. It is an experimentally-oriented survey of research and theory on animal and human motivation. In the first edition I noted that it is difficult to maintain a completely logical and consistent conceptualization of motivation without sacrificing a large amount of material which many people consider important to the topic. This is still true. Motivation theorists and researchers are still fragmented in their efforts to understand motivation. Much of the reason for this, it still seems to me, is that *evolution* has not been a logical and consistent process. Consequently, theoretical principles developed in the context of one species or motivational problem, say eating behavior in omnivores (like humans and rats) may not be applicable to a different set of motivational problems, or to the same problems in different species (such as eating in herbivores or carnivores). The end result is a great diversity of approaches to motivation, none of which may be *the* correct approach but all of which may have some usefulness. For such reasons as this, the first chapter is still devoted to discussion of the nature of scientific *theory*, just so the student can gain insight as to why a theory can be good and useful without being universally true.

Motivation, 4e reflects the above diversity, as it must, while still trying to provide an unbrella approach which sets motivation off as a distinct area of psychology. Conceptually, motivation is much more than a series of questions about why organisms behave as they do. It is a distinctly definable and useful concept for understanding behavior. Although this point seems to have been lost (or at least misplaced) in the enthusiasm surrounding the "cognitive revolution," it seems to be regaining a foothold there. Cognition might be "cold" and emotionless but the reasons for engaging in cognitive processing are often highly charged. This is demonstrated even among the exchanges of those advocating different theoretical views of motivation. These advocacies are indicative of the goals, as well as passions, of the people who put their views forth. It may be too easy to overlook the motives of those who mount seemingly rational arguments. And, of course, the cognitive revolution is a human enterprise; just how it would apply to animal food preferences without parallel discussions of the "value" of different foods is not at all clear.

Given the same ambitions as the previous editions, there are similarities with the previous editions as well as differences. One of these similarities is to try to give some historical perspective to topics. Some older concepts and theories may not be as important as they once seemed (such as drive theory) but such concepts have a way of reappearing under new names. The strengths and weaknesses of the earlier concepts may apply to the new concepts and it seems to me there is much to be gained by at least familiarizing students with the older concepts.

There are also many changes in the structure and content of this edition to reflect in the ten years since the previous edition appeared. Chapter 2 (Emotion) has been extensively revised to take into account the burgeoning research of the last decade. More than ever, an understanding of emotion helps us understand motivation. It seems not unlikely that the two areas will eventually become one. Research on the role of pleasure, and of the underlying dopamine and endorphin systems, in mammalian activities ranging from feeding behavior to psychological disorders is burgeoning. Positive affect has come into its own as an equal "partner" with the negative affects that has so long concerned psychologists. Hedonism is no longer "just psychological" or "subjective." There are clear physiological mechanisms underlying pleasure and distress and these are being exploited by many researchers at both human and animal levels. One point of consensus in the area of feeding research, for example, is that eating is under the control of many factors, not the least of which are learning and pleasure. Interest in homeostatic mechanisms has not disappeared, but the importance of homeostatic mechanisms in day to day survival is no longer considered all-important. The pleasure from eating some foods may play a long-term role in homeostasis, but is not in itself necessarily an immediate response to homeostatic upset. Pleasure and aversion are once more major concepts to account for the choices organisms make among the activities available to them.

I would like to thank a number of people for their assistance. Will Fleeson, Batja Mesquita, and Terry Blumenthal critically read chapters one, two, and four, respectively, and made many helpful comments. Sandra L. Schneider of the University of South Florida reviewed this edition. I would again like to recognize my intellectual debt to four great teachers and psychologists who are no longer with us: J. McV. Hunt, O. H. Mower, Lawrence I. O'Kelly, and Paul Thomas Young. They hardly ever seemed to agree on much theoretically, but all were inspirations and the diversity they provided was a stern warning not to take any idea as "the" truth. Ideas are living things; they are born, evolve, sometimes die, and sometimes are resurrected. It is good to know when an old idea is reborn.

Robert C. Beck

CHAPTER ONE

The Nature of Motivation Theory

——•——

INTRODUCTION

What Is Motivational Psychology About?

On August 1, 1966, Charles Whitman, twenty-five years of age, climbed to the observation deck of the Tower Building at the University of Texas. In two hours he killed fourteen people and wounded twenty-four others before he himself was slain by the police. The question raised for all psychology, and especially for motivation theory, is why? By any common meaning of the term, Whitman was not rational, even though his actions seemed carefully planned. There were numerous interesting little twists in the accounts that followed. Many people thought him a fine young man. He liked children, worked hard, and had been an Eagle Scout at the age of twelve. He had a good sense of humor, and most of his friends and acquaintances seemed to regard him highly. And the night before, he had also killed his mother and father.

There are many possible explanations for Whitman's spree. He had a need for achievement, particularly to surpass his father, but was frustrated by not doing as well in school as he had hoped. He was continually stressed by overwork; he carried heavy academic loads and part-time jobs. His family had an abiding interest in guns, which reporters saw in every room of his parents' house after the incident. And there was possibly a specific biological disorder: He was reported (upon autopsy) to have a brain tumor in an area known to be related to aggressive behaviors. Any of these factors, as well as others not considered here, might have led to the final tragic outcome. We cannot really know the answer to this particular drama, because the central character is gone. This much we do know: The answer is not simple. But it is the kind of mystery that psychologists are supposed to help unravel.

We also see in this example the possibility that there are many motives. Sometimes a *single* motivational concept seems to provide adequate explanation, such as "I eat when I am 'hungry' but do not eat otherwise." But to explain a situation as complex as Charles Whitman's, we might find ourselves discussing drives, goals, incentives, frustration, conflict, aggression, and needs for achievement or power. We might also wish to consider brain damage or drug use as possible factors.

Motivation is one of the explanations we use when we try to account for the variability of behavior. Motivational concepts are supposed to help explain the fact that under virtually identical external circumstances, there are great variations in individual behavior. For example, why do some kids do well in school when equally talented ones fail? This dilemma suggests that there may be differences in motivation for achievement. Why do some children steal, when others of equal social status or income are scrupulously honest? Why do some people take drugs, when others under similar living circumstances ignore them? How can we get people to work harder? Why do we have wars and killings? Why do people create? Why would anybody repeatedly eat until they vomit or starve themselves when food is easily available? The individual variations in these activities suggest the need for motivational explanations and the possibility of producing change for the better.

A Preliminary Definition of Motivation

Let us start with a very general definition of what we mean by motivation. Motivation is a **theoretical concept** that accounts for why people (or animals) choose to engage in particular behaviors at particular times. Why do we eat rather than drink, play rather than work, read rather than exercise? We do not assume that organisms are inert unless prodded into action by some motive. The nervous system is continually active, sometimes violently, even as we sleep. The motivational problem is how to account for fluctuations in the choices made among the possible things an organism might do. Hunger helps explain why I eat sometimes, but not at others. We shall phrase this slightly differently, however, and say that I eat when I have the **desire** for food. Or, I don't eat some foods because I find them unpleasant or **aversive** (e.g., broccoli).

Our basic motivational premise is that organisms **approach** goals, or engage in activities that are expected to have **desirable outcomes,** and **avoid** activities that are expected to have unpleasant or **aversive outcomes.** This premise is psychological hedonism. We must use this premise with caution, however. First and foremost, we must define desire and aversion objectively. We cannot rely on individual impressions of what is or what ought to be desirable or aversive. A common criticism of hedonistic approaches is the claim that what is considered pleasant or unpleasant depends on subjective experience, and that subjective experiences cannot constitute objective scientific data. Therefore, it is argued, desire and aversion are not useful scientific concepts. This argument is quite simply not correct. Later we shall see in detail how desire and aversion can be defined objectively and related to behavior.

SCIENTIFIC THEORY

Why We Must Have Theory

The daily lives of most of us are not fraught with murder and mayhem, but we do have motivational questions about things that are important to us. You might ask, "How could I have done better on my last exam?" Or, "Why does Suzy have so many friends when Mary has so few?" "How can I get the job I want?" "How can I reduce the stress in my life?" In order to answer the many such specific questions that people might ask, we must have some general psychological principles to apply to specific situations. To apply a psychological (or any other) principle means to use a general principle to explain a specific situation. This, of course, requires that we know what the relevant general principles are and that we have a theory. Discovering general principles and weaving them into theory is what psychological research is all about. When theory has been sufficiently developed, we can apply it to such specific problems as aiding clients with weight disorders, helping a manufacturer sell his or her product, helping an athlete perform better, or helping an unhappy marriage. Our purpose in this section is to see what a theory actually is and how to distinguish a good theory from a bad theory. Applying a bad theory is worse than applying no theory at all.

Nature of Scientific Theory

A scientific theory is like a map. We commonly refer to theories as being like models. We use the word *model* in a broad sense, referring to an actual physical model, to a set of blueprints, to a set of mathematical equations, or to a map (Toulmin, 1953). Let us think of a theory as a map of some part of the world of interest to us. A theory is a *representation* of real things and places in the world, and it relates those things to each other by a set of rules. It organizes some part of the world and guides us.

A map has objectively definable names for places (e.g., North America is such and such; Mount Rushmore is such and such; Kernersville is such and such). Figure 1–1 shows a map with different places linked together so that we can relate them to each other (e.g., Kernersville is seventeen miles east of Winston-Salem on I-40). If we follow the map and actually get to where the map says we should be (e.g., Kernersville), then we have evidence that the map is good. If we follow the map and arrive in Statesville rather than Kernersville, we know that the map has some serious flaws. It is thus pretty easy to tell when we have a good or a bad map.

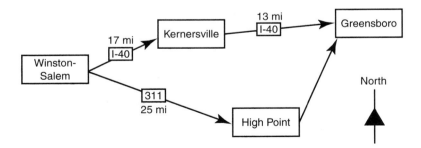

FIGURE 1–1.   A theory of how to get from Winston-Salem to Greensboro in North Carolina. This rough mapping of distances and directions from Winston-Salem to Kernersville and on to Greensboro should be accurate enough to get us there in a predicted amount of time, if we know what the names refer to and have established the distances accurately. If the map is to scale, we should even be able to estimate traveling time by the alternate High Point route. Note that the map leaves out a lot. Are the omitted things important?

Even a very accurate map is an incomplete representation of the world, but useful for some purposes. A map of the United States will not tell us how to get to the Psychology Building on our campus, and a highway map doesn't help a lot if we want to go someplace by boat. There may be many different maps of the same area, corresponding to different aspects of the environment. There are road maps, geodetic maps, temperature maps, ocean-floor maps, and so on. None of these maps is completely right, none may be completely wrong. They are merely different because they organize different things in different ways and have different uses. Similarly, there many be many theories of motivation (or, of learning or perception), none of which explain everything but each of which is useful for explaining some things. For example, theories of feeding, achievement motivation, and fear all have to do with motivation but deal with different domains of behavior. We develop and use the theories that are appropriate to the situation at hand.

Making measurements.   The classic method of mapping is to send out an explorer, compass in hand, who measures distances and directions, recording what she or he finds. Different ways of measuring the "same thing" may give different results, however. Suppose that there are two rivers separated by a mountain and that we ask what the distance is between the rivers? Is the distance the walking distance going straight up and down over the mountain? Is it the distance walking around the mountain? Is it the distance as the crow flies in a straight line? (And if this, how was this distance measured before we had aircraft and could not actually travel in a straight line? Think about it.) If we are measuring people's attitudes, do we record what they say about things if asked directly? Do we use attitude scales? Do we use physiological measures? Clearly, we have options about how to measure the things that interest us, and depending on the method of measurement, we may end up with quite different maps. New and improved methods produce new and improved maps. Satellite mapping systems and PET scans give us dramatically improved methods for looking at the earth and at the brain, respectively. Digital computers allow us to look at and organize psychological data in ways never before possible.

Objectivity in observation.   Several times we have used the word *objective* to refer to observations. We hear this word so often that we think we know what it means, but do we really? Most people probably think of objective observation as being "perfect," free from any subjective bias on the part of the researcher. But a moment's reflection tells us that this definition cannot be entirely true. Counters and clocks all have to be read by someone, and this reading can be biased. All observations are potentially subject to some kind of error, and *objective* and *subjective* are just relative terms. Objective simply means that several people are in high agreement about what they observe. It is easier to agree on what an automatic counter says than to agree on a number that we have had to count in our heads. We may be satisfied that a single person reading a counter is adequate because we have previously established that people usually agree on such readings. In psychology we often must make observations in situations where it is necessary to demonstrate that there is high agreement among observers. Suppose that we are watching an infant's face and are recording smiles over a period of time. If we were doing this for research, we would want to have more than one observer doing the recording and to verify that their recordings are similar. Or we might videotape the infant for later counting of smiles by two or more observers.

Drawing a map.   Given that we have obtained the data from which to make a map (or theory), how are we to draw the map? Again, there are choices. If we draw a rectangular map, we run into problems when we try to represent the whole earth, because areas near the poles will be disproportionately large on the map. If we try to represent the globe on a flat surface, in the way it would look if we made cuts in a ball and flattened it out, we get a map that is very difficult to follow, and so on. Instead of a drawing, our representation of the world may be linguistic. The title to a particular piece of property is both pictorial (a diagram of land shape with locations indicated) and a purely verbal description in terms of latitude and longitude and particular landmarks. We can also map behavior over time and space just as we map the orbits of planets over time and space (see Figure 1–2a). For example, we may measure "general activity" of animals over days as we study circadian rhythms. Or we can describe behavior over both time and space, as with the dances of honey bees that show the distance and direction of food from the hive, as illustrated in Figure 1–2b. These *dynamic maps* might be described mathematically rather than verbally or graphi-

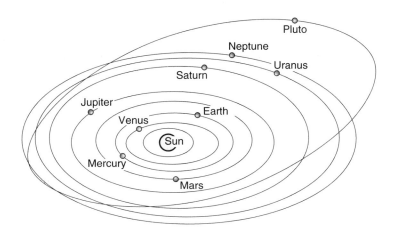

FIGURE 1–2A.   Dynamic mapping of the solar system, showing the orbits of the planets around the sun. The orbits can be described mathematically as well.

Round Dance

Tail-wagging Dance

FIGURE 1–2B.   Dances of bees to show location of food. The round dance shows only that food is nearby. A worker bee returns to the hive and just goes around in circles, exciting the others to go get food. The tail-wagging dance shows the direction of the food (by the direction of the wavy line in the middle), and the speed of the dance indicates distance. The faster the dance, the closer the food is. A classic book on the dances of bees is Von Frisch (1967).

cally. Once we have drawn a map or developed a theory, however, how do we know it is a "good" map or theory?

Criteria for Goodness of a Theory

Four qualities distinguish a good theory: testability, fruitfulness, simplicity, and comprehensiveness.

- **Testability.** Most people might say that a good theory is one that cannot be proven false. In fact, however, the single most important characteristic of a good theory is that it *can* be shown wrong (Popper, 1959). A good theory makes predictions specific enough to be "risky," so that some outcome other than the predicted outcome can possibly occur and disconfirm (falsify) the theory. A theory that cannot be falsified is not a good theory, because it cannot be tested. Suppose I propose the theory that I am being followed by little green men who are known only to me and who disappear when I turn around to look at them. This "theory" is a very bad theory, because there is no way to find out whether it is right or wrong, no way to test it. Compare this with the theory that gravity on the moon is only one-sixth of the gravity on Earth. We've had a theory of gravitational pull for about three hundred years, and it has worked very well in accounting for planetary motion, but we could not test it with human beings on the moon until thirty years ago. Unlike the little-green-men theory, however, the moon's gravity was testable in principle as soon as it was proposed by Isaac Newton in the seventeenth century. We just had to wait for technology that would get us to the moon. In the meanwhile, of course, there was much other evidence to support the theory, and what a surprise it would have been had we been wrong when we got to the moon!
- **Fruitfulness.** A fruitful theory generates research so that more knowledge is gained. Hull's (1943) theory of behavior (which we look at in more detail later) generated a great deal of research, much of which showed the theory to be

wrong in many ways. The theory was thus also good because it was falsifiable. Built-in obsolescence as a result of being fruitful and testable is a mark of good theory. Sometimes a theory is proposed that sounds good at the time but that generates virtually no further research and does not aid in development of the field. Such a theory is inevitably assigned to the dustbin of history.

- **Simplicity.** If there are two explanations for an event, the simpler of the two is preferable. This principle of parsimony is commonly called "Occam's razor." The term *simplicity* may refer to the number of concepts in a theory (the fewer the better if they are adequate) or to the complexity of the relationships among the concepts. A variation of this is called Lloyd Morgan's Canon. Morgan was a comparative psychologist at the turn of the century, studying many different kinds of animals. His law was that you should not apply more complex mental activities to explain animal behavior than are necessary to account for the behavior. To use a very simple example, consider the tendency of moths to fly into flame (a phototropism). One might say that, like Icarus of Greek mythology, the moth was trying to reach the sun and thus burned its wings. Or one might say that the moth had a death wish. But one might also say that a moth has photoreceptors in its wings that automatically make it fly toward light and that it is quite accidental that the moth flies into the flame. Which theory is simplest? Which makes more sense, and why?

- **Comprehensiveness.** The better a theory is, the greater number of observations it explains. Einstein's theory of relativity was more complicated than Newton's theory of gravity, but it was also more comprehensive. Newton's theory is still quite adequate for many practical purposes, such as working out the trajectories of shells fired from cannons. Einstein's theory would be of no practical use in improving gunnery on earth, but is certainly better for understanding many mysteries of the universe. In motivation there is a theory called **expectancy-value theory,** which says that we make decisions on the basis of the value to us of possible outcomes of our choices. This theory has been applied to animals foraging for food, economic decisions, choice of a mate, and satisfaction with one's job. It is one of psychology's most durable and comprehensive theories.

Explanation

We want to develop theory so that we can "explain" past observations or predict future ones. But what does it mean to "explain" something? One kind of scientific explanation is to identify a specific event as an instance of a more general principle or law. One principle in psychology is the serial position effect in verbal learning. Words in the middle of a list are harder to learn than words at the beginning or end of the list. If someone were having trouble learning the middle of a list, we could explain his or her difficulty as an instance of the serial position effect. Identifying something as an "instance" of a particular phenomenon would be considered a "low-level" explanation. A higher-level explanation would explain the serial position effect itself, as well as other facts of verbal learning. Hull, Hovland, Ross, Hall, Perkins, and Fitch (1940) proposed such a theory, using the concepts of "excitatory" and "inhibitory" response tendencies to derive the serial position effect and other learning phenomena.

Turner (1967) distinguished between explanations that are logically satisfying and those that are psychologically satisfying. A psychologically satisfying explanation may be pleasing to hear, familiar, or even mystifying, but not necessarily accurate. To say that "aggression wells up in a person until it spills into behavior like water overflowing a tank" may be appealing (both Sigmund Freud and Konrad Lorenz have used such an analogy), but the appeal is based on our familiarity with water tanks and has little to do with the facts of behavior or of the nervous system. Witchcraft, astrology, and magic might be psychologically satisfying explanations of events to some people, but not to scientists.

THE ASSUMPTION OF DETERMINISM

The Problem of Freedom

Let us ponder for a moment one of the most important ideas implied by the very existence of psychological theory, which is the implication that human behavior can be predicted. This must mean that behavior has causes. If behavior has causes, we are not free to choose our behaviors in any way we want. Indeed, if we know the causes of a behavior, then we could make the behavior occur by producing those causes.

The conclusion that behavior has causes has powerful implications for life in general, as well as for psychological science. We all like to feel free to act as we choose; however, determinism challenges that feeling of freedom. From a scientific point of view, though, total freedom to choose poses a problem: If we can do anything we wish at any time, then we could not predict behavior. Science aside, if we could not predict the behavior of others, how would we ever know how to interact with them? Would not utter social chaos arise? Obviously, we actually do a pretty good job at predicting the behavior of others, and we do not always have total chaos.

Society as a whole deals inconsistently with the question of freedom, however. On the one hand, a person may be imprisoned because she "chose" to commit a crime. But on the other hand, if we assume complete freedom of choice of behavior, then such punishment should not deter future crimes. Punishment would be nothing more than a retributive "eye for an eye." Punishment makes sense only if we expect it to alter (determine) future behavior. Even the argument that punishment sets an example for others assumes that the threat of punishment will partly determine their behavior. Because of such inconsistencies in the freewill argument, as well as because of the impossibility of having a science of behavior without assuming determinism, determinism is considered to be as necessary for the behavioral sciences as it is for the physical sciences.

Determinism

Stated simply, determinism means that if Cause A occurs, the Effect B will follow. If I suddenly make a loud sound behind you, you will jump. If I am hungry, I will eat. In mathematical terminology we would say that **Effect** = f **(Cause).** In psychological terminology we might say that **Response** = f **(Stimulus, Organism)** or **Behavior** = f **(Person, Environment).** In the psychology laboratory, we can repeatedly do experiments with human subjects and obtain the same results under the same conditions. Indeed, most undergraduate experimental psychology laboratories use at least some "tried and true" demonstration experiments that almost always work, such as simple experiments in human learning or perception. We depend on the predictability of behavior to make such demonstrations reliable.

Behavior is affected by many different conditions, however, and to the extent that we do not know what conditions are prevailing at a given time, our predictions are less reliable. A psychologist is unwilling to predict the behavior of a person at a party for the same reason that a physicist balks at predicting the behavior of a handful of confetti thrown at that party: In neither case are known all the conditions bearing on the behaviors. Prediction in psychology is also made more difficult, because some of the variables influencing behavior are *internal* variables, not open to direct observation by outsiders. These are the "organism" or "person" variables in the equations presented earlier. The "impressions" of past experiences are obviously important, but we can neither recall all our own past experiences nor know all those of other people.

"Freedom," then, often comes down to **lack of predictability.** Freedom of behavior is perceived differently according to where the cause(s) of a particular behavior are located. If a particular behavior is mainly controlled by external, observable events, we tend to say that it is determined. If the behavior is primarily controlled by internal, unobservable events, we might say that it is free. As Tomkins (1981) also points out, the more choices we have, the "freer" we seem. Failure to predict behavior with perfect accuracy is not the same thing as freedom, though. It is just failure to predict perfectly.

There are several possible meanings of determinism, however:

- **Hard determinism.** If we knew enough, perhaps we could predict all the behavior of a person with mathematical precision. This is an untestable hypothesis, however, since we never have this much information. Such precise prediction, or hard determinism, is thus an ideal, but not an immediate, practical goal.
- **Soft determinism.** This is the view that some behaviors are determined and others are not. This is perhaps the worst approach to the problem, because it provides no rules for saying whether an inaccurate prediction about behavior means that the behavior is "free" or whether today we are simply ignorant of important variables that tomorrow we might understand. Predictions of behavior can go wrong for many reasons. We may have poor measurement procedures, use sloppy research technique, or simply be studying the wrong variable for predicting a behavior of interest.

- **Probabilistic determinism.** This concept approaches prediction as insurance companies do (Vorsteg, 1974). If we can predict with a respectable level of probability that people will perform a certain way under certain conditions, we believe that we have predicted rather successfully. We have statistical techniques (inferential statistics) to help evaluate our success in such probabilistic situations. Probabilistic prediction, then, is no denial of determinism; it is just a realistic recognition of the fallibility of science and scientists.

The question of social freedom or control is not the issue here. Belief in freedom does not change the laws of behavior, and belief in determinism does not imply any particular kind of social control. A **belief** in freedom, however, could be an internal determinant of behavior with different effects than those which follow a belief in determinism. Political leaders who believe in determinism may try to exert different social controls than the leaders who believe in freedom. By the same token, anyone asking for improved teaching methods, cures for mental illness, or less violence is asking, "What can we do to *produce* those ends?" These questions assume determinism since they imply that if we had the answers, we could *make* things happen the way we want.

A Closer Look at Causation

We do research to find the causes of events. Explanations often involve statements of causation. "Why did George's knee jerk?" "Because the doctor struck him below the knee with a rubber hammer." The blow caused the knee jerk. Or if a child started crying when a dog approached, we might say that the dog caused the child to cry. But what is a cause? Remember that all we can know about in the world is the impression of the world that is on our sense organs, either directly or indirectly by means of instruments. We perceive that some events occur closely in time and space (the dog appeared, and the child cried), and we make a statement of causality based on the observation, (the dog caused the child to cry). But perhaps the child's parent said something that made the child cry, and the innocent dog just happened on the scene at a bad time. Causes are what we perceive or think them to be, and nothing more. Scientists do not find ultimate truths or ultimate causes. Rather, on the basis of observations, they write statements, called *laws,* about observed events. The causality is in the statements, the language of science, rather than directly in the physical world. That is one of the reasons why we want to be as precise as we can with language.

THE MIND-BODY PUZZLE

If we accept the principle of determinism, which we must do if we are to believe that psychological science and theory is possible, then we have another problem. We often see psychology defined as the science that uniquely studies both mind and body. We might be inclined to say that our mind causes our body to engage in certain actions. But such a causal relationship raises problems that have puzzled critical thinkers for literally thousands of years. What do we mean by mind? What do we mean by body? And how are the two related?

For the average person, the relationship of mind to body probably is clear. The "official doctrine" (Ryle, 1949) is that "body" is physical and material, that it is limited in space, time, and size, and that it is objectively observable. "Mind," on the other hand, bears the opposite of all these qualities. It is subjective, directly known only to the individual possessing it, unlimited in physical dimensions, and, perhaps, everlasting. This distinction is essentially the same doctrine generally accepted in Western theology to maintain the separation of "body" and "soul." It goes back to the Greek philosopher Plato around 400 B.C., came into Christianity with St. Augustine about seven hundred years later, and reemerged in seventeenth century with the French philosopher René Descartes.

As a "person on the street" might view it, we are aware of our circumstances, feelings, and ideas. Faced consciously with several possible courses of action, we *consciously* and *freely will* ourselves to take this or that action. This one brief statement assumes that the separation of mind and body is real and that we are free to make any choice. It is important to scrutinize these assumptions, however. We have already seen that "free will" is not the direction in which we want to head. But what are the alternatives to the mind-body relation?

There are two general classes of opinion regarding mind and body. The proponents of **dualism** assume that mind and body are qualitatively different. The **monism** camp assumes that the mind and body really are qualitatively the same.

Dualisms

Interactionistic dualism.   This is the view developed by Descartes, commonly called Cartesian dualism. Mind and body are considered qualitatively different categories, immaterial and material, and what the body does depends on the mind. That is, there is a causal relation between mind and body, which is illustrated in Figure 1–3. However, where and how do these qualitatively different substances interact? Descartes ([1650] 1892) suggested the pineal gland in the brain as the point of interaction and developed a physical model based on reflected light rays. He proposed that light energy comes into the eyes and activates "spirits" that are reflected one way or another by the pineal gland, which he saw as something like a pivoting mirror. Depending on where the spirits are reflected, different movements of the body occur. The term *reflex*, referring to an automatic movement following a particular stimulus (such as a knee jerk when the patellar tendon is struck),

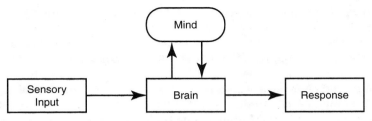

A. Cartesian dualism. Arrows indicate causal
relationship between mind and brain.

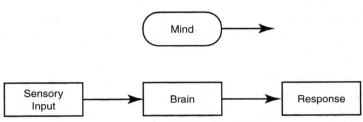

B. Parallelism. No causal relation between mind
and brain. They just run in parallel.

C. Idealistic monism (idealism). There is nothing but mind.

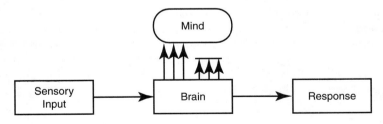

D. Materialistic monism (identity theory). Mind is a
function of brain processes and has no causal
properties. All mind states have corresponding
brain states, but not all brain states have
corresponding mind states.

FIGURE 1–3.   Possible causal relations between mind and body. The brain is the most important aspect
of body here.

comes from Descartes's description of the "reflection of spirits." We would now call these "spirits" neural impulses. According to Descartes, animal behavior consists entirely of reflexes; humans were also said to have reflexes, but, in addition, the human mind could will various behaviors.

The logical problems with such a theory are painfully difficult. If our minds and bodies really are so unlike each other, how could they interact? How can an immaterial mind cause any behavior to occur? At a physical level, we know that it takes energy to make the body move and that if the mind has no energy, there is no way it can make the body move. We also know that the pineal gland serves no function like the one that Descartes imagined. Actually, his speculation was based only on the fact that unlike other parts of the brain, the pineal gland was not duplicated in the two hemispheres. Most scientists, as well as philosophers, have rejected Descartes's system for these reasons.

Parallelistic dualism.   This approach retains a mind-body dualism without getting into the sticky issue of how mind could play a causal role in behavior. Suppose we set two atomic clocks to exactly the same time and then leave them to run out their separate existences. Whenever we look at the first clock, we will be able to tell what the second says. The German philosopher Gottfried Wilhelm Leibniz proposed such a view of mind and body (Duncan, 1890). Just as the first clock does not cause the second to tell a particular time, so the mind does not cause the body to do a particular thing. There is a high correlation between the two events in question, however. This view recognizes the dual existence of mental life and of the body, and the correlation between experience and behavior, but it does not raise the problem of how they could interact in any causal way.

Parallelism may indeed simply make a practical distinction between mind and body. The methods for studying mental activity (such as recording what people say about their experiences) are sufficiently different from the methods of studying bodily action (such as physical recordings) that the mind-body distinction is worth maintaining for this reason alone. This principle is called a methodological dualism.

Monisms

Monism is the idea that there is only a single "substance," encompassing both mind and body. This view completely does away with any problems of interaction because there are not two different substances to interact. As one might expect, however, this view has its own problems, depending on what view of monism one proposes: mentalistic or materialistic.

Mentalistic monism.   How do we know about the existence of a world outside our own minds? It seems obvious that we know about this world through our consciousness of it, through our minds. But what proof could we offer that things exist outside our minds? Our dreams in all their terror or sensuousness seem real when they occur, but we know they are not "real." Neither are hallucinations. Mentalistic monism is the view that we do not have to assume any external world if our only knowledge of it is from our experience. If we know the world only from experiences, perhaps experience is all there is. This view was proposed by the British philosopher Bishop George Berkeley ([1710] 1939). The great German physiologist Johannes Mueller proposed a similar view in the early nineteenth century, but in biological terms. We are not directly aware of the external world, said Mueller, we are aware only of the activity of our own nervous systems.

Another British philosopher, David Hume ([1748] 1939), proposed an even more extreme view, called **solipsism.** Hume's logical extension of Berkeley is the possibility that there is but a single mind and that any other apparent minds are only the experience of this mind, just as apparent objects are the experience of this mind. There are no physical objects, no bodies, no other minds. The logic is undeniable. Someone may cry, however, "Why do thorns pain me unless thorns exist?" The direct answer to this question is that the existence of thorns has to be *assumed* before the question can even be asked. The assumption that thorns exist is built into the question. The solipsistic argument assumes the opposite, that such things as thorns (or anything else) do *not* exist outside the mind. The burden of proof falls on you to show that they *do* exist as separate entities. If the experience of pain accompanies the experience of thorns, that is just the way experiences are. None of the experiences constitute proof of a separate existence outside experience. "But," may come another objection, "surely a mind would not produce pain for itself." This is irrelevant. The mind does not pick and choose its experiences, they just happen. Indeed, even the objections to my argument do not exist outside my own mind because there is no separate "you" outside my own mind. The mind-body problem disappears since there is only the mind.

Materialistic monism.   This view holds that the single underlying reality is material. The mind represents the functioning of the brain. Let us use the analogy of a dump truck. The truck moves about, picks up and drops things, generally acting as a dump truck should. We do not, however, talk about these functions of the truck as causing the truck to behave in its ordained manner or as existing separately from the truck. From this point of view, the body, especially the nervous system, is so constructed that one of its functions is consciousness. This *function* does not cause behaviors to occur, however; the nervous system causes them to occur. This process is illustrated in Figure 1–3.

One variation of materialistic monism, called **neural identity theory,** says that the material nervous system can be viewed in two different ways, just as we view two sides of a coin differently. The physiologist's description of the brain and a person's report of his or her own experience are both symbolic statements about the same thing (Pepper, 1959). Both describe the activity of the brain, but from different points of view and with different languages. For example, the person talks about seeing the color red, whereas the physiologist talks about certain neurons firing when the eye is stimulated with a certain wavelength of light. This theory is also sometimes called *double aspectism* in reference to looking at two aspects of the brain (from the inside, so to speak, and from the outside).

According to neural identity theory, for every conscious mental event, there is a corresponding brain event, but the converse is not true. That is, we are not aware of everything that goes on in our nervous systems, for example, the neural activities that control breathing. Nor at a given moment are we aware of all of the things we can possibly remember. Neural processes involved in motivation, emotion, and memory may influence our behavior without our being aware of them at the moment. Neural activities of which we *are* aware may be especially important for such activities as learning, but this is speculation, and its validity must be determined by research. (Considerable research does show, for example, that we can learn little or nothing while sound asleep.)

The close identity of conscious experience and brain function is increasingly shown in neurophysiological research. Here are three examples:

- Some individual neurons in the visual part of the brain respond only to lines with vertical orientations, others to horizontal lines, and some to both orientations. Other neurons respond only to moving stimuli, not to stationary ones. Such relationships have been found in frogs, cats, and monkeys, and it is reasonable to assume that they also exist in humans.
- If the two hemispheres of the brain are surgically separated, there are two independent "minds," whereas before there was only one mind. Each half of the brain is now an independent unit, and things learned in one half are unknown to the other half (e.g., Gazzaniga, 1967). Reason or logic based on just our conscious experience would never have predicted that splitting the brain into two hemispheres would produce two minds.
- Many drugs have mind-altering effects, such as producing hallucinations, making us more sleepy or alert, reducing our anxiety, or making us feel more happy.

Here is one final point on the mind-body problem. By nature and definition, science deals with observable events. For psychology these observable events are behaviors, body activities ranging from filling out attitude-survey questionnaires to throwing baseballs to describing drug experiences. Do we need to infer something behind those behaviors that is uniquely different from what the nervous system can reasonably be expected to do? The answer would seem to be no. This is not to say that all experience is expressed in behavior or that behavior tells us everything about a person. From a scientific point of view, however, the minds of other people are inferred from their behavior, including the things they say. We do not question the existence of consciousness here but do argue that the immediate experience of consciousness is not usable scientific data, open to observers other than the self.

In summary, the popular view that mind and body are different and that mind controls body is but one of several logical possibilities. The particular belief anyone has in this matter may have important practical consequences—deciding how to go about studying and treating "mental" disorders, for example. Indeed, what could be the possible reason for using drug therapy for mental disorders if the nervous system were not related to the mind? But there is no way to know which view is "really" correct.

THE LANGUAGE OF SCIENCE

A characteristic of science is that it is as precise as it can be at any given time. One of the greatest steps forward in the history of science came with the beginning of actual measurement of times, speeds, distances, weights, and temperatures. There is a big difference, for example, between saying that water freezes when it gets cold and that water freezes at a specific temperature that can be measured. We carry this precision into the language of science so that we can speak and think more precisely.

The philosopher Charles Morris (1938) has provided a system for understanding scientific language, called **semiotic.** The three subareas, illustrated in Figure 1–4, are **syntactics** (the relations of different signs to each other), **semantics** (the relations of signs to the objects to which they refer), and **pragmatics** (the relations of signs to their users). Signs are any linguistic conventions, words, or numbers. We are interested here in syntactics and semantics.

Syntactics: Rules for Using Signs

Syntactics is concerned with the establishment and use of agreed-on rules by which we can relate signs (symbols or words) to each other. Every language, including logic and mathematics, has such formal rules. In English,

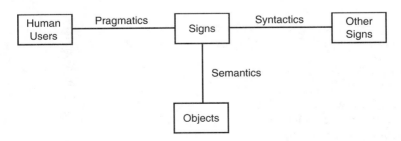

FIGURE 1–4. Three areas of semiotic: syntactics, semantics, and pragmatics.

for example, the rule is generally that nouns come before verbs, but in German the verbs all come at the very end of the sentence, and so on. In mathematics we can apply the basic rules of arithmetic and algebra to manipulate the formula $M = \Sigma X/N$ in various ways, including $NM = \Sigma X$ or $N = \Sigma X/M$. As any psychology student would recognize, this is the formula for the arithmetic mean, in which M equals the mean, ΣX is the sum of the individual scores, and N is the number of scores. Using the formal rules, however, we can move the signs around into different combinations even if the signs do not actually refer to anything in the real world. No matter what the symbols refer to, all we need to manipulate them is knowledge of the rules.

Semantics: What Shall Our Words Mean?

Semantics refers to the rules by which we assign symbols to objects or events; these are the rules for **defining** terms. The simplest definition is the **ostensive**, or pointing, definition. For example, we may say "That is what I mean by dog," while pointing to a dog. All definitions eventually have to appeal to some kind of sense observation in this way. We might read that a "dog" is "a four-legged animal that barks and is commonly used as a house pet," but we then have the problem of knowing what is meant by the words "four," "legged," "animal," and "barks," and we are back to observation. The individual reading the definition must know the meaning of these more **primitive** terms, on the basis of observation, before the definition makes sense. We usually assume that everybody knows what is meant by color names, simple numbers, and so on, and we progress from there to build more complex definitions via language. As another example, if we say that "a group is two or more people," we assume that our reader knows already what the words "two," "more," and "people" mean.

OPERATIONAL DEFINITIONS

The physicist P. W. Bridgman argued that we define the meaning of a concept in terms of how we measure it. The procedures for measuring length are what we mean by the term *length* just as the procedures for measuring temperature are what we mean by *temperature*. The meaning of any concept is synonymous with the corresponding set of measurement operations (Bridgman, 1927, p. 5). Without measurement procedures, such concepts as length, weight, and time are empirically meaningless words, not related to the "real world." If we talked about length but had no way to measure it on real objects, then it would not have any meaning in relation to real objects. We can measure length, of course, by laying down a standard rod repeatedly and counting the number of times it takes to go from one end of an object to the other. A soccer field is a hundred and twenty meters long, and a meter is the length of a rod kept in the International Bureau of Standards. The meter gives us an objective way of defining the length of a field that we can all agree on. But what about situations in which we cannot perform this operation? The diameter of the sun, the diameter of an atom, or the distance of the stars cannot be measured by "laying down a rod." Neither can the length of an object moving at high speed (such as a photon) be measured in this manner. We have to have new kinds of measurement procedures for these situations, and when any new measurement procedure is introduced, we may be led to changes in fundamental concepts, whether in physics or in psychology. The development of modern statistical methods (such as factor analysis) has had a profound impact on the way psychological measurements, such as personality tests, are constructed. These new tests, in turn, strongly impact our understanding of human personality and intellect.

Operational Definitions of Psychological Concepts

There is an old saying that "intelligence is what intelligence tests measure." In a trivial sense, this remark denies that we have any understanding of intelligence. Operationally, however, it means that our understanding of intelligence depends on the procedures (operations) by which intelligence is measured. If intelligence is defined in terms of some vague hypothetical property like "problem-solving ability," we do little to understand it and nothing to measure it. But if we set up a series of problems and measure the ability to solve them (such as how fast they are solved), we have taken a step in the right direction. Alfred Binet did just this when he defined mental age in terms of successful completion of various tasks. Now someone might want to argue that a particular intelligence test is a poor way to measure intelligence or to say, "That's not what I mean by intelligence." That is all to the good, but at the same time, it is incumbent on the critic to say what her or his alternative way of measuring intelligence would be. The critic's way of measuring intelligence would give us her or his operational definition of intelligence.

Circular Definitions

Suppose that two rats run down an alleyway to a goal box where there is water. One rat runs very quickly to the water, the other runs slowly. How would we account for the difference in running speed? We might be inclined to say that one rat runs fast because it is thirsty and that the other runs slowly because it is not thirsty. But what is the evidence for their being thirsty or not? The evidence is that they run fast or slow! This is a **circular definition,** in which something is defined in terms of itself. We would be saying that the fast animal runs fast because it runs fast. This, of course, is no definition at all. It is simply giving a name (thirst, in this case) to something observed. As another example, we might see a flock of sheep gathered together and ask why they are doing so. An answer might be that "they have a herding instinct."

How do we know that they have a herding instinct? The answer is because they are gathering together. Again, the definition is circular and simply involves putting a name (herd instinct) to the observed behavior (gathering together). Circular definitions are dangerous to theory because they deceptively appear to be saying something when they are not. This dilemma is avoided by defining concepts as intervening variables.

Intervening Variables

Let us go back to the two rats running down the alleyway to water. Suppose that upon inquiry, we found that the fast-running rat had been without water for a day and the slow-running rat had actually drunk all it wanted just before being tested. If we asked why one rat ran faster, we might say because it was thirsty. And how do we know it was thirsty? Because it had been without water for a day (not because it ran faster). In technical terms the **concept** (thirst) is defined by observable **antecedent** and **consequent** conditions, as shown in Figure 1–5.

The antecedent condition is operationally defined as hours without water, and the consequent condition is operationally defined as speed of running. That is, the concept is "anchored" on the antecedent and consequent sides. The anchors are the objectively measured conditions. In an experiment, antecedent and consequent conditions correspond to the familiar independent variable that the experimenter manipulates and the dependent variable that the experimenter measures.

The two disciplines of scientific psychology. Lee Cronbach (1957), in his presidential address to the American Psychological Association, argued that there are "two disciplines of scientific psychology," **experimental** and **psychometric** (measurement and comparisons of individual differences). Spence (1944) had made a similar point with regard to kinds of intervening variables, which Kimble (1994a,b) has recently brought to the fore again. The distinction is that experimental psychologists **manipulate** variables to study their effects on behavior, whereas psychometric psychologists **correlate** measures of different variables of interest. Intervening variables can be approached in these same two ways, as experimental intervening variables and psychometric intervening variables.

Antecedent Condition	Intervening Variable	Consequent Condition
24-Hour Water Deprivation········· Thirst··Running Fast		
No Water Deprivation ··························· No Thirst·· Running Slow		

FIGURE 1–5. Defining an intervening variable (thirst) in terms of antecedent and consequent conditions.

Antecedent Condition (Stimulus)	Intervening Variable	Consequent Condition (Response)
Threat of Shock ··· Fear ······························ Fast Response to Signal		
No Threat of Shock ······························· No Fear ·························· Slower Response to Signal		

FIGURE 1–6. Experimentally defined (manipulated) intervening variable. The intervening variable is defined in terms of experimentally manipulated antecedent condition (threat of shock) and is therefore under experimental control.

Experimentally defined intervening variables. In the previous example, the intervening variable was defined by a stimulus (experimenter controllable) condition. There are many such examples. Suppose we wanted to study the effect of fear on speed of response to a signal. We might manipulate level of fear by telling some subjects that they will get shocked if they do not respond quickly (having previously determined that such a threat is fear-arousing). This situation is illustrated in Figure 1–6.

Psychometrically defined intervening variables. In this approach, instead of using some stimulus manipulation as an antecedent condition, some response measure or test score is used as the antecedent condition. Suppose we are interested in the effects of anxiety on performance but were not able to manipulate anxiety level in an experimental group. For example, we might hypothesize that anxiety can interfere with test performance in the classroom. We want to set up a learning study to test this hypothesis. Since our hypothesis is about students who bring their anxiety with them into the testing situation, we could set up our study to distinguish among subjects who normally differ in level of anxiety. We administer an anxiety scale to all of them and then compare their memory test scores with their anxiety test scores. We must, of course, be careful to control for such extraneous factors as intelligence, year in school, and the like. The research design would then look like Figure 1–7.

We would correlate the anxiety scores and the test performance scores. If there were a significant correlation between anxiety scores and test performance (subjects with higher scores performing more poorly), we could at-

Antecedent Condition (Response 1)	Intervening Variable	Consequent Condition (Response 2)
Scores on Anxiety Scale ··················· Anxiety Level··································· Test Performance		

FIGURE 1–7. Psychometrically defined intervening variable. The antecedent condition is defined by one set of responses (scores on anxiety scale), and consequent condition is defined by a different set of responses (test performance). The antecedent condition is not manipulated; it is measured and is not under experimental control.

tribute the difference to anxiety. We should have somewhat less confidence in our interpretation here, however, because this is a *correlational* procedure, not an experimental procedure. We are not manipulating anxiety as an experimental variable (as we did with threat); rather, we are comparing subjects with already-existing differences in level of anxiety. It is always possible that some unknown third factor accounts for the correlation.

A variation of the psychometric approach is to select and compare subjects who are high and low on a variable of interest. We might do this simply as a matter of efficiency, so that there might be a smaller number of subjects to deal with. Or the task that the selected subjects have to perform might be very time-consuming and expensive, and costs should be kept down. We might then, for example, administer the anxiety test to a large number potential subjects and then use only the subjects getting the top 25 percent of the scores and those getting the bottom 25 percent. We could then compare subsequent experimental task performance by the two groups, but using only half as many subjects as we would otherwise. This method is shown diagrammatically in Figure 1–8.

This method gives the appearance of using an experimental intervening variable in an experimental study because there are two groups differing in anxiety level. But, of course, it is still just a correlational procedure. We have grouped subjects into high and low scorers for comparison, but we are still just measuring anxiety level, not manipulating it. Therefore, we still have the same reservations about interpreting anxiety as the cause of differences between the groups.

Converging operations.   A single set of operations seldom isolates a single concept as an account of a behavior. Rather, we *converge* on a concept by using different operations (Garner, Hake, & Eriksen, 1956). For example, an experiment by McCleary and Lazarus (1949) showed that emotion-arousing words had to be flashed in front of a subject for longer periods of time to be accurately recognized than did neutral words. One interpretation was that emotion-arousal "blocked" *perception* of the words (McGinnies, 1949). On the other hand, it is possible that a *response bias* was involved, that is, lesser willing-

Antecedent Condition (Test Scores)	Intervening Variable	Consequent Condition (Task Scores)
High Anxiety Scale Scores ·············· High Anxiety ······························· Test Performance		
Low Anxiety Scale Scores ·············· Low Anxiety ······························· Test Performance		

FIGURE 1–8. Psychometrically defined intervening variable with subject selection. Scores are gathered from a large group of subjects, but only those subjects who score high or low on this antecedent measure (an anxiety scale in this example) are actually used for measurement of the consequent condition (task scores). This may be a more efficient use of subjects, but even though it may look like an experiment, it is not. The antecedent condition is not manipulated.

ness to report the "emotion-arousing" words. Thus, college students of the 1950s might have hesitated to *say* out loud such "dirty words" as *bitch*, which were flashed at them in a psychology laboratory, unless they were absolutely certain that they were correct about what the words were. Saying more neutral words would not be held back by subjects, however. Experiments involving other operations were conducted to converge on this response-bias interpretation. Postman, Bronson, and Gropper (1953) told different groups of subjects that it was a sign of good or poor mental health to recognize such words readily. The "good health" group was quicker to "recognize" (report) the words than a group given no instructions, and the "poor health" group was slowest. The results, therefore, did converge on the response-bias interpretation as the correct one. Converging operations have also been used in experiments attempting to distinguish between learning and motivational influences on behavior.

Putting Together a Theory

Let us look at an example of a theory. Consider first the formal structure of a theory in abstract terms, as illustrated in Figure 1–9.

The concepts of the theory are defined in terms of observable events, and the theory states how these concepts are related to each other. Predictions about the real world are made on the basis of the syntax of the theory, which is determined by both observation and logic. This example uses a completely arbitrary syntax just for the purpose of showing what syntax is. A, B, and C are theoretical concepts defined by specific experimental control procedures (operations) a, b, and c. Concept D, however, is defined by the syntax of the theory $D = (A \times B) + C$. If we know the values for A, B, and C (the independent variables in the experimental situation), then we can predict the value for D, which is measured as the *dependent* variable in the situation. If we hold A and B constant, changing only the value of C, the measured outcome tells how C affects the dependent variable. If the theory does not predict accurately, we will change its syntax, add new concepts, or eliminate old ones. We may have to scrap the theory if it never works right.

Level of Theoretical Concepts	(A)	×	(B)	+	C	=	D
Definition	↑		↑		↑		↓
Level of Observations	(a) Control		(b) Control		(c) Control		(d) Measure

FIGURE 1–9. Formal structure of a theory. Theoretical concepts (A, B, and C) are defined in terms of observations. They are intervening variables. Concept D is defined according to the syntax of the theory ([A × B] + C = D). D is measured in terms of some appropriate response. If any two of A, B, and C were held constant, then D would reflect the change in the variable not held constant. For example, if A and B were held constant and C were varied, then D would reflect the variation in C.

Level of Theoretical Concepts	H	×	D	=	E
Definition	↑		↑		↓
Level of Observations	Number of Learning Trials		Hours of Deprivation		Speed of Running

FIGURE 1–10. Hull's theory. Habit and drive (*H* and *D*) are defined as intervening variables, and excitatory potential (*E*) is defined by the syntax of the theory ($E = H \times D$). The strength of *E* is measured by some appropriate response, in this example the speed of running.

As a specific example, Hull (1943) proposed that learning multiplies with motivation to determine performance. He symbolized learning as *H* (for habit), motivation as *D* (for drive), and performance potential as *E* (for excitatory potential). The syntax for these was

Excitatory Potential = Habit × Drive, or $E = H \times D$

He defined the magnitude of *H* operationally in terms of number of previous learning trials (the more trials, the greater is *H*), magnitude of *D* in terms of hours of food deprivation (more hours of deprivation produces greater *D*), and *E* as $H \times D$. Putting this into the preceding format, provides the theoretical concepts defined as shown in Figure 1–10.

Given the concepts and the syntax, we can make many specific predictions about experimental outcomes. For example, the theory says that running speed depends on the multiplication of habit and drive. If a particular response has not been learned (*H* = *O*) or if there is no drive (*D* = *O*), then *E* = *O*. If *E* = *O*, there would be no performance; the subject would not run. To make exact predictions, we would need exact numerical values for the concepts, such as numerical values for habit and drive. In psychological research there is seldom such high precision, and therefore we usually deal with inequalities. Thus, we might say that twenty-two hours of food deprivation produces *more* "drive" than two hours, and performance should be better (running faster to food) at twenty-two hours. We cannot predict exact speeds, however, because there are too many other variables that would affect speed. For example, running speed might be affected by the age, sex, and species (or, strain) of subject, as well as by the particular experimental task used to test the subject. Still and all, however, the theory is testable.

DEFINING MOTIVATION

Regulatory versus Purposive Approaches

The single most difficult task for a motivation theorist is to define motivation, and it is doubly difficult to define motivation to everyone's satisfaction, partly because there are different approaches to motivation, each with its own proponents. Two major differences in emphasis are represented by the regulatory and purposive approaches to motivation.

- The **regulatory approach** emphasizes the body's responses to such disruptive internal forces as hunger and pain and the way that the body tries to restore internal equilibrium. This process is commonly referred to as **homeostasis.** The emphasis is on what happens in the body when an organism needs food or water, for example, and is closely tied to physiology.
- The **purposive approach** emphasizes the goal-directed nature of behavior. This approach is more cognitive and relatively less concerned with the physiology of regulation.

It must be emphasized, however, that these are extremes of these positions and that the distinction may break down in a particular case. For example, a physiologist studying hunger (regulation) may also be interested in the kinds of food (goals) that an animal chooses when it is hungry. To further complicate things, the two approaches sometimes share the same terms, but with different meanings. For example, to the regulatory theorist, *need* refers to a life-threatening physiological deficit or excess. To the purposive theorist, however, needs may also refer to such goals as striving for affiliation, power, or achievement, which are hardly lethal if unmet. These equally legitimate approaches to motivation are deeply rooted in different historical traditions.

Background of the regulatory approach.   The regulatory approach has a biological tradition, traceable to Darwin's theory of evolution and to experimental medicine. At the turn of the century, the functional school of psychology developed and was led by such intellectual luminaries as William James and John Dewey. The question they raised was, How does mental activity help organisms adapt to their environment? About the same time, however, under the influence of Pavlov in Russia and Sherrington in England, the study of reflexes became popular. Such reflex responses as salivating were behaviors simple enough to be analyzed in detail. Complex behaviors were interpreted as "strings" of reflexes, and so, it was theorized, understanding reflexes could also lead to understanding complex social behaviors. The most extreme position was John B. Watson's **behaviorism.** Watson denied any role for "mental" events in the determination of behavior, and had no use for the notion of purpose.[1]

At their inceptions the functionalist and behaviorist approaches relied solely on stimuli as causes of behavior, without a separate motivational concept. Behavior was said to flow from one stimulus to the next. Some stimuli

---

[1]More sophisticated modern forms of behaviorism say that we infer mental activities from behavioral observations. Contemporary psychologists who might deny any strong allegiance to a behavioristic point of view would generally admit to this methodological limitation on how we go about studying internal events.

were **motivating stimuli,** however. In 1918, Robert S. Woodworth added the term **drive** to psychology's dictionary. He argued that like an automobile, behavior had a driving mechanism and a steering mechanism. The driving mechanism provided the power or energy to make an otherwise motionless organism run. Environmental stimuli helped to guide or steer the organism in one direction or another. A biologically adaptive act, then, consisted of the following sequence:

Internal Need → Drive → Activity → Goal → Quiescence

Need for food drives an organism to be active until it finds and consumes food, after which it is quiet until some new need rearouses drive. The motivational emphasis of the regulatory approach is on the need/drive aspect of the process and on the underlying physiology of need/drive. Goals come into play in the service of internal disturbances.

Background of the purposive approach. The origins of the purposive approach are found in ancient philosophical views about *choices* of goals and behaviors, often couched in terms of choices between good and evil. Scientifically, the question is phrased in terms of what makes a person choose any kind of goal over some alternative. Why choose steak rather than fish for supper? Why select this person for a spouse, and not that person? According to the purposive approach, we look to the *future,* at the potential outcomes of choosing different possible courses of action. Then we strive towards goals which we anticipate will be of the greatest *value* to us. Given the choice between two spouses, we choose the one who we anticipate will provide the greater satisfaction. There is no *necessary* concept of internal need or drive from the purposive point of view.

The regulatory and purposive approaches both have important things to say about motivation, and the problem for the modern motivation theorist is to bring them together in such a way that they fit under a common definition. In effect, doing this means that the definition has to be rather "loose," including a large number of specific concepts under the umbrella of motivation.

Motivational Concepts as an Intervening Variable

We previously saw that intervening variables are defined in terms of antecedent and consequent conditions, and we saw "drive" as an intervening variable in the example of Hull's theory. Let us now see how we can define desire and aversion operationally as intervening variables, thus avoiding the criticism of being subjective. We begin with what Tolman (1938) called the *defining operations* for an intervening variable. Suppose that there is a pair of rats, which we let run a number of times in a T-maze having food in one arm of the T but not in the other. One of the animals consistently runs to the

Antecedent Condition	Intervening Variable	Consequent Condition
Food Deprivation ···································· X ···························		Greater Preference for Food
No Food Deprivation ······························ No X ·······················		Less Preference for Food

FIGURE 1–11.   An intervening variable, which is just called X for the moment, defined in terms of food preference.

food and eats. The other animal runs randomly to either side and does not eat. We might conclude that being hungry produced a change in the animal that led to a preference for food.

If this conclusion is set up as an intervening variable, there are (1) an **antecedent condition,** such as hours of deprivation and (2) a **consequent condition,** such as preference for food. Keeping such conditions as amount of prior experience in the apparatus constant, we define our intervening variable, which is shown diagrammatically in Figure 1–11.

The more hours of food deprivation, the greater X is, and the greater the preference for food. In this example, we have not yet attached a name to X, because the arbitrary term "X" really says all there is to say thus far. This example is so simple that hesitation in giving a name to the intervening variable may not make sense. In other situations the need for caution in naming an intervening variable begins to make more sense. Suppose that we frustrate a person (antecedent condition), so that the person acts aggressively (consequent condition). Can we then argue that frustration produces anger, which leads to an aggressive act? It might be that a person has just learned to act aggressively to get something without being angry at all. We need to be careful in assigning names to intervening variables and in using them at all. We do not want to imply something more or different than what we have defined operationally

Criteria for calling an intervening variable motivational.   At what point do we say that an intervening variable is a motivational variable rather than, say, learning or fatigue? The criterion is this: **If a difference in the level of an intervening variable, X, is related to a difference in preference, persistence, or vigor of behavior, the intervening variable is motivational.** Depending on the nature of the difference, the variable might be classified as **desire** or **aversion.** Other variables, such as learning or fatigue, would be defined differently.

Desire and Aversion as Intervening Variables

The hedonic axiom.   All theories start from some very basic assumptions. The first assumption here is that, at any given moment, there is an ordering of events along a continuum ranging from very aversive, through neutral, through very desirable. This is called the **hedonic continuum.** The

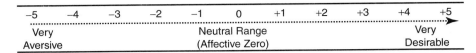

−5	−4	−3	−2	−1	0	+1	+2	+3	+4	+5

| Very | | | | Neutral Range | | | | | Very | |
| Aversive | | | | (Affective Zero) | | | | | Desirable | |

FIGURE 1–12. Hedonic continuum and hedonic axiom. Objects or events can be placed on the hedonic continuum from very aversive to very desirable (illustrated with the arbitrary numbering from −5 to +5). According to the hedonic axiom, organisms strive to move from more aversive to less aversive conditions and/or to gain more positive conditions.

hedonic continuum may vary from one organism to another or for the same organism from one time to another. At any given moment, however, it is assumed to be fixed. Our second assumption is the **Hedonic Axiom,** which states that **organisms direct their behaviors to minimize aversive outcomes and maximize desirable outcomes.** This axiom has been held by all hedonic theorists, from ancient times on up to P. T. Young (1961) and Frank Irwin (1971), whom we follow most closely. According to the hedonic axiom, organisms always make choices in favor of the direction of the arrow, as shown in Figure 1–12.

The concepts of desire and aversion both hinge on the idea of **neutrality,** or **affective zero.** If a behavioral outcome, *A*, is preferred to a neutral outcome, then *A* is desirable. If a neutral outcome is preferred to *A*, then *A* is aversive.

Symbolically, where > means "is preferred to":

If *A* > neutral, then *A* is desirable
But, if neutral > *A*, then *A* is aversive

Obviously, then, the fact that something is preferred does not necessarily mean that it is desirable. Suppose we have made preference tests for six different foods and found the order of preference from *A* to *F*, with *A* the most preferred and *F* the least preferred. Which of the outcomes are desirable, and which are aversive? This question can be answered only with reference to a neutral point. In Figure 1–13 a neutral point has been inserted, and we can see that *D, E,* and *F* are aversive and that *A, B,* and *C* are desirable.

In another example consider how we might be misled if we uncritically equate preference with desire. An instructor teaches a course that every semester has a high enrollment. He concludes that he is a superb instructor teaching a fascinating course. His course is obviously desirable because students flock to it in preference to all the other courses they might take. Then the requirements for a major are changed, and the course enrollment plunges. His course had not really been very desirable to most students; instead, it had only been preferred to a more aversive alternative, not graduating. With reference to the diagram, his course might have been *E*, taken in preference to *F*. With the new requirements, even a mildly aversive course is preferable.

The critical question for determining desire and aversion, then, is this: In very concrete and specific terms, how do we find a neutral point or zone of

Preference Test:	F	E		D		C			B	A	
−5	−4	−3	−2	−1	0	+1	+2	+3	+4	+5
Very Aversive				Neutral Range (Affective Zero)					Very Desirable	

FIGURE 1–13. Preference alone does not tell us whether something is desirable or aversive. We can determine this only in relation to some neutral point. A desirable object is preferred to neutral, but an aversive object is less preferred than neutral. *D* is preferred to *E*, but *D* is still aversive.

neutrality in a real situation? In many situations, including the example just given, perhaps we cannot. We cannot change a curriculum structure just to answer such a question (although we might find some other ways to answer it). Technical difficulty in determining a neutral point is not a fatal flaw in the definitions of desire and aversion, however, and in research we can overcome the difficulty. Figure 1–14 illustrates a classic problem in choice, a rat turning right or left in a T-maze. We can operationally define desire and aversion in terms of this situation.

Operationally defining desire and aversion. There are two possible outcomes in this situation, 01 and 02, which occur when the rat turns either left or right. The rat has chosen 02, which follows the right turn. What we don't know is *why* the animal has chosen to turn right. There are several possible explanations: 02 is less aversive than 01, 01 is aversive and 02 desirable, or 01 is desirable and 02 more desirable. If we can establish a neutral point, we can distinguish among these alternatives. Establishing a neutral point is done as follows:

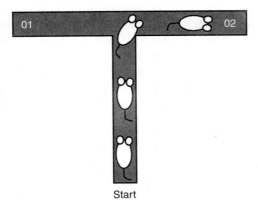

Start

FIGURE 1–14. Why does the rat turn right? All we know at the moment is that 02 is preferred to 01. The motivational problem is to determine the difference between 02 and 01, which will tell us why.

- **Neutrality.** First, we determine that the rat is indifferent between outcomes O1 and O2 at the beginning of the experiment, shown by its turning left or right equally often. For example, we could put it into the empty maze several times and record its choices. No matter which choice the animal makes, the outcome is essentially neutral, in that the two goal boxes are empty. And even if the two choices are not exactly neutral, their outcomes are *equal*, such as getting out of the maze. Let us assume that the rat is indifferent between the outcomes of the two choices: O1 = O2 = Neutral. We can then define desire and aversion as outcomes.

- **Desire: An outcome is desirable if it is preferred to a neutral outcome or some other already-known desirable outcome.** If without changing the left side (O1), we added food to the right side (O2) and the animal preferred O2 over a number of test trials, then we could conclude that the food is desirable. Food (O2) is preferred to the neutral outcome (O1).

- **Aversion: An outcome is aversive if a neutral or less aversive outcome is preferred to it.** If we put electric shock in the floor of the left side, without changing the right side, and if the animal prefers to go to right side, we can conclude that the left side (O1) is aversive because a neutral outcome (O2) is preferred to it.

Other measures of motivation.   We have taken preference as the behavioral measure for defining desire and aversion. For practical purposes, however, other correlated measures may be more useful, such as speed, vigor, or persistence in responding. The different measures are not always highly correlated, however, because more than one variable can influence a measure. For example, if an animal were already responding as quickly as possible, giving it a more desirable reward could not increase its response speed. A measure of preference, however, could show that the new reward is more desirable.

As Atkinson and Birch (1978) have argued, we cannot take any single behavior in isolation from other behaviors. A child washing dishes is easily tempted away by ice cream, but a child playing a favorite game may be harder to lure with ice cream. Much motivational research, especially with animals, has not been approached with such multiple responses in mind, perhaps because arousal and vigor of behavior have been considered *the* important motivational problems, not the choice of behaviors. A response like running in an alleyway provides little opportunity for shifts in activity or preference since it offers little opportunity for alternative behaviors. Multiple response measures have been elegantly discussed by Atkinson and Birch (1978), as well as by Premack (1971).

Vigor of response (such as speed or force) may also be difficult to interpret because it can be part of what is learned. Even the rat will run or lever-press fast or slow if it is selectively rewarded for responding fast or slow (Logan, 1960). Capaldi and Davidson (1979) even got rats to run more rapidly with a short period of food deprivation than with a long period. They just did not reward the rats with food if they ran too vigorously when very hungry. The rats learned to take it easy when they were most hungry.

Desire and aversion as classes of variables.   Many different operationally defined concepts can be put under the broad headings of desire or aversion. But this is not to say that they are all the same concepts or subject to manipulations of the same variables. For example, sweet food, sex objects, and good music may all be desirable and approached, but they are hardly the same thing otherwise. Similarly, pain, foul odors, and screechy noises are aversive, but not otherwise identical. The following list illustrates some motivational concepts that fit under the umbrellas of desire and aversion:

DESIRE	AVERSION
need for achievement	fear of failure
positive incentives	negative incentives
rewards	punishers
cognitive consistency	cognitive dissonance
love	fear
hope for power	fear of power
relaxation	stress

Motives are hierarchical.   Each of us strives towards some goals more persistently than towards others. If such goals are ranked in order of importance, there is a *hierarchy of motives.* The concept of a motivational hierarchy was popularized by Abraham Maslow (1970), who argued that motives are ordered from more basic to less basic as follows: (1) physiological (hunger, etc.), (2) safety, (3) belongingness and love, (4) esteem (e.g., achievement), and (5) self-actualization (fulfilling one's unique potential, whatever it may be). The concept of a hierarchy is precisely what the hedonic continuum represents: The ordering of outcomes from left to right is a hierarchy of desirability. Harder to accept are Maslow's stipulations that higher level needs do not come into play until lower needs are satisfied, and that the same hierarchy applies to all individuals. There is little evidence for either of these assertions. But it is arguable that each individual has her or his own hierarchy of motives. For example, a student wishing strongly to graduate from college would choose activities that lead to this goal or that at least do not conflict with it. Similarly, a presidential candidate may select every behavior for years with the goal of the presidency always in mind. Such goals can change, and rearrangement of hierarchies occurs, but for some people there are indeed long-persistent, highly dominant goals.

SUMMARY

1. Motivation is a **theoretical concept** that accounts for why people (or animals) choose to engage in particular behaviors at particular times. Our basic motivational premise is that organisms approach goals or engage in activities that are expected to have desirable outcomes and that they avoid activities that are expected to have unpleasant or aversive outcomes. This is psychological hedonism.

2. It is necessary to have psychological theory if we wish to use psychology to explain particular events. **A theory is a like a map;** it represents real things and events in the world, and relates these things to each other by a set of rules.

3. Theories are "good" to the extent that they are testable, fruitful (generate new ideas and research), simple, and comprehensive.

4. Psychologists assume that behavior is determined by causes that can potentially be known. We cannot freely choose to do anything we wish at any given time. This assumption underlies every science. Some causes are internal, however, and difficult to discover or analyze.

5. A fundamental question concerns the relationship between mind and body. We assume that mind is the functioning of the body (brain). **The mind is what the brain does.** According to neural identity theory, for every conscious mental event, there is a corresponding brain event. Not every brain event has a corresponding event in consciousness, however.

6. It is important to use language as precisely as possible. **Semiotic,** one type of linguistic analysis, involves **syntactics** (the rules for relating signs to each other, as in grammar), **semantics** (the relations of signs to objects, the definitions of signs), and **pragmatics** (relations of signs to their users).

7. **Operational definitions** define concepts in terms of the procedures (operations) used to *measure* the concepts. For example, aggression may be defined as the number of times one child pushes another on the playground.

8. Objectivity is the extent to which different observers *agree* about observations of the same events. Explanation is the application of general principles to account for specific events. A cause is a verbal statement of what is perceived to be a unique set of conditions preceding some observed event.

9. Defining motivation is made more complicated by the fact that there are different approaches to motivation. Two of these are the **regulatory** approach (emphasizing the body's physiological reactions to such disruptive forces as hunger) and the **purposive** approach (emphasizing the goal-directed nature of behavior). These different approaches are rooted in different historical backgrounds.

10. Motivational variables are defined as **intervening variables,** explained by antecedent and consequent conditions, in order to avoid circular definitions, which only give behavior a different name. There are experimentally defined and psychometrically defined intervening variables. The former use experimental manipulations as antecedent conditions, and the latter use measurements of behavior as antecedent conditions (e.g., test scores).

11. Two major **classes** of motivational variables are **desire** and **aversion.** Desire is defined as a preference for a behavior whose outcome is more preferred than a neutral outcome. Aversion is defined as a preference for a behavior whose outcome is less preferred than a neutral outcome. Many different specifically defined motivational intervening variables may fall within these two classes.

12. The **hedonic axiom** states that organisms work to minimize aversive outcomes and to maximize desirable outcomes. It is an objective and empirical question whether an outcome is desirable or aversive, however, and not a subjective decision on the part of an observer.

13. **Preference** is considered the most basic motivational index, but **persistence** and **vigor** of behavior are often correlated with preference and, under particular conditions, may be better measures.

CHAPTER TWO

Emotional Foundations of Motivation

——•——

INTRODUCTION AND HISTORICAL BACKGROUND

In Chapter One we operationally defined desire and aversion as motivational concepts, and described how we would use these terms and concepts in a preference situation. Desire and aversion can be used as objective terms and do not depend on subjective reports of liking and disliking. The very selection of the words *desire* and *aversion,* however, adds what the philosophers call **surplus meaning** to the concepts. These words imply a relationship between motivation and emotion. This chapter begins to clarify this relationship by examining emotion broadly. We conclude by indicating how emotion relates to motivation throughout the rest of the text.

Philosophical Background

Throughout the history of Western thought, philosophers have asked, Why do people choose to act the way they do? Socrates in the fourth century B.C. taught that people do what they perceive to be the right thing to do, that is, a rational analysis of a situation automatically leads a person to do the right thing. It may be difficult to determine what the right thing is, as the sometimes tortured Socratic dialogues show, but reason ultimately prevails. Such passions as love and hate only cloud our reason.

Other Greek philosophers, such as Epicurus and Aristotle, argued that reason alone is not enough to determine behavior. They believed that we act to maximize our pleasure and minimize our discomfort. Reason helps us to determine whether our actions will be to our benefit (pleasure) or harm (discomfort). This hedonistic, emotional approach carried forward to Thomas Hobbes and Alexander Bain in the seventeenth and nineteenth centuries and into contemporary psychology. It therefore behooves us to give some attention to emotion theory and research. As we shall see, emotion is regaining its previously central role in motivation theory.

Wundt and Titchener

Early scientific psychologists often looked at emotion as a *content* of experience, to be studied by introspection. Research subjects, often the experimenters themselves, "looked into their own minds" and reported what they were aware of. Wilhelm Wundt, the man credited with founding the first psychology laboratory in 1879, proposed a tridimensional theory of emotion. He said that all emotional experiences could be produced by some appropriate combination of feelings of pleasant-unpleasant, tension-relaxation, and excitement-depression.

Edward B. Titchener, the Englishman who carried Wundt's psychology to the United States, argued that the single dimension of pleasant-unpleasant was sufficient to describe the totality of emotional experience. Affections (emotions) had several attributes in common with sensory experiences, such as quality, intensity, and duration. The affects were vague, however, whereas sensations could be sharp and clear. Titchener's student, Paul Thomas Young (1936, 1961), carried the concept of emotion into the contemporary realm of American motivation theory. Young's basic tenet was that organisms work to "maximize delight and minimize distress."

James and Lange

It was William James in the 1880s who really started the ball rolling, however. The common view that emotion is aroused in us by some event and that we then act in accordance with the emotion is wrong, he said. It is wrong to say that we run because we are afraid. Instead, according to James (1884), **emotion is the perception of bodily changes that have already occurred in response to an event.** That is, our response to an emotion-arousing situation (such as running away) comes *before* the emotional experience. The emotional experience is the perception of the response to the situation. To use his famous example, we do not see a bear, become afraid, and then run. Rather, we see the bear, run, and then are afraid. The emphasis is on the response to the bear, which might be only the physiological arousal that we identify as fear, without running. Just as physiological and behavioral responses to a situation may be variable from person to person, so may the details of emotional experience. James especially emphasized the sympathetic nervous system and the visceral responses it controls, such as heart rate, blood pressure, perspiration, and gastrointestinal functions. James did *not* deny the importance of skeletal muscular movements and the perception of them, but over a period of time, his theory became identified almost solely with visceral activity. A Danish physiologist, Carl Lange (1885), proposed a similar theory, restricted to vascular system changes. The theory has since been known as the James-Lange theory. Recently, Robert Zajonc (Zajonc, 1985; Zajonc, Murphy, & Inglehart, 1989) has revitalized the idea that the vascular system is critical to emotion.

The immediate importance of the James-Lange theory was that, since it made emotion dependent on specific identifiable portions of the body, it seemed to be testable by use of the surgical techniques available at the time. One could cut the sympathetic nervous system, which lies outside the spinal cord and brain, with a scalpel and then observe whether animals still behaved emotionally. Figure 2–1 shows the brain, sympathetic nervous system, and viscera. It also followed from James's theory that different emotional experiences have their unique physiological counterparts; otherwise, emotions would be indistinguishable. This has been referred to as the **identity theory of emotion;** there is a one-to-one relation between experienced emotion and physiology. In one sense, this relation is axiomatic. If we can tell the difference between two events, there must be bodily differences between the two events, reflected in the activity of the brain. Saying this, however, is not the same thing as doing the research to demonstrate it is so.

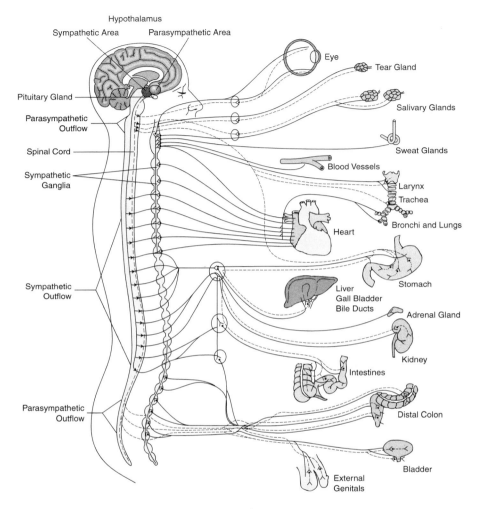

FIGURE 2–1. The autonomic nervous system and the body organs it controls. The limbic system is a set of brain structures surrounding the hypothalamus. (Reprinted from Krech, Crutchfield, & Livson, 1970. Copyright 1970 by Alfred A. Knopf. Used by permission.)

Cannon and Bard

The inevitable attack on James' theory of emotion came from Walter Cannon (1927), who proposed the following five arguments against James:

1. Separating the viscera from the nervous system does not change emotional behavior.

2. The same visceral changes occur in different emotional states as well as in such nonemotional states as violent activity.
3. The viscera are relatively insensitive structures.
4. Visceral changes occur too slowly (a matter of seconds) to be the source of sudden emotional changes.
5. Artificial induction of the visceral changes typical of strong emotions does not produce these same strong emotions.

Cannon's alternative proposal was a **central neural theory,** supported by research in Philip Bard's laboratory. Cannon suggested that neural impulses from the sense organs, flowing into the thalamus (not at that time clearly distinguished from the hypothalamus), were experienced as emotion as they were routed "upstream" to the cortex, and slightly later produced visceral changes as they were routed "downstream" to the autonomic nervous system and viscera. In other words, neural activity in the brain alone is sufficient to produce emotional experience. This view contrasts with James's view that such impulses first excite the viscera and that feedback from the viscera to the cortex is experienced as emotion.

Cannon's own arguments have since been criticized. In some of the experiments he cited, it is not clear that all the connections between viscera and nervous system had actually been severed. Furthermore, these experiments were with animals, usually dogs. But James had said that emotional **experience** was produced by feedback from the viscera, but not necessarily that emotional **behavior** was so produced. This distinction made the relevance of the animal research questionable. There have been several relevant studies with humans, however. Hohmann (1966) reported that amount of spinal cord damage was correlated with amount of loss of emotional experience. This finding seemed to support James. Two more recent studies with better methodology have contradicted Hohmann's results, though. In both studies, patients with severe cord damage and very limited body feeling commonly reported experiencing emotions even *more* intensely than they had prior to their injuries (Chwalisz, Diener, & Gallagher, 1988; Bermond, Nieuwenhuyse, Fasotti, & Schuerman, 1991). This finding lends more support to Cannon than to James, since it indicates that the many visceral responses that typically occur during emotion-arousing situations are not absolutely necessary for experienced emotion.

Elizabeth Duffy

Elizabeth Duffy (1934) argued that emotion consists of mobilization of energy of the body for strong activity. Energy mobilization **is** emotion. This view is similar to what Cannon called the **emergency theory of emotion,** preparation of the body for fight or flight. Duffy's premise was that behavior can be described in terms of its **direction** (approaching or avoiding objects or situations) and **intensity** (fast or slow, vigorous or sluggish). The most important departure from previous theories was that Duffy did not deal with "desire" and "aversion" or "pleasantness" and "unpleasantness," but only with the direction and intensity of *behavior.* This approach was subsequently picked up by the activation theorists in the 1950s, who argued that the amount of neural activity in the brainstem determined emotion (e.g., Lindsley, 1951). Chapter 5 discusses activation theory in more detail.

The Papez Circuit and the Kluver-Bucy Syndrome

In 1937 two monumental publications changed our way of looking at the neuroanatomy of emotion (Kluver & Bucy, 1937; Papez, 1937). James Papez, in a masterful integration of much seemingly unrelated evidence, theorized that a set of pathways in the core of the brain constitute the neural circuitry underlying emotional experience and behavior. This **Papez circuit** (now generally referred to as the **limbic system,** Figure 2–2) runs from the **hippocampus** via the **fornix** to the **anterior thalamus,** then to the **cingulate cortex,** the **amygdala,** and back to the hippocampus. This emotional circuitry is buried deep inside all mammalian brains, and it accounts for most of the brain mass of reptiles. The more recently evolved brain structures, such as the neocortex, may exert control over the primitive limbic systems, but the Papez circuit may still not be fully adapted to life in modern civilization (Malmo, 1975). The brain mechanisms that evolved for such strong actions as fight or flight in primitive animals still produce strong physiological arousal in civilized people in situations in which strong action is inappropriate. Such arousal, if maintained for a long time, is stressful and may produce health problems.

About the same time that Papez's work became known, Heinrich Kluver and Paul Bucy (1937) described the effects of experimentally removing the temporal lobes of rhesus monkeys. In particular, after damage to the hippocampus and amygdala, they found the following bizarre pattern of behavior that is now known as the **Kluver-Bucy Syndrome:**

1. A "psychic blindness," in which the animals apparently could not remember things visually, although there was no apparent damage to the primary visual system.
2. Heightened orality, which consisted of licking, biting, chewing, or touching with the lips almost everything with which they came into contact.
3. A strong tendency to respond to all visual stimuli indiscriminately and compulsively.
4. A disappearance or great reduction of reactions usually associated with fear and anger.
5. A great increase in sexual activity, including masturbation and attempts to mate with members of other species.

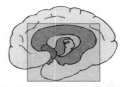

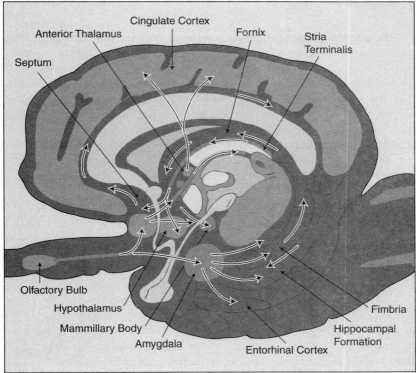

FIGURE 2–2. Schematic and simplified representation of the limbic system. (From Carlson, 1987. Copyright © 1987 by Allyn and Bacon, Inc. Used by permission.)

This syndrome was unexpected because no one previously had any idea that the temporal lobes were involved in such a diversity of motivational, emotional, and perceptual functions. Half a century later it appears that most of these effects actually resulted from damage to the amygdala and reflect a general loss of ability to attach emotional significance to objects (LeDoux, 1993). The point, however, is that whereas earlier emotion research had been predominantly concerned with the autonomic nervous system, the groundwork was now laid for study of the role of the "reptilian brain" in the control of emotion.

CONTEMPORARY STUDY OF EMOTION

Structure of Affect

The term **affect** refers to experiences that have the quality of being either pleasant or unpleasant. We may then define three different aspects of affective experience, as follows.

Temperament.   Temperament refers to very stable tendencies toward certain kinds of affective experience. These tendencies endure over years, suggesting a genetic basis (Goldsmith, 1993; Oatley & Jenkins, 1996). The most notable genetic tendency is along a dimension of introversion/extraversion, or shy versus outgoing. Children who at an early age are recognized as withdrawn tend to remain so throughout life (Kagan, Reznick, & Snidman, 1988). Genetic studies suggest that something between 25 percent and 50 percent of the variability in extraversion across people is genetically determined. Personality and temperament are not totally unchangeable, but there are clear enduring tendencies (see Chapters Three and Twelve for related discussions).

Moods.   Moods are typically characterized as being relatively weak but pervasive affective experiences, without a specific recognized object, and relatively enduring (e.g., minutes to hours). We may "get out of bed on the wrong side" and be irritable for half the day or have a "blue Monday." These moods are a low-level background of affect that "color" our thoughts and behaviors. Indeed, we may not ourselves recognize that we are in a "bad mood" until it is pointed out to us. Moods are often researched in terms of their being positive or negative, usually referring to happy and sad, but also to other moods. Positive moods may include elation and tranquillity, whereas negative moods may include sadness, irritation, and anxiousness.

Emotions.   In contrast to temperament or moods, emotions are typically described as relatively brief and stronger, and as having some specific object toward which there is a tendency to act (approach or avoid). We are happy *with* someone, sad *about* something, angry *at* someone, or afraid *of* something.

Emotions as Intervening Variables

Following the outline of how to define concepts in Chapter One, we may think theoretically of emotions as intervening variables so that we can avoid the problem of circular definitions and can distinguish among various emotions as objectively as possible. For example, in William James's illustration, if a person sees a bear (antecedent condition) and his heart rate accelerates and he runs away (consequent conditions), we may infer that he is afraid (emotion). If a person sees a bear and approaches the bear, we would infer that either he is not afraid or that he has some more powerful reason to approach the bear. (In June 1998 a mother hiking in Big Bend (Texas) State Park with her three children held off an attacking cougar with a knife as they slowly worked their way back to their car. The mother's concern for her children kept her from running away.) The way that we distinguish among different emotions and determine their different characteristics is by analyzing antecedent and consequent conditions. Table 2–1 summarizes some antecedent and consequent conditions that define different emotions. This table is not

TABLE 2–1. Potential antecedent and consequent conditions used to define emotions as intervening variables. We may commonly think of these as causes and effects of emotion. The table is intended to show how we go about distinguishing emotions, not to indicate that the list of emotional names is the list that all theorists would use.

ANTECEDENT CONDITIONS	INTERVENING VARIABLES	CONSEQUENT CONDITIONS
WHAT CAUSES A PARTICULAR EMOTION?	WHAT EMOTIONS ARE DEFINED BY ANTECEDENT AND CONSEQUENT CONDITIONS?	WHAT ARE THE EFFECTS OF EMOTIONS?
Environmental Events Home team's winning ball game Sight of loved one Snarling dog Loss of fortune Sight of someone throwing up **Cognitive Events** Memories Evaluations of events **Body Changes** Biochemical changes (e.g., drugs) Fatigue Disease Physical activity (e.g., running)	**Positive Emotions** Happiness Interest Surprise Sexual arousal Love **Negative Emotions** Fear Sadness Anger Disgust	**Feelings** Verbal self-report scales **Behaviors** **Expressive Behaviors** Facial expressions Body language **Approach/Avoidance** **Task Performance** Work Sport **Cognitive Processes** Attention Thinking Learning Memory **Physiologic Events** Central nervous system Autonomic nervous system Neurohormones (e.g., endorphins) Neurotransmitters (e.g., dopamine, adrenaline, noradrenaline, etc.)

meant to be exhaustive; its purpose is to show how we can organize our thinking about emotion in such a way that we can see what questions about emotion become important.

The Measurement of Emotion

Verbal behavior.   We cannot feel other people's feelings, but we can record what they say about their emotional experiences. Psychotherapists use this approach extensively, as did early scientific psychologists in their laboratories. Modern researchers also use psychological tests and scales as somewhat more quantifiable indicators of emotional experience. Verbal behavior is subject to many biases, however, and has to be assessed cautiously. The research subject, the clinical patient, and the person-on-the-street often may say what they think is expected or is socially desirable, rather than just what is felt. That is, words may not accurately convey a person's felt emotion or may indicate emotion when there is none.

Nonverbal behavior.   This is any behavior, besides talking, that a person or animal might engage in that can readily be seen by the naked eye, such as changing facial expression or making particular body movements. If I clench my fist, someone watching me could infer that I am angry. There is the possibility of error, though; I might have clenched my fist for emphasis while speaking. We have to be just as careful in interpreting behaviors as we are with speech.

The study of escape and avoidance behavior in animals is particularly useful because these are analogous to many human "neurotic" behaviors. Animals can, for example, learn to avoid electric shock in an experimental apparatus and may successfully do so for hundreds of trials. We would surely be astounded at seeing an animal compulsively moving back and forth in an apparatus if we came upon it without knowing its history. If we know how a behavior came to be learned, however, the behavior makes sense, and we can form ideas about how to change it. Psychologists have long been concerned with giving accounts of adult neurosis so that the "strange" behavior of humans could be as understandable as the behavior of persistently avoiding rats. Classical conditioning of "emotional" responses has also been extensively studied.

Physiology.   A large number of physiological activities and anatomical locations have been described in relation to emotion and motivation, as indicated in Table 2–1. Although most of the body changes related to emotion are impossible to observe with the naked eye, many are observable with the aid of electronic amplification. The most common measures of emotion are (1) heart rate; (2) blood pressure; (3) galvanic skin response, an increase in the electrical conductivity of the skin during emotional arousal; (4) respiration (breathing) rate; (5) blood volume change, easily recorded at the tips of the fingers; (6) perspiration; (7) muscle tension, measured by means of electrodes placed over specific muscles; and (8) skin temperature, an indirect measure of blood flow, through the fingers, for example. Just as with verbal or behavioral measures, physiological measures have to be interpreted with caution. One major concern is that such measures are not unique to emotion; all these measures also increase with such body activity as running. Other useful measures, such as of hormone levels, can be obtained from blood and urine samples. With animals, experimental surgery is also possible. Moreover, human brain damage from accidents or disease occurs with such frequency that we can learn a great deal about emotion from clinical cases.

THE BIOLOGY OF EMOTION

At this point we describe in general terms some of the anatomy and physiology of the nervous system that is important for both motivation and emotion. In later chapters we go into more specific details in relation to such particular topics as hunger, thirst, aggressive behavior, and stress.

Divisions of the Nervous System

Table 2–2 outlines the divisions of the nervous system. The nervous system is divided into **central** (brain and spinal cord) and **peripheral** portions (everything else). It is also divided into **somatic** and **autonomic** portions. The somatic nervous system regulates interactions with the environment: sensory inputs and muscle movements.

The **autonomic nervous system** (ANS) is particularly important for emotion. It regulates internal body activities involved in maintaining and replenishing the body. Also, it controls heart muscle, the smooth muscle of the body cavity, such as stomach and intestines, and the release of hormones from glands such as the pituitary and adrenal glands. The **parasympathetic** portion of the ANS is concerned with digestive activity. The **sympathetic**

TABLE 2–2. Divisions of the nervous system. The somatic nervous system is involved in interactions with the external environment. The autonomic system is more involved with the regulation of the internal activity and chemistry of the body.

	SOMATIC	AUTONOMIC
Central	Brain and spinal cord	Limbic system, hypothalamus, and brain stem
Peripheral	Nerves to skeletal muscles and from sense organs	Sympathetic, parasympathetic

portion of the ANS is concerned with emergency functions, such as preparation of the body for fight or flight (Cannon, 1939a). The intense activity we feel in our bodies when we are very active, angry, or frightened reflects the activity of the sympathetic nervous system and the arousal of the internal organs.

The parasympathetic and sympathetic systems (see Figure 2–1) each affect every visceral organ and are generally antagonistic to each other. When the sympathetic system is strongly aroused, the parasympathetic system is relatively suppressed, and vice versa. We thus understand why we have indigestion when we are upset: The sympathetic system partly suppresses the parasympathetic system, which controls digestion.

We commonly speak of "adrenaline flowing" during excitement. This and related hormones are circulated through the body via the bloodstream. They are also released from nerve endings in the sympathetic system. This double-barreled action produces both quick and widespread arousal, which prepares the body for emergency activity. This preparation includes the release of blood sugar into the body, more rapid breathing, quicker circulation of oxygen, and perspiration for cooling. Continued emotional arousal over a long time may produce the so-called psychosomatic or stress diseases discussed in a later chapter.

Hemispheric Differences in Emotion

It is well established that there are reliable differences in the functioning of the right and the left cerebral hemispheres of humans. Speech, for example, is almost always localized in the left hemisphere. As a generalization, the left hemisphere is concerned with such sequential, analytic activities as language. The right hemisphere is relatively more concerned with "holistic impressions," a more immediate grasp of a spatial situation. The right hemisphere also controls emotion recognition and expression better than the left (Kalat, 1988; Rinn, 1984). If a humorous visual stimulus is presented to the right hemisphere but not to the left, a research subject may smile but will not be able to say why she is smiling. The emotional quality of the stimulus has been detected by the right hemisphere but cannot be put into language, since the left hemisphere has not gotten the information. Lesions in the right hemisphere, but not the left, impair the ability of the affected person to detect emotion in other people. There is still some controversy about such generalizations, however (Leventhal & Tomarken, 1986).

It may be that both hemispheres contribute to emotion, but in different ways. This possibility is suggested by evidence that there is right hemisphere dominance for negative emotions and left hemisphere dominance for positive emotions. Thus, left hemisphere damage or sedation by a drug injected into the hemisphere is associated with excessive worry, pessimism, and crying. Conversely, right hemisphere damage or suppression is associated with euphoria or laughing (Tucker, 1981). It is now clear that there are right and left hemisphere differences ("asymmetries") in brain wave activity related to positive and negative affect (Davidson, 1994; Tomarken, Davidson, Wheeler, & Doss, 1992; Jacobs & Snyder, 1996; Spence, Shapiro, & Zaidel, 1996; but also see Collet & Duclaux, 1986). These differences are shown by people with different personality characteristics, such as extraversion versus introversion, and are demonstrated with experimental manipulations of positive versus negative affect. Harmon-Jones and Allen (1998) point out that positive affect and approach motivation usually occur together, so it is possible that approach and withdrawal tendencies are being confounded with positive and negative affect in this type of research. In support, they found that self-report measures of anger, usually considered a negative affect, were correlated with left frontal EEG activity but that measures of positive and negative affect were not. A characteristic of anger is that it is related to approach, but not for the same reason that food or a loved one is approached. In any case, studies of hemispheric differences help us to clarify the nature of emotion.

THEORIES OF EMOTION

Discrete Emotion Theories

The number of emotion-related words in the English language runs into the thousands. The richness of poetic description depends partly on the use of many emotion words differing in sound, number of syllables, and other linguistic characteristics. Obviously, however, not all of these words represent different emotions. Many of the words are synonyms (e.g., joy, ecstacy), and others represent different intensities of the same emotions (e.g., irritation, anger, rage, fury). Discrete emotion theories assume that there is some small number of core emotions and that emotion words apply to these core emotions and their combinations. The core emotions are thought to be specific, biologically determined emotional responses whose expression and recognition is fundamentally the same for all individuals and peoples. This is a Darwinian evolutionary viewpoint running counter to many previously accepted notions of cultural anthropologists who argued for culture-specific emotions.[1] The number of such emotions is in the range of seven to ten, depending on the particular theory (e.g., Ekman & Oster, 1979; Izard, 1977; Plutchik, 1980; Tomkins, 1981). Table 2–3 shows the discrete emotions identified by various theorists. The particular emotions proposed by modern theories are not much different than those proposed by René Descartes in the seventeenth century or Charles Darwin in the nineteenth. The evolutionary argument is that particular emotions and their expressions have survived in

[1]Paul Ekman has commented on this history in the recently published third edition of Charles Darwin's *The Expression of the Emotions in Man and Animals* (Darwin, 1998).

TABLE 2–3.   Discrete emotions according to several theorists.

IZARD	TOMPKINS	EKMAN	PLUTCHIK
1. Interest-excitement	Interest	—	Expectancy
2. Joy	Joy	Happiness	Joy
3. Surprise	Startle	Surprise	Surprise
4. Distress-Anguish	Distress	Sadness	Sadness
5. Anger-Rage	—	Anger	Anger
6. Disgust	—	Disgust	Disgust
7. Contempt-Scorn	—	Contempt	—
8. Fear-Terror	Fear	Fear	Fear
9. Shame-Shyness	—	—	—
10. Guilt	—	—	—
11. —	Laughter	—	—
12. —	—	—	Acceptance

the progression of animal development because they have adaptive value. Darwin's contribution was to show the cross-species similarities and suggest principles to account for the continued presence of these emotions.

Sylvan Tomkins (1962, 1981), to whom many contemporary discrete emotion theorists recognize an intellectual debt, argued that the genetically programmed emotional responses serve to amplify biological need states. He says, for example, that an animal or a person may *detect* hunger or thirst but that this recognition is just a cue to produce emotion, and it is the emotion that "energizes" behaviors for getting food or water. Need states do not directly energize behavior except insofar as they are amplified by emotions. This finding clearly indicates one theorist's view of the link between motivation and emotion. Two of Tomkins's students, Paul Ekman (e.g., 1994) and Carroll Izard (1991) have been highly productive researchers and supporters of the discrete emotions approach (although not necessarily of all the details of Tomkins's theory).

Robert Plutchik's (1980) approach to discrete emotions has been more directly evolutionary than most. He noted that most "definitions" of emotion depend on the reader's already knowing what is to be "defined." That is, if the reader's emotional experience corresponds to some particular description of an emotion, the emotion is said to be defined for that reader. Plutchik tries to be more objective by approaching emotions from the evolutionary perspective. He proposes that common to all organisms, there are eight adaptive **behaviors** necessary for survival but that higher mammals also have **emotional** states corresponding to the behavioral activities. The specific terms for these activities are **functional** and do not necessarily refer to any specific form of movement. For example, a great number of different behaviors might be involved in the **protection** of oneself or one's offspring (note the earlier example of the woman defending her children from the cougar). Different behaviors might serve the same function, or the same behavior might serve different functions. Running, for example, might serve both approach and avoidance functions at different times.

Plutchik described each of the adaptive acts in terms of four different kinds of languages that psychologists use:

- **Subjective language** is the language of human introspection. For example, "I feel afraid" or "I am angry."
- **Behavioral language** refers to the behaviors we might observe in humans or other animals, from which we might infer a particular emotion.
- **Functional language** refers to the life-sustaining functions on which the theory is based, such as reproduction or protection.
- **Trait language** is that commonly used to describe personality characteristics, such as "He is timid" or "She is gregarious."

Evidence for Discrete Emotions

Facial expression in humans.   Figure 2–3 on page 48 shows six different posed emotional expressions. Can you identify them? Research on facial expressions goes back to the nineteenth century. Darwin himself (1872/1998) observed that many species show similar expressions of emotion. Dogs, cats, and monkeys draw back their lips and bare their teeth when angry, much as people do, and such emotional *displays* may replace actual fighting. In humans such displays are often pale reflections of those shown by lower animals, but the evolutionary relationship to our animal ancestors seems clear enough. In recent years facial-expression research has been dominated by the work of Paul Ekman and his colleagues (e.g., Ekman & Friesen, 1975; Ekman & Friesen, 1986). Evidence from such diverse cultures as preliterate mountain natives of New Guinea, as well as from more developed cultures, indicates universal recognition of expressions of **happiness, anger, sadness, disgust, surprise, fear,** and **contempt.** People who have neither seen Caucasians nor been exposed to photographs or television can correctly identify specific facial expressions as indicative of the emotions that a person in a story would express (Ekman & Friesen, 1971). Deaf and blind children also show the typical facial expressions for these emotions (Ekman & Oster, 1979). It has been suggested that emotional expressions may be universal because they are biologically valuable forms of communication for infants, arousing care-taking by adults.

Anatomy of facial expression.   Facial expressions are determined by contractions of muscles in the face that contort the skin to form the visible expression. It is possible to catalog the specific muscles that contract during different facial expressions. Once these are known, it is possible to distinguish spontaneous expressions from faked ones and to learn more about the details of emotion. Such a catalog has been developed by Ekman & Friesen (1978), in what they call the **Facial Action Coding System.** Figure 2–4 shows a

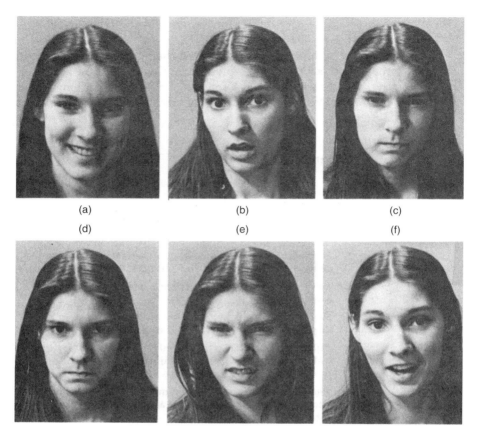

(a)   (b)   (c)

(d)   (e)   (f)

FIGURE 2–3. Facial expressions of emotion like those used in research on emotion. These six are common around the world. Can identify them?

(a) Happy, (b) fear/surprise, (c) anger, (d) sorrow, (e) disgust, (f) surprise/happy.

simplified diagram of some of the muscles that are important for the facial expression of emotion. The **frontalis** muscles produce wrinkles in the forehead; the **corrugator** muscles produce frowning eyebrows; the **orbicularis oculi** muscles produce the "crow's-feet" that characterize smiling; and the **zygomatic major** and **orbicularis orbis** muscles around the cheeks and mouth produce smiling. When we change moods from negative to positive, activity of the corrugators decreases, and activity of the zygomatic and orbicularis orbis increases (Cacioppo, Petty, Losch, & Kim, 1986). Not surprisingly, then, zygomatic activity is also greater during the presentation of sexual stimuli than of nonsexual stimuli (Sullivan & Bender, 1986). To what extent is facial expression a determinant of experienced emotion, as William James suggested? Can we make ourselves feel better by "putting on a happy face"?

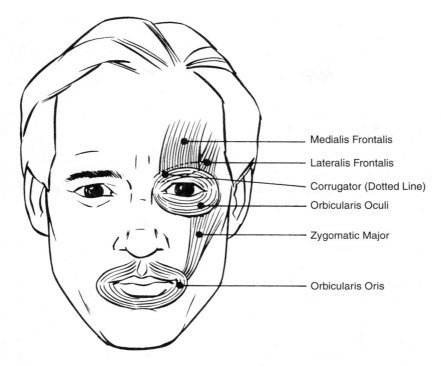

Medialis Frontalis
Lateralis Frontalis
Corrugator (Dotted Line)
Orbicularis Oculi
Zygomatic Major
Orbicularis Oris

FIGURE 2–4.   Important muscles involved in pleasant and unpleasant facial expressions.

The facial feedback hypothesis.   William James's theory of emotion stated that the experience of emotion is the perception of one's responses to the environment. This led him (1890) to consider whether actors, for example, actually felt the emotions that they were mimicking with their faces. He concluded that the evidence on the question was ambiguous, probably because the actors could not easily produce the appropriate visceral changes to go along with the facial expressions. Tomkins (1962) and Izard (1971) argued, however, that the facial musculature is complex enough that the feedback produced is adequate to produce the experience of different emotions. If this is true, then artificial manipulation of facial expressions should modify emotional experience.

Artificial manipulation of facial reactions has been studied with two different approaches, by directly manipulating facial muscles or by instructing subjects to express or hide a particular emotion (Leventhal & Tomarkan, 1986). Indirect manipulation has also been done by using such cues as "canned laughter" to facilitate such humorous responses as smiling and laughing. Laird (1974) reported that subjects instructed to frown also reported feeling aggressive in response to photographs but that smiles induced positive feelings toward the same photos. The evidence is ambiguous, however. Tourangeau and Ellsworth (1979) produced appropriate facial expressions of fear or sadness in their subjects, but these expressions did not affect the subjects' reports of their feelings while watching fearful or sad movies and did not produce any other physiological changes in the subject.

Leventhal and Tomarken (1986, p. 580) conclude that expressive changes can alter subjective states but that such effects are very small. Matsumoto (1987) analyzed the data from sixteen experiments on manipulation of facial expression and found that facial feedback accounts for only about 12 percent of the variation of reported emotional change. This 12 percent is equivalent to a correlation of .35, however, which is typically what researchers consider to be a meaningful correlation in personality research. Artificially manipulated facial feedback may not produce large changes in experienced emotion, but the effect seems to be as large as is found with many other variables in personality research.

Carroll and Russell (1997) have challenged the notion that specific facial muscles automatically mean certain emotions, at least as they are described by the FACS. They had subjects identify emotions portrayed by actors without regard to any particular muscles. Film clips of Academy Award winning performances were shown to subjects who were asked to identify the emotions being portrayed. There was a high amount of agreement about the portrayed emotions but except for upturned corners of the mouth for happiness, the facial musculature did not correspond to the Facial Action Coding System. This finding does not rule out the possibility of genetically determined responses for particular emotions but does call for more solid proof. Carroll and Russell (1996) also revived the old idea that facial expressions of emotion are judged by the context in which they appear. They found that "most observers judged the expresser [the person expressing the emotion to be judged] to be feeling the emotion anticipated from the situation rather than the one allegedly signaled by the face (p. 215)." They believe that any distinctive facial features are related only to pleasure and arousal. Aronoff, Woike, and Hyman, (1992) conducted several experiments indicating that anger is shown by diagonal facial features and happiness by rounded ones. Thus, a facial structure of \ / around the forehead and eyes suggests anger, where as O O suggests happiness. In a classical conditioning study in our laboratory (Beck & Godfrey, 1998), subjects anticipated that the \ / configuration was more likely to be followed by an aversive loud noise than was the O O configuration. Apparently they thought there was something relatively "bad" about the \ / configuration.

Emotional expression as social communication: Display rules.   Even if facial expressions of emotion were genetically programmed, there are variations. Ekman (1972) argues that these are due to cultural "display rules" that tell us when and how we *ought* to express grief, joy, and other emotions and that may therefore interfere with "basic" emotional expressions. Thus, if I win a lottery, I will feel happy and communicate that happiness. If I were to feel happy at someone else's misfortune, however, I probably would **not** want to communicate that joy and would try to mask it. Ekman and Oster (1979) reported that Japanese people watching a movie controlled their facial expressions if they knew they were being observed more than Americans did. The stereotypes of the "stoic" Britisher, the "inscrutable" Oriental, or the "excitable" Latin may have arisen because of such specific cultural influences on the expression of emotion. Overt expressions of emotion may be aroused more readily by social cues than by other events. Bowlers, hockey fans, and people strolling down the street were more likely to smile in response to other people than to cues regarding sports results that should have made them happy, such as good bowling scores (Kraut & Johnston, 1979). The concept of display rules has been criticized, however, as an attempt to save discrete emotions theory. Thus if a person shows some theoretically "appropriate" emotional response (e.g., facial expression), it is considered support for the theory. If the person does not show this, display rules are invoked to account for the failure to observe the "appropriate" response. The theory then becomes nearly untestable until we are given the rules which govern whether or not display rules are to be invoked.

Moderator variables also affect social communication. One such variable is the degree of spontaneity of expression. Spontaneous reactions to stimuli are stronger in terms of both facial expression and reported feelings than are artificial reactions. In fact, voluntary and involuntary (spontaneous) emotional responses appear to "originate" in different motor systems in the brain (Rinn, 1984). Involuntary emotional responses operate through the **extrapyramidal motor system** in the brain, and voluntary responses through the **pyramidal motor system.** A person with damage to the extrapyramidal system may laugh or cry uncontrollably, expressing emotion inappropriate to the situation. Voluntary expression of emotion, however, is not affected. Conversely, a person with pyramidal damage has difficulty making voluntary expressions of emotion but shows appropriate involuntary responses. This dual control system would account for the fact that there is sometimes **emotional leakage.** When people try to disguise their emotions (pyramidal control), their "true" emotion may still "leak" through in facial expression (extrapyramidal control). An angry person may try to hide his anger, but some component of the involuntary emotional response cannot be inhibited and leaks through so that the anger can be detected by others.

Development of facial expression.   The facial muscles of newborn humans are fully operative, and adultlike expressions occur early. In the first few hours of life, infants show expressions of distress, disgust, and startle. Imitation of adult facial expressions may occur as early as two or three weeks of age. At about three months, smiling begins to occur reliably, and infants begin to distinguish adult facial expressions and respond differently to them

(Ekman & Oster, 1979). Preschool children know most of the common facial expressions and what elicits them, although this knowledge continues to grow until at least age ten.

Dimensional Theories of Emotion

In contrast to the discrete emotion approach is the dimensional approach, exemplified by Wundt's theory. Wundt said that all emotional experiences could be considered as combinations of **pleasant-unpleasant, tense-relaxed,** and **excitement-depression.** Since Wundt's time, virtually every study of emotional expression or recognition looking for dimensions has found pleasant-unpleasant as the most important and level of arousal as the second most important. Several of these are summarized in Table 2–4. In this approach, emotions are described as lying somewhere along two or more dimensions of affect and can be located in a geometric space defined by those dimensions. Figure 2–5 (Russell, 1980) shows the data from one study. Because such emotion plots form a circle, such a geometric model is called a **circumplex model of emotion.**

Dimensions of emotion are discovered by studying similarities and differences in recognition of different facial expressions or in emotion words. In starting with many words or pictures representing emotions, the problem is to find a smaller number of threads running through these. For example, if the word *joy* is used similarly to the word *euphoria,* there is overlap in the meaning of the two words, and they do not represent entirely different emotions. When appropriate statistical analyses (such as factor analysis or multidimensional scaling) are applied to such data, we obtain sets of words that vary qualitatively (such as **good** versus **bad, pleasant** versus **unpleasant,** or **happy** versus **sad**). Other sets of words vary quantitatively (such as **irritation, anger,** and **rage,** which represent progressively stronger degrees of the same emotion).

TABLE 2–4.   Dimensions of emotion found by a number of different researchers.

NAME	DIMENSIONS		
	FIRST	SECOND	THIRD
Wundt (1902)	Pleasant-Unpleasant	Tense-Relaxed	Excitement-Depression
Titchner (1910)	Pleasant-Unpleasant	—	—
Schlosberg (1954)	Pleasant-Unpleasant	Tense-Relaxed	Acceptance-Rejection
Osgood, Suci, & Tannenbaum (1957)	Evaluative (Good-Bad)	Activity (Fast-Slow)	Potency (Strong-Weak)
Davitz (1970)*	Hedonic Tone (Comfort-Discomfort)	Activation	Competence
Russell and Mehrebian (1977)	Pleasure-Displeasure	Degree of arousal	Dominance-Submission

*Davitz also identified a fourth dimension that he termed "relatedness."

FIGURE 2–5. Russell's circumplex model of emotion. A representation of 28 emotion-related words on the two dimensions of pleasant-unpleasant and level of arousal. (From Russell, 1980, Figure 2. Copyright 1980 by the American Psychological Association. Reprinted by permission.)

Whether or not there are important emotional dimensions beyond pleasant-unpleasant and level of arousal is still unanswered. Thayer (1978) has distinguished two dimensions of arousal, not just one: **tense-relaxed** and **energetic-sleepy.** The former is characterized by the tension that builds up during a day full of hassles, following which a person may just want to relax. The latter is characteristic of hard work or play, following which a person is sleepy. Other researchers have reported other dimensions as the third. One such dimension, which may be called **control-lack of control,** has appeared under such names as **competence** (Davitz, 1970), **dominance-submission** (Russell & Mehrabian, 1977), and **potency** (Osgood, Suci, & Tannenbaum, 1957). Russell (1979) suggests that a feeling of control is not a separate dimension but only a determinant of whether an event is experienced as pleasant. In recent years, the feeling of control has been extensively studied in research on motivation, emotion, stress, and anxiety.

Bipolar versus Unipolar Representations of Affect

Bipolar. In the circumplex model, affect is described as a single bipolar dimension of pleasant-unpleasant. That is, pleasant affect is at one pole (end) of the dimension, and unpleasant affect is at the other. In this model, then, pleasant and unpleasant emotions are not independent. The model clearly says that if you are feeling bad (experiencing unpleasant emotion) you cannot be feeling good (experiencing pleasant emotion) at the same time. Conversely, if you are feeling good, you cannot simultaneously feel bad.

Independent unipolar dimensions.   It is also possible, however, to describe positive and negative affect as separate (unipolar) and independent dimensions. Affect ranges from zero to very positive on one dimension, and zero to very negative on the other dimension. This model says that positive and negative affect can be aroused with any level of intensity at either the same or different times. The "felt emotion" is the sum of the positive and negative affective arousals. This model is summarized in Figure 2–6 (see also Cacioppo & Berntson, 1994; or Cacioppo, Gardner, & Berntson, 1997). Which of the two models is better supported by data?

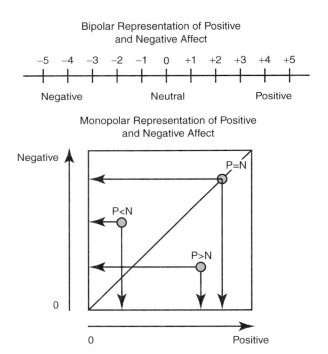

FIGURE 2–6.   Bipolar and monopolar representations of positive and negative affect. With the bipolar, a person's affect is located at a point along the line from negative to positive, and it cannot simultaneously be positive and negative. With the monopolar, the underlying biological systems for positive and negative affect could be aroused simultaneously and independently in any degree. The affect experienced depends on the relative strengths of the positive and negative affect. If positive is greater than negative (P>N), there would be a positive experience. If positive is less than negative (P<N), there would be negative experience. (See text for discussion.)

Evidence comparing the two models. *Statistical evidence.* According to the bipolar model, if a person reports feeling very good, then that person should also report not feeling very bad, and vice-versa. Such reports should be highly negatively correlated. In fact, however, if people are asked to report on separate scales how good and how bad they feel (neutral to very positive and neutral to very negative), the two sets of scores show near-zero correlations. Almost any degree of feeling good may be accompanied by any degree of feeling bad. This finding, in turn, implies that there are two separate systems underlying positive and negative affect rather than a single bipolar dimension. Green, Goldman, and Salovey (1993), in support of the bipolar approach, suggested that the usual lack of correlation results from using scales with low reliability. Low scale reliability would not account for more basic biological data, however.

Biological evidence. An avalanche of evidence gathered over the past few years supports the idea that there are two basic biological emotion systems corresponding to positive and negative affect. First of all, there are hemispheric differences for positive and negative emotion discussed earlier (Davidson, 1994). Second, there are different subcortical systems in the brain corresponding to positive and negative emotion. In particular, the positive system is the ventral tegmental dopamine system (Wise, 1989), and the negative system is related to the amygdala (LeDoux, 1994) and perhaps the neurotransmitter serotonin. Measures of affect in animals show that these systems can function independently (Berridge, 1996; and see Chapter Four). The biological evidence strongly favors two different underlying systems for positive and negative emotions even though we may experience only one affect, which is a combination of the activities of the underlying systems.

Importance of dimensional analyses. First, regardless of which particular dimensional analysis might be correct, the dimensional analysis sheds light on certain problems. For example, we have a clue to the great difficulty in finding specific physiological bases for *discrete emotions*. There are none. That is, what appear to be discrete emotions share a common physiological basis (combinations of activity in the two neural systems), so that discrete emotions cannot be distinguished very well physiologically. This finding may or may not turn out to be true, but it does help guide research.

Second, in practice, many types of emotional research are based on a dimensional approach. Research on mood, for example, generally assumes that people have good and bad moods that affect how they think and behave (e.g., Isen, 1984).

Third, if there is in fact only a small range of physiological differences in relation to many experienced emotions, cognition may be accorded a greater role in emotion. Our experienced emotions might depend on our appraisal or interpretation of the situation we are in, as well as on differences in internal arousal. Eventually we want to relate the biological bases of cognition to the biological bases of emotion (LeDoux, 1994). Finding such connections is fundamental to understanding such disorders as depression, as well as to understanding everyday thought and emotion.

Cognitive Theories of Emotion

According to cognitive theories, emotion depends on how we appraise or evaluate situations. Frijda (1993) argues that emotion is related to our readiness to act in a certain way, depending on how the situation might affect us. Such **action-readiness** partly defines different emotions. If a person hears footsteps in the dark, he may appraise them as bad (a burglar) and be anxious or may appraise them as good (a friend or loved one) and be relieved or happy. In the former case, he is prepared to escape from the intruder, whereas in the latter, he is prepared to approach the intruder. The "objective situation" may be the same in either case, but the responses may be entirely different. Psychologists do not question that cognition has a role in emotion but have disputed over just what that role is.

Is cognition necessary for emotion?   One dispute is whether cognitive appraisal is necessary for emotion to occur. Robert Zajonc (1984) argued that cognition is not necessary for emotion. Emotional responses to stimuli can be immediate and do not require cognitive appraisal. For example, people report liking stimuli more if they have previously been exposed to those stimuli, even though they do not remember the earlier exposure. This is called the **mere exposure effect.** Since the change in liking occurs without awareness, Zajonc concludes that cognitive appraisal is not a necessary condition for all emotional responses. In a rather striking set of experiments, Murphy and Zajonc (1993) reported that emotional responses could be **primed** with stimuli presented too briefly to be recognized. They flashed pictures of male and female faces expressing either happiness or anger for either 4/1000 of a second (4 msec) or for 1000 msec (1 second). These pictures were followed immediately by Chinese ideographs, which are affectively neutral stimuli. The question was whether the happy and angry faces (primes) would induce positive and negative affect into the ideographs. The subjects rated their degree of liking/disliking on a 5-point scale (1 = did not like, 5 = liked a lot). The result was that when the faces were exposed for only 4 msec, the ratings for the ideographs changed appropriately in comparison with a control condition with no primes. When the faces were exposed for a full second, however, there was no effect. Figure 2–7 shows the results. The authors interpreted their data to mean that affective responses were aroused by stimuli presented too quickly to be consciously recognized, hence supporting Zajonc's argument. Why was there no change in liking for the ideographs with the 1-second primes? One possibility is that the longer presentations gave subjects enough time to attach the emotion expressed in the faces to the faces themselves. Therefore, they did not transfer to the ideographs. With the

4-Msec Exposure

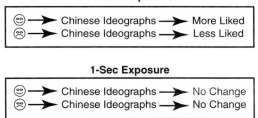

1-Sec Exposure

FIGURE 2–7. Summary of Murphy and Zajonc's (1993) results. When positive and negative faces were presented so rapidly (4-msec) preceding the Chinese ideographs that the subjects could not identify them, the faces affected subsequent reports of liking for the ideographs. If the faces were presented long enough so that they were easily identified (1-sec), they had no effect on subsequent reports of liking for the ideographs.

brief presentations, however, emotional responses were aroused but not associated with any discernible stimuli. Therefore, these responses became attached to the first discernible stimuli to occur, the ideographs.

There is a multitude of other problems for the theorist who argues that appraisal is absolutely necessary for emotion. For one, there are the emotional effects of music (Ellsworth, 1994). We do not appraise our stereo loudspeakers as beneficial or threatening before being emotionally aroused by the sounds they emit. There is something in the music itself that produces an emotional effect. There are theorists who argue that all emotional responses to music are learned, but this seems unlikely since upon first hearing, we find some selections either pleasant or unpleasant. Also, there are emotional rebounds, which lie at the heart of the **opponent-process theory** of emotion (Solomon & Corbit, 1974; Solomon, 1980). Specifically, the theory states that when a strong emotion is aroused (pleasant or unpleasant), the opposite experience occurs when the stimulus for that emotion is removed. For example, there is an emotional letdown, a feeling of sadness, following a prolonged positive experience. This opponent process is considered to occur automatically, without appraisal. This theory is discussed in more detail in later chapters. Frijda says (1994, p. 198): "I believe that nobody contests the essentially noncognitive determination of the likes and dislikes for particular smells, tastes, and bodily sensations, at least for certain ones. Nothing other than direct prewired determination appears to be involved in the practically universal liking for moderately sweet substances, caresses, and sexual climaxing." In brief, the evidence for emotional arousal without appraisal seems convincing.

Richard Lazarus (1984) argues in favor of cognition's being necessary for emotion by pointing to extensive research from his own lab and others. For example, subjects viewing rather grisly accident scenes in a movie can have a physiological response (GSR) exaggerated or attenuated according to the narrative that accompanies the film. Lazarus then argues that appraisal is necessary for emotion but is not necessarily conscious. The debate, then, seems to hinge on the question of how we are to define appraisal. If appraisal, by definition, is a conscious process, then appraisal may not be necessary. But if appraisal, by definition, can sometimes be unconscious, then appraisal may be necessary. One way this might work is as follows, and illustrated in Figure 2–8. Sensory inputs come into the brain and follow two

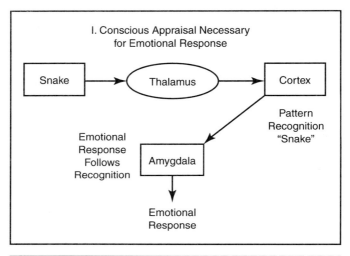

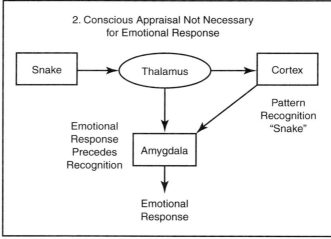

FIGURE 2–8.   The upper part of the figure shows a "long" pathway by which a stimulus goes through the visual cortex and is consciously recognized before being routed to the amygdala, where an emotional response is activated. The lower part of the figure shows a second and more direct pathway to the amygdala. This allows for an emotional response to a stimulus before it is consciously recognized. Research indicates that people can respond to stimuli emotionally without conscious recognition of the stimuli.

pathways (LeDoux, 1993). A very short path goes to the amygdala in the limbic system, where there may be emotional appraisal. A longer path goes to the sensory cortex and on to other parts of the brain before the stimulus is consciously identified. For those brief presentations of stimuli that produce emotional effects without stimulus recognition, the longer pathway may never be completed. Hence, there may be an emotional response without awareness. Appraisal, such as it is, is just for the positive or negative character of the stimulus, without reference to its other distinguishing features.

Suffice it to say that the role of cognition in emotion is still unsettled because we do not have an exact definition of cognition, because we do not clearly understand what roles "conscious" and "unconscious" factors play in cognition, and because we are not certain which neurological structures and processes are involved in cognition. We can safely say, however, that whether or not cognition is necessary for emotion, there is little question that cognitive processes are important to emotion.

Attribution theory and emotion.   By the 1960s, psychology was ripe for a new approach to emotion. Activation theory had become the major theory of emotion, but many psychologists found it difficult to believe that differences in level of activation alone could account for all the perceived differences in reported emotional experience. The new approach grew out of the developing **attribution theory** in social psychology. Attribution theory is concerned with how people seek and find causes for behavior. It was a short step to propose that people also seek causes to account for how they feel and to interpret their feelings in terms of the situation(s) in which they find themselves. If a person feels herself becoming aroused, she might interpret this arousal in any of several ways. If a large, unfriendly dog is approaching, she might interpret the arousal as fear. If someone has just insulted her, she might interpret the arousal as anger. If a friend is approaching, she might interpret the arousal as joy. Mandler (1962) and Schachter and Singer (1962) simultaneously proposed that such interpretations are crucial to emotional experience. The latter were more influential, however, because they also presented an experiment purporting to show that the same state of internal arousal could be interpreted as either happiness or anger, depending on environmental circumstances. The theory was compelling, not because of their data, which had all kinds of inconsistencies and alternative interpretations, but because the theory filled a theoretical vacuum in which psychologists had been foundering for half a century.

Cognitive-arousal theory.   Schachter and Singer's theory was that perceived emotion is a joint function of internal arousal and an appropriate cognition with which to label the arousal. The labeling, such as referring to the arousal as fear, is a cognitive activity (in this case, an attribution). The arousal and the cognition are both necessary for the experienced emotion. If either the arousal or the cognition is not present, an emotion is not experienced.

Schachter and Singer tested this hypothesis by giving subjects injections of adrenaline (to produce general arousal) and then putting them into different situations calculated to produce different cognitive labeling of the arousal. Some subjects were subjected to conditions calculated to make them happy, others to make them angry. They reported positive results, and a happy reading public eagerly embraced the theory (but see Beck, 1990, for detailed analysis of the shortcomings of their data).

Unfortunately, subsequent research did not support the theory very well. Reisenzein (1983) concluded that the only adequate support came from research involving misattributed arousal from an irrelevant source, such as attributing exercise-induced arousal to sexual arousal in the presence of sexual cues. He further concluded that there was no evidence that unexplained arousal instigates a search for the cause of such arousal. Leventhal and Tomarken (1986, p. 574) agreed that research testing predictions from cognitive-arousal theory yielded disappointing results. In addition, Maslach (1979) and Marshall and Zimbardo (1979) found that subjects described the arousal produced by adrenaline injections as unpleasant under any condition. They did not describe it as "happiness" when placed in the happy experimental condition previously used by Schachter and Singer.

Excitation-transfer theory. The one area of support for cognitive-arousal theory, noted before, involves what is called excitation transfer (Zillman, 1978). According to this theory, when arousal occurs, it takes some period of time for the arousal to decay. While arousal is still decaying, a person may incorrectly identify the source of arousal. Thus, for example, already-existing feelings of anger, aggression, or sexual arousal might be intensified by irrelevant arousal produced by exercise.

Excitation-transfer theory differs from cognitive-arousal theory in important ways (Leventhal & Tomarken, 1986). First, excitation-transfer theory does not assume any causal search for the source of unexplained arousal. Misattributions (mistaken attributions) occur by accident, not as a result of a search for the cause of unexplained arousal. Second, excitation-transfer theory assumes that misattribution is most likely to occur when people are actually becoming *less aware* of their arousal. For example, Cantor, Zillman, and Bryant (1975) studied the effect of prior physical exercise on self-reports of sexual arousal from erotic films. They had separate groups of subjects view a film entitled *Naked Under Leather* at either zero, five, or nine minutes after exercising, when the exercise-induced arousal is high, imperceptible, or back to preexercise baseline. Actual arousal level was measured by heart rate change from baseline. Only subjects in the five-minute group, who had imperceptible residual arousal, rated their level of sexual arousal higher. Presumably, the zero-delay group recognized that much of their arousal was attributable to exercise and the nine-minute group was no longer aroused by the exercise and so had no excitation to transfer. Results from this line of research seem robust.

Valins's Attribution Theory.   Valins (1966, 1970) extended the Schachter-Singer approach by suggesting that the **perception** of physiological change is a sufficient condition for experienced emotion, whether or not the perception is accurate. If we only *think* we have been aroused, we can *interpret* this apparent arousal as emotion. Valins (1966) tested his hypothesis by giving male subjects false information about their heart rates as they viewed slides of *Playboy* centerfolds. Slides associated with either an increase or a decrease in heart rate were rated more attractive than those not associated with change. Overall, the results supported Valins's hypothesis that when subjects heard the fake heart rate changes, they searched the slides for characteristics of the models (such as parts of the anatomy) that might have caused the cardiac changes and then attributed the changes to these "attractive" features. In short, subjects reached the attribution that they had made emotional responses to slides that were more attractive. Unfortunately for the hypothesis, the effect can readily be obtained under conditions that do not correspond to the attribution search hypothesis. It appears that just calling attention to slides makes them more attractive. Beck et al. (1988) found, among the results of several experiments, that tourist slides of Rome, Italy, could be made more attractive simply by bringing subjects' attention to them. There is little emotion in this activity. Beck et al. interpreted the results as due to experimental demand. Given the experimental situation in which some slides are selected for more attention than others, a subject looking at nude slides might say to himself: "What am I expected to do here? I am in an experiment on emotional arousal, looking at pictures of naked women; they tell me my heart rate is higher for some pictures than for others, and I am supposed to rate the pictures. Perhaps I should give higher ratings to pictures where my heart rate changes." Quite apart from emotional arousal, the situation may set up a *demand* to rate repeated slides as more attractive.

We conclude that cognitive factors, including attributions, can affect emotional responses. However, the evidence does not support cognitive-arousal theory as a general theory of emotion, nor does it support the attribution-search hypothesis very well. The false-feedback experiments seem to indicate more about conditions under which a person will make particular ratings about any stimulus than about what might be true emotional responses.

RELATION OF EMOTION TO MOTIVATION

Jeffrey Gray (1994) makes the point that emotion theorists generally agree that emotion is concerned with reactions to rewards and punishments, learned or unlearned. He also stresses that there are specific emotion systems, although few in number (probably three or four). Given considerable agreement on these two points, however, emotion theorists still have widely differing points of view on many issues. Thus, we have seen theories of emotion ranging from those which argue for a number of discrete, biologically determined emotions, through emotional dimensions and nonspecific arousal and its interpretation, to purely cognitive (attributional) interpretations. Without any "standard" theory of emotion, there is no complete integration of motivation and emotion that satisfies all theorists. We can, however, point out how each of the three main approaches to emotion that we covered (discrete, dimensional, and cognitive theories) can relate to motivation.

Discrete theories. Throughout the text we will make reference to particular emotions, e.g., love, happiness, anger, anxiety, depression, and fear, thereby implying that there *are* such discrete emotions. What we have learned from this chapter is that the number of such emotions is small and that the degree to which they are biologically fixed is debatable. Some concepts, such as fear, are equally central to both emotion and motivation theory.

Dimensional theories. Dimensional theories divide emotions into pleasant and unpleasant, which is a particularly good fit to the hedonic approach to motivation as it was outlined in Chapter One. The motivational concept of desire corresponds to the anticipation of a pleasant emotional outcome, and the motivational concept of aversion corresponds to the anticipation of an unpleasant emotional outcome. These anticipations are based on prior pleasant or unpleasant experiences, and we try to re-create the pleasant experiences and avoid the unpleasant. Such anticipations are **motives** and approach and avoidance are motivated behaviors.

Cognitive theories. Cognitive theories are concerned with the effect that appraisal or evaluation of a situation has on what emotion is aroused, pleasant or unpleasant. Such appraisals determine whether a situation is approached or avoided. We may also relate appraisal to other theoretical approaches. For example, if I *appraise* a situation as dangerous (cognitive theory) I may be *afraid* (discrete theory) and try to reduce this *unpleasant* state (dimensional theory) by running away. Or, if I interpret a slight to me as intentional I may become angry and perhaps aggressive, whereas if I perceive the slight as accidental I do not become angry and behave entirely differently. In the area of achievement theory, some theorists have emphasized that our interpretations about the causes of our successes and failures play a major role in our subsequent achievement motivation.

In summary, emotion and motivation are intimately related regardless of what theoretical approach to emotion we may favor. At a particular time, one approach may be more appropriate, whereas at a different time, another approach may serve better.

SUMMARY

1. Most contemporary motivation theorists consider motivation and emotion to be intimately related. This chapter examines theories and data from emotion research in order to define this relationship more thoroughly.

2. Early psychologists considered emotion a content of mind, like perception or thought. Emotion was studied by **introspection,** or "looking into one's own mind" and reporting its contents. The primary emotional characteristics were reported to be feelings of **pleasantness** and **unpleasantness.**

3. The **James-Lange theory** proposed that emotion is the perception of bodily activity that is aroused as a response to some environmental event. This theory emphasized the visceral activity controlled by the autonomic nervous system. The **Cannon-Bard theory** emphasized activity in the thalamic area of the brain as the core of emotion and led to extensive research on the brain and emotion.

4. Emotions can be considered theoretically as **intervening variables** defined by antecedent and consequent conditions. This view helps us to avoid circular definitions and to clarify the meaning of emotion concepts.

5. Contemporary research on emotion combines research on **verbal behavior, nonverbal behavior,** and **physiology.**

6. Parts of the nervous system particularly important for emotion are the **limbic system** of the brain and the **autonomic nervous system,** which controls the viscera. There also appear to be important differences between the right and left **hemispheres** of the brain. The left seems relatively more involved with positive emotion, and the right with negative emotion.

7. **Discrete emotion theories** assume that there is some fixed number of genetically programmed emotional reactions to specific kinds of situations. Six have been reliably identified across many cultures: happiness, anger, sadness, disgust, surprise, and fear. Others have been reported less consistently. Facial expressions are among the most reliable indicators of emotion, but many expressions are also blends of the "basic" emotions, and expression of even these basic emotions can be modified by experience. The **facial feedback hypothesis** proposes that a person's *felt emotion* is partly due to facial expression.

8. **Dimensional theories** of emotion assume that all emotional experience can be accounted for by combinations of different intensities of some small number of emotional dimensions. Much research shows that the most important dimension is **pleasant-unpleasant,** followed by **level of arousal** (tension). Increasing evidence suggests that there are two basic underlying emotional systems (positive and negative) and that felt-emotion is a combination of the arousal of these.

9. **Cognitive theories** emphasize that emotional responses are largely determined by how we **evaluate** or **appraise** situations. A controversial issue is whether such evaluations are necessary in order to have any emotional experience at all, and if so, whether such evaluations are necessarily conscious.

10. **Cognitive-arousal theory** proposes that both visceral arousal and an attribution of the cause of the arousal are necessary for emotional experience. Different interpretations of the same arousal are said to produce different emotional experiences. Research has not supported this theory very well, but it has supported a limited variation called **excitation transfer theory.**

11. Different motivational concepts can be related to the different major theoretical approaches to emotion: discrete theories, dimensional theories, and cogni-

tive theories. For example, some motivational concepts are concerned only with positive versus negative experiences and approach or avoidance of these, which fall within the dimensional approach. Others are concerned with such specific emotions as fear or anxiety, rather than with all unpleasant situations. These fall within the discrete emotions approach. Other aspects of motivation depend heavily on cognitive activity, such as the way we interpret events, e.g., whether harm to us was intentional or accidental. The interpretation may determine whether we respond aggressively.

CHAPTER THREE

Instinct and Species-Specific Behavior

———•———

INTRODUCTORY EXAMPLES

The Curious Case of the Cowbird

Cowbirds are a curiosity because they never raise their own young. They lay eggs in other birds' nests and then depart forever. The unwitting foster mother hatches the egg and cares for the cowbird baby until it can go out on its own. There are a number of such **brood parasites,** but cowbirds stand out among this group because they parasitize the nests of over two hundred other species. This behavior raises numerous questions (West, King, & Eastzer, 1981). How do the females go about exchanging eggs? How can the baby cowbirds get so many different kinds of mothers to care for them? And most important of all: How do cowbirds recognize other cowbirds and know with whom to mate? It has generally been assumed that birds learn appropriate species-recognition songs from their parents, but this is clearly not so with the cowbird.

Songs by cowbirds reared in isolation. Shortly after cowbirds leave the foster parent's nest, they manage to seek out other cowbirds and travel in flocks. They obviously recognize each other, but not necessarily by song. In the case of mating, however, song plays a demonstrably important role. When a male sings his song of love, the female adopts a specific and identifiable posture that can be used to judge the effectiveness of a male's song. And the result is striking. Male cowbirds reared in isolation from all other birds from two days after hatching until adulthood are more successful at evoking the female copulatory posture than are males who have lived with other cowbirds. We thus have a specific behavior that appears to be unlearned but is more effective than the same behavior with opportunity for learning. Isolate-reared cowbird songs, played to females on a tape recorder, evoke copulatory responses about 60 percent of the time, whereas normally reared males are only about 25 percent effective. However, if the isolates are now placed with other males, the isolates' songs are degraded to the lower effectiveness of normally reared birds. Or if normally reared birds are isolated in adulthood, their songs become more effective. In short, socialization has the perverse effect of making male cowbird songs less appealing to female cowbirds. Finally, the cowbirds with the most effective songs actually do mate more than those with less effective songs. Why, then, does socialization lead to less lovable cowbird males?

Isolation, dominance, and aggression. The elegant studies of West and King and their associates show that isolate cowbirds have a particular frequency component in part of their song that is especially attractive to females. Socialized birds do not have this component because it evokes attack on them by other males. Only those birds that are at the top of the dominance hierarchy in a group can sing the most effective song with impunity and can mate most often. In terms of natural selection, this ability does tend to guarantee that the most fit males breed. Isolate birds have not learned to suppress the critical song component and are attacked and even killed if they sing it when introduced to a group. Conversely, birds put into isolation learn that they will not be attacked and start to sing the most happy song. If a dominant bird from one group is put into another group, he is no longer dominant, but he does not know this. He therefore sings his best song, is attacked, and either changes his ways or is killed.

The conclusion, then, is that the male cowbird comes out of its shell equipped to sing a highly enticing mating song but learns **not** to sing it unless he becomes a dominant bird. The female comes into the world prepared to respond to this song during the mating season. There is, therefore, a complex set of genetic, hormonal, and social learning experiences that operate on natural selection. It is the genetic component, the apparently prewired ability to sing on the one hand and to respond appropriately to the song on the other, which keeps the notion of "instinct-as-specific-response" alive. Biologists, of course, are less interested in calling this instinct than in finding out the exact sensory-neural-muscular mechanisms that can account for such behaviors. For this kind of study, we turn to a simpler organism, the cricket, whose song is less lyrical than that of the birds but effective for its purpose.

Cricket Song

Research on cricket song by Bentley and Hoy (e.g., Bentley, 1977; Bentley & Hoy, 1972; Hoy & Casaday, 1979) has identified a very specific neural location for controlling the mating song of the cricket. The cricket's song is produced by opening and closing the wings. The rough end of the wing (the **scraper**) rubs against a row of ridges (the **file**) under the cover of the opposite wing. This rubbing produces the familiar summertime chirping sound. The cricket song is limited to different temporal patterns and intensities, and the males of different species identify themselves solely by their own species-specific variation in these. What humans normally hear is the calling song, which loudly proclaims the singer as an adult male of a particular species, with a territory of his own and ready for action. Sexually receptive females respond to the unique male song of their species. In order to mate, the cricket must precisely control its wing movements. The question is, How?

The cricket wings are controlled by muscles in the thorax, which in turn are connected to a nerve bundle called the **thoracic ganglion.** The delicate wing timing is controlled by a single neuron in the brain, the **command interneuron.** Direct electrical stimulation of this neuron produces neural impulses, which have the appropriate species-specific rhythm. These neural impulses stimulate the thoracic ganglion, thus stimulating the thoracic muscles and wing movement and subsequent chirping. The correct calling song can be produced by such artificial stimulation even in otherwise brainless crickets. Under normal conditions, brain cells probably put together such information as time of day and weather, and if everything is "right," the command interneuron fires, and so on. Crickets reared in isolation through the ten moultings preceding adulthood still sing the right song. By isolating males and females of different species together, it is possible to produce hybrid offspring that have a greater variety of calls. These are apparently the result of having more than one command interneuron, each with its unique timing control (Alcott, 1979). Again, both genetics and experience are involved in species-specific behaviors, but the relative contributions of these sources of behavior variation differ according to the species and the behavior in question.

The cowbirds and the crickets illustrate why the instinct concept survives: Every so often someone researches a behavior that just does not seem accountable in terms of standard learning theory principles. Besides different physical characteristics, each species has unique behaviors that set it apart. Spiders construct webs that are even specific to subspecies of spiders, and different species of birds build their own peculiar nests. Such behaviors are often called instinctive, usually to imply they are not learned. William James (1890, p. 393) said that instinct was the "faculty of acting in such a way as to produce a certain end without foresight of that end, and without the individual's having previous education in that performance." More recently, the biologist Nikolaas Tinbergen (1951) defined instinct by four criteria: (1) the behavior is stereotyped and constant in form; (2) the behavior is characteristic of the species; (3) the behavior appears in animals reared in isolation from each other; and (4) the behavior develops fully formed in animals prevented from practicing it. The main questions here are whether the concept of instinct is actually useful in explaining such behavior and whether other explanations might fit better.

THE PROBLEMS OF INSTINCT THEORY

Meanings of Instinct

Whether we should consider "instinct" a **motivational** concept depends on how we use the term. Unfortunately, the term *instinct* is so loosely used, sometimes in contradictory ways, that there is no clear-cut meaning to the term, either motivational or nonmotivational.

Instinct as universal behavior.   We may apply the term *instinct* when a particular behavior occurs very commonly in a species, including humans. Maternal behavior may be said to be instinctive, since most mothers engage in something called maternal activities. William James (1884) thought no hen could resist the charm of an egg-to-be-sat-upon and that no woman could resist the charm of a small, naked baby. John B. Watson (1924), however, noted that in hospitals where they could be closely observed, new mothers were very awkward with their first child and did not do all those tender, loving things that supposedly characterize the "maternal instinct." Watson pointed out the pitfalls of attributing any behavior to a universal instinct.

Instinct as unlearned behavior.   A second way in which the term is applied is to activities that seem to occur without much forethought. The prizefighter who is quick to dodge his opponent's jabs may be said to "duck instinctively," but very little imagination is necessary to see that one either learns to duck or gets out of the business. In this kind of example, the term *instinct* is used as if some people have it (the capacity to respond quickly) and some do not. Thus, it seems to be used as an account of differences within a species rather than as an explanation for the *universality* of a species behavior. This is just the opposite of the use described in the preceding paragraph or in Tinbergen's definition.

Instinct as urge versus instinct as behavior.   Another kind of confusion arises in treating instinct as an urge toward some activity (thus being like a motive or an emotion) as compared with referring to such specific behaviors as web building. James and Freud both talked more in terms of urges than of behaviors. In fact, what are usually referred to as instincts in Freudian theory (sex and aggression) come from the German word *Trieb,* which can be translated as either "instinct" or "drive." As it happened, the term *instinct* was originally used and hence picked up connotations that Freud did not necessarily intend. Freud talked about instincts as having **source, impetus, aim,** and **object,** implying that either internal or external stimulation (source) produces "instinct"; that the instinct carries some degree of force (impetus) that is related to the intensity of behavior; that the person tries to reduce the tension (aim); and, finally, that this process is all ended by some object. Freud saw neither fixed behaviors nor invariant objects related to instincts; both, in his view, are subject to change because of particular individual experiences. For Freud these built-in urges might find their outlets in very disguised forms, because of social pressures. He saw many behaviors as being apparently irrational because they are stimulated by instincts that the individual cannot identify but that can be studied and their causes determined.

William McDougall (1923) argued that instincts were innate tendencies to engage in certain actions under certain conditions but that the goal of actions should be taken into account. Thus one animal might follow another with the goal of either mating, fighting, or eating (prey). In order to identify the instinct, one must know the behavioral outcome. McDougall also believed that each separate instinct had its own unique emotional experience accompanying it.

Most serious theorists have argued that as far as specific responses are concerned, the term *instinct* should be limited to some very small segments of behavior, almost at the level of reflexes. All major instinct theorists have believed that there were some inborn tendencies or urges but that these are overshadowed by learning. James, for example, described instinct as being without the foresight of its end, but he also said that once an instinctive activity occurred, there would be foresight of its end on future occasions. This foresight would either facilitate or block the expression of the instinct. James (1890, p. 395) even referred to the idea of invariable instincts as "mystical" and observed that "the minuter study of recent years has found continuity, transition, variation and mistake wherever it has looked for them," and decided that what is called an instinct is usually only a tendency to act in a way of which the *average* is pretty constant, but which need not be mathematically 'true.' McDougall believed that instincts were often more permanent than James believed, but that they still could be modified.

History of the Instinct Concept

Origins. Given the considerable agreement that so-called instinctive behavior is never as invariant as supposed, how did the concept gain such a foothold and still maintain such a grip on popular opinion? One reason is that it keeps getting revived by people like Lorenz (1965) and Ardrey (1966), who argued, respectively, that aggression and territorial behaviors in humans are instinctive. Although most biologists have been skeptical of these views, they have had great popular appeal.

A deeper running current, however, is that the instinct concept derived from theology rather than biology (Beach, 1955).[1] The line of reasoning, still applicable today in some circles, is as follows: People get to heaven or hell according to their earthly choices. If they make the correct moral decisions, their reward is paradise; if not, their "reward" is perdition. But the whole problem is meaningless unless we assume that people are free to choose. This capacity to make moral choices was considered to be a unique property of the rational soul of humans, just as an afterlife was said to be reserved to them. But without a capacity to make rational decisions, how could animals carry on the complex activities that they obviously do? It was simply postulated that animals are not rational and do not have to make decisions because their behavior consists of predetermined responses to particular situations. This view of theology is still widely held, as we saw in Chapter one, and still lends credence to the concept of instinct in animals.

---

[1]The early confusion between theology and actual animal behavior is nowhere more dramatically illustrated than in the medieval "bestiaries," or books of beasts. One story reported by White (1954) says, for example, that lion cubs are born lifeless, and after three days the father lion breathes life into them just as God the Father resurrected Christ the Son after three days.

The anti-instinct revolt. Darwinian biology partly bridged the gap between animals and humans by proposing that humans also have instincts. Both William James and William McDougall believed that humans actually have more instincts than other animals. And though they saw these more as urges than specific behaviors, less sophisticated writers proposed human instincts running into the hundreds. By about 1920 a number of psychologists became alarmed by this proliferation, which in effect was nothing more than putting names to behaviors without further explanation. Knight Dunlap (1919) and Zing Yang Kuo (1922) were particularly strident in their attacks on the practice, arguing for the greater importance of environmental determinants on behavior.

Kuo went further in undertaking a productive program of research on what were commonly thought to be instinctive behaviors. He showed that not all cats do "naturally" kill rats and that such factors as familiarity are involved (1930). From his extensive investigation of the development of the embryonic chick, he also made a convincing argument (1932) that the "instinctive" pecking and swallowing of the newborn chick has its origins in embryonic movements that are "forced" in the course of morphological development. For example, after the embryonic heart starts to beat, the chick's head is moved back and forth in the egg, the mouth opens and closes, and there is some swallowing. As a result of many such attacks on the instinct concept, it fell into ill repute in American psychology in the 1920s.

Resurgence of interest at midcentury. In 1938, Karl Lashley spoke out in favor of instinct. He gave fifteen examples of what he believed were "confirmed" instinctive behaviors, most of which involved mating or maternal activities. But as Beach (1955) pointed out, few American psychologists had ever seen any of the behaviors listed (responses of the sooty tern to her nest and young, for example). And Beach once more made the point that the more closely any behavior is studied, the less likely it is to be considered automatic. Gradually, however, increasing numbers of examples of species-specific behaviors, such as the mating of the stickleback fish, caught the attention of both psychologists and biologists, particularly after World War II.

A paper by Breland and Breland (1961) was particularly interesting to learning-oriented psychologists. Entitled "The Misbehavior of Organisms," a switch on the title of Skinner's classic *Behavior of Organisms* (1938), it attracted attention in part because it was an insider's account of the difficulties of doing operant conditioning with many different species. Originally students of Skinner's, Keller and Marian Breland were so impressed by the power of operant conditioning that they started a business training animals for shows. They reported that certain behaviors simply could not be trained with some species. In one act, for example, a pig was supposed to carry a large, simulated gold coin to a piggy bank. This behavior was learned, but then, in spite of continued reward for success, the pigs began dropping the coin on the ground, rooting around at it, and never got it to the bank anymore. It seemed as if the pigs were trying to "root" the coin, much as they would root for food in the ground. Similarly, racoons had great difficulty in letting go of objects that they were supposed to deposit someplace else, tending to hold them in their hands and to "wash" them. The Brelands referred to such problems as a drift from learned to instinctive behavior. To avoid the difficulties of this "instinctive drift," they eventually built all their acts around what the animals would do reliably rather than trying to train responses arbitrarily selected.

Present status of the instinct concept.   Psychologists and biologists agree that behavior is in part genetically determined, but the actual term *instinct* rarely appears in the biological literature on behavior, except perhaps to put it into historical perspective (e.g., Eibl-Eibesfeldt, 1975). Instead, it is argued that **genes establish the potential for species-specific behaviors** and that this potential is fulfilled to greater or lesser degree under different environmental conditions. The problem, then, is to determine what specific mechanisms are inherited and what environmental conditions bring them into play. This kind of analysis proceeds nicely without any concept of instinct, except as it may refer generally to such motivational systems as hunger or reproduction.

A sophisticated differentiation of the concepts of **instinct** and **motivation** has been proposed by Epstein (1982), however, who argues that a large amount of animal behavior *is* unlearned. If we look at a wide spectrum of animal life, we find that most of the earth's animal population is far less complicated than primates, or even vertebrates, and that it is among the masses of insects, mollusks, and arachnids that instinctive **behaviors** are most likely to occur. Epstein distinguishes instinctive and motivated behaviors in terms of behavioral characteristics (Epstein, 1982), summarized in Table 3–1. Briefly stated, motivated behaviors are characterized by **variability, foresight,** and **emotion,** but instinctive behaviors lack these features. There are species-specific behaviors at all levels of complexity, however. Species vary genetically in their behavioral capabilities.

THE ETHOLOGICAL APPROACH TO BEHAVIOR

Ethology is a part of biological science concerned with animal behavior, initiated largely in Europe under the leadership of Konrad Lorenz, Nikolaas Tinbergen, and Karl von Frisch. Tinbergen (1951) considered the main question of ethology to be, Why does the animal behave as it does? His answer was that behavior is the joint product of environmental events and internal conditions, which is also the psychologist's standard answer to the same question. The difference is that the ethologists place more emphasis on (1) detailed study of animal behavior in natural settings, (2) closer attention to the development of behavior, (3) genetics and the phylogenetic development of a

TABLE 3–1.   A comparison of instinct and motivation (adapted from Epstein, 1982).

I. COMMON CHARACTERISTICS

1. Both employ innate mechanisms for behavior.
2. Both employ acquired (learned) components.
3. Both are organized sequentially into highly variable goal-seeking behavior, followed by more specific consummatory responses.[1]
4. Both are drive induced (i.e., induced by some physiological imbalance).
5. Both contribute to homeostasis.

II. DIFFERENCES

A. INSTINCT

1. Species-specific in terms of the kinds of stimuli that *release* the behavior and the specific organizations of behaviors.
2. Goal-seeking (appetitive) behavior not changed by expectancy (i.e., is not changed by learning).
3. Nonemotional.
4. Biologically common, occurring across many different phyla and orders.

B. MOTIVATION

1. Goal-seeking behavior that can be modified by learning.
2. Anticipating goals.
3. Accompanied by expression of emotion.
4. Biologically rare (very few animals show it).

Source: A. N. Epstein, 1982. Copyright © 1982 Springer-Verlag. Used by permission.
[1]These are commonly referred to as *appetitive* and *consummatory* phases.

species, and (4) studies of birds, fish, and insects, as well as mammals. Psychologists have also incorporated these approaches into their research.

The Ethogram

The first step in the ethological analysis of behavior is to map out the typical behavior of a species in its normal environment. Activities are observed, recorded, and counted, as are the circumstances under which they occur. This behavioral map is the ethogram. The description of the cowbird's behavior is an ethogram, valuable because it gives a baseline of normal behavior against which the effects of changing the organism or its surroundings can be evaluated.

Erbkoordination

The general name given to an "instinctive" pattern of behavior is **Erbkoordination.** It is a core of more or less complex and fixed "inborn" movement forms. This fixed core is also referred to as a **fixed action pattern** (FAP). The

FAP does not involve all the behavior in any such sequence as feeding or mating; instead, it generally refers to the terminal, or **consummatory,** behavior[2] that is the final phase of a "motivated act." An animal may engage in widely variable movements, or **appetitive** behaviors, which bring it into contact with food or a sexual partner. As the animal gets closer to the end of the sequence, the behavior is relatively more stereotyped. As an example of such stereotypy, the drinking rate of a rat licking from a water tube is relatively constant, at about six licks per second. This number may vary with circumstances, but under any normal conditions, it is never reported as low as three nor as high as ten per second; the range is small. The distinction between appetitive and consummatory behaviors is essentially the same as the distinction that psychologists usually make between instrumental (or operant) and consummatory behaviors. The FAP constitutes only a small fragment of an overall sequence of motivated behavior.

The early Lorenz-Tinbergen analysis emphasized that **reaction-specific energy** (RSE) builds up in the organism much as water fills a tank. The RSE was so called because it was considered specific to particular kinds of behavior such as feeding, mating, or aggressive activities. The concept of RSE is a motivational concept, separate from specific behaviors but attempting to serve as an explanation for their occurrence. A particular behavior was said not to be stimulated by external events, but released by them. Until a specific stimulus called a **releaser,** or **sign stimulus,** is presented to the organism, the RSE is internally blocked and is not expressed overtly. The releaser is a "key" that fits the "lock" of the **innate releasing mechanism** (IRM). When a releaser (such as the gaping mouth of a baby bird) is presented, the appropriate behavior is released (the parent putting food into the mouth).

Hierarchical Ordering of Action

A crucial concept is that the neural centers storing the RSE are ordered in a hierarchy according to complexity. At the highest level, there are "moods," which correspond to such broad kinds of behavior as are involved in feeding, mating, sleeping, or aggression. Within each mood, there are successively "lower" levels of hierarchy corresponding to more and more specific kinds of behaviors involved in the total activity, down to the movements of specific muscle groups. Figure 3–1 (Tinbergen, 1951) shows the nature of this hierarchical structure in the specific example of stickleback mating behavior. The hierarchical concept has been given support in research described by von Hoist and von St. Paul (1962), using electrodes permanently implanted in chicken brains so that behavior could be artificially stimulated.

---

[2]The word *consummatory* comes from the verb "to consummate," not from "to consume." To consummate something is to complete it, not to consume it. Eating and drinking are both consumatory and consummatory acts, but sex and aggression are acts that are consummated.

Level of the
Major Instinct

Next Lower
Instinctive Level

Level of the
Consummatory Act

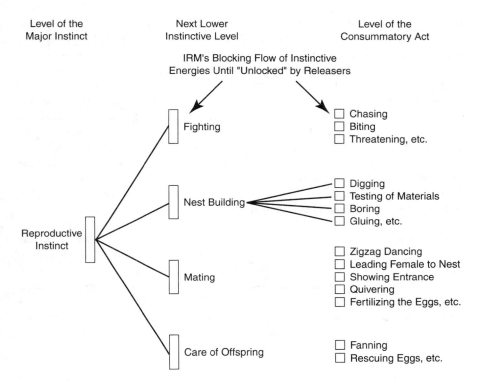

FIGURE 3-1.   The reproductive instinct of the male three-spined stickleback, showing the hierarchical ordering of action, with different levels of instinct indicating innate releasing mechanisms. (Modified from Tinbergen, 1951, p. 104.)

Depending on exact electrode placement, either an overall "mood" or very specific behaviors could be produced. The sleepy chicken, for example, goes through a standard ritual in preparation for sleep, including standing on one leg and putting the head under a wing. Von Hoist reported that, at one electrode site, the entire "sleepy" mood could be stimulated, with all the behaviors in sequence and the chicken actually going to sleep. Presumably, the electrode had tapped into a fairly high position in the hierarchy. With other locations, only very specific parts of the overall behavior pattern were evoked, such as putting the head under the wing, but the other behaviors did not occur, and the chicken did not sleep.

Vacuum Reactions and Displacement

If a releasing stimulus is not presented to "unblock" the IRM, the buildup of a particular RSE may be so great that the reaction occurs anyway. The reaction is called, in German, a **Leerlaufreaktion** (vacuum reaction).

Continuing the previous hydraulic analogy, the "water tank" overflows so that an FAP occurs, such as "spontaneous" aggressive behavior or inappropriate sexual activity, perhaps with an animal trying to mate with an inanimate object or a member of another species. Or if two incompatible reactions are simultaneously released, as with courtship and aggressive activities, the animal cannot really complete either. In such a case, there may be an alternation between attack and enticement, and some unexpected response may suddenly appear. A chicken may suddenly start pecking at the ground, for example. This is called **displacement activity** and is thought to be caused by released energy from the conflicting (and blocked) RSE's "spilling over" to release other behaviors. Both vacuum and displacement reactions, including reactions to unusual stimuli, are based on the "full water-tank" model. Although it is an interesting analogy, biologists do not take the hydraulic model seriously as an explanation of behavior. There is no known neurological mechanism that has the properties of such a model. In the case of displacement, moreover, Zeigler (1964) showed how specific kinds of stimulation could determine what behaviors would occur when conflicting activities block each other. In the courtship-fighting conflict, a bird might start to preen because of the engorgement of blood close to the skin. Similarly, "vacuum" reactions do not occur completely in isolation from the environment; they are also responses to some kind of stimulation.

THE EVOLUTION OF BEHAVIOR

Darwin's Theory

Charles Darwin's *Origin of Species* ([1859] 1936) was not the first attempt to describe continuously evolving life, but it was certainly the most influential. Based on a myriad of observations during his worldwide travels on the *Beagle*, Darwin's thesis was that there is a natural selection of organisms based on their fitness to reach maturity and reproduce themselves. Or as Wilson (1975) more recently has put it, natural selection is the process whereby certain genetic material gains increased representation in the following generation. Such "survival of the fittest" does sometimes depend on savagery and cunning, but not always. The opossum, which exhibits neither of these characteristics in great amount, has survived for over sixty million years. So has the cockroach.

Specific survival rules are not laid down in advance, however. Evolution is opportunistic, and whatever assists survival at a given time and place is the physical or behavioral character selected in a species. Some animals survive by being inconspicuous, their form and coloring providing **camouflage** that allows them to blend almost invisibly into their environment. Insects are particularly adept at this, but the spotted coat of the fawn, the stripes of the zebra, and the white fur of the polar bear are also protective. Other animals show **mimicry,** looking like different species that are more dangerous than they are. For example, one species of butterfly *(Limenitis archippus)* survives in part because it looks like the Monarch butterfly, which feeds on poisonous plants and is rejected by such predators as the bluejay because it tastes bad. Many animals have **rituals** that make them appear more dangerous and threatening than they really are, such as spreading feathers or puffing up the cheeks.

Selection itself, however, depends on two other factors: **genetic variation** (which Darwin simply referred to as "natural variation") and **environmental pressure.** Darwin recognized that there could be no selection unless there were alternatives to be selected from and reasons for them to be selected. Unless organisms differed from their parents, and hence from each other, all the members of a species would be equally likely to perish or survive. As an example of such pressure, in England the industrial revolution led to cities that became black with coal dust and smoke. Moths that were darker could survive and multiply in the cities, where they literally blended into the walls (camouflage) and were protected, but the lighter colored moths of the same species could not. In more rural areas, however, lighter colored moths were less conspicuous and continued to survive better than the darker ones. If there had been no variation among the moths, with complete adaptation to the country living, city survival would not have been possible. This would have been an instance of **over-specialization** in natural selection.

Abrupt environmental changes may provide pressures that a species cannot withstand because it does not possess sufficient variability among its members. It then becomes extinct. Shifting land masses and bodies of water possibly had such effects on the dinosaur. Sometimes the introduction of a new species plays havoc because the new species is better adapted to survival in the environment than the established inhabitants. Thus the placental jackrabbit was better adapted to life in Australia than the indigenous marsupials and rapidly multiplied when introduced there. The incessant movement of humans into wilderness areas has caused extinction of numerous species and endangered many others. Sometimes, however, environmental changes in the form of such geographic upheavals may give new life to a species. Some of Darwin's most important observations were made of the variations of finches among the different Galapagos Islands of volcanic origin. The finches experienced different environmental pressures on these different, suddenly appearing islands and therefore developed along different lines.

Mendel's Theory

Gregor Mendel did his work on inheritance in the middle 1880s, but it was about 1900 before it became evident that this was the mechanism of Darwin's natural variation. An organism passes some of its characteristics to its offspring. The mechanism of transmission is the *genes* (Mendel himself just referred to "factors"). A particular organism has a **genotype,** the actual genes it receives from its parents, and a **phenotype,** that part of its genetic inheritance that is actually expressed in observable characteristics under appropriate environmental conditions.

Each adult individual has *pairs* of genes for a particular character, such as eye color. The genes may be of the same kind, or they may be different. Such different forms of the same gene are called **alleles.** When reproductive cells, or **gametes,** are formed in the adult individual, only one member of each gene pair goes into the gamete. In the combination of gametes from each parent, the offspring gets a full complement of genes; the exact combinations depend on which genes from a particular parent went into the gamete and on which adults happen to mate with each other. If one allele, which we may call A, is **dominant** over another allele, A', which is **recessive,** then an individual receiving A from one parent and A' from the other will have the phenotype of A. Suppose that A represents the allele for brown eyes and A' for blue, and that A is dominant (which it is). We may then ask what the eye color of the offspring will be on the basis of the parental phenotypes and genotypes.

Figure 3–2 shows some of the possibilities. We show here the combinations of the two phenotypes, but with different underlying genotypes. If one parent is AA, then the offspring will be brown-eyed, because no matter what allele the other parent brings to the situation, A will always be dominant in the combination. If both parents are AA', they will have brown eyes, but it is expected that one out of four offspring will be blue-eyed (an A'A' combination).

If both parents are blue-eyed, then we know immediately what the genotype of the offspring will be. Both parents have to be A'A', so there is no way for the offspring to be anything but A'A' and hence blue-eyed. Such genetic crosses as we have described produce these particular phenotypes in the specific cases in which dichotomous characters (such as eye color) are controlled by a particular gene and are unrelated to other genes. If the genes in question interact with other genes, the outcomes may be quite different. As it happened, the garden peas that Mendel studied did show such simple dominant and recessive characters. Other genetic crosses may show "blends," or combinations of the phenotypic characters of the parents. For example, in flowers a red male and a white female may produce a pink offspring. Two pinks may produce either red, white, or pink. Somewhere along the way, however, there may be a genetic error. Perhaps a gene is not reproduced correctly or is not passed on to the offspring. An offspring that does not get the normal genetic complement from each parent is a **mutant** (there is a **mutation,** or genetic change). Usually this is lethal, sometimes harmless, and only rarely advantageous. Advantageous mutations have had time in their favor, however—millions of years to occur, to be selected, and to become part of the gene pool of a species. It is through gene mutations that the necessary

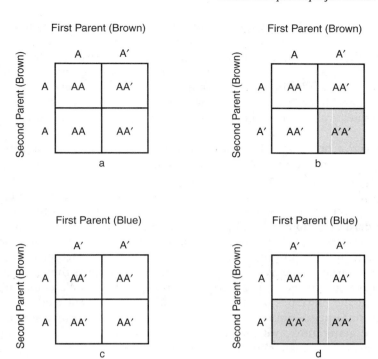

FIGURE 3–2. Illustrative genetic tables for brown-eyed and blue-eyed parents and their offspring. The margins of each table show the genotypes of the parents (A = Brown, dominant; A′ = Blue, recessive). Blue occurs only when two recessive blue genes are paired. The phenotypes of the parents are indicated in the marginal parentheses, and the blue phenotype for offspring is in the stippled cells in (b) and (d). Note that the parental phenotypes are the same in (a) and (b) (both brown), but the genotypes are different, and 1 out of 4 offspring in (b) is expected to be blue-eyed. In (c) and (d) there is one blue-eyed and one brown-eyed parent, but only in (d) are there blue-eyed offspring.

variability in species is maintained, which is necessary for the operation of natural selection.

Genetic versus Environmental Contributions to Behavior

The problem of "nature versus nurture" or "heredity versus environment" generates heated discussions on topics such as personality, intelligence, and criminal tendencies. At various times, the pendulum has swung in favor of the one or the other view. The inevitable conclusion, however, is that both factors are involved and that the problem is to determine the conditions under which one or the other is relatively more influential. We cannot judge by simple observation the extent to which a particular behavior is caused by nature or nurture. By using appropriate analytic and/or experimental procedures, however, we can estimate the relative amounts of variation in behavioral or other characteristics caused by genetic and environmental factors in **groups** of animals. These techniques may involve experiments with selective breeding of particular individuals, comparisons of monozygotic twins (from a single egg and hence with identical genes) with dizygotic twins or other relatives, or statistical studies of behaviors in populations of individuals.

Selective breeding.   If we take an unselected sample of subjects from some population and measure a specific behavior, we find that there is a distribution of scores for that behavior around some average (mean) value. The amount of variation among the scores, how widely they spread, can be determined by calculation of a statistic called the **variance** (which is the square of the **standard deviation**). This population variance, **Vpop,** consists of two components: (I) the individual differences caused by genetics, or the genetic variance, **Vgen,** and (2) differences caused by environmental factors, or the environmental variance, **Venv.**[3] Now we take a group of subjects that are, say, very close to the group mean and selectively inbreed them. (We could inbreed subjects at the extremes of the distribution.) With each succeeding generation, we continue to inbreed those subjects closest to the group average. Over successive generations, we will find that the variance of the inbred groups gets progressively smaller until, after about twenty generations, it reaches a stable value and is no longer reduced by further inbreeding. At this point, we have a homozygous group (all the members have virtually identical genotypes with regard to the character being bred for). There is still some variability, however, that must be caused by environmental factors. Now, we have already said that **Vpop = Vgen + Venv.** In our experimental breeding procedure, since we reduced **Vgen** to zero, any remaining variability is attributable to environmental factors and thus constitutes **Venv.** We then can determine **Vgen** by this simple formula: **Vgen = Vpop − Venv.**

This process is illustrated in Figure 3–3. Suppose that the initial unselected population variance was 10 and that the twentieth generation variance was 3. Then **Vgen** = 10 − 3 = 7. The final step would be to obtain a **heritability coefficient,** which is calculated as **Vgen/Vpop** = 7/10 = .70.[4] This ratio is the proportion of the unselected population variance that is caused by genetic factors. It does not say that 70 percent of the behavior of any **particular** animal is caused by genetics and 30 percent by environmental factors, but it does

[3]There is also a third term, *interaction variance,* which is a measure of the *interaction* between genetic and environmental variance. Genetic potential is realized one way in one environment and a different way in a different environment. In order to determine this, we would have to do selective breeding experiments in several environments. Since our purpose here is just to illustrate the general approach, we have simplified things by ignoring such interactions.

[4]There are a number of ways to arrive at heritability coefficients. This one is illustrative.

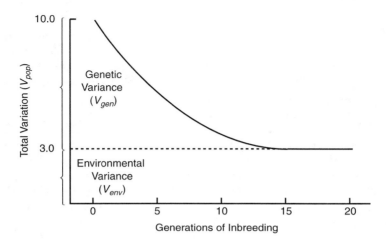

FIGURE 3–3. Stylized representation of change in population variance over successive generations of inbreeding. When further inbreeding produces no further reduction in variance of the bre 'ing characteristic, it is assumed that only environmental variance remains. The proportion of variance that is genetic in this examine is the 10.0–3.0 = 70 percent. See text for details.

say that for the group as a whole, 70 percent of the variance among animals is genetic and 30 percent is environmental.

Many such selective breeding experiments have been done, both in laboratories and in agricultural situations. The latter are often less quantitative, but from them we know that animals can be bred for specific features. Horses, cattle, chickens, turkeys, hogs, and others can be bred for commercially desirable characteristics. Dogs can be bred as gentle pets for children, as hunters, or for sheepherding. In laboratories, fruit flies have been bred for such characteristics as phototaxis (tendency to approach a light), and mice have been bred for aggressiveness or for either high or low emotionality (fearfulness). The common laboratory rat, intentionally or not, has been bred for tameness. In one of the early studies of behavior genetics, Tryon (1940) inbred rats that quickly learned a standard maze and rats that were slow to learn the maze. Within twenty generations, he had bred virtually nonoverlapping populations of animals for the maze task.

Twin studies. Identical twins are homozygous because they come from a union of the same sperm and egg. Nonidentical twins or siblings do not have the same genes because the eggs and sperms from which they come are not genetically identical. The closer the familial relationship, the more similar are the genetics of two individuals, however. Using a **coefficient of concordance,** one can compare the likelihood of one identical twin having a certain characteristic if the other has it and so on through the rest of the familial relations. For example, if one member of every pair of one hundred twins has a particular characteristic and if eighty of the second members have it, the coefficient of concordance is .80. If a particular characteristic is genetically determined, then identical twins should have the highest coefficients, siblings next, and randomly paired members of the population as a whole should have the lowest. Using this approach, Kallmann (1946) found that schizophrenia seemed to have a large genetic component. One might argue that this might be due to more closely related members of a family also having more similar environments. The answer to this challenge lies in demonstrations that identical twins reared in very different environments have higher concordance ratios than nonidentical twins reared in the *same* general environment. We could also calculate a heritability coefficient from twin data. If we assume that any variation between identical twins is environmental, then we could compare this variance to the total population variance. Thus, **Vgen = Vpop − Twin.** We could go from there to calculate the heritability coefficient: **Vgen/Vpop.**

Population genetics.   Selective breeding is not feasible with humans, and the occurrence of particular phenotypic characteristics with twins may not be frequent enough to be enlightening about the genetic basis of a particular human characteristic of interest to us. Data on the frequency of particular phenotypic characters in families or other genetically close groups can give us much information, however. A variety of characteristics are thus found to be hereditary, including blood type, extra fingers, the Rh factor in blood, some forms of mental retardation, color blindness, and hemophilia (excessive bleeding). Some genes may be carried by both sexes but be sex-linked in their expression. Thus, color blindness occurs almost exclusively in males.

A particular group, because of its geographic or social isolation, may contain a gene virtually unknown in other groups. For example, in the United States, sickle cells in the blood are found only among African-Americans and are pathological (sickle-cell anemia). In Africa, however, sickle cells were apparently naturally selected because they are resistant to malaria and hence had a positive value in prolonging life. Similarly, the Jewish population carries a recessive gene for Tay-Sachs disease (a lethal central nervous system disorder) and shows a much higher incidence than in other populations. At the same time, however, a genetic defect called phenylketonuria (PKU), which produces mental retardation, is virtually unknown among Jews. Other religious groups (like the Amish and the Muslems) also have particular recessive pathological genes that are uncommon in other populations. Hemophilia is caused by a recessive gene and although occurring rarely in any broad population, is found with considerable frequency in European royal families. These families have intermarried so frequently over the years that the probability of two recessives mating is much higher than the chance pairing in the general population.

Recent research indicates that cognitive abilities also have a genetic component that appears only after adolescence (Plomin, Fulker, Corley, & DeFries, 1997). This finding was made in a twenty-year longitudinal adoption study that compared 245 adoptive children, their adoptive and biological parents, and 25 matched nonadoptive parents and children. On several measures of cognitive ability, adoptive children are never like their adoptive parents but become more like their natural parents as they pass through adolescence. Eventually they have the same degree of similarity to their biological parents as do children raised with their own biological parents. In general, it appears that somewhere between 20 percent and 50 percent (depending on the study and the characteristics measured) of the variation in human personality is genetically determined (Hamer, 1997).

Evolutionary Psychology

Edmund Wilson (1975) popularized the term **sociobiology** in his widely cited book of the same name, but his application of biological principles to sociological events was not a new idea. Indeed, for higher-life forms, social interaction is the sine qua non of evolution and obviously dates back to Darwin and earlier. The evolutionary process of natural selection is based on variation and genetic transmission, which among animals usually requires some degree of social interaction, i.e., mating. The question of who mates with whom and how this affects survival requires examination of aggressive male behavior, development of mating rituals, attractiveness, coloration, seasonal estrus, and on and on. All of these problems have been studied for many years by biologists and psychologists under the general rubric of adaptation.

Adaptations.   Adaptation to conditions of life is the key to evolution. An adaption is an inherited characteristic that appears through natural selection because it enhances survival and facilitates reproduction. Although an adaptation is inherited, the expression of an adaptation depends on many events in the life of the individual organism. Intrauterine conditions affect development of intelligence (e.g., measles during pregnancy), as can extreme social isolation after birth. Along with adaptations there may be incidental **by-products** that are not part of the adaptive solution. For example, bones are white because of the calcium they contain (which adds strength), not because whiteness solves any evolutionary problem (Buss et al., 1998). Whiteness of external coloration (e.g., on polar bears) obviously does have adaptive value in camouflaging the bear as it hunts prey. Sometimes there are just random effects in reproduction, neutral with regard to adaptation and not linked (as with whiteness of bones) to some adaptive effect (calcium in bones). Although adaptation is the key to evolution, some newer concepts have been added.

Expanded adaptation theory.   Gould (1991) has argued that many present functions of organisms were not initially selected because they were adapted for these present functions. For example, feathers are important for bird flight but seem initially to have evolved because of their thermal properties. Evolved first for one function (keeping warm), they began to be used ("co-opted") for a different function (flying). Gould calls this **exaptation.** A feature that now enhances fitness for one function (feathers for flying) was originally adapted because it enhanced fitness for a different function (keeping warm). In both cases the feathers are functional. Another example is handgrip, which evolved for one function but is now used for holding hammers, tennis rackets, and ski poles.

Another concept of Gould's is **spandrels.** A spandrel is an incidental by-product that subsequently became a functional adaptation. Gould suggests that the human brain was adapted for just one use but that reading, writing, fine arts, commerce, and war are incidental by-products of brain evolution. Adaptation is still the key to evolution, but the evolutionary road is more like a back-country trail than a superhighway. It has many twists and turns, ups and downs. Table 3–2 summarizes some of the characteristics of these evolutionary concepts (from Buss et al., 1998, Table 2, p. 545).

Buss et al. (1998) cite what they consider to be "thirty recent examples of empirical discoveries about humans generated by thinking about adaptation and selection," but were unable to find examples of discoveries about humans based on the concepts of exaptations or spandrels. In any case, the main point is that a broader view of evolution may reap a richer harvest of applications to psychology, and new concepts are needed. In the evolution of science, not all new concepts survive, but new concepts are necessary for the evolution of science to occur at all.

Inclusive fitness theory.   One concept that seems to bear fruit is inclusive fitness. We generally think of fitness in terms of individual genetic characteristics that are passed on directly by that individual to his or her offspring. Other characteristics may indirectly serve this function, however. For example, one man may be able to protect his small family so that his children live longer than those of a man with a large family who cannot protect them. The former may have his genes passed on with greater frequency because he helps his offspring to survive longer and hence to mate more. Similarly, a person who protects his extended family (brothers, sisters, nieces, nephews), which shares his genes, also helps more of these shared genes to be passed on. Inclusive fitness (Hamilton, 1964), then, refers to a person's own reproductive success plus the effects of his or her behavior on the reproductive success of genetic relatives.

In summary, Darwin's principle of natural selection is still the basic mechanism for evolutionary change, but other principles build on it. It remains to be seen whether some of the newer approaches are going to prove out as major contributions to the study of behavior.

TABLE 3.2 Criteria for evaluating concepts of adaptations, exaptations, spandrels, and functionless by-products.

DIFFERENTIATION CRITERIA	ADAPTATION	EXAPTATION (CO-OPTED ADAPTATION)	CO-OPTED SPANDREL	FUNCTIONLESS BY-PRODUCT
Definition	Natural selection is due to fitness of structure/function or through inclusive fitness	Natural selection is for a different function than a current function	Present feature is a by-product of other evolved features	Feature is an accident with no particular functional advantage
Examples	Moth coloration matches surround (individual) or care of offspring (social)	Evolution of feathers was for warmth, but now used for flying	Human speech may be based on evolution of brain for other sensorimotor activities	Whiteness of bones is due to calcium
Origin and maintenance	Adaptation based on history of selection for fitness	Selection operates on previous adaptation	Selection operates on previous by-product	Selection was for mechanism that produced by-product
Role of fitness	Present fitness is correlated with fitness in the past	Adaptation is correlated with present fitness	Adaptation is correlated with present fitness	Adaptation is not directly related to fitness
Critical features	Present function solved an adaptive problem in the past	Adaptation has a new function	Adaptation has a new function	No previous or current function

Source: Adapted from Buss, D. M., Haselton, M. G., Shackelford, T. K., Bleske, A. L., & Wakefield, J. C. (1998). Adaptations, exaptations, and spandrels. *American Psychologist, 53*, 533–548. (Table 2). Copyright 1998 by American Psychological Association. Used by permission.

STIMULUS CONTROL OF SPECIES-SPECIFIC BEHAVIOR

Examples

Of the many energy forms in the environment, living organisms are sensitive to only a few. An animal's sensory system operates as a filter that lets some energy forms "pass" into the animal's nervous system but excludes others. If an animal has a receptor mechanism for transducing a particular environmental energy into neural activity, it is sensitive to that energy. The kinds of receptors that an animal has, and the kind and complexity of neural machinery for processing the sensory inputs, determine that animal's perceptual world. We may all occupy the earth, but we do not all live in the same perceptual world; for example,

1. Humans can hear from about 20 hertz (Hz) to 20 kilohertz (kHz; hertz is the term for cycles per second) sound waves, but dogs and rats hear up to about 40 kHz, and bats and porpoises into the range of 80–100 kHz.
2. Migrating birds are sensitive to the earth's magnetic fields, but humans are apparently not.
3. Bees and some birds are sensitive to polarized light, to which humans are blind.
4. Humans are sensitive to light wavelengths in the range of 400 to 700 millionths of a millimeter but are blind to infrared and ultraviolet wavelengths just on either side of the visible spectrum, as well as to radio frequencies. Many mammals seem to be color-blind, but birds typically have excellent color vision.
5. Sea animals, such as sharks, do not have particularly good vision, but have highly developed smell, which is essential to them for the location of food. A variety of land animals also have excellent smell and utilize body secretions called *pheromones* to communicate with other members of the species, particularly for sexual attraction. Male butterflies can detect and locate female odors at distances of up to several miles. According to Wilson (1975), such chemical communication is virtually universal among living organisms.

Such a list could go on and on, but the general point is made: There are large differences in perceptual sensitivity, and on the basis of our own perceptions, we cannot make any assumptions about what nonhumans are perceiving.

Given that a particular species is **sensitive** to a particular range of stimuli, the species then has to **respond** appropriately to stimulus configurations within that range. Such responding may be based on inherited neural mechanisms for responding in relatively specific ways to specific configurations and/or may depend on prior experience. We may refer to these respectively as **releasing stimulus control** and **acquired stimulus control.**

Releasing stimuli.   Many species may be *sensitive* to a particular stimulus pattern, but only some are uniquely *responsive* to them. Thus, releasing stimuli[5] depend on species-specific sensorimotor organizations for their effectiveness, in addition to stimulus sensitivity per se. For example, many species are sensitive to other organisms looking at them, but primates are especially aggressive in response to being stared in the eye. Rhesus monkeys bare their teeth, scream, and may attack. Male squirrel monkeys, on the other hand, make penile displays as a ritualistic response that has apparently replaced fighting. As another kind of social interaction, baby birds gape in response to particular stimuli from the parents; the gaping is, in turn, a releaser for the parents to feed the babies.

Both mother love and love for mother suffer at the hands of the ethologists, however, because it turns out that the **effective stimuli** for releasing many social behaviors are only a small fraction of the total stimulus input from another organism. We find out what the effective stimuli are by making models with varying degrees of similarity to living organisms, or parts thereof, until it is determined what minimal aspect of the natural stimulus will release a particular behavior. The following examples illustrate such minimal stimuli:

1. For the stickleback, a wooden model on a stick lowered into the water tank will release male sexual behavior, but all that is required of the model is that it look vaguely like the swollen belly of a female with eggs.
2. The gaping behavior of hungry baby birds can be released by a stick with a spot on it (in some cases, a ring around it), similar to the bill of the parent.
3. Male turkeys get excited by a model of a female turkey head, although a real head is better (whether or not attached to a body).
4. The squirrel monkey's penile display is released by a mirror reflection of nothing more than its own eyeball.
5. A cardboard model of a "hawk" produced fearful behavior in chickens when the model was "flown" over the flock, but the same model "flown" in reverse (now having a long neck on the leading edge and looking more like a goose) did not. The exact interpretation of this phenomenon is controversial, but it seems well established that such a phenomenon occurs.
6. Frogs strike out at any small, buglike objects in motion, but not if the stimuli are stationary. Frogs respond to large, dark stimuli by escaping.
7. There are also supernormal stimuli, which are artificial stimuli that are better releasers than natural ones. Thus gulls will take care of oversize artificial eggs in preference to their own.

Desmond Morris (1967) tried to make the argument that human female breasts and lips are sexual releasers because of their similarity to the

---

[5]The concept of releasing stimuli, or releasers, is still a kind of holdover from the concept of reaction specific energy that is blocked until a particular stimulus releases it. If this view of motivation is wrong, which it certainly seems to be, then we have to think of releasing stimuli in somewhat different terms. For our purposes we shall simply view releasing stimuli as any stimuli that evoke specific response patterns, based on some prewired perceptual-motor organization. The terms *stimulate* or *arouse* would then be equivalent to *release*.

female buttocks and genitalia. The argument was that in the course of the evolution of walking erect, women minimized the display of those sexual releasers that are obvious in the more typical bent-over primate position; therefore, new releasers were evolved. As Eibl-Eibesfeldt (1975, p. 495) notes, however, "the artificially up-lifted breast of a movie star may evoke such an association, but a normal breast is as dissimilar from a buttock as lips are from the labia." Besides which, men also have lips.

Interaction of Internal States and Releasers

A stimulus that will release a behavior such as sexual activity at one time may not do so at another time. Responsiveness depends on internal hormonal conditions that may be present only at a particular time of the month (estrus, for example) in cyclic fashion or at certain seasons of the year (as with ungulates). In the case of seasonal mating, sex hormone changes are initiated by the pituitary gland, which, in turn, is under the control of dark-light cycles. Sexual arousability by members of the opposite sex is therefore under the control of complex organismic and environmental interactions. Only in the human species do females seem prepared to mate at any time, and even here the common restrictions against intercourse during menstruation are based on social taboos rather than on biological factors. Human females are also more sensitive to musk odors (as in perfumes) during their childbearing years; men are sensitive to them only if injected with estrogen prior to the odor test. We shall have much more to say about the interaction of internal states and external stimuli in subsequent chapters.

Acquired Stimulus Control

Besides the innate releasing mechanisms, organisms **learn** to use stimuli as cues. They learn that a particular food is good or bad, that a particular event is painful, or that a stimulus signals a pleasant or an unpleasant situation to come. Depending on the individual circumstances of learning, the range of stimuli to which an animal responds in a particular way may be widened or narrowed. A child may learn to be afraid either of all dogs or of only one special dog. But again depending on the particular structural characteristics of a species, some things are learned more readily than others. Presumably in the course of evolution, animals have developed mechanisms for responding to stimuli that are biologically important to them. In the case of releasers, there was *phylogenetic* selection for such responsiveness. Even in the case of learning, there appears to be some preprogramming so that there is a bias in **ontogenetic** selection as well; that is, there is greater ease of learning some things than others. Seligman (1970) has referred to this as "preparedness." In humans, for example, Valentine (1930) reported that it was easy for a child to learn to be afraid of caterpillars but that children did not readily become conditioned to fear opera glasses or a bottle. As Hebb (1955) suggests, there may be a latent fear of certain things that makes it easy to condition them. Such a "latent fear" is a genetic predisposition. We discuss such dispositions in more detail later.

Imprinting.   William James (1890) described the phenomenon we now call imprinting. It is a particular kind of learning occurring most reliably with precocial birds, such as chickens and ducks, which are born with down and are active immediately after hatching. The behavior usually studied is the **following response** of newborn precocial birds. These birds follow any object that moves in front of them on the first day or so of life, but there is a **critical period** of time after hatching during which a permanent attachment to the moving object can develop. Mallard ducklings follow a duck-mother model or a ball or a box that moves, and they are imprinted most strongly at about sixteen hours after hatching (Hess, 1962). In the normal course of duckling events, fortunately, the most likely moving stimulus is the real mother.

For different species there are different critical periods for imprinting, but in all cases there is considerable variability. Hinde, Thorpe, and Vince (1956) found imprinting in coots as late as six days after hatching and were able to correlate the end of the imprinting period with the onset of a **flight period.** That is, the birds would imprint until they reached an age at which they became afraid of strange objects and would not follow them, hence they did not become "attached." There apparently is no unique physiological process involved in imprinting; it is just that after a while, birds (or other animals) become afraid of novel stimuli and do not become "attached" to them. This same view of attachment behavior in mammals has been expressed by Scott (1962) and may be seen in humans. For about the first three months of life, human infants show little response to parental billing and cooing; then they begin to smile and make answering noises. At about six months of age, the infants suddenly become frightened by unfamiliar stimuli, including new faces. This response is often to the chagrin of grandparents or friends who arouse screaming and crying when they expect laughing and smiling. Eventually, of course, most children lose their extreme fear of unfamiliar stimuli.

Lorenz (1966) had argued that imprinting is very nearly irreversible, citing the case of an adult shell parakeet that made sexual advances toward a human to whom it had been imprinted in early life. He believed that this aberrant sexual behavior had been caused by imprinting when the parakeet was young, and he did not believe it represented instrumental conditioning, because the response had not occurred at the time of imprinting. What does more systematic research indicate, however?

Permanence, or irreversibility, of imprinting can refer either to (1) lack of generalization of the imprinted behavior to other stimuli, so that the response is only to a very specific stimulus, or (2) a failure of the strength of the imprinted response to decline. The evidence seems to be largely negative in either case. Hinde, Thorpe, and Vince (1956) found that coots would follow objects very dissimilar to the one on which they were imprinted, and Fabricius (1951) found that, although he could establish a strong following response in tufted ducks, shovellers, and eiders, the following response gradually diminished beginning at about three weeks of age. The most likely explanation for the attractiveness of humans to parakeets is that they were in each other's company over a long period of time, during which a strong attachment developed. Furthermore, as Moltz (1960) suggests, what is "imprinted" may be primarily an emotional response that leads to generalized approach behavior toward a given stimulus rather than a specific response toward that stimulus. Gallagher and Ash (1978), however, report that imprinting of Japanese quail to an albino hen during the first ten days of life is strong, being demonstrated by adult sexual preferences of the imprinted males for albino hens. Post-imprinting experience with hens different from the imprinted hen can change this preference. But lacking later experience, the early establishment of a social bond does last into adulthood. Perhaps the learning is persistent because of lack of interference by other stimuli. At any rate, the general conclusion from research on imprinting is that it is not a unique process but is a fairly typical kind of learning that happens to occur at a particular stage in life.

SUMMARY

1. Species-specific behaviors are those activities unique to a particular species and that have at least partial genetic determination.

2. Species-specific behaviors have often been called *instinctive,* but early in this century, the indiscriminate use of the term *instinct* brought it into disfavor among both biologists and psychologists. Historically, American psychologists have placed greater emphasis on learning than on genetic factors, but there is a rising increase in interest in genetics as it is found that even personality characteristics have a significant genetic component.

3. The term *instinct* has been applied both to *universal* and to *unique* behaviors, and to *urges* (like sex). The usage most closely approximating a motivational concept is that of the urge to do something, rather than any particular behavior.

4. A revival of interest in species-specific behaviors began after World War II, under the influence of the *European ethologists,* especially Konrad Lorenz and Nikolaas Tinbergen.

5. The primary motivational concept in ethology for a long time was that of **reaction-specific energy** (RSE). A system of "energy reservoirs" was conceived to underlay each specific behavior, or **fixed action pattern** (FAP).

6. The various RSEs were said to "build up" spontaneously, and if not released by a **sign stimulus** (also called **releaser**) in the environment, the reservoir for a particular FAP would "overflow" into the behavior appropriate to that energy but not necessarily appropriate to the situation. Such spontaneous activities are called **vacuum reactions** or **displacement** behaviors. Evidence does not generally support the notion of RSEs.

7. Charles Darwin's theory of evolution argued that organisms best adapted for survival would reproduce more often and gain increased representation over successive generations. Survival thus involves **selection** of individuals who can respond behaviorally with the most efficiency in their particular historical time and place.

8. Gregor Mendel's postulation of specific **genetic inheritance** and of **gene mutation** provided the basis for which variation among organisms upon natural selection could work.

9. Any behavior is the joint product of genetic and environmental effects (including the intrauterine environment). Heredity versus environment arguments always reduce to the question of "How much variability in any species characteristic (including behavior) is due to genetic differences, and how much to environmental differences?" Such questions are studied in animals by **selective breeding,** and in humans by studies of **twins, families,** and other genetically related groups.

10. **Evolutionary psychology** is the application of evolutionary concepts to social behaviors, also referred to as **sociobiology.** The concept of **inclusive fitness** is that an organism can help pass on its own genes by protecting its own family members, which carry its genes. Other concepts that have been proposed to expand beyond the idea of adaptation to the environment are **exaptation, spandrel,** and **functionless by-product.**

11. **Releasing stimulus control** of behavior refers to responsiveness to particular stimulus configurations due to genetically programmed stimulus-response connections, such as the gaping mouth of a baby bird eliciting feeding from a parent. The **effective** releasing stimulus is often only a small fragment of the total stimulus. Responsiveness to such stimuli often depends on internal states, such as the level of circulating sex hormones.

12. **Acquired stimulus control** refers to any kind of learning that involves responding to stimuli. Considerable evidence indicates genetic predispositions that make it easier for a given species to learn some things rather than others.

13. A form of learning called **imprinting** is exemplified by the **following behavior** of ducklings. It is said to occur only during a **critical period** after birth and to be very enduring. Evidence indicates that critical periods vary a great deal, that imprinting is reliably found mainly with precocial birds, and that it is not as permanent as has often been stated. It is questionable whether imprinting is a unique kind of learning at all.

CHAPTER FOUR

Eating, Taste, and Addiction

———•———

Over the last thirty years, there has been a revolution in the study of consumatory behavior, which is still gaining momentum in both research and theory. The new view emphasizes the roles of pleasure, learning, and environmental and social factors in the control of feeding and drinking. This chapter reflects the new outlook and the way that it reorganizes our thinking about how we survive.

CLASSIC HOMEOSTATIC THEORY

Constancy of the Internal Environment

Biological approaches to motivation have largely grown out of Darwin's theory of evolution by natural selection. If complex organisms are to reproduce, they must survive. To survive, they must monitor the status of their **internal environments** so that they can make necessary behavioral adjustments to keep healthy, such as eating and drinking. The internal environment (*milieu interieur*) consists of the fluids that bathe our body cells, bringing nutrients and removing metabolic waste. Claude Bernard ([1865] 1967), often called the father of experimental medicine, developed the dictum that **the necessary condition for a free life is constancy of the internal environment.** An animal is "free" when it can carry its internal environment around without undue threat of cell destruction. When all the controls necessary for life become portable and are protected from the environment by the skin, an animal is free.

Homeostasis

Walter Cannon (1939b) built on Bernard's ideas by developing the concept of **homeostasis,** which he called "the wisdom of the body." Cannon described homeostasis as the automatic adjustments the body makes to restore stability when there is a departure from the narrow tolerance ranges of temperature, acidity, glucose concentration, salt and water balance, and so on. Homeostatic mechanisms are under the control of the autonomic nervous system, but this system can do only so much until behavior becomes necessary. For example, when the body becomes overheated, perspiration promotes evaporative cooling, but at the cost of losing body water. Automatic mechanisms come into play to conserve water, but eventually the organism must take action to replace lost water and/or to cool itself without evaporation. The study of such regulatory actions is part of the study of **motivated behavior.**

Homeostatic Signals

A deficiency in the body can be corrected by motivated behavior only if the body sends signals of the deficiency to trigger appropriate compensatory activities. These activities, in turn, must generate "stop" signals to terminate the behavior when the deficiency has been offset. One of the major problems, then, is to determine what the "start" and "stop" signals are and where they are generated.

Peripheral theories.   In the 1930s, Walter Cannon (e.g., 1934) argued for a **peripheral** theory of motivation, which says that start and stop signals arise outside the central nervous system. Cannon proposed that the signals for eating and drinking were contractions of the stomach and a dry mouth, respectively. Experiments by Anton Carlson, in which stomach balloons were used to record stomach contractions, seemed to support Cannon's theory. It was also shown, however, that animals or people without stomachs still ate normal amounts of food and that a man without salivary glands drank normal amounts of water (Steggerda, 1941). Furthermore, stomach contractions measured from electrodes on the abdomen do not correlate with experienced "hunger pangs." Thus, although peripheral start signals may exist, they cannot be the whole story. Evidence for peripheral stop signals appears strong and is discussed later in this chapter.

Central theories.   Other researchers emphasized start signals generated within the central nervous system. Karl Lashley (1938) said that instinctive behaviors (including feeding) were controlled by the brain, and Frank Beach (1942) said the same about sexual behavior. Clifford Morgan (1943, 1959) proposed the concept of a **central motive state** (CMS), a hypothetical system of brain centers and pathways concerned with particular kinds of motives. A specific CMS was defined in terms of the kinds of environmental stimuli to which an animal responds. Responsiveness to food indicates a hunger CMS, responsiveness to water indicates a thirst CMS, and so on. Morgan attributed three properties to a CMS. Once it is triggered, the CMS **persists** for some time without further stimulation; it **predisposes** an organism to act in a certain way to particular stimuli (e.g., to approach food) but not to other stimuli; and it **directly emits** certain behaviors. For example, the sexual movements of a female rat in heat might occur as a direct response to a CMS and its hormones. Morgan held that hormones were probably more important than external stimuli in arousing and maintaining CMSs because circulating hormones could maintain a state of excitability over a long period of time.

Elliot Stellar (1954) proposed more specifically that motivated behavior results from arousal of excitatory centers in the hypothalamus of the brain. The activity of these centers is determined by (1) **inhibitory centers** that depress the excitatory centers; (2) **sensory stimuli;** (3) **humoral factors;** and (4) **cortical and thalamic centers** that can produce either excitatory or inhibitory effects on the hypothalamus.

HUNGER AS A HOMEOSTATIC NEED

Once an animal begins a meal (the amount an animal eats in a "bout" of feeding), it continues to eat until something stops it. This response (eating) depends on opposing signals for starting and maintaining behavior and for stopping behavior. These are now often called **positive and negative feedback** signals. Whether the animal eats or not depends on the relative strength of the two sets of signals. It is not clear where or how these signals are measured or compared by the brain, but it is likely that such "computations" would occur, if at all, in the general region of the hypothalamus.

Positive Feedback Signals

The mouth and nose are the primary sites of positive feedback for eating. Food-seeking activity may be triggered before food stimuli reach the mouth or nose, but once an animal can smell or taste food, approach to food and eating are intensified. The dopamine and endorphin systems in the brain (discussed later) are major components of positive feedback. Opiate drugs enhance eating, and drugs that counteract opiates reduce eating.

Negative Feedback Signals

Negative feedback signals are generated as food passes through the mouth, stomach, and small intestine. These signals are anticipatory and tell the animal to stop eating before food can be absorbed and homeostasis is restored. Stomach distention may be one such signal, but it cannot be the only signal. Even if the vagus nerve from the stomach is severed, animals still stop eating after normal-size meals; hence, there must be other signals. There are species differences in negative feedback (what does stomach distention mean to a cow with its four stomachs?), but because of the great similarity of rat and human in most aspects of feeding, it would appear that similar mechanisms are involved for these two species.

A major source of negative feedback signals appears to be the release of hormones from the stomach and intestinal walls. In particular, **cholecystokinin** (CCK) and **bombesin** are involved in negative feedback. It appears that CCK reduces the pleasure felt from the ingested food so that the animal stops eating. It is also possible that there are even more specific chemical satiety signals, since we may become satiated ("full") for one food and immediately start consuming another.

Energy monitoring. Early theories treated hunger as a *single* motivational state involved in the control of the body's energy. However, evidence indicates that specific food deficits initiate searches for specific kinds of food, such as sugar, salt, fats, and amino acids. This finding suggested that there is more than one kind of hunger. Smith and Gibbs (1995) flatly state to the contrary that only one **physiological** control of the initiation of eating has been identified in the rat. This control is a decline of blood glucose of about 12 percent, which occurs about five minutes before the rat spontaneously begins to eat. It is not clear that this is a cue in humans.

Current research suggests that the brain may monitor the overall energy status of the body, regardless of the particular food being utilized (Bernardis & Bellinger,1996; Ramsay, Seeley, Bolles, & Woods, 1996). For example, oxidation rate in the liver is correlated with the uptake of free fatty acids in the lateral hypothalamus (LH). Sugars, proteins, and fats all contribute to this, and specific receptors for each food type are not needed. When energy production in the body declines (as shown by decreased liver activity), there is a change in LH neurons that triggers feeding. As the organism eats, metabolic activity in the liver increases, fatty acids in the hypothalamus increase, and feeding declines. This is a nice homeostatic account, which says that the constancy of the internal environment is maintained by monitoring energy level rather than by monitoring particular food deficits. By and large, though, it appears that organisms use such energy signals as a last resort, in emergencies that arise when body needs have not been anticipated in some other way.

Feedforward Signals

Woods (1991) has argued convincingly that the act of eating must in itself be highly disruptive to homeostasis, because it produces large internal changes rather suddenly. We usually think of the parasympathetic division of the autonomic nervous system as having a calming influence as food is digested and of the sympathetic system as being dominant during exciting fight-flight episodes of activity. Actually, the sympathetic system is active, and epinephrine, norepinephrine, and other stress hormones are released into the blood as we eat. It would therefore seem that at least some aspects of feeding should be aimed at protecting the organism from this stress. A separate set of **feedforward signals** may warn the animal to act before feeding disruption becomes overly severe. Consider the case of body temperature. The homeostatic problem is to keep the **core** of the body within a narrow temperature range. As the body starts to cool, our hands get cold before core temperature drops. This is a signal that we should do something to get warm, and it occurs before there is a truly dangerous drop in core temperature. Most feedforward signals appear to be learned.

Cephalic insulin.   One feedforward signal related to feeding is **cephalic insulin** (Woods, 1991). Insulin is released from the pancreas into the blood in response to increases of glucose, fat, or amino acids. Insulin release is a homeostatic mechanism that helps the body return to its normal blood glucose level by removing the newly consumed foods from the bloodstream and into body cells. If the insulin supply is inadequate, as in the case of **diabetes mellitus,** there is a surplus of unabsorbed glucose in the blood. Insulin release is triggered not only by food in the mouth but also by such external cues as the sight, taste, and smell of food. It can also be conditioned to such arbitrary external stimuli as lights and sounds. This anticipatory release of insulin by such cues is what is meant by cephalic insulin. In this case, insulin begins to appear in the blood before the animal/person actually starts to eat, and the homeostatic-disruptive food can thus be moved more quickly from the blood (Woods, 1991).

Inherent Limitations of the Homeostatic Model

George Collier and his associates (e.g., Collier, Kanarek, Hirsch, & Marwine, 1976; Collier, Hirsch, & Hamlin, 1972) have argued that animals or people rarely eat because they are depleted. Rather, they eat to prevent depletion. Eating or drinking increases with deprivation, but we seldom see such deprivation in nature, and laboratory animals are not normally starving when they eat in their home cages. The homeostatic model predicts that feeding should be correlated with amount of time since the last meal (or until the next one), but such correlations are rarely found. Each kind of animal in its own particular ecological niche comes to know what to do to keep from getting overly hungry. De Castro, in a study of over three hundred human adults, also found that the types of food or beverage that people consume within a meal or over a day is more influenced by nonhomeostatic factors than by any responses to homeostatic imbalance (De Castro, 1993).

Does nature know best? All animals must meet certain minimal dietary requirements to maintain health. For humans, three major food components are **fats,** which break down into fatty acids and glycerol; **carbohydrates,** which break down into the sugars glucose and fructose; and **proteins,** which break down into the twenty or so different amino acids. Fats are found in meats, milk products, and oils; carbohydrates are found in breads, pasta, and fruits; proteins are found in vegetables, meats, and beans. In addition, we need vitamins and minerals. A nutritionally balanced diet contains about 15 percent protein, 65 percent carbohydrates, and 15 to 20 percent fats. Vitamins and minerals are typically in these foods rather than having separate sources. But how do animals, including humans, go about selecting a balanced diet from all the possible choices available? Has nature "hardwired" us with this ability so that we just automatically select proper foods, or is something else involved?

Some animals are feeding **specialists,** and others are **generalists.** Specialists, like koala bears, which feed exclusively on eucalyptus leaves, do have a genetically determined capacity to select the proper food. They eat only the leaves, which are a proper diet for them. The koalas' only problem is getting enough to eat. Generalists, like omnivores, can find an adequate diet among many foods and must make wise feeding choices from among the many foods available to them. Evolution provided the generalists with a particularly important genetic decision-making aid: taste. Good-tasting things tend to be healthy, and bad-tasting substances tend to be deadly. The correlation between taste quality and degree of toxicity is about +.80 (Scott, 1990). We have a chance to find out whether something is good or bad for us before it goes to the stomach, and we can either continue or stop eating it. But does this, or any other automatic mechanism, guarantee good nutrition?

For nearly a century, there has been a running debate between those who believe that "nature knows best" and those who believe that "nature is fickle" when it comes to self-selected diets. In early "cafeteria studies," animals (or children, Davis, 1939) were given all the foods necessary for a well-rounded diet and allowed to eat freely whatever they wanted. The animals tended to eat appropriately over a period of time. This finding seemed to support the "nature knows best" argument. Cafeteria diets are successful, but only if the necessary foods are available and if there is not some high-preference food in the mix, such as a delicious desert. When high-preference foods are available, animals do not eat any more wisely than humans; they eat what tastes good. Young and Chaplin (1945) found that rats deprived of protein preferred a high-protein food in comparison with a regular laboratory chow diet, but not in preference to a sugar-laced diet. Galef (1991) also points out that half the cafeteria studies have *not* shown that animals "naturally" select a nutritionally adequate diet and that even in the wild, animals are not guaranteed nutritionally adequate diets. Many wild animals do not survive to adulthood because they do not eat properly. Nature can be a very fickle mistress.

P. T. Young (1966) took a strong stand against the homeostatic approach as the sole explanation of food selection. He said that food acceptance is determined by at least four groups of determinants:

- **Organic conditions.** These include metabolic needs such as those that are induced by deprivation, but also include other organic states. Illness, for example, overrides deprivation and often abolishes any desire for food.
- **Peripheral stimulations.** These involve not only the immediate impact of food on the head receptors (taste, smell, touch, vision, audition) but also complex social and cultural factors.
- **Previous experience.** This includes dietary history, as well as feeding habits, attitudes, and expectancies.
- **Bodily constitution.** This includes not only types of taste receptors, which vary from species to species, but also more complex body differences. Thus, if a feeding specialist like the koala bear is limited to eating eucalyptus leaves, then its body must be able to derive all its nutritional requirements from these leaves. Other animals cannot do this.

Herman (1996) points out that the homeostatic depletion-repletion model is often kept in its dominant theoretical position by simply ignoring "other" factors that affect eating or by considering them "exceptions" to the homeostatic rule. These include sensory pleasure, previous individual experience with foods, family history, cultural background, and emotional and immediate social factors. Herman suggests that all these factor together may lead to food selection that is adequate and that gives the appearance of homeostasis because the organism survives. Modern research on feeding has taken these factors into greater account, making a more complicated story, but one that better fits the data.

BRAIN MECHANISMS FOR FEEDING

Many parts of the brain must be involved in feeding. For example, sensory systems must help locate and discriminate among possible foods. Muscle systems must be activated to collect and eat food, and so on. It is in the limbic system and brain stem, however, that the crucial components specific to feeding seem to be located. The hypothalamus and surrounding areas have received the most attention.

The Dual Hypothalamic Theory of Hunger

According to the dual hypothalamic theory of hunger, the **lateral hypothalamus** (LH) is an **excitatory** area for feeding, and the **ventromedial hypothalamus** (VMH) is an **inhibitory area** for feeding (see Figure 4–1).

Lateral hypothalamic syndrome. Direct electrical stimulation of the LH leads to *stimulus bound eating*, which lasts only as long as the stimulation is on. When the lateral hypothalamus is destroyed by passing an electrical current through it with carefully placed electrodes, animals stop eating and drinking for times ranging from days to weeks, depending on the size and locations of the lesions. As the animals recover, they go through a sequence of feeding changes called the lateral hypothalamic syndrome. Initially, they have to be tube fed because they will not eat or drink anything. Then the animals begin to accept such highly palatable foods as chocolate chip cookies ground up in milk but will not eat regular lab chow (which is similar to dry dog food). Finally, they will voluntarily eat enough lab chow and drink enough water to maintain their body weight, apparently regulating their food and water intake according to their need (Teitelbaum & Epstein, 1962). As it turns out, however, the animals get enough water only accidentally, as a side effect of drinking while eating. Unlike normal animals, they do not respond to water deprivation by increasing their water intake, because their thirst system is permanently impaired.

The LH contains its own nerve cells but is also part of the ventral tegmental dopamine pathway, which is discussed in more detail later. Some of the pathways running through the lateral hypothalamus go to a motor area

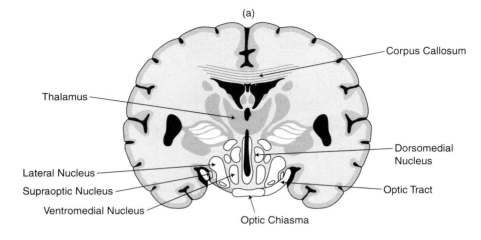

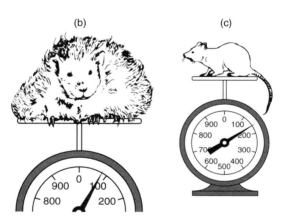

FIGURE 4–1. Hypothalamic nuclei. The cross-section of the brain (a) shows several of the hypothalamic nuclei. The obese rat (b) has lesions in the ventromedial nuclei. A normal rat (c) is shown for comparison. A rat with lesions in the lateral nuclei starves itself. (From Schneider & Tarshis, *An Introduction to Physiological Psychology*, 1975, p. 278. Reprinted with permission of Random House, Inc.)

of the forebrain (the **globus pallidus**). Since LH animals were very sloppy eaters, as if they could not eat and swallow food normally, it was suggested that the lesions may have produced a deficit in muscle coordination rather than in motivation. Other experiments showed, however, that if the animals were required to press a lever to get food, they showed the same sequence of recovery as animals who had only to eat the food available. This finding means that even if the acts of grasping, eating, and swallowing food had been impaired, there was also a motivational deficit, because a behavior not disturbed by the lesions (bar pressing) was also affected. The motivational hypothesis was favored also by the fact that during recovery, animals could and would eat highly palatable foods but would not eat lab chow, suggesting that the palatability of the regular diet was altered by the lesions.

Ventromedial hypothalamic effects. Electrical stimulation of the VMH puts a stop to eating, and destruction of the VMH produces animals that eat voraciously, to the point of doubling or tripling their body weight. Figure 4–2 shows how animals gain weight. Stimulation of the VMH also inhibits just about anything an animal might be doing, however, so that the VMH is not involved just in the control of eating. In addition, VMH-lesioned animals have shown other food-related changes. They overeat to the point of gross obesity and are overreactive to good and bad tastes. Compared with normal animals, they eat more of sweet-tasting food but less of bitter-adulterated food. Furthermore, in spite of their ravenous appetites and responsiveness to good tastes, they often will not work as much as normal animals to get food.

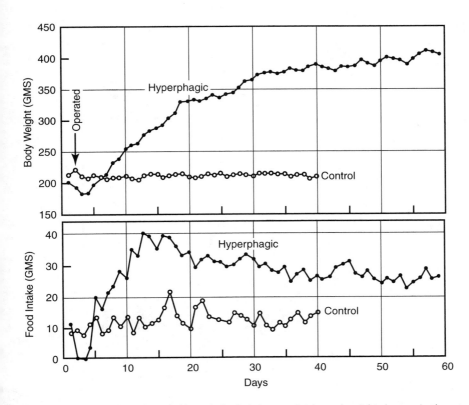

FIGURE 4–2. Effects of ventromedial hypothalamic lesions on intake and weight changes in the rat. (From Teitelbaum, 1961. Reprinted from 1961 *Nebraska Symposium on Motivation,* by permission of University of Nebraska Press. Copyright © 1961 by University of Nebraska Press.)

Pleasure Centers and Feeding

In 1954, James Olds and Peter Milner reported that a tiny amount of electric current, which was put into the brain of a rat by means of a permanently implanted electrode, was a powerful reward. They subsequently proposed that there is a "pleasure center" in the brain and that any stimulus exciting this area of the brain would be rewarding. This research immediately seemed to be incompatible with the then-influential drive reduction theory of reinforcement. This extension of homeostatic theory said that all rewards are effective because they reduce body needs. Instead, the Olds-Milner experiment seemed to be more compatible with classic hedonic theories that said that pleasurable stimulation is rewarding.

Figure 4–3 illustrates an animal pressing a lever for brain stimulation reward, and Figure 4–4 illustrates the power of such reward. We see a cumula-

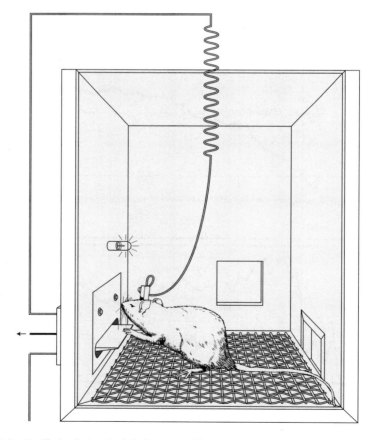

FIGURE 4–3. A self-stimulation circuit is diagrammed here. When the rat presses on the treadle, it triggers an electric stimulus to its brain and simultaneously records action via wire at left. (From Olds, 1956, p. 108. Copyright © 1956 by Scientific American, Inc. Reprinted by permission.)

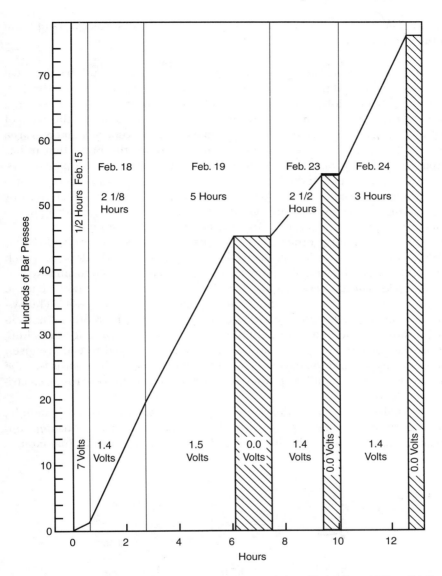

FIGURE 4–4. Smoothed cumulative response curve for a rat. (From Olds & Milner, 1954, p. 424. Copyright © 1954 by the American Psychological Association. Reprinted by permission.)

tive lever-pressing curve for a single animal tested over thirteen hours. The animal pressed steadily when it was rewarded by brain stimulation, but stopped pressing when the current was eliminated. Olds (1958) showed data from an animal that responded about 2,000 times an hour for twenty-four consecutive hours before collapsing from fatigue. However, as fascinating as these results are in their own right, we do not find animals with electrodes in the brains running around in the wild. How do the pleasure centers operate in the natural brain?

Loci of pleasurable stimulation effects. Anatomical and biochemical studies over the next thirty years revealed that locations ranging from the neocortex and frontal lobes all the way down to the brain stem can be rewarding with electrical self-stimulation of the brain. These locations are in the areas of the **medial forebrain bundle, lateral hypothalamus,** and **ventral tegmental area** (VTA), shown in Figure 4–5. They are those parts of the brain that utilize dopamine as a neurotransmitter (Stellar & Stellar, 1985). The dopamine system is also where such addictive drugs as cocaine and the amphetamines produce their pleasurable effects. Whether the dopamine system is activated by such natural causes as pleasant food, by such unnatural causes as drug ingestion, or by direct electrical activation, the end effect is pleasurable.

At the same time, other areas of the brain must also be involved (Kalat, 1988). The brain stimulation electrode must be placed in a dopamine-rich area of the brain, but the dopamine system connects to the **endorphin** system in the **nucleus accumbens** (Figure 4–5). The endorphins, the brain's natural opiates, may be the key neurotransmitters for reward (Wise, 1989). This system may be involved in all forms of addiction. Furthermore, if other "motivating" stimuli are added to brain stimulation, animals work more for the stimulation (Hoebel, 1969). For example, if animals are allowed to eat, are given the odor peppermint, or have sucrose put directly into their mouths by tube when they are self-stimulating, they respond more for the rewarding electrical stimulation.

It is also clear that endorphins and sweet tastes interact. For example, administration of opiates prior to feeding enhances sucrose consumption. But if animals are injected with a drug that counteracts opiates **(naloxone),**

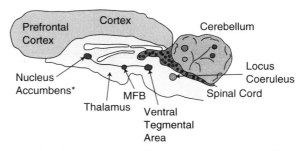

*Stimulation is reinforcing along pathway between n.a. and VTA.

FIGURE 4–5.   The dopamine "pleasure system" in the rat brain, running from the ventral tegmental area (VTA) through the hypothalamus and medial forebrain bundle (MFB), and on to the nucleus accumbens. When electrically stimulated, this area produces a highly pleasurable effect. It is involved in feeding and drug addiction.

they consume less sucrose. Lateral hypothalamic lesions may damage this system so that the pleasurable effects of eating regular lab chow are diminished. Thus after the animals begin to recover, they eat only highly palatable foods for a while before they begin to eat lab cow again.

Brain differences in liking and wanting.   We typically think that animals like what they want and want what they like. The rat that likes sucrose also wants it, as shown by how much it is willing to work for it. Kent Berridge (1996) demonstrated that the functions of liking and wanting are separable in the brain and have different characteristics. To show this, however, we need independent measures of liking and wanting. Fortunately for this purpose, animals have head movements that indicate liking or disliking of foods, and these movements can be distinguished from the amount of work that an animal will do to get something.

Liking and disliking are shown by the way laboratory rats consume fluids. They drink tasty fluids eagerly. They lick steadily at the drinking tube, are careful to swallow all they can get, and so on. They show similar signs if the fluid is injected directly into the mouth so that they can taste and swallow it without having to drink from a tube. Conversely, if they do not like the fluid, they try to spit it out, withdraw from it, let it dribble from their mouths, or wipe it away from their mouths with their paws. These highly stereotyped acceptance and rejection behaviors can be recorded on videotape for later analysis and are readily distinguished by observers. Human infants show similar signs of acceptance and rejection. These reactions (illustrated in Figure 4–6) are determined in the brainstem and do not require conscious recognition. Various experimental manipulations that alter human perception of palatability, such as food deprivation, have similar effects on the affective reactions of rats.

If dopamine in the tegmental system is temporarily "wiped out" by injection of **6-hydroxydopamine,** animals will not work for sweet foods because they do not want them. If, however, a sweet solution is injected into the mouths of these same animals, they show the head movements that indicate liking. Administration of naloxone eliminates these liking responses. Liking thus appears to be related to the endorphins, and wanting (anticipating and working for an incentive) is related to the dopamine system. This separation of liking and wanting has important implications for much of motivation theory and gives us a new way to look at many problems. For example, Berridge (1991) showed that the positive affective reactions to food were reduced when the animals became satiated but that the aversive reactions did not increase. This finding indicates that the decline in palatability that occurs with satiation is a reduction in liking (endorphin related) rather than actual aversion to food.

The caudal brainstem.   Many parts of the brain must be involved in the complex web of factors that determine **food selection.** We may ask, however,

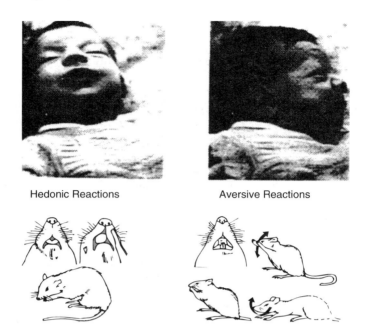

FIGURE 4–6. Affective reactions to taste. Hedonic reaction of a 3-week-old infant to a sweet solution (left; 1 M sucrose) versus aversive reaction to an unpleasantly salty solution (right; 0.15 M NaCl) are shown in videotape frames at top. Various hedonic and aversive reactions of rats, which would be elicited by the same tastes, are drawn below. Hedonic reactions include tongue protrusions, lateral tongue protrusions, and paw licks. Aversive reactions include gapes, headshakes, face/paw wipes, and forelimb flails. Infant video from unpublished observations collected by G. Harris, D. Booth, and K. Berridge at the University of Birmingham, England [following Stiner (130,131)]. Rat drawings of taste reactivity components follow Grill and Norgren (63). (From Berridge, 1996, Figure 2.)

what is the lowest level of brain organization sufficient to account for the facts of consummatory behavior? The caudal brainstem seems to do the job. This is the brainstem that is disconnected from the diencephalon (thalamus and hypothalamus) and the cerebral hemispheres. A rat cannot survive this operation without being tube fed. However, if food is squirted into its mouth through a tube that runs into the top of its mouth, it responds to different taste stimuli the same way a normal animal does. Tasty fluid is flicked toward the throat by the tongue, much as a normal animal laps at solutions from a drinking tube. The animal does this at the same rate as normal licking (about six licks per second). It responds more for higher concentrations of sucrose; it responds more for sucrose when food is deprived and less after being stomach-loaded with glucose; it responds less following injection of CCK. It rejects quinine. By all tests thus far devised, the caudal animal acts just like a normal animal as far as accepting and rejecting tastes (Grill & Kaplan, 1990).

Once an animal has food in its mouth, it hardly seems to miss the parts of its brain above the brainstem. Organization of activities for approaching and learning about foods, however, presumably involves a higher level of brain organization than found in the brainstem.

TASTE AND FEEDING

Palatability

Palatability refers to many features that make food more or less appetizing, which is to say, pleasurable. These features include taste, odor, texture, temperature, color, and even shape. Some of these are genetically determined, others are learned. Food manufacturers have fine-tuned palatability and have provided us, for example, with such palatability highlights as fruit- and sweet-flavored cereals that have bright colors and interesting shapes, and that don't get soggy in milk.

Taste Qualities and Their Stimuli

The single most important palatability factor is probably taste. In humans, there are four commonly recognized taste qualities: **sweet, bitter, salty,** and **sour.** The prototype stimuli for these are sucrose (table sugar), quinine, sodium chloride (table salt), and citric acid (as found in citrus fruits). Other taste qualities seem to be either a combination of these four or a mixture of taste and smell. Other species may have more or fewer tastes than humans. Rats are equally responsive to the same stimuli as humans but also appear to have a receptor for **polyglucose,** a more complex sugar (Sclafani, 1991). Some of the food specialists have taste receptors for very particular substances and are taste-blind to all else, e.g., the koala bear's responding only to eucalyptus leaves and the tomato worm's responding only to tomato leaves. Dogs love sweets, but cats are indifferent to them.

Sweet taste is produced by a variety of organic compounds, including sugars, glycols, and alcohols, with no specific chemical similarities among them yet known. Salty taste is produced by water-soluble salts, with both positive and negative ions contributing to the taste. Sour taste is correlated with the concentration of hydrogen ($H+$) ions, with a number of different acids having the same taste. Alkaline substances are bitter, but there is no known specific chemical structure for all stimuli that have a bitter taste.

Primary Taste Qualities and Hunger

It would appear to be no accident that the primary taste qualities are so important to feeding. They are tuned to stimuli that play important roles in survival, not all of which are nutritional.

Sweet.   The body's most important source of energy is glucose, which is a sugar, and sugars are some of our most motivationally potent stimuli. Common table sugar, sucrose, breaks down into glucose and fructose. Glucose provides energy to the muscles, but the body's most gluttonous user of glucose is the brain. Consider, then, the following:

- Food deprivation increases animals' liking for sugars, so that they consume more (e.g., Collier & Myers, 1961), a phenomenon known as **allesthesis** (Cabanac, 1990).
- If glucose is injected directly into the blood of a hungry animal before it eats, it eats less sugar.
- Glucose in the mouth stimulates firing of sweet-taste receptors on the tongue, which leads to firing of "sweet" neurons in the brain, thereby signaling that something in the mouth is good. But if glucose is injected directly into the blood, these brain responses are inhibited; the brain detects that the body has enough glucose.
- Diabetic humans tend to overeat because they have a strong liking for sweets, which are not being absorbed because of lack of insulin. Their bodies then continue to signal that they are hungry. Injection of insulin also inhibits neural responses to a glucose taste stimulus.

Salt.   Salt is needed by the body for regulating the amount of water in the body and for normal nerve and muscle activity. Severe salt deficit is a health-threatening problem. Most people like food a little salty, and wild animals will travel miles to get to a salt lick. Laboratory rats normally prefer about a 1 percent solution of salt water to plain water. If their adrenal glands are removed so that the salt-regulating hormone **aldosterone** is lost, they drink more salt solution and prefer a higher concentration (3 percent), which is normally very aversive. People with **diabetes insipidus,** a disease of the adrenal gland, lose massive amounts of salt in their urine and subsequently consume large amounts of salt. Why?

Kurt Richter (1936), a pioneer in the study of behavior and homeostasis, suggested that adrenalectomized animals become more sensitive to the taste of salt. This suggestion turned out to be wrong, however. The minimal concentration of sodium chloride sufficient to activate the taste system is the *same* for normal and adrenalectomized animals (Pfaffman & Bare, 1950). Even a normal rat *can* discriminate between water and saline, if it is motivated (by punishment) to do so. We therefore conclude that salt deprivation affects salt **preference** rather than sensitivity. The evidence that this is a genetic mechanism is strong. For example, after a single salt depletion, animals show greater preference for salt. No experience is necessary (Krieckhaus & Wolf, 1968; A. N. Epstein, 1967; Falk, 1961). Even more interesting, Scott (1990) measured the activity of individual neurons in the brain and found that salt-responsive neurons had different patterns of firing than sugar-responsive neurons. When animals were salt deprived, however, salt-responsive neurons began to behave more like sweet-responsive neurons. Increased preference for salt may thus be explained by the fact that the brain begins to treat salt more like sugar. Young and Christensen (1962) showed that aversive concentrations of salt become more palatable if sugar is mixed in with them.

Bitter.   The prototype bitter taste is that of quinine, once the standard treatment for malaria. There is no concentration of quinine that animals prefer to deionized water, the standard "neutral stimulus" in taste research. Quinine is always avoided by the animals that can taste it. Could such a strong aversion be reversed by early experience with quinine? Both rats and guinea pigs have been exposed to quinine immediately after birth and throughout infancy. It becomes tolerated at low concentrations, but as soon as animals are given the choice of water, they avoid the quinine in the same way as animals that have never tasted quinine. The aversive reaction to quinine is genetically determined, just as the approach reaction to sugar and salt is genetic. The only way yet discovered to make a bitter taste more attractive is by introducing the taste in a social context with another person or animal (Galef, 1996).

Sour.   Sour tastes are generally aversive but can become attractive under some conditions, especially in combination with sweet, such as in sour candy or lemonade. The sour taste of pickles is enjoyed by some, but as with bitter, this characteristic seems to develop in a social context.

Fat.   Although fat is not a basic taste, it is such an important determinant of food preference that we put it with the others. Fat is important because it and sugar are the most highly preferred human tastes and because excess fat produces health problems. Fat combined with sugar makes a potent taste package, no secret among cookie manufacturers.

LEARNING AND CONSUMATORY BEHAVIOR

In order to understand how our experience is related to feeding behavior we must first understand a few of the basic principles of *classical (Pavlovian) conditioning*. Conditioning is not the only form of learning that affects our eating, but it has been studied in the laboratory for well over a hundred years and accounts for phenomena ranging from learning what foods are good or bad to promoting political candidates by associating them with good events.

Classical Conditioning

While doing research on salivary reflexes, Ivan Pavlov normally put food on the tongues of dogs and recorded the amount of salivation stimulated by the food. He observed that the dogs sometimes began to salivate before food was placed on the tongue, even as they were being put into the experimental apparatus. The salivary reflex had been conditioned to cues in the environment. Pavlov then spent the next thirty years studying what he called "psychic secretions" (Pavlov, 1927).

Classical conditioning is a form of **associative learning,** which means that the relationship between two events is learned because they occur closely in time; Figure 4–7 illustrates these relationships. The following four terms are basic:

- **Unconditioned stimulus (UCS).** Any stimulus, such as food, that will reliably elicit a response before conditioning occurs.
- **Unconditioned response (UCR).** The response elicited by an unconditioned stimulus, such as a salivary reflex by putting food in the mouth.
- **Conditioned stimulus (CS).** Any stimulus that gains the power to evoke the response produced by the UCS by closely preceding the UCS in time. For example, the sound of a buzzer (CS) could come to evoke salivation (CR) if paired with food presentation (UCS).
- **Conditioned response (CR).** The response, such as salivation, evoked by the CS. The CR may not be exactly like the UCR, but it has some of the characteristics of the UCR.

The processes described in the following paragraphs are basic to classical conditioning.

Acquisition.   This is the process of learning to associate the CS with a meaningful stimulus (the UCS). The process is diagrammed in Figure 4–8. If you use an electric can opener to open food for your dog, the dog will eventually associate the whirring sound with food. You may not see the salivation, but you can see that the dog "perks up" when it hears the sound, just as it perks up when it smells the food. The conditioned response becomes

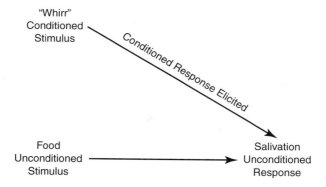

FIGURE 4–7.   The basic arrangement and terminology to describe classical conditioning of salivation. The "whirr" of the can opener is associated with food and comes to elicit salivation as the food does. See text for more details.

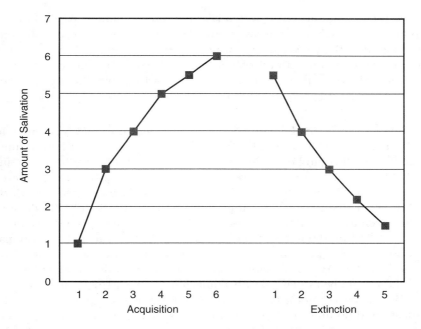

FIGURE 4–8. Acquisition and extinction of a conditioned salivation response over six acquisition trials and extinction over six trials. Curves are illustrative, and amount of salivation is in arbitrary numbers.

"stronger" with more pairings of the CS and UCS (called **trials**). The magnitude of the response (amount of saliva) is measured. Other possible response measures are speed of responding or probability of responding.

Extinction. This is the decline of the conditioned response when the CS is presented without the UCS. If you stopped feeding the dog after using the can opener, the dog would lose interest and stop salivating when the can opener sounded. Extinction is not the same as forgetting, however. If one day you suddenly started feeding your dog again after using the can opener, the dog would almost immediately start salivating again.

Stimulus generalization. When we are conditioned to one CS, we are also conditioned (less strongly) to similar stimuli. This process is stimulus generalization, which protects us from having to learn everything anew. If someone is hit by a Buick, she may associate her pain with Cadillacs, Chevrolets, or even Hondas.

Discrimination. If we always generalized to other stimuli, generalization would be as maladaptive as if we never generalized at all. A second process then comes into play, which is called discrimination. We continue to respond to the CS, but responses to other stimuli extinguish because they are not followed by the UCS. If a large white dog first growled and then bit someone, he might become afraid of this dog and generalize his fear to other dogs. As he discovers that other dogs do not growl and bite, however, his fear of other dogs would probably decline.

The CS-UCS interval.   The CS must come before the UCS in order for reliable conditioning to occur. But just how close in time must the two stimuli occur? If stimuli could be conditioned completely without regard to the time between them, then just about every stimulus would be associated with every other stimulus. This result would be terribly chaotic, but, of course it does not actually happen. The "best" time interval between CS and UCS depends on the specific stimuli and responses involved. With simple reflex responses, a time interval of about 0.5 seconds works very well. With such "emotional" responses as a change in heart rate, a longer delay works better (e.g., 2 to 5 seconds). With very strong stimuli, even longer intervals are effective. The taste of food can be associated with stomach upset occurring hours later.

What is learned in classical conditioning? Psychologists once believed that classical conditioning involved nothing but specific responses being conditioned to specific stimuli, such as the salivary reflex becoming conditioned to a new sound. It was believed that **contiguity** (presenting CS and UCS close to each other in time) was sufficient for this conditioning. Now it appears that in many situations, a stimulus is more likely to become an effective CS if it reliably **predicts** that another stimulus (the UCS) will follow (Rescorla, 1987; Gordon, 1989). This relationship is called the **contingency theory** of conditioning; the occurrence of the UCS is contingent on the occurrence of the CS. The whir of the can opener is an effective CS because it reliably informs the dog that dinner is on the way. If the can opener sounded randomly in relation to feeding, the sound would not become a CS because it would not reliably tell the dog anything.

Learning and Feeding Behavior

As earlier noted, feeding generalists eat a variety of foods but have the problem of selecting the right foods for a nutritious diet. A great number of specific taste preferences have been uncovered among the omnivores, leading us to ask whether *every* apparent dietary deficiency has a mechanism to make some substance more preferred. One answer to this question, in terms of homeostasis, may be that the body responds to changes in energy use. Another possibility is that there may be general processes by which a preference or an aversion for *any* food might be learned. Taste-aversion learning and learned safety are two such general processes. Both involve preference changes that relate to the general health of an animal.

Taste aversion learning. If you ask, most people, they will tell you that they have an aversion to some food that made them sick. In several survey studies, over half the respondents had developed such an aversion to some food (Schafe & Bernstein, 1996). Such aversions are typically learned in a single experience, with delays of minutes or hours between eating and getting sick, and the aversions occur more readily with new foods.

In the first report of taste aversion conditioning in the laboratory (Garcia & Koelling, 1966), there were four experimental conditions, indicated in Table 4–1. In two conditions the CS was water accompanied by lights and noise, and in two others the CS was saccharine-flavored water. For each CS, there were two aversive UCSs: drug-induced illness and foot shock. The test was the amount of solution consumed after conditioning, a measure of degree of aversion to the CSs. Aversion to the saccharin taste occurred with illness as the UCS, but not shock; and aversion to the lights and noise occurred with shock, but not illness. The experiment not only demonstrated taste aversion learning but also showed that some stimulus combinations are more readily associated than others. In a similar experiment, Garcia and Ervin (1968) found that animals learned to discriminate between two sizes of food pellet with shock as the UCS, but not illness. However, animals did not learn differential aversion to one of two sizes of food pellet with illness as a UCS. Garcia and Ervin hypothesized that it is easy to develop external (size)–external (shock) associations or internal (taste)–internal (illness) associations, but not external–internal associations. Quail, which are more visually oriented animals than rats, show aversion to colors that precede illness but not to tastes (Wilcoxin, Dragoin, & Kral, 1971). This finding suggests that the ease of association of different stimuli varies across species, a conclusion subsequently well-supported by much research.

Taste aversion conditioning experiments challenged two conventional principles in classical conditioning. The first principle was that short intervals between CS and UCS are necessary for conditioning. When the initial laboratory reports of taste aversion learning appeared in the 1960s, some psycholo-

TABLE 4–1. Taste aversion conditioning experiment. Saccharin-flavored water was a good CS when illness was the UCS, but not when shock was the UCS. Bright, noisy water was a good CS when shock was the UCS, but not when flavor was the UCS. See text for more details. (From Garcia & Koelling, 1966.)

CONDITIONED STIMULI	UNCONDITIONED STIMULI	CONDITIONING OCCURS
Saccharin flavor	Illness	Yes
Saccharin flavor	Shock	No
Bright, noisy water	Illness	No
Bright, noisy water	Shock	Yes

gists simply did not believe that learning with delays of minutes or hours between CS (food) and UCS (illness) was possible. One prominent learning theorist publicly remarked that conditioning with such long delays was about as likely as finding bird dung in a cuckoo clock. Hundreds of subsequent taste aversion conditioning experiments have since forced a radical revision in learning theory to accommodate long CS-UCS intervals. The second principle challenged was that all CSs and UCSs can be associated with equal ease. As we saw in the experiments previously described and in Chapter Three, some events are more readily associated than others. The ease with which different kinds of stimuli can be associated differs from species to species (see reviews by Rozin & Kalat, 1971; Revusky & Garcia, 1970). It appears that in the course of evolution, different species developed somewhat different mechanisms of learning that are specific to their own needs.

Learned safety.   All rats approach new stimuli timidly, and wild rats are especially **neophobic.** A new food associated with illness is dangerous and is avoided. But if nothing dangerous happens, the new stimulus is considered safe, and the animal returns to it. The rat thus learns to eat new foods as it discovers they are safe. According to learned safety theory, then, animals avoid foods that are associated with illness and tentatively try out new foods until they find one that is safe. The new food becomes associated with well-being and is attractive (Rozin & Kalat, 1971). This mechanism allows for development of a "specific hunger" for practically any food that turns out to be safe. The theory requires only that the animal be able to recognize differences between foods so it can associate them with either danger or well-being. In probably the first of such studies showing this, it was found that vitamin B deficiency was corrected by dietary choice only if the vitamin were tagged with a distinctive licorice flavor (Harris, Clay, Hargreaves, & Ward (1933).

Social Factors in Eating

The manager of a college cafeteria told me that he could never satisfy his customers because all the students wanted food like what their own mothers made. Even rats learn to prefer foods that they were first exposed to as infants, which would typically be foods associated with the mother (Galef, 1971; Galef & Henderson, 1972). Infant rats actually prefer foods that their mothers ate while they were still in the womb. Food tastes are transferred to the fetuses through the placenta, familiarizing the offspring with tastes that they will later encounter. Young rats thus become familiar with "safe" tastes and subsequently prefer them.

Among humans, whole cultures have "eating habits" that seem so natural to them that they reject the equally popular eating habits of other whole cultures. Many foods that we prize or abhor (chili peppers, eyeballs, raw octopus, lizards, monkey brains, corn on the cob) have become pleasurable or aversive because of the way they are treated within our own culture (Rozin, 1996). This is not just a matter of exposure to foods, because animals do not always share the food preferences of the human cultures in which they live. In one instance, an expressive cat kept begging for food as several people ate dinner. They put some food in a bowl for her and set it on the floor. She took one smell, turned around, and tried to cover it with her back paw. She was not acculturated enough to eat chili. Additional social influences are necessary.

Direct social influences. These require that another person or persons be present during eating. For example, the more people there are present at a meal, the more each individual tends to eat (de Castro & Brewer, 1991). Children prefer foods eaten by admired others (Birch & Fisher, 1996) as well as those eaten by members of their peer group. In a social context, humans will develop a liking for otherwise unpalatable foods. Bitter substances like coffee, quinine water, and burnt food become popular as do such irritants as alcohol, chili pepper, ginger, and raw garlic or onion (Rozin, 1996). In the case of chili peppers, young children are exposed to the burning sensation in the atmosphere of family and friends, and these positive situations encourage a liking for the burning sensation. Dogs in the same family context do not develop such a liking, indicating that it is socialization, not just familiarity, that produces the liking.

Even with the rat, social factors are powerful influences in food preferences. For example, young rats prefer foods found in the presence of just an adult rat that has been anesthetized and lays near a food source. Preferences for foods associated with adults have been found with rats, cats, sheep, and chickens. Galef argues that the physical presence of one individual at a location attracts others and makes it more likely they will eat the food found there. An animal learns to eat (or not to eat) foods by observing other members of its species eating the foods and not becoming (or becoming) ill (Galef, 1996).

Indirect social influences. Indirect effects of culture on eating and nutritional adequacy occur without the intervention of another person. The cuisine that is characteristic of a particular culture is used whether other individuals are present or not. "Cuisines are defined by the basic ingredients they employ (e.g., rice, potatoes, fish), the characteristic flavors (flavor principles) employed (e.g., a combination of chili pepper with either tomato or lime for Mexico, a varied mixture of spices called "curry" for India), and particular modes of food preparation (e.g., stir-frying for China)" (Rozin, 1996, p. 236). Each culture has its rules about how foods are prepared, what foods are served in combination, what is appropriate for special occasions, what is appropriate at each time of day, and so on.

As an example, corn is a staple in Mexican cuisine but is inadequate as a nutrient because it is low in niacin (a B vitamin) and calcium, and it does not have an adequate pattern of essential amino acids. Making corn into tortillas solves a number of these problems because the corn is soaked in a solution of lime that increases the level of niacin, improves the amino acid pattern, and adds calcium. Since the tortilla is usually eaten along with beans and chili peppers, there is an adequate protein source. If you ask Mexican women why they soak the corn, however, they say that it makes the tortillas easier to roll out. In other words, a cultural tradition promotes a healthy diet, but the participants don't even know what the problem is that the technology solved (Rozin, 1996).

Beliefs and attitudes also play a major role. In Hindu culture the sacredness of cows prohibits eating them and Hebrews shun pork. Such beliefs affect the way food is perceived, commercialized, and eaten.

EATING DISORDERS AND THEIR TREATMENT

Definition of Eating Disorders

An eating disorder is any change in eating behavior that leads to impaired physical or psychological health. "Typical" eating disorders are obesity, anorexia nervosa, and bulimia nervosa. "Atypical" eating disorders may have some of the characteristics of anorexia and bulimia but also include overeating or vomiting associated with other disturbances and eating unusual substances (such as feces or chalk). Otherwise unspecified eating disorders are also included here (Fairburn & Walsh, 1995).

Obesity

Definition.   Obesity is usually defined as a body weight that is 20 percent greater than the ideal weight for a given height, as established by life insurance norms (L. Epstein, 1990). This excess weight is associated with the storage of fat. Somewhere between a third and a quarter of the United States population over age thirty is obese by this criterion. The social acceptability of obesity varies with cultures. In some places obesity is a sign of success (eating more food than the minimum for survival). In others it is a negative characteristic with regard to appearance, especially for women. The prevalence of obesity in this country may well reflect dietary habits more than anything else. Experimental research on obesity is relatively new, however.

Causes.   According to Drewnowski (1996, p. 304), "The question of who becomes obese and why remains unsolved." Increases in average national weight found in large-scale studies reflect obese persons' becoming fatter, not everyone's becoming fatter. A large part of the population is resistant to getting fat. A number of hypotheses about the causes of obesity, or differences between normal weight and obese people, have been proposed, tested, and rejected over the last twenty-five years. Three of these hypotheses are the externality hypothesis, taste changes with obesity, and set point theory.

- **Schachter's externality hypothesis.** Stanley Schachter and his associates compared eating by obese humans with that of hypothalamic hyperphagic rats in a series of creative laboratory and field studies (e.g., Schachter, 1971a, b). The animal research indicated that fat rats eat faster, are more finicky about what they eat, but will not work more for food. In one of Schachter's studies, overweight subjects were found to prefer eating unshelled almonds but that normal-weight subjects were indifferent between shelled and unshelled. Similarly, 20 percent of normal-weight American patrons of Chinese and Japanese restaurants were observed to eat with chopsticks, but only five percent of obese patrons did so. Presumably using chopsticks is more work for Americans than using a knife and fork. These studies seemed to support the failure-to-work hypothesis. Schachter suggested that obese people are more reactive to external food-related stimuli, whereas normal-weight people are more reactive to internal cues for eating. Rodin (1981) reviewed subsequent human obesity research and found that normal and obese individuals respond equally to environmental cues, refuting Schachter's generalization that obese people are more responsive to external cues.
- **Taste preferences in obesity.** Obese individuals have a substantial preference for foods that are high sweet and/or high fat, and there are some sex differences. Men prefer meats more than do women (97 percent versus 86 percent); both prefer carbohydrates/fats equally (93 percent versus 92 percent); and women prefer high-fat sweets more than men (81 percent versus 68 percent) (Drewnowski, 1996). However, taste preferences between normal or overweight groups are overshadowed by the great variation within each group. Hence, taste preferences do not predict who will be obese.
- **Set point theory.** According to set point theory (Keesey & Powley, 1986), different people have different biologically determined "set points" for body weight. The main line of support for this theory is that although there are fluctuations in body weights, most people have a relatively stable body weight after they reach maturity. A set point operates like the thermostat on a furnace. When our body detects that we are below the set point, it "turns on" the eating system just as the thermostat turns on the furnace. A fat person is said to have a very high set point and therefore has to eat more than a skinny person just to keep his or her weight at the set point. Being "fat" may actually be "normal" for some people, if they are maintaining their weight at their own set point. The set point idea is appealing because it is like the control systems concept often used with reference to homeostatic mechanisms. Also, it may make some people more comfortable if they believe that "biology is destiny" and that it is not their fault they are overweight. Actual evidence for a body weight set point is scanty, however.

Other factors gaining support include the following:

- **Genetics and obesity.** There are genetic differences in *susceptibility* to obesity among humans, as well as among rodents. An example is that the Pima Indians of the southwest United States have an unusually high prevalence of obesity. Another is that identical twins reared apart are more similar in obesity than are nonidentical twins reared together. (Van Itallie & Kissileff, 1990). Given free access to food, some strains of mice become obese, and other strains do not. Even this tendency interacts with the specifics of diet, however. Genetically obese animals gain weight on a diet of standard lab chow, whereas other strains become obese only with intensely sweet, high-fat diets (Drewnowski, 1996). This finding strongly suggests that there is no single genetic factor accounting for obesity.

- **Food cravings involve endorphin release.** Beta-endorphins are associated with overeating in genetically obese mice and rats. In humans, administration of naloxone, an opiate antagonist, suppressed consumption of sweet, fat foods for binge eaters but not in nonbingers. Overall food intake was not reduced (Drewnowski et al., 1992). Since not all obese individuals overeat on highly palatable foods, the endorphin hypothesis does not account for all obesity.

Weight control programs.   The best way to control weight is to back away from the dining table sooner. In addition, regular exercise helps reduce the craving for food, making dieting easier. The problem is that some people cannot stay on diets, cannot exercise, and cannot do anything else long enough to reduce weight significantly. Some kind of psychological intervention is called for when the simpler, more obvious solutions do not work. **Behavior therapy** appears to be the most successful psychological treatment and is now part of most obesity programs (Epstein, 1990). The behavioral approach assumes that, unless there is a true medical disorder, obesity is mainly a problem of bad eating habits and that the solution is to change these habits (Ferster, Nurnberger, & Levitt, 1962). This has been one of the major success stories of an area of laboratory animal research (operant conditioning) moving to a significant human clinical problem. By 1983 behavioral programs had progressed to the point where the average weight loss was in the range of fifteen to twenty-five pounds.

Behavioral treatment is done in a graduated series of steps with the individual, may involve family members, and extends to general lifestyle problems in addition to just eating. The first step is for the patient to keep track of when and how much she or he eats. This step alone is very useful, because many obese people simply do not realize how often they snack or "finish off a plate" before washing it. Can you remember everything you have eaten in the last twelve hours? The patient also keeps a careful record of her or his weight so that she or he will be reinforced for eating less by the satisfaction of seeing body weight go down. This process is not unlike standing in front of a mirror so that you can see your muscles bulge as you exercise. Eating is done only at specific times and places, such as in the dining room at mealtime, using a clean tablecloth and silverware. Doing this cuts down on snacking and eating right out of the refrigerator or cupboard. The patient may have a contract with the therapist, having to donate a specified amount of money to charity any week that the weight loss contract is not met. The behavior therapy approach is both effective and less dangerous than some of the faddish diets that have been promoted in best-selling books or touted on television. Medical treatment of some form may be required for any kind of weight disorder if the individual has reached a life-threatening weight level.

Anorexia Nervosa

Anorexia nervosa (self-starvation) is characterized by refusal to maintain an appropriate minimum body weight, intense fear of becoming fat (even though underweight), disturbance in the perception of one's own body size or shape, and amenorrhea (absence of menstrual cycles). This self-starvation is seen mostly in intelligent young women who may take on the appearance of starved prisoners of war. The cause is not clear, but it is thought that they may be responding to social pressure to look thin and that in their own eyes, they may appear to look heavier than they actually are. Professional models and beauty pageant contestants weigh less than average for their height, and so if a women judges herself against such standards, she is likely to perceive herself as overweight.

The most effective treatment for anorexia also appears to be behavior therapy. The therapist rewards the client with whatever is effective only when the client eats. The reward may simply be to talk to the client when the client takes a bite of food. Opportunity for exercise is often an effective reward, which is rather surprising in light of the client's state of health.

Anorexia Bulimia

Anorexia bulimia is characterized by repeated episodes of binge eating (an inordinate amount of eating in a short period of time). Often called the "binge-purge" syndrome, bulimia is characterized by excessive eating followed by such inappropriate compensatory behaviors as self-induced vomiting, misuse of medications (e.g., laxatives), fasting, or excessive exercise (Garfinkel, 1995). During an average binge, a bulimic eats 2,000 to 3,000 calories, usually of junk food. Persons of any weight, from anorectic to obese, may behave in this manner. The typical bulimic individual, however, is a slender female who is college educated and working, who may take care of a house and children, and who is highly achievement-oriented. Bulimics may suffer from a number of serious health problems resulting from the repeated binge-purge cycle, such as ulcers and other intestinal difficulties. There may be dental problems, and the sudden chemical imbalances in the body caused by bingeing and purging may lead to heart attacks (Mitchell, 1986). Bulimics typically fear the shame and embarrassment of being caught bingeing or purging.

Although social factors seem obviously important in the etiology of both anorexia and bulimia, more basic physiological factors may also be involved. Are food taste and pleasure actually different for people with eating disorders? We know that taste plays a role because bingeing involves good-tasting foods.

Rodin, Bartoshuk, Peterson, & Schank (1990) suggested that taste abnormalities might be implicated in the development and/or maintenance of the disorder or might be produced by the disorder. They, as well as Garfinkel, Molodofsky, and Garner (1979), found in experiments that hedonic ratings of sucrose did not decline following a high calorie lunch or glucose load (a glucose solution), although ratings typically decline with normal-weight subjects. This finding suggests that bulimics do not have the normal experience of satiation following food ingestion. Whether this taste modification causes bingeing or results from purging is not known. The acid reflux from purging does damage taste receptors, and this effect may facilitate purging by making it less obnoxious to taste. The binge-purge cycle is thus easier and more frequent, and this change may affect post-ingestional satiety mechanisms.

The causes of bulimia are not clearly different from those of anorexia, and the most promising treatments are behavioral. Close medical supervision may be required because of the bulimic's poor state of health.

ADDICTIONS

A drug addict has an overwhelming craving for the drug to which he or she is addicted, and this craving is a two-headed motivational monster. Initially the addict seeks the pleasure produced by the drug, but then must seek relief from the pain and torment of not having the drug. These tandem motivational factors make it difficult to break away from even a life-threatening addiction. The two primary classes of addicting drugs are the central nervous system *depressants* and *excitants*. The major addictive depressants are alcohol, the barbiturates, the tranquilizers, and the opiates. The major excitants are the amphetamines and the various forms of cocaine. Caffeine and nicotine are less potent addictive excitatory drugs. Although drug addictions are hardly new, the need to study and treat them has assumed a new importance because the use of cocaine and crack has dramatically increased. Addictions to opium, morphine, heroin, and alcohol have been around longer and are still major problems. The reason for looking at addiction in this chapter is that the brain mechanisms involved in feeding have a great deal of overlap with those involved in drug addiction. The so-called hallucinogenic drugs, which produce bizarre perceptual experiences, are not generally addictive.

One of the great paradoxes of pharmacology is that the very drugs that produce the greatest relief from suffering can themselves produce some of the greatest suffering. The opiate drug morphine not only is one of the most powerful drugs for the relief of pain but also has some of the greatest abuse potential, along with other opiates (such as heroin) that are completely illegal. This association between analgesia and abuse potential provides major clues as to the nature of pleasure and of pain and its relief.

General Principles of Drug Action

The way that drugs influence neural transmission.   A neurotransmitter is a chemical released at the synapse by one neuron to affect the activity of another neuron when it goes to a **receptor site** on the receiving neuron. The neurotransmitter is stored in the axon of the neuron until released. Following release, any excess transmitter substance is either broken down chemically in the synapse and/or reabsorbed into the axon. Of the fifty or so different neurotransmitters, the most commonly known are **adrenaline, noradrenaline, acetylcholine, serotonin, dopamine,** and the **endorphins.** The neurotransmitter effect may be **excitatory** (causing other neurons to "fire") or **inhibitory** (making it harder for other neurons to fire).

A particular drug affects the process by which neurotransmitters function in one of several possible ways. Some drugs have chemical structures similar to those of naturally occurring transmitters. These drugs **mimic** the effect of the transmitter and "fool" the receptor neuron into firing. Heroin may do this by mimicking the **endogenous** neurotransmitters, the endorphins. Or just the opposite, a drug might block out the neurotransmitter substance and prevent the neuron from being fired. Maisto, Galizio, and Connors (1991) list eight different ways by which a drug may alter normal neural activity: by (1) increasing or decreasing synthesis of neurotransmitters, (2) interfering with the transport of neurotransmitter molecules to the axon terminals, (3) interfering with the storage of neurotransmitters in the axon terminal, (4) producing premature release of neurotransmitters into the synapse, (5) influencing the breakdown of neurotransmitters by enzymes, (6) blocking the reuptake of neurotransmitters into the axon terminals, (7) activating a receptor site through mimicry, and (8) blocking a receptor site. Which of these specific actions of drugs will occur and what will be the psychological effects depend on what parts of the brain are affected.

Nonspecific Factors Affecting Drug Actions

In addition to the specific effects that different drugs have, there are **nonspecific** effects that apply to many different kinds of drugs. For example, drug effects may be modified by such **organismic variables** as age, size, sex, biological rhythms, genetics, diet, personality, or general state of health. Two drugs taken at or near the same time may *interact* with unexpected results. They may cancel each other out, have much more powerful effects than just adding their individual potency, have toxic effects, or have no effect at all. As a rule, drugs that have similar psychological effects add together. Central nervous system depressant drugs, for example, have additive effects.

Repeated administrations of the same drug may lead to **tolerance,** so that larger doses of the same drug are required to produce the same effect, or **cross-tolerance,** so that drugs of the same general class, such as central nervous system depressants, produce a tolerance for other drugs in the same class. For example, barbiturates would produce a cross-tolerance for alcohol.

The **environmental conditions** under which drugs are taken may influence the perceived effects of drugs. Lighting, music, odors, or social interactions may influence drug effects. Three beers at a party would probably have a very different effect than the same three beers in a hospital waiting room, a sterile research lab, or a police station. Our **expectations** of what a drug should do may have a powerful influence on its actual effect. This tendency is generally called the **placebo effect.** Virtually all drug research controls for placebo effects by the use of **double-blind** procedures so that neither the person getting the drug nor the person administering the drug know what the drug is. The subject might be getting a real drug or a placebo (e.g., a substance that looks, feels, and tastes just like the drug but that is inert—such as a sugar pill). Only if the drug shows a stronger effect than the placebo can we conclude that there is a drug-specific effect.

Through the process of classical conditioning, stimuli associated with drug administration become conditioned stimuli for drug effects. For example, a drug addict may have addiction symptoms conditioned to environmental stimuli, people, hypodermic needles, and the like so that the craving for the drug is heightened in the presence of these stimuli. This situation makes it difficult to get addicts off a drug if they remain in an environment full of conditioned stimuli for the withdrawal symptoms. A drug addict may be "cured" in a hospital and then may quickly relapse when sent back to the same cue-rich environment where the addiction originally occurred.

Addiction Characteristics

Addiction is generally defined by two major symptoms, **tolerance** and **withdrawal** symptoms. Tolerance means that more of the drug must be taken to produce the same effect, usually a pleasant or exciting experience. Withdrawal symptoms are feelings and physiological effects essentially the opposite of whatever the addicting substance produces, which occur if the addicted substance is withheld. If a person is addicted to a drug that excites the central nervous system, such as **amphetamine,** the withdrawal symptoms are a depression of central nervous system activity. Some of the most addictive drugs are central nervous system depressants, the barbiturates, commonly used as sleeping pills. A person who had never taken the drug before would normally become sleepy with a single tablet. If the drug were taken repeatedly, however, an increasingly larger dose would be required to produce the same degree of sleepiness, the tolerance effect. If an addicted person were suddenly to stop taking the drug altogether, great central nervous system excitation—including possible seizures—would occur.

Theories of Addiction

Opponent process theory. This theory is covered in more detail in Chapter Six; however, the basic principle of the theory (Solomon & Corbit, 1974; Solomon, 1980) is that when the circumstances producing a strong emotion are removed, a person does not feel just neutral, but strongly feels the opposite emotion. If the person has been feeling joyous, then she feels sad. If the person has been feeling depressed or afraid, then she feels happy. This same principle has been used to account for drug addictions.

Suppose a person takes a "recreational" drug that makes him feel euphoric. He gradually requires more of the drug to get the same good feeling, and then the drug supply is cut off. Without the drug he feels very bad, very depressed, and very ill. His new experience is just the opposite of that which he felt while taking the drug, but it is just as much determined by the drug as the earlier good experiences were. According to opponent process theory, with successive drug experiences, the negative effect of the drug becomes stronger and stronger until it begins to cancel out the positive emotional experience. This effect is the opponent process beginning to work. A stronger stimulus (more drug) is needed to produce the same level of positive emotion or excitement previously experienced. This effect is the addiction. When the positive effect of the drug wears off, the opponent process, the negative effect, persists and is so strong that the addicted person feels he must have the drug to relieve this unpleasant experience, so that vicious cycle develops. The more the drug is taken, the greater the tolerance, and the more unpleasant the opponent process when the drug wears off. When the addict goes off the drug, the system eventually comes back into "balance," unless permanent damage has occurred.

The dopamine depletion hypothesis. As we have seen, the dopamine system is closely related to pleasure. Cocaine addiction is hypothesized to occur in relation to dopamine depletion. Dackis and Gold (1985) outline the following sequence of events as a possible explanation for cocaine addiction. If cocaine is put into the body, it quickly migrates to neuron areas where dopamine is the neurotransmitter, those same areas that underlie the pleasurable effects of reward. The cocaine triggers the release of dopamine (producing the pleasurable experience) but also blocks the normal reuptake of dopamine into the neuron from the synapse. This process is illustrated in Figure 4–9. As the drug wears off, the brain has a shortage of the dopamine neurotransmitter, and there are some withdrawal effects because the brain cannot respond pleasurably to the stimuli that are normally effective. Consequently, there is a craving for more of the drug in order to re-create even normal pleasant experience. The addict may progress from "snorting" the drug up the nose to "freebasing," dissolving the drug and injecting it. The euphoric "rush" from freebasing occurs literally within a few seconds of injection.

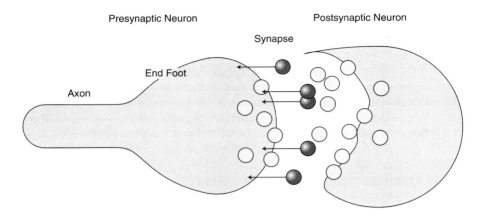

(a) Dopamine is released from the presynaptic neuron into the synapse and enters into the postsynaptic neuron. Some of the dopamine molecules are taken up from the synapse back into the presynaptic site.

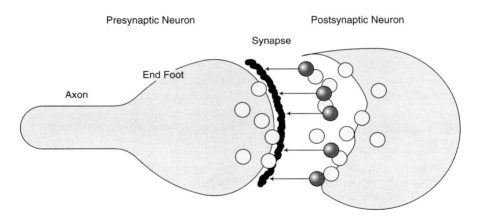

(b) Dopamine reuptake is blocked by cocaine so that dopamine remains more active in the synapse, heightening the effect of dopamine.

FIGURE 4–9.   Effect of cocaine at the synapse in the dopamine system.

If the very strong craving of the addict is to be reduced, the brain must start manufacturing more dopamine while the addict is not using the drug. Of course, it is difficult for the addict to abstain, since the craving for the drug is so intense. The addict needs considerable social support for abstaining and certainly freedom from temptations to use the drug lest immediate relapse occur. All sorts of stimuli (such as social situations in which the drug has been taken) may become conditioned stimuli to increase the craving and lead to relapse. The power of the drug is evidenced by several highly publicized examples of multimillion-dollar-a-year athletes whose careers have been ruined or jeopardized by cocaine addiction.

It is also likely that endorphins are involved in addictions (Kalat, 1988). In terms of brain chemistry, there may be multiple forms of addiction, but quite possibly all of them involve the endorphin system.

Liking, wanting, learning, and addiction.   Learning plays a crucial role in wanting, but less in liking (Berridge, 1996). The stimuli in the addict's environment have become conditioned stimuli signaling that a wanted substance is available and that initiate the addictive behaviors. We can thus see why people so readily relapse into drug use if they return to the same environments where the drug addiction occurred. With lesions in the dopamine system, the animals do not respond to these learned signals, although they show the signs of liking. In the case of abused substances (e.g., cocaine and heroin), the brain is **sensitized** to the wanting cues, so that animals (or people) will do all kinds of things to get the drug (wanting) even though they may not like it after they get it. Thus drug addiction involves an increase in wanting without necessarily involving liking.

A major point of this sensitization theory of addiction is that people are not necessarily **conscious** of the reasons why they seek a particular substance or of why they like or dislike a particular substance. These systems operate at the level of the caudal brainstem, well below the level of consciousness. When a person says that she "just likes" something without knowing why, that is probably the truth. Evaluations of objects can take place, as we also saw in Chapter Two, without a person's necessarily being conscious of their occurrence.

SUMMARY

1. **Homeostasis** refers to the automatic adjustments the body makes to maintain a constant internal environment, the body fluids surrounding individual cells. For example, the body can store fat or sugar and release it as needed. Eventually, however, food must be sought and consumed. Thus some behaviors are at the service of homeostasis.

2. Homeostatic behaviors must be triggered by cues that signal departures from homeostatic balance, signals to **start** eating and then to **stop** eating. According to **peripheral theories,** these signals are initiated outside the central nervous system, such as stomach contractions to initiate eating and stomach distention to stop eating. According to **central theories,** the brain detects homeostatic imbalances and their restoration such as changes in blood sugar level. It appears that both peripheral and central events are involved in hunger.

3. **Positive feedback** signals to initiate and maintain eating involve taste and smell. **Negative feedback** signals are generated as food passes through the mouth,

stomach, and small intestine. These signals are anticipatory and tell the animal to stop before food is actually absorbed and can restore homeostasis. The release of hormones that go to the brain, as well as more direct neural connections from the stomach and intestines, are negative feedback signals.

4. A drop in **blood glucose level** is the only specific physiological signal known to reliably precede eating in the laboratory rat. Another possible signal is the **uptake of fatty acids** in the brain, which is correlated with the amount of work the liver is doing in breaking down foods. The brain's activity may thus reflect energy production, as shown by liver activity, as the basis for stopping and starting eating.

5. **Feedforward signals** anticipate body needs and initiate compensatory activity before strong needs arise. For example, insulin release is triggered by the taste and smell of food (as well as by other learned signals for food) so that it is in the blood prior to the delivery of glucose to the blood by digestion.

6. Limitations to the homeostatic model revolve around the fact that food intake is controlled by many **nonhomeostatic factors,** including sensory pleasure, previous individual experiences, family history, cultural background, emotional, and immediate social factors. These seem to control feeding more than does hemostatic imbalance, but they contribute to homeostasis by regulating feeding.

7. The multitude of external factors in control of feeding may lead to bad feeding and may work against homeostasis. For example, the pleasurable tastes of non-healthy foods may override the nutrition provided by other foods. Neither humans nor other animals always eat wisely if left to their own choices.

8. According to the dual hypothalamic theory of hunger, the **lateral hypothalamus** is an **excitatory** area of feeding, and the **ventromedial hypothalamus** is an **inhibitory** area for feeding. When the lateral hypothalamus is damaged, animals stop eating and only gradually recover in a progression called the **lateral hypothalamic syndrome.** When the ventromedial area is damaged, animals show large weight increases.

9. So-called **"pleasure centers"** in the brain are involved in feeding. This system involves neurons that have **dopamine** as a neurotransmitter and are related to the release of **endorphins** in the brain. Animals will work harder for electrical stimulation of this area more than any other known reward.

10. Two aspects of eating and other motivations have been distinguished, called **liking** and **wanting,** that are related to the pleasure system. Liking is shown by preference for foods, and wanting is indicated by the amount of effort put forth to obtain food. Liking is related to the endorphin system, and wanting to the dopamine system. Preferential responses to tastes can be shown by animals with only the brainstem intact.

11. Innate taste preferences and aversions are related to the **four primary taste qualities: sweet, salty, bitter, and sour.** Salt is normally preferred only in low concentrations, but salt-deprived animals prefer higher concentrations.

12. **Classical (Pavlovian) conditioning** is related to feeding in several ways. New **taste preferences** or **aversions** can be learned by associating tastes with "good" consequences (e.g., sugars or fats) or bad consequences (illness following consumption of a particular taste substance).

13. According to the **learned safety principle,** animals come to prefer food tastes that they associate with well-being. If an animal becomes ill because of dietary deficiency, it can associate a particular taste with the well-being that follows eating the needed substance (e.g., vitamins).

14. **Social factors,** including both familial and cultural eating habits, have a strong influence on food likes and dislikes. Foods considered delicacies in one culture may be considered disgusting in another. Social reinforcement seems to be the only way to get people to like bitter/sour tastes.

15. **Obesity** is a common eating problem whose causes are not well understood, but that may involve genetic and taste factors. Obese individuals may not be sensitive to the "stop cues" for feeding in the same way that "normal weight" individuals are. The most successful weight loss programs involve **behavior therapy.**

16. **Anorexia nervosa** and **bulimia nervosa** are eating disorders most commonly found in young, well-educated women. In the former, eating is so reduced that the individual may become emaciated. In the latter, there are periodic eating binges followed by vomiting and dieting. Again, the most successful treatments have been behavior therapies.

17. Drug addictions are defined by **tolerance** (more drug needed to obtain a particular level of effect) and **withdrawal symptoms** that are opposite to whatever the effect of the drug is. The most commonly addicted drugs are central nervous system depressants (including alcohol and opiates) and excitants (including cocaine and amphetamines). Addictive drugs operate through arousing the dopamine and endorphin systems, as do pleasurable foods.

18. According to the **opponent process theory,** a drug has a particular effect (e.g., pleasurable) that is automatically followed by an unpleasant effect. With repeated exposures to a drug, the aftereffect (the opponent process) gets stronger and begins to cancel out the pleasurable experience, requiring a larger dose of the drug. This effect is tolerance. If the drug is withheld, the opponent process is very active, producing the withdrawal symptoms.

18. According to the **dopamine depletion hypothesis** of cocaine addiction, cocaine triggers the release of dopamine (producing the pleasurable experience) but also blocks the normal reuptake of dopamine into the neuron from the synapse. The pleasurable effect produced by dopamine is therefore longer lasting.

CHAPTER FIVE

Drinking, Thermoregulation, and Reproduction

——•——

DRINKING BEHAVIOR

Our bodies are about 70 percent water, and we begin to get thirsty with as little as a 2 percent loss. People may survive for weeks without food, but in a hot, dry environment, a person without water may die most unpleasantly within hours. Our bodies neither store surplus water nor completely halt its loss through evaporation as we breathe and perspire, or through urination. Without sufficient water, our bodies become a hostile environment for the cells within.

The problem of regulating the amount of water in the body has been "solved" in different ways by different species. Some desert animals, such as the kangaroo rat, metabolize water from dry seeds and survive without ever drinking. Most land animals must rely on drinking to replenish water, however. Ultimately, water consumption, whether by drinking water or other fluids, or by obtaining water in food, is the way humans control the body's water supply. The factors influencing how we get fluid are as variable as are those for getting food. Drinking is not controlled just by some homeostatically determined need for a certain amount of water (Toates, 1979).

Regulatory Drinking

Start cues for drinking.   Animals can be induced to drink or to work for water, by water deprivation, eating dry food, working in a hot environment, consuming excess salt, or losing blood. It would seem, however, that there must be some smaller number of internal start cues activated by these various conditions. Contemporary theory is dominated by a two-factor theory of stimulation called the **double depletion hypothesis.** This hypothesis says that there are two independent mechanisms for stimulating us to drink. The first depends on what happens to the fluid within cells, an **intracellular** mechanism. The second depends on changes in the volume of body fluid, an **extracellular** mechanism.

The osmotic gradient: an intracellular mechanism.   Body fluids are normally about 0.9 percent salt, and if a more concentrated solution is injected into an animal, it drinks. This occurs without any change in fluid volume. In Figure 5–1 we see a body cell and its **intracellular fluid** surrounded by **extracellular fluid,** which is all body fluids not found inside cells. When salt is put into the extracellular fluid, water is pulled by osmosis from the less concentrated fluid inside the cell. Water easily passes through the cell membrane, but salt does not. Gilman (1937) demonstrated that this difference in concentration inside and outside the cell was critical for drinking. He injected dogs with **urea,** a substance that readily passes into the cell so that there is an equal increase in concentration both inside and outside the cells. Urea produced very little drinking, whereas injections of saline produced a lot.

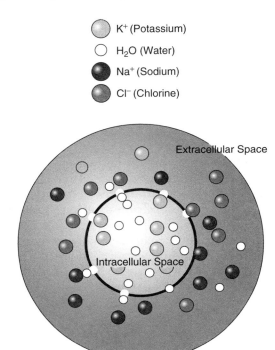

○ K⁺ (Potassium)

○ H₂O (Water)

● Na⁺ (Sodium)

● Cl⁻ (Chlorine)

FIGURE 5–1.   Intracellular and extracellular water spaces. Small water molecules easily move across the cell membrane to and from the intracellular space. Potassium ions are trapped inside the cell, and sodium and chlorine ions are kept outside. If water is lost from the extracellular space, there is a higher concentration of sodium and chloride, so that water moves from inside the cell to outside the cell by the process of osmosis. The cell therefore shrinks and provides a stimulus to drinking.

Specialized brain cells, called **osmoreceptors,** are thought to detect the concentration difference and signal the brain to initiate appropriate action.

Any mechanical distortion of the "osmoreceptors" may trigger drinking, however. If salts are *removed* from the extracellular space, water moves *into* the cell and makes it swell. This process can lead to a condition called **water intoxication,** characterized by excessive drinking and urination, and mental aberration. The treatment, paradoxically, is to give the patient *more* salt. The water then leaves the cells, which return to normal size, and excessive drinking is no longer stimulated.

The site of the osmoreceptor.   The hypothalamus and surrounding areas are crucial to water regulation, which involves *conservation* of water as well as increased intake. In the normal animal, the **supraoptic nucleus** of the hypothalamus manufactures **antidiuretic hormone** (ADH), which is released when the animal is water deprived. This hormone increases the rate of reabsorption of water from the kidneys, so that less is lost by excretion. Without ADH, the animal urinates excessively and has to drink excessively to make up the loss, a clinical condition known as **diabetes insipidus** (Ranson, Fischer, & Ingram, 1938). Direct injections of very small quantities of saline into the hypothalamus induce voracious drinking (Andersson, 1952). A one-milliliter (1/1000 of a liter) injection of saline may induce a goat to drink a gallon of water. Drinking can be elicited also by electrical stimulation of the hypothalamus and limbic system, as well as by various drugs placed in small quantity into the limbic system (e.g., Fisher, 1964).

Fluid volume: the extracellular mechanism. Thirst often accompanies blood loss, vomiting, or diarrhea, even though these do not change osmotic pressure (Wolf, 1958). Fitzsimmons (1972) and others have shown that if the blood supply to the kidneys is reduced, drinking increases. This condition occurs if the aorta is tied off above the renal arteries (which carry blood to the kidneys) or if the vena cava (going directly to the heart) is blocked. There appear to be independent sets of **pressure receptors** in the heart and in the renal blood supplies (Carlson, 1980). These receptors may send direct signals to the brain, but they also initiate a major chemical mechanism. When the venous pressure drops, the kidneys release **renin** into the bloodstream, which is in effect a "thirst hormone." The renin reacts with another substance to form **angiotensin,** which acts on brain receptors to incite drinking. Injected directly into the brain, angiotensin is the most powerful stimulus to drinking yet found. The location of the brain receptors for angiotensin has provided a lively dispute among those interested in the problem, but the two prime candidates (the **subfornical organ** and the **organum vascularis of the lamina terminalis**) both lie near the *ventricles* of the brain, in the vicinity of the hypothalamus.

Stop cues for drinking. According to the homeostatic model, when an animal has drunk enough water to offset its deficit, it should stop drinking. In support of this, after injections of saline that increase salt concentration in the body, rats accurately drink enough to restore proper concentrations of body fluids. That is, they drink enough to dilute the injected saline to normal body-fluid concentration, which is just less than 1 percent (Corbit, 1969). There must be some kind of "meter" running, to tell the animal when it has had enough and to stop drinking. There is no specific brain area yet known to be a satiety area for drinking, but there are several possible cues for the animal.

Mouth metering. If a normal dog is deprived of water, it offsets its water deficit with nearly 100 percent accuracy by drinking. If a fistula (tube) is inserted into the esophagus of the dog so that ingested water runs out of the tube and does not reach the stomach, the dog may drink twice as much as it needs to offset its deficit. Its intake is still proportional to the number of hours it has been without water, however (Bellows, 1939). This finding tells us that the process of lapping and swallowing water cannot be the only stop mechanism. There is, however, evidence for water receptors in the mouth (Nicholaidis, 1968), so that water passing through the mouth may also "turn off" the stimuli to drinking.

Stomach distention. To determine if a "full" (distended) stomach might be a cutoff cue for drinking, Towbin (1949) put balloons into the stomachs of thirsty dogs. He found that as more air was pumped into the balloon, the dog drank less. On the other hand, if a thirsty dog had enough water tubed directly into its stomach to offset its deficit, it would immediately drink the same amount of water all over again. It is as if the dog did not know that water had been put into its stomach. If drinking were delayed for just a few minutes after tubing water into the stomach, however, the animal did *not* drink. This whole sequence is just the *opposite* of how stomach distention should work. If distention were the cue, the animal should not drink just after tubing but should drink after a delay. Stomach distention does not then seem to be a major cue for cutting off drinking. Water by itself is not actually good for producing distention because water drains through the stomach very quickly as the animal is drinking. Substances with more bulk (like solid food) or with greater concentration (like sugar solutions) do not clear the stomach as quickly as water. These may produce more stomach distention and inhibit consumption, but this is not the same as distention by consumed water.

Reversal of the initiating stimulus. Water ingestion has often been thought to cease before there is time to reverse the stimulus that triggered drinking. In fact, however, about 25 percent of water tubed into the stomach of the rat is absorbed within fifteen minutes (e.g., O'Kelly & Beck, 1960). Novin (1962) recorded changes in electrical resistance of fluids in the region of the hypothalamus and found them to change within ten minutes of the onset of drinking by the rat. In other words, water was getting from the intestine to the brain within ten minutes, several minutes before the rats voluntarily stopped drinking. Reversal of the initiating stimulus, then, may be another cutoff cue.

Nonregulatory Drinking

Drinking elicited by eating. Eating and drinking usually occur together. In the normal animal, insulin is released upon eating, and the insulin, in turn, stimulates the release of **histamine** from endocrine-like cells in the gastric lining. Histamine receptors in the intestines are activated, and drinking occurs (Kraly, 1984). **Serotonin**, another neurotransmitter, may also be released when the rat eats, and it also stimulates drinking in its own right. Histamine and serotonin effects on drinking are due to two independent mechanisms that together produce greater drinking than either by itself (Kraly, Simansky, Coogan, & Trattner, 1985). The histamine and serotonin effects are eliminated if the vagus nerve from the stomach is cut, so that there is no signal from the stomach to the brain via the autonomic nervous system.

Taste factors.   The rat *can* regulate its water balance without smelling or tasting water, by pressing a lever that produces a squirt of water directly into its stomach (Teitelbaum & Epstein, 1962). A normal animal, however, *does* have taste and smell to guide it, and behavioral studies show that these are important in water-regulatory behavior. Humans drink great quantities of soft drinks for taste alone, which reduces the need to drink water at other times. Thus, taste indirectly serves to maintain homeostasis.

For an animal not water deprived or not eating, water does not seem to be very palatable, and animals do not drink much of it. If nonthirsty rats are forced to lap water from a tube to avoid shock, they let the water dribble out of their mouths without really swallowing it (Williams & Teitelbaum, 1956). Neal Miller (1959) developed what he called the "quinine test" for thirst. If thirsty animals have their drinking water adulterated with a small amount of quinine, they drink less. The more water deprived they are, the more quinine they will tolerate. We might conjecture, then, that when an animal is thirsty, water tastes better, and the "good" taste overcomes the "bad" taste of quinine. Water-deprived animals consume water avidly and show less of a preference for sugar water over plain water (Sclafani & Nissenbaum, 1987; Beck & Bidwell, 1974; Beck, Nash, Viernstein, & Gordon, 1972). Under some conditions water may even be preferred to sugar solution (Cohen & Tokieda, 1972). Recall, also, that LH-lesioned animals early in their recovery drink only sweet solutions, as if a mechanism for making water taste good to the normal animal had been impaired. We begin to piece together the picture of an animal that generally finds water not very palatable until it becomes thirsty. Desire for water then overrides the bitterness of quinine and competes with the sweetness of sugar.

Mouth cooling.   Both rat and human data suggest that mouth cooling is a major factor in drinking. Mendelson and Chillag (1970) found that thirsty rats would lick at a drinking spout that delivered a stream of cool air instead of water. Boulze, Montatruc, and Cabanac (1983) studied the effect of water temperature on both the pleasantness ratings of water and the amount consumed by dehydrated humans. Subjects either were sweating profusely or had been mountain climbing. As water temperature increased from 32° F to 56° F, the subjects drank more, but above 56° intake went down as temperature increased. Water never became more pleasant with temperatures above 56° and was considered unpleasant at higher temperatures. It is curious that pleasantness and intake were not correlated, since pleasantness and intake of substances are generally correlated.

Ecology, effort, and satiation. A simple regulatory theory would say that animals should drink until they restore water balance, but a more ecologically oriented argument takes other factors into account. Thus even when there is an unlimited supply of water available, rats consistently drink less when more effort is required to obtain the water (Toates, 1979). For example, if animals have to press a lever to obtain water, they take less water when more presses are required. Similarly, when rats were required to run six feet to obtain each sip of water, they stopped running after obtaining far less water than animals required to run only two feet (O'Kelly & Beck, 1960). The amount of water required to "satiate" an animal therefore depends on factors other than just the amount of water needed to offset a deficit. These other factors include effort and taste, and perhaps other variables.

Learning to Prevent Thirst

Fitzsimmons and LeMagnen (1969) reported data suggesting that rats learn to *anticipate* the osmotic water deficit that results from eating thirst-arousing food. Specifically, they shifted rats from a high-carbohydrate (low thirst-arousal) diet to a high-protein (high thirst-arousal) diet. In the first few days, the animals drank more *after* the meal but gradually began to drink more *during* the meal, as if anticipating thirst. This finding suggests that animals learn behaviors that prevent a departure from homeostasis so that homeostatic mechanisms do not come into play as strongly, much as Woods (1991) proposed for eating.

THERMOREGULATION

Extremes of temperature, whether high or low, are aversive, and we work hard to escape or avoid them. The largest energy use of the year comes during summer heat waves when air conditioning is at its peak. The second largest is in winter cold spells. In the extreme, we all know of the failures of temperature regulation, death by freezing or heatstroke. In fact, however, these are rare events, and animals and people survive very well in extreme environments. Polar land animals survive in subzero temperatures, and sea animals survive in subfreezing waters (because of its salt content, seawater freezes below 32° F). A combination of anatomical characteristics (such as fat and fur insulation), homeostatic mechanisms, and behaviors combine to keep body temperature within the range required for survival. Temperature regulation is important because temperature plays a major role in the chemical reactions necessary for life. The proper utilization and transfer of substances within the body, including nerve transmission, involve chemical reactions that must occur within an appropriate temperature range if they are to occur at all.

Cold-blooded animals, such as fish, amphibians, and reptiles, are **poikilothermic**, which is to say that their body temperature is usually just slightly higher than that of the surrounding environment. Warm-blooded animals, such as mammals and birds, are **homeothermic**, maintaining a nearly constant internal temperature in spite of changing environmental temperature. The "constant" temperature actually fluctuates regularly with the time of day in accordance with the **circadian rhythm** of the animal, the so-called **biological clock.** Many of our body processes wax and wane with approximately a twenty-four-hour cycle. The "normal" temperature for humans is slightly higher in the afternoon (about 37° C) than during the night (about 36° C) (Kalat, 1988). A constant body temperature also permits animals to be equally active at many different environmental temperatures. Cold-blooded animals are more sluggish when the temperature is low.

Mechanisms of Temperature Regulation

One of the body's first rules of temperature regulation is to protect the brain and vital organs at the expense of peripheral parts. When the temperature goes down, peripheral blood vessels contract so that less blood is exposed to cold air and less heat is lost. We are all aware that our fingers and hands get cold before our bodies do, sometimes with frostbite resulting. About half of our body cooling occurs from exposure of the head and neck to the environment; hence, the admonishment, if your hands get cold, put on a hat. Cold hands are a signal that body temperature is going down, and covering the head slows down the loss of body heat. Other responses of the body include generation of heat by shivering and fluffing of the fur (with furry animals).

When we get too hot, the opposite reactions occur. Peripheral blood vessels expand so that more blood passes under the surface of the skin and is cooled, and we perspire so that we are cooled even more when the perspiration evaporates. Cats lick their fur and cool themselves by evaporation of the saliva. Dogs cool primarily by evaporation from the mouth and tongue when they pant.

Brain mechanisms of thermoregulation. The hypothalamus plays a major role in thermoregulation, just as it does in hunger and thirst. The **preoptic area** of the hypothalamus monitors body temperature and activates homeostatic mechanisms for raising or lowering temperature. If a device called a **thermode** is inserted into the preoptic nucleus, thermoregulatory mechanisms can be manipulated experimentally. The thermode can be warmed or cooled, thereby fooling the preoptic nucleus into believing that the body is warming or cooling. If the thermode is cooled, an animal shivers; if the thermode is warmed, the animal pants or perspires. These effects occur within a constant laboratory environment. If the preoptic nucleus is damaged, animals do not show appropriate thermoregulation and have large fluctuations (e.g., 10° C) in body temperature. However, the preoptic nucleus is not the only part of the brain or body involved in temperature regulation. There are also temperature receptors in the skin, spinal cord, and areas of the brain other than the hypothalamus.

Eating and drinking are also affected by temperature regulatory systems. When the preoptic nucleus is cooled, animals eat more and drink less, but when it is warmed, they drink more and eat less. Reduced food intake in warm environments may occur because the increased specific dynamic action of food ingestion may generate an uncomfortable increase in body temperature.

For a number of years, the preoptic nucleus seemed to fit the ideal model of a thermostat because it is set at 37° C. If the temperature goes down, the preoptic nucleus instigates warming activities; if temperature goes up, cooling activities are instigated. A problem for this notion (Satinoff, 1983) is that when there is preoptic damage so severe that shivering, sweating, or other automatic mechanisms do not go into action, animals will still thermoregulate behaviorally. They will, for example, press a lever to warm or cool themselves. This activity means that thermoregulation is not destroyed, only that one aspect of it is changed (Satinoff, 1983).

Thermoregulatory behavior.   Within limits, warm-blooded animals can maintain constant body temperature with homeostatic mechanisms, but what happens with cold-blooded animals or warm-blooded ones in more extreme environments? Poikilothermic animals have only their behavior to fall back on, and what they do is move to warmer or cooler environments. Fish can move to shallower or deeper water to warm or cool, and desert reptiles can move about seeking sunnier or shadier spots. Some desert animals, having to face extreme temperature differences between night and day, burrow into the ground at night and slowly come out into the sun in the morning. As the day heats up, they burrow again to keep cool.

Satinoff (1983) points out that psychologists generally think of behavior as being more complicated than homeostatic regulatory mechanisms but that physiologists often think of behavior as being simpler. In the case of thermoregulation, Satinoff says (1983, pp. 461–462), "the responses to thermal stress are many and varied, but in the beginning was behavior . . . all species tested, from insects through humans, show behavioral temperature selection." Even single-celled organisms show **thermotaxis,** moving toward or away from areas of extreme water temperatures to areas of more moderate temperatures. There is no simpler response.

Organization of Thermoregulatory Responses

Satinoff (1983) argues against the notion that there is a single "thermo-stat" in the preoptic nucleus because there is simply too much evidence to the contrary. In particular, destruction of the preoptic nucleus does not lead to complete failure of temperature regulation. What the preoptic nucleus seems to do in the normal course of events is *organize* or *integrate* the activities of a number of different thermoregulatory responses, including behavioral. If the preoptic nucleus is made inoperative, these specific thermoregulatory responses are still available, and thermoregulation can still occur. For example, shivering may not occur, but moving to a warmer location may occur.

Satinoff also points out that thermoregulatory mechanisms did not evolve only as thermoregulatory mechanisms. Panting, for example, cools a dog that has been running but also increases the amount of oxygen consumed. Alligators also have greater heat loss if their mouths are open than if they are closed, a variation on dog panting. Such variation suggests that there is no reason to believe that a single thermoregulatory center in the brain should have evolved. Rather, various specific responses evolved. Individually these responses may operate at the level of the spinal cord, but they also came under the control of higher brain centers, such as the hypothalamus. Destruction of the higher control centers does not destroy the responses, it just destroys their integrated control system. Thermoregulation can and does still occur; however, it does not occur as a single response that is turned on by a hypothalamic thermostat.

Fever

When someone feels sick, the first thing the person does is take his or her temperature to determine how serious the illness is. If oral temperature is much above 98.6° F (37° C), we consider taking some action. With infants, one of our first actions is to try to reduce the body temperature, by washing the baby with lukewarm water, for example. But why does temperature go up at all when we are sick? Fever is not the illness—it is a symptom of the body's response to infections by viruses or bacteria. When foreign substances enter the body, white blood cells are mobilized to fight those substances. The white blood cells (**leukocytes**) release a protein called **leukocytic pyrogen,** which causes production of **prostaglandin E,** which acts on the preoptic nucleus to increase body temperature.

Does a fever in itself do us any good? Again, temperature is an important variable in chemical reactions, and some bacteria grow less well at elevated body temperatures (Kluger & Rottenberg, 1979). Therefore, fever may have direct value in fighting disease. From a strictly motivational point of view, however, fevers (or the conditions with which they are associated) are usually unpleasant, and we do all we can to get rid of them. At the same time, we may lose our appetite or the energy to engage in other motivated activities.

REPRODUCTIVE BEHAVIOR

In terms of species survival, sex is as important as hunger or thirst. Sexual behavior, however, is not entirely "driven" by internal states any more than eating or drinking are entirely driven by internal states. Such external incentives as other people, pictures, or the written word play a major role in arousing and sustaining sexual motivation. We may presume that sex evolved into such a powerful motive because animals with higher levels of this motivation reproduce more and hence were favored by natural selection.

Stimulus Factors in Sex

Many different stimulus elements determine sexual attraction. Among birds, for example, there are complex courtship rituals. Male birds are usually more flamboyant in plumage and coloration than are females, and the males use these characteristics to attract females. Different species also have their own specific mating signals. Crickets have their calls, frogs have theirs, and mockingbirds have theirs. Obviously these animals do not respond to calls of the other species. Mockingbirds are an unusual case of signaling. They have about five *hundred* different calls during mating season and a different five hundred calls during the "off" season. It is not clear just what they do with all the information-sending capacity, but it would seem to be sex-related.

Visual stimuli. Visual stimuli, whether from living people, photographs, drawings, or videotapes, are among the most potent sources of human sexual arousal. Many magazines, such as *Playboy* or the *Sports Illustrated* swimsuit issue, rely on the sexually exciting quality of more or less explicit nudity for their sales. Videotape rentals testify strongly to the value many people place on sexual arousal through visual stimulation.

Chemical stimuli. Some animals, such as moths, have powerful airborne chemical sex attractants called **pheromones** to entice potential mates. These are effective for distances as long as a half-mile. The effects of pheromones may depend on hormones in the recipient. For example, castration decreases a male hamster's interest in female odors (Gregory, Engle, & Pfaff, 1975). It appears that male sex hormones excite neural circuits in the amygdala so that these brain circuits respond to the odor of vaginal secretions (Carlson, 1987).

Smell plays a role in primate sexual behaviors, but there do not seem to be any pheromones that excite specific unlearned sexual behaviors in either humans or other primates (Carlson, 1987). Swabbing a female monkey with strange odors increases the interest of a male, even when the odor is like green peppers and bears little conceivable relation to normal sexual attraction. Such novel odors probably just arouse curiosity. Familiar odors may play a role in sexual attraction because they are associated with particular situations. Perfumes, for example, may be arousing to some people because (rightly or wrongly) they associate perfumes with availability for sex.

Touch.   The skin is the largest sense organ of the human body, and touch is one of the most immediate triggers for sexual arousal. Being touched on any part of the body may produce arousal, but the genital areas of either sex are the most sensitive. Touching the body of a partner also triggers arousal in the person doing the touching. This arousal may be due at least in part because of the fantasies aroused by the touch.

Sexual fantasies.   With or without the aid of pictures or other stimuli, sexual fantasies play a major role in sex. Romantic novels lacking explicit sexual passages may nevertheless produce sexual arousal because of the fantasies triggered by the story. Similarly, photographs have much of their impact because they trigger fantasies that go far beyond the photo content, such as the viewer's fantasizing having sex with the person in the picture. Such fantasies occur almost invariably with masturbation but also occur frequently during intercourse. Intercourse fantasies frequently involve a different partner than the one present at the moment or having other kinds of sex than that being engaged in at the moment (Sue, 1979).

Stimulus variation.   It is well-demonstrated with animals that stimulus variation plays a role in sexual attraction and even has a name, the **Coolidge Effect.** The story is that President and Mrs. Calvin Coolidge were taking a tour of a farm. Mrs. Coolidge observed that there was only one rooster but a hundred hens. One rooster is enough, she was told. "Tell that to Mr. Coolidge," she said. When told this, Mr. Coolidge asked whether the rooster served one hen a hundred times or a hundred hens once. Informed that it was the latter, he said, "Tell that to Mrs. Coolidge." Under experimental conditions, male animals that have copulated to the point of exhaustion with a particular female partner will immediately resume their activity if a new partner is presented. In fact, Beamer, Bermant, and Clegg (1969) provided a ram with a new female after each ejaculation and found the animal able to ejaculate in less than two minutes with each of twelve different females. This response is not typical, even for a ram. What it tells us is that the "exhaustion" found with repeated intercourse is not just a physical inability to perform but that it involves a "psychological" factor, perhaps akin to boredom. Among humans, it is not uncommon to find that stimulus variation produces an increase in sexual activity. The variation may be in the form of time, place, behavior, or partner. Marriage counselors often recommend introducing variation into the love lives of clients who have "gotten in a rut" or seemed to have lost interest in each other.

Individual differences in sexual attraction.   There are individual differences in what appears attractive to human males and females, and even with dogs. Frank Beach (1969) found not only that male beagles had reliable but different preferences for particular females but also that the females also had their own preferences. Some females rejected the amorous advances of particular males even though other females accepted those same males. We do not know why the animals had the preferences they did, but it is clear that a mutual attraction between male and female had to be present before things progressed any further. We discuss such issues in more detail in Chapter Fourteen.

Internal Factors

Arousal versus arousability.   Whereas arousal refers to the level of actual arousal, arousability refers to the ease with which arousal occurs (Whalen, 1966). Hormones may set different levels of arousability, but some external stimulus triggers arousal. An animal not aroused with a particular partner may be easily aroused by a new partner. We would conclude that the animal was previously arousable, even though not aroused by the previous partner.

Among such "lower" mammals as rodents, arousability is largely determined by sex hormones, the **androgens** (primarily **testosterone**) in males and **estrogens** in females. Castrated farm animals lose their interest in sex and do not engage in sexual activity, and laboratory experiments clearly show the role of sex hormones in this activity. If castrated animals are given hormone replacement therapy (injections of testosterone), they resume sexual activity as long as the hormone lasts. Interest again wanes until further injections.

Human males, on the other hand, may be sexually aroused and may display sexual interest long after castration. Similarly, some men show considerable sexual activity at advanced ages when testosterone levels are very low. Human females are also sexually aroused and engage in sexual behavior after hormones have been reduced to very low levels, for example, following menopause. This behavior indicates that human sexual arousal is controlled by the nervous system more so than in other animals and may be due to greater cognitive abilities, such as engaging in sexual fantasies, which presumably requires a complex brain. We do know from such surveys as the Kinsey reports (Kinsey et al., 1948, 1953), from sales of popular magazines, and from videotape rentals that humans do actively engage in sexual fantasies.

Hormone effects.   Human sexual behavior is influenced by hormones but is not fully determined by them. For example, if a male had female hormone replacement therapy, he would not act like a female just because of this. Conversely, testosterone treatment will not cause a woman to lose sexual interest in men (Carlson, 1987). Excessive exposure to androgens during the prenatal period has, however, been associated with somewhat different social characteristics in adult females. They consider themselves more "tomboyish" and are more athletic. But they also show the same level of satisfaction with a female sex role and its activities as do nonandrogenized control subjects (Money & Ehrhardt, 1972). The interpretation of the androgen effects is itself questionable. Androgens may lead to greater physical activity and hence to more malelike behaviors (Carlson, 1994). None of these are "abnormal" behaviors and may be worthy of comment only because they don't fit a "feminine" stereotype. Women may engage in many nonstereotypical activities if given the opportunity and encouragement to do so. So may men.

Emotions and Sex

Positive emotion is obviously related to sex, but sometimes there are negative emotions, particularly anxiety and guilt. At some point in the history of humanity, it was apparently considered necessary to make certain sexual activities taboo, perhaps so that sex would be limited to reproduction that was necessary for social survival. Strong moral codes prohibiting such activities as masturbation, homosexuality, and artificial contraception developed. These are still major points of contention in such institutions as the Roman Catholic church. The problems raised by these prohibitions are that situations may change, such as overpopulation rapidly overtaking the world, but the old rules are retained (Baron & Byrne, 1977). Each generation has to teach the next generation the "rules," and the teaching generation may not hold up its end of the bargain very well. For example, in its attempt to regulate sexual activities, the teaching generation may pass along such misinformation as that masturbation leads to insanity.

Because of differences in background and experience with sex, different people develop completely different attitudes about any given sexual activity. For example, Wallace and Wehmer (1972) found that people who were "sexually liberal" or "sexually conservative" were equally aroused by sexually explicit pictures of different activities. But whereas the "liberal" group considered the pictures entertaining, the "conservative" group considered them disgusting. Individuals who are more emotionally negative toward sex are also more restrictive in what they consider "permissible" sexual acts and in what they actually do in their own sex activity. The emotion of guilt seems to be particularly important; the greater the guilt associated with sex, the smaller the range of sexual activities a person is likely to engage in. People with strong negative emotions toward sex are also more likely to have difficulty in achieving successful orgasm, **frigidity** in females and **impotence** in males. These are usually psychological problems rather than physical, and psychologists have devised a variety of therapies for successfully dealing with them.

The Human Sexual Response

The most dramatic breakthrough in human sexual research came with the pioneering studies by Masters and Johnson (1966). Using direct observation of behavior as well as color cinematography and physiological recordings, they arrived at some general characteristics of sexual responses. Both male and female responses are divided into the following four phases, characterized by general body changes as well as reactions of sex organs. Not all of these occur with every individual, and some may be so brief that they are not noticed without the aid of recording instruments.

Excitement.   Sexual excitement may be produced by fantasy, looking at pictures, physical contact, or a variety of other stimuli. Nipple erection is common in females but also occurs in some males. There is sometimes a reddening of the skin of the chest and head, called a "sex tension flush." In females this may spread to lower parts of the body. Males show penile erection, which may occur in seconds (and reverse just as fast), and females have vaginal lubrication and thickening of the vaginal walls. Female breast size may begin to increase.

Plateau.   Arousal increases with sustained stimulation. There is an increased frequency of sex tension flush, general muscular tension, spasmodic movements of wrists and ankles, hyperventilation, and increased heart rate (100 to 160 beats per minute). Female breast size may increase as much as 25 percent above prestimulation baseline, along with other changes in the sex organs. The circumference of the corona of the penis may increase twofold, change to a purplish color, and emit from the Cowper's gland a fluid that deacidifies the interior of the penis, making a safer pathway for the sperm and providing lubrication.

Orgasm.   At the peak of sexual excitement, there are specific muscle contractions, related to pelvic thrusting as well as to abdominal and facial muscles. In males there is contraction of the various accessory organs necessary for ejaculation. The female shows corresponding contractions of the uterus and genital area. The actual climax, expulsion of semen by the male and vaginal contraction by the female, takes only a few seconds, and once started is not under voluntary control. These are the fixed action patterns, or consummatory responses, discussed in Chapter Three. The behaviors leading up to them are highly variable, but the final responses are highly stereotyped.

Resolution.   After climax there is often a sweating reaction by both male and female, but this is related to autonomic nervous system arousal and separate from physical exertion. There is also hyperventilation and high heart rate, which may largely be due to physical exertion. Males show a "refractory period," with reduced penile erection and a lower level of arousability. During this refractory period, which may last from minutes to hours, the male cannot readily be rearoused. Females, clearly showing the greater dura-bility of their half of the species, can maintain continuously high levels of sex-ual arousal with no refractory period. A female may reach climax many times during a sexual episode, whereas the male climaxes only once.

The Masters and Johnson type of research has been criticized on the grounds that it deals only with the mechanical aspects of sex, ignoring the roles of love and affection. This criticism is true, and the reason is simple: Any research can deal with only a limited number of questions at a time. The Masters and Johnson research was not intended to answer all possible ques-tions about interpersonal relations. Many other researchers have addressed those questions (Chapter Fourteen).

Sexual Orientation

Most people experience sexual attraction and arousal toward members of the opposite sex, but a significant minority (about 4 percent of males and 1 percent of females) are exclusively attracted to persons of the same sex. The percentages are higher if we include people who have a bisexual orienta-tion (i.e., toward both sexes). Homosexuality has long been a hotly debated topic. It has been viewed as sinful, as deviant, as an illness, and as perfectly normal activity. What is clear is that the male homosexual population, for ex-ample, has a wide range of members whose only common characteristic seems to be homosexuality. The male homosexual is not necessarily effemi-nate. Alexander the Great of Macedonia, conqueror of the ancient world, was bisexual, and some stars of the National Football League have "come out" and reported themselves to be homosexual. Similarly, female homosexuals are not necessarily masculine in appearance or behavior. The great range of appearance and behavior among homosexuals is interestingly shown in the participants in gay parades or rallies.

The biological, psychological, and social factors that might affect sexual orientation have all been explored extensively, but thus far there is no single factor, or even a set of factors, known to produce heterosexuality or homo-sexuality (Kalat, 1995; Carlson, 1994). Indeed, it is just as reasonable to ask why someone is heterosexual as to ask why someone is homosexual. If the de-terminants of heterosexuality are found, so probably will be the determinants of homosexuality.

It contributes nothing toward answering the question to say that hetero-sexuality is "natural." All this tells us is that most people are heterosexual, but we already know that. It does not tell us why the majority are heterosexual. Supposed biblical exhortations against homosexuality (which may be matters of interpretation) are not much help, either. In spite of the protestations of the "moral majority," there is no evidence that homosexuality is just a "lifestyle choice" that can be "corrected" in the way that a person would shift his or her diet from French cuisine to Mexican. What does the evidence indi-cate?

1. **Genetics.** Some evidence suggests a genetic predisposition toward homosexuality. In one study of male homosexuals, there were concordance ratios of 52 percent for monozygotic twins, 22 percent for dizygotic twins, and 11 percent for adopted brothers (Kalat, 1995), and similar ratios for female homosexuals. Self-reports of homosexual interest appear early in life and are not related to parental upbringing or any other known social factor. It should be noted that a concordance ratio of 52 percent for homosexuality in monozygotic twins also means that in 48 percent of twin pairs, one twin was homosexual and the other was not. Thus, there is no clear-cut biological basis in these data. In a family that had three pairs of identical twins, two pairs were homosexual, but the third pair were heterosexual. This finding would seem to eliminate environmental factors as sole determinants of homosexuality, since all the twins might be expected to be of the same sexual orientation if reared in the same family. The reason for searching for such biological factors is that social factors do not seem to account for homosexual orientation (Storms, 1983 a,b). There simply is no strong evidence that interpersonal relationships within a family, such as a domineering mother and a weak father, lead to male homosexuality.

2. **Hormones.** Homosexuality is not due to a preponderance of a particular hormone. A castrated male who is injected with female hormones does not become homosexual, nor does a female who is ovariectomized and given male hormones become homosexual. Homosexual males have normal levels of androgens, although two lines of evidence suggest the possibility of a hormonal factor. First, many homosexual men show a female type of hormonal response if injected with estrogen (Gladue, Green, & Hellman, 1984). Second, abnormally high levels of testosterone injected into a pregnant sheep at a critical time during gestation may produce a lesbian offspring (Money, 1987).

3. **Behaviors.** Carlson (1994) points out that homosexuals and heterosexuals engage in the same kinds of behaviors. It is just the sex of the object of those behaviors that is different. He speculates that there might be subtle differences in brains that are based on differences in sex hormones during prenatal development. These differences may then determine what is sexually attractive.

The best correlate of homosexuality is which sex a person says he or she is attracted to. This attraction may have partial biological (genetic) determination. Consider a couple of facts that we know about sexual behavior of animals. First, nonhumans show fluctuating interests in members of the opposite sex, related to variations in hormone level. Second, when attraction occurs, it is to members of one's own species, not to others. The latter point is so obvious as to be easily overlooked. If attraction were based solely on learning, we might expect more cross-species sexual activity than we seem to observe.

SUMMARY

1. Our bodies are about 70 percent water, but we cannot store surplus water. We must get water, typically by drinking, in order to restore water lost through evaporation, urination, or blood loss.

2. According to the **double-depletion theory** of thirst, there are two sources of start cues for regulatory drinking, **intracellular** and **extracellular**.

3. The **intracellular** cues to drinking result from increased salt concentration of body fluids outside the cells, resulting in cell shrinkage. This is detected by "osmoreceptors" in the hypothalamus, which trigger some degree of water conservation in the body as well as drinking if water is available.

4. The **extracellular** mechanism involves activation of **pressure receptors** in the vascular system. Reduced pressure triggers a chemical reaction, which leads to stimulation of hypothalamic cells by a chemical called **angiotensin,** which elicits drinking behavior. Drinking is also stimulated by **histamine** and **serotonin,** which are released when food is ingested.

5. Drinking is **terminated** by stop cues from the **mouth** and **stomach,** and by rapid **absorption of water,** which turns off the cues that initiated drinking.

6. Since termination of drinking is also determined by such behavioral factors as the amount of **effort** required to get water, satiation is not determined by some fixed quantity of water consumed.

7. An important **nonregulatory** factor in drinking is the **palatability** of fluid. This involves **taste** but also seems to involve **cooling.** People or animals may drink fluids because they taste good and hence get enough fluid without necessarily getting thirsty.

8. In order for animals to survive, their body temperatures must be protected, sometime in the face of extreme shifts in environmental temperature. Cold-blooded animals have the same temperature as the surrounding environment and regulate temperature by selecting environments. Warm-blooded animals keep the same temperature in spite of changes in environment, utilizing a combination of behavioral and homeostatic mechanisms.

9. When temperature drops, heat is first conserved for the internal organs of warm-blooded animals by constriction of peripheral blood vessels. When temperature rises, these vessels expand, producing evaporative cooling through perspiration.

10. The **preoptic** area of the hypothalamus monitors body temperature and activates homeostatic mechanisms for raising or lowering temperature. If this area is damaged, there are large fluctuations of body temperature. Even without the preoptic nucleus, however, warm-blooded animals can still regulate temperature behaviorally.

11. The preoptic nucleus seems to organize a number of different thermoregulatory responses, both homeostatic and behavioral. If there is damage to part of the system, other parts can still function. Most thermoregulatory responses (e.g., panting in dogs) are also parts of other functions (getting more oxygen), so that thermoregulation can be maintained in the normal course of other events.

12. **Fever** occurs when white blood cells stimulate the release of **prostaglandin E,** which acts on the hypothalamus to increase body temperature. Increased temperature may directly help fight disease by altering the body's chemical reactions to viruses or bacteria.

13. Sex is a powerful biological motive for survival of the species, but it does not involve homeostatic mechanisms. Sexual deprivation is not life-threatening but does involve complex interactions between environmental stimuli and internal states.

14. Many kinds of visual, auditory, chemical, and tactile stimuli affect sexual arousal, depending on the particular species. Chemical substances called **pheromones** are released by many species and serve as olfactory sexual attrac-

tants, as perfumes are said to do. It is not clear that pheromones function among primates as they do among lower animals, however. Simple stimulus variation appears to be an important factor in sexual arousal for humans or other animals.

15. Internal factors, mainly sex hormones, affect sexual **arousal** and **arousability.** Arousal refers to the level of sexual motivation at the moment; arousability refers to the ease or rapidity of arousal. Two animals may be equally nonaroused at the moment, but one may be much more easily aroused than the other.

16. The sexual behavior of nonhumans is more controlled by hormones than is human behavior. Human sexual behavior is influenced by hormones but not fully determined by them. Thus males or females injected with hormones of the opposite sex still behave much as they did before. The main effect of **androgens** (male sex hormones) on women may simply be to increase the amount of physical activity and hence give the appearance of malelike behavior.

17. The human sexual response has been divided by Masters and Johnson into four phases that are said to characterize both males and females: (1) **excitement**, (2) **plateau,** (3) **orgasm,** and (4) **resolution**. Each phase is described in terms of specific physiological changes.

18. Sexual preferences, especially homosexuality, have engendered a great deal of heated debate, but *the basis of homosexuality is not known*. Two facts seem clear, however. Homosexuality is not caused by a dominance of one or another sex hormone and is not related to any specific family constellation, such as a weak father and a domineering mother. There is some evidence for partial genetic determination, but other factors are apparently important.

CHAPTER SIX

Drive and Activation

——●——

DRIVE THEORY

Drive theory developed out of the regulatory approach to motivation, emphasizing homeostasis and a general energization of behavior; however, it has expanded far beyond its biological origins into personality theory and social psychology. Therefore, the student of psychology generally needs to be conversant with drive theory in order to understand its wide influence. Like the homeostatic approach in general, we shall find problems with drive theory but also find instances when it continues to be useful.

Background

Homeostasis. If our hunger is so severe that we cannot compensate for lost energy by using what is already in our body, we must actively do something to restore homeostatic balance. Internally aroused by a state of imbalance, an organism does what it can to reduce the internal tension and to restore balance. The critical question is, How do internal imbalances result in the *particular* behavioral adjustments that restore balance?

Adaptive acts. Evolutionary approaches to psychology emphasized the **adaptation** and **adjustment** of organisms to the environment. Harvey Carr (1925), one of the leaders of the American functional school of psychology, as well as others before him, argued that the basic animal behavior was the **adaptive act.** When an organism needs food or water, there is a persistent internal stimulus that arouses adaptive activity until the need is satisfied. A number of key concepts emerged from this view.

1. **Need.** Need is an excess or a deficiency of some product related to survival. Need is defined on the antecedent side in terms of deprivation (such as food) and on the consequent side in terms of health or survival. Needs frequently lead to activity that restores the appropriate balance, but not necessarily. Some needs, such as some vitamin deficiencies or oxygen deficit, do **not** stimulate compensatory activity. Therefore, the concept of drive is introduced.
2. **Drive.** The antecedents for drive could be the same as for need (e.g., deprivation), but its consequent conditions are behaviors. It is drive, not need, that goads the animal to activity; drive provides the persistent stimulus to behavior. Miller (1951b) suggested that any strong and persistent stimulus can have drive properties. Need and drive may be correlated, but the fact that they are not always correlated is why there are two concepts and not just one.
3. **Goal.** A goal is some commodity that will reduce the drive that initiated the activity. A hungry animal consumes food and for a while thereafter, it is inactive as far as food is concerned.

The whole sequence then is as follows:

Need → Drive → Activity → Goal → Reduced Drive → Reduced Activity

Hull's Drive Theory

One of America's most prestigious psychologists, Clark Hull, was noted early in his career for work on aptitude testing and hypnosis. About 1930, however, he began to develop a general theory of behavior, culminating in the *Principles of Behavior* (1943). Research related to the *Principles,* whether supportive or contradictory, dominated the fields of motivation and learning for twenty years. Many features of the theory have not well stood the test of time, but some aspects are still considered to be useful. The *Principles* was meant as the beginning of a complete theory of behavior, but Hull died before he could extend the theory to human social activity as he had envisioned. We shall consider only those parts most relevant to motivation.

Drive as an intervening variable.   Hull, like others, distinguished between performance and the variables that *determine* performance. The two main variables were **habit strength** (sHr), which is the strength of association between a given stimulus and response,[1] and drive (D), which "activates" habit into performance. Hull argued that drive does not direct, guide, steer, or select responses. Instead, Hull proposed, drive equally energizes *all* responses. In a specific situation, the response that has the strongest association (i.e., habit strength, sHr) to the stimuli present would be the response most likely to occur.

In the more precise language of the theory, drive *multiplies* habit to produce the **excitatory potential** for a particular response. Thus,

Excitatory Potential = Habit × Drive,

or, symbolically:

$$sEr = sHr \times D, \text{ or just } E = H \times D$$

E, H, and D are **intervening variables,** with different antecedent conditions. The strength of H is defined in terms of number of learning trials, increasing with the number of S-R associations. The strength of D is defined, for example, in terms of number of hours of food deprivation or intensity of a noxious stimulus. The value of E is defined according to the **syntax of the theory,** in terms of the relation between H and D. On the consequent side, these intervening variables are *measured* in terms of amplitude, frequency, probability, or latency of responding. This concept is illustrated in Figure 6–1. Observable events are outside the box, and intervening variables are inside the box.

---

[1]The assumption that learning involves only S-R associations is considered one of the major flaws of Hull's theory overall, but this does not necessarily negate everything Hull has to say about the relation between learning and motivation.

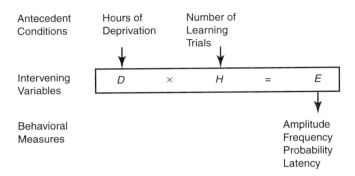

FIGURE 6–1. Antecedent conditions, consequent conditions, and intervening variables in Hull's (1943) theory.

The multiplicative relationship between *H* and *D* was arrived at partly by logical considerations and partly by research. Logically it would make little sense to propose that $E = H - D$ or that $E = H/D$, since either of these statements says that performance (*E*) would get *weaker* with increasing drive. Either $E = H + D$ or $E = H \times D$ makes more sense, since either of these formulations says that performance will improve with increasing drive. On the basis of data from previous experiments, Hull selected the $H \times D$ formulation. The general prediction from the multiplicative formulation is illustrated in Figure 6–2. Many subsequent researchers have used such diverging curves as illus-

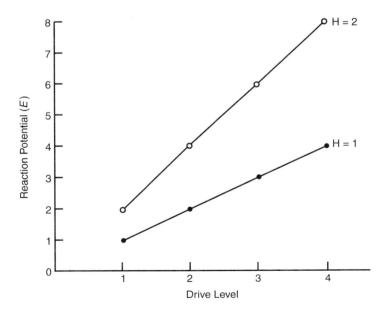

FIGURE 6–2. Habit and drive interaction in Hullian theory ($E = H \times D$).

trated in Figure 6–2 as evidence for the operation of motivational variables (e.g., Zajonc & Sales, 1966; Cooper & Fazio, 1984).

Different predictions for simple and complex responses.   We make different behavioral predictions from the theory depending on whether the responses to be made are simple or complex. A **simple** response is a **clearly dominant response,** and the theory predicts that such a response will become even more dominant with a higher level of drive as Figure 6–2 indicates. If an animal has learned the simple response of running down a straight alleyway to get to food, the animal should run faster with longer deprivation (higher drive).

Drive would also energize **unlearned** response tendencies if the stimuli for those responses were present and more dominant than learned response tendencies in the same situation. Thus $E = sUr \times D$, where sUr is a stimulus-response relationship that does not require learning. Examples of sUr would include simple reflexes but would also presumably include "spontaneous" or "random" activity, which we shall discuss shortly.

In a **complex** response situation, however, there are several possible responses with habits of near-equal strength. These different habits conflict with each other and produce **competing responses.** If such competing responses are simultaneously activated, we would expect error and confusion. Suppose that a machine operator has several similar levers to pull in order to perform different job functions. If the operator is not careful, he or she might "accidentally" pull a wrong lever at any time. If the operator's drive is very high, such as during an emergency, the chances of making an error are even greater because all the responses are more strongly energized. In sum, the theory says that at high levels of drive, dominant responses become even more dominant but that competing responses interfere with each other even more and performance gets worse. For example, to drive a car with a manual transmission, one must push in the clutch pedal, move the stick to change gears, operate the brake and gas, all in a well-timed sequence. Initially these different responses compete with each other, and in an emergency situation, the new learner may panic and make the wrong response. The predictions for these two situations are summarized in Table 6–1.

What Makes a Variable Motivational?

In Hull's theory how do we decide that an intervening variable is motivational rather than, say, learning? The following criteria have commonly been used to identify drive:

1. **An increase in the level of the variable energizes a wide range of responses.** This criterion distinguishes drive from a specific stimulus that evokes a specific response, such as a reflex response. Food deprivation energizes eating, running to food, pressing a lever to get food, and so on. When such a variety of responses is energized, a specific *S-R* connection is ruled out, and a more general "motivating" variable is indicated.

TABLE 6–1. Performance of simple and complex responses under conditions of low and high drive according to Hull's theory.

	SIMPLE RESPONSES	COMPLEX RESPONSES
Low drive	Worse	Better
High drive	Better	Worse

2. **A decrease in the level of the variable is reinforcing.** If pain is reduced following a particular response and if that same response occurs more frequently in the future under similar circumstances, the variable (pain) may be said to be drive. Reduction of pain drive reinforces (strengthens) the association between the situation and the response.

3. **An increase in the level of the variable is punishing.** If a response is followed by increased pain, the response is less likely to occur; it has been punished. Pain meets this criterion for drive, but hunger and thirst have not.

Evaluating Drive Theory

Persistence in responding. Since drive theory predicts stronger responding with higher drive, hungrier animals should respond more for food, thirstier animals should respond more for water, and so on. Research consistently shows this result. Warden (1931), for example, studied strength of drive in an **obstruction box,** where an animal has to cross an electrified floor to reach food, water, or other goal. With longer deprivation, animals would cross the electrified floor more times, or would tolerate stronger shocks to get at the food.

The problem for a drive theory interpretation is that the animals were running *to* some goal, and the effect of deprivation could be on **responsiveness to the goal,** not just an energization of behavior. A less ambiguous demonstration of a drive effect would be on behavior where there is no clear goal. One idea is that drive energizes "random" activity ($D \times sUr$), which should facilitate **finding** an appropriate goal. Thus, a hungry animal should be more active in its search for food.

Drive and activity. In 1925, John F. Dashiell reported that hungry rats explored a "checkerboard" maze more than satiated rats. This finding was confirmed in many subsequent experiments and was taken by a generation of psychologists to mean that drive energizes activity. But does drive energize all kinds of activity, as Hull said it should? There are many equally "good" ways to measure activity. For example, the **activity wheel,** commonly used for pet mice or hamsters, can be rigged so that each revolution of the wheel is counted and activity thereby measured. A **jiggle cage (stabilimeter)** is mounted on springs so that when an animal in the cage shifts its weight, the cage, moves, and electrical contacts open and close. Or we can record the number of times an animal moves across the midline of a cage, or the number of squares on the floor that an animal crosses in an "open field." Each of these measurement procedures provides an operational definition of "activity." Do higher levels of deprivation increase activity by all these measures?

The answer, in a nutshell, is no, deprivation does not affect all kinds of activity equally. Campbell (1964) used albino laboratory rats to compare food and water deprivation in three different apparatuses (activity wheels, stabilimeters, and mazes). The animals were continuously in their respective apparatuses for several days. The results (as seen in Figure 6–3) were that

- Food-deprived rats in activity wheels increased their activity to a peak of about 1,200 percent of the baseline measure but increased only about 500 percent in the other two apparatuses.
- Water-deprived rats increased about 500 percent in the activity wheels, but not at all in the other apparatuses.
- The amount of activity depends on the kind of deprivation (food or water) and the particular measure of activity used. Campbell, Smith, Misanin, and Jaynes (1966) found that deprivation affected differently the activity of chicks, guinea pigs, hamsters, and rabbits. The exact effects depended on the species, the type of deprivation, and the type of measure. For example, hungry hamsters were more active in the wheel than satiated hamsters, but thirsty hamsters were less active than satiated hamsters.
- Animals can *learn* to become more active. If rats are fed immediately after they have been running in an activity wheel, they become more active than if their food is delayed an hour (Finger, Reid, & Weasner, 1957; Hall, 1958). Activity is to a large extent learned and to some extent unlearned (Campbell & Cicala, 1962; Finger, 1965).

The generalization that "drive increases activity" is subject to so many qualifications as to be almost useless.

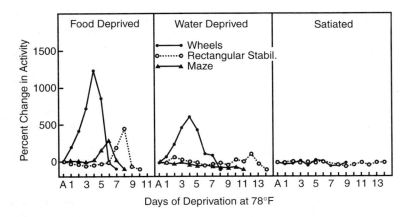

FIGURE 6–3. Percent changes in activity of food-deprived, water-deprived, and satiated rats in activity wheels, rectangular stabilimeter cages, and an automatic Dashiell maze at 78°F. (From Campbell, 1964, p. 330. Copyright © 1964 by Pergamon Press. Reprinted by permission.)

Irrelevant drive.   According to Hull's theory, **any source of drive should energize any response tendency.** For example, thirst should energize a habit originally learned with food deprivation and food reward. In such a case, hunger is called a **relevant** drive because it is relevant to the food that reduces the drive. Thirst is called an **irrelevant drive** because it is not relevant to the hunger and food used to establish the response. In general, irrelevant drive refers to internal motivational states that are not relevant to the goal available at the moment. Hull's equation for excitatory potential is then expanded as follows:

$$E = sHr \times (Dr + Di), \quad \text{where } Dr = \text{relevant drive and } Di = \text{irrelevant drive}$$

The concept was originally developed by Hull (1943) to explain why animals satiated for food made a large number of responses during extinction of the food-getting response (Perin, 1942). Hull felt that this behavior could mean only that some source of drive other than hunger was present, since according to the theory, the animals should not respond without some drive. Hunger, thirst, pain, fear, or any other source of drive could serve as either relevant or irrelevant drive. A variety of experiments involving combinations of hunger and thirst give little support to the irrelevant drive concept, however. Depriving animals of food and water, for example, does not "energize" behavior more than either form of deprivation by itself (see Bolles, 1975; or Beck, 1983, for summary). Hunger and thirst do not combine in the way Hull's theory said they should.

Nonspecific arousal.   Many different behaviors can be elicited by **nonspecific arousal,** however. For example, Valenstein and Kakolewski (1970) reported that electrical stimulation of the *same* brain area produced different behaviors on different days, partly depending on the environment. If food was available, the animals would eat; if water was available, they would drink. Even a pinch to the tail of the animal elicited such behaviors as eating, drinking, or attacking another animal. In short, when an animal is aroused by any of a large number of stimuli, it may engage in whatever behavior the environment "supports" at the moment (Carlson, 1987). This finding could be interpreted in terms of a nonspecific drive that energizes a wide variety of responses, lending some support to a general drive theory.

Human Applications of Drive Theory

Paradoxically, perhaps, drive theory has not worked as well with animals as its proponents had hoped (Miller, 1959; Spence, 1956), but it has provided useful predictions and explanations in human research.

Classical conditioning. In classical conditioning experiments with human subjects, the eye blink is a commonly used response. A soft tone may be used as the conditioned stimulus (CS), followed by a brief puff of air to the cornea of the eye as the unconditioned stimulus (UCS). The eye normally blinks in response to the air puff. Conditioned responses—those eye blinks to the CS that occur without the air puff—become a dominant response. Higher intensities of air puff are considered to produce higher levels of drive, and the level of conditioning is in fact higher with stronger air puffs (Spence, 1956). Taylor (1953) further hypothesized that anxiety would also function as an irrelevant drive. Anxiety level was measured by a self-report scale of anxiety symptoms, such as "I am often sick to my stomach" and "My sleep is restless and disturbed." By manipulating intensity of air puff, we can *produce* high or low levels of drive; and by measuring anxiety (using the Taylor Manifest Anxiety Scale), we can *select* subjects who are high or low in irrelevant drive (anxiety). Spence and Taylor combined these procedures in a single experiment, with the results shown in Figure 6–4. As predicted, (1) subjects getting 2 pounds of pressure per square inch (psi) in the air puff conditioned better than subjects getting 0.6 psi, and (2) high-anxious subjects conditioned better than low-anxious subjects. Both of these results

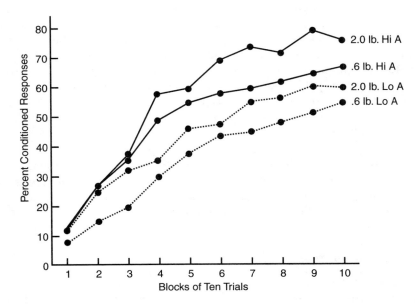

FIGURE 6–4. Eyeblink conditioning as a function of UCS intensity (pounds of pressure per square inch of the air puff) and level of anxiety (measured by the Taylor Manifest Anxiety Scale). (Originally from Spence & Taylor, 1951, adapted from Spence, 1958. Copyright 1951 by the American Psychological Association. Reprinted by permission.)

follow directly from drive theory predictions for dominant responses. This experiment is very good support for drive theory.

Paired associates learning.   Whereas the classical conditioning procedure establishes a single dominant response, a paired-associates learning procedure can be used to set up competing, nondominant responses. A subject views a series of word pairs. The first member of a pair is the stimulus word, the second is the response word. The task on successive presentations is to give the correct response word when only the stimulus word is shown. The experimenter can set up word pairs that have very strong initial associations (such as dog-cat) or very weak ones (like zov-dax). Drive theory predicts that high-anxious subjects should perform better than low-anxious subjects on lists with strong associations (highly *dominant* responses to the stimuli) and worse on lists with weak associations (where there are competing responses). The results have been positive often enough to be provocative, although far from conclusive (see Bolles, 1967; or Byrne, 1974).

Social facilitation.   Social facilitation refers to the effects that observers have on individual performance (Tripplet, 1897). Robert Zajonc (1965) proposed that an *audience* arouses an irrelevant drive in an *actor*. He predicted that performance of dominant responses should be facilitated by an audience and that performance of nondominant responses should become poorer; the predictions were supported in his experiments. The theory can be extended to explain a wide range of social phenomena (Weiss & Miller, 1971; Guerin & Innes, 1984). A highly trained professional athlete, whose responses to virtually every situation in his sport are well practiced, performs better in a stadium full of fans. A young child, who is just learning the same sport and having few well-learned (dominant) responses, may perform more poorly in front of an audience.

Aggression.   Sexually arousing stimuli (pornographic movies), loud sounds, and the presence of weapons have all raised the level of aggressive behavior shown by laboratory subjects. Leonard Berkowitz (1974) argued that this result occurs because these conditions produce a higher level of irrelevant drive.

Drive Stimulus Theory

If general drive activates all responses, why do hungry animals eat, and thirsty ones drink? As obvious as these differences are, they are *not* predicted by general drive theory, because according to the theory, the "same" drive is aroused by all drive-producing operations. One solution to this dilemma is to say that **specific drive-producing procedures also produce specific stimuli in the organism.** These internal stimuli, called **drive stimuli** (S_D), serve as cues for specific responses (running to food or water) just as external stimuli are conditioned to specific responses.

$$\text{Drive Operation (e.g., Deprivation)} \begin{cases} \text{Drive} \\ S_D \end{cases}$$

Animal motivation. S_D is a specific internal stimulus, such as invoked by food deprivation ($S_{D\,\text{Hunger}}$) or by water deprivation ($S_{D\,\text{Thirst}}$), and D is general drive, which would be aroused by either food deprivation or water deprivation. Such internal stimuli are presumed to have the same properties as external stimuli: They can be **discriminated** (we can tell them apart), they can serve as cues, and they can be **conditioned** to responses. The general drive, D, would multiply the habits associated with the internal cues. Whichever cue is present at the time, $S_{D\,\text{Thirst}}$ or $S_{D\,\text{Hunger}}$, would determine the response. For example, if an animal gets food in the right arm of a T-maze and water in the left arm, it learns to go left or right according to whether it is hungry or thirsty on a given day. This activity is illustrated in Figure 6–5. On the very **first trial** on a day when the animal is thirsty, for example, it turns left to the water. Since all aspects of the apparatus are the same every day, the animal appears to be using its own hunger or thirst to guide its behavior (Bailey, 1955; Leeper, 1935).

Capaldi and Davidson (1979) found that rats easily discriminated among different *levels* of deprivation. Capaldi, Vivieros, and Davidson (1981) had rats run in a straight alleyway, with *kind* of deprivation (food versus water) or *amount* of deprivation (short versus long) signaling the *presence or absence* of reward on a given day's trials. For example, a particular animal might get food reward on days when it had short deprivation might but not get food on days when it had long deprivation. This process directly pits the "higher drive" against the internal cue for no reward, and vice versa. Their animals did learn to run faster under low deprivation than high deprivation, if low deprivation signaled reward and if high deprivation signaled no reward.

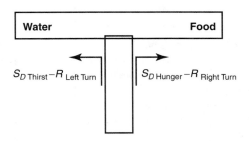

FIGURE 6–5.   The general drive produced by water or food deprivation energizes both right and left turn responses. The drive stimuli, $S_{D\,\text{Thirst}}$ and $S_{D\,\text{Hunger}}$, are distinctive cues that have become conditioned to left-turning and right-turning responses. Since the maze cues themselves are the same under either hunger or thirst conditions, the drive stimuli provide the only cues for which response to make.

Mood dependent memory.   People tend to remember things better if they are in the same mood as when they learned them. For example, if a list was learned while a person was in a sad mood, there is a slight tendency to remember the list better at a later time if in a sad mood rather than in, say, a happy mood. Since moods are internal states, it appears that, other things being equal, moods can serve as memory cues and hence are much like drive stimuli. The phenomenon has been difficult to obtain in the laboratory, for unknown reasons, but appears to be real (Eich, 1995).

Learned Drives

Hunger, thirst, and pain are often called **primary drives,** to indicate their biological primacy and to indicate there is little learning involved in their arousal. But much animal behavior, including human, is *not* directed toward reducing hunger, thirst, or pain. Consequently, drive theorists have postulated that behavior is also motivated by **learned drives** (also called **secondary** or **acquired drives**). A learned drive is one that is aroused by stimuli previously associated with a primary drive. We need to distinguish clearly between learned **drives** and learned **goals (incentives, rewards, reinforcers)**, however. *Drive* refers to an internal state of arousal in the organism; *goal* refers to some external stimulus toward which behavior is directed. Secondary reinforcers are discussed in more detail in Chapter Seven. The most widely examined learned drive has been **fear**.

Fear as an acquired drive.   Many psychologists have believed that animal laboratory analogs for human anxiety and neurotic behavior can shed light on human clinical problems. Therefore, they have developed experimental procedures for producing animal equivalents of human anxiety, conflict, frustration, and even love and affection. These procedures allow for the experimental control necessary to determine causes, which in turn we apply to the human situation.

Fear as an intervening variable.   We treat fear as an intervening variable as indicated in Figure 6–6. A previously conditioned aversive stimulus is the antecedent condition; and verbal reports, nonverbal behaviors, or physiological responses are consequent conditions. Physiological measures might seem the most direct measures of fear, but the exclusive use of such measures would assume that fear is entirely reducible to the particular response(s) being measured and that the measures are accurate. The behavior of the whole animal as it escapes or avoids a fearful situation is often the most sensitive index of fear (McAllister & McAllister, 1971).

If fear is a learned drive, then it should meet the criteria that define any other drive. Fear should **energize** a variety of responses, fear reduction

Antecedent Condition	Intervening Variable	Consequent Conditions
Previously ································· FEAR ································· Conditioned CS		Verbal Response Nonverbal Behavior Physiological Response

FIGURE 6–6.   Fear as an intervening variable.

should be **reinforcing,** and fear increase should be **punishing.** There is good evidence for all of these.

Fear as an energizer.   Fear-drive should energize many responses, but a reflex response should be of special interest because it should be inherently less variable than a learned response (Brown, Kalish, & Farber, 1951). Brown et al. reasoned that fear should energize the startle response, a reflex common to all mammals that occurs when a loud, sharp sound is presented. They placed rats in a small apparatus mounted on a postage scale, so that when an animal was startled by the sharp sound of a cap pistol, it jumped. The magnitude of this startle-jump was recorded by the pressure against the scale. Over a series of trials, a tone was paired with foot shock, and periodically the animals were tested for startle when the fear-arousing tone was on. As predicted (Figure 6–7), the magnitude of startle response increased with the number of

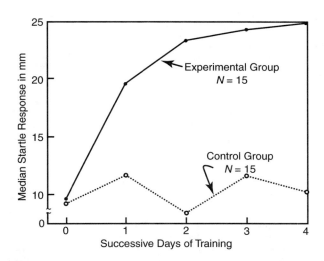

FIGURE 6–7.   Median Amplitude of startle responses of fearful and nonfearful rats to a loud, sharp sound. The upper curve shows that experimental animals presumed to be fearful jumped more vigorously to the sound as the number of fear-conditioning trials increased. The responses of control (nonfearful) subjects, however, did not change progressively or significantly during the same period. (From Brown, Kalish, & Farber, 1951, p. 321. Copyright © 1951 by the American Psychological Association. Reprinted by permission.)

fear-conditioning trials. Control animals, on the other hand, did not show any change in the startle response, suggesting that fear was indeed energizing the startle response. Many subsequent studies (with much more sophisticated apparatus!) have supported the Brown et al. results (Davis & Astrachan, 1978; Davis, 1986).

Fear reduction as reinforcement. The reference experiment for fear reduction was conducted by Neal Miller (1948). The apparatus is illustrated in Figure 6–8. Rats were shocked in one compartment of a two-compartment apparatus and escaped into the other compartment. After this training, the escape route was blocked, but no more shock was given. A wheel was made available to the animals, and when they turned it, the door blocking their escape was opened, and the animals ran to the "safe" side of the apparatus. After wheel turning had been learned, the wheel was made inoperative, and pressing a lever became reinforced by escape. Wheel turning extinguished, and lever pressing increased. The conclusion was that escape into the safe compartment was fear reducing, and this fear reduction reinforced the learning of the two instrumental responses.

Many, many experiments since Miller's (see Mowrer, 1960, for a review) point to the interpretation that fear reduction is reinforcing. Davis and Miller

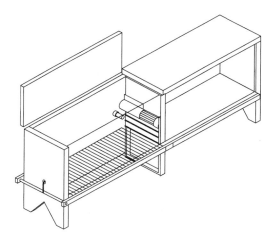

FIGURE 6–8. Acquired drive apparatus. The left compartment is painted white, the right one black. A shock may be administered through the grid that is on the floor of the white compartment. When the animal is placed on the grid that is pivoted at the inside end, it moves down slightly, making a contact that starts an electric timer. When the animal performs the correct response, turning the wheel or pressing the bar as the case may be, it stops the clock and actuates a solenoid that allows the door, painted with horizontal black and white stripes, to drop. The experimenter can also cause the door to drop by pressing a button. The dimensions of each compartment are 18 × 6 × 8½ inches. (From Miller, 1948, p. 90. Copyright © 1948 by the American Psychological Association. Reprinted by permission.)

(1963) even found that rats would press a lever more for an intravenous injection of sodium amytal, a nervous system depressant, in a situation in which they had previously been shocked than would nonshocked control animals. They argued that the drug was reinforcing for the previously shocked animals because it reduced their fear but that the drug did not reinforce the control animals because they had no fear to be reduced.

Fear as a punisher.   Stimuli associated with pain clearly can suppress ongoing behavior, but punishment is a broad topic and is addressed in appropriate detail in Chapter Nine.

An application of learned drive to humans.   To exemplify how learned drive could account for a human phenomenon, Judson Brown (1961) analyzed miserliness, or "desire for money," in terms of anxiety and anxiety reduction. Brown proposed that stimuli associated with *not having money* become conditioned stimuli for fear arousal. A child may hear his parents argue about not having money, expressing anxiety over where money for food and rent is going to come from, and so on. The arguments and fears expressed by the parents are unconditioned stimuli for fear on the part of the child, and such words as "We have no money" become conditioned stimuli for arousing this fear. The child may then learn that *this fear is reduced by getting and having money.* Therefore, whenever the cues for *not* having money are presented, the adult does what she or he has learned as the means of reducing this fear (eliminating the cues): The adult gets money. This kind of fear, as well as a conspicuous consumption that serves to hold down the anxiety cues of poverty, has been described poignantly by the great American playwright Moss Hart in his autobiography, *Act One.*

Other kinds of compulsions may have similar bases. Excessive sexual activity is frequently interpreted in this fashion: Not being loved may serve as an anxiety-arousing cue that is temporarily removed by having sex. Such an interpretation helps the clinician account for behaviors that otherwise seem to have no common explanation.

ACTIVATION THEORY

Background

In Chapter Two we discussed activation as a dimension of emotion, but activation theory has broader motivational implications. Like drive theory, activation theory has been used to account for the **energization** of behavior, but not its **direction.** Elizabeth Duffy (1934), who originally proposed activation theory under the name of **energy mobilization,** emphasized the autonomic arousal that characterizes Cannon's **fight-flight,** or **emergency reaction.**

Subsequently, the role of the **reticular activating system** (RAS) of the mid-brain (e.g., Berlyne, 1960; Duffy, 1962; Hebb, 1955; Lindsley, 1951; Malmo, 1959; Woodworth & Schlosberg, 1954) was emphasized. Much of the early enthusiasm for the theory occurred because it seemed to provide a physiological account of drive while at the same time solving many problems faced by drive theory.

RAS Activation

Beginning in the 1950s, the basic activation mechanism was considered to be the reticular activating system (RAS) in the brainstem, illustrated in Figure 6–9. The RAS receives inputs from all sensory systems except smell and then distributes these diffusely to all parts of the cerebrum via the **ascending** RAS. Specific sensory information is lost in the RAS, but the widespread distribution of RAS output "tones up" the cortex in preparation for further input and attention to the environment. Simultaneously, impulses sent to motor neurons via the **descending** RAS serve to maintain muscle tonus over long periods of time.

Increased RAS activity is seen in the electroencephalogram (EEG, electrical activity of the brain, or brain waves, recorded from various locations on

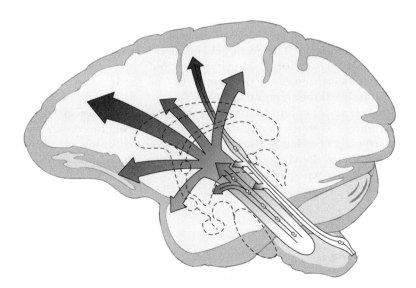

FIGURE 6–9. Schema projected upon a monkey brain showing ARAS, including the reticular formation in the central core of the lower brain stem with multisynaptic relays and its upward diffuse projections to all parts of the cortex. To the right a single afferent pathway with a relay in the thalamus proceeds to the postcentral cortex, but gives off collaterals (arrows) to the reticular formation. These are respectively the unspecified and specific sensory systems. Source: Magoun (1954). Used by permission of the publisher.

the scalp). There is a shift from a "resting" alpha wave pattern (8 to 12 Hz; Hz is the abbreviation for hertz, or cycles per second) to an "activated" beta pattern (15 Hz and up, with lower amplitude and greater irregularity). This shift in EEG pattern, illustrated in Figure 6–10, is widely spread over the cortex and may be conceptualized as something like a fire alarm that gets people into action but does not really say where the fire is. For a determination of where to go or what responses to make, more specific environmental information must come through the sensory channels that run directly to the sensory cortex of the brain.

The alpha pattern, which has a relatively high amplitude and low frequency, is said to be "synchronized" and represents an awake but relaxed state. The beta pattern, of higher frequency and lower amplitude, is "desynchronized" and represents an aroused or excited state. Alpha and beta normally fluctuate as we go about our daily activities. Moruzzi and Magoun (1949) showed that direct electrical stimulation of the RAS through permanently implanted electrodes produces this same desynchronization.

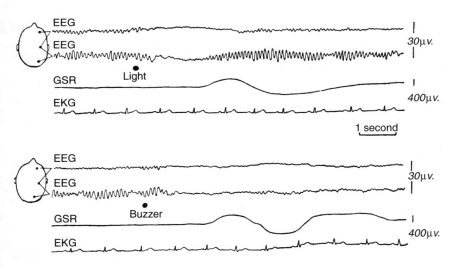

FIGURE 6–10.   Arousal effects of unexpected light and sound stimuli on the electroencephalogram (EEG), galvanic skin response (GSR), and heart rate (EKG). Electrode placements for the EEG are indicated from the top of the head. Note that the posterior electrodes show a large-amplitude, low-frequency alpha wave before the presentation of light or buzzer. This is a typical, relaxed, waking record. After the light or buzzer, there is a transition to a low-amplitude, high-frequency beta wave that is typical of a more alert or excited subject. The alpha is "blocked" by activity from the brain stem reticular system following presentation of the light and buzzer. The buzzer in this illustration was obviously a more "exciting" stimulus, since the alpha blocking lasted longer and there was a larger GSR change as well. HR is not obviously faster after stimulation, but the naked eye is not a good indicator of HR records shown in this manner. Source: Lindsley (1950). Used by permission of the publisher.

Early research of the 1950s indicated that destruction of the RAS had effects opposite to those of stimulation. Severe RAS damage left animals comatose and unresponsive to stimulation, with a continuous highly synchronized EEG. Electrical records showed that stimuli reached the sensory cortex but that no overall desynchronization of the EEG appeared, and there was no overt response to the stimulation. Energizing drugs like amphetamines increase RAS activity and alertness, and central nervous system depressants like barbiturates decrease activity and alertness. Such data supported the idea that the RAS is an important, if not completely critical, area of the brain for attention and consciousness.

Although EEG activity is heavily emphasized in activation theory, the more classic measures of autonomic nervous system arousal are still commonly used for practical reasons. These include heart rate, blood pressure, muscle tension, and the galvanic skin response. It is presumed that all such physiological activity should increase or decrease in unison under conditions of stress or relaxation, reflecting greater or lesser energy expenditure by the organism. Figure 6–9 also shows the effect of a sudden stimulus on some of these other measures.

Optimal Level of Arousal Theory

The inverted-U function. The primary motivational proposition of activation theory is that there is an optimal level of arousal for behavior, an inverted-U function, as shown in Figure 6–11. Some intermediate level of

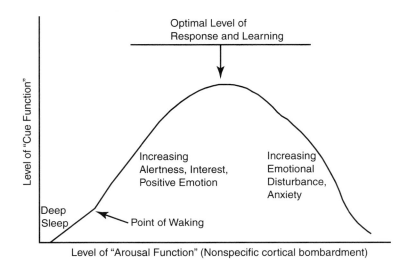

FIGURE 6–11. Relationship between level of arousal (in the ascending reticular activating system) and effectiveness of responses to cues in the environment. (From Hebb, 1955, p. 250. Copyright © 1955 by the American Psychological Association. Reprinted by permission.)

arousal is said to be better for performance than either lower or higher levels. It is generally implicit that such a medium level of arousal is also desirable and sought (Hebb, 1955; Malmo, 1959).

The Yerkes-Dodson law. The concept of an **optimal level of arousal** for performance dates back to Yerkes and Dodson (1908). These investigators reported that when a brightness discrimination problem was made more difficult for animals (they used "dancing mice" in their research), the optimal level of punishment for errors was lower. That is, more-difficult problems were learned better with lower levels of punishment. This concept is illustrated in Figure 6–12. Broadhurst (1957) deprived rats of different amounts of air by holding them under water for different periods of time. When the rats were released to swim to safety, there was an inverted-U function for a difficult brightness discrimination problem, but an optimal level was not clearly shown with problems of simple or moderate difficulty. Anderson (1994) found support for the law when she compared performance on an easy (letter cancellation) and a hard (verbal abilities) task under conditions of five different dose levels of caffeine. As predicted, performance on the easy task improved with increasing levels of caffeine. With the harder task,

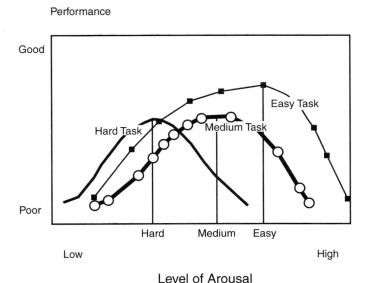

The Yerkes-Dodson (1908) Law

FIGURE 6–12. The Yerkes-Dodson law. As the difficulty of the task increases, the optimal level of arousal for performance decreases. The optimal levels of arousal for each type of task are shown by the vertical lines.

however, performance declined at the higher dose levels for subjects who were more easily aroused. This experiment was particularly interesting because all subjects got every dose level of caffeine, enabling a very sensitive test of the law. It has also been found, however, that almost *any* response can potentially be inhibited at a high enough level of arousal, not just nondominant, competing responses or difficult task behaviors. An individual may simply freeze, as with stage fright. There is a brainstem inhibitory mechanism that paralyzes motor activity when there is a high level of arousal (Morrison, 1983).

A major impetus for the optimal level of arousal view came from studies of sensory isolation (e.g., Bexton, Heron, & Scott, 1954). Following many hours of severely reduced sensory input, normal college-age subjects had difficulty in concentrating and solving problems. They showed abnormalities even in their ordinary perceptions. Printed lines refused to stay in place, walls bowed outward, and objects seemed to retreat as one looked away from them. Such data suggested that insufficient sensory input had a detrimental effect on perception, which Hebb (1955) thought to be due to reduced RAS activity. Later experiments with **stabilized retinal images** gave further support to this conjecture (e.g., Pritchard, 1961). A tiny, high-frequency (25/sec) vibration of the eyes normally produces constantly changing retinal stimulation. By various mechanical means, such as mounting a miniature slide projector on a contact lens, the visual stimulus can be made to vibrate right along with the eye. The image is stabilized on the retina because the eye is not moving with reference to the visual stimulus. Such stabilized images *disappear* within a minute or so, and it is clear that **stimulus change** is important for normal perception. What all this says is that the lowest possible level of arousal is not a viable biological goal.

The Easterbrook hypothesis.   J. A. Easterbrook (1959) developed a perceptual hypothesis of why high levels of arousal may impair performance. He said that arousal reduces the range of cues in the environment that an organism can attend to. In a state of low arousal, all cognitive units are equally activated, but with increasing activation, there is progressively more narrow focusing and less attention to peripheral elements. This **spotlight** effect is illustrated in Figure 6–13. Reduced cue availability may either help or hinder performance. Thus,

- Arousal should **improve** performance if there are many peripheral stimuli that are **irrelevant** to the task at hand. In a noisy environment, for example, a person may become aroused by irrelevant peripheral noise but also more focused on the task. The student who claims to study better with rock music in the background may actually do so, if he becomes more focused with the music. This is no surefire way to improve studying, however!
- High arousal should **impair** performance if there are many **relevant** peripheral stimuli that should be attended to. In a problem-solving task requiring the person to be aware of all sorts of cues around her, narrowing the focus to just those

Worse
A

Better
B

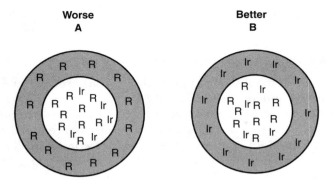

FIGURE 6–13. Easterbrook's spotlight model for the effects of arousal on attention. The whole area of the circle (dark plus light) is what is noticed under low arousal. The smaller white area is what is noticed under high arousal. R and Ir represent relevant and irrelevant cues, respectively. In A, more relevant cues (Rs) go unnoticed in the periphery, and performance is worse. In B, more irrelevant cues (Ir) go unnoticed in the periphery, and performance is better.

immediately in front would impair performance. This hypothesis would account for some of the same effects that the Yerkes-Dodson law does. That is, insofar as complex tasks involve more relevant cues, some of these cues are more likely to be missed under high arousal.

The following experiment illustrates the theory. Subjects with different levels of arousal studied a list of words while also hearing an incidental (extraneous) list of words being played on a tape recorder. Subsequently, they did anagrams in which some of the incidental words were anagram solutions. The low-arousal subjects used more of the incidental words heard on the tape than did the high-arousal subjects.

In summary, our capacity to attend to environmental cues varies according to our internal state. If this capacity is reduced by arousal, stress, or emotion, we have less capacity for attending to peripheral (incidental) stimuli. Whether performance is aided or impaired depends on the relevance of the peripheral cues to the task at hand.

Comparison of Drive and Activation Theories

Drive and activation theories both deal with an intensity dimension of motivation, but whereas drive theory assumes that the lowest possible level of drive is the "ideal" state of the organism, activation theory assumes nirvana to be at some intermediate level of stimulation. To reach this intermediate level, we may have either to increase or to decrease stimulation, depending on our momentary level. If the momentary level of arousal is low, an even lower level would be aversive. Therefore, a higher level is sought—pushing toward the optimum. Conversely, if the momentary level is very high, an even higher level would be aversive, and a lower level is sought.

Problems with RAS Activation Theory

The hope that the RAS might underlie a unitary arousal dimension was crushed soon after intense research on the RAS was begun. It was found that (1) if animals survived RAS destruction, they could show normal fluctuations in activity and responsiveness to stimuli (Lindsley, Schreiner, Knowles, & Magoun, 1950); (2) if RAS destruction is done in a series of small steps, even a temporary comatose state is forestalled (Adametz, 1959); and (3) massive lesions of sensory pathways, without direct damage to the RAS, produce many of the same overt behavioral effects as do RAS lesions (Sprague, Chambers, & Stellar, 1961). Other areas of the brain may be more important for arousal than the RAS. What appears to be likely is that there are multiple systems of arousal, as implied by evidence that EEG arousal, autonomic arousal, and behavioral arousal can be distinguished.

Sleep and Waking

Early activation theories assumed that sleep represents a low state of arousal. The discovery of **rapid eye movement** (REM) sleep changed our entire view of sleep and dreaming, however, because sleep and dreams involve very active brain processes (Aserinsky & Kleitman, 1953; Dement & Kleitman, 1957). Figure 6–14 shows EEG changes during sleep. As the individual goes to sleep, the amplitude of **alpha** waves decreases, then the record becomes relatively flat and irregular, possibly interspersed with **theta** waves (4 to 8 Hz) in some parts of the brain. In very deep sleep, **delta** waves (1 to 3 Hz) are prominent. Respiration is deep and regular, heart rate is slow and regular, the eyes are relatively still, and there is some muscle tension. This is **nonrapid eye movement** (NREM) sleep.

After about nintey minutes, the EEG becomes more active, showing the **beta** waves of an alert waking person. There is pronounced movement of the eyes, breathing becomes shallow and irregular, heart rate is faster, muscle movement is inhibited, and males have erections. This is REM sleep, also called **paradoxical sleep** (Jouvet, 1967) because the person is harder to wake up in spite of the intense brain activity and autonomic arousal. If human subjects are awakened during REM sleep, they are much more likely to report dreaming than when awakened from NREM sleep. As the night goes on, REM and NREM sleep fluctuate, with REM periods becoming gradually longer, culminating with a REM period of about ninety minutes in early morning. The dream most likely to be remembered in the morning is this last one.

Virtually all animals with brains more complicated than reptiles show REM and NREM sleep, with about 22 percent of a normal adult's sleep in

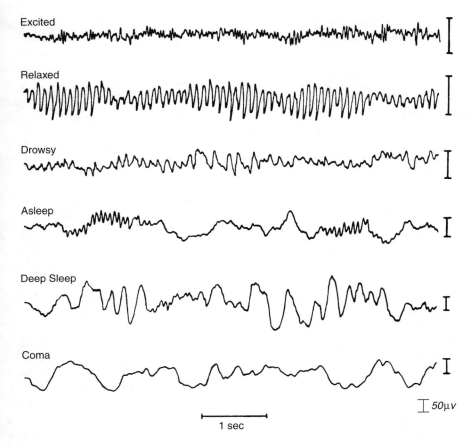

Excited

Relaxed

Drowsy

Asleep

Deep Sleep

Coma

50μv

1 sec

FIGURE 6–14.   Typical EEG records from normal subjects in different states of arousal and from a comatose subject. (From Penfield & Jasper, 1954, p. 188. Copyright © 1954 by Little, Brown, Co. Reprinted by permission.)

REM. Newborn infants spend about half their sleeping time in REM, and premature infants even more than that. Thus a consistent pattern in humans is that with longer sleep or with developing brains, there is more REM. Such evidence suggests that REM sleep might be important for the development and maintenance of normal brain function. Vertes (1986) proposed that **slow wave sleep** (NREM) is primarily for rest and recuperation. Thus brain neurons discharge more slowly, protein synthesis is increased, and strenuous activity increases the duration of such sleep. Vertes's theory, then, is that the brain requires periodic reactivation from slow wave sleep in order to maintain its normal functioning, as well as to ensure that the unconsciousness of sleep does not drift into a comatose state from which the individual may not recover.

Vertes relates his theory to two fatal, sleep associated syndromes, the **sudden infant death syndrome** and the **Oriental nocturnal death syndrome.** In the former, infants die during sleep for no apparent reason. Vertes suggests that they simply do not have sufficient REM sleep to reactivate them from slow wave sleep. In the latter, apparently healthy males of Oriental descent suddenly die in their sleep, also from no discernible disorder. There is evidence that the death results from ventricular fibrillation (an arrhythmic pattern of heartbeat that keeps the heart from pumping blood properly) during the first three hours of sleep. This may occur *before* REM sleep appears during a night, and the cause of death may therefore be the same as for infant death.

Dreaming

Freud's psychoanalytic theory of dreams. In his monumental *The Interpretation of Dreams,* Freud ([1900] 1938) recognized that most dreams are simply replays of the previous day's events, which he called "day residues." The more dramatic and puzzling dreams, however, were thought to represent the same principles of anxiety and anxiety reduction characteristic of many overt behaviors.

The theory runs as follows. People have desires (e.g., sexual or aggressive) that run into conflict with social norms or other people. If we directly expressed these wishes in dreams, they would make us anxious, and we would wake up. We therefore disguise the real meaning of the dreams by using symbols, for example. A policeman might substitute for an authoritative parent. Thus an argument with a policeman might be the **manifest content** of a dream. The "real" meaning of the dream, its **latent content,** would be conflict between parent and child. The dream allows the individual to fulfill the wish of resisting a parent but without arousing anxiety, therefore allowing sleep. Freud referred to dreams as the "guardians of sleep." Sleep research discloses, however, that the symptoms of anxiety (autonomic nervous system arousal) occur *during* dreams, not before dreams. Freud's theory would say that dreams should have a calming effect because their very function is to reduce anxiety. Since just the reverse happens, it appears that something is seriously wrong with the theory.

The Hobson-McCarley activation-synthesis theory. This theory is closely tied to the physiology of dreaming, which was unknown to Freud at the turn of the century. The electroencephalograph for measuring brain activity was not invented until about 1930, and REM sleep was not discovered until the 1950s. The theory (Hobson, 1988) says that after a certain amount of sleep, neurons in the brain stem become active and that they **randomly activate** visual images. The brain then synthesizes these images into a more or less coherent story. There is no hidden or latent content in dreams. Many dreams may be about the previous day's events because these events are the easiest ones to activate. These activities may be synthesized with other randomly aroused images and produce bizarre dream content. But bizarre is just bizarre; it is not a fancy way to disguise the "real" meaning of dreams.

In summary, then, dreams may actually represent part of the brain's self-excitation to keep itself alive and well. In any event, it is abundantly clear that sleep is *not* just a low level of activation, even though NREM sleep might be described this way.

Environmental Stimulation and Arousal

Stimulus intensity and stimulus complexity. Intense stimuli, such as loud noises and frightening experiences, produce arousal. Our concern here, however, is with a more psychological dimension of stimuli, **complexity.** Daniel Berlyne (1960) used the phrase **ludic behavior** to refer to those activities we usually call "recreation, entertainment, or 'idle curiosity,'" as well as art, philosophy, and pure (as distinct from applied) science" (p. 5). The most notable characteristic of such behavior is that it is not driven by homeostatic need, it "does not have a biological function that we can clearly recognize" (p. 5). The common thread among these activities is that they involve seeking stimuli that have one or more of the following characteristics. First, there is **novelty,** which may include the characteristics of **surprisingness** and **incongruity,** both of which involve expectations that are not fulfilled, that is, we expect one thing, but something different happens. Second, there is **uncertainty,** which refers to the amount of **information** carried by a stimulus. A plain gray sheet of cardboard, for example, is simpler and carries less information than the same cardboard painted like a checkerboard or a person. Third, there is **conflict,** the tendency of some stimuli to arouse different responses from a viewer (of visual stimuli) at the same time. Finally, there is **complexity,** which increases with the number of distinguishable elements, the dissimilarity among elements, and the degree to which the elements are responded to as a unit. Figure 6–15 illustrates these variables.

Stimuli that are more novel, uncertain, conflicting, or complex also produce more arousal. Berlyne (1970) hypothesized that positive affect is aroused by stimuli that produce some medium level of arousal. Relationships between stimuli, arousal, and affect are illustrated in Figure 6–16. Here we see stimuli ranging from simple and familiar (not novel) to complex and novel. Such stimuli are therefore sought out by people or other animals. Stimuli that are too far above or below the optimal level are aversive and so are escaped or avoided. We thus have approach and avoidance behavior that is "motivated" by something other than homeostatic imbalance and that is reinforced by something other than restoration of homeostatic balance. Following activation theory more generally, organisms seek some level of arousal greater than zero, not too high and not too low—just right.

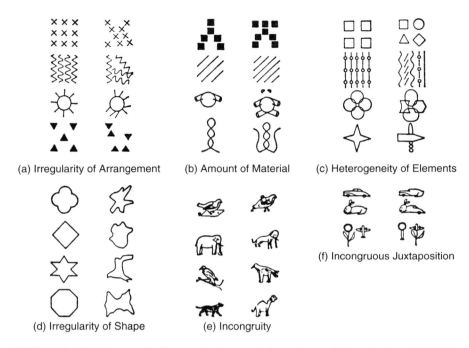

(a) Irregularity of Arrangement   (b) Amount of Material   (c) Heterogeneity of Elements

(f) Incongruous Juxtaposition

(d) Irregularity of Shape   (e) Incongruity

FIGURE 6–15. Variables contributing to stimulus complexity and arousal. (From Berlyne, D. E., 1958. Copyright 1958 by the American Psychological Association. Used by permission.)

Environmental load. Environmental load refers to the amount of information an individual must use to deal with the environment. A **high load** environment is a complex, changing environment, full of novelty and surprises, and it requires much effort in responding. A **low load** environment is relatively unchanging and simple, with little novelty or surprise, and it requires little effort to track. The perceived amount of load in an environment has been measured by rating the environment on such stimulus dimensions as uncertain-certain, complex-simple, surprising-usual, and crowded-uncrowded (Mehrabian, 1976, p. 12). New York City is typically a high-load environment; a small rural town would typically be a low load environment. There are, naturally, many little pockets of variation in either the large city or the small town.

Individual differences: screeners and nonscreeners. Mehrabian distinguished what he called screeners and nonscreeners. Screeners are people who are very sensitive to selected parts of their environment and to load changes. They are quickly aroused, but their arousal also subsides quickly when the load reduces. The nonscreeners are less selective in what they respond to. They take in more stimuli, are aroused by a greater variety of

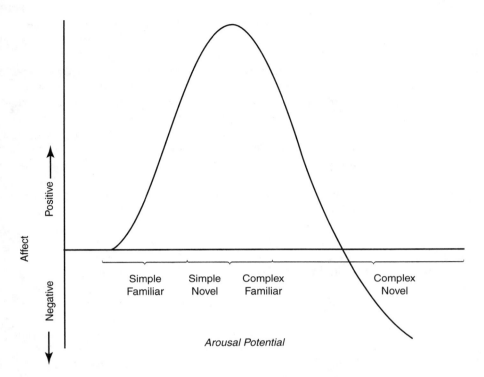

FIGURE 6–16. The hypothesized relation between affect and the arousal potential of a stimulus as proposed by Berlyne. Note that positive affect is greatest when a stimulus is moderately complex or moderately novel. (From Berlyne, 1970.) Copyright 1970 by the Psychonomic Society. Used by permission.

things, and stay aroused longer after the load has been reduced. A screener recovers more quickly from an environmental load than a nonscreener and is ready to "take on" the environment again sooner. People try to average out situations so that over some period of time, such as a day or a week, the average load best suited to them is achieved. Even without this detailed information, however, we can understand why some people want vacations full of excitement and why others just want to have a quiet two weeks away from everything.

Humor and Aesthetics

Humor. The importance we attach to humor can be seen in the eagerness with which we approach and pay for the privilege of exposure to variety and incongruity. Humor often involves incongruities or unexpected twists, even with very simple words. For example, Henny Youngman's "Take my wife, please" first leads us to think that he is going to use his wife as an example of something, and then he switches to a very literal meaning of "take." The *Far Side* cartoons emphasized the incongruity of animals doing what humans commonly do. The accompanying cartoon illustrates this as well.

The "comeback line" also involves an unexpected twist. When Woodrow Wilson was governor of New Jersey, he reportedly received a phone call from a politician who wanted to be appointed replacement for a just-deceased United States Senator. "That's perfectly agreeable with me," said Wilson, "if it's agreeable to the undertaker." Humor is, of course, a complex subject, and any explanation for all forms of humor depends on more than incongruity. Jack Benny, for example, was funniest and most famous for doing things that he was fully expected to do, such as assuming his quizzical expression and saying "Well!" He was funny because of his predictability. Nonetheless, incongruity must be considered an important component of humor.

Aesthetics.   The nature of beauty, as found in any sensory modality (visual art, tactual art, or music) is also a demanding topic, and our cursory treatment here is limited to the arousal aspect. Great art or music or writing is ultimately determined by its longevity, which is due in part to the technical skill of the artist or composer or writer and in part to the degree to which the art in question has "universal" appeal. That is, great aesthetic works seem to "speak" to many people, to carry messages that are attracting to many people over many years. On repeated exposure to the same work, observers or listeners see or hear different things from what they saw or heard before. People keep finding new things in a great work

Put in psychological terms, great aesthetic works carry more information than is processed in a single viewing or listening. As different information is detected from one viewing/hearing to another, there is stimulus variation. In a very real sense, each time we hear a great piece of music, we are

Courtesy of David Hills.

hearing something different from the previous times. For a particularly in-sightful discussion of aesthetics and psychology, Berlyne (1960, 1971) and Platt (1961) are recommended.

If medium levels of arousal are desirable, we might expect that "artistic" stimuli that produce medium levels of arousal should also be more desirable. The trick is to define stimuli so that they can be numerically scaled in terms of arousal properties. Smith and Dorfman (1975) did this by using a basic concept from information theory. The amount of information in a stimulus is defined as the amount of uncertainty about that stimulus, what has been called "surprisal value." A complex stimulus has more surprisal value than a simple one. The more information a stimulus contains, the greater its sur-prisal and arousal value. Smith and Dorfman used black-white checkerboard stimuli of low, medium, and high complexity. The subjects rated these for lik-ing after one, five, ten, and twenty exposures. Smith and Dorfman also as-sumed that on successive exposures, subjects would adapt to the stimuli so that the stimuli would be perceived as less complex after repeated viewing.

The results are shown in Figure 6–17. The most complex stimulus (highest arousal) was least liked upon initial exposure, and the simplest stim-ulus (lowest arousal) was most liked. This finding would indeed provide an inverted-U function for liking after the first exposure. As the subjects became more familiar with the stimuli, however, there was an orderly change. The simplest stimulus quickly became least liked, as with many popular songs that are "catchy" at first hearing but that quickly become boring. The most

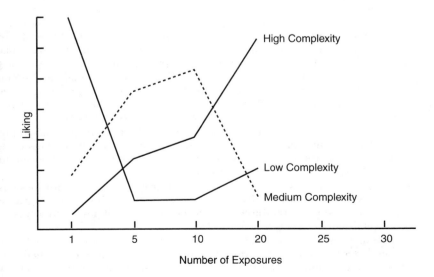

FIGURE 6–17. Liking of visual stimuli as a function of stimulus complexity and number of exposures. (From Smith & Dorfman, 1975, p. 152. Copyright © 1975 by the American Psychological Association. Reprinted by permission.)

complex stimulus increased steadily in liking as subjects became more familiar with it, as it presumably moved from a highly arousing to a less arousing (and more optimal) position on the inverted U curve. The medium complexity stimulus first increased in liking, apparently shifting from highly arousing to optimally arousing and then to less liked, with further exposure to it. This experiment rather dramatically substantiates activation theory predictions taken in conjunction with adaptation principles. Vitz (1966) performed a similar experiment, but with auditory stimuli. He concocted six different tone sequences ranging from simple to complex on the basis of number of pitches, durations, and volume levels. He then had subjects of high and low musical experience rate each of the six sequences for pleasantness. The highest preference for musically inexperienced subjects was for relatively low stimulus complexity, whereas the pleasantness of the stimulus sequences was much more equal for the experienced subjects. The results of these two experiments support the idea that as we gain more experience with a particular type of stimuli, we also begin to prefer more complex stimuli.

SUMMARY

1. According to **drive theory,** disruptions of homeostatic balance **energize** an organism into action. The most influential drive theory (Hull's) holds that drive is a **general energizer** and that particular responses are determined by learning. Responses are said to be learned if they are reinforced (rewarded) by **drive reduction.**

2. The effect of drive on behavior depends on the kind of response involved. If a response is a **simple, dominant** response, a high level of drive **facilitates** the response. If the response is **complex** or not the dominant response in a particular situation, high drive may make performance **worse.**

3. Tests of predictions from drive theory in animal research have met with variable success. Hunger and thirst do not generally produce an increase in "random" activity, as suggested by the theory. With humans, high anxiety does facilitate a simple conditioned response but interferes with more complex tasks.

4. In Hull's theory, drive cannot **direct** or **select** behavior, but internal stimuli called **drive stimuli** can do so. Drive stimuli are specific stimuli accompanying particular drive-producing operations. Hunger and thirst have unique stimuli that can help direct behavior to appropriate goals.

5. **Learned drives,** such as **fear,** are drives that are aroused by stimuli previously associated with such **primary drives** as **pain.** Fear has been shown to **energize** responses, fear-reduction **reinforces** the learning of new responses, and increased fear is **punishing.**

6. **Activation theory,** like drive theory, is concerned with the energization of behavior, not the direction of behavior. Activation theory is more concerned with **physiological arousal,** however, in either the brain or the autonomic nervous system.

7. The major **behavioral prediction** of activation theory is that behavior is less efficient at either very low or very high levels of arousal than at some medium level

of arousal. This is the **optimal level of arousal hypothesis,** which has been influential in motivation theory. The hypothesis has received only limited support in research, perhaps because it is difficult to control or measure arousal levels accurately and because there seem to be several kinds of arousal.

8. The **Yerkes-Dodson law** is an old variant of optimal level of arousal theory, which says that the more difficult a task is, the lower is the optimal level of response.

9. The **Easterbrook "spotlight theory"** says that the focus of attention is narrower under high levels of arousal than under low levels of arousal. This tendency impedes performance if peripheral stimuli are relevant to the task at hand but improves performance if irrelevant stimuli are excluded.

10. **Sleep** is not just a lower level of arousal. In **rapid eye movement (REM) sleep,** there is a high level of brain and autonomic nervous system activity, including dreams. In non-REM (NREM), or slow wave sleep, the brain and viscera are less aroused, and dreaming is infrequent.

11. The brain appears to require periodic activation (REM sleep) in order to maintain its normal function and to ensure that the individual does not drift off into a coma. Two lethal sleep disorders, **sudden infant death syndrome** and **Oriental nocturnal death syndrome,** have been associated with NREM sleep.

12. Freud's **psychoanalytic theory of dreams** posited that dreams allow us to sleep by letting us fulfill anxiety-arousing impulses (e.g., sex or aggression) in a nonthreatening manner. Modern sleep research contradicts this theory by showing that dreams generally occur when our autonomic nervous system is most aroused during REM sleep.

13. The Hobson-McCarley **activation-synthesis theory of dreams** says that dream images are randomly activated via the brain stem and then are synthesized into the more or less meaningful sequences that we recall. Dreams are not disguises for anxiety-arousing wishes.

14. Stimuli that **are novel, are uncertain, produce conflict, or are complex, all produce arousal.** Stimuli that produce medium levels of arousal are sought, whereas stimuli that produce high or low levels of arousal are escaped or avoided.

15. **Environments differ** in the degree to which they produce arousal. High load environments are complex and require much effort to deal with; low load environments are simple and repetitive.

16. People vary in how aroused they are by the environment. **Screeners** are quickly aroused by selective stimulus events, but their arousal subsides quickly. **Non-screeners** are aroused by a much greater range of stimulus events, and their arousal persists longer.

17. **Humor** and **aesthetics** can both be characterized in terms of their arousal effects. Incongruity is a major factor in humor. Stimulus complexity is a major factor in aesthetics.

CHAPTER SEVEN

Rewards as Reinforcers

——•——

Rewards are behavioral outcomes that are desirable and worked for. Psychologists have looked at rewards in two different ways, however: (1) as **reinforcers** for learning new behaviors, and (2) as **incentive stimuli** that motivate approach behaviors. These different accounts of rewards grow out of their use in everyday life and with a laboratory procedure known as instrumental conditioning. In order to understand the differences in these accounts, we must first understand some of the basic concepts of instrumental conditioning.

INSTRUMENTAL CONDITIONING

Instrumental conditioning has generally taken on two different sets of methods, exemplified by the work of E. L. Thorndike at the beginning of the twentieth century, followed by the innovations of B. F. Skinner in the latter half of the century.

Thorndike and Connectionism

Instrumental conditioning refers to the effect on a behavior when that behavior is followed by reward or punishment. Edward L. Thorndike (1913), an educational psychologist who did some of the pioneering research in this field, developed what he called the **Law of Effect.** Behavior is modified by the effects it produces. If the effect is satisfying (rewarding), the behavior will be "strengthened" and repeated in similar circumstances. If the effect is annoying (punishing), the response is less likely to occur again. These were old ideas even in Thorndike's time, but Thorndike took the crucial next step of going into the laboratory with them.

Thorndike put a cat inside a "puzzle box" (Figure 7–1), and the cat had to learn to get out of the box to reach food. Since the cat initially knew nothing about the situation, the first correct response (such as pressing a lever or pulling a string) was made accidentally. When it made the response, however, the door was opened, and the cat immediately fed. On successive trials, cats got out of the box faster and faster. If we plot the time to get out of the box on each trial, we have an instrumental learning curve, illustrated in Figure 7–2. A faster response indicates "stronger" conditioning. Thorndike's experiments were forerunners of thousands of other experiments on instrumental conditioning, with many different species, responses, rewards, and apparatuses.

Thorndike argued that learning consists of forming a connection between a specific stimulus and a specific response. He called such a connection an "S-R bond." During learning, said Thorndike, an S-R bond is "strengthened" so that the stimulus will evoke the response in reflex fashion. The evidence is now overwhelming, however, that most instrumental learning does not consist of such S-R bonds. We can readily illustrate why this is so.

179

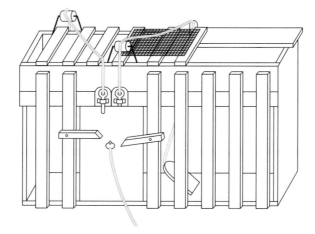

FIGURE 7–1. Thorndike's puzzle box for studying learning in cats. The box is 20 inches long by 15 inches deep by 12 inches high. The cat is put into the box, and when it pushes the pedal on the floor, the door is unlocked and the cat can get to the food. (From Thorndike, E. L. 1898. Animal Intelligence: An experimental study of associative processes in animals. *Psychological Review Monograph Supplement, 2*(8).)

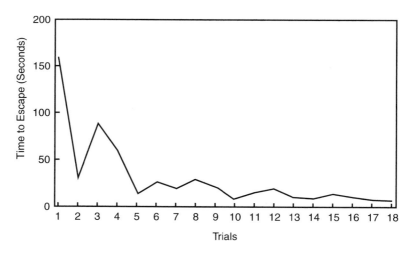

FIGURE 7–2. A typical learning curve for one cat in Thorndike's experiments. The cat is slow to get out of the box to food in early trials but finally levels off at about 8 seconds to do so. Rapid improvement in early trials followed by more gradual improvement in later trials is typical of learning. (From Thorndike, E. L., 1898. Animal intelligence: An experimental study of associative processes in animals. *Psychological Review Monograph Supplement, 2*(8).)

If you have never written your name in the sand with your big toe, do you think you could do it? If you put a pencil in your mouth, do you think you could scratch out your name with it? Probably so. If you *can* do these things, never having done them before, it is clear that learning to write your name involves something more than making a specific muscular response to a particular stimulus. More to the point, Karl Lashley (1950) taught monkeys to work mechanical puzzles with one hand literally tied behind their backs. The monkeys then proceeded to work the puzzles without difficulty when the untrained hand was freed and the trained hand was immobilized. Since the learning transferred from one hand to the other without further training, the learning must have involved more than the response of the initial hand. Many other experiments have made the same point.

Skinner and Operant Conditioning

B. F. Skinner (1938, 1953) coined the phrase **operant conditioning** for his version of instrumental conditioning. He also developed an apparatus that he called the operant conditioning chamber, more popularly known as the Skinner box shown in Figure 7–3. Other types of apparatus usually require that the animal be removed after the reward is received—at the end of a maze, for example—and placed back at the beginning of the maze for each new trial. The Skinner box automatically presents rewards and records responses, making it possible to study behavior continuously over many hours or days without disturbing the animal. The results are like those of time-lapse

FIGURE 7–3. Skinner's operant conditioning chamber for studying behavior of the rat.

photography with which we can see the petals of a flower opening in the morning and closing at night. With the Skinner box and continuous recording, psychologists can see slowly developing behavior patterns that would not be observable otherwise.

Nature of reinforcers and punishers. Skinner used a fourfold classification of reinforcers (Skinner's term for rewards) and punishers, as follows:

Positive reinforcer. Any stimulus (such as food or praise) that will increase the occurrence of a response that it follows.

Negative reinforcer. Any stimulus (such as pain) whose termination will increase the occurrence of a response that it follows.

Punisher 1. Any stimulus, such as pain, that will decrease the occurrence of a response that it follows.

Punisher 2. Any stimulus, such as social contact or television viewing, that will decrease responding if removed after a response.

Skinner's definitions do not tell us what stimuli will be reinforcers or punishers. This is determined by trial, not by some preconceived notion about what stimuli ought to be reinforcers or punishers. Thus all people do not find the same events rewarding. Even such a commonly used reinforcer as money may be an insult if it is less than the recipient expects or is offered to a friend who has done a favor. Wise old Brer Rabbit pleaded against being punished by saying, "Don't throw me into the briar patch," and immediately was rewarded by being tossed exactly where he wanted to go.

When to Deliver Rewards

The rule of thumb here is simple: Rewards are more effective the more quickly that they are given after a response. If a child does something to please her parents but the approval is slow in coming, the child may not even realize she was rewarded for her earlier behavior. She is more likely to associate the reinforcer with some irrelevant response that occurred just before the reinforcer was given. Long delays of reinforcement may produce confusing results for parents, who cannot understand why the child does not learn to act in the way that they want when they are "rewarding" good behavior. So-called superstitious behavior may develop when behaviors are accidentally reinforced. A coach who wins a big game while wearing his red socks may continue to wear these socks "for luck" in future games, as if wearing the socks was the behavior that won the game.

Bridging Delay Between Response and Reinforcement

Long delays between behavior and reinforcement are often inevitable but can be spanned with a **secondary reinforcer,** which is a stimulus that has been associated with some other reinforcer and becomes reinforcing itself. For example, if a sound precedes food, the sound becomes a reinforcer in its own right because it can reinforce new responses, but it can also bridge a delay until some other reinforcer is given. Wolfe (1933) established poker chips as secondary reinforcers for monkeys by letting the monkeys trade the chips for grapes or raisins. The monkeys would then work for chips as people work for money, eventually trading them for something "really" valuable. Many **social reinforcers** are secondary reinforcers, such as good grades in school, high performance evaluations at work, and trophies for winning tournaments.

Extinction

Extinction means that responding declines when rewards cease coming. If you are working at a job and then stop getting paid, you might work for a while longer but would eventually stop. Working has extinguished. Again, however, extinction is not the same as forgetting. If you get paid again, you may immediately return to your previous work level. How long an animal or a person will persist in responding without reinforcement depends on a number of factors, but the pattern of reinforcement is especially important. We usually persist longer during extinction if our behavior has been **periodically reinforced** (partial reinforcement) than if is continuously reinforced. Under appropriate partial reinforcement training conditions, laboratory animals have been known to give many thousands of responses without further reinforcement.

Generalization and Discrimination

When we reinforce a child with praise for saying "please" and "thank you" at home, we hope that the child will **generalize** this behavior to other social situations and are happy when he does so without prompting. The same behaviors should not have to be learned anew for every specific situation.

At the same time, however, the child learns the difference between situations when responses are and are not reinforced. This perception is **discrimination.** Children, for example, learn that they can get many favors from their grandparents more easily than from their parents, so that they ask their grandparents more often for favors (for ice cream or candy or staying up late). In our daily lives we learn many cues that tell us when or when not to respond: Fire alarms, telephone bells, traffic lights, police sirens, and clocks are all stimuli that signal that we should do something only when those stimuli occur.

Building Behavior by Shaping

It is Alice's first day in the shop, and we have to teach her how to operate the "Old No. 6" machine. Initially we may talk her through it, along with a demonstration. She then goes through the steps. First, she turns on the machine. She is reinforced twice, once when the whirring of the motor tells her that she has done it right and a second time when we say "good."

The next step might require feeding a piece of wood into the machine. Alice might hold the wood improperly, making an accident likely. We immediately give her feedback about this danger and then have her do it again. When the wood is fed correctly, we immediately say so. It might not be fed exactly right, but we accept the approximation. Over successive practice runs, we require closer and closer approximations to the correct procedure before saying "good" or "okay" to reinforce Alice. Such **selective reinforcement of successive approximations** is what we mean by **shaping behavior.** Shaping is particularly important when instructions alone are not adequate, as with motor skills that are very hard to describe or with people (especially children) who cannot use language well. The instructor who is dispensing reinforcers must know in advance what behavior is finally desired and what approximations may be reinforced, leading to the desired behavior.

Maintaining Behavior: Schedules of Reinforcement

A schedule of reinforcement is a rule for presenting reinforcers. At first, we reward children with praise every time they say "please," but we can progressively reduce the frequency of praise and the behavior will still occur, for two reasons. First, the behavior is maintained because it is reinforced when the child gets what he wants after saying please. Secondly, the behavior is maintained because it was learned on a partial reinforcement schedule. Saying please does not extinguish immediately if not reinforced. In general, behavior that is partially reinforced is more "resistant to extinction."

Cumulative recording.   Animals and people learn to perform in very consistent ways on different schedules, but we may have to keep records over a period of hours or even days in order to see the consistencies. Skinner devised the cumulative recording system to do just this. The frequency of a given response, such as a laboratory rat's pressing a lever or a pigeon's pecking at a disk, is measured over time on a cumulative recorder, as illustrated in Figure 7–4. A pen makes a small step across continuously unrolling paper every time a response occurs. If the animal presses the lever rapidly, there is a steep line across the paper. When the animal is not responding, there is just a horizontal line. A blip mark shows when a reinforcer is given. Responses and reinforcers would usually be counted automatically. This process can all be done now with a computer, which allows for complex analyses of the data.

The basic schedules.   There are many possible schedules of reinforcement, but four basic ones illustrate the principles involved. Each schedule produces its own particular pattern of responding. The reinforcer always follows a response (e.g., lever pressing) very closely, but the schedule determines *which* lever presses are to be reinforced.

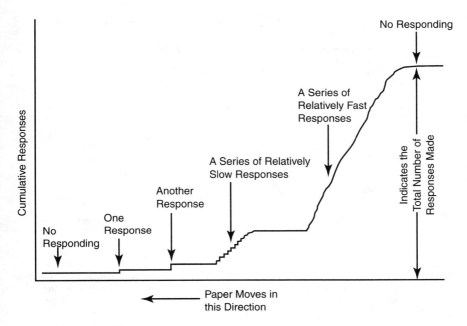

FIGURE 7–4. A cumulative recording. The pen moves a step up the paper each time a response is made. The steeper the line, the faster the rate of responding. A line parallel to the baseline indicates no responding at all. (From Hergenhahn, 1976. Used by permission of Prentice Hall, Inc.)

Fixed ratio (FR) schedule. A response is reinforced every x-number of times it occurs, such as after every tenth response. Every tenth response would be immediately reinforced, but no others. Large ratios are built up gradually so that the subject does not extinguish while waiting for the next reinforcer. A shop worker paid for every twenty widgets assembled would be working on a fixed ratio schedule. The FR schedule generates a highly reliable behavior pattern over time. The person (or animal) makes a fast run of response to get a reinforcer, and then pauses before beginning the next run. Figure 7–5 shows this behavior pattern, along with the other basic schedules.

Variable ratio (VR) schedule. With the VR schedule an unpredictable number of responses must be made to obtain a reinforcer. For example, a door-to-door salesperson might learn that a sale is made after an average of every twenty calls, but the actual number of calls between sales might range from one to thirty. This schedule produces a high response rate with little pause between reinforcement and the next response. The salesperson's very next call might be a sale. The schedule is demanding, however, and may often be considered unpleasant. One explanation for why some people gamble exorbitantly is that they are on a variable ratio schedule. They get

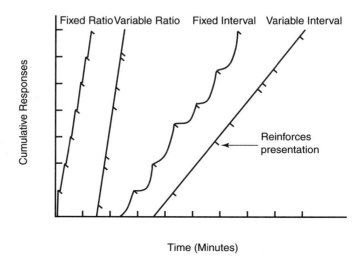

Time (Minutes)

FIGURE 7–5. Stylized cumulative response records for each of the four basic schedules of reinforcement discussed in the text. Each has its characteristic pattern and relative rate of responding compared with the others. Vertical marks show when reinforcers were presented.

reinforced by winning periodically. The more they gamble, the more they get reinforced, so that they keep gambling even more.

Fixed interval (FI) schedule.   Ratio schedules are defined in terms of the number of responses made, but interval schedules depend on elapsed time since the previous reinforcement. The first response made at the end of a set time, such as five minutes, is reinforced. No further response is reinforced until another five minutes has passed. The characteristic response pattern is a slow rate of response during the early part of each interval, gradually increasing until the end of the interval. This pattern is called a **scallop** on the record. People often put things off until the last minute, then work hard to meet a reinforcing deadline. A teacher who checks work only at the end of the hour would probably have many students on this schedule.

Variable interval (VI) schedule.   Here the time between reinforced responses is unpredictable. Responding is steady, but slower than with the variable ratio schedule. An example might be a department store clerk's waiting for customers to appear; the time between sales is unpredictable.

By gradually increasing the number of responses required for a reinforcer, all the preceding schedules can generate many responses with few reinforcers. The author has had rats, which are on a VI one-minute schedule, press a lever consistently from day to day at about 2,000 response per hour.

Pigeons commonly peck thousands of times per hour with only a few seconds' access to grain every ten or fifteen minutes.

THEORIES OF REWARDS AS REINFORCERS

Now we come to the nitty-gritty issue of rewards. We have seen that they can be used to modify behavior, an interesting and important point in child rearing, animal training, psychotherapy, and life in general. However, the more fundamental question is, What do rewards *do* that produce their behavioral effects?

Rewards are commonly called reinforcers because a response followed by a reward is "strengthened," or more likely to recur. Thorndike's phrase "law of effect" refers to the fact that the effect of a behavior (its consequences) determines whether the behavior will be repeated. A **weak** law of effect says only that reinforcers change behavior, without concern for *how* they work. Skinner's (1938) approach to operant conditioning represents this view. We can study schedules of reinforcement, for example, without having a theory of how reinforcers work. A **strong** law of effect says that some specific feature of the process of reinforcing is a **necessary** condition for reinforcing effects to occur. It is such strong laws of reinforcement that we are interested in now.[1] The various theories of rewards as reinforcers are classed as **response, motivational,** or **stimulus** theories.

Response Theories

Functional analysis.   Skinner and his followers have defined reinforcers **functionally,** saying that **any stimulus following a response that increases the probability of that response's recurring is a reinforcer.** The functional approach has considerable practical utility, because it is often difficult to say *in advance* what will be a good reinforcer for a given person in a given situation. Years of experience may tell us that money or praise will be a good reinforcer, but even these tried-and-true stimuli sometimes fail to modify human behavior in the way we expect them to.

The Premack principle.   David Premack (1959) proposed a more systematic functional analysis and a strong law of reinforcement. He said that **any Response A will reinforce any other Response B, if A has a higher response rate than B.** If a rat licks at a water tube at a higher rate than it presses a lever,

---

[1]Some authors (e.g., Postman, 1947) have argued that the concept of reinforcement is circular, that a reinforcer is known only by its effects on behavior. This concept would be true, however, only if the concept were applied to a single response in a single situation. If a stimulus such as food is reinforcing in many different situations for many different responses, as food is, then there is no circularity (Meehl, 1950).

then licking can reinforce lever pressing, but lever pressing cannot reinforce licking. This example seems trivially obvious, but Premack also performed a number of other experiments to test his hypothesis, including the following. Schoolchildren were given their choice of operating a candy machine or a pinball machine, and according to their choices were designated as "eaters" or "manipulators." Subsequently, getting candy reinforced playing pinball for the eaters, and playing pinball reinforced getting candy for the manipulators. Premack himself (1971) eventually concluded that the **hedonic** properties of stimuli provided a simpler account of reinforcers than did the response rate theory. Nevertheless, Premack's original analysis was highly influential among workers in applied behavior modification. It follows, for example, that the sequencing of activities during a daily classroom routine can be arranged to advantage. Unpopular academic activities can be scheduled earlier and reinforced by popular activities that come later. Arithmetic might be followed by reading, which in turn might be followed by drawing.

Elicitation theories.   Denny and Adelman (1955) proposed that all that is required for reinforcement is that a response be repeatedly **elicited** by some stimulus. For example, if an animal gets food following lever pressing, it goes to the food and eats it. Going to the food reinforces lever pressing, and the response of eating reinforces going to the food. Thus,

Lever Pressing → Running to Food → Response (Eating Food)

Each response reinforces the preceding response. The only relevance of food is that **food reliably elicits eating.** The main weakness with the theory is that stimuli can be reinforcing even when no reliable responses are elicited by the stimuli.

Sheffield (1966) proposed a similar theory, but it was limited to **consummatory** responses. Although a number of provocative experiments supported Sheffield's position, it should be kept in mind that this theory was mainly pitted against drive reduction theory. For example, Sheffield, Wulff, and Backer (1951) showed that male rats would learn responses reinforced by copulation (a consummatory response) without ejaculation (drive reduction). The consummatory response interpretation is less convincing if we consider sexual arousal reinforcing in itself, but the experiment was in fact another nail in the coffin of drive reduction theory. Sheffield and Roby (1950) also reported that rats would work hard for nonnutritive (and non–drive-reducing) saccharin solution. This result is also better interpreted in terms of taste, however, because the reinforcing effect is correlated with the concentration of the reinforcer, but not with the rate of licking at the reinforcer (Kraeling, 1961). Rats lick at a nearly constant rate of about 6 licks per second whenever they lick at all.

The Glickman-Schiff biological theory.   The preceding theories require that the "reinforcing responses" (e.g., eating) actually occur. Glickman and Schiff (1967) suggested that a stimulus would be reinforcing if it just **activated the neural systems underlying responses even if an overt response did not occur.** Thus, for example, animals will normally eat if the lateral hypothalamus is electrically stimulated and food is available. Stimulation to the lateral hypothalamus is also a powerful reinforcer for lever pressing even when food is *not* available, however. This finding suggests that stimulation of the response system in the brain is adequate for reinforcement. Since we now know that reinforcing brain stimulation triggers the release of pleasurable brain opiates, it is less clear that stimulation of a *response* system is critical to reinforcement. The endorphins may produce positive affect, which is reinforcing.

Motivational Theories

Drive reduction theory.   Drive reduction theory directly ties reinforcement to motivation by saying that drive reduction is a necessary condition for reinforcement (Hull, 1943). Without drive there can be no drive reduction. It is necessary to distinguish between **need reduction** and **drive stimulus reduction,** however. Thus, Miller (1951a, 1959) argued that **any strong stimulus has drive properties, but not all need states produce strong stimuli.** For example, oxygen deficit is not discomforting and by itself has no identifiable drive properties. By this analysis, **drive stimulus reduction** is the reinforcing event, whether the drive stimulus is generated by some internal need such as hunger or comes from an unpleasant external stimulus. Miller and Kessen (1952) supported this view by showing that milk *drunk* by a hungry rat was a better reinforcer in a T-maze than milk *tubed directly into the stomach.* Tubed milk was more reinforcing than tubed saline solution. They argued that if **need reduction** were the critical factor, the milk should be equally reinforcing whether drunk normally or tubed into the stomach. Therefore, drinking was reducing both drive stimulus intensity *and* need, whereas tubing reduced only need. Saline reduced neither. Such analytical experiments as this are important because the observation that food or water reinforce hungry or thirsty animals does not *necessarily* support the drive reduction theory. The palatability of ingested food might be the critical reinforcing factor, not hunger (drive) reduction, and the trick is to separate palatability from need/drive reduction. Tubing of different solutions into the stomach does this.

Evidence for drive reduction.   Drive-reduction theory is supported by research on pain reduction, fear reduction, and reward-by-fistula (as in the Miller-Kessen experiment). Pain reduction is the clearest example, however. Pain (as from electric shock) is easy to control, and its termination, like getting rid of a toothache, is a powerful reinforcer. Since there is no observable incentive external reinforcer that corresponds to food or water, shock reduction is often considered a "pure" case of drive reduction. Termination of almost any uncomfortably intense stimulus is demonstrably reinforcing.

Animals will also learn new responses if reinforced by opportunity to escape from a fear-arousing environment (Miller, 1948). Escape from a fear-arousing compartment increases with such variables as the intensity of the shock used to condition the fear and the number of fear-conditioning trials given before testing the escape response (Kalish, 1954).

The sensory qualities of foods (taste, texture, etc.) can be eliminated as possible reinforcers by inserting a plastic tube (a fistula) directly into the stomach or bloodstream so that nutritive material bypasses the mouth and nose. Such injected foods are reinforcing, but there is also evidence that the temperature of fluids passing through the tube may be critical for reinforcement (Holman, 1969; Mendelson & Chillag, 1970). The fistula experiments therefore may not be "pure" tests of drive reduction.

Evidence against drive reduction.   The preceding evidence suggests that drive reduction may be a **sufficient** condition for reinforcement but not that drive reduction is the only or necessary condition. Research shows that **exciting** events are also reinforcing. We have already seen that Sheffield's sex and saccharin studies challenge drive reduction theory, so let us look at what has been called the **pain-fear paradox** (Mowrer, 1960).

The paradox is that **whereas the presentation of a painful stimulus reinforces the learning of fear, pain punishes other responses.** Furthermore, a drive reduction theorist would have to say that it is the **end of pain** that reinforces fear learning. The paradox is resolved by experiments showing that the **onset of pain,** not the termination, reinforces fear learning (Mowrer & Aiken, 1954; Davitz, 1955). This finding led to the development of **two-factor theory,** which says that some responses are reinforced by **drive induction** (increase) and others by drive reduction.

Arousal theory.   Since arousal theory was discussed in detail in Chapter Five, suffice it to say that according to the theory, either **increases** or **decreases** in internal arousal can be reinforcing as long as they lead to a more optimal level of arousal.

Stimulus Theories

Hedonic reinforcers.   Animals that are not under any known dietary deficiency and that never have been deprived of food or water will press levers or run through mazes for sweet-tasting substances (e.g., Young, 1959). Taste, not drive reduction, seems to account for this behavior. Drive reduction theorists have argued, however, that the sweet-tasting substances used in such experiments actually were drive reducing. This is a weak argument, however, since it must make the undocumented assumption that the animals in such experiments were under some level of drive. It has also been argued that sweet tastes may have become **conditioned reinforcers** through their previous association with drive (hunger) reduction, especially during nursing. In fact, however, sweet substances **are preferred by newborn infants** before there is association of the sweet substances with hunger reduction (Jacobs, 1964; Lippsitt et al., 1976). Newborn rats and newborn humans lick at and swallow sugar solutions placed on the lips almost immediately after birth, but they reject bitter solutions. Furthermore, even months of exposure to a bitter taste from birth on does not change the preference for sweet substances with guinea pigs (Warren & Pfaffman, 1958). Direct evidence for genetic differences in taste preference also argues against the learning interpretation (e.g., Ramirez & Fuller, 1976). Learning *can* be involved in taste preferences, as shown in Chapter Four, but not all reinforcing tastes depend on previous association with drive reduction.

Sex and brain stimulation.   We shall put here only some previous commentary into context. First, sexual **arousal** appears to be very reinforcing. Second, electrical stimulation of the brain produces excitement in animals and is highly reinforcing.

Stimulus change and information.   Harry Harlow (1953) said, "It is my belief that the theory which describes learning as dependent upon drive reduction is false, that internal drive as such is a variable of little importance to learning, and that this small importance steadily decreases as we investigate learning problems of progressive complexity." He then went on to point out that he usually fed his laboratory monkeys *before* the experimental session. The monkeys stored food in their cheek pouches and then proceeded to swallow a little food after every response they made, whether the response was right or wrong. But the animals learned the correct responses. "It would seem" said Harlow, "that the Lord was simply unaware of drive reduction learning theory when he created, or permitted the gradual evolution of, the rhesus monkey." In general, Harlow made the point that external stimuli are more important sources of motivation than are internal drive states and suggested that the "main role of the primary drive seems to be one of altering the threshold for precurrent responses." That is, certain of the responses already available are simply made more likely to occur when an animal is deprived.

Monkeys will work for hours on puzzle-type problems without deprivation or external reinforcement. They will also work inside a dark box at a task that permits no more than a window opening so that they can see out of the box. Also, they are very active in exploring their environments. Indeed, even rats will choose the arm of a T-maze that leads to an explorable checkerboard-type maze rather than a plain box, and food deprivation actually reduces this tendency to explore (Montgomery, 1953).

When rats are run in a T-maze with no reward at all, they tend to alternate running to one side or the other on successive trials. That is, they tend *not* to go to the goal box that they entered on the previous trial. This tendency is called **spontaneous alternation behavior.** Two explanations that have been proposed to account for alternation behavior are **response inhibition** and **stimulus satiation.** Response inhibition theory says that the animal tends **not to repeat the same response,** whereas Stimulus satiation theory says that the animal tends **not to go to the same stimulus.** The animal becomes satiated for the stimulus just experienced and so goes to the alternate stimulus on the next trial because it is either more novel or more informational. Since both theories account equally well for simple alternation, the following critical test of the theories has been conducted.

Animals are run without reinforcement in a T-maze where the left goal arm is white and the right goal arm is black (with appropriate controls for brightness in various groups). Assume that on Trial 1, the animals run to the *right*, choosing the *black* goal arm. On Trial 2, the animals are run in the maze with the colors of the goal boxes reversed. In which direction should they turn? According to response inhibition theory, they should go to the *left*, since that would be opposite their right turn on the previous trial. According to stimulus satiation theory, they should repeat the same response and go to the *right*, because that is now where the alternate stimulus is. A large number of experiments indicate that they go to the right and generally alternate with reference to stimuli, not responses. Interestingly, it has also been found that animals alternate with reference to **absolute direction** (such as east versus west), not just light versus dark. This tendency is still alternation with reference to stimuli, however.

As with most other research stories, even such an apparently simple phenomenon as spontaneous alternation quickly becomes more complicated (Dember & Richman, 1989; Richman, Dember, & Kim, 1986–87). First, if the choices are side-by-side and readily visible from the same position, animals alternate with reference to **goal box brightness.** But if the choices are more discrete, alleys going in different directions in a T-maze, animals alternate with reference to **direction** (e.g., east versus west). And under some conditions, it also appears that animals *do* alternate with reference to responses (Dember & Richman, 1989; Richman, Dember, & Kim, 1986–87). If animals with four hours' food deprivation can obtain a food pellet following the choice of **either** arm in a T-maze, they alternate with reference to stimuli in early trials of "training." After many trials in the apparatus, however, they switch to alternating responses. It is as if the animals "switched off" environmental information that was useless to them and let their bodies run on automatic pilot. Indeed, most of us do this with such highly routine tasks as driving—until something goes wrong to attract our attention again.

A number of authors have proposed that **exposure to complex, changing stimuli is reinforcing** (Dember & Richman, 1989). Dember and Earl (1957) proposed that there is an optimal level of stimulus complexity that is reinforcing and that varies from one individual to another. They further argued that organisms tend to respond to stimuli that are just a little more complex than the optimum. These are called **pacer stimuli.** Once an individual's preferred complexity level is established, any change in preference will be in the direction of greater complexity, not less. Psychological growth—the capacity to deal with progressively more complex stimuli—is built into the theory.

The informational approach says that stimuli can be reinforcing simply by virtue of telling an organism, human or otherwise, something it did not already know. An experiment by Bower, McLean, and Meacham (1966) exemplifies this. Bower et al. asked whether **information** about the delay of reward would be reinforcing to pigeons even though this information could not change the delay. Given their choice of either of two keys to peck at, the birds pecked more than 90 percent of the time at a key that signaled whether a short or long delay was coming (by red or green light) and less than 10% at a key that turned on a white light whether the delay was long or short. The birds clearly preferred to know what was going on. Whether good news or bad, there is undoubtedly considerable survival value in knowing what is happening in the environment.

Secondary Reinforcement

Background. Just as such "primary" biological drives as hunger and thirst do not influence our behavior much of the time, neither do their corresponding primary reinforcers, food and water. As a consequence, the concept of **secondary (acquired, conditioned) reinforcement** was devised. A secondary reinforcer is **a formerly neutral stimulus that, through association with a primary reinforcer, takes on some of the same functions as a primary reinforcer.** Although a primary reinforcer may be any established reinforcer, we usually think of things like food and water as primary reinforcers. A buzzer previously associated with food may reinforce lever pressing. Secondary reinforcement has been used to account for much human behavior. Money, for example, is one of the most general secondary reinforcers, useful only in relation to some other commodity.

Four different **functions** are ascribed to secondary reinforcers: (1) reinforcing the learning of new responses; (2) maintaining behavior during extinction; (3) mediating long delay of reinforcement by presenting a secondary reinforcer between the time a response is made and the delivery of a primary reinforcer; and (4) establishing and maintaining schedules of reinforcement (Wike, 1966; Hendry, 1969; Mowrer, 1960). If a secondary reinforcer is periodically "reconditioned" (associated with its primary reinforcer), it may retain its potency almost indefinitely (Wike, 1966; Zimmerman, 1957; 1959).

The power of a secondary reinforcer depends on variables similar to those that affect the strength of classical conditioning (Wike, 1966). These include **number** of associations with a primary reinforcer, the **amount** of primary reinforcement, close **temporal association** with primary reinforcement, and **probability** that the secondary reinforcer will be followed by the primary reinforcer.

Theories of secondary reinforcement.   Theories of secondary reinforcement also fall into response, motivation, and stimulus categories.

Response theories say that a secondary reinforcer is just another stimulus that comes to elicit a response. If a clicking sound **elicits the response** of running to get food, it is an effective secondary reinforcer (Denny & Adelman, 1955; Bugelski, 1956).

Motivational theories are stretched, however, because secondary reinforcers **cannot reduce need** in the way that the primary reinforcers can (the sound of a buzzer is not likely to make us less hungry). A secondary reinforcer *might* reduce drive stimulus intensity, however (Mowrer, 1960). A somewhat critical test is whether a stimulus paired with shock termination can become a secondary reinforcer. There is virtually no evidence demonstrating that this result can occur (Beck, 1961; LoLordo, 1969; Siegel & Milby, 1969). However, a stimulus that **signals a shock-free period of time** can become a secondary reinforcer (Moscovitch & LoLordo, 1968; Rescorla, 1969). The signaling property of the stimulus is apparently reinforcing, however, not drive stimulus reduction. Such a reinforcer may signal a period of **relaxation.** Denny (1971) argued that **relief** (decreased tension) occurs immediately after shock ends, but a **qualitatively different relaxation response** starts about fifteen to thirty seconds later. Denny suggested that a stimulus paired with relaxation can be reinforcing but that a stimulus paired with relief cannot.

Stimulus theories say that a stimulus becomes a secondary reinforcer if it provides **reliable and unique information** about a forthcoming primary reinforcer, such as a buzzer signaling that food is coming. A **redundant stimulus,** coming after another signal has already informed an animal that food is coming, is *not* a good secondary reinforcer (Egger & Miller, 1962, 1963). The most widely accepted theoretical view now is that a secondary reinforcer is a stimulus that is **positively correlated** with the occurrence of a primary reinforcer (Rescorla, 1987).

INTERACTION OF EXTRINSIC REWARDS
AND INTRINSIC MOTIVATION

Industrial psychologists commonly distinguish between **intrinsic motivation** and **external rewards.** Intrinsic motivation refers to factors that make certain activities rewarding in themselves, such as hobbies, games, puzzles, creative endeavors, and so on. Extrinsic rewards refer to those rewards given us by other people for our behavior. This is the standard approach of operant conditioning and behavior modification. We might expect that if external reward were combined with intrinsic motivation, a person would perform even better at an activity that he or she already likes. This result does not always seem to come about, however. In some situations external rewards for an already interesting task may actually *reduce* performance on the task, or even liking for the task.

As an example of this phenomenon in a study of nursery school children, Anderson, Manoogian, and Reznick (1976) compared the effects of money, a "good-player" award, and verbal praise as reinforcers. The children were first pretested for the amount of time spent drawing with magic markers. They were then rewarded for drawing. Finally, they were posttested, without reward, for drawing. Both the money (pennies) and the good-player award produced a drop in amount of time spent drawing, but the praise produced a slight increase. Similar results have been produced in a variety of experiments, with both children and adults (Notz, 1975; Deci, 1975; Lepper & Greene, 1978; Deci, 1980). Given the importance generally attached to external rewards in the control of behavior, such "hidden costs of reward" call for clarification.

This line of research was stimulated by DeCharms's (1968) suggestion that there should be an **interaction** of intrinsic motivation and external motivation, not just an additive effect. DeCharms believed that this interaction would be based on a person's perception of whether he or she was the controlling agent in getting rewards or was at the mercy of outside agents. If the person sees himself or herself as the causal factor in getting desirable outcomes, then the behavior producing those outcomes is intrinsically motivating and desirable. The individual will continue to do things over which there is personal control. On the other hand, if the person sees rewards as depending on someone else, the activities necessary to get those rewards will be less intrinsically motivating. A person may continue to work at his or her job because money is needed to live, but the work is likely to be of little intrinsic interest.

Deci (1978) concluded that intrinsic motivation and external rewards interact in the following way:

1. External rewards *facilitate* behavior when (1) they primarily convey information that a person is competent and the rewards are not perceived as controlling behavior, and (2) they are given for routine, well-learned activities. The first instance fits the "praise condition" in the Anderson et al. experiment with nursery school children, and the second fits an assembly-line type of job.

2. External rewards tend to *impair* performance when (1) they are obvious and given for activities already of high interest, and (2) they are related to such open-ended activities as problem solving. The first instance is like the use of money in the Anderson et al. experiment. The second instance is closer to the creative activities of managers, artists, musicians, or others who do not know in advance just what they are going to do or how they are going to do it.

People often are not even striving for predetermined rewards but *discover* the rewards as they go along. Highly creative visual artists, for example, do not have preset notions about what a picture *should* look like before they start. Rather, they change their ideas as the work progresses. Much the same holds for writing; a book begins to take on a "life of its own" as it develops, often in a very different form from that initially projected by its author. Similarly, small children may pile blocks on top of each other with no idea of what they are trying to build, but they are reinforced at various steps by characteristics of the block tower that appeal to them. Not only is the motivation (reward) intrinsic, but it is also actually discovered moment by moment (Csikszentmihalyi, 1978).

Deci's theory of **cognitive evaluation** (Deci, 1980; Deci & Ryan, 1985) says that rewards have a **controlling** aspect and an **informational** aspect. If the controlling aspect is more salient, a person will perceive control as external. If the informational aspect is more salient, control will be perceived as internal, and feelings of competence and self-determination will emerge. It should follow, then, that external reward can in fact facilitate *any* behavior if the reward informs a person that she or he is doing well. As a character in a movie once said, business is a game and money is how you keep score. Money is not *always* controlling.

Other theorists have looked at the problem somewhat differently. Kruglanski (1978), for example, distinguished between activities that are ends unto themselves and activities that are the means to some other goal. In this view, an activity is perceived more favorably if it is an end rather than a (perhaps unpleasant) means to something else. It has also been argued from an operant conditioning point of view, that the performance decrement that occurs after reward, happens simply because **reward has been omitted.** In other words, it is an **extinction** effect. Considerable research is still needed in this area to sort out many problems.

Control and desire for control.   If the perception of self-control (or personal causation) is truly important, we might ask whether external rewards would be more detrimental to the intrinsic motivation of people with a high desire for control. People not concerned about control would presumably be less affected by low perceived control than would those with high concern for control. Burger (1980) tested this hypothesis by paying or not paying subjects who were either high or low in need for control according to a scale devised by him. The results are shown in Figure 7–6. Payment of $2.00 for doing a task reduced the intrinsic motivation of the task in high-desire-for-control subjects but not in low-desire-for-control subjects.

Are Rewards Truly Detrimental?

Eisenberger and Cameron (1996) mounted an attack on the general idea inherent in the literature discussed before, that when rewards are removed, behavior tends to be less likely than before rewards were introduced

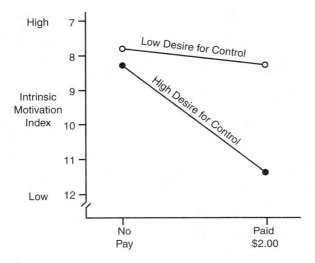

FIGURE 7–6. Effect of paying subjects with high and low desire for control on intrinsic interest in the task. (From Burger, 1980.)

in the first place. They note the very important practical implications of this concept, such as illustrated by an article entitled "Why Incentive Plans Cannot Work" (Kohn, 1993a) and by a book entitled *Punished by Rewards* (Kohn, 1993b). Similarly, a report in *U.S. News and World Report* indicated that programs that reward children for reading actually were making them nonreaders by destroying their enjoyment of reading. The question then is, Do the existing data actually support such strong conclusions? Or have existing data been magnified by some romantic idealism inherent in the American psyche, stressing the importance of self-direction and independence?

Meta-analysis of research. Meta-analysis is a statistical technique for combining the results of a large number of studies on a topic to arrive at some conclusion about the whole set of studies. This method is preferable to doing counts of studies showing positive results, no results, negative results, and so on. Cameron and Pierce (1994) analyzed a total of 96 studies in which a control group and an experimental group with withdrawn reward were compared. The data showed virtually no effect of removing reward on attitude toward the previously rewarded task. Eisenberger & Cameron (1996) interpreted the data to indicate that the only effects on behavior were those involving an expected, tangible reward. And, certainly, none of these effects are all-or-none.

Learned industriousness. An argument against the use of rewards to foster creative behavior is that rewards only increase repetition of responses that get the reward. This argument belies the fact that one can selectively reinforce any aspect of responses that one so chooses, including variation (Skinner, 1953). We can selectively reinforce animals for responding at high or low rates in a Skinner box, for example. Eisenberger's (1992) learned industriousness theory says that the perceived effort involved in doing a task acquires secondary reinforcing properties when the effort is successfully reinforced. It then follows that reinforcing creative behavior, such as attempts to search for unusual solutions to problems, would result in continued effort at creative behavior. In other words, there is nothing inherent in the use of reinforcers that says they will necessarily restrict behavior. It depends on how the reinforcers are used. One can shape creativity as much as one shapes repetitiveness.

EXPANDED REINFORCEMENT THEORY: BEHAVIORAL ECONOMICS

Psychologists have traditionally developed their theories of reinforcement in laboratory settings, with tight experimental control, and then extrapolated their findings to nonlaboratory settings. This process has been done most elegantly within the framework of Skinner's operant conditioning approach, where practical applications abound. Skinner's novel *Walden II* (1948) described a Utopian society based on operant conditioning principles; and small-scale "token economies" of the kind Skinner described in his novel have actually been established in such institutional settings as psychiatric hospitals, prisons, and classrooms. These economies use tokens for reinforcers, which can later be traded for food, special privileges, or other commodities.

A very different approach comes from viewing reinforcers as commodities or money in **open** economies where there are many choices, as contrasted to the **closed economy** of the traditional laboratory experiment, where subjects seldom have choices about what reinforcers they get or what it takes to get them. Over the past two decades, psychologists have begun to explore reinforcers in broader contexts than the usual Skinner box or T-maze environments. One reason is the recognition of the possibility that the "standard" laboratory methods for studying reinforcers have an artificiality about them, so that the **concepts** derived from such research may be too specific to those situations. A number of psychologists have become interested in **economic theory** in relation to reinforcement. The Skinner box provides a nice analogy. An animal gets **paid** (reinforced) a certain amount for a given amount of work (lever presses, key pecks). How does an animal adjust its behavior as the **price** (work required) for a commodity changes?

The mathematical curve that relates the **amount** of a commodity sought to the **price** of the commodity is called a **demand curve**. For example, the number of food pellets a rat will "buy" (work for) varies with the price, such as the number of lever presses required for a reinforcer. The number of presses required per pellet is one characteristic of a schedule of reinforcement. A reinforcer requiring ten presses is more expensive (greater cost) than one requiring only five presses. The demand for a commodity is said to be **elastic** if the animal works *less* as the cost increases. Conversely, a commodity is **inelastic** if the demand remains relatively constant in spite of increasing cost. This concept is illustrated in Figure 7–7. "Luxury" items tend to be more elastic than such necessities as food, but such "luxuries" as coffee are very inelastic. Governments also tax "sin" (such as alcohol and cigarettes) with foreknowledge that these commodities are very inelastic; they sell at nearly the same volume even at the higher prices resulting from the added tax.

The effect of a price change can be divided into two parts, however: the **income effect** and the **substitutability effect.** The income effect is the extent to which a price change affects the real income of a person, the total amount of goods a person can buy with his or her money. If an increase in price is balanced by an increase in income (inflation), there may be no effect of price on demand. Conversely, if price goes up while income goes down, the unhappy situation with high inflation and low employment, there may be a greatly reduced demand with higher price. The substitutability effect refers to the availability of a *similar* commodity at a lower price. If there is no substitute, as with oil for automobiles, there is a smaller effect of price increase on consumption than if there were a substitute. The demand for butter, however, changes with price because a number of good substitutes are available (margarine, cooking oils). In like manner, with the influx of foreign products selling at lower prices than American-made products, there is great substitutability, therefore great elasticity in demand for American goods.

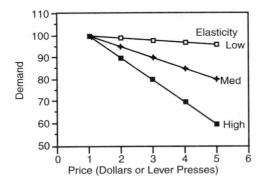

FIGURE 7–7. Demand curves varying in elasticity. A demand curve with low elasticity shows little change in demand (sales) with increasing price. A demand curve with high elasticity shows a large drop in sales when there is increasing price. In economics, cost is typically measured in monetary units, such as dollars. In animal research, cost is given by the amount of work, such as the number of lever presses required to obtain a fixed amount of food. Arbitrary units are used on both axes.

Another principle, called the **complementarity effect,** works opposite to the substitutability effect. Complementarity means that an increase in the demand for one product also produces an increased demand for another. A rise in the sales of pretzels increases the sales of beer, and increased air travel increases the sales of flight insurance.

These principles have been shown to work to some extent in the animal laboratory. For example, in one study, rats pressed either one lever for food and another for water, or one lever for Tom Collins mix and another for root beer. As the price (number of presses) required for a morsel of food increased, the animals did not switch to pressing for water (no substitutability); they paid more (pressed more) for food. When the price of Tom Collins mix went up, however, the rats readily switched their allegiance to root beer. The two commodities were substitutable (Lea, 1978).

If animals have **free access** to food for a certain amount of time daily, they will press a lever in a Skinner box for food anyway—until the cost becomes too high. When this event happens, the animals simply stop "eating out," no longer pressing the lever if free food is available. The free food is substitutable for the food bought with lever presses. If, however, the only food available has to be bought by lever pressing, the demand for the food is much less elastic than if there is free food. The animals keep responding until they spend virtually all their time working to get food (e.g., Collier et al., 1976).

It is not yet clear whether the application of human economic principles will further our understanding of reinforcers or whether there is simply a new set of words for already established principles. Additional research will decide that question. Meanwhile, it is worth considering that human economic principles may have developed as they have **because they do in fact represent broad biological principles of reinforcement.**

SUMMARY

1. **Instrumental conditioning** refers to the effect on a behavior when that behavior is followed by reward or punishment. We consider rewards as reinforcers when we look at their relationship to the learning of behaviors.

2. Thorndike argued that learning consists of forming a connection between a specific stimulus and a specific response. He called such a connection an "S-R bond." Most instrumental learning does not consist of such S-R bonds, however, since most behaviors learned with one response to a stimulus can be transferred to other responses without further training.

3. B. F. Skinner coined the phrase **operant conditioning** for his approach to instrumental conditioning. He developed an apparatus called the operant conditioning chamber that automatically presents rewards and records responses, making it possible to study behavior continuously over long periods of time without disturbing the animal.

4. Skinner defined a reinforcer as any stimulus following a behavior that **increases the probability** that the behavior will occur again. A punisher is any stimulus following a behavior that **decreases the probability** that the behavior will occur again. In the terminology of this text, reinforcers are desirable outcomes of behavior, and punishers are aversive outcomes of behavior.

5. Reinforcers are most effective if given **immediately** after a response and are progressively less effective with longer delays. The delay between a response and a reinforcer can be bridged by a **secondary reinforcer,** a stimulus that gets its reinforcing power by previous association with some reinforcer.

6. A **schedule of reinforcement** is some rule for when to deliver reinforcers in relation to responses. Schedules can be **response-based**, such as delivering a reinforcer after every tenth response (a **fixed ratio schedule**) or can be **time-based,** such as reinforcing the first response after some minimum amount of time has passed since the last reinforcement (a **fixed interval schedule**).

7. A **functional analysis of behavior** involves determining what rewards are effective for a given individual. No theory of reinforcement is necessary beyond saying that rewards are sufficient for learning to occur.

8. **Response theories** of reinforcement say that the effective rewarding events are the responses made, not the subsequent stimuli. Food is effective because it elicits the response of eating. Actual responses may not be necessary; activation of brain processes underlying responses may be adequate.

9. **Motivational theories** emphasize increases or decreases of drive or arousal as reinforcing events.

10. **Stimulus theories** say that stimuli that produce positive emotion or provide information are reinforcing.

11. **Secondary reinforcers** are formerly neutral stimuli that have gained reinforcing capacity of their own by being associated with such primary reinforcers as food. A good secondary reinforcer provides reliable information about a forthcoming primary reinforcer.

12. External rewards for behavior sometimes reduce **intrinsic motivation** to engage in those behaviors. Deci's theory of cognitive evaluation says that rewards have **controlling** and **informational** aspects. When rewards are perceived as controlling behavior, intrinsic motivation is said to decrease. The generality of this effect has been challenged by some researchers.

13. External rewards are more detrimental to the intrinsic motivation of people with a **high desire for control**, presumably because external rewards are perceived as *not* being under the individual's control.

14. **Behavioral economics** is the application of economic principles to laboratory research on rewards. **Demand curves** (effects of increasing cost for commodities) have been studied, using the number of lever presses required to obtain a reward as a definition of cost. This approach has made some verifiable predictions in the animal laboratory.

CHAPTER EIGHT

Rewards as Incentives

——————●——————

INCENTIVE MOTIVATION

The Concept of Incentive

Having examined the idea that rewards work "backward" to reinforce responses, let us now explore the alternative notion that the **anticipation** of rewarding stimuli (incentives) is what affects behavior. Incentives, like drives, are said to "motivate" behavior, but drives differ from incentives in that primary drives like hunger are biologically **inevitable** and are **cyclic,** automatically occurring at periodic intervals. Incentive motivation is not so inevitable, because it develops through experience and can be aroused whenever the appropriate stimuli are present, not depending on a cyclic process.

Importance of the Incentive Concept

Laboratory evidence favoring the importance of incentive motivation of behavior has been developing for well over half a century, providing data that are not easily accounted for by even the most strident drive theorist or the most liberal interpretation of drive theory. The following five different kinds of data are especially compelling.

Amount of reward and reward shifts. Animals reliably perform better (faster, more vigorously, more accurately) for large rewards than for small ones (see Black, 1969, for a review). This behavior could mean either that the animals are more motivated or that they have learned better with large rewards. When animals are **shifted** from small to large rewards, however, their performance improves much more quickly than we would expect on the basis of response learning principles. Nor are the sudden changes accounted for by a change in drive, because drive (amount of deprivation) is held constant. This situation leaves incentive motivation the most viable alternative account.

The classic incentive shift study was by Crespi (1942). Rats received 1, 4, 16, or 256 small food pellets as reward at the end of a straight runway. The more pellets they received, the faster the animals ran. When the number of pellets was increased or decreased, the animals ran faster or slower, respectively. Figure 8–1 shows the shift effect resulting from a hypothetical experiment patterned after Crespi's. Following the shift upward is an **overshooting** effect, which Crespi called the **elation effect.** The upshifted animals perform better at the new reward level than do animals that have been at the same large-reward level continuously. Conversely, there was an **undershooting** effect for downshifted animals, known as the **depression effect.** These exaggerated shift effects are important because they cannot be accounted for by changes in drive level or by response learning (the animals already know the response). Crespi (1944) suggested that the animals developed different amounts of anticipatory excitement, which he called **eagerness,** and said that this was related to learning only to the extent that the animal had to find out

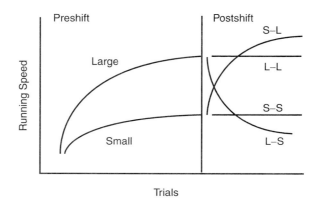

FIGURE 8-1. Idealized presentation of the Crespi shift effect. During original training (preshift) animals run faster to large rewards than to small ones. After the shift, animals switched from small to large rewards (S-L) quickly increase their speed to a level even higher than that of animals continuously trained with large rewards (L-L). Conversely, animals shifted from large to small rewards (L-S) drop below the level of animals continuing to get small rewards (S-S).

how much incentive it was getting before it exhibited the appropriate amount of eagerness. Many experiments (e.g., Zeaman, 1949) have replicated Crespi's general results.

Incentive contrast effects. By **contrast effect** we mean that if different incentives are presented simultaneously or successively to the same animal, the animal will respond differently to them than if each were presented alone, as illustrated in Figure 8–2. This principle is also exemplified by the elation and depression effects in the Crespi experiment. Animals respond more positively to the "better" of two stimuli and more negatively to the "worse" of two stimuli when the stimuli are contrasted. This finding holds true for either consummatory or instrumental responses (Flaherty, 1982).

Quality of reward. Different kinds of rewards have different incentive motivational properties. In 1924, Simmons showed that rodents performed better in a maze if rewarded with bread and milk than they did if rewarded with sunflower seeds. In general, substances that are more highly preferred are also better incentives. Guttman (1953; 1954) separated quality from quantity of reward by giving animals fixed amounts (quantity) of different concentrations (quality) of sucrose or glucose solution when they pressed a lever. Response rate was highly correlated with concentration of reward, as shown in Figure 8–3. Therefore, quality was important separate from quantity.

Deprivation effects. Incentive theorists argue that deprivation does not directly energize behavior. Rather, as we saw in our earlier discussion of feed-

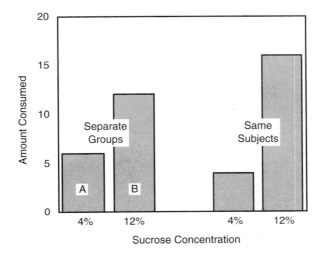

FIGURE 8–2. Incentive contrast effect. Bars on left represent amount of sucrose consumed in a fixed amount of time by separate groups, A and B, when each gets only one solution. Bars on right represent amount consumed when the same subjects have both solutions available simultaneously. Animals drink more of the higher concentration and less of the lower when they can directly compare the two solutions.

ing, deprivation enhances incentives. Hunger makes food a better incentive, and so on. Even Pavlov observed that dogs had to be food deprived in order for salivary conditioning to take place. Such enhancement is further illustrated by the fact that preference for a specific flavor food increases if that food has been eaten when the animal is very hungry (Revusky, 1967; 1968). Curiously, however, one report found that animals tended to *avoid* foods consumed while very hungry, as if they did not want to be reminded of the long deprivation (Capaldi & Myers, 1982). Positive enhancement is the more frequently reported effect, however.

Deprivation effects are sometimes more spectacular when we compare different *kinds* of deprivation rather than different amounts. For example, given the choice between 6 percent sucrose and water, hungry rats virtually always choose the sucrose, but thirsty rats are almost indifferent between the two choices. Preferences are reversed simply by making the thirsty rats hungry and the hungry rats thirsty, as shown in Figure 8–4 (from Beck & Bidwell, 1974).

Latent learning and latent extinction.   Tolman and Honzik (1930) were perhaps the first to demonstrate that learning and performance are not the same thing. They had three different groups of rats learn a complex maze. One group was rewarded with food in the goal box after each run and

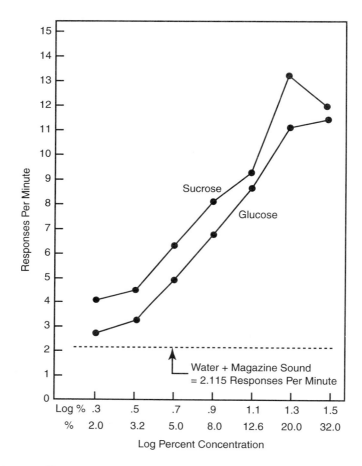

FIGURE 8–3. Rate of bar pressing as a function of concentration of reinforcing agent. (From Guttman, 1954, p. 359. Copyright © 1954 by the American Psychological Association. Reprinted by permission.)

showed progressively fewer errors. A second group was never rewarded and showed no improvement. A third group ran the maze for several days without reward and did not improve during this time. Reward was then introduced, and the performance of the third group improved almost immediately to the level of the first group (see Figure 8–5). This result showed that reward was not necessary for *learning* the maze but was necessary to get the animals to *perform* better. The learning was **latent,** not demonstrated in performance until reward was introduced. Many subsequent experiments validated the principle of latent learning (Thistlethwaite, 1951).

In the latent learning experiment, learning occurs without reward. In the **latent extinction** experiment, extinction occurs (at least partly) without the animal's performing the response to be extinguished. Thus two groups of

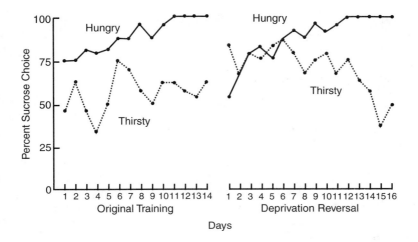

FIGURE 8–4.   Preferences for 8 percent sucrose over water by hungry or thirsty rats in a maze choice situation. The animals were run six trials a day and were forced to go to the nonpreferred side, if necessary, in order to equalize number of trials to each side. Equal experience with each incentive each day was thus guaranteed. After fourteen days of original training, each group was switched to the opposite deprivation condition (deprivation reversal) for the next sixteen days of training. In each case, the animals adjusted to the new deprivation condition by responding similarly to the behavior of the other group in the original deprived condition (sucrose preference increased quickly for the now-hungry animals and declined for the now-thirsty animals). (From Beck & Bidwell, 1974, p. 331.)

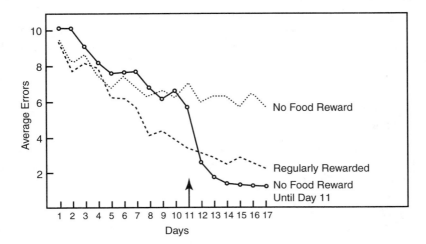

FIGURE 8–5.   Evidence for the latent learning in the maze. With no food reward, there is some reduction in errors, but not as great a reduction as with regular food reward. Despite the higher error scores prior to the introduction of food, the group rewarded only from the eleventh trial immediately begins to do as well as the group that had been regularly rewarded. The interpretation is that some learning went on within the first ten trials, which did not show in performance until the food incentive activated it. (After Tolman & Honzik, published in 1930 by The Regents of the University of California; reprinted by permission of the University of California Press.)

animals are trained to run in a straight runway with food reward. One group is then placed in the goal box a number of times without food, the other is not. The running response is then extinguished in both groups by having the animals run to the empty goal box, the normal extinction procedure. The result is that the placement group extinguishes faster than the control group. Since drive was the same for the two groups and since the placement animals did not actually do any running during latent extinction (goal box placement) trials, the results are attributed to a lower level of incentive motivation. The placement group learned not to expect reward.

These five lines of evidence converge on the idea that incentive motivation is very important, perhaps the most important motivational determinant of performance. Incentive motivation is in turn influenced both by experience and by internal states of the organism. We now turn to theories that attempt to explain how incentive motivation works. One type of theory assumes that incentive motivation develops out of **responses**, the other assumes that incentive motivation is a **central nervous system process** that does not depend on overt responses.

RESPONSE MEDIATION THEORY

The essence of mediation theory is that some internal event in the organism occurs between, or mediates, an overt stimulus and an overt response. Early behavioristic theories did not include such mediation—they were simply S-R theories. Robert S. Woodworth (1938) emphasized that organismic events should be taken into account, and he proposed the expanded formula S-O-R. There is little doubt that there are such mediators. The question is, how do they work?

Classically Conditioned Responses as Mediators (r_g Theory)

On the basis of the Crespi data, Hull (1952) added an intervening variable for incentive motivation to his system, symbolized as the letter K. The new formulation then read:

$$E = H \times D \times K$$

The antecedent conditions for manipulating the strength of K were the amount, quality, and delay of reinforcement (longer delays produce weaker incentive motivation).

Kenneth Spence (1956) suggested that K itself might be derived from Hull's concept of the **fractional anticipatory goal response**. Hull (1933a) had used this concept to account for purpose and expectation in terms of stimulus-response theory. We may describe the mechanism as follows: When an animal is rewarded with food after making a response, it *eats* the food. Eating is a **goal response** (R_G), and occurs only when there is food. When the animal eats, however, there are also **fractional goal responses** (r_g's) that may occur with or without food, such as small chewing or licking movements, or salivation. These fractional responses are considered to be conditionable just like other responses. For example, maze stimuli preceding the goal response (R_g, eating) could become conditioned stimuli for the fractional goal responses (r_g's.). The r_g's could then be aroused by stimuli in the maze *before* the animal reaches the goal box and the food. Similarly, *internal stimuli* (drive stimuli accompanying deprivation) could also be conditioned to the r_g's. After a number of training trials, the maze cues and internal stimuli could arouse conditioned r_g's at the *beginning* of the maze. The r_g's have become anticipatory goal responses, occurring in anticipation of the goal response of eating.

The anticipatory r_g's become motivational by virtue of the fact that they have **stimulus consequences**. Any response that we can "feel," for example, has stimulus consequences that feed information about the response back to the brain. The stimulus consequences of r_g's are s_g's. The s_g's in turn can become conditioned to overt responses. We then have the following sequence:

$$S \rightarrow (r_g\text{--}s_g) \rightarrow R,$$

or more specifically

$$(S) \text{ Apparatus Cues} \rightarrow (r_{salivation}\text{--}s_{salivation}) \rightarrow (R) \text{ Running to Food}$$

where S is an environmental stimulus, R is an overt response, and r_g--s_g is the anticipatory goal response and its stimulus. In this instance we are assuming that salivation is the r_g. S is a maze stimulus, and R is running in the maze, then r_g--s_g is conditioned to running in the maze. The stronger the r_g, the stronger the s_g, and hence the stronger the effect of s_g on behavior.

Applications of r_g theory to incentive phenomena. The r_g--s_g mechanism accounts for some of the major incentive phenomena as follows.

Incentive shifts. When rewards are shifted from small to large, there is a larger R_G, and therefore a larger r_g--s_g. Since r_g--s_g was already conditioned to responses in earlier training, a sudden increase in the intensity of r_g--s_g could produce a sudden "improvement" in behavior.

Latent learning. Incentive motivation could not develop in nonrewarded animals because there is no R_G (eating) and hence no r_g--s_g related to eating. When food is introduced, r_g--s_g occurs and can be conditioned to various maze stimuli, and performance improves. Hull (1931) explained the elimination of maze errors in these terms. He argued that r_g-s_g is most strongly conditioned to responses that get the animal to the reward faster. Correct responses get the animal to food faster than do incorrect responses. Therefore, correct responses are more strongly conditioned to r_g-s_g than are errors, and the errors are eliminated.

Latent extinction.   During training, the r_g-s_g is conditioned to goal-box stimuli, as well as other apparatus cues. When the animal is placed in the goal box without food, r_g is aroused but not reinforced by the presentation of food. Therefore, r_g extinguishes to the goal box cues and to some extent to other apparatus cues. During regular extinction that follows, these animals stop running sooner because stimulation for running (r_g-s_g) has already been partly extinguished.

Quality of reward.   A more-preferred reward arouses a strong R_G and hence a strong r_g-s_g. The stronger r_g-s_g stimulates more vigorous performance.

Theoretical problems with r_g theory.   This line of theory is beset with serious problems both in theory and in related evidence.

- **Theoretical ambiguity about what r_g-s_g does.** The apparent simplicity of the r_g-s_g mechanism is somewhat deceptive. On the one hand, s_g might facilitate responses because it is an **intense stimulus** and therefore has drive properties like any other intense stimulus. This characteristic would quite nicely account for situations in which **vigor** of response is measured, such as running speeds in the Crespi experiment. On the other hand, s_g might facilitate responding because it is just another stimulus to which responses are conditioned. This is an associative (learning) interpretation, however, not a motivational interpretation.

  Some theorists have argued for the associative interpretation for incentive effects on the grounds that there is little direct evidence that positive incentives are internally arousing. However, it has been found that both rodents and human infants have higher heart rates when drinking higher-concentration sucrose solutions (Beck and Meinrath, 1978; Lippsitt, Reilly, Butcher, & Greenwood, 1976). This finding is in line with a motivational interpretation. After considerable experience with the solutions, however, the animals in the Beck and Meinrath research did not show differential heart rate to higher concentrations even though the animals continued to press a lever more for higher concentrations. It may be that the "motivational" (arousal) effect dropped out, leaving only an associative effect for the different incentives.

- The r_g mechanism is supposed to account for very rapid behavioral changes, following incentive shifts, for example. Supposedly this concept negates a learning interpretation for the shift effects. But since r_g itself is learned (conditioned), how can it be evidence against learning? One answer is that r_g's are learned more rapidly than other responses. Within the context of Hull-Spence theory, this is a weak answer. The best that can be said is that there are two kinds of learning, incentive learning and response learning (Logan, 1968; Young, 1959).

Empirical problems with r_g theory. R_g theory had a seductive appeal for S-R theorists because it seemed to account for incentive motivation while still relying on observable stimuli and responses rather than on mentalistic concepts. The main empirical problem is the lack of tangible evidence that such fractional responses either occur or are conditioned to environmental cues. Two specific problems are illustrative:

- Vigor of consummatory and instrumental responses should be highly correlated if strong r_g's stimulate stronger responses. Such correlations are small at best, however (e.g., Black, 1969; Robbins, 1969).
- The r_g's should be conditioned to start-box cues if the theory is to account for the well-documented fact that with "better" rewards animals are much quicker to leave the start box of the apparatus. This conditioning simply has not been observed (Sheffield, 1966).

In conclusion, r_g theory was ingenious but seems inadequate because of lack of evidence that r_g's either occur or function as the theory says. We are therefore pushed back into the central nervous system. In fairness to Hull's theory, however, his addition of incentive motivation to his basic formulation ($E = H \times D \times K$) does not require the r_g-s_g formulation. The r_g interpretation was added by other theorists.

TOLMAN'S PURPOSIVE BEHAVIORISM

E. C. Tolman championed the incentive view before it was generally popular among American psychologists. We examine Tolman in some detail because of his historical priority, the generality of his concepts to many areas of psychology, and the contemporary usage of many of his concepts.

For many years Tolman and his followers at the University of California were the primary antagonists to the Hull and Spence groups at Yale and Iowa. The active controversy often clouded the fact that Tolman's approach was every bit as behavioral as Hull's. In fact, Tolman (1938) introduced intervening variables into psychological theory, insisting on the importance of tying theoretical concepts to observable events. However, Tolman was concerned with what he called **molar behavior,** not with specific "muscle twitches." Thus, if an animal turns to the right in a maze, "turning right" is the response. It makes little difference which exact muscles do the job. Tolman was a strict behaviorist, but not an S-R theorist in the sense of believing that learning consists of S-R connections, as Hull believed (Tolman, 1932; 1938).

Tolman, like Hull, was concerned with **purposive,** or **goal-oriented** behavior, but Tolman's theoretical concepts had more mentalistic-sounding names than Hull's, and these names grated on the ears of S-R theorists. For example, two of Tolman's early concepts were **expectancy** and **demand.** An expectancy is the anticipation that under given circumstances, a particular behavior will lead to a particular outcome. Going to the store will result in getting food. A demand is the motivation *for* food. Whereas Hull had an S-R concept of learning (habit is the association between an S and an R), Tolman had an S_1R_1-S_2 theory. S_1R_1-S_2 is an expectancy that in this situation (S1) if I make a particular response (R1), then some event (S2) will follow. For Tolman, the *S*'s were environmental places or events, and behavior was simply how a person or an animal got from one place or event to another.

Demand, the motivation component, is related to the outcome of behavior. I might **expect** that if I go to the refrigerator there will be a piece of chicken to eat, but unless I have a **demand** for food, I will not go to the refrigerator, and the chicken will have no value for me. Demands are determined jointly by internal and external events, such as being hungry and liking the taste of chicken. There are demands both for and against events. We have demands *for* desirable outcomes and *against* aversive outcomes.

Cognition in Tolman's Theorizing

Tolman believed that expectancies were central brain processes, not requiring overt responses. What distinguished his approach from the "mentalistic" approach of some earlier psychologists was that he worked only with observable events and *inferred* underlying expectancies and demands from his objective observations. Studying laboratory rats, he showed that it was possible to discuss purpose, foresight, and expectation, using objective events as the primary data rather than depending on human introspective reports. Purpose, foresight, and expectation were intervening variables. Much contemporary cognitive research takes a similar approach.

Cognitive maps. If a person or an animal has expectancies about "getting from here to there," the person or animal must have some notion about where "here" and "there" are. Tolman (1948) argued that animals have environmental "maps" in their heads, which they follow. He likened the brain to a map room, in contrast to the telephone switchboard analogy used by S-R theorists. The telephone analogy says that incoming sensory information is automatically switched to outgoing motor lines, with little information processing in the head. Modern information processing theorists emphasize to a much greater extent what goes on in the head. The cognitive map concept has turned out to be important to modern **environmental psychologists,** who are much concerned with how people perceive, learn about, and locomote through their environments.

Tolman's Systematic Theory

We shall use Tolman's own final presentation of his theory (1959) for our remaining discussion, but MacCorquodale and Meehl (1954) provided the most detailed analysis of his system ever available.

The following formula is modified from Tolman (1959, p. 134), but neither his symbolism nor the entire formula is used.

$$\text{Performance Tendency} = f\binom{\text{Expectancy, Drive Stimulation,}}{\text{Incentive Valence}}$$

Each of these is an intervening variable that has a rough equivalent in Hull's theory. The basic concepts in the two theories are compared in Table 8–1. Tolman defines his concepts differently, of course, and attributes different characteristics to them.

Performance tendency is the strength of the tendency for an expectancy S_1R_1–S_2 to be expressed in behavior, just as sEr in Hull's theory is the tendency for sHr to be expressed in behavior. Performance tendency is a function of many variables, as is sEr.

Expectancies were of two kinds. Tolman considered the S_1R_1–S_2 expectancy more important, since it involves behavior. The second kind was an S_1–S_2 expectancy, that one stimulus event will follow from another. This is the general form of classical conditioning, where S_1 and S_2 correspond to CS and UCS.

A concept closely related to expectancy is **means-end-readiness,** or **belief.** When a particular S_1 occurs, there is "released" an expectancy that a particular response will lead to a particular outcome, or that an S_2 will follow. A belief is more enduring than an expectancy. Thus, I may have an enduring **belief** that with certain temperature and cloud conditions, it will snow. But only when these conditions actually prevail will I **expect** it to snow.

Incentive valence refers to the **value** of S_2 to the organism. If a tasty food has a high positive value now, I expect it to have a high value in the future. This *expected value* is the *valence* of the food. Valences are learned from experiences with objects of particular values. The combination of drive stimulation and valence is what Tolman had earlier called **demand.**

Evidence for Tolman's system.   Tolman (1959) saw evidence for the correctness of his theory throughout all experiments in instrumental learning. His approach simply looks at everything differently from an S-R approach like Hull's. Problems that nagged at Hull's theory simply dissipated in Tolman's.

TABLE 8–1.   Comparisons of concepts in Hull's and Tolman's theories.

CONCEPTS	HULL	TOLMAN
Performance	Excitatory potential	Performance tendency
Learning	Habit (H)	Expectancy
Internal state	Drive (D)	Drive stimulation
Incentive motivation	Incentive (K)	Incentive valence

Such issues as drive reduction reinforcement and the possibility of whether learning can take place without responding simply did not bother Tolman. He also believed that his view was more likely to be a fruitful approach to human cognition than was S-R theory, a view vindicated in modern cognitive theory.

CENTRAL STATE THEORIES

Central state theories assume that **incentive motivation is a central brain process directly aroused by positive or negative stimuli.** Some stimuli produce *unconditioned* arousal of a central process, whereas other stimuli can be *conditioned* to evoke arousal. Young's hedonic theory was one such theory. These theories agree that instrumental responses are learned by a process that is different from that involved in incentive learning. Incentive stimuli provide the motivation for selecting one response over another but do not reinforce behavior in the sense of an "S-R gluing" process, as discussed earlier.

Central Motive State

Going into the 1940s, a number of theorists began to suggest that central brain processes were important for motivation. As we saw earlier, Morgan (1943; 1959) proposed that a variety of circumstances lead to a central nervous system change that he called the **central motive state** (CMS). Its theoretical importance at that time was that it departed from the prevailing views that drive states are aroused by peripheral events: hunger by stomach contractions, thirst by a dry mouth, and so on.

Bindra (e.g., 1969; 1978) further elaborated the CMS concept, saying that the CMS is generated by the interactions of "neural representations of organismic state and incentive object" (1969, p. 12). A "reinforcing" stimulus does not produce any specific response selection (by "reinforcing" one response and not others). Instead, it arouses a motivational state that influences *many* subsequent behaviors. The CMS alters the value of incentive objects and changes the likelihood of appropriate approach and consummatory responses. Stimuli associated with incentives control approach responses, but not consummatory responses (for example, food controls eating responses, not stimuli paired with food).

An experiment by Bindra and Palfai (1967) illustrates the theory. Thirsty rats had the click of a metronome paired with water while they were confined in a small cage where locomotor activity was impossible. The animals were then divided into three groups (low, medium, and high water deprivation) and, in a larger cage, the activities of locomotion, sitting, and grooming were recorded before, while, and after the metronome was turned on. Locomotion was generally higher under medium or high deprivation, but presence of the metronome, the conditioned stimulus signaling water, further increased perambulation only under medium or high deprivation.

Two-Process Learning Theory

Two-process learning theory concerns the *interaction between classical and instrumental conditioning*. It asserts that Pavlovian conditioned emotional responses (CRs) can *directly* affect instrumental behavior (Bolles & Moot, 1972; Mowrer, 1960; Rescorla & Solomon, 1967). Consider the situation in which an animal runs down a runway to get food. The animal's running is reinforced when it obtains food (instrumental conditioning), but the various runway cues come to predict that the food is on the way (classical conditioning). The cues to food (CSs) arouse a conditioned response (CR), which is a central emotional state labeled "hope." If the animal anticipated getting shocked, the CS would arouse an emotional state commonly called "fear." A signal that a positive event is to be terminated arouses an aversive state of "disappointment," and a signal that an aversive event is about to end arouses a positive state of "relief." These are summarized in Table 8–2.[1] The interesting facts are how these emotional states affect other behaviors.

Transfer of control experiments. The essential idea here is that even if classical and instrumental conditioning have occurred in different situations, the classical conditioning can affect instrumental responding because *both classical and instrumental conditioning involve hedonic arousal*. Classical conditioning involves hedonic arousal by the UCS, and instrumental conditioning involves hedonic arousal by the reward (or punishment). If the classically conditioned hedonic arousal has the *same valence* (positive or negative) as the instrumental outcome, the classical CR will facilitate the instrumental response. Conversely, if the emotional response has the opposite valence, then it should inhibit the instrumental response. Emotional states are mutually excitatory if of the same valence, but mutually inhibitory if of the opposite valence. Hope quells fear, and fear dashes hope. Table 8–3 summarizes eight different combinations of unconditioned stimuli and type of reinforcement.

---

[1]This terminology was first used by Mowrer, but to help keep the historical record straight, Mowrer himself never thought of hope as anticipation of a positive event. Rather, he considered hope to be the anticipatory reduction of fear. Mowrer never considered pleasure as a source of motivation separate from fear. In one of Mowrer's 1950s seminars on "revised two-factor theory" in which the author participated, Mowrer was challenged on this point by a student who asked why fear was necessary in order to explain all approach behaviors. Mowrer's answer was enlightening, both theoretically and clinically. "Why," he replied, "I wouldn't know what to do without my fear." Mowrer's personal history of depression is well known.

TABLE 8–2.   Emotional states involved in classical conditioning.

CONDITIONED STIMULUS	UNCONDITIONED STIMULUS	
	APPETITIVE (FOOD)	AVERSIVE (SHOCK)
CS+	Hope	Fear
CS–	Disappointment	Relief

What Table 8–3 shows us is that appetitive (approach) responses are facilitated by appetitive CRs and inhibited by aversive CRs. Conversely, escape and avoidance responses are facilitated by aversive CRs and inhibited by appetitive CRs. Thus, for example, when a stimulus previously paired with food is presented while a dog is responding with regularity for food in a Skinner box, presentation of the food signal will increase the rate of responding (#3 in Table 8–3). If a signal for shock is presented, however, responding will decrease (#4). If an animal is engaged in an avoidance response, however, the food signal reduces the rate of responding (#6) (Rescorla & Lolordo, 1965; Bolles & Moot, 1972). Conversely, if a signal associated with shock is presented while the subject is making avoidance responses, the rate of responding increases.

Extension to moods.   Two-process learning theory has interesting extensions to human research on moods. Two-process theory would predict that positive or negative moods should have different effects according to the kind of stimulus situation in which they occur. For example, if a particular behavior (e.g., altruistic) is normally rewarded, a positive mood will facilitate such behavior in the future because it has the same valence as that produced when the behavior was rewarded. More generally, the theory would predict the following:

- Positive mood should facilitate rewarded behavior.
- Negative mood should facilitate avoidance or escape.

TABLE 8–3.   Effects of classically conditioned stimuli on rate of instrumental behavior.

CONDITIONED STIMULI	AVERSIVE UCS		APPETITIVE UCS	
	CS + (FEAR)	CS – (RELIEF)	CS + (HOPE)	CS – (DISAPPOINTMENT)
Instrumental Schedule				
Positive reinforcement	1. **Decrease**	2. Increase	3. **Increase**	4. **Decrease**
Negative reinforcement	5. **Increase**	6. **Decrease**	7. **Decrease**	8. Increase

Note: **Boldface** means that there is good evidence for the prediction.

- Positive mood should inhibit avoidance or escape.
- Negative mood should inhibit rewarded behavior.

Two-process learning theory can serve as a guide for laying out many predictions about the effects of mood that might not otherwise be obvious. Learning theory also raises certain questions that might not be so readily asked otherwise. For example, the effects of positive mood on prosocial behavior seem well founded, but the learning theorist would ask how the prosocial behavior got established in the first place. The answer would tell us the stimulus conditions under which prosocial behavior is more or less likely to occur in the future. Clearly, prosocial behavior occurs without a prior mood-altering intervention, and all that good mood can do is to change the likelihood of the behavior. Two-process theory suggests that good mood should automatically increase the likelihood of behavior previously rewarded in similar circumstances.

Lang's Affective Modulation Theory

Startle response. The presentation of a sudden intense stimulus to any mammal produces a startle response, which is a whole-body set of reflexive movements. The most studied component of these movements is the eye blink, which can be measured by placing recording electrodes on the **orbicularis occuli** muscle under the eye. This muscle contracts within one-tenth of a second of startle stimulus onset and "drives" the eye blink. The most commonly used startle stimulus is a brief burst of high frequency noise at about 95db, but a visual stimulus, such as an electronic flash or an electrical stimulus, is also effective. Psychologists have traditionally studied the eye-blink reflex in the context of classical conditioning, but Lang, Bradley, and Cuthbert (1989) take a different approach to emotion and reflex responses that has some similarities to two-process theory. Basically, the theory shows how internal states (positive or negative) affect a wide range of responses, including reflex responses.

Startle modification. Lang's approach defines emotions as **action dispositions,** founded on brain states that organize behavior along a basic approach-avoidance dimension. All affects are assumed to be associated with behavioral tendencies to approach (movement toward, attachment, and consummatory behaviors) or to escape, avoid, or defend against aversive stimuli. The whole motor system is "tuned" in terms of the central affects. Thus reflexes associated with appetitive behaviors (e.g., the salivary reflex to food) would be enhanced if activated when a subject was already in a positive emotional state. Conversely, the startle reflex to a sudden loud noise is viewed as an aversive or defensive response and would be enhanced if the organism was already in a negative emotional state when the startle was elicited.

The reflex eye blink has been studied extensively in humans and found to be modifiable by positive and negative toned "foreground" stimuli, such as hedonically positive or negative pictures. In the context of aversive foreground stimuli (e.g., while looking at unpleasant slides), the defensive startle reflex would be enhanced, but with pleasant slides would be inhibited. These predictions, much like those that two-process theory would make, have been repeatedly confirmed. The startle response has been reduced or augmented with pleasant versus unpleasant slides, pleasant versus unpleasant mental imagery, and pleasant versus unpleasant music. Figure 8–6 shows some illustrative results.

These results are important for several reasons. One is that unlike other measures of emotional arousal, the startle probe is sensitive to the valence of the foreground stimuli. That is, it can be either greater or lesser than with emotionally charged stimuli than with neutral stimuli. The galvanic skin response, in contrast, just goes up in the presence either of pleasant or of unpleasant stimuli. Indeed, the startle response appears to be one of the most reliable physiological measures of affective valence (positive or negative) presently available. The only other reliable indicators seem to be records of facial muscle activity during positive and negative emotional experiences. Furthermore, pleasant and unpleasant mental imagery and music have also been widely used to induce positive and negative moods in experimental set-

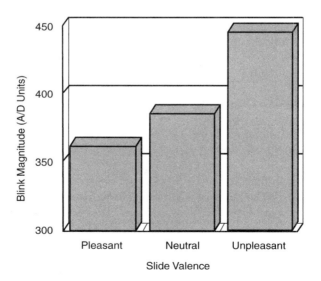

FIGURE 8–6. Magnitude of startle response to auditory stimulus while watching slides with different valences. Unpleasant slides increase the startle magnitude as compared with control (neutral), and pleasant slides reduce startle magnitude. See text for details. (Source: Vrana, S. R., Spence, E. L., & Lang, P. J. 1988. Copyright 1988 by the American Psychological Association. Used by permission.)

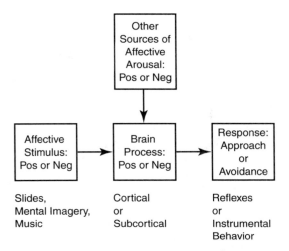

FIGURE 8–7. Model for affective modification of stimulus input. A stimulus arouses positive or negative affective brain process and leads to approach or avoidance behavior. Independent sources of affective arousal can either enhance or inhibit the stimulus-aroused emotional process and thereby facilitate or impede behavior, even though never previously associated with that behavior.

tings. In effect, then, many experiments with the startle probe have had subjects induced into positive or negative moods, and the startle probe is then presented during the mood. Pleasant moods inhibit the startle, and negative moods facilitate it. Again, the predictions are much like those of two-process theory.

We then have the model shown in Figure 8–7, which summarizes both two-process theory and affective modulation theory.

YOUNG'S EXPERIMENTAL HEDONISM

Paul Thomas Young has been referred to by one noted psychologist as the "solitary hedonist" (Bolles, 1991) Throughout the entire era when Hull's drive theory was at its peak of popularity, Young continued to work independently on his hedonic theory. Even within his own department at the University of Illinois, however, none of a highly renowned faculty took his work very seriously. As the flaws of drive theory were gradually exposed, however, more and more psychologists did take notice of Young's work. This trend was particularly true among researchers in the areas of hunger, thirst, and taste. As we saw in Chapter Four, it has become increasingly apparent that organisms do not often seem to eat and drink just to restore homeostasis. Instead, they eat things they like. As one researcher put it, Young became "like a god" to a new generation of researchers. Young's research, primarily on taste prefer-ences in the rat, was insightful and carefully done, and his principles of hedo-nism were objective.

Young (1959, 1966, 1968) set forth a system of principles of experimen-tal hedonism. At the time of Young's major writings, little was known about the details of the neural systems underlying approach and avoidance, so he had little to say about them. Contemporary knowledge about brain structure, function, and chemicals provides more detailed elaboration of hedonic the-ory. Some of this was covered in Chapter Four. In this section, we outline Young's principles (last published thirty years ago) and update them with re-gard to more recent knowledge. This updating involves elaboration of his stated principles and the addition of some others that fall in the spirit of his approach.

Young began by assuming the existence of a hedonic continuum and the hedonic axiom, as was done in Chapter One. Young's principles were out-lined by him as empirical facts, not theoretical concepts.[2] Each was bolstered by specific experimental data, largely from taste studies with rats. There could be little challenge to the objectivity of his data, although others some-times tried to reinterpret his results in terms of drive theory (e.g., Mowrer, 1960). Young repeatedly pointed out that the animals in his experiments were never deprived of food and water, were sleek and healthy, and eagerly sought the tasty solutions he provided them in his experiments. Where was the homeostatic imbalance or any source of drive?

Principles of Experimental Hedonism

1. **Stimulation has affective as well as sensory consequences.** As the con-centrations of salt solutions are increased, recording of neural activity in the taste system shows continuously increasing rates of neural firing. Animals' preferences for such solutions also increase, up to a point, but then decline. Sensory consequences (neural firing rates) and affective consequences (pref-erence) are therefore different processes.

2. **Organisms orient toward stimuli that produce positive affective arousal and away from those that produce negative affective arousal.** Animals or people approach good-tasting foods, for example, and avoid excessively bitter or sour foods. The definitions of desire and aversion developed in Chapter One apply here.

3. **Motives develop out of affective arousals.** Young distinguished be-tween what he called Primary and Conditioned Affective Arousals. Primary arousal, positive or negative, is directly produced by a stimulus (e.g., taste of

---

[2]In correspondence with Professor Young, shortly before his death in 1978, I pointed out that I had defined motivation in terms of the concepts of desire and aversion in the first edition of this book (Beck, 1978). He replied that it was interesting that I considered them concepts, be-cause he considered them empirical facts.

food in the mouth), and conditioned affective arousal is the anticipatory arousal produced by stimuli previously associated with primary arousal. Young uses the term **motive** to refer to the **anticipation** of future primary hedonic arousal. Motives take some amount of time (experience) to develop, so that behavior following initial exposure to a substance may not be an accurate index of the final level of motivation that substance provides.

Berridge's distinction between liking and wanting, which we saw in Chapter Four, seems to be very similar to Young's distinction between primary and conditioned affective arousals. Liking refers to the immediate experience of a stimulus, which may be pleasant or unpleasant. This is a primary affective arousal, associated with the endorphin system. Wanting is the motivation to approach a stimulus and is associated with the dopamine system. Also, wanting is conditioned to stimuli associated with the liked stimulus, which appears to be Young's conditioned affective arousal. Berridge's distinction is based on knowledge about brain function unavailable to Young.

4. **The strength of motives depends on the intensity, duration, frequency, and recency of previous affective arousals.** These parameters are generally the same as those involved in the establishment of classically conditioned stimuli or learned rewards (Wike, 1966). The more often primary affective arousals are associated with particular stimuli, the stronger are the conditioned affective arousals and motives to approach.

5. **Affective processes regulate behavior by influencing choice.** Organisms approach stimuli that produce positive affective arousal and withdraw from those that produce negative affective arousal.

6. **Behavior is organized according to the basic hedonic principle of maximizing positive and minimizing negative hedonic arousal.** This is the hedonic axiom of Chapter One.

7. **The affective value of stimuli is modified by internal states.** Young (1966, p. 60) defined palatability as "the hedonic characteristic of a food dependent upon stimulation of the head receptors by a foodstuff and/or its surroundings when other determinants are held constant." What we suggest is that hedonic quality (rather than just "acceptability") changes with deprivation and satiation, for example. One of the reasons that Young worked with nondeprived animals was that they are more discriminating in their food preferences. Deprivation increases the acceptability of more foods. It does not do so equally for all substances, however, and it is this interaction that, we think, reflects changing affective value rather than just general acceptance of any food.

8. **Positive and negative hedonic stimuli combine.** In a series of experiments in Young's laboratory at the University of Illinois, different combinations of taste stimuli were compared. For example, Kappauf, Burright, and DeMarco (1963) compared preference for combinations of sucrose and quinine with different fixed concentrations of sucrose (1, 4, 16, or 40 percent). A specific experimental question would then be as follows: How much su-

crose do you have to add to a particular amount of quinine to make a combination equal in preference to 4 percent sucrose? Obviously, the more quinine you have, the more sucrose you have to add to make the combination equivalent to 4 percent plain sucrose. The most interesting aspect of such data is that the addition of quinine *enhances* sucrose preferences. For example, when .003 percent concentration of quinine is added to 16 percent sucrose, it is equal in taste preference to 40 percent plain sucrose. Valenstein, Kakelewski, and Cox (1967) also showed that a combination of sucrose and saccharin was consumed in much greater quantity than a simple combination of the two would predict.

9. **Approach behaviors are enhanced by hedonically positive states and inhibited by negative ones.** Conversely, withdrawal or avoidance behaviors are enhanced by hedonically negative states and inhibited by positive. We have added this principle on the basis of theoretical and empirical developments that have occurred since Young's death. Most notably, the development of two-process learning theory and its related research is critical. For example, organisms are more likely to engage in previously rewarded behaviors when in a positive hedonic state but are inhibited by a negative state.

10. **Positive or negative hedonic states automatically arouse their opposite states.** This is the addition of the Solomon-Corbit opponent process theory to Young's postulates, not one of his own statements. Opponent process theory was introduced very near the end of Young's career, and he never had opportunity to incorporate it into his principles. Clearly, however, it should be among them.

Solomon and Corbit's (1974) new principle of hedonism has subsequently been used to account for a wide range of behaviors. Previous theories assumed that particular stimulus could arouse either a pleasant or an unpleasant state, but not both. Similarly, a stimulus associated with positive or negative arousal would also come to produce the same type of arousal (positive or negative) according to classical conditioning principles. Opponent process theory says that there is a **nonassociative effect of experience on hedonic processes** such that a situation that arouses positive (or negative) affect also automatically leads to the opposite affect (Solomon & Corbit, 1974; Solomon, 1980).

Consider this illustration. A woman discovers a lump in her breast and is immediately fearful of cancer. She makes an appointment with her doctor but frets about it until he reports that the tumor is benign. Her strong anxiety is then replaced by great elation. An opposite example would be the sudden loss of something or someone that has brought us great pleasure; we are then depressed. The crux of the opponent process theory, then, is this: **Every affective state, whether pleasurable or aversive, tends to arouse the opponent state.** Extreme fear arouses the opponent process, which is pleasure, and when the source of the fear is removed, the pleasure process becomes dominant and lingers for a while. At any given time, the affective experience of the individual is the algebraic sum of the two processes. The process directly aroused by a stimulus situation is dominant while the situation lasts, but the opponent process becomes dominant when the primary stimulus for emotional arousal is changed.

The initial affective process aroused is called an **A-state,** whether positive or negative. The opponent process is automatically aroused by the A-state is called the **B-state.** It is said that the B-state is a **slave** to the A-state. The person who does something very frightening, such as jumping out of an airplane, initially has a fearful A-state aroused, and the joyful B-state automatically follows. The A-state is dominant until the person lands safely on the ground and the danger is over. The joyful B-state is then very strong for a while.

The A-state and B-state are the **underlying affective processes.** They combine to produce a single positive or negative affective state, the **manifest affect,** which is what we experience. If the A-state and B-state were exactly equal, there would be a neutral effect. The strength of the B-state increases with the number of times that the A-state has occurred. This characteristic means that the B-state has an increasing neutralizing effect on the manifest affect. Stronger arousal of the A-state is necessary just to get the same degree of pleasure from the positive A-state that was initially obtained. If the stimuli arousing the A-state are removed, the B-state remains. This effect explains why the theory applies so well to drug addiction. A tolerance builds up (the increasing B-state counteracting the A-state), and so there are withdrawal symptoms when the drug is not taken (the B-state occurs). Figures 8–8 and 8–9 illustrate the temporal course of events with the A-state and B-state as a function of the number of times the A-state has occurred.

In summary, Young's principles are still solid, but the addition of some new principles uncovered since his last writings on the topic make them even more potent. Much of what we know about the facts of motivation can be encompassed within his framework.

INCENTIVES AND FANTASY

Commitments and Concerns

The final approach to incentives that we review was developed by Eric Klinger (1975; 1977). Klinger's basic concepts are **commitment to goals** and **current concerns** about achieving goals. Current concerns are considered to persist over time, even when there are numerous interruptions in striving for a particular goal. For example, as I write, I am interrupted by the telephone and then return to the computer. Then there is a meeting, a different concern, after which I again resume writing. This behavior persists intermittently

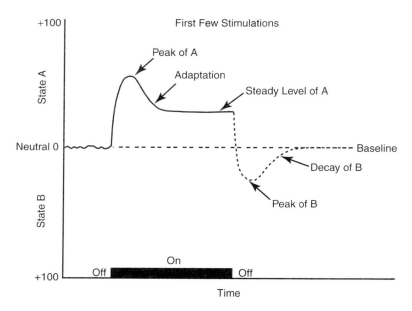

FIGURE 8–8. The manifest temporal dynamics generated by the opponent process system during the first few stimulations. (The five features of the affective response are labeled.) The curves are the algebraic summation of the opponent processes. Note the high level of A relative to B. (Solomon & Corbit, 1974, p. 128. Copyright © 1974 by the American Psychological Association. Reprinted by permission.)

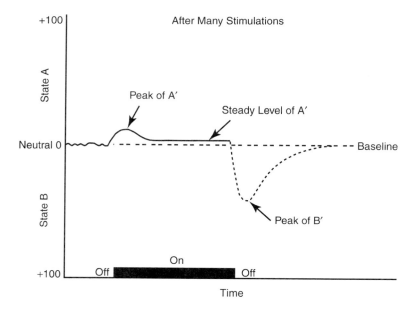

FIGURE 8–9. The manifest temporal dynamics generated by the opponent process system after many repeated stimulations. (The major features of the modified patterns are labeled.) Compared with the curves in Figure 8–8, note the low level of A and the relatively high level of B.

for perhaps a year or two, at which time I become **disengaged** from the particular writing goal and have a different set of concerns. Once there is commitment to a goal, Klinger (1975, p. 4) suggests, there are at least four kinds of consequences.

1. **Actions.** The anticipation of obtaining incentives (commitment to goals) is vital in instigating, directing, and maintaining action.
2. **Content of thoughts and dreams.** A person is most likely to think or dream about something while it is related to one of the person's current concerns. These thoughts, dreams, or fantasies may involve achievement, power, affiliation, fear, sex, aggression, and so on. If you know what someone's current concerns are, you can likely predict rather well that person's fantasy life.
3. **Sensitization to goal-related cues.** People are more sensitive to stimuli associated with themselves and their current concerns. For example, people hear their own names when they do not detect other stimuli.
4. **Perceptual qualities of goal-related stimuli.** Stimuli related to current concerns are more prominent or noticeable.

Disengagement from Incentives

The value of incentives and commitment to them is, of course, not permanently fixed. The value of a graduate degree may change with the economy or the availability of jobs for people with that degree, and our commitment stops after a goal has been achieved. But what happens when commitment to a goal ends?

First, even if a goal is achieved, we may feel let down, and perhaps somewhat depressed, unless we have other ongoing concerns and incentives. Indeed, this is said to be a major problem with retirement.

Second, more devastating circumstances may come when we fail to achieve the incentive that we are committed to. Klinger sees five phases of the incentive disengagement cycle.

1. There is **invigoration,** a stronger attempt to achieve the goal. This happens in frustrating situations (see Chapter Eight).
2. Second, there may be **aggressive** behavior, as when aggression follows frustration.
3. Third, there is a **downswing into depression,** a giving up when an important incentive, or incentives, remain(s) unachieved.
4. Fourth, there is **depression,** characterized by apathy toward a great many normally attractive incentives.
5. Fifth, there is **recovery,** which seems to occur commonly after **reactive** depressions (those related to specific life events).

One may find other concepts to explain this cycle. The opponent process theory, for example, can explain many of these phenomena, such as depression following the pursuit of exhilarating goals. Our concern at this point, however, is to emphasize the role of cognitive processes, including fantasy and perception, in relation to incentive motivation. The kind of cognitive theory that Tolman applied to rats can be considerably expanded when applied to humans.

SUMMARY

1. The concept of **incentive motivation** is based on the idea that rewards do not necessarily affect specific responses. Rather, the **anticipation** of rewards arouses whatever responses might be effective in obtaining the rewards.

2. A variety of experiments shows that **changes** in incentive value, increasing or decreasing, quickly produce appropriate changes in performance even though not associated with particular responses. In latent learning experiments, animals show no sign of learning a maze after many trials if they are not rewarded for running accurately, but they suddenly perform very well when reward is introduced.

3. Hull added incentive motivation (K) to his theory, so that his expanded formula read: $E = H \times D \times K$. Spence proposed that incentive motivation grows out of **goal responses**. A fraction of the eating response, for example, can be conditioned. This fractional goal response, $r_g\text{--}s_g$, is conditioned to environmental cues and has drivelike properties. The $r_g\text{--}s_g$ mechanism then has incentive motivational properties. The theory accounted for many facts of incentive motivation, but there is little evidence for the existence of such responses.

4. **Tolman's purposive behaviorism** is much like the approach we took in defining motivation in Chapter One. In Tolman's system, organisms are said to learn **expectancies** about incentives. Incentives have positive or negative **valence,** which is their motivational power to attract or repel organisms.

5. **Central motive state** (CMS) theory proposes that incentive stimuli, in conjunction with internal states, produce a central motivational state that influences many behaviors. Since the central state may persist for some time, it seems likely to have a neurochemical or hormonal basis.

6. **Two-process learning theory** concerns the interaction between classical and instrumental conditioning. It asserts that Pavlovian conditioned emotional responses (CRs) can directly affect instrumental behavior. For example, a tone associated with food can stimulate lever pressing for food even though the tone was never previously associated with lever pressing.

7. Two-process theory postulates four kinds of conditioned emotions, called **hope, fear, relief,** and **disappointment.** These are aroused by stimuli associated with the presentation of a positive stimulus (hope) or negative stimulus (fear) or the removal of a negative stimulus (relief) or positive stimulus (disappointment).

8. Lang's **affective modulation theory** is a central theory that has a number of similarities to two-process theory. It says that behavior, including reflexes, would be augmented or diminished if aroused in the context of an ongoing emotion. For example, negative emotional arousal would enhance the defensive startle reflex that occurs when a sudden loud stimulus is presented. Conversely, an ongoing positive emotion would inhibit the startle reflex.

9. Young's **experimental hedonism** says that organisms act to "maximize delight and minimize distress" but also has a set of specific principles for how affective arousals are learned and how they function.

10. Solomon and Corbit's **opponent-process theory** postulates that every positive or negative emotion automatically arouses an opponent emotional process. Thus, a stimulus arousing a positive emotion indirectly also arouses a negative emotion, and vice-versa. The opponent process emotion persists for a time after the original emotion declines and is dominant. Thus, depression may follow the loss of a loved one.

11. **Human incentives** are also related to **fantasy.** Klinger has proposed that we have **commitment to goals** (incentives) and that this commitment is reflected in our **current concerns** that persist over time. Current concerns are shown in fantasy, dreams, and thoughts.

CHAPTER NINE

Escape, Fear, Avoidance, and Punishment

——●——

In the previous two chapters we looked at behavioral outcomes that are desirable and sought. In this chapter we look at aversive events that are escaped, feared, avoided, and punishing.

INSTRUMENTAL ESCAPE LEARNING

Instrumental escape learning refers to any response that is reinforced by a reduction of aversive stimulation. An obvious escape response is running away. It is also escape if we end an unpleasant conversation even though we do not physically leave the situation. Although electric shock has been the most-used aversive stimulus in the animal laboratory, cold water, loud noises, and bright lights are also effective aversive stimuli. The most commonly used aversive stimuli with human research now are loud noises and threats of various kinds, such as threat of shock or some kind of negative personal evaluation.

Variables Affecting Animal Escape Learning

Amount of reinforcement. Amount of reinforcement is just as important in escape learning as it is in reward learning. Campbell and Kraeling (1953) had rats run in a straight alley to escape from 200, 300, or 400 volts of grid shock to a lower level of shock. Early in training, higher shock produced faster running, although all groups eventually converged to the same level of rapid escape. It was also found that early running speed depended on the *proportion* of shock intensity that was reduced, not the absolute amount of reduction in the goal box. For example, a 100-volt reduction was very effective if the change was from 100 volts to no shock, but less effective going from 200 to 100 volts, and still less effective going from 400 to 300 volts. The data were an approximation to Weber's law in perception:[1] Amount of reinforcement depends on percentage change, not just absolute change (Campbell & Masterton, 1969).

There is an even more important implication of these data from a motivational point of view. If animals are running faster from 400 volts to 100 volts than from 400 volts to 300 volts, then they must be *anticipating* the amount of shock reduction to come. If their running speed were determined only by the shock in the alleyway, they would have run at the same speed. Thus there seems to be an incentive effect with escape learning.

"Drive" and "incentive" effects have been studied in some detail with rats swimming to escape cold water (Woods, Davidson, & Peters, 1964). Drive was manipulated by varying temperature in a "runway" tank, and incentive was manipulated by adjusting temperature in the "goal" tank. Goal tank tem-

---

[1]According to Weber's law, the minimum amount of stimulus intensity change, in any stimulus dimension, is some constant proportion of the reference stimulus. For example, if the value of the proportion were .10, it would take a change from 10 to 11, or from 100 to 110, to be noticed.

perature turned out to affect swimming speed much more than runway tank temperature, further lending emphasis to the incentive aspects of escape learning. Other investigators have reported similar results (Stavely, 1966).

Delay of reinforcement.   Immediacy of reinforcement after a response is also important for escape learning. Fowler and Trapold (1962) had rats run from a 250-volt runway shock to a goal box where shock termination was delayed between 0 and 16 seconds for different groups. Running speed was faster with shorter delays of reinforcement (Figure 9–1). When shock levels are high, however, long delays are less detrimental to running than short delays (Bell, Noah, & Davis, 1965).

Incentive shifts. The pièce de résistance for an incentive interpretation for shock reduction reinforcement would be to show incentive shift effects like those found by Crespi for amount of food. Bower, Fowler, and Trapold (1959) did exactly this. They had rats run from a 250-volt alleyway shock to a goal box where shocks of 200, 150, or 50 volts were continued for 20 seconds after the animal had entered. The animals escaped faster when there was greater shock reduction and when the goal-box shock level was adjusted upward or downward the animals rapidly adjusted their running speeds accordingly. The results (Figure 9–2) look very much like those found in the positive incentive shift experiments discussed in Chapter Eight. Woods (1967) reported similar results when goal-tank water temperatures were lowered or raised for escape from a cold-water alley tank.

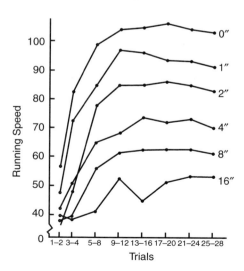

FIGURE 9–1.   Running speed (100/time in seconds) as a function of the delay (in seconds) of shock termination in the goal box. (From Fowler, & Trapold, 1962, p. 465. Copyright © 1962 by the American Psychological Association. Reprinted by permission.)

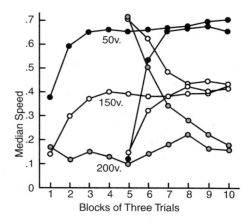

FIGURE 9–2. Group median speed (1/time in seconds) as a function of goal-shock voltage. (From Bower, Fowler, & Trapold, 1959, p. 483. Copyright © 1959 by the American Psychological Association. Reprinted by permission.)

Unlike results with positive incentive shifts, however, the elation and depression effects were not found with escape. For example, animals going from a lower amount of reinforcement to a larger one did not run faster than animals continuously on larger reinforcement. In general, contrast effects have not been reported for escape learning.

Theories for Escape Learning

Drive theory. For a long time, drive theory seemed such an obvious interpretation for escape learning that alternatives were not seriously considered. An intense stimulus produces drive; the more intense the stimulus, the harder an animal will work to escape, and the greater is the reinforcement when the animal does escape. Thus, shock produces a drive, and shock reduction is the reinforcer. In the experiments just reviewed, however, in which animals ran to different amounts of shock in the goal box, the animals were clearly responding to **anticipated** shock levels in the goal box, as well as to the shock they encountered in the alleyway. At the very least, then, we need to supplement a drive interpretation with an incentive interpretation.

Incentive theory. **Hope** and **relaxation** are similar concepts to explain escape learning in incentive terms (Mowrer, 1960; Denny, 1971). When a painful stimulus ends, there is an *internal change* that can be conditioned to stimuli preceding the end of the stimulus. We shall simply denote this conditioned change as **anticipatory relaxation.** When an animal finds its way to the shock-free goal box, the "goal response" is relaxation, and the conditioned component of the goal response is anticipatory relaxation. Anticipatory relaxation is stronger as the animal gets closer to the goal box, and the animal makes responses that increasingly maximize anticipatory relaxation until it obtains "real" relaxation.

What is the role of shock intensity in an incentive theory of escape learning? Just as deprivation increases the incentive value of food, intense stimulation should increase the amount of anticipatory relaxation: the stronger the shock, the greater the anticipatory relaxation. Without shock, there should be no anticipatory relaxation, so that "poor" performance should result. Increasing or decreasing either alley shock or goal shock changes the amount of anticipated relaxation, and behavior changes appropriately: the incentive shift effect.

An exception to the previous predictions can occur as a result of fear learning. The alleyway stimuli could become conditioned stimuli for fear because they have been paired with shock. Even without shock in the alleyway, the animal would be fearful, and anticipatory relaxation would still occur as long as this fear persists. The fearful subject would continue to escape at least until the fear extinguished to a low enough level that anticipatory relaxation was too weak an incentive to arouse behavior.

CONDITIONED AVERSION: FEAR

Historical Background and Clinical Importance

In 1920, Watson and Raynor reported their classic experiment with Little Albert. An eleven-month-old child, Albert, was initially exposed to a series of objects, including a white rat, a rabbit, a dog, a monkey, masks with and without hair, cotton, wool, and so on. "Manipulation was the most usual reaction called out. At no time did this infant ever show fear in any situation" (Watson & Rayner, 1920, p. 2). Albert was then shown a white rat while a steel bar behind him was struck with a hammer. The rat was the conditioned stimulus (CS), and the loud noise the unconditioned stimulus (UCS). After seven trials that were spread over several days, "the instant the rat was shown the baby began to cry" and to try to get away. Five days later Albert was fearful not only of the rat but also of the rabbit, the dog, a seal-fur coat, and a Santa Claus mask. A fear response had been classically conditioned and generalized to other stimuli. Watson pointed out that the results demonstrated that not all anxiety was related to sex or unconscious conflicts, as Freud had claimed.

Shortly thereafter, another of Watson's students, Mary Cover Jones (1924), studied the elimination of children's preexisting fears rather than fears experimentally induced in the laboratory. Describing her most effective technique for doing this, she said, "By the method of direct conditioning, we associated the fear object with a craving object and replaced the fear by a positive response" (p. 390). Food, for example, was presented along with the feared object. In contemporary terminology, this process is **counterconditioning.**

In these two experiments, the foundations of contemporary behavior therapy could well have been laid, and we might have expected an outpouring of further research of this type. Instead, the Freudians held the day, and it remained for Mowrer (1939), fifteen years later, to focus on the problem of aversive conditioning and neurosis in a way that was to have real impact on psychological research and theory. We have already seen part of this development in the study of learned drives (Chapter Six), but the study of fear has not been limited to drive theory. Because of the clinical importance of fear, anxiety, and phobias (intense fears of specific objects), fear has been approached from many different directions.

Unlearned Sources of Fear

Genetic/Maturational. Intense or pain-producing stimuli are obvious sources of fear, but not the only ones (Hebb, 1946; Gray, 1971). A common phobia, for example, is fear of snakes. Jones and Jones (1928) reported that young city children who had never encountered snakes in the wild did not have a fear of snakes but that a large percentage of adults reared in the city did have this fear. Hebb concluded that snake phobia is the result of maturation and does not require specific experience with snakes for its occurrence.

Not only are snake phobias common in adults, but they are also a common theme in visions produced by hallucinogenic drugs throughout the world. It is possible that fear of snakes (as well as insects, lizards, and other "creepy, crawly" animals) is a kind of species-specific reaction left over from a period of evolutionary development when it was adaptive to avoid snakes without having to be bitten first. Ancestors who ran first and "asked questions later" may have lived to love more frequently than those who waited around for attack. Such genetically determined fear might indeed account for the evil attributed to the serpent and for the worldwide use of dragon and serpent symbols in mythology. One line of research concerned with such genetic bias has studied the relative ease of aversive conditioning to pictures of snakes or lizards, as compared with pictures of bunnies and flowers (Öhman, 1986). If shock or loud noise are used as the unconditioned stimulus, galvanic skin responses conditioned to such animal stimuli are more resistant to extinction than are responses to neutral stimuli.

Hebb claimed that "psychologically" there is little in common among the many events that arouse fear. For example, loud noises arouse fear, but so does darkness. We may conjecture, however, that these are all stimulus conditions in which emotional responses have enhanced survival (Gray, 1971). Loud noises call for attention and make us wary, and we may need to be more attentive in the dark because we do not have the use of vision, our major source of information about the environment.

Hebb (1946) also noted that fears could occur because of direct changes to the nervous system. For example, people affected by the nutrition-deficit disease pellagra show psychotic fears that disappear on treatment with nicotinic acid. The individual may recall the fears that he or she had while sick and be at a loss to explain them. Hormones can also produce unexpected emotional responsiveness. For example, pregnant women or women getting injections of estrogens may inexplicably break into tears. Such responses disappear after the pregnancy is completed or hormone treatment is discontinued.

Fear of the unfamiliar.   At about three months of age, human infants begin to make positive responses to people by smiling and cooing. But at six months, they often show a strong negative reaction towards strangers (or even towards people to whom they have previously shown positive responses, such as grandparents). Hebb (1946) suggested that this reaction is based on experience but not on classical conditioning. Rather, the child becomes familiar with certain people, and therefore when an unfamiliar face appears, the child is afraid. This kind of fear involves the violation of an expectation. As an example of such an expectancy violation with an adult, the author was startled one morning when he got off the elevator at his accustomed floor, and the hallway was not there! It took a few troubled seconds to realize that earlier that morning, physical-plant employees had placed a number of tall metal cabinets in front of the elevator door, where they blocked off all the familiar signs of the hallway. Had this been the first trip ever to this floor, there would have been no startle, since the author would have had no expectation about what the hall should look like when the elevator door opened.

Emotional Conditioning

Fear can be readily conditioned in the general manner described by Watson and Raynor, but more subtle factors than those indicated in that experiment are involved. Recall that according to the contingency theory of conditioning, a stimulus becomes an effective CS if it reliably and uniquely predicts the occurrence of some other stimulus, the UCS. The theory does not say that an organism has to be consciously aware of such a relationship, but there is good evidence with human subjects that often this may be the case. For example, Fuhrer and Baer (1965) presented one stimulus as a CS+ (followed by shock) to human subjects and a different stimulus as CS– (not followed by shock). This process is a **differential conditioning** paradigm, which controls for such factors as sensitization to all stimuli as a result of a UCS being presented. If the response being measured is elicited more strongly by CS+ than by CS–, there is evidence of conditioning. In the Fuhrer and Baer experiment, differential conditioning of the galvanic skin response occurred only with those subjects who reported that the CS+ meant that shock was coming on. If they were not aware of this relationship, differential conditioning did not occur. Other experiments have reported similar results. Recent research is beginning to report conditioning without awareness more reliably under certain procedures, however.

Preattentive Conditioning

Backward masking. **Preattentive** refers to stimulus processing that goes on in our brain without our being aware of the stimulus. If a word, such as *dog*, is briefly flashed on a computer screen (for about 40 milliseconds), a human subject can readily identify the word. But if the word is presented and immediately followed by a string of Xs overlaying the screen position where the word appeared, the subject reports that no word was presented, that she saw nothing. This **backward masking procedure** is a way of studying preattentive processing; the procedure is illustrated in Figure 9–3. Obviously, the word got into the brain, since without the backward masking, it could be identified. The question then is this: Does such a masked word have any influence on thinking or behavior?

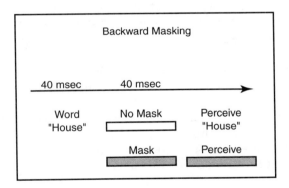

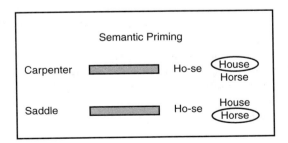

FIGURE 9–3. Backward masking (upper): A 40-msec stimulus is recognizable by itself, but if followed by a masking stimulus (cross-hatched bar), it is not consciously recognizable. Semantic priming (lower): A backward-masked stimulus that is not consciously visible can still affect behavior by "priming" responses. See text for details.

Semantic priming. To determine whether a backward-masked word has an effect on us, we turn to another research technique called **semantic priming.** If we have seen or heard a particular word, phrase, or sentence, we are primed to make a certain response. Suppose that you are shown the word CARPENTER, and then to make a complete word, you are asked to fill in the blank space in HO_SE. You would be primed to complete the word HOUSE. On the other hand, if you were shown the word SADDLE and asked to fill in the blank, you would probably complete the word HORSE. The question then is, Would semantic priming work with a backward masked stimulus? Would completion of HO_SE be different depending on whether CARPENTER or SADDLE was presented with a backward mask? If the response bias in favor of HORSE or HOUSE is about the same with masked words as it is with clearly visible words, then we would have strong evidence that unconscious perception has a predictable effect on conscious processes; in fact, the results do show this. In general, laboratory evidence indicates that stimuli that are at or below the threshold for identification can influence other thoughts. Recall, also, the Murphy and Zajonc experiments (1993) described in Chapter Two. They presented pictures of happy versus angry faces for 4 msec, followed immediately by Chinese ideographs. Although subjects could not recognize the faces presented so rapidly, they nevertheless made more positive ratings for the ideographs preceded by the happy faces than by the angry faces.

Conditioning. Arne Öhman and his colleagues then asked whether a backward-masked CS+ would evoke a conditioned GSR response? That is, would a conditioned response occur to a stimulus of which a subject is not consciously aware (e.g., Öhman, 1986; Esteves, Parra, Dimberg, & Öhman, 1994). Their general procedure is outlined in Figure 9–4. Subjects were first trained with the differential conditioning procedure just described, where neither CS+ nor CS– was masked. The subjects were then tested when both CS+ and CS– were masked. The results indicate that the backward-masked CS+ evoked the GSR but that the backward-masked CS– did not do so. At a level below conscious awareness, it appears that subjects were able to tell the difference between CS+ and CS–, responding with a larger GSR to CS+. This experiment and similar ones from other laboratories lead to the tentative conclusion that a conditioned emotional response can be evoked without the subject's being conscious of the conditioned stimulus. Some authors believe that these effects may be limited to stimuli that are genetically prepared to be fearful (e.g., snakes, spiders, angry faces), but other authors doubt this is the case (e.g., Kirsch & Boucsein, 1997).

Phobias

Phobias are intense, irrational fears of specific stimuli, such as a fear of high places, open or closed spaces, flying, or such objects as snakes or insects. Phobias are resistant to change and may have such debilitating effects as

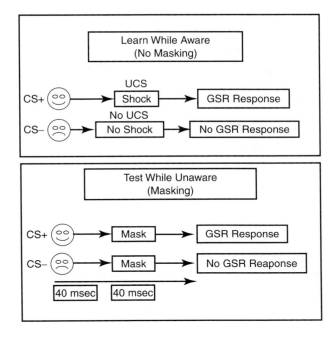

FIGURE 9–4. Ohman's backward masking paradigm for classical aversive conditioning. In the learning phase, one facial stimulus (CS+) is paired with shock, but the other (CS–) is not. There is a greater GSR response to the CS+ than the CS–. In testing, CS+ and CS– are presented but immediately followed by a masking stimulus so that the subject does not consciously recognize them. Nevertheless, the subject shows a greater GSR response to the CS+ than to the CS–, indicating that at some preattentive (unconscious) level, the two stimuli were recognized and distinguished.

keeping a person from going outside or always having to avoid animals. According to classical psychoanalytic theory, a phobia is nonspecific anxiety attached to some specific object. Anxiety is vague and difficult to deal with, whereas a phobia can be dealt with, for example, by avoiding the situation that arouses the phobia. The psychoanalytic treatment would be to try to find the underlying conflict, or source of anxiety, leading to the phobia and then to reduce that anxiety.

Behavior theorists have taken a different approach to the origin of most phobias, arguing that they are acquired through classical conditioning (Wolpe & Rachman, 1960; McNally, 1987). An important question, however, is whether phobias presented to clinicians by their patients really are the same kinds of fear as those established by laboratory conditioning. Seligman (1971) pointed out that phobias differ from conventional conditioned fears in that they (1) are acquired very quickly, (2) persist in spite of the patient's "objective knowledge" that the phobic object is harmless, (3) relate to objects (such as animals) that rarely pose a threat in modern life, and finally, (4) are resistant to extinction by normal Pavlovian procedures.

Seligman's **preparedness** theory (Seligman, 1970; 1971) maintains that organisms are "prepared" or "predisposed" to learn associations that have had survival value in past millennia but that are no longer appropriate. The common phobias of snakes, lizards, spiders, insects, and the like represent stimuli whose forms are supposedly readily conditionable to humans. McNally (1987) concludes that there is not a great deal of empirical support for the preparedness theory of phobias. Some experiments have shown faster GSR conditioning with "phobic" stimuli as CSs than to such neutral stimuli as triangles (e.g., see Öhman, 1986), but many experiments have not done so. The best evidence for preparedness theory is that extinction of the GSR conditioned to such prepared phobic stimuli as snakes is consistently slower than extinction to neutral stimuli. Upon examination, however, the difference in laboratory research is a mere handful of trials. Evidence for other aspects of preparedness theory and phobias is ambiguous at best.

Modifying Fears

Several approaches to modifying fears (or phobias) have been utilized in **behavior therapy,** the application of learning principles to therapeutic problems.

Extinction.   One treatment, called **systematic desensitization,** is to present a phobic stimulus repeatedly to a patient, showing that it has no ill effects and, hopefully, producing extinction. This treatment is often done in conjunction with a **fear hierarchy,** gradually presenting a client with stimuli that are progressively more similar to the phobic stimuli. When the client's fear of the generalized stimulus has extinguished, another stimulus more like the phobic stimulus is presented until fear of that stimulus extinguishes, and so on. For example, the word *snake* may be presented first, followed in progression by a picture of a snake, a model of a snake, a real snake at a distance, and finally a real snake to be touched and held. This kind of treatment has been found to be quite effective (Rimm & Masters, 1979).

Counterconditioning.   A phobic stimulus, which arouses a fearful response, is presented in conjunction with a stimulus that arouses an incompatible response. For example, a phobic stimulus might be presented along with food that arouses a pleasant response, so that the phobic stimulus becomes associated with the food. This result has also been reported for pleasant music (Eifert, Craill, Carey, & O'Connor, 1988). It is also common practice to do extinction in conjunction with relaxation exercises, the relaxation presumably being incompatible with fear-related tension.

Flooding.   Flooding refers to presenting repeatedly or intensely a fear-arousing stimulus to a client. Thus a person with a snake phobia might be "bombarded" with pictures of snakes. Fear responses may extinguish when no harm follows the phobic stimuli.

Cognitive changes. Foa and Kozak (1986) argue that emotional changes, such as reduction of phobic responses, result from exposure to emotional stimuli because of changed meanings of the phobic stimuli. The therapeutic tactic then is (1) to activate the fear by facing the client with those stimuli/situations that arouse fear, and (2) while the fear is still aroused, to incorporate information about a stimulus that is incompatible with the fear-arousing elements. The phobic stimuli may be imagined by the client or be real stimuli. Just presenting a phobic stimulus repeatedly may not in itself be sufficient to produce change (because adequate new information may not be conveyed), and just giving new information may be inadequate (if the fear is not aroused at the time). The new information may be both cognitive (such as a different interpretation of the stimulus that arouses the fear) and emotional (fear-reducing, pleasure-arousing) at the same time.

AVOIDANCE LEARNING

Most of us tend not to stick metal objects into electrical outlets or to walk indiscriminately in front of speeding automobiles. We are careful to avoid dangerous or threatening activities, including unpleasant social situations. Such avoidance behavior can be debilitating, and because of its clinical importance, avoidance learning has been studied intensely in animals.

Laboratory Avoidance

If we put a rat into a grid-floor apparatus and sound a buzzer, the animal will make little noticeable response. If we electrify the grid sufficiently five seconds later, however, the response is immediate. The rat may jump about and will probably urinate or defecate, all strong signs of emotional arousal. In a few seconds the animal crosses the midline of the box to the other side, where there is no shock. The animal has **escaped** the shock. We repeat the buzzer-shock sequence a number of times, with a minute delay after the animal has successfully responded. The escape response becomes swift and precise.

After about thirty trials or so, however, something new happens. The animal crosses the midline of the box in less than five seconds and therefore does not get shocked. It has made its first **avoidance** response. On an increasing percentage of trials, the animal responds before the shock comes on, thus becoming a proficient avoider. Figure 9–5 illustrates the performance of a single animal during the course of avoidance training. Two important elements seem to be involved in this situation: (1) The animal learns to become afraid when the buzzer sounds, and (2) the animal learns to run to the other

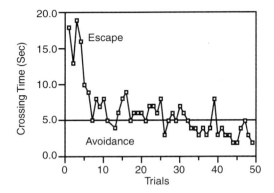

FIGURE 9–5. The course of avoidance learning. A 5-second signal forewarns the animal of impending shock. Early in learning, the animal escapes from shock, taking more than 5-seconds to make the appropriate response. Later, it avoids shock by responding in less than 5-seconds after the signal is presented.

side of the box before it gets shocked. These events have been quantified in a number of experiments (e.g., Hoffman & Fleshler, 1962).

Many factors determine just how fast an animal learns to avoid and how proficient it becomes, but a basic question has always been, *What keeps the animal avoiding?* Fear conditioning seems to be involved, but if the animal successfully avoids getting shocked, why doesn't the fear extinguish and the animal stop avoiding? Yet dogs in such a situation have been found to keep on avoiding for literally hundreds of trials without getting shocked; it was the experimenters who wore down, not the dogs (Solomon & Wynne, 1954). This is not to say that extinction never occurs, only that under some experimental conditions, it can take a very long time.

Interpretations of Avoidance Behavior

The most popular interpretation of active avoidance has been two-factor learning theory. The two factors are (1) **classical conditioning** of fear to the CS as a result of shock coming on after a buzzer sounds, and (2) **instrumental conditioning** of the escape and avoidance behaviors. A two-process theory seems to be demanded because neither classical nor instrumental conditioning alone provide adequate explanation of avoidance (Mowrer, 1960; Rescorla & Solomon, 1967). Let us see why.

Avoidance is not just classical conditioning. Brogden, Lipman, and Culler (1938) showed why classical conditioning could not account for avoidance. Placing guinea pigs in a revolving cage, they used a buzzer as the CS, and shock as the UCS. For a classical conditioning group, the buzzer was always followed by shock. The shock typically evoked running. For an avoidance conditioning group, however, shock was delivered only if an animal failed to run when the buzzer sounded. According to Pavlovian conditioning principles, the classical conditioning group should have run more reliably when the buzzer sounded. In fact, however, this group's best performance (Figure 9–6) was only about 50 percent. The avoidance group, on the other hand, quickly learned to run on every trial when the buzzer sounded. The reason for the poor performance by the classical conditioning group was clarified by Sheffield (1948). The animals in that condition are sometimes *already moving* when the shock comes on. The shock is *punishment for their moving,* therefore they run inconsistently. The death knell to the classical conditioning interpretation was sounded in an experiment by Mowrer and Lamoreaux (1946). They trained rats to *run* to escape shock and to *jump off the floor* to avoid shock in the same situation. The escape and avoidance responses were very different, and the avoidance response was not even the same as the unconditioned response to shock. Classical conditioning of the avoidance response was thus ruled out, but the animals nevertheless learned the problem without difficulty.

Avoidance is not just instrumental conditioning. The inadequacy of the instrumental conditioning explanation is brought out in the question, What is the reinforcer if the animal is successfully avoiding the shock? It cannot be shock reduction, since the animal is not getting shocked. We can postulate that fear reduction is the reinforcement, but then we would also have to postulate that fear had been conditioned. This seems to be the case and so leads us back to the two-factor theory of avoidance.

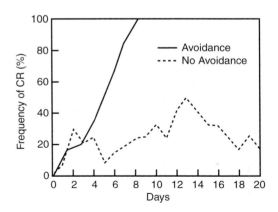

FIGURE 9–6. Learning curves showing the performance of animals for whom the response to the CS was not followed by shock (avoidance) and those for which the CS was always followed by shock (no avoidance). These results show that avoidance learning is not just classical conditioning. (From Brogden, Lipman, & Culler, 1938, p. 110. Reprinted by permission of The University of Illinois Press.).

Two-factor interpretation of avoidance.   According to two-factor theory, an animal first learns to become afraid of the buzzer through classical conditioning (buzzer paired with shock). Simultaneously, the animal learns to escape from shock. The animal then transfers the running responses from the shock stimulus to the fear stimulus. This transfer can occur because the shock aroused both fear and pain in earlier training, and thus the fear also was a stimulus for running at that time. The animal is reinforced on successful avoidance trials because the fear-arousing buzzer is turned off when the avoidance response is made. The fear in this case functions as both a drive and a cue, and fear reduction is the reinforcer. This theory solves many problems, but questions have been raised about the role of fear and the CS. All available evidence would indicate that avoidance learning does not seem to occur without some measurable amount of fear (Mineka, 1979). Beyond this, the evidence on the role of fear is much less certain. If the role of fear is questionable, then any theory requiring fear (such as two-factor theory) is equally in doubt.

Evidence for Fear in Avoidance

Cutting the sympathetic nervous system.   If we reduce the autonomic aspects of the fear response by cutting the sympathetic nervous system, we would expect avoidance behavior to be disrupted. The results of such an experiment (Solomon & Wynne, 1950) are more intriguing than this, however. If the operation is done *before* avoidance training, avoidance learning is much poorer. This result supports the theory that fear is important to avoidance. If the operation is performed after the animal has already learned to avoid, however, performance is not affected; the animals continue to avoid quite adequately. This finding suggests that once the behavior is well-learned, the CS may be only a **cue** to make the response and will not arouse fear the same way as it does in the early training. This is also supported by research showing that fear is greatly reduced in animals that have learned an avoidance response well. In this research, fear and avoidance responding are measured independently of each other (Hoffman & Fleshler, 1962). Solomon and Wynne (1954) proposed, however, that even slight amounts of fear might be aroused by the CS and that avoidance then occurs so quickly that a large amount of fear is not necessary. Since the fear response does not occur fully on such trials, it is "protected" from extinction. Cutting the sympathetic nervous system might greatly reduce fear, but not completely eliminate it, so the animals can still avoid. McAllister, McAllister, Scoles, and Hampton (1986) supported this proposal by showing that conditioned fear could motivate escape responding in animals for literally hundreds of trials after the last fear-conditioning trial had been completed. Their animals had twenty-five pairings of a light and an electric shock prior to any escape. The animals then had hurdle-jumping escape trials in response to light onset, without any further shock. Speed of escape increased sharply in the first 50 escape trials, then slowly declined over the next 250 trials, illustrated in Figure 9–7.

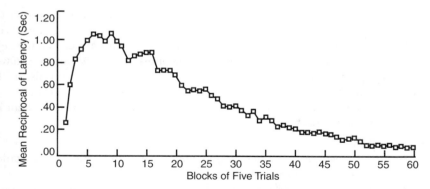

FIGURE 9–7. Mean speed of hurdle jumping over 60 blocks of five trials. (From McAllister, McAllister, Scoles, & Hampton, 1986. Reprinted by permission of the American Psychological Association.)

Curare experiments.   Suppose that we conditioned fear when no overt response could be made. If fear arousal facilitated avoidance at a later time, we would have to conclude that fear was important to avoidance. In such an experiment, dogs were first given standard avoidance training with a light as the CS. Then, while immobilized by the paralyzing drug curare, the animals were given differential classical conditioning with one tone as CS+ and a different tone as CS–, and shock as the UCS. Subsequently, these stimuli were presented as CSs in the avoidance apparatus. The animals made avoidance responses to CS+ but not to CS–. Since the fearful CS+ had never before been paired with the avoidance response, we conclude that the fear aroused by CS+ is important to avoidance (A. H. Black, Carlson, & Solomon, 1962; Solomon & Turner, 1962; Leaf, 1964). At the very least, fear seems to increase the likelihood of avoidance responding.

Tranquilizing drugs.   Tranquilizing drugs, such as Valium (diazepam) operate selectively to suppress avoidance and other fear-related behaviors, but they have relatively little effect on positively motivated behaviors (Ray, 1963; Gray, 1982a, b). This finding indicates that fear is involved in avoidance.

Dissociation of Fear and Avoidance

Fear declines during avoidance learning.   As avoidance learning progresses, animals become less fearful, as shown by various measures of fear (Mineka, 1979). This decline has something to do with *responding*, because control animals getting the same shocks (but not avoiding) do not show the fear decrement (Starr & Mineka, 1977). The importance of declining fear is the theoretical problem it poses, namely, Why does avoidance response improve at the same time that fear is declining? Furthermore, if fear were critical to avoidance, we would expect that during extinction of avoidance responding, fear would also decline. This response does not happen reliably, either: Animals that show significant extinction of avoidance responding have been shown to be just as fearful as animals without extinction trials at all (Kamin, Brimer, & Black, 1963). Why then do animals extinguish at all, if fear is not being reduced during extinction? Some insight on this problem is found with response prevention and flooding.

Response prevention and flooding techniques.   Two-factor theory would predict that if animals had extensive nonreinforced exposure to the CS, fear should extinguish, and avoidance responding should decline. Flooding refers to exposure to fear stimuli when there is no way for the subject to get rid of the stimuli. Page (1955) had animals learn an avoidance response, then prevented them from making this response when put into the apparatus without shock (response prevention). This response prevention facilitated subsequent regular extinction, as predicted. After extinction of avoidance responding, however, animals *refused to go back* into the avoidance apparatus when given the opportunity to do so. They were still afraid, even though they had stopped avoiding. The continued presence of fear in such situations was also shown in an experiment in which rats had been kept from responding and stopped avoiding, but their heart rates were still as elevated as when they were avoiding (Werboff, Duane, & Cohen, 1964). In short, when animals undergo extinction of an avoidance response, they are not necessarily free of fear.

Flooding results are further complicated by the fact that extinction of avoidance is facilitated by simply confining animals in either a novel or a fearful place that is not related to the place where avoidance learning occurred. Crawford (1977) suggested that this result was due to the emergence of a new response, **freezing.** Specifically, when an animal is fearful during the course of confinement, it may engage in what Bolles (1972) called a **species-specific defense reaction** (SSDR). For the rat, freezing would be a typical response in such a situation. When it is placed back into the avoidance apparatus, the animal might now show its new dominant response, freezing.

The Role of the CS in Avoidance

Fear is clearly involved in avoidance learning, but what exactly does the CS do? In the early avoidance learning experiments, the CS was left on until the animal made an avoidance response, at which time the CS was terminated. It was argued that onset of the CS aroused the avoidance response, which was then reinforced by turning off the fearful CS. With this experimental procedure, however, both shock avoidance and CS termination occurred and hence were confounded. Kamin (1956) tried to separate the effects of

CS termination and UCS avoidance, and concluded that both were important aspects of avoidance learning.

A variation on the theme that the CS arouses fear is one that we saw in Chapter Seven under the discussion of two-process theory. This is the notion of fear as **Pavlovian conditioned excitation** (Rescorla & Solomon, 1967). A CS signaling the onset of shock will increase the rate of avoidance responses even though it has never been specifically paired with those responses, as was shown in the curare experiments. The CS presumably increases fear. Conversely, a signal that indicates that no shock is forthcoming produces **conditioned inhibition** of fear, and reduces the rate of avoidance responding.

A third idea is that the CS for avoidance is a *discriminative stimulus,* or *cue,* for responding. Herrnstein (1969) argued that a CS is not necessary for avoidance learning. All the animal has to learn is that it gets shocked less often when it makes the avoidance response than when it does not make the response. The CS just tells the animal *when* to respond to keep down the amount of shock. If this view is correct, then it should be possible for an animal to learn avoidance *without* any external signal as a CS.

Unsignaled avoidance. An avoidance learning experiment without an external signal is conducted in the following manner (Sidman, 1966). Animals in a Skinner box with an electrifiable grid floor are given brief shocks (0.5 second) that cannot be escaped. These shocks are programmed according to two different schedules. If the animal never responds at all, it is automatically shocked every so often (say, 20 seconds). This is the **shock-shock interval.** If, however, the animal presses the lever *during* the shock-shock interval, the clock is reset, and the next shock is *postponed* for a set length of time (say, also, 20 seconds). This is the **response-shock interval.** If the animal were to press the lever just once every 20 seconds, it would never get shocked. But, pity to say, animals never respond quite this way.

If the shock-shock and response-shock intervals are equally long, there is great variability in how rapidly and well animals learn unsignaled avoidance. Figure 9–8 shows the performance of one "typical" learner and one "fast" learner. Note that the sessions are eight and six *hours* long, respectively, and that each blip represents a shock. Even the fast learner gets many, many more shocks than is typical for the shuttle box situation. The animals never seem to "wait out" an interval and respond just before the next shock is due. To the contrary, the animals are as likely to respond in the first half of the shock-shock interval as in the last half. By special training procedures, animals can be taught to wait until the last part of the shock-shock interval to respond, but they do not seem to learn this spontaneously. The animals' overall rate of responding can be manipulated by changing the length of the response-shock interval, however. If the response-shock interval is much shorter than the shock-shock interval, animals learn not to respond much more quickly. In effect, they are pun-

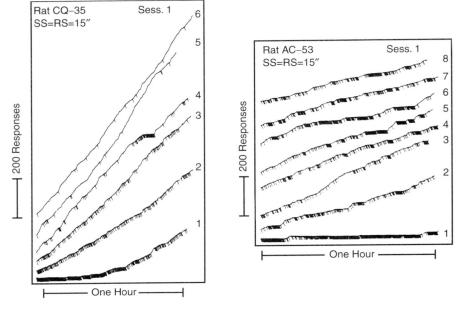

FIGURE 9–8. Cumulative records for two rats in their first sessions of Sidman avoidance learning, about six and eight hours long, respectively. To condense the figures, the records have been cut into segments of approximately one hour each and are numbered in temporal order. The oblique "pips" on the record indicate shocks. Rat CQ-35 learned more rapidly than did Rat AC-53, but CQ-35 had a few minutes in the fourth hour when it got a large number of shocks. (From Sidman, 1966, pp. 451, 452, 453. Reprinted by permission of Prentice Hall, Inc., Englewood Cliffs, New Jersey.)

ished for responding. Conversely, if the response-shock interval is much longer than the shock-shock interval, they learn to respond more readily.

Since there is no external CS in Sidman's situation, the importance of a CS in avoidance is questioned. It has been argued, however, that the CS for responding is an internal "stimulus trace" from the previous avoidance response (Anger, 1963; Mowrer, 1960). When the animal makes an avoidance response, there is strong feedback from the muscles, and this feedback gradually gets weaker after the response is made. A strong feedback trace is thus associated with no shock, because the animal is never shocked immediately after responding. As the trace weakens, however, shock becomes more likely, and *this weaker trace becomes a CS* for fear. Over the course of the response-shock interval, the fear builds up to a level where it triggers the animal to respond. This response is followed by fear reduction, and the whole cycle starts up again. In the Sidman situation, a Pavlovian conditioned fear CS (never previously associated with the avoidance response) increases the rate of Sidman avoidance responding, and a conditioned inhibitor will reduce the rate of responding. This finding indicates that fear is playing some role in unsignaled avoidance.

Cognitive Interpretations of Avoidance

At the time that research on avoidance learning was undertaken, the primary researchers were strongly behavioristic and wary of cognitive concepts. Therefore, they emphasized classical and instrumental conditioning. Quite early, however, Osgood (1950) proposed a cognitive interpretation based on Tolman's theory. Osgood said that the buzzer becomes a signal of shock and that the animals do whatever is required to avoid shock. A problem for cognitive theory is why avoidance should ever decline. Unless the animal fails to make the avoidance response, how will it find out that shock will not follow the buzzer? Osgood simply assumed that the *demand* against shock declines with successful avoidance. Occasionally, the animal will fail to respond in time to avoid shock. Then, either (1) it will get shocked, its expectation of shock will be reconfirmed, and it will start avoiding again; or (2) it will not get shocked (as with extinction), a new expectation of no-shock will be established, and avoidance will cease.

Seligman and Johnston (1973) proposed a cognitive theory of avoidance based on Irwin's (1971) theory of intentional behavior, as follows. At the peak of avoidance learning, an animal acquires two expectancies: (1) If it responds in a given time after CS onset, it will *not* get shocked; and (2) if it does not respond fast enough, it *will* get shocked. The animal prefers not getting shocked and therefore makes the avoidance response.

These cognitive interpretations may have a certain appeal, but neither of them has been fruitful and generated any research. Therefore, these theories have contributed little to our understanding of avoidance and are rarely referred to.

PUNISHMENT

Punishment takes such varied guises as physical pain or its threat, social sanctions, isolation, and withdrawal of privileges. All of these are supposed to suppress "undesirable" behavior. Events that are supposed to be punishing are often ineffective, however. Sometimes "punishment" increases the very behavior it is expected to eliminate and sometimes suppresses many different behaviors indiscriminately. Thus while it is true that "punishment suppresses behavior," our understanding of exactly what is involved requires more detailed study (Campbell & Church, 1969; Dunham, 1971).

Defining Punishment

Stimulus definition. According to a stimulus definition, punishment is the delivery of an aversive stimulus to an organism following a response. The organism is expected to suppress the response as a means of avoiding punishment. This behavior is sometimes referred to as **passive avoidance,** as compared with the active avoidance that we discussed earlier. This definition would require that in the study of punishment, we must use stimuli that are demonstrably aversive; otherwise, the definition cannot apply.

Response definition. A response definition of punishment says that punishment is the delivery of *any* stimulus that effectively suppresses the preceding behavior, whether or not the stimulus is demonstrably aversive otherwise. Such a stimulus could be punishing in some situations but not others. This explanaton does not define for us in advance whether a particular stimulus will be a punisher, but it does encourage us to look for effective punishers. For example, a retarded child who stuck out her tongue several times a minute was resistant to all kinds of attempted punishment until the therapist hit upon putting lemon juice on the child's tongue whenever she stuck it out. Doing this was an effective punisher; it suppressed the behavior. For the sake of consistency, we will hereafter assume a response definition of punishment unless otherwise indicated.

Suppressive Effects of Punishment

It is clear from much research and practical experience that *punishment does not eliminate behaviors.* Instead, it suppresses behaviors in certain situations. According to the **alternative response theory,** punished behaviors are less likely to occur because they have been replaced at least temporarily by other, alternative behaviors. Skinner (1938), in one of the earliest laboratory reports of punishment of free operant behavior (lever pressing), slapped a rat's paw when it touched the lever to get food. Lever pressing was suppressed for a while but came back because there was no other way the animal could get food. Estes and Skinner (1941) went on to show that even electric shock following a response suppressed lever pressing only temporarily, and for the same reason: The only way to get food was to press the lever. Dunham (1971) tested the alternative response hypothesis with Mongolian gerbils as subjects. Given the opportunity, isolated gerbils will spend most of their waking time doing just three things: shredding paper, eating food pellets, and drinking water. Each of these is easily measured (amount of paper pulled from a roll can be recorded automatically), so it is possible to get normal baseline measures for each and then to see how all the responses change when one of them is punished. As predicted by the alternative response theory, a punished response (any of the three) declined, but then one of the other alternative responses would increase.

Response Factors in Punishment

The nature of the response elicited by punishment is very important, since the elicited response may either **interfere with** or **facilitate** the punished response. We saw this outcome with the guinea pigs in avoidance learning. If an animal is punished while running, the automatic response is to stop. If an animal is punished while standing still, the response may be to run. In order to predict the effects of punishment, then, we have to know what response the punishment evokes. Fowler and Miller (1963) studied this by having animals run down a straight runway to get food. They found that when animals had their *hind paws* shocked just as they entered the goal box (thereby facilitating forward movement), they ran *faster*. On the other hand, animals that had their *forepaws* shocked as they entered the goal box (thereby facilitating backing up) ran *slower*. Shock by itself did not determine how the animals responded; the response elicited by the shock determined how they would respond.

Stimulus Factors in Punishment

Immediacy of punishment. If one has an effective punisher available, the single most basic rule for using it is that the punisher should follow an undesirable response as quickly as possible. The longer the delay between response and punishment, the less effective the punishment is. Figure 9–9 shows the results of an experiment in which punishment of lever pressing by

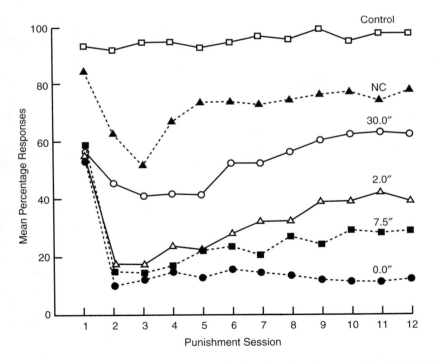

FIGURE 9–9. Mean percentages of responses as a function of sessions for groups with .0, 2.0, 7.5, 30.0 seconds delay of punishment, noncontingent shock, and unpunished control group. (Failure to press the lever within 10 seconds of stimulus onset was defined as a nonresponse.) (From Camp, Raymond, & Church, 1967, p. 121. Copyright © 1967 by the American Psychological Association. Reprinted by permission.)

electric shock was delayed from zero to thirty seconds (Camp, Raymond, & Church, 1967). The zero-delay group was most suppressed, and the thirty-second delay the least. Note also in Figure 9–9 that even a noncontingent punishment group (NC), which received shocks randomly, showed less suppression than the thirty-second-delay group.

What is meant to be response-contingent punishment may, because of bad timing, become either **noncontingent** or **stimulus-contingent.** By stimulus-contingent we mean that the punishment is associated with a particular stimulus (as in classical conditioning) rather than with a particular response. For example, instead of punishing a child immediately for some indiscretion, suppose a parent waits until the spouse comes home to have the spouse punish the child. In this case, the punishment may become stimulus-contingent. Instead of the bad behavior's being associated with the punishment, the punishing parent becomes associated with the punishment. The expected result would be fear of the parent but little suppression of the undesired behavior. With older children or adults, long delays between response and punishment may be mediated by verbal warning, such as discussing the behavior to be punished and the reason for punishment.

Effects of noncontingent punishment. A noncontingent punishment procedure called the **conditioned emotional response (CER)** procedure has been used to study punishment of free operant behavior. The punishing stimulus follows some signal, rather than a response, but such behavior as lever pressing is suppressed when the signal is turned on. The CER procedure has a number of different effects from those of response-contingent punishment, however (Hunt & Brady, 1955; Church, 1969). For example, the CER procedure suppresses many different behaviors, is slower to extinguish, and is harder to counter condition with positive reinforcement. And, as we have seen, even delayed response-contingent punishment is more effective in suppressing specific responses than is noncontingent punishment.

Stimulus intensity and adaptation. More intense punishing stimuli have greater suppressive effects (Azrin & Holz, 1966), and if the punishing stimulus is strong enough, the effects may be nearly irreversible. For example, cats that had received strong punishment for eating refused thereafter to eat in the experimental apparatus (Masserman, 1943). If experimental animals are gradually adapted to increasingly strong shocks, however, the suppressive effect is considerably weakened (Miller, 1960). This weakening is not due to simple sensory adaptation to the shocks, however. Control animals that were exposed to the same intensities of shock *outside* the primary experimental apparatus did not show the effects of this adaptation when they were inside the apparatus. The adaptation in some sense was "psychological." Possibly, when shock was increased gradually in the apparatus, the animals may have learned to cope with it by responding in particular ways. Increasing shock levels outside the apparatus would not have allowed this kind of learning. Therefore, the shock was more suppressive when the animals were introduced into the apparatus. This phenomenon may be related to the learned helplessness phenomenon, discussed in detail in Chapter Ten.

Potential Problems Using Punishment

Since punishment is used widely, although not necessarily wisely, it is worthwhile to point out some very specific general rules for effective use.

1. **Make sure that the punishment is associated with the undesirable behavior.** Punishment should be delivered promptly, whether in the form of a reprimand, a slap on the wrist, or withdrawal of privileges. This advice is especially true with small children or nonverbal organisms. With older children, one can make the association verbally after a delay, but it is better made immediately.

2. **Make sure that the punisher is punishing.** A slight word of discouragement that may stop one child from an activity may be completely ineffective with a different child. It may be necessary to work at finding what is punishing for a particular individual.

3. **The punishment should not contain concealed rewards.** For example, if a child is sent to his room as punishment, where he plays his stereo, watches TV, and phones his friends, the "punishment" is not likely to have much effect.

4. **Watch out for side effects of punishment.** Strong punishment may produce excessive emotional responses and/or escape behavior. These are minimized by careful response-contingent punishment, which is more effective and less disturbing than delayed or stimulus-contingent punishment.

5. **Reinforce alternative behaviors.** The role of punishment may be just to suppress undesirable behavior long enough for desirable behavior to occur and be rewarded. The problem is to change behavior, not just to deliver punishment. If desirable behaviors are rewarded at the same time that undesirable behaviors are punished, then the effects of punishment are likely to be more satisfactory. In fact, when alternative behaviors are rewarded, punishment may not be necessary. If a child gets hold of a dangerous kitchen utensil to play with, the child may be praised for giving the utensil to the parent, who is at the same time giving her a toy to play with. The child can learn alternative behavior without punishment.

SUMMARY

1. **Instrumental escape learning** refers to any situation in which responses are reinforced by reducing the level of aversive stimulation. Almost any intense stimulus is potentially aversive. Any response that removes the animal from the aversive situation is escape.

2. Speed of escape is determined by such variables as *amount* and *delay* of reinforcement. **Incentive shift effects,** varying amount of aversive stimulation reduction following escape, have been found, just as with reward learning.

3. Drive and drive reduction theory account for much escape learning but fail to account for the **anticipation** of the amount of stimulus reduction shown by animals in escape learning situations. The concept of **anticipatory relaxation,** an incentive point of view, does account for such anticipatory responses.

4. Fear, an aversive emotional state, may be aroused by intense or painful unconditioned stimuli, by such specific stimulus patterns as snakes or insects, or by unexpected events. Unlearned fearful responses to some stimuli might have evolved as an adaptive survival mechanism. Some fears are also related to direct changes in the nervous system, such as during illness.

5. Fear is readily **conditioned** in accordance with Pavlovian principles with either humans or animals. Human fear conditioning appears to be possible under limited conditions when subjects are not aware of the conditioned stimuli.

6. **Phobias** are intense fears of specific stimuli, which are quickly acquired, difficult to eliminate, and often unrelated to objects that pose a real threat. Treatments for the elimination of phobias have involved **extinction** and **counterconditioning** procedures. Intense exposure to feared stimuli ("flooding") has also been effective in reducing or eliminating phobias, as clients discover that their fears are unfounded.

7. **Avoidance behavior** consists of any response that prevents the occurrence of an anticipated aversive event. A major question is why animals or people continue avoiding, since they do not experience the aversive stimulus if they successfully avoid it.

8. The most widely used interpretation of avoidance is **two-factor learning theory.** This says that organisms first learn to be fearful in the situation according to **classical conditioning** principles and then learn to reduce fear according to **instrumental conditioning** principles. Neither process alone accounts for avoidance.

9. Fear is clearly important in the initial learning of avoidance responses but is less clearly involved in their long-term maintenance. Fear and avoidance become **dissociated** during the course of avoidance learning. Avoidance responses may also undergo extinction without any marked reduction in fear.

10. The CS for avoidance generally has been considered important because it arouses fear and because CS termination is reinforcing. Avoidance can be learned without any external stimulus to signal oncoming shock, however, and the CS may serve only as a cue to tell the organism when responding will prevent an aversive stimulus. In such situations, however, a fear stimulus from a completely different situation will increase the rate of avoidance responding.

11. **Punishment** involves the **inhibition** of responses by presenting aversive stimuli when such responses occur. As a practical matter, whatever stimuli suppress behavior may be considered punishers. Removal of some stimuli, such as withdrawing privileges, is also punishing.

12. **Response** factors are important in punishment, because a punisher may arouse responses that either **compete with** or **facilitate** a punished response. To be effective, punishment should arouse responses that compete with the punished response.

13. The **alternative response theory** says that punishment stimulates organisms to make some response other than the punished response, and this alternative response is reinforced.

14. **Stimulus** variables affecting power of punishment include **delay** between response and punishment, **intensity** of the punishment, and **adaptation** to the punishing stimulus.

15. Effective use of punishment involves making sure that (1) the punishment is associated with the undesirable behavior, (2) the punishing stimulus is in fact punishing, (3) the punishment contains no concealed rewards, (4) the side effects of punishment are not worse than the behavior being punished, and (5) alternative behaviors are reinforced.

CHAPTER TEN

Frustration, Anxiety, and Stress

——•——

FRUSTRATION

A student told me a story about a friend who was supposed to meet his wife at the airport before she left on a flight. He was delayed and arrived at the airport too late for the meeting. He thereupon beat in the hood of his rented car, and had to pay for the damage out of his pocket. This example indicates rather extremely what we commonly mean by frustration: negative emotion aroused when an anticipated desirable goal is not attained. Frustration is an important explanatory concept because it involves the arousal of aversive states when there is no prior aversive stimulus. Frustration grows out of positive expectations that are not fulfilled.

The Frustration/Problem Solving Situation

Figure 10–1 illustrates the situation in which frustration occurs. There is an organism striving to reach some goal but that is blocked from the goal by a barrier. Frustration is a form of emotional arousal that may occur in such situations. We can look at the situation from two different perspectives, however. On the one hand, we may focus on the frustration aspect of not achieving a goal and the effects of frustration on thought and behavior. On the other hand, we may focus on the problem aspect of trying to reach a blocked goal and on the way in which a person will go about trying to solve the problem. In addition, there may be attempts to regulate the amount of emotion that one experiences in such a situation. Such **coping** has two aspects, **emotion-focused** coping or **problem-focused** coping. Emotion-focused coping is concerned with controlling the level of emotion produced in the situation by dealing directly with the emotion. Problem-focused coping controls emotion by effectively working on problems and involves problem solving skills.

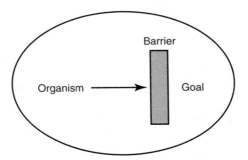

FIGURE 10–1. The frustration/problem solving situation. An organism striving to reach a goal is blocked by some kind of barrier. This obstruction produces frustration, a state of internal arousal that is aversive at high levels. At the same time, it is a situation in which problem-solving skills are needed to overcome or circumvent the barrier.

Definition of Frustration

In defining frustration as an intervening variable, there is blocking of a goal as an antecedent condition, and there is some response as a consequent condition. This situation is illustrated in Figure 10–2.

Failing to reach the airport on time was the antecedent condition for the woebegone spouse, and beating in the car hood was the consequent condition. Had we only seen him beating in the car hood, we would have no firm justification for saying he was frustrated. There might be many reasons for this behavior. Knowing that he beat the car hood just after he had failed to reach his goal, however, we *are* justified in inferring frustration. We must keep in mind, however, that responses to frustration are as variable as responses to any other aversive motivational condition, or drive. The responses depend on what an animal or a person has learned to do in such a situation, as well as upon the motivation (Brown & Farber, 1951). Earlier in this century, considerable effort was spent trying to find specific responses unique to frustration, but such responses have not been found (Lawson, 1965; Yates, 1962).

Problem-Solving Response versus Response to Frustration

We need to distinguish between the effects of the problem solving situation per se on behavior and the effects of induced frustration on behavior. The problem solving situation is the circumstance in which strong frustration might occur. Frustration is the **emotional** state that may occur when a goal is blocked. A particular behavior may simply be a problem solving behavior, without any strong emotional response being involved. For example, I once had a TV set that in its declining years had a very snowy screen. The temporary cure was to hit the set until the screen cleared. This cure usually worked and was cheaper than repairing the set. But how would a stranger interpret my behavior? She might infer that in response to frustration, I became emotional and lashed out angrily at the TV set. She would be interpreting my behavior in terms of an emotional state that she presumed to exist. My interpretation, however, is that in this situation I simply did what usually worked for me. I hit the set because hitting the set was reinforced by getting rid of the snow. Even vigorous behavior in an apparently frustrating situation does not

Antecedent Condition	Intervening Variable	Consequent Conditions
Blocking of Goal Behavior → (Failure to obtain expected goal)	Frustration →	Responses (a) Emotional/Motivational (b) Behavioral (c) Cognitive

FIGURE 10–2. Defining frustration as an intervening variable.

always mean strong frustration. It may simply mean that vigorous behavior is the learned response. To infer that there was necessarily frustration would be overinterpreting the situation.

Frustration as Drive

Nonreward frustration. Many years ago a psychologist named Tinklepaugh (1928) was training a monkey with standard monkey rewards—raisins and grapes—which the animal came to expect for its efforts. Tinklepaugh then substituted a piece of lettuce for the expected reward, and this substitution obviously disturbed the animal. This observation has three important elements. First, the monkey had to learn to **expect** a particular reward. Second, the monkey got something **less attractive** than expected. Third, the change in reward produced a disturbance in the animal's behavior, from which frustration is inferred. Presumably, Tinklepaugh's monkey felt something like an upset student who has gotten a C after expecting an A. The antecedent condition for **nonreward frustration** is like that just described, except that no expected reward at all is given. Amsel (1958; 1962; 1992) developed **nonreward frustration theory** in the context of Hull's drive theory.

Amsel's theory. Amsel assumed that nonreward frustration has the properties of aversive drive. Frustration energizes behavior, its onset is punishing, and its termination is reinforcing. For example, rats frustrated by nonreward (after having been rewarded) in an apparatus goal box subsequently learned to escape faster from the goal box than did nonfrustrated control animals (Daly, 1974). Speed of escape in such a situation is a function of variables that should produce greater frustration. Thus larger rewards produce more nonreward frustration than small rewards, and high concentration sucrose rewards produce more frustration than low concentration. In both cases, animals trained with the "better" reward learn to escape faster from the goal box when the reward is omitted than do animals trained with the lesser reward.

Frustration theory does not say that instrumental responses are necessary for frustration, however. The only requirement is that the *expectation* of reward be frustrated. The frustration effects that follow instrumental responding should also be found after simply consuming food in a particular environment. Daly also demonstrated such frustration by directly placing animals into a goal box with food (but no running) during training. Then, when food was omitted, the animals learned to get out of the goal box faster than no-food control animals. With humans, you can tell people that they are going to get something they want and then not give it to them. This treatment may produce frustration. They may then find stimuli associated with this frustration aversive. The person who has made a promise and not kept it may become aversive and disliked.

Frustration also serves as a **cue** because it has drive stimuli ($S_{D \text{ frustration}}$). Recall that in Hullian drive theory, the drive itself does not give direction to behavior; it is drive stimuli that do this. Frustration may thus **evoke** responses or **guide** behavior. These stimulus properties are very important, as we shall shortly see.

Energizing effect of nonreward frustration. Suppose that we put an animal into an apparatus called a **double runway,** two separate runways strung together so that the goal box for the first runway is also the start box for the second runway. This apparatus is illustrated in Figure 10–3. The animal runs down the first runway to get food in the first goal box; then when a door is opened, it runs down the second runway to get food in the second goal box. After the animal has thoroughly learned the task, we ask this question: If food is omitted in the *first goal box,* what will be the effect on running speed in the *second runway?* Frustration theory predicts that the animal should run *faster* than usual because **nonreward in the first goal box is frustrating** and produces a higher level of drive. This increased drive should energize running in the second runway. And that is exactly what happens. The increase in running speed following nonreward is called the **frustration effect** (Amsel & Roussel, 1952). Control subjects that are *never* rewarded in the first goal box run *slower* in the second runway than do frustrated animals (Wagner, 1963). In line with the discussion of incentives in Chapter Eight, Amsel proposed that during training, an anticipatory goal response (r_g–s_g) is conditioned to apparatus cues. As r_g–s_g becomes stronger, there is more frustration if reward is omitted. The frustration is a source of drive, and hence the animal runs faster.

Frustrative nonreward and extinction. If an animal is trained in a simple runway with one goal box, it learns to expect reward and then is frustrated when the reward is omitted. This is the same frustration effect that occurs in the double runway. In this case, however, the goal box cues are associated with the aversive frustration and arouse **conditioned frustration,** which is aversive. As the animal approaches the goal box, the conditioned aversion gets stronger, and the animal slows down. The animal extinguishes running to the goal box

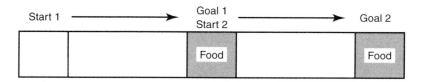

FIGURE 10–3. The double-runway apparatus for studying nonreward frustration. The animal is placed in start box 1 and runs to goal box 1 for food. It then runs from goal box 1 to goal box 2 for food. The amimal learns to run quickly from each point to the next. If food is then omitted in goal box 1, the animal runs faster to goal box 2. It is "energized" by omission of food in goal box 1, the frustration effect.

both because it learns that food is not there and because it is frustrated. How do we know that frustration is involved? Experiments that manipulate frustration reveal this tendency. For example, suppose that one animal is trained with a large reward and another with a small reward. Since a large reward is a better incentive, we might expect the large-reward subject to extinguish more slowly. But according to frustration theory, omission of a large reward should be more frustrating (more aversive) than omission of a small reward. Therefore, the large-reward animal should extinguish faster. And that is what happens—the large-reward animals extinguish faster. A similar result occurs when animals are shifted from a larger to a smaller reward, as we saw with the Crespi effect in Chapter Eight. The animals run more slowly than do animals that have been continuously trained with a small reward. Crespi's "depression effect" is usually interpreted in terms of frustration.

Persistence following frustration: partial reinforcement effects. One of the more puzzling effects of rewards is that they produce greater resistance to extinction if *not* given for every response. Animals rewarded after every trip down a runway or after a lever press (100 percent reinforcement) extinguish *faster* than animals rewarded only part of the time (partial reinforcement). This is called the **partial reinforcement extinction effect (PREE)**. The obvious question is, How can a response rewarded part of the time be "stronger" than one rewarded all the time?

According to frustration theory, following 100 percent reinforcement during training, omission of reward in extinction produces the animal's first nonreward frustration in the situation. This is the same as the interpretation of extinction previously given. With partial reinforcement training, however, the animal is frustrated on each nonreinforced trial during training. This primary frustration (R_F) also has a *conditionable component* (r_f) that has a stimulus component (s_f). How does this affect behavior? Early in training, partially reinforced animals run more slowly than 100-percent-reinforced animals, because the partially reinforced animals have some frustration conditioned to the goal box (Wagner, 1963). As frustration (and r_f-s_f) occurs more often, however, s_f becomes one of the stimuli to which running is conditioned. Eventually, r_f-s_f facilitates running:

Apparatus Cues → (r_f-s_f) → Running.

As a consequence, when extinction is begun and reward is omitted altogether, the animal's performance does not suddenly fall apart. The animal has learned to run and be reinforced when the frustration cues (r_f-s_f) are aroused on non-reinforced trials. Such an interpretation accounts for persistence of behavior in many situations in which there is emotional arousal (Amsel, 1992).

Some athletes, for example, seem to thrive on emotional outburst and controversy when they are frustrated. The frustration interpretation is that their performance has become conditioned to the emotional arousal and that the emotional arousal is a "support stimulus" for their performance. In addition, of course, their motivational arousal may be a drive that energizes their performance. The partial reinforcement effect also accounts for what is called **frustration tolerance** in humans. People who have learned to persist in the face of frustration use frustration as a cue to keep on working. If they keep on working, they are more likely to succeed. Instead of having nonproductive emotional responses to frustration (as a "spoiled" child might have), they engage in productive behavior. We often consider the development of such frustration tolerance to be a sign of maturity. Amsel (1992) has shown a number of instances in which frustration theory applies to human behavior.

Frustration and the small-trial PREE.   By Amsel's account, anticipation of a goal (r_g–s_g) has to develop before there would be frustration, and r_g–s_g was said to develop slowly. It was found, however, that the PREE could be obtained with only *two* acquisition trials, nonreinforced and reinforced (Mc-Cain, 1966). Brooks (1969) argued that the small-trial PREE is better analyzed in terms of the frustration that develops during extinction than in terms of the conditioning of frustration during training. Brooks tested this argument by giving one group of animals six goal-box placements with a large reward (30 seconds' access to wet mash) and another group a small reward (one 45 mg food pellet). Half of each group got food on all trials, and half on 50 percent of the trials. The 100 percent, large-reward group learned to escape faster when food was omitted than did the other three groups, which performed the same as a group never fed in the goal box. With large rewards there is indeed a partial-reinforcement frustration effect with a small number of trials. In any case, what we see is that frustration can lead to more persistent behavior, whether the emphasis is on training or extinction.

Results in **choice situations** do not fit the frustration model as well. Suppose that we train animals in a choice apparatus, like a T-maze, with 100 percent reinforcement on one side and 50 percent on the other side. The animals eventually choose the 100 percent side every time. In extinction, the animals still choose the 100 percent side for many, many trials, which is *exactly opposite* to what should happen according to frustration theory (Logan, 1968). The 100 percent side should become more aversive than the 50 percent side and hence be chosen less often. It would appear that frustration theory does not apply here. Other, nonmotivational, accounts have been developed to explain such results.

Conflict as a Source of Frustration

A conflict situation produces frustration when one goal is "blocked" by a **competing goal.** Virtually all behavior involves some degree of conflict because we are always making choices among competing goals. Conflict has long been considered a basic problem in neurotic behavior. In Freudian theory, for example, conflicts between the **id** (such biological "drives" as sex or aggression) and the **superego** (socialization) are particularly important. Clinical problems have been a rich source of research ideas about conflict. The most dominant theory of conflict has been that of Neal Miller.

Miller's Theory of Conflict

The theory.   Miller and his associates (e.g., Dollard & Miller, 1941; Miller, 1959) progressively developed the theory of conflict. Miller (1959) begins with six assumptions:

1. The closer an organism is to a positive goal, the stronger the motivation to approach that goal. This is called an **approach gradient.**
2. The closer an organism is to an aversive goal, the stronger the motivation to escape or avoid the goal. This is called an **avoidance gradient.**
3. The avoidance gradient is **steeper** than the approach gradient. It drops off more rapidly than the approach gradient as the organism is further from the goal.
4. The level of either approach or avoidance gradients can be raised or lowered by appropriate manipulations of approach and avoidance motivation (such as changes in degree of hunger or level of fearfulness).
5. The approach or avoidance tendencies increase in strength with number of trials.
6. When two incompatible responses are in conflict, the one with the stronger motivation (approach or avoidance) will occur.

Figure 10–4 illustrates the typical conflict situation in laboratory research. The strength of approach or avoidance is a function of both *learning* and *motivation,* so Miller's concepts are more like Hull's excitatory potentials (Chapter Six) than just motivational concepts.

Evidence for Miller's theory.   Judson Brown (1948) tested the first four assumptions. He tethered rats to a calibrated spring with a harness so that he could record the strength of the rats' pull toward or away from a goal. Some animals were trained to run down an alleyway to food and then were stopped by the tether either "near" (30 cm) or "far" (170 cm) from the goal. The results, which are shown in Figure 10–5, were that

1. The rats pulled harder when they were in the near position.
2. Other animals, shocked but not fed at the end of the runway, pulled away from the shock area harder when in the near position.
3. The slope of the escape gradient was steeper between the two points than was that of the approach gradient. The results, which are shown in Figure 10–5 (a), are as predicted, but the gradients are not necessarily linear (it's just that two points can define only a linear function). The only real requirement of the theory, however, is that the gradients cross.
4. Figure 10–5 (b) shows the results of testing the animals under strong versus

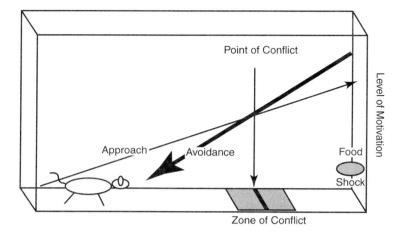

FIGURE 10–4. Conflict situation. The animal is first trained to run down the apparatus (left to right) to get food. Doing this establishes the approach motivation gradient. It then receives shock at the food source. This establishes the avoidance motivation gradient and produces an approach-avoidance conflict. The "point of conflict" is where the two gradients intersect. See text for further details.

weak avoidance. The overall gradient is lower with weak avoidance. Other animals, tested at forty-six hours of deprivation, showed stronger approach than animals deprived for one hour. However, since these animals were tested only at the near distance, we can only assume that the overall approach gradient was lower for one group than the other.

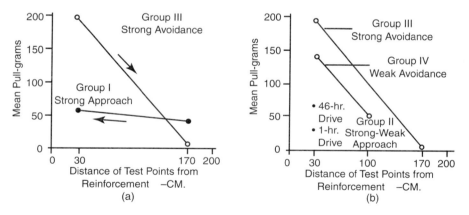

FIGURE 10–5. (a) The approach gradient represents the mean force exerted by 46-hour motivated rats when restrained at two points in the alley. The avoidance gradient reveals the force exerted by rats in their efforts to avoid a region where strong shock has been given. Although the experimental points in this figure and in (b) have been joined by straight lines, no assumption is intended with respect to the linearity of the gradients. (b) This section illustrates the effect of reduced shock and reduced hunger upon the strengths of the avoidance and approach responses, respectively. (From Brown, 1948, pp. 457 and 459. Copyright © 1948 by the American Psychological Association. Reprinted by permission.)

5. Kaufman and Miller (1949) supported the fifth assumption by showing that with more approach training trials, the animals were more likely to go to the goal after having been shocked there.
6. The primary evidence for this assumption is the fact of conflict resolution. That is, animals do ultimately approach or avoid.

Types of conflict. Psychologists generally distinguish four kinds of conflict, diagrammed in Figure 10–6, in terms of Miller's gradient theory.

- **Approach-Approach.** This involves two discrete positive alternatives, Goal A and Goal B. As the animal moves toward A, the tendency to approach A is even stronger, and the tendency to approach B is less. Therefore, the conflict is easily resolved. The fable of the indecisive jackass that starved to death between two bales of hay is charming but unlikely.
- **Avoidance-Avoidance.** This involves two aversive goals. As the animal moves away from one, it necessarily moves toward the other and then is forced back to-

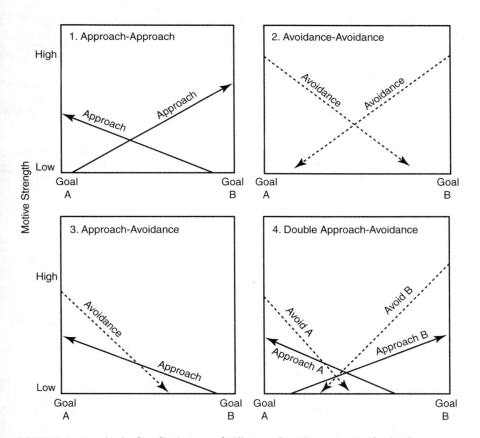

FIGURE 10–6. Four kinds of conflict in terms of Miller's gradient theory. See text for details.

ward the first, and so on. Such conflict gives rise to sayings such as "between the devil and the deep blue sea." If the animal has to stay in the situation, it should eventually become more or less immobile at the point of minimal aversive stimulation, where the two gradients intersect. This behavior is commonly seen in the laboratory when an animal (for example, a rat) is shocked at either end of a runway and settles down in the middle.

Given the chance to get away from such a totally disastrous situation, animals will attempt to get out of the situation, either physically or psychologically. Amnesia is often thought to have this motivational basis: A person in an intolerable situation may escape by "forgetting." Such forgetting is not consciously intentional but nevertheless serves the purpose. Some people escape by sleeping, others by taking drugs.

- **Approach-Avoidance.** This conflict involves goals with both desirable and aversive features. As in Brown's experiment, an animal is trained to run down an alleyway to food, and then the food container is wired so that the animal gets shocked if it touches the food. The animal then vacillates in the runway because of its simultaneous motivation to approach and to avoid the same goal. The area in which vacillation occurs is the "conflict zone," the region in which the approach and avoidance gradients intersect. Approach-avoidance conflicts have received considerable experimental attention because they are so common. Usually such a conflict is resolved in some way, and we must assume a shift in the relative strengths of approach and avoidance so that the individual goes either all the way to the goal or so far away that the approach motivation is no longer effective.

- **Double Approach-Avoidance.** This conflict involves two goals, each having positive and negative features. The choice of one goal results in the loss of another, and this loss is a negative feature of the chosen goal. For example, you might have the choice of buying a large, comfortable, and expensive car or of a smaller, less comfortable car that costs less. To gain the good feature of one, you inevitably lose the good feature of the other. This type of conflict, perhaps better called **multiple approach-avoidance** because the alternatives may be more than two, is more typical of real-life situations but is also more difficult to analyze experimentally.

ANXIETY

Most psychologists would agree about the following aspects of strong anxiety:

- High anxiety is an unpleasant emotional experience.
- High anxiety is strongly motivating, sometimes pushing people to extreme thoughts and behaviors to control it.
- Long periods of high anxiety and the attendant upheaval of the autonomic nervous system can be bad for our health, producing so-called stress disorders. Cardiovascular disorders are prominent among these.

For these reasons, anxiety has probably received more attention than any other emotion in terms of both research and theory. A theory of anxiety is, of course, a theory of emotion, or at least one aspect of emotion.

Anxiety versus Fear

The distinction between anxiety and fear is often not obvious. Freud, for example, distinguished between **objective anxiety** (what we call **fear**) and **neurotic anxiety**. Objective anxiety is directed toward some specific object that causes it, whereas neurotic anxiety is fear without a (recognized) cause. Neurotic anxiety has also been characterized as out of proportion to the actual threat to the individual.

S. Epstein (1967; 1986) has suggested a distinction between fear and anxiety that is based on *perception of control* rather than recognition of the cause. Anxiety, he says, is a qualitatively different experience from fear and arises when a person *cannot cope* with threat. Such an inability to cope might, of course, occur because a person does not recognize the source of the threat. Anxiety might also occur, however, when a person knows exactly what the threat is but can do nothing about it. For example, a soldier might specifically be afraid of the mortar shells he sees and hears dropping around him but might also be anxious because he cannot cope with them. The critical element is ability to cope with a fearful situation, not whether the cause is recognized.

It is not always easy to maintain a definitional distinction between fear and anxiety, however, and in animal research such a distinction is virtually meaningless. What would we mean by "fear without a cause" in reference to a rat or a dog? Such distinctions therefore shall be limited here to humans.

State versus Trait Anxiety

State anxiety (A-state).   State anxiety is the anxiety an individual experiences in a specific situation at a specific time (Cattell & Scheier, 1961; Spielberger, 1966; 1976). An example of state anxiety would be when a person who is fearless in many situations becomes highly anxious when giving a speech to a group or when a student becomes highly anxious only when taking tests.

Research has repeatedly shown that whether a person reports being anxious depends on the *person*, the *situation*, and the type of "*anxious response*" being reported (Endler, Hunt, & Rosen, 1962; Endler, 1998). Endler et al. devised the *S-R Inventory of Anxiousness*, consisting of eleven different situations (such as starting on an auto trip or climbing on a mountain ledge) and fourteen kinds of responses (such as heart beats faster, feels uneasy). A given person tends to rate himself or herself as more or less anxious according to the situation and the response. This tendency carries the important implication that if anxiety is specific to situations and responses, then treatments may have to be equally specific. For example, test anxiety would be treated differently from fear of heights or fear of flying. This, of course, has been the approach taken by behavior therapists.

Trait anxiety (A-trait).   Trait anxiety is a relatively enduring personality trait, a *disposition* to be anxious in many different situations. It is commonly distinguished from state anxiety by means of the *State-Trait Anxiety Inventory* (STAI; Spielberger, Gorsuch, & Lushene, 1970). In personality theory, trait anxiety may also be referred to as **neuroticism** or **negative affectivity.** It is one of the most commonly described personality traits (see Chapter Twelve), is generally considered a "basic" emotion (i.e., fear), and is a major concern in clinical psychology (M. Eysenck, 1997). Twelve different anxiety disorders are identified in DSM-IV (1994).

Biological Approaches to Anxiety

Biological theories of anxiety (e.g., Gray, 1982a,b; H. Eysenck, 1967) assume that physiological differences account for the difference in anxiety levels that people experience, and that there is a genetic basis for individual differences in anxiety. A number of genetic studies, especially of twins, indicate that perhaps 30 percent to 50 percent of the variance in trait anxiety may be genetic (M. Eysenck, 1997). Although this is not a trivial amount, it accounts for only half the variance, at best. Furthermore, as we saw in Chapter Two, no one has yet been able to distinguish among emotions solely on the basis of physiological measures. It would then seem that other factors must be brought into play. We assume that these other factors also have a basis in the brain, but of a different sort than we usually attribute to emotion.

Gray's theory.   Fear and anxiety are generally conceded to involve arousal of the sympathetic nervous system and related hormones. Gray (1982a,b) proposed a theory that more specifically relates "anxious behavior" to particular brain locations and neurochemistry. Gray argues that there is a **behavioral inhibition system** (BIS), which is located in a **septal-hippocampal system** (part of the limbic system) in the brain. In Gray's theory, *activation of the BIS is anxiety.* Gray proposes that the BIS responds to several kinds of stimulus inputs with several kinds of response outputs, which are illustrated in Figure 10–7.

When a person is engaged in some goal-oriented behavior and faces threatening (punishing) stimuli, frustrative nonreward, or unexpected (novel) stimuli, the BIS is activated. This activation inhibits the ongoing behavior and produces increased arousal, and the organism attends to the dis-

Input		Output
Signals of Punishment		Behavioral Inhibition
Signals of Nonreward → Behavioral Inhibition System →	Increased Arousal
Novel Stimuli		Increased Attention

FIGURE 10–7.   Gray's behavioral inhibition system. See text for details.

ruptive elements. Anxiety is experienced. Much of the evidence for Gray's theory is from research with **antianxiety** (tranquilizing) drugs. These drugs reduce each of these three kinds of responses. Gray suggests that these drugs reduce anxiety because they facilitate the effects of **gamma aminobutyric acid (GABA),** an inhibitory neurotransmitter.

Gray also brings **cognitive** factors into the theory. He says that an organism is continuously comparing its plans for the future, its predicted outcomes of its present behavior, and stored information about the way the world works. The septal-hippocampal system (known to be involved in memory) compares internal plans, predictions, and stored information with what is going on in the environment. As long as plans and expectations are being met, there is no anxiety and no behavioral inhibition. If, however, progress toward an expected outcome is interrupted by threat, frustration, or novel event, the BIS becomes active, and anxiety is experienced.

In Gray's theory, signals of punishment or nonreward are anxiety-provoking. The perceived threat, however, is thought to depend on the individual's *interpretation* or *appraisal* of signals in the environment. A person has to perceive that a particular signal means danger before the person responds to it as a threatening stimulus. Research shows that clinical patients with anxiety neuroses express exaggerated thoughts about danger and exaggerated fear of the consequences of their behavior. They appraise life events as more dangerous and threatening than a more objective observer would (Beck & Rush, 1980). Recall from Chapter Two, however, that people can discriminate between "good" and "bad" stimuli without consciously recognizing them. Not all appraisals are necessarily conscious.

Cognitive Approaches to Anxiety

The physiological approach to trait anxiety tends to neglect environmental factors, changes in personality over time, the multidimensional nature of trait anxiety, and individual differences in cognitive functioning (M. Eysenck, 1997). Cognitive approaches take these factors into account. Contemporary research on cognitive processes involves methodologies that are designed to tease out **preattentive** (unconscious) effects from **attentive** (conscious) effects, to detect **selective attention** to some events rather than others, or to detect **selective memories** or distortions of memory. Once dominated by psychoanalytic interpretations, the study of anxiety has become enveloped by the cognitive revolution.

Cognitive theories of trait anxiety emphasize several aspects of cognition, not just appraisal of threat (Williams, Watts, McLeod, & Mathews, 1997; M. Eysenck, 1997). For example, there are individual differences in the **schemas** that people have for interpreting events. Some people are more prone than others to see stimuli as dangerous or threatening, and hence they are biased in the way they attend to events. An "emotional" stimulus triggers cognitive appraisal, but a person high in trait anxiety is more likely to perceive an event as dangerous. This biased cognitive appraisal determines the level of **physiological activity** (e.g., sympathetic arousal), **action tendencies** (e.g., to run away or otherwise be defensive), and **cognitions** (e.g., likelihood of worrying about the situation).

Selective attention.   M. Eysenck (1991) studied bias in attention by high and low trait anxious subjects. He used a standard **dichotic listening task,** in which subjects have different messages sent to the two ears through headphones. Subjects had a mix of emotionally neutral and threatening words presented to the attended ear and were supposed to "shadow" the words by repeating them as they heard them. Emotionally neutral words were presented to the unattended ear, and subjects were instructed to ignore these. The measure of attention was how fast a subject responded to a tone presented to one of the ears. A faster response when the tone is presented to one ear rather than the other indicates that the subject is paying closer attention to that ear. High anxious subjects responded more quickly to the emotional stimuli in the attended ear, whereas the low anxious subjects responded more rapidly to the neutral stimuli in the unattended ear. The high anxious subjects were more attentive to threatening stimuli than were low anxious subjects.

Interpretive bias.   Several studies have shown that high anxious subjects will make more threatening interpretations of what they hear. For example, Eysenck et al. (1987) presented subjects orally with *homophones,* words with the same sound but different meanings, such as *pain* and *pane,* or *die* and *dye.* The subjects' task was simply to write down the word they heard. Anxious subjects were more prone to make negative interpretations of what they heard (e.g., writing down "pain" rather than "pane"). There was a strong correlation ($r = +.60$) between level of anxiety and number of threat-related interpretations.

Negative memory bias.   An example of this bias is that there is a tendency for high anxious subjects to remember negative words that they had previously used to describe themselves rather than positive words. There is a general account of such memory bias, called **mood congruent memory** (Blaney, 1986). People tend to remember events that are congruent with their present mood. People in a sad mood remember sad events, and people in a happy mood remember happy events, and so on. Such biased memories are thought to help perpetuate whatever the mood a person is in at the time.

STRESS

The General Adaptation Syndrome

The concept of stress has subsumed much of the subject matter of frustration, conflict, and anxiety in recent years. This focus is largely due to the prodigious efforts of Hans Selye and his concept of the **general adaptation syndrome** (GAS). Selye (pronounced Sel-yea) considered the GAS to be common to many different "stress situations" and characterized it in three stages (Selye, 1956), which are summarized in Figure 10–8.

1. **Alarm reaction.** When an organism faces a **stressor,** such as disease, extreme temperature, or injury, the body shows an alarm reaction, such as a sudden drop in blood sugar level followed quickly by a counterresponse, such as an increase in blood sugar. Other typical changes are in blood pressure, heart rate, and release of adrenal hormones.

2. **Stage of resistance.** Following the alarm, the body uses its resources to keep its physiology on a normal course during stress. Since the body has to work harder than usual to maintain itself, it is especially susceptible to the effects of additional stress. If this effortful resistance continues long enough, the body may "wear down" and go into the third stage.

3. **Stage of exhaustion.** This stage, possibly life threatening, is characterized by **enlarged adrenal glands, shriveling of the thymus and lymph glands** (necessary to fight disease), and **gastrointestinal ulcers.** Other effects specific to particular stressors may also occur, but the three described here are widely found regardless of what the stressor is. Hence the name "general adaptation syndrome."

A major advantage of the stress concept is that it provides medical and psychological researchers a common theoretical framework. So-called **psychosomatic disorders,** illnesses sometimes said to be "in the head" and therefore not "real," make sense in terms of stress. We need only assume that stress has both psychological and physical origins. This assumption also forces a more psychologically oriented definition of stress than that originally provided by Selye.

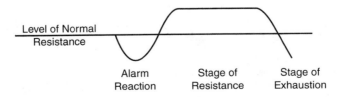

FIGURE 10–8. The time course of stress. (From Selye, 1956. © 1974 by McGraw-Hill Book Co. Used with permission of publisher.)

Definitions of Stress

As we look at stress more closely, we see that some definitions that have been proposed (including Selye's) are just too simple:

1. **Stimulus definition.** Stress is defined in terms of specific environmental (stimulus) conditions that produce arousal, such as danger or loud noise. These same conditions are not equally stressful for all individuals, however, so that the stimulus definition has limited value.
2. **Response definition.** Selye (1956) used a response definition, saying that stress is a state manifested by the pattern of symptoms (responses) that characterizes the emotional fight-flight reaction. We infer stress from the symptoms (responses). The problem is that this definition does not tell us what situations will produce stress, and the definition easily becomes circular: "This must be a stressful situation because this person is stressed." Experience tells us that some things frequently produce stress, such as surgical anesthesia, pain, cold, or loss of blood, but this knowledge does not *define* stress for us.
3. **Interactive definition.** Most psychologists now define stress in terms of stimuli *and* responses, an organism-environment interaction. Stress occurs when the demands of the environment are too great for the organism to cope with (McGrath, 1970, p. 17). This definition of stress includes our definition of frustration, that is, an internal state produced when there is goal blocking, but it also includes the fear/anxiety aroused in danger situations, as well as sympathetic arousal that accompanies noise or rapidly changing stimulation. The imbalance is partly subjective, depending on whether a person *perceives* that he or she can respond effectively to the environment and on whether it is *important* to do so. A person perfectly capable of responding effectively may not perceive that she or he can do so and is therefore "stressed." Conversely, a person may perceive that he or she is "invincible" and is therefore not stressed, even though objectively is no more capable than the person who is stressed.

Sources of Stress

Traumatic events.   Being caught in a fire, being raped, witnessing a gory crime, or being held prisoner of war are examples of traumatic stressors. Sometimes, even though a victim seems to be coping with the immediate situation, a delayed stress reaction may appear weeks or months later. A victim may begin to feel depressed and have nightmares about the event, or may have flashbacks and briefly relive the horror of the earlier experience. This condition is called **post-traumatic stress disorder** (PTSD).

Recent life changes.   Holmes and Rahe (1967) devised a scale to quantify the degree of stressfulness of many different life changes, as shown in Table 10–1. They suggested that the effects of life changes cumulate so that if the life change units exceed three hundred in a year, illness is more likely to occur. Such details are controversial, however. First, not all life changes mean the same thing to all people. One person's only divorce after thirty years of marriage would not mean the same thing as another's sixth divorce in six

TABLE 10–1. Life change events and stress values of their corresponding life change units (LCU's).

EVENT	LCU VALUE
Family:	
Death of a spouse	100
Divorce	73
Marital separation	65
Death of close family member	63
Marriage	50
Marital reconciliation	45
Major change in health of family	44
Pregnancy	40
Addition of new family member	39
Major change in arguments with wife	35
Son or dauthter leaving home	29
In-law troubles	29
Wife starting or ending work	26
Major change in family get-togethers	15
Personal:	
Detention in jail	63
Major personal injury or illness	53
Sexual difficulties	39
Death of a close friend	37
Outstanding personal achievement	28
Start or end of formal schooling	26
Major change in living conditions	25
Major revision of personal habits	24
Changing to a new school	20
Change in residence	20
Major change in recreation	19
Major change in church activities	19
Major change in sleeping habits	16
Major change in eating habits	15
Vacation	13
Christmas	12
Minor violations of the law	11
Work:	
Being fired from work	47
Retirement from work	45
Major business adjustment	39
Changing to different line of work	36
Major change in work responsibilities	29
Trouble with boss	23
Major change in working conditons	20
Financial:	
Major change in financial state	38
Mortgage or loan over $10,000	31
Mortgage foreclosure	30
Mortgage or loan less than $10,000	17

Source: Holmes and Rahe, 1967, pp. 213–218. Copyright © 1967 by Pergamon Press. Used by permission.

years. Second, some of the changes in the scale are themselves illnesses and hence would probably contribute more to stress. Third, a person's score on the scale often depends on the memories of the person involved and so may not be entirely reliable. Research also suggests that only the negative events contribute to stress, not the positive ones. Details aside, however, life changes do contribute to stress.

Hassles.   The stresses that face us most often are the hassles of everyday life (Lazarus, 1981), which may cumulate to high levels of stress. Many parents spend hours weekly getting children to and from school, parties, and lessons; taking care of the family; and dealing with countless small family emergencies. As such hassles continue, stress increases, and ability to cope with stress may go down. Long-term accumulation of small frustrations, hassles, and stress may occur in any occupation, for either men or women. People do lead lives of quiet desperation, and all their stresses may not be obvious to the outsider.

Stress and the Environment

Environmental load.   We saw the concept of environmental load in Chapter Six in the discussion of arousal. A high-load environment is complex and changing, a low-load environment is simple and unchanging. A high load makes more demands on the individual, with greater chance of stress. Crowding and noise, among many other factors, add to environmental load.

Crowding and stress.   Animals and people tend to distance themselves from each other, maintaining **personal space**, which is often described as a "protective bubble" around the individual. Other individuals are kept at distances appropriate for certain kinds of activities: close for intimate activities, further away for business activities, and so on. A person moving too close to conduct business would be violating personal space, producing discomfort and stress. Personal space is said to be maintained for **protection** from overstimulation and for **communication** about the relationships between people (Bell, Fisher, & Loomis, 1978).

We try to protect ourselves from overstimulation produced by too-close contact with others. Although animal research is not always directly applicable to human situations, animal populations are thought to rise and fall because population growth produces greater stress from excessive interanimal contact. Calhoun (1962) showed that if rodents are allowed unlimited food and water but have limited space in which to live and breed, the population will level off at a number well below the limit to which it could rise. There is a disastrous drop in birth rate, high infant mortality rate, homosexuality, greater aggressiveness, and cannibalism. A **behavioral sink** is established, usually around a food source, where there is a high density of animals and where many social problems occur. In the wild, heavily crowded conditions can also produce population decrements.

The communication function is that by maintaining a distance between ourselves and others, we send the message that we are *controlling* our space. Schmidt and Keating (1979) suggested that the term **crowding** is a label we put on a situation when density results in a loss of personal control. A place becomes crowded when we perceive we are losing freedom because of the number of people. People with an external locus of control feel more crowded under given conditions than do people with an internal locus of control. The externals presumably are more responsive to crowding, as they are to other environmental factors. Studies in prisons also indicate that the greater the crowding, the higher the blood pressure and the greater the number of illnesses reported by inmates (Cox, Paulus, McCain, & Karlovac, 1982). Individuals in dense urban environments seem to maintain control partly by ignoring much of the environment, thereby reducing the amount of stimulation to be responded to. It is harder for prisoners to ignore each other.

Noise and stress. About one American in three lives in a neighborhood so noisy that there is general annoyance and interference with communication (Cohen, Krantz, Evans, & Stokols, 1982). The noise comes from traffic, aircraft, construction, neighbors, children, pets, and so on. High-intensity noise can impair hearing, increase cardiovascular risk, and produce disturbing psychological symptoms (Cohen & Weinstein, 1981). Laboratory research indicates that high-intensity noise narrows the focus of attention, reduces perceived control, and increases physiological arousal. In the **Los Angeles Noise Project,** Cohen et al. (1982) compared the performance and blood pressure of children attending school near the Los Angeles International Airport with children at more distant points. Aircraft were taking off and landing an average of every two-and-a-half minutes during school hours, with peak noise intensities as high as 95 db. Mean systolic and diastolic pressures for the high-noise subjects were two to four points above the low-noise subjects, although still well within a normal range. The high-noise subjects were also poorer at solving puzzles than the low-noise subjects. The effects of the noisy environment were (to this reader, at least) surprisingly small, a testimonial perhaps to the resilience of children. Unwanted noise is nevertheless a great irritant to many people.

In a similar study, third- and fourth-grade children living near the Munich (Germany) International Airport were compared with those living in a quiet suburban neighborhood (Evans, Hygge, & Bullinger, 1995). Their results were compatible with those of the earlier Los Angeles study but added to it importantly in showing that the children living near the airport had higher levels of both epinephrine and norepinephrine, measured in urine collected overnight at home. There was little difference in blood pressure, but the differences in catecholamines indicated a higher stress level. Further-

more, the children near the airport performed significantly less well on both
memory and reading tests.

Individual Differences in Susceptibility to Stress

Genetic differences.   In both applied and experimental settings, we
have bred animals of very different temperaments. Some dogs (e.g., retriev-
ers) are normally calm and relatively unresponsive to stimulation, whereas
others are highly excitable (e.g., Pekingese). Laboratory mice have been bred
for high or low levels of emotional reactivity, indexed by both physiological
arousal and behaviors (e.g., crouching in a corner).

Early experience.   Early experience may be either *prenatal* or *postnatal,*
exemplified in the research of Seymour Levine, Victor Denenberg, and
J. McV. Hunt.

Levine's research.   According to psychoanalytic theory, early infantile
trauma should produce later emotional disorders. Levine (1960) put this hypothesis to the test with rat pups in their first ten days of life. Contrary to expectation, he found that pups that were left entirely in the care of their mothers were more anxious as adults in new situations than were pups that had been
either "traumatized" by being shocked or handled ten minutes a day by the ex-
perimeter. Levine argued that either the mild shock or the daily handling facilitated provided stimulation, which facilitated emotional stability. It was also
found that escape learning was faster with nonhandled animals but that avoidance learning was faster with handled animals. This finding is explained in
terms of the kinds of behaviors required. Escape is usually a simple response,
and the greater the fear arousal, the faster the escape. Avoidance, on the other
hand, requires a more delicately timed response in the presence of a cue. Nonhandled animals might be too emotional to respond efficiently. Furthermore,
the adrenalcorticosteroid levels of the nonhandled animals rise and fall more
slowly when shock is presented and terminated than the levels do with shocked
or handled animals. The autonomic responses of the nonhandled animals simply do not respond very efficiently to environmental changes.

Denenberg's research: genetics-experience interactions.   Animals with
the same genes may develop different degrees of emotionality because of different social interactions. Denenberg (1963) made female rats emotional or
nonemotional by Levine's procedure of differential early handling. He then
reared the offspring of these animals with either emotional or nonemotional
mothers and did the same with the offspring of nonemotional mothers.
Birthing and parenting by emotional mothers produced the most emotional
offspring, and birthing and parenting by nonemotional mothers produced
the least emotional offspring, the other two combinations falling between.

Being born to an emotional mother is thus different from being born to a nonemotional mother. The fetus of the emotional mother may become more emotional because it is "sensitized" by maternal adrenal hormones, for example. It was also found that the offspring affected the mothers. Babies of nonemotional mothers had a calming effect on an emotional foster mother, whereas offspring of emotional mothers had "upsetting" effects on a calm mother (Gray, 1971).

Hunt's orphanage research. Hunt (1984) found that infants in orphanages had high incidence of health problems that were not due to poor health care. Instead, they resulted from lack of stimulation in a dull and unchanging environment. This had previously been described clinically under the name **miasmas,** as well as being found in Harry Harlow's experimental research with monkeys (e.g., Harlow, 1958). The basic phenomenon reported by Harlow was that monkeys reared from birth in almost complete isolation were seriously deficient in social skills as adults.

Emotional conditioning. As we saw in Chapter Nine, emotional responses can be classically conditioned. Many internal "stress responses" can be conditioned to external stimuli (e.g., Bykov, 1957; Razran, 1961). This being the case, then stress responses can be aroused in otherwise nonstressful situations if the appropriate conditioned stimuli are present. For example, a person who as a child was punished by an authority, may experience anxiety in dealing with authority figures in entirely different situations in later life.

Stress and Control

The concept of control has been pursued with considerable success in research with both human and animal subjects. The physiological effects of lack of control are especially noteworthy.

Decision making and ulcers. Folklore has it that the conflict of making decisions takes its toll through the ulcerated stomach if not the palpitating heart. Research has repeatedly shown, however, that *animals that do not have control over aversive events are the ones that develop ulcers* (Weiss, 1972, 1977). If two animals are simultaneously hooked up to an apparatus in such a way that only one of the animals controls the amount of shock received by both of them, the animal in charge does *not* develop ulcers.[1] The animal *without control* gets them. Figure 10– 9 illustrates such an experimental arrangement.

---

[1]A study by Brady (1958) on "executive monkeys" indicated that the decision making monkey, the one that had to make responses in order to avoid shock for itself and for a control animal, developed ulcers. Flaws in this research were subsequently discovered, and it has not been replicated.

EXP   Yoked
                       Control

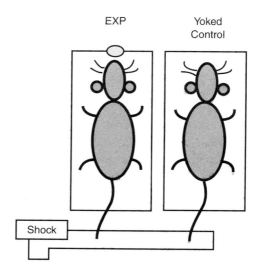

FIGURE 10–9. Experimental arrangement for yoked-control procedure. Both animals receive shock through the tail simultaneously, but only the experimental animal (EXP) can turn off the shock for itself and for the control animal by pushing a button at the front of the apparatus. The control animal is helpless.

Control in human research.   In animal research it is relatively easy to say what we mean by control: An animal can or cannot terminate or postpone shock by its behavior. In human situations it can be more difficult to determine what constitutes control. Humans devise many methods to gain *what they perceive as control,* and perceived control is often the critical factor in stress.

Perceived control is not a simple idea, however; even learned helplessness may be a kind of control (Rothbaum, Weisz, & Snyder, 1982). The stereotypical Southern belle of the *Gone With the Wind* genre tyrannizes others with her "helplessness" just as some babies tyrannize their parents. Rothbaum et al. argue that people first try to **control events** (primary control), and if this fails, they **adjust themselves to events** (secondary control), with much of life being a compromise between the two. Secondary control takes on many guises.

- **Predictive control** is achieved even in failure situations; failure becomes a predictable outcome and can be dealt with.
- **Illusory control** is achieved even in chance situations; a person may attribute chance outcomes to personal skill. Even the luck that one might have at throwing dice becomes a kind of personal skill.
- **Vicarious control** can be gained by identifying with powerful others. The most intolerable situations, including prison camps, can be tolerable to a person who believes that God is on his or her side.

- **Interpretive control** can be gained if a person can find **meaning** in uncontrollable events, such as "This is a test of my faith, so I shall accept it." All these variations on control help alleviate the stressfulness of a situation.

Thompson (1981) sees **meaning** as the unifying element in many different kinds of control in aversive situations. She defines control as the belief that one can do something to reduce the aversiveness of an event. Meaning may affect a person's perception of control by making events seem more **endurable,** by interpreting bad events as forerunners of **future good events,** or by perceiving misfortune as a **part of some greater plan.** The lesson to be learned from the preceding recitation of kinds of control would seem to be that methods of gaining control may be just as variable and idiosyncratic as methods of getting food or of getting rid of pain. Put another way, methods of control may be any thoughts or behaviors that reduce stress and are reinforced.

Predictability and control. If a person or an animal has control, it has "mastery" or "power" over the environment. If the organism has power, it can *predict* the outcome of its actions because its expectancies are fulfilled. We may, then, ask whether predictability alone is sufficient to confer the perception of control and thereby reduce stress (Arthur, 1986; Fisher, 1984; Mineka & Henderson, 1985). Considerable evidence shows that animals prefer to know that an aversive event is coming. Specifically, they prefer *signaled shock* to *unsignaled shock.* One interpretation for this is that the foreknowledge gives an animal a chance to prepare for the oncoming aversive event, such as by assuming a body posture that will make the shock less painful. Miller et al. (1983) found that animals preferred a strong, signaled shock to a weaker shock that was unsignaled. An information theory interpretation of this phenomenon says that even information about bad events is still information and that it is reinforcing (see Chapter Six for more on rewards). In line with this interpretation, D'Amato and Safarjan (1979) found that animals preferred a situation in which one signal predicted a long shock and a different signal predicted a brief shock, rather than signals that did not say which shock was coming. There are alternative interpretations for such phenomena (Mineka & Henderson, 1985), but the basic facts remain the same.

Research with humans (e.g., Miller & Managan, 1983) suggests that whether information about a forthcoming stressful medical procedure will reduce stress depends on how an individual typically copes with such situations. If a person's habitual style is to "blunt" the situation by distracting himself, then information may *not* alleviate stress. If a person uses the information to prepare for the forthcoming event, then it may alleviate stress. Weiss (1977) suggested that if an animal *fails* while attempting to control a predictable shock, the value of predictability is lost, and stomach ulceration may occur just as it does in other uncontrollable shock experiments.

A particularly poignant experiment on control was conducted by Rodin and Langer (1977) in a nursing home environment. Using standard institutional procedures as a baseline condition, a series of additional small responsibilities were given to the residents of one floor of the home. For example, they had more responsibility for room arrangements and had a houseplant to take care of if they wanted one. These residents then had a greater feeling of enjoyment in this environment than did residents who had less control over their lives.

In summary, helplessness and control are important concepts related to the interactive definition of stress, which says that stress occurs when a person faces environmental challenges that he or she perceives cannot be met. A person may consider himself or herself unable to meet challenges because he or she is helpless and lacks the capacity to gain control.

Learned Helplessness

Learned helplessness.   Some people are helpless and anxious in new situations, appearing to be at a loss to do anything. How does such helplessness come about? According to learned helplessness theory, organisms learn that their behavior is ineffective and therefore do nothing. Mowrer and Viek (1948) demonstrated an effect of helplessness in an experiment involving what they called **fear from a sense of helplessness.** Some subjects (laboratory rats) experienced a tone followed by an electric shock to the feet, which they could terminate by jumping off the floor. Other subjects could not end the shock by their own responses. The tone, a conditioned stimulus for fear, was then shown to be a more effective punisher for the animals previously unable to escape the shock. Mowrer and Viek suggested that the tone aroused greater fear for these animals because of their helplessness in the previous shock situation.

Many subsequent *learned helplessness* experiments show that inescapable shock greatly interferes with later escape and avoidance learning (Overmier & Seligman, 1967; Seligman & Maier, 1967). Specifically, dogs shocked helplessly while in a harness would subsequently just sit and take shocks in a shuttle box They did not even learn to escape from shock, much less avoid it. Figure 10–10 (Maier, Seligman, & Solomon, 1969) shows the escape latencies for "helpless" animals in the shuttle box compared with animals without earlier exposure to shock. Two-thirds of the 82 dogs given inescapable shock did not learn to escape from shock in the shuttle box, as compared with only 6 percent of animals not shocked previously. Lack of control over shock while in the harness is the critical element, because animals that can turn off the shock while in the harness later learn escape and avoidance responses normally (Seligman & Maier, 1967). Learned helplessness is found with many species (cats, dogs, mice, monkeys, and humans), with several forms of aversive stimulation (electric shock, loud noise, forced swimming), and with dif-

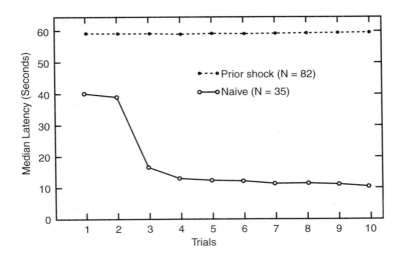

FIGURE 10–10. The effects of inescapable shocks in the Pavlov harness on escape responding in the shuttle box. This figure shows that there is rapid escape learning by 35 naive dogs that received no shocks in the harness. In contrast, the median for 82 dogs that received inescapable shocks in the harness, prior to escape training in the shuttle box, shows failure to escape shock. The arbitrary failure criterion was 60 seconds a shock (a latency of 60 seconds after onset of the S+). (From Maier, Seligam, & Solomon, 1969, p. 321. © 1969. Reprinted by permission of Prentice Hall, Inc., Englewood Cliffs, New Jersey.)

ferent tasks (lever pressing, shuttle box avoidance, or, for humans, solving anagrams). It is not an isolated phenomenon.

Learned helplessness in humans. The procedures used to establish learned helplessness in laboratory animals quickly caught the attention of researchers interested in human clinical problems. Hiroto (1974) pointed out the similarity of the learned helplessness concept to that of **locus of control** (Rotter, 1966) and studied learned helplessness in subjects with high versus low external locus of control.[2] Using an analog of the animal procedures, Hiroto exposed his subjects to loud bursts of aversive noise. Some subjects could stop the noise by pushing a button, while others could not. Subjects could then move a knob to avoid a signaled noise, simulating the shuttle box.

The subjects with previous uncontrollable noise learned to avoid more slowly and had more trials without responding at all. In addition, subjects with external locus of control performed more poorly than those with internal locus, and subjects led to believe that their success was due to chance did less well than those who believed that skill could be effective. Hiroto and

[2]Locus of control refers to the extent to which a person believes that his or her success depends on his or her own actions (internal locus) or on outside forces or other people (external locus).

Seligman (1975) subsequently reported similar results using solutions to anagram problems as the response. Other investigators have not always been able to replicate these results, but these experiments were important to the development of learned helplessness theory.

Helplessness and depression.   Seligman (1975) proposed that learned helplessness might be a cause of depression. The difficulty with this interpretation is that many individuals in a "helpless" situation do *not* become depressed, whereas many individuals who are not in "helpless" situations *do* become depressed. This tendency suggests that whether a situation is "helpless" depends on a person's perception of whether she is in control of the situation and thus led to the **attributional theory of depression** (Abramson, Seligman, & Teasdale, 1978). The new theory was also intended to account for the observations that (a) lowered self-esteem is a common symptom of depression, (b) depressed individuals frequently blame themselves for their failures, and (c) helplessness generalizes across many situations and times.

Attribution theory (Heider, 1958) is an account of how people search for **causes** for their own behavior or that of other people. A particular cause is **attributed** to some person, thing, or event. Within their theory, Abramson et al. defined the following three major dimensions of attribution that would be related to helplessness:

1. **Internal versus external locus of control.** A particular event, such as success or failure at a job, is attributed to oneself (internal) or to some outside event (external), such as to another person or to the difficulty of the job at which one succeeded or failed.
2. **Stable versus unstable causes.** A stable cause is one that is enduring, such as a person's intellectual ability. An unstable cause is one that can vary from time to time, such as how much a person is motivated to study for an exam or whether the questions on the exam happen to match what has been studied. Stable factors can be either internal or external.
3. **Global versus specific.** An attribution may apply to a wide range of events or to a particular event. Thus, I might attribute my failure on an exam to such a global factor as "I always fail exams" or to some specific characteristic of this particular exam, such as "I did not study for this exam."

Table 10–2 summarizes the preceding dimensions and the type of attributions that might be given for failing an examination. The attributional dimensions relate to depression as follows: (1) Lowered self-esteem occurs when a person attributes failure, which is a lack of control over the situation, to an **internal** dimension, such as lack of ability; (2) attributing lack of control to **stable** factors produces a **generalized expectancy** of no control, thus extending helplessness and depression to other times and situations; and (3) **global** attributions extend helplessness over situations, just as stability extends helplessness over time. The most helpless and depressing attribution

TABLE 10–2.   The attributional model of depression in relation to examination failure.

	INTERNAL		EXTERNAL	
DIMENSION	STABLE	UNSTABLE	STABLE	UNSTABLE
Global	I always fail examinations.	I often don't study for exams.	Exams are always too picky.	I usually get the hard exam questions.
Specific	This subject is too hard for me.	I did not study for this exam.	This exam was too hard.	The questions on this exam weren't what I studied.

should then be an **internal, stable, global attribution for lack of control** (failure).

Seligman and his colleagues developed the *Attributional Style Questionnaire,* a self-report measure designed to score attributions in terms of the three attribution dimensions (Seligman, Abramson, Semmel, & von Bayer, 1979). As predicted, undergraduate students who were more depressed according to the Beck Depression Inventory (Beck, 1967) attributed bad outcomes more to internal, stable, and global factors than did the less-depressed students. Seligman and his colleagues argue that the depressive attributional style is a *cause* of depression, but attributional style may be more involved in the *maintenance* of depression after it has been initiated by some other factor (Munton, 1985–86). Robins (1988), noting the inconsistent conclusions about attributional style in previous reviews (Coyne & Gotlib, 1983; Hammen, 1985; Sweeney, Anderson, & Bailey, 1986) concluded that in studies in which there were enough subjects to obtain significant results with a "medium-size" difference between depressed and nondepressed groups, there were fairly consistent attributional differences between the groups. The question of causality is not yet answered, however.

The attribution model assumes, of course, that an individual has experienced negative life events so that depressive attributions can be made. The question is whether people with depressive attributional styles are more likely to become depressed after such events than are individuals with different attributional styles. Several studies of real-life negative events provide only modest support for the attributional style interpretation (Munton, 1985–86, p. 339). Feather and Barbor (1983), for example, found that attributional style accounted for less than 10 percent of the variation in depression inventory scores of unemployed young Australians. The attribution model might be correct in the kinds of attributions important for depression, but data demonstrating the attribution-depression relationship are not very reliable (Munton, 1985–86).

Personality Moderators of Stress

Type A behavior pattern.   Friedman and Rosenman (1974) distinguished between what they called the Type A and Type B behavior patterns. The Type A person is characterized by anger or hostility, and excessive achievement striving. Type A has also been called the "hurry sickness," trying to get more and more done in less and less time and responding aggressively when there is failure. The Type B is defined by the absence of Type A characteristics. The distinction between Type A and Type B caught the fancy of researchers because it appeared that Type A people might have greater susceptibility to coronary heart disease. Coronary heart disease includes the building up of fat deposits in the arteries (atherosclerosis) and high blood pressure.

The evidence linking Type A behavior and heart disease is not nearly so strong as commonly reported in the popular press or even in many textbooks. Moreover, to the extent that such a link does exist, all the evidence points to the anger/hostility component of Type A behavior, not to the time orientation or achievement components (e.g., Hecker, Chesney, Black, & Frautschi, 1988). One investigator (Williams, 1994) suggests that people who are generally cynical (distrusting the motives of others or tending to attribute malicious motives to others) are more likely to develop coronary heart disease. For example, if caught in a line at the checkout counter of the supermarket, a person with a "cynical heart" might take the delay as a personal affront, an attempt by others to delay him, and react physiologically with an "aggressive" cardiovascular response.

Krantz and Manuck (1984) cautioned that cardiac reactivity per se should not be regarded as a proven risk factor for cardiovascular disease. But until some other risk factor is found, autonomic reactivity is likely to remain a good candidate for cardiac risk because a number of kinds of data converge on that hypothesis. For example, Sherwood, Allen, Obrist, and Langer (1986) showed that subjects pressing a telegraph key to avoid shock took in more oxygen than the task itself required. This finding suggested that large amounts of oxygenated blood were getting into the tissues, producing a reflexive constriction of blood vessels, which increases blood pressure. This reflex response to control level of blood oxygen might in the long run lead to cardiovascular problems. The chronically angry or hostile person may be emotionally overresponsive to frustrating situations and more susceptible to cardiovascular disorders for the same reason (Diamond, 1982).

Hardiness.   Another personality type that supposedly buffers the effect of stress is the **hardy personality.** Proposed by Suzanne Kobasa (1979), the hardy personality is said to be **committed** to goals rather than alienated from life, to treat life's frustrations as **challenges** rather than threats, and to feel in **control** of his or her own life. Kobasa and others have reported some evidence that "hardy" individuals show less illness of various kinds (Kobasa, 1979). Other research indicates some problems with the concept, however. First, factor analyses of various test scores have not produced the three dimensions of hardiness postulated by Kobasa (Funk & Houston, 1987; Gainer & Beck, 1987). Second, there is a high negative correlation between hardiness scores and measures of neuroticism (also an indicator of anxiety). This finding indicates that hardiness is not really a new concept but is simply a different way of getting at the personality trait of **neuroticism.** People who are said to be high in hardiness are low in neuroticism, and vice-versa. People who score high on tests of neuroticism have long been known to have more health problems than people low in neuroticism (Funk and Houston, 1987). "Hardiness" is a warmer, fuzzier sounding word than "low neuroticism," but both terms appear to refer to the same personality characteristic.

Extraversion and optimism. Extraversion is characterized by a person being open, talkative, adventurous, and sociable as opposed to being secretive, silent, cautious, and reclusive. Extraverts are generally happier and more optimistic than introverts. Optimists appear less prone to stress problems than pessimists (Taylor, 1989). In part, extraversion and optimism are inherited traits, with about 50 percent of the variation of either characteristic being genetic. Studies showing greater resilience to stress of optimistic individuals may therefore be mirroring the genetic differences, since such studies are correlational.

A Brighter Outlook on Stress

The present discussion, as with most discussions about stress, have emphasized the bad effects. There are other considerations, however. First, depending on the exact definition of stress, some amount of stress is probably good. If we never had any stress, how would we learn to cope with it? Recall the notion of frustration tolerance, which develops out of experiences with frustration. We could talk about stress tolerance in the same way. Second, even highly traumatic stress events may have long-term good effects. Suedfield (1998, p. 164), having interviewed many survivors of stressful situations, including concentration camps, says: ". . . the fact is that most survivors have demonstrated surprising ability to endure, recover from, overcome, and even be strengthened by, events that to outside observers seem overwhelmingly destructive. We must recognize that trauma and damage are not inescapable consequences of the many vicissitudes that life can put in our way."

We should make a couple of points here. First, going to a concentration camp would not be the recommended way to build emotional stability. Second, many of the examples that Suedfield gives are indeed from survivors (what about the nonsurvivors?) or sometimes from people who volunteered themselves into such situations as wintering over in the arctic regions. In either case, the examples given are from highly selected subjects who may not be at all typical of the general population. Describing the horrors of World War II prisoner-of-war camps, Bettleheim (1960) observed that when new prisoners were brought to a camp, it was obvious to the "old" inmates who among the newcomers were going to be survivors and who were not. The nonsurvivors had a look of hopelessness about them; they had already given up, whereas the "survivors" showed more of a fighting spirit.

Having said this, however, we would completely agree with the point that moderate stress, especially in early life, promotes successful coping later. Neither children nor adults should be protected from all frustration, conflict, or stress. Without opportunity to experience stress, how could they learn to cope with frustrating, stressful situations? Suedfield's point is not that we should be unsympathetic toward people with problems, rather it is that in recent years, society seems to have taken the view that "human beings are predominantly weak and vulnerable creatures, who need protection from, and professional intervention after, almost any unpleasant experience" (p. 169). Instead of thinking about how getting through a stressful situation might strengthen someone (and researching that possibility), we emphasize posttraumatic stress disorder as a clinical entity to be cured or prevented. Reiterating the earlier point, people are made stronger by facing and overcoming limited-stress situations. They should not be deprived of the opportunity and benefits of this experience.

COPING

Nature of Coping

Coping refers to any way that we may voluntarily try to control stress or anxiety in ourselves. Coping activities are *self-regulatory*. The individual *consciously* does something to deal with his or her own situation. Historically, psychologists have talked a great deal about **defense mechanisms** (such as repression, reaction formation, projection, and denial), whose function is also to reduce anxiety, but not consciously. One important aspect of newer approaches is that in contrast to the classic mechanisms, there is no hint of "abnormality" in their use.

Classification of Coping Mechanisms

Lazarus and Folkman (1984) distinguished the two kinds of coping noted earlier. **Problem-focused** coping seeks to improve a stress situation by working on the cause of the stress. A person feeling the stress of overwork might try to reduce the workload, go on a vacation, use time more efficiently, and so on. **Emotion-focused (palliative)** coping activities do not change the situation, but instead just aim to make one feel better. These might involve denying that there *is* a problem, engaging in vigorous exercise, or taking drugs or alcohol. Obviously, some emotion-focused behaviors (e.g., taking drugs) may produce worse problems than those that initiated the coping. As Monat and Lazarus (1985) also point out, people do not exclusively employ one form of coping response.

Stress Management Techniques

Monat and Lazarus (1985) summarize stress-management techniques in three categories: changing environment and lifestyle, changing personality and perceptions, and directly modifying biological responses.

Changing environment and lifestyle. This includes such activities as time management, getting proper nutrition, exercising, stopping smoking and drinking, finding alternatives to frustrated goals, and so on. Many of the activities in this category are things that our grandmothers might have advised, but in the more technical jargon of modern health psychology, many of these are **immunogenic behaviors.** That is, they protect us from the potential ravages of too-severe stress. Other stress management techniques may be **pathogenic behaviors** (such as alcohol consumption or poor sleeping habits) that have ill effects.

Changing personality and perceptions. These might include such activities as assertiveness training (to achieve goals more successfully) or changes in cognitive activities. As we have seen, theories of stress emphasize the importance of the *perception* of a situation as threatening. If two people are in a sinking boat, one may appraise the situation as dangerous (he cannot swim and believes the water to be deep), but the other appraises the situation as safe (she knows the water is only three feet deep). One effective way to cope with dangerous situations sometimes, then, is to *change our appraisals* of them. Throwing out the anchor would indicate the depth of the water and lead to a reappraisal of the situation (if the water is in fact shallow). Changes in appraisals are not always effective, but it is useful to explore different appraisals to find out whether new ones might be more appropriate.

Lazarus (1968) showed how different appraisals of a situation can affect emotional responses. He recorded the GSR of subjects before and during a movie showing a primitive male puberty rite known as subcision, which consists of making several cuts on the underside of the initiate's penis. The movie uniformly produces emotional reactions in the viewers, with GSR peaks corresponding to each of the cuts. Lazarus asked whether different kinds of cognitive appraisals of the situation would diminish the emotional reactivity of different kinds of subjects. In one experiment, college students and relatively uneducated middle-management businessmen were compared. Three different soundtracks accompanied the otherwise silent film. In the first, there was no sound. In the second, the narrator said that the operation was not really unpleasant or painful and that the young man looked forward to it. In the third, a narrator described the scene objectively as just an interesting bit of anthropological data. The first narration involved the defense mechanism of **denial,** whereas the second involved the mechanism of **intellectualization.** Lazarus predicted that the college students would cope better (as indicated by lower GSR) by intellectualizing along with the soundtrack but that the businessmen would show less stress with the denial. The results came out as predicted. Another experiment showed that just presenting different introductions to the film was about as effective as narrations that continued throughout the film.

Modifying biological responses.   A person might try to control stress responses through the use of relaxation exercises, meditation, hypnosis, or biofeedback. The difference between this overall approach and those listed earlier is the emphasis on *directly* modifying the physiological responses to stress, without necessarily changing the stressful situation or the perception of it.

1. **Meditation.** There are many different forms of meditation (Ornstein, 1986), but the best-known in the United States is **transcendental meditation** (TM), a simplification of Zen Buddhism. Its primary *guru* (teacher) is Maharishi Mahesh Yogi. Under the guidance of a trained teacher, the initiate is given a *mantra*, a particular word or phrase that is said repeatedly. The mantra is a word or syllable, like "om," which has a soft rolling sound to it. The individual relaxes as much as possible in nondistracting conditions and concentrates on the mantra to the exclusion of other stimuli or thoughts. Two 20-minute periods of meditation a day are claimed to make one happier, healthier, more loving, more energetic, and more able to use one's mind creatively. Many devotees are satisfied that they have indeed become better people through the use of TM, and quite possibly this is so. The question is whether TM does this, and, if so, is there anything unique about it?

There is no compelling evidence that meditation is associated with any cognitive or physiological state that is unique to meditation. The effects of meditation are comparable to those produced by relaxation (Delmonte, 1984). Moreover, Holmes (1984) found that subjects who meditated showed just as strong somatic responses to stressful situations as did nonmeditators. Speech-anxious subjects assigned to a meditation condition did not show any lower heart rate during a subsequent speech than did subjects in three different control conditions (Kirsch & Henry, 1979). Meditation may be an especially effective way for some individuals to achieve relaxation, and it has some merit in that regard. Our existing knowledge does not show that TM (or any other form of meditation) produces a clearly different physiological state than other methods of achieving relaxation, however, and other relaxation techniques may be better for some people.

2. **Biofeedback.** Biofeedback instruments are amplifiers specialized to convert such physiological signals as skin temperature, blood pressure, heart rate, muscle tension, or EEG into readily identifiable visual or auditory stimuli that tell us what is happening. For example, a light may come on only when our brain is producing alpha waves, or a tone may change pitch upward or downward as muscle tension increases or decreases.

The therapeutic logic behind the use of biofeedback is generally that high levels of physiological activity are associated with tension (beta waves in the EEG, low skin resistance, high blood pressure and heart rate, and tense muscles). Biofeedback techniques can help us to learn what it feels like to relax by telling us when we relax even a tiny bit. Muscle tension, for example, often creeps up on us over a period of time so that we do not notice that we are getting tense; then suddenly we have headaches, muscle aches, or tics, or we grind our teeth. From electrodes placed on the appropriate muscles, we can see or hear from the biofeedback instrument when there is an increase or decrease in tension. We may thereby learn to discriminate tension from relaxation and be able to control tension. The 1970s wave of almost uncritical enthusiasm for biofeedback has now subsided as the limitations of the technique have become apparent. Biofeedback works well for some kinds of problems but not so well for others. For example, it has been difficult to obtain reductions of heart rate or blood pressure of clinically significant magnitude that will last outside the laboratory setting. Feedback can be very effective for any problem (including headaches) that are related to muscle tension.

SUMMARY

1. Frustration is an **aversive state** that occurs when an anticipated desirable goal is not attained. Theoretically, it is an intervening variable that has blocking of a goal as the antecedent condition, and cognitive, behavioral, and physiological events as the consequent condition. There are no unique frustration responses.

2. Frustration may have both **cue** and **drive** properties. As a cue, frustration helps select or guide behavior. As a drive, frustration energizes behavior, and escape from a frustration situation is reinforcing.

3. Frustration theory accounts for the greater **persistence** of responding by animals during extinction if they have received **partial reinforcement** during training. Frustration becomes conditioned to responses and helps maintain behavior in the absence of reward.

4. **Conflict** is a special category of frustration, involving choices among incompatible responses so that achieving one goal precludes achieving another.

5. The best developed **experimental** theory of conflict is that of Neal Miller. Miller assumes that the closer one is to a positive or negative goal, the stronger is the tendency to approach or avoid, respectively. These increasing tendencies are

called **approach and avoidance gradients,** with the avoidance gradient being **steeper** than the approach gradient.

6. Four basic kinds of conflict are **approach-approach, avoidance-avoidance, approach-avoidance,** and **multiple approach-avoidance.** Most research has been done on approach-avoidance conflicts, where it is assumed that approach and avoidance gradients **intersect.** This point of intersection is the point of maximal conflict.

7. Anxiety may be considered an aversive fearlike state that occurs when the cause cannot be controlled. **Trait anxiety** is an enduring disposition to be anxious in many situations. **State anxiety** refers to anxiety aroused in a very specific situation.

8. Gray has proposed a **biological theory of anxiety,** which says that when ongoing behaviors are interrupted by signals of punishment or nonreward, or by novel stimuli, activity in a **behavioral inhibition system** is aroused. This activity *is* anxiety and produces inhibition of the ongoing behavior, increases physiological arousal, and increased attention to the threatening stimuli.

9. **Cognitive approaches** to anxiety involve methodologies that are designed to tease out **preattentive** (unconscious) effects from **attentive** (conscious) effects, to detect selective attention to some events rather than others, or to detect selective memories or distortions of memory.

10. The **general adaptation syndrome** (GAS) is a physiological response to many kinds of environmental stressors. In the **stage of exhaustion** the organism's physiological defenses break down, and illness or death may ensue.

11. The **interactive definition** of stress says that stress occurs when the environment makes demands on the organism that the organism cannot meet. This definition accounts for individual differences in susceptibility to stress.

12. Stress may occur as a result of **traumatic events,** accumulated **life changes,** or accumulated daily **hassles. Noise** and **crowding** are also stressful. Animals and people try to maintain **personal space** between themselves and others, protecting the individual from overstimulation and informing others that the "owner" of the space is in control.

13. Individual differences in susceptibility to stress depend on **genetics** and **early experiences,** both prenatal and postnatal. Early exposure to changing stimulation is important in developing resistance to stress. Emotional conditioning also occurs.

14. **Lack of control** in aversive situations can produce such stress disorders as gastrointestinal ulcers. Humans develop many strategies for gaining **perceived control** in situations in which there may be no real control. This technique helps to reduce the stressfulness of uncontrollable aversive events

15. If an organism is repeatedly unable to be effective in its interactions with the environment, **learned helplessness** may result. This failure to respond is presumed to occur when the organism perceives that it has no control over the environment.

16. The **attributional theory of depression** says that human depression occurs when a person perceives that his or her failures are due to causes that are **internal** to the person, are **global** (occurring across many situations), and are **stable** across time.

17. A number of personality characteristics are thought to moderate the effects of stress, including they **Type A behavior pattern, hardiness,** and **extraversion.**

18. **Coping** refers to any way in which we more or less consciously try to control stress or anxiety in ourselves. **Problem-focused coping** seeks to change the cause

of the stress. **Emotion-focused coping** tries to change the emotional response to the stressful situation.

19. Stress management techniques include changing the environment or one's lifestyle, changing one's perceptions (especially by reappraising the stressful situation), and changing biological responses (physiological arousal).

20. **Meditation** is a way of reducing physiological responsiveness by producing relaxation. There is little evidence that meditation does anything beyond producing general relaxation.

21. **Biofeedback** involves electronic amplification of physiological responses as a technique for learning how to control those responses. Biofeedback works best for relaxation of specific skeletal muscle groups and for disorders resulting from muscle tension. Feedback has not been found to be an effective procedure for reducing blood pressure.

CHAPTER ELEVEN

Aggression and Altruism

——•——

The simultaneous presence of aggressive and altruistic behaviors within at least one species, *homo sapiens,* provides an interesting biological and social puzzle. From the point of view of natural selection, aggressive behavior would seem to have great value. Aggressive males of many species have access to more females and hence disseminate their genes more widely. Among humans, unfortunately, aggressive behavior can quite literally lead to "overkill." Most of us are familiar with the German and Soviet atrocities under Hitler and Stalin during the 1930s and 1940s, but these now spark only dim awareness in many people and even denial of their occurrence by others. Less easy to deny are the 1990s attempts at genocide occurring between the Hutu and Tutsi tribes in Africa, and warfare between the Serbians and Croatians in deconstructed Yugoslavia. These examples suggest the philosophical view held by the British philosopher Thomas Hobbes, that men are inherently evil and that it is the duty of the state to keep their violent impulses in check. The other side of the coin provides foundation for Jean-Jacques Rousseau's view of the "noble savage," that men are inherently good but are corrupted by society. People do engage in apparently selfless acts of heroism, as well as everyday kindnesses to others, which would not seem to promote self-interest. Why, for example, would a person donate his or her own blood to a faceless blood bank? It is to such questions as good and evil that we now turn.

AGGRESSION

What Is Aggression?

No amount of definition seems to cover what everyone means by aggression. What has been called aggression ranges from attack and killing, on the one hand, to verbal descriptions of Rorschach inkblots, on the other. Table 11–1 is a set of examples that may or may not be considered aggressive. Check the ones you think represent aggression. If you compare notes with someone else, the difficulty soon becomes obvious. For example, a definition including all *actual harm* would include item 1 (Boy Scout) and item 3 (flowerpot), as well as item 21 (hired killer). If actual harm and intent to harm are both considered necessary, then we eliminate items 1 and 3, among others. If *intent alone* is deemed sufficient, even for a failed act (e.g., item 2, assassin misses target), then we have yet another set of aggressive behaviors. If we exclude food-getting behavior (item 4) or an act committed under someone else's orders (item 6), the picture changes again.

We conclude from the preceding that no single circumstance can satisfactorily characterize everything that might be considered aggressive. This point is further emphasized when we look at cross-cultural definitions of "crime." In some societies, for example, the killing of a newborn child is an aggressive act punishable by law, as is abortion. In other societies, "infanti-

TABLE 11–1.   Behaviors that might be considered aggressive.

1. A Boy Scout helping an old lady across the street accidentally trips her, and she sprains her ankle.
2. An assassin attempts to kill a presidential candidate, but his shot misses.
3. A housewife knocks a flowerpot off a fifth-story window ledge, and it hits a passerby.
4. A farmer kills a chicken for dinner.
5. In a debate, one person belittles another's qualifications.
6. A soldier presses a button that fires a nuclear missile and kills thousands of people whom he cannot even see.
7. A policeman trying to break up a riot hits a rioter on the head with a club and knocks him unconscious.
8. A cat stalks, catches, tosses around, and eventually kills a mouse.
9. A wife accuses her husband of having an affair, and he retorts that after living with her, anyone would have an affair.
10. A frightened boy, caught in the act of stealing and trying to escape, shoots his discoverer.
11. One child takes a toy away from another, making him cry.
12. A man unable to get into his locked car kicks in the side of the door.
13. A man pays 25¢ to beat an old car with an iron bar, which he does vigorously.
14. A football player blocks another player from behind (clipping) and breaks his leg.
15. A businessman hires a professional killer to "take care of" a business rival.
16. A woman carefully plots how she will kill her husband, and then does so.
17. Two students get into a drunken brawl, and one hits the other with a beer bottle.
18. A businessman works vigorously to improve his business and drive out the competition.
19. On the Rorschach inkblot test, a hospitalized mental patient is scored as being highly aggressive, although he has never actually harmed anyone.
20. A young boy talks a lot about how he is going to beat up others, but he never does it.
21. A hired killer successfully completes his job.

cide" is taken for granted and justified on the same grounds that abortion may be justified, such as having too many children or being unable to afford to take care of a child (Segall, Ember, & Ember, 1997). Behaviors that are called aggressive may represent many different underlying processes, as well as be subject to differences in definition.

Multiprocess Views of Aggression

Biologists generally talk about **agonistic behaviors** rather than aggression. These are any kind of attack, fighting, escape, or avoidance behaviors. Three common types are predatory behavior, attack behavior, and defensive fighting. Predatory behavior is seldom considered aggressive because it is not between members of the same species and is usually unemotional, such as the quiet stalking behavior of the cat. Attack behavior between cats, on the other hand, involves a lot of noise, back arching, and hair fluffing. Defensive fighting also has a desperate and highly emotional quality.

Moyer (e.g., 1971) distinguishes eight forms of aggression, differentiated by specific behaviors and by what Moyer believes are different physiological bases. These are (1) predatory, (2) intermale, (3) fear induced, (4) irritable (such as pain induced), (5) territorial defense, (6) maternal, (7) sex related, and (8) instrumental. The last involves harm-doing behaviors rewarded by something other than the aggressive behavior itself. Moyer believes that each form of aggression in lower animals has a different brain circuitry but that the circuits may overlap—as they obviously must, if they result in common behaviors. At any given time, more than one circuit may be active, such as with intermale and territorial defense. With people, however, Moyer argued that there is no good evidence for differences in brain circuitry for different kinds of aggressive behavior. The human's refined capacity for learning and using symbols provides an indefinitely wide range of possibilities for arousing aggressive behavior through the same circuitry.

ANIMAL AGGRESSION

Antecedent Conditions for the Arousal of Aggression

Aversive stimuli.   Most of us get irritable when we are in pain, and in the laboratory we can arouse fighting behavior in animals by application of a variety of aversive ("irritating") stimuli (Vernon, 1969). A young mouse, for example, tries to bite anything that pinches its tail; and when a monkey in a restraining chair is struck on the tail, it will bite a ball held in front of its head. Hutchinson (1972) classified antecedents of animal aggression as (1) an increase of intense, noxious, or painful stimuli; or (2) the decrease or offset of pleasant, beneficial, or rewarding stimuli. The *delivery* of physical blows, tail shock, intense heat, noxious brain stimulation, air blasts, foot shock, loud noise, and aversive conditioned stimuli, or the *withdrawal* of food, morphine, mobility, rewarding brain stimulation, money, and conditioned stimuli for rewarding events lead to attacks on conspecifics, rubber hoses, toy animals, contraspecifics, response panels, and tennis balls. As a rule, attack increases with stimulus intensity, duration, and closeness in time of multiple aversive stimulations, and it is weaker with repetitive weak stimulations or more frequent stimulations. The species studied include barn wasps, boa constrictors, snapping turtles, alligators, opossums, foxes, ferrets, pigeons, rats, monkeys, and humans.

Shock-elicited aggression.   The most widely used procedure for obtaining unconditioned attack is to deliver foot shock to a pair of rats placed together in a grid-floor box. The shocks are presented for a half-second at repeated intervals. The initial response is to attempt escape, but the animals quickly begin to assume a stereotyped position, standing on the back paws and biting at each other when the shock is turned on (O'Kelly & Steckle, 1939; Ulrich & Azrin, 1962). Such fighting increases in proportion to shock frequency and intensity. The size of the box is also important. In a 0.25-square-foot space there is almost 100 percent fighting between two rats, but when the area is increased to 2.25 or 4.0 square feet, shock-induced fighting is almost zero.

Conditioned reflexive fighting.   Since it is possible to instigate reflexive fighting every time two animals are put together, could such "reflexive fighting" be conditioned to other stimuli? Vernon and Ulrich (1966) paired a sound with shock, but over hundreds of trials there was never more than about 50 percent fighting. Reflexive fighting in the rat, then, is *not* readily conditionable. The highly pugnacious Siamese fighting fish (*Betta splendens*), however, show more reliable conditioning of an aggressive display (e.g., Thompson & Sturm, 1965). Thus, some aspects of aggressive behavior can be readily conditioned.

Punishment of shock-induced aggression.   Nature built a clever biological trap here. If we try to stop shock-induced fighting by punishing it, the punishment simply arouses further unconditioned aggression. If rats are given continuous shock as long as they fight, they fight more (Ulrich & Craine, 1964). Similarly, punishment of reflexive biting by monkeys leads to more biting and hence more punishment, and so on. Pain-elicited aggressive responses may be inhibited by punishment under specific conditions, but these conditions are not yet clearly identified.

Proximity to other animals.   Proximity is one of the most important antecedents for aggression (Marler, 1976). Crowding results in more fighting, with either birds or mammals, and the closeness of a same-sex conspecific is especially important. Male chaffinches start fights with other males when they are farther away than they do with females. But if the females have their breasts dyed red like the males, the females are also attacked when they are farther away. There may have been selection for fighting with same-sex conspecifics because they are the strongest competitors for resources and mates.

Dominance, rituals, and peaceful coexistence.   Many animals develop dominance hierarchies, usually with one male at the top that gets first chance at food and his choice of females. Positions in the hierarchy are sometimes determined by actual fighting and sometimes by ritual fighting—aggressive displays such as spreading out feathers, baring teeth, or making noise. High rank may also be attained "by cunning or even by accident if the critical encounters with opponents occur at a time when something else in their recent past predisposes them to be subordinate to whomever they meet" (Marler, 1976, p. 239). One can be born into a high-status position, even among monkeys. If one's mother is of high status, then the offspring enjoys the same status. A hierarchy remains stable until some animal is challenged for its place. Actual fighting also may be reduced by establishment of territories. Some species fight at territorial boundaries, but others tend not to. Shrews, for example, "give a chirp of alarm, turn tail, and run" when they meet at the common boundary of their territories (Marler, 1976, p. 240).

Ritualized aggression, dominance hierarchies, and territorial control have been said to be nature's way of preserving life. The apparent calm may mask the destruction of uncountable numbers of animals forced to live in marginal habitats, however. Ritualized aggression still favors the victor. The loser has fewer chances at food or mates. In evolution it matters not how you play the game, but whether you win or lose.

Reinforcement. There are also *subsequent-stimulus* causes of aggression; aggressive behavior may increase if it is rewarded. This behavior is called instrumental aggression. Rewards include the delivery of target contact (being allowed to aggress against some particular target), food, and rewarding brain stimulation. The removal of conspecific attack, tail shock, or attack from some other species is also rewarding (Hutchinson, 1972). Conversely, delivery of a noxious stimulus elicits attack, and its removal following attack is rewarding. Or removal of a rewarding stimulus elicits attack, and presentation of a rewarding stimulus after attack is rewarding.

Inhibition to Aggression

Animals can do many things to avoid aggressive encounters, some of which are under social control. These include

- Keeping a distance from the antagonist.
- Arousing a noncompetitive response, such as making a sexual display so that the antagonist is distracted.
- Avoiding provocation of others, including not fighting back.
- Producing rapid familiarity, which includes making the animal's own smell, taste, sight, and sound as familiar as possible to the other animals with which it must remain in close contact. Animals are more likely to attack "strangers" than "friends." Animals sprayed with deodorants to hide a familiar smell, for example, are attacked by normally friendly members of their living group.
- Diverting attack elsewhere. A victim might attack a third animal and have its own attacker then become an aggressive partner. Such coalitions are found among both human and nonhuman primates. Lorenz has repeatedly claimed that defeated wolves inhibit further aggression by baring their throats to their victors. Other authors (e.g., Scott, 1958) strongly disputed this claim, however.

HUMAN AGGRESSION AND INTENT

Intent is a nebulous concept in the discussion of animal aggression but is widely accepted in definitions of human aggression. We may say that **aggressive behaviors are behaviors intended to do physical or psychological damage to someone.** Let us clarify this definition.

First, there is intent to harm. Did the defendant, with malice aforethought, intend to kill the victim? The jury's answer to that question is of vital interest to the defendant, but how can intention be determined? Francis Irwin (1971) illustrated a way to determine intent with an episode from *Bullivant and the Lambs* (Compton-Burnett, 1949). The father of two young boys walks by a place in a garden where the boys are building a hutch, speaks with them, then continues walking on a path toward a footbridge over a deep ravine. The bridge had been so weakened by a storm the previous night that it would not support a man's weight, but this danger was not immediately visible. A warning sign had been posted, but the father (in the context of the story) concludes that his sons wanted him to die because they knew of the danger but did not tell him about it. Irwin analyzes the episode in terms of his criteria for intentional behavior, which were discussed with regard to desire and aversion in Chapter One. The father realized that the sons expected that (1) he would *not* be hurt if they told him of the danger, and (2) he *would* be hurt if they did not tell him, and they preferred (2) over (1). The sons preferred his being hurt to his not being hurt. Intent is inferred from the choice of one act over another when the expected outcome of each act is known. In the list in Table 11–1, we assume that the Boy Scout does not expect that helping the old lady will harm her, so the unfortunate result is neither intentional nor aggressive. The man who employs an assassin, however, expects that this act will result in harm, and the employment is therefore an aggressive act.

The distinction between physical and psychological harm is straightforward. We may harm people by physically hitting them or by damaging their self-esteem. We make "cutting remarks" with "sharp tongues," verbal barbs as ruthless as metal ones.

Much "aggression" research does not meet these definitional criteria, however. Tedeschi, Smith, and Brown (1974) even challenge the usefulness of intent as a research criterion because laboratory studies almost never establish aggressive intent in their subjects and frequently involve elaborate cover stories to seduce subjects into harmful behaviors. Laboratory subjects generally intend to carry out the experimenter's wishes, not to harm someone. This disclaimer should be kept in mind while reading the pages that follow.

THEORIES OF HUMAN AGGRESSION

Drive Theory

The frustration-aggression hypothesis.   The idea here is that there may be some kind of aggressive drive. Although Sigmund Freud made the first modern statement that frustration leads to aggression, Dollard, Doob, Mowrer, Miller, and Sears (1939) translated the theory into behavioral terms and made it more testable. They illustrated the theory with the following example. Four-year-old James hears the ice-cream-truck bell and says he wants some ice cream. He is refused and so becomes aggressive. The following concepts are used to explain James's possible aggressive behavior:

1. The bell **instigates** the response of trying to get ice cream.
2. A **goal-response** (such as eating the ice cream) reduces the instigation to make the goal response.
3. Prevention of the goal response produces **interference;** not letting James have ice cream is interference.
4. Interference with the goal-directed response produces **frustration,** an internal state.
5. Frustration instigates **aggressive behavior** that is intended to harm someone. If the instigated aggressive behavior is itself interfered with, this interference is further instigation to aggressive behavior.
6. Aggressive behavior may be **inhibited,** particularly by fear of punishment.
7. Aggressive behavior may be **direct** (aimed at the source of the frustration) or **indirect (displaced)**. Indirect aggression may involve a change in the **object** of aggression (perhaps a more vulnerable target than the direct object) or a change in the **form** of aggression (such as from physical to psychological).
8. According to the concept of **catharsis** (from the Greek word for "cleansing" or "purging"), aggressive acts are assumed to reduce further instigation to aggression.

Role of anger.   The frustration-aggression hypothesis says that blocking a goal instigates the intention to harm someone. Many theorists believe that this is correct; however, it is correct only when the frustration produces *anger* or *hostility*. In turn, it is thought that a person's anger in a frustrating situation depends on her or his interpretation of whether the interference was *justified* (Berkowitz, 1988; Averill, 1978; 1982; 1983). People tend to become angry when they perceive that someone has unjustly or arbitrarily deprived them of some anticipated gratification. Pastore (1952), for example, presented research subjects with various frustration scenarios, and the subjects reported they would not become angry if interference were appropriate to the situation. A person might be disappointed at 12:15 if a store had closed at its usual 12:00 time and thus desirable refreshment could not be obtained, but would not be angry. If admittance were refused at 11:55, however, a person might become angry at this arbitrary frustration five minutes before the stated closing time. Arbitrary frustrations produce stronger anger than justifiable or uncontrollable frustrations, but is arbitrariness a *necessary* condition for anger?

It turns out that uncontrollable, nonarbitrary frustrations can produce anger. In one study, research subjects imagining themselves caught in a traffic jam on the way to a job interview reported that they would become very angry (Berkowitz, 1988). In another study, subjects overtly indicated hostile reactions toward a person who frustrated them by repeatedly misunderstanding and asking questions. Subjects did not show overt hostility toward a person who was said to be hard-of-hearing but who engaged in the same behaviors. Subsequently, however, the same subjects indicated disliking for the hearing-impaired person if they could do so privately (Burnstein & Worchel, 1962). In short, a nonarbitrary frustration produced hostility that was not publicly expressed. This finding presumably reflects social rules about when it is appropriate to become angry.

Anger reduction.   We often hear it said that holding in our anger is bad for our mental health, that we should *release* it, get it out. This "ventilationist" point of view holds that expressing anger is cathartic, that anger will be reduced faster if it is expressed. Holding in anger is said to be bad because we are stuck with the emotional arousal of anger, including autonomic arousal. Tavris (1983), however, argues that venting anger simply makes people angrier, raises the noise level of our lives, and does not do any particular good most of the time.

How fast anger subsides depends on many factors, and venting anger may indeed sustain or increase anger rather than reducing it. Hokanson (1970) found that male laboratory subjects intentionally angered by the experimenter tended to show a quicker drop in blood pressure if they responded in an angry manner but that female subjects showed a more rapid drop if they responded in a conciliatory manner. Hokanson then went on to show that male subjects could be *taught* to respond in a more conciliatory manner and females in a more aggressive manner, and that blood pressure came down more quickly with the new mode of responding. Either angry or friendly responses could be "cathartic," if properly learned.

Tavris also argues that "talking out" anger does not reduce anger, it *rehearses* it. Couples who yell at each other usually get more angry, not less. In a study of aerospace engineers and technicians who had been laid off from their jobs, interview responses were compared with those of other employees who had voluntarily resigned. When fired employees targeted the company or a particular supervisor whom they could blame for their predicament, they became more angry and hostile toward their target as a result of talking about the *target*. If they picked on a supervisor, they became more angry at the supervisor but not at the company in general, and vice versa. Tavris suggests that getting angry is cathartic only if you get a sense of *control* from the anger, whether control of your own internal arousal or of the situation that was anger-provoking. The main points here are that anger is not an invariable result of frustration, anger may be lowered or raised by expressing anger, and the degree of anger we feel or express is in large part determined by the social context in which we have learned to respond to other people.

Criticisms of the frustration-aggression hypothesis.   The first criticism of the hypothesis was that it simply is not always correct. Aggression has other causes, and frustration has other effects. A second difficulty is that the hypothesis seems to require two unseen processes: frustration and tendency to aggression, but without independent operations for each. If aggressive behavior occurs, we have to speculate that there was prior frustration. A frustrating situation, however, may simply arouse an **aversive state,** without any behavior effects specific to frustration per se. We have already seen, for example, that whether people respond aggressively depends partly on whether they perceive the goal interference as justified. In any event, the frustration-aggression hypothesis has faded as a major theory in its own right, but elements of it are found in many discussions of aggression.

Social Learning Theory

The difficulties with the frustration-aggression hypothesis led to the development of a different line of theory, social learning theory (Eron, 1994). Social learning theory (e.g., Bandura, 1973) emphasizes all the possible sources of stimulation and reinforcement for behaviors that a social environment provides. It assigns special importance to **imitation and modeling** with humans, however. A child sees an adult doing something ("modeling") and copies the behavior ("imitation").

In one of the classic studies of imitation of aggression, Bandura, Ross, and Ross (1963) compared aggressive behaviors of nursery school children after the children had observed aggressive behavior by live adults, in a film of adults, or in a film of cartoon characters (adults dressed in cat costumes). Control subjects were not shown any of the aggressive sequences. The groups were further subdivided according to whether models were the same or opposite sex of the child. The main aggressive behavior was hitting a three-foot-tall inflatable rubber doll. The model sat on the doll, hit it with a fist or mallet, threw it up in the air, and kicked it about the room. The model also said such things as "Sock him in the nose" or "Hit him down." Such specific behaviors by the model were intended to be behaviors that could clearly be identified as imitative on the part of the child. Each child was then mildly frustrated by being allowed to play for a little while with an attractive toy and then being told that he or she could not play with it anymore. Toys in a different room, including a Bobo doll, could be played with, however. In each five seconds of a twenty-minute test period, the child was scored for aggressive responses, a total of 240 possible scores. The response categories were imitative aggression, partially imitative aggression, mallet aggression, sitting on the doll, nonimitative aggression, and aggressive gun play (a gun was among the toys in the test room). Certain results were clear-cut:

1. Aggressive-model groups were more aggressive than the control group.
2. Boys were more aggressive than girls.

3. Girls were more aggressive with female models, and boys more aggressive with male models.
4. Live models or film models, real people or cartoon characters, were equally effective models.

In another study (Bandura et al., 1963), children who saw an aggressive model rewarded were subsequently more aggressive than control subjects, but children who saw the aggressive model punished were less aggressive. The children later identified the models as "good" (nonaggressive) or "bad" (aggressive), *but they preferred the aggressive model when he succeeded but not when he failed.* Their reasoning was quite frank: The aggressive, rewarded model got what he wanted. Aggressive behavior was therefore viewed as a successful, instrumental behavior.

Modeling and imitation are particularly important when we look at the role of television as an instigator or inhibitor of aggressive behaviors. It is well known that television is a source of *information* about aggressive activities, although it is less clear that television viewing is in itself an instigator of aggressive behaviors. For example, a hoax following the story line of a television program was perpetrated on an airline. A bomb was said to be planted on an airliner and set to go off at any altitude less than 5,000 feet. The plane was rerouted to Denver, Colorado, which has an airport above 5,000 feet. Even more violent instances of imitation have been reported, such as dousing an innocent victim with gasoline and striking a match, after having seen such an act on television. Berkowitz (1984) has recorded many instances of epidemic violent behavior that were apparently copied. One such example during the Viet Nam war was a brief flurry of self-directed aggression, setting oneself on fire in protest of the war. In all such examples, however, it is not clear whether the individual aggressors were stimulated to imitate aggressive acts when they would not have been aggressive otherwise or whether they have simply been provided with information that helps them do something they were already motivated to do for other reasons.

Social Cognitive Theory

In the tenor of the times, as problems arose with the notion that external events solely control behavior, there was a movement toward more cognitive theories of aggressive behavior, which built on previous motivational and reinforcement theories. These cognitive theories differ in detail, but all agree that "the way the individual perceives and interprets environmental events determines whether he or she will respond with aggression or some other behavior" (Eron, 1994, p. 7). Three of these theories are neoassociation theory, attribution theory, and script theory.

Neoassociation theory. Berkowitz (1984) argued that television or other media events can instill ideas into an audience that are then carried into action—the contagion of violence. Gabriel Tarde, a French sociologist writing in 1912, said that "epidemics of crime follow the line of the telegraph." Tarde reported that the infamous Jack the Ripper murders in London led to eight imitations in London itself, and others elsewhere. Berkowitz follows the **associative network theory** (e.g., Bower, 1981). Briefly stated, the theory says the following: Memory is a series of **networks** that consist of **nodes** (representing thoughts, feelings, and actions) that are interconnected by **associative pathways.** It is assumed that these nodes and pathways are represented in brain structures, but there is no specific brain reference. Such a network is illustrated in Figure 11–1. Memories are aroused when a stimulus activates a particular node and this activation spreads to other nodes. The more nodes that are interconnected, the more memories that this **spreading activation** will arouse.

According to this theory, then, when an aggressive idea is suggested by a violent movie, the idea spreads from its particular node to other nodes. The associative strength will be greater among aggressive nodes, so that other aggressive thoughts, feelings, or actions are more likely to occur. Thus in one experiment, different groups of subjects constructed sentences out of either aggressive words or nonaggressive words. Subjects exposed to the aggressive words were subsequently more likely to give a negative evaluation to a person on the basis of a brief description than were subjects who made sentences from nonaggressive words (Wyer & Hartwick, 1980). The aggressive nodes

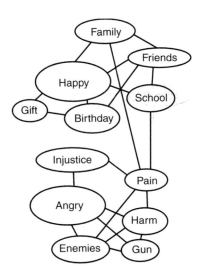

FIGURE 11–1. An associative network. The closer together two nodes (shown as ellipses) are, the more likely that when one is activated, the other will also be activated. A happy mood is more likely to activate happy thoughts and actions, and an angry mood is more likely to activate angry thoughts and actions.

aroused negative affect, which then became associated with the target of the evaluation.

Berkowitz points out that a difficulty for a social learning theory is that aggressive (or other) acts ought to be physically similar to the portrayed behavior (e.g., a knifing) but in fact rarely are. Most experiments record aggressive behaviors that are *physically different* from the behavior modeled. Associative network accounts for this by saying that portrayed violence would activate a node in an associative network and that the spreading activation from this node could reach nodes for a number of different aggressive behaviors, not just the one depicted. Thus a subject in a laboratory, seeing a gun, would have the "gun node" activated. The activation would spread to other associated nodes, such as to a node for "hurting" someone. This event could then facilitate the subject's pressing a button to deliver shocks. This explanation is more adequate to account for the weapons effect than the rather oversimplified classical conditioning interpretations that had previously been used.

This line of theory leads to another possibility, namely, that what we see on television does not just activate a preexisting associative network, *it becomes part of the associative network.* Television violence then may become part of the reality of the viewer, so that the viewer "gets used to it" and thinks that the TV viewing *is* part of reality and should be treated that way. This is basically the argument used in connection with pornography and violence against women, that there is a kind of desensitization because pornography and violence are accepted as reality.

Attribution theory. We saw earlier that whether a person becomes angry in response to frustration depends partly on whether the frustrated party attributes intent to the frustrating agent. Thus if I am walking down the aisle of a theater and someone inadvertently trips me in the dark, I am less likely to be angry than if I think the trip was intentional.

Script theory. Huesmann and Eron (1984) hypothesized that social behavior is to a large extent controlled by "programs" for behavior that have been learned during early development. These programs, or scripts, are used to guide behavior and to solve social problems. Thus on the basis of his experience, a child may develop the script that whenever he doesn't get what he wants, he becomes aggressive. Therefore, an innocuous situation might evoke aggressive behavior on the part of an individual whose script for dealing with most situations was to be aggressive. The typical "aggression-inducing variables" would not need to be present because the child had learned to be aggressive regardless of the details of the situation. To the extent that the aggression script continues to be reinforced, the individual continues to behave aggressively.

VARIABLES INFLUENCING HUMAN AGGRESSION

Biological Factors

Genetics.   Genetics plays a role in aggressive behavior as shown by selective breeding in animal husbandry and in laboratory research. An interesting example is the Norway gray rat (*Rattus norvegicus*) so commonly used in psychological research. An albino strain of this species has been selectively bred for ease of handling by researchers who must frequently pick up and move the animals. These animals are gentle, rarely bite, and are relatively nonresponsive to stimuli. As a rule, only a female with a litter is likely to bite. A wild gray rat brought into the laboratory is an entirely different story. It is highly responsive to the slightest noise and ready to bite at anything. Only a daring experimenter wearing heavy gloves would think of handling one of these beasts. In a similar vein, some dogs have been bred to be attacking watch dogs and others to be gentle children's pets.

Brain mechanisms.   The limbic system and hypothalamus are particularly important for the arousal or modulation of aggressive behavior. **Stimulation** of some hypothalamic and midbrain areas can produce attack behavior, such as mouse-killing behavior by rats or cricket-killing behavior by mice. Extensive research by Flynn (1972) has shown how stimulation of very specific brain sites can produce parts of the attack sequence or the entire attack. Aggressive behavior is organized hierarchically, as illustrated in Figure 3–1 of this text. Stimulation of one part of the amygdala facilitates attack behavior, but the general function of the amygdala seems to be to modulate the effects of hypothalamic arousal. The septal area of the brain seems to work opposite to the amygdala. Septal stimulation has a calming effect, and septal lesions produce a more vicious animal (Carlson, 1987).

Hormones and neurotransmitters.   Their effects are as follows:

1. **Testosterone.** In many species, males are more aggressive than females. The hormonal basis for this (testosterone) is indicated by the fact that males are more aggressive during the mating season when male hormones are at their highest level and are least aggressive after castration (as with a gelding steer or horse). Testosterone is related to a variety of competitive activities in humans. For example, there is the phenomenon of **steroid rage,** shown by athletes' taking hormones in order to "bulk up" their bodies. The testosterone increases muscle size but also increases aggressive behavior. The aggressive effect may have some on-field advantage in a contact sport like football, but the effect is unfortunately not limited to on-field activities. Since the research is correlational, we cannot be certain that the steroids cause

more aggressive behavior (Carlson, 1994), but given the dangerous health side effects of such hormones, it seems wise to restrain from their use. Furthermore, testosterone levels are higher in the winners than the losers of competitions, whether among humans or other animals. This phenomenon is shown particularly in animals at different levels of dominance hierarchies in their social groups.

2. **Serotonin**. Serotonin (5-hydroxytryptamine) is an inhibitory neurotransmitter in the central nervous system, which is to say that its major role is to inhibit the effects of other neurotransmitters. Low levels of serotonin have been implicated in higher levels of aggressive behavior in both animals and humans. For example, serotonin deficits have been associated with antisocial traits, suicide, aggressive/hostile traits, and impulsive violence (Finn, Young, Pihl, & Ervin, 1998; Berman & Coccaro, 1998). In addition to these stable behavior characteristics related to chronic levels of serotonin, there is also evidence that experimentally manipulated levels of serotonin are related to aggressive behavior. Animals whose diets have been manipulated by varying the amount of **tryptophan** (an amino acid precursor of serotonin) in the diet indicate that increases and decreases, respectively, lead to lower or higher levels of aggressive behavior in animals and mood changes in humans. In the experiment by Finn et al. (1998), the data suggested that people who are normally high in trait hostility may be more responsive to manipulation of tryptophan treatment.

Environmental Factors

Impulsive aggression. Impulsive aggression refers to aggressive acts that were not preplanned. Berkowitz (e.g., 1974; 1988) maintains that environmental situations (including the actions of other people) provoke impulsive attack behaviors. Most homicides, for example, are not premeditated but are spontaneous and passionate, often arising from disagreements about relatively trivial matters. The threat of capital punishment has little deterrent value because in the heat of the moment, the consequences of killing simply are not anticipated. A variety of stimulus events may facilitate, if not entirely provoke, impulsive aggressive behaviors.

Painful stimuli. As we saw earlier, painful stimuli frequently provoke escape and avoidance behaviors, but may also provoke attack. Fighting is more likely to occur if escape is not permitted, the confining space is small, and the shocks are frequent or intense (Ulrich & Azrin, 1962).

Crowding. Proximity to other animals is one of the main precursors of fighting among either birds or mammals (Marler, 1976). Crowding among rats has produced disastrous consequences, including low birth rate, high infant mortality rate, homosexuality, heightened aggressiveness, and cannibalism (Calhoun, 1962).

Human research does not bear out all the pessimistic implications of animal research, however. The fact that some cities of very high population density (e.g., Hong Kong, Tokyo) have much less crime than cities of lower density indicates that the aversive consequences of crowding can be overridden or inhibited by social controls. For example, in the Far East there is a greater emphasis on collectivism than on individualism. The amount and/or kind of aggressive behavior may vary according to this emphasis (Triandis, 1994). Thus members of collectivist cultures find aggressive behavior more tolerable when it comes from an in-group authority than when it comes from a low-level in-group member or an outsider. Overall, there are wide cultural differences in the prevalence of crime. Some indications of the aversive consequences of crowding, which might lead to more hostile behaviors, are the following (Bell, Fisher, & Loomis, 1978):

- People working under crowded conditions report more discomfort, and males more so than females.
- Males show increased physiological arousal under crowded conditions, but females do not.
- People living under crowded conditions are less attracted to others, again more true for males than females.
- People tend to withdraw from high-density situations.
- The greater the population density, as in an apartment building, the less likely people are to help each other.

What makes crowding unpleasant? One possibility is that crowding produces a very high level of arousal, which is aversive. Another is that personal freedom is restricted and that this reduced freedom is aversive.

Temperature. The weather provides a good example of a nonarbitrary source of aggressive acts; the weather does many things, but it does not select particular individuals to treat unfairly. Working under the dashboard of a car on a hot summer day, head upside down, glasses falling off, perspiration flooding into one's eyes, can lead to frustration and hostility quite apart from any culpability of the weather. There is a phenomenon known as the "long hot summer effect," wherein crime rates are apparently higher during long sieges of hot weather. This effect has been used to account in part for urban riots (Carlsmith & Anderson, 1979), and such violent crimes as homicides and assaults (Anderson & Anderson, 1984). Laboratory studies have also indicated that high temperatures, smoke, and bad odors heighten aggressive activities (Berkowitz, 1983). Figure 11–2 illustrates the effect.

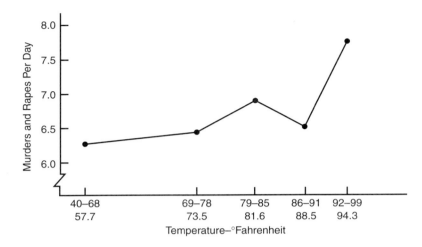

FIGURE 11–2. The long hot summer effect. In this study, the numbers of rapes and murders were correlated with temperature in Houston, Texas, over a two-year period. There were more
of these crimes during very warm weather, but this fact does not necessarily mean that
high temperatures caused the crimes. There may have been other important factors
that were not recorded. (From Anderson & Anderson, 1984, pp. 91–97. Copyright 1984
by the American Psychological Association. Reprinted by permission.)

The weapons effect.   Suppose you were asked to serve in an experiment studying physiological reactions to the stress produced by mild electric
shocks. You and another subject are to evaluate each other's performance on
a problem solving task by giving each other electric shocks. You get evaluated
first and receive seven shocks out of the ten possible—not very good. In your
experimental room, there is a telegraph key for delivering shocks to your
partner, along with a rifle and a pistol left by a previous experimenter from
an unrelated experiment. You deliver six shocks to your partner as your evaluation of his performance.
    You, of course, were in just one of a number of experimental condi-
tions, and your "partner" was really the experimenter's assistant. Your treatment was intended to anger you by giving you a large number of shocks and
to provide aggression-arousing cues (the guns). Both of these factors were expected to make you more aggressive so that you would give more shocks than
if you were less angry or did not have cues for aggressive behavior. Table 11–2
summarizes the results of this experiment by Berkowitz and Le Page (1967).
Subjects getting seven shocks gave back more shocks than subjects getting
only one shock, supporting the anger-arousal part of the hypothesis. Subjects
seeing the guns gave more shocks than those not seeing the guns, supporting
the cue-arousal part of the hypothesis.
    Berkowitz originally spoke of this cue property in terms of classically
conditioned aggressive responses. By prior association with anger, weapons

TABLE 11–2.   Mean number of shocks given in each condition of the Berkowitz and Le Page (1967) experiment.

CONDITION	NUMBER OF SHOCKS RECEIVED BY THE SUBJECT	
	1	7
Associated weapons	2.60	6.07
Unassociated weapons	2.20	5.67
No object	3.07	4.67
Badminton rackets[a]	—	4.60

[a]There was no one-shock group with badminton rackets.
Source: From Berkowitz & Le Page, 1967, p. 205. Copyright © 1967 by the American Psychological Association. Reprinted by permission.

become conditioned stimuli for anger. The anger then serves the twofold function of being a **cue** for making particular responses and of being a **drive** to intensify responses. Like fear or frustration, anger is a conditionable response with drive and cue properties. In his more recent theorizing, however, Berkowitz suggests that weapons tap into an associative network that can trigger any behavior that might be associated with anger. In some situations, anger may be a more direct cue for a particular response. If someone has previously learned to fire a gun while angry, the sight of the weapon might be a conditioned stimulus to anger, and the anger might be a cue for firing the weapon. Diagrammatically:

Gun → Anger Response → Anger Stimulus → Firing Gun

Other factors in the situation, such as fear of retribution, would also help determine whether the gun will be fired.

Berkowitz and his associates have manipulated many variables that heighten aggressive responses toward the target (the fictitious other subject). For example, when the target was said to be a college boxer and subjects had been shown a boxing film, the target got more shocks. Subjects shown an exciting, but nonaggressive, track race did not give more shocks to the target. There is also evidence that generalized arousal may facilitate aggressive response, in line with Zillman's excitation-transfer theory, discussed in Chapter Two. Thus subjects frustrated when working a jigsaw puzzle subsequently delivered more shocks to the confederate (Geen & Berkowitz, 1967), a loud noise made subjects more aggressive (Geen & O'Neal, 1969), and a sex film led to more punishment of an antagonistic partner (Tannenbaum & Zillman, 1975). Finally, subjects seeing Kirk Douglas beaten up in a fight movie (*The Champion*) subsequently delivered more shocks to the confederate if told that the beating was *justified*, as if this information produced some generalized justification for aggressive actions.

The research just described is dramatic and obviously bears on such important issues as gun control and television violence. Nevertheless, serious reservations have been raised about its meaning. First, in at least two sets of experiments, the effects could not be repeated. Buss, Booker, and Buss (1972) reported five experiments in which neither firing guns nor the presence of guns enhanced shocking a confederate. Page and Sheidt (1971) could not reproduce the weapons effect and suggested that the effect is due to an **experimenter demand** to behave aggressively. Given the situation, they suggest that the subject does what the subject thinks he or she is supposed to do—act aggressively. Page and Sheidt report that subjects receiving seven shocks were no more angry than subjects getting one shock. On many occasions the present author has outlined the experimental procedure to a class and then asked how many shocks class members would give back after receiving one shock or seven shocks. The class estimates are very close to the results obtained with real subjects getting real shocks, suggesting that under these experimental conditions, subjects do have some expectations about what is appropriate.

Berkowitz (1974) argued in defense of the weapons effect by saying that the way in which weapons are *perceived* and *interpreted* by subjects is critical. If a subject thinks a gun is terrible and frightening, it might arouse more anxiety than aggression and even lead to *fewer* shocks being delivered. Even granting the validity of this argument, however, it is difficult to see why the meaning should have been so different in Berkowitz's experiments from those reported from other laboratories.

Social Factors

Victims may provoke attack upon themselves.   This is in the category of impulsive aggression. Most murders are committed by people who know the victim well, the victim is often a relative, and the homicide is likely to have been preceded by an argument that escalated into a killing. The well-known popular singer Marvin Gaye was killed by his own father under such circumstances. In one study, a fourth of six hundred homicides were at least partly provoked by the victim (Wolfgang, 1957). Toch (1970) also found from interviews with police, from interviews with prison inmates, and from police records that about 40 percent of violent sequences were initiated when an arresting officer notified a person of his or her arrest and was treated contemptuously. In some 27 percent of the cases, violence already existed, and police action tended to inflame rather than dampen this violence. The moral seems to be clear: One of the most effective ways to avoid being attacked is not to provoke attack on oneself by returning hostile actions. An argument for gun control is that even a robbery victim is less likely to get shot if the victim does not have a gun to provoke attack by an intruder. An acquaintance of the author, a night manager of an all-night market, was killed when he picked up a gun and followed a robber out into the night. In another instance with which the author has some firsthand knowledge, a man asked his neighbor, over the back fence, for a cigarette but was refused. This refusal escalated into an argument, culminating in the shooting death of the man who had refused the cigarette.

Aggression and coercive power.   Tedeschi, Smith, and Brown (1974) view what is called human aggression as just another way that people try to get what they want, just another kind of instrumental behavior. When other methods fail, people threaten violence and sometimes back up the threat. Tedeschi et al. then suggest that the main problem is to determine conditions under which society *says* behavior is aggressive. Socially justified acts are not considered aggressive; unjustified ones are. Since no specific response is unambiguously aggressive, researchers decide what they shall call aggressive. This situation can also involve a misunderstanding of law. Many people seem to believe that it is justifiable to shoot (and possibly kill) an intruder into one's home. The law is more likely to treat this as aggressive behavior.

The scientists' labeling of a particular behavior as aggressive may ignore **negative reciprocity** and **equity.** Negative reciprocity is a social norm that gives a person the "right" to retaliate for harm done. Equity is a social norm that says you can have an eye for an eye, but no more. Kane, Doerge, and Tedeschi (1973) illustrated this point by having subjects rate the aggressiveness of participants in various conditions of a hypothetical Berkowitz-type experiment. The result was that someone receiving seven shocks was not considered aggressive for giving back seven—that number was perfectly equitable. Only if a person gave back more shocks than received was she or he considered aggressive. On average, subjects in the Berkowitz experiments never gave back more than they received. Therefore, it may have been equity that was demonstrated, not aggression.

Negative reciprocity and equity have considerable social importance, for if a person can change the meaning of his or her action, it may be judged nonaggressive. For example, German troops dressed as Polish soldiers "attacked" German installations along the Polish-German border in 1939. Hitler then "justified" the invasion of Poland as a countermeasure. Most of us try to make our actions look necessary or defensive so that they will be labeled nonaggressive.

Obedient aggression.   In this century alone, many major atrocities have been well-documented: Nazi attempts to exterminate the Jews (12 million dead); the terrorism of the Stalinist regime (at least 20 million dead); atrocities in World War II; terrorist activities related to civil strife in Ireland, Israel, Pakistan, Chile, various African countries; and the My Lai massacre by Americans in Viet Nam. When such activities come to trial, however, it is very difficult to fix blame. It is often said that the "little guys" who pull the triggers are the scapegoats for the "big guys" who give the orders. But what are these little guys like that they follow such orders? Stanley Milgram (1974) made this question into a laboratory experiment.

How far, asked Milgram, will a normal person go in following repugnant orders? Using a good cross-section of the adult population, not just college students, Milgram set up a situation in which subjects were supposed to give a "learner" increasingly strong electric shocks every time the learner made a mistake in memorizing a list of words. The "learner," an experimental assistant, was a friendly, middle-aged man whom the subjects met prior to the experiment. The fake shock apparatus was clearly marked in thirty levels, ranging from 15 to 450 volts, and with such written labels as "Slight Shock" (15 to 60 volts), "Danger: Severe Shock" (375 to 420 volts), and "XXX" (435 to 450 volts). The learner followed a set routine: He was wrong about 75 percent of the time and complained of how painful the ever-increasing shocks were. The learner and subject were in different rooms. The subjects looked to the experimenter for guidance as they became unsure about what they were doing, but they were told to continue and even to treat failure to respond as an error and to give another shock.

Before the experiment began, the anticipated results were rather innocuous. Milgram's students estimated that only about 3 percent of subjects would continue to shock the learner up to the maximum. In the very first experiment, however, **no subject stopped below 300 volts, and 26 of 40 subjects went the limit to 450 volts.** Various checks indicated that the subjects really did believe they were delivering highly painful, perhaps dangerous, shocks to the learner. For example, subjects judged the intensity of the strongest shock as 13.4 on a 14 point scale. These results are astonishing in their suggestion of how easy it is to get one human to hurt another, especially since the subjects came from all walks of life, varied in age from 20 to 50 years, and (perhaps unlike college students) were likely to believe what they were told about their participation in "an experiment on learning and memory" conducted by Yale University. In another experiment (Sheridan & King, 1972), the learner was a puppy. The stated shock levels were highly exaggerated, but they were sufficient to evoke obviously negative responses from the puppy. Most subjects, male or female, shocked the puppy all the way to the top of the shock scale.

Milgram replicated the preceding results but also found some important modifying variables. For example, the closer the contact between subject and learner (having complete isolation of the two from each other, hearing the learner's voice, being in the same room, and touching), the less likely the subject was to give the strongest shock.

The most serious criticism of the experiments per se is the possibility of experimenter demand; the subjects may have been aware of what they were expected to do. This possibility was tested in one experiment, for example, in which subjects were read the method section of an "experimental proposal" for the Milgram experiment. The method section clearly stated the shocks were not real (O'Leary, Willis, & Tomich, 1969). The subjects were then told to role-play as if they were real subjects in the experiment. The results were virtually the same as Milgram's, supporting the experimenter demand interpretation. Strangely, however, the subjects also showed many of the same signs of tension as Milgram's subjects, as if they really thought the learner was being shocked. The validity of any of the specific experimental results just described may be challenged, but there is no argument about the reality of obedient aggression and its importance. It does seem clear that people do get themselves into situations in which they feel compelled to carry out orders and do highly repugnant things, either because of their commitment or because of fear of punishment for not doing so. It is also possible that by shifting responsibility to someone who gives the orders to behave aggressively, fear of retaliation is reduced, and some people may do things they have wanted to do anyway.

Television Viewing and Aggression

Because of the great amount of exposure that people (especially children) have to television and the violence it portrays, much concern has been expressed about TV as a contributor to real-life violence. There are individuals and groups who claim that it is obvious that the massive amount of violence shown on TV produces an increase in violence outside the box. This belief reflects the social learning view. The cathartic view (see later) would say just the opposite, that TV violence may protect society by providing a harmless outlet for aggressive tendencies. There certainly is no dispute that there is a large amount of wanton killing, fighting, and property damage shown on TV. We then have two questions to face. First, what data are there to show that TV violence *is related* to real-life violence? And second, if there is such a relationship, how do we *interpret* the data that show it? For example, are the data *only correlational,* or do they indicate a *causal* relationship?

First of all, it does *not* appear that increased television viewing has *reduced* the crime rate, as predicted by catharsis theory. Catharsis theory presumably would predict a negative correlation between TV violence and real-world violence, and no research has shown this. What does the evidence show?

Correlational studies of TV viewing and violence. In one of the major studies of the effects of TV violence, data relating TV viewing and aggressive behavior were collected for 427 children over a period of ten years (Eron, Lefkowitz, Huesmann, & Walder, 1972). In Grade 3, the original group of 875 children (every third-grader in town) were judged by their peers as to how aggressive they were. At the same time, data on other variables potentially related to aggressive behavior of the children were collected from parents, such as children's preferences in TV viewing. Each parent was asked the child's three favorite TV shows, and these were given violence ratings based on an independent judge's ratings of all the TV shows mentioned.

The ten-year follow-up data are referred to as Grade 13. At this time, there were three measures of aggressiveness: peer ratings, subjects' self-reports, and a personality test. Other data, such as favorite programs, were also collected by self-reports. It is important to note that all the Grade 13 measures were obtained independently of the Grade 3 measures. The results for boys are shown in Figure 11–3; the data for girls showed no significant trends.

Figure 11–3 shows a **cross-lagged correlation,** a method for using correlational data to get at causal relations. First, there was a low (.21) but significant relation between TV preference and aggressive behavior in Grade 3. This finding, of course, is ambiguous as regards causality. There was an even higher correlation between Grade 3 and Grade 13 aggressive behavior, which tells us only that the same people were violent ten years later. Two other correlations tell us more about the effect of TV viewing on violence: Grade 3 aggressiveness did *not* predict Grade 13 TV preference ($r = .01$), but Grade 3 TV preference did predict Grade 13 violence ($r = .31$). From this it appears that Grade 3 TV preference played a *causal* role in Grade 13 violence, but not the other way around. Television viewing habits are obviously not the only factor involved in Grade 13 aggression, since the correlations are not tremendously high, but it is remarkable that there are any significant correlations at all over a ten-year period. The data are, however, weakened by the lack of any relationship for the females.

Reviewing all the published literature to date, Freedman (1984) concluded that there is a small but consistently positive correlation (somewhere between .10 and .20) between viewing TV violence and aggressiveness. This conclusion was based on research involving thousands of subjects, in several

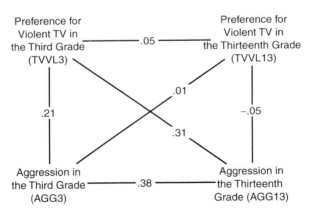

FIGURE 11–3.   The correlations between a preference for violent television and peer-rated aggression for 211 boys over a 10-year-lag. (From Eron, Lefkowitz, Huesmann, and Walder, 1972, p. 257. Copyright © 1972 by the American Psychological Association. Reprinted by permission.)

different countries. At the same time, it should be noted that this finding means that only about 4 percent of the variation in aggressive behavior can be accounted for by variation in television viewing. The most generous interpretation possible, based only on the highest of such correlations (on the order of .30), would account for only about 10 percent of the aggression variability in terms of TV viewing. It is important to note, however, that similar results have been found in several other countries, lending credibility to the research conducted in the United States (Segall, Ember, & Ember, 1997).

Field experiments on TV viewing and violence. These are studies in natural settings, with some degree of experimental control over television or movie viewing so that the effects of the kind or amount of viewing on behavior can be interpreted causally. Residential schools have been one of the more-used settings. There have been a number of reviews of such studies, with the reviewers not always in agreement. Freedman (1984) concluded that there were found at *best* only a few modest relationships between TV viewing and aggressiveness. Friedrich-Cofer & Huston (1986) argued that there is a more consistent relationship between violent TV viewing and aggressive behavior than Freedman's analysis would make it appear. Wood, Wong, and Chachere (1991) analyzed the results of twenty-eight laboratory and field experiments in which children or adolescents were randomly assigned to groups exposed to violent or nonviolent presentations of movies, and their subsequent spontaneous social interactions were analyzed for aggressive acts. The results showed with statistical reliability that groups watching violent films were more aggressive in their social interactions than were control subjects.

Control of Aggression

Biological control. Behavior that is called "aggressive" (1) may be socially defined, (2) is often hard to identify as unambiguously aggressive, (3) is affected by noxious events in the immediate environment, and (4) is heavily influenced by the specific ways in which an individual has learned to deal with situations. Given all these caveats, do we know enough about brain mechanisms to justify doing anything permanently to the brain when there might be serious side effects? In some cases the answer is clearly yes. Surgeons operate on the brain for tumors, for extremely severe epilepsy, or other physically definable pathologies in which the benefits to the patient outweigh the potential risks. Aggressive behavior might be secondary to these brain disorders and reduced by their treatment. Without a clearly defined brain pathology, however, there is little justification for surgical intervention to modify aggressive behavior (Valenstein, 1973).

Catharsis versus social learning. Konrad Lorenz (1966), among others, considered aggression to be instinctive, following the water-tank (hydraulic) model. Aggressive "energy" is said to well up inside the individual, like water in a tank, until it overflows spontaneously into aggressive behavior unless "drained off" harmlessly (catharsis). Lorenz also claimed that animals have instinctive inhibitions to aggression, so that a species does not kill itself off. For example, a dog defeated in a fight stops fighting and adopts a vulnerable position that tends to inhibit further attack by the winner. Humans, on the other hand (says Lorenz), do *not* have these inhibitions. Therefore, without some other outlet for the spontaneously building aggressive energy, humans will inevitably fight among themselves. Lorenz's solution was to provide alternative aggression outlets so that aggressive energy does not build up too much. Such **displacement** (indirect) activities as athletic events would presumably be cathartic because they would drain off aggressive energy harmlessly and hence reduce the likelihood of serious aggressive activity. This view is the same as the ventilationist view of anger.

The instinct model has not been taken seriously by either biologists or psychologists for many years (e.g., see Bandura, 1973). There is no known physiological mechanism by which there could be a buildup of instinctive energy as described by the model. Energy can be stored, of course, but it is in the form of fat or glycogen that is available for all behaviors, not just aggressive behaviors. As Scott (1971) pointed out, anger is aroused by external stimuli, not by some aggression-specific energy. Furthermore, internal arousal eventually dies out in the absence of further stimulation. It does not accumulate indefinitely, as the hydraulic model says. Neither is there real evidence that animals are kept from fighting by inhibitions that humans do not have. We saw earlier that either aggressive or nonaggressive responses may lead to a reduction of emotional arousal, depending on previous experience. Further, in the face of such events as a 1964 soccer championship in Peru where fans got into a riot resulting in three hundred deaths and five hundred injuries, it is difficult to believe that vicarious participation in violence is cathartic. Indeed, fan violence is some of the most visible evidence against the cathartic view. Finally, research on the effects of television viewing have consistently shown positive correlations between watching violent television shows and aggressive behavior. Sometimes the results are negligible. But from the point of view of catharsis, it appears that *no research has shown a negative correlation* between watching violent television and aggressive behavior. Yet, this is exactly what the catharsis hypothesis would predict.

Social learning.   The alternative view from social learning theory, however, is exactly the opposite of the cathartic view. The learning view says that aggressive behavior occurs because it is rewarded and that successful aggression is *more likely* to occur again, not less likely. If either of these views were entirely correct, it would obviously be socially disastrous to try to control aggression on the basis of the *wrong one,* either instinct or social learning. It becomes critical, then, to evaluate as best one can the evidence pro and con on these views. It is also possible that both views have some validity under partic-ular circumstances. If so, the circumstances should be clarified.

ALTRUISM

Altruism, helping, and prosocial behavior are equivalent terms referring to behavior intended to benefit others without obvious benefit in return. Such behavior commonly characterizes people in love, but it is broader than just that. The question we ask is, Under what conditions are people more likely or less likely to help someone else?

Bystander Apathy

The single event that more than any other sparked interest in helping behavior was the 1964 case of Kitty Genovese. As she returned to her home in Queens (New York City) about 3:00 A.M., she was attacked and repeatedly stabbed over a half-hour period, all the while screaming until she was finally killed. Thirty-eight neighbors watched the gory episode without so much as calling the police. The horror of this scene highlighted the dramatic *failure* of people to help a fellow person. An immediate interpretation was that "big city people" had become callous and indifferent to the plight of anyone else. At best, however, this is just one of many factors that determine when some-one will help. We may divide these factors into characteristics of the situation, of the helper, and of the victim.

Situational Influences

Latane and Darley (1970) argued that the presence of other bystanders makes it less likely that any one person will help. They staged elaborate "emergencies" in laboratories and public places, and observed bystander be-havior. For example, they had smoke pour into a room where students were working, arranged for subjects to hear an apparent accident over an inter-com, staged an epileptic seizure, and pulled a fake robbery in a liquor store (with the manager's permission). Their results consistently indicated that people were more likely to help if they were alone than if someone else were present. Latane and Darley proposed three complementary explanations for this behavior:

1. **Audience inhibition.** If others are present, we are slower to act because we are concerned about their evaluation of our behavior. Perhaps the smoke is not re-ally an emergency, and we would look foolish if we treated it as such.
2. **Social influence.** We watch others to see how they are acting. If *everyone* is trying to be cool and nonchalant, then a whole group may fool itself into believing there is no emergency.

3. **Diffusion of responsibility.** Psychologically we may feel that if there is a single person present at an emergency, it is more imperative to help. When more people are present, there is less pressure for any single individual to help. Hence, nobody may act.

Latane and Darley found that a person alone would help someone about 95 percent of the time, but helping dropped to 84 percent if a second person were present. The percentage dropped to 50 if another person present failed to respond to the emergency. Fortunately, people will sometimes help in the presence of others. Piliavin, Rodin, and Piliavin (1969) faked the collapse of a person on a subway train and found that 70 percent of the time bystanders helped immediately. The authors believed that this response occured because the emergency was unquestionable to the bystanders and that there clearly was no one else to help except them.

The diffusion of responsibility phenomenon has subsequently been studied under the rubric of **social loafing** and turns out to be a very general phenomenon (Latane, 1981). The idea here is that people will generally work less hard if the work is shared than if they are working alone. For example, in a tug of war, each individual on a team works less hard than if just one person on each team were pitted against one person on the other team.

Costs and benefits of helping. In an informal manner, people weigh the relative costs and benefits of getting involved with any particular activity. The potential costs of intervening in a situation are inconvenience, unpleasantness, and possible danger. The costs of not helping may be feelings of guilt and possible scorn from others. Benefits of helping may be feeling greater self-esteem, being praised by others, or receiving thanks. Sometimes people do jump in and help without thinking at all, as did a bystander when a plane crashed into freezing waters in Washington, D.C. Research shows that

- Bystanders are more likely to help someone neat and well-dressed than an apparent derelict or drunk or troublemaker.
- Bystanders are more likely to help someone with a cane rather than an apparent drunk carrying what appears to be a bottle in a brown bag.
- Bystanders are less likely to help if there is some person apparently more capable present (such as someone in a hospital uniform).

Modeling. Bryan and Test (1967) had two disabled cars with women as drivers along the side of a busy street. Under one condition someone was helping the first woman driver, but under another condition not helping. Fifty-eight motorists stopped to help the second driver when they saw the first driver being aided, as compared with thirty-five when the first driver was not being aided. Similar results were obtained with people who saw another person donate to Salvation Army solicitors. If the model is too generous, however, potential donors might be scared off because they might be embarrassed by their own small contributions.

Being a Good Samaritan may be discouraged for many reasons. Physicians may refrain from spontaneously helping accident victims for fear of malpractice suits. Within large cities there is also an element of trying to keep a certain amount of social distance between oneself and others. The hurried activity in a city may also make it more difficult to attract attention for help. Darley and Bateson (1973) found that if subjects were told to be someplace in a hurry, they were less likely to stop and help someone in apparent difficulty. The subjects were theology students told to go to a lecture on Good Samaritanism!

Severity of the emergency. Severity is not an overriding factor, else Kitty Genovese would have gotten help. The costs associated with helping seem particularly important in such situations. For example, in one study a bloodied victim was *less likely* than a nonbloodied victim to receive direct help. The bloodied victim did get more help indirectly, however, such as by a phone call.

Characteristics of the Victim

A reputable looking victim has a better chance of getting help than a disreputable victim, but people are also more likely to help others who are like themselves. For example, in the early 1970s a "hippie-looking" person and a more conservative-looking person solicited money from "hippies" and "straights" on the street. The person-on-the-street was more likely to help the solicitor who was more like himself or herself (Enswiller, Deaux, & Willits, 1971).

There is also the so-called **just world hypothesis,** which says that people bring their problems on themselves and that they get what they deserve. Some people are unwilling to help others because they believe, rightly or wrongly, that people in trouble are getting what they deserve. The "just world" belief has strong implications for such social issues as welfare, and it has certainly played a role in attitudes towards AIDS. Since AIDS has been more widespread among homosexuals and among intravenous drug users sharing needles, there have been people (including public figures such as the Reverend Jerry Falwell) who have proclaimed the disease a just retribution for a sinful life style.

Finally, the **norm of reciprocity** comes into play. If a person has given help to someone in the past, this "helping person" is more likely to get help in the future. Goranson and Berkowitz (1966) found that experimental subjects were more likely to help a laboratory supervisor if they believed that the supervisor had previously volunteered to help them than if the supervisor had refused to help or if the help had been mandatory.

Characteristics of the Helper

Personality variables. Several personal characteristics distinguish helpers from nonhelpers. Schwartz found that high scorers on his **Ascription**

of Responsibility Scale (those who tended to ascribe responsibility to themselves rather than others) were more likely to take action in a fake emergency situation (Schwartz, 1968; Schwartz & Clausen, 1970). Similarly, people who feel competent are more likely to help, even if this feeling has only just been engendered in an experimental situation by success at an experimental task. Conversely, it has also been suggested that people with low self-esteem may be more likely to help if they can thereby raise their self-esteem.

Mood. A large amount of research shows that people in a good mood are more likely to help than are people in a bad mood (Morris, 1989; Salovey, Mayer, & Rosenhan, 1991). For example, a person in a shopping mall is more likely to help a stranger pick up a spilled bag of items after the helping person has just received a small gift. There are a number of explanations to account for this behavior. According to **mood maintenance theory,** people in a good mood are more likely to help others because it helps maintain the good mood that they are in. It has also been reported, albeit less often than with positive mood, that people in a negative mood are also more likely to help someone. This behavior is accounted for in terms of **mood restoration.** Helping someone else gets a person out of a bad mood into a more neutral or positive mood. Both theories are incentive theories, saying that people engage in activities that they anticipate will make them happier (by maintaining or improving their good mood) or less unhappy (by getting rid of a negative mood). Both these hypotheses seem to assume that people are thoughtful and calculating about helping others. Although this may be true for some situations, the little helpful things that people do every day do not seem to involve much forethought.

Theories of Prosocial Behavior

Freud's psychoanalytic theory. Freud divided personality into three parts—**id, ego,** and **superego.** The id refers to such "basic" drives as hunger, thirst, sex, and aggression. Superego is equivalent to "conscience." Ego is the rational part of the personality that tries to "referee" between the demands of the id for immediate gratification and the hesitancy on the part of the superego. These are not separately identifiable parts of the brain but are Freud's metaphorical way of looking at the mind. Our interest here is in superego, or conscience.

According to Freud, the superego develops as a child learns values (what is good and what is bad) from his or her parents and culture. These values are "internalized" and become part of the individual, serving as ideals and internal sources of reward and punishment. In a sense, the child develops a set of imaginary parents who, like Jiminy Cricket in *Pinocchio,* direct the child's behavior. If we do something we have learned is "wrong," we may be punished by feeling guilt and anxiety. If we do something that is "right," we are rewarded by feeling good. If certain ideals are strongly internalized, we may, for example, do almost anything rather than lie or cheat. Martyrs appear to be people who would give up their lives rather than their ideals.

Reinforcement theory. Reinforcement theory is similar to psychoanalytic theory, but reinforcement theorists would tend to emphasize reward and punishment for *specific* behaviors. Altruistic behavior would in this view occur only if it had been rewarded in the past. The anticipation of future rewards and punishments for helping (or not helping) are of course also important. Anticipations of punishment (inconvenience, possible danger) are weighed against possible rewards (being thanked, getting money, or receiving intangible reward in the hereafter).

Moss and Page (1972) studied the effect of reward for helping on future helping. They approached passersby on the street and asked directions to a particular department store. The strangers were either rewarded with a smile and a thank you, were punished by being rudely told the direction did not make sense, or were left neutral (with just an "okay"). Farther down the street, a female confederate dropped a small bag as the same passerby approached. Only 40 percent of the just-punished individuals picked up the bag for her, but 82 percent of the neutral subjects and 85 percent of the rewarded subjects did so. The rude response clearly had a detrimental effect, but the neutral subjects were about as helpful as the rewarded. Perhaps the simple acknowledgment of their previous help was sufficient reward to carry over.

Kohlberg's theory of moral judgment. Kohlberg (1964) proposed a theory of moral judgment that depends on the increasing ability of a child to understand complex situations. At the **preconventional** level, the child is primarily influenced by the consequences of her or his actions. That is, the child's behavior is determined by rewards and punishments, just as reinforcement theory says. The young child obeys adults because adults mete out punishment. At the **conventional** level, the older child becomes concerned with what others expect of her or him and tries to behave in a conventional way. This is a kind of conformity for the sake of conformity, having respect for authority because such respect is right and proper. At the **postconventional** level, which some adults never achieve, there is a mature level of conscience that is more influential than society's laws. The individual becomes concerned with moral values and the basis for laws. This level is important for any change in a system of justice. It does not represent a flagrant disregard of all of society's rules, but it is concerned with the basis of these rules and their moral correctness. For example, someone may intentionally break a law in order to test its constitutionality in court. Nonviolent methods of breaking the law as a matter of principle have been effective around the world, such as in bringing discriminatory laws to test in the civil rights activities starting in the 1960s.

Latane and Darley's cognitive analysis.   Latane and Darley (1970) approached the problem of helping behavior from a perception-cognition point of view. They suggest that the potential helper has to go through five steps.

1. You must **perceive** that something noteworthy is happening. If you do not hear gunshots, you are not going to rush to help someone who might be shot.
2. You must **interpret** what you have perceived. Having heard several loud sharp sounds, you might interpret them as gunshots or a car backfiring. Only if you interpret your perception as a real danger are you likely to help someone; otherwise, you might appear foolish.
3. If you correctly interpret that someone needs help, you must **decide** that it is *your* responsibility to help. If you think it is someone else's responsibility, you may do nothing.
4. You must decide **what to do.** Should you call the police or fire department, take things into your own hands, or what?
5. You must **actually do** what you have decided is the best action.

Each of these five steps is influenced by many factors that we have already discussed.

SUMMARY

1. Biologists commonly talk about **agonistic behaviors** (attack, fighting, escape, fleeing) rather than aggression. Animal attack/fighting behavior is aroused by a variety of aversive stimuli, including pain. Other animals, especially male conspecifics, provoke fighting with each other. Actual fighting is reduced by the establishment of dominance hierarchies.
2. Human aggression is commonly defined in terms of **intent to do physical or psychological harm to someone.** No single circumstance satisfactorily characterizes every behavior that might be considered aggressive, however.
3. A drive-theory account of aggression is the **frustration-aggression hypothesis,** which states that frustration instigates aggression. Aggressive acts directed toward the blocking agent or toward a substitute are said to reduce the instigation to aggression. Reduction of the instigation is called **catharsis.** Direct aggressive acts may be **inhibited** by threat of punishment.
4. Many theorists believe that frustration leads to aggressive behavior only if the frustration arouses **anger.** It is often said that we should **vent** our anger rather than hold it in because expressing the anger is cathartic, and expression of anger will reduce it faster. Another view, however, is that venting anger makes people angrier. Research suggests that anger and anger reduction are learned responses that can be changed with training.
5. **Social learning theory** assigns especial importance to **modeling** and **imitation** in the development of aggressive behavior. A child sees someone else (e.g., an adult) act aggressively and imitates that behavior. Television is thought to be a particularly important source of modeling.
6. **Social cognitive theories** emphasize individual differences in the ways people

perceive and interpret environmental events. **Neoassociation theory, attribution theory,** and **script theory** emphasize different aspects of such individual differences. An important fact addressed by these theories is that people do not use exactly the same aggressive behaviors that they have seen modeled.

7. **Biological factors** influencing aggression involve genetics, brain structures, hormones, and neurotransmitters. Animals can be selectively bred for greater or lesser readiness to fight. Electrical stimulation of specific brain areas can trigger fighting. The male sex hormone, **testosterone,** is positively correlated with aggressive behavior, as is the neurotransmitter **serotonin.**

8. **Environmental factors** that are especially related to **impulsive** (unpremeditated) aggression include painful stimuli, crowding, temperature, and the presence of weapons. Aggressive acts may be facilitated by the presence of aggressive cues in the environment, such as weapons.

9. **Social factors** related to aggression also include the facts that victims may provoke attack on themselves, that aggressive behavior is a form of power people use to get what they want, or that people may obediently carry out orders to be aggressive. A given behavior may not be interpreted as aggressive if it is perceived as equitable reciprocation for previous aggression. **Instrumental aggression** is harmful behavior rewarded by something other than the harm, such as a boxer's fighting for pay or a person's being obedient to orders.

10. A large number of studies (both correlational and experimental) have been done in attempting to determine whether watching violent behavior on television increases violent behavior by viewers, especially children. Taken as a whole, the research indicates there is a causal relation.

11. Two major and opposing approaches to the control of aggression are (1) **catharsis theory,** which says that **vicarious** aggression will reduce the occurrence of truly harmful behavior, and (2) **social learning theory,** which says that social acceptance of aggressive acts rewards such acts and that aggressive acts (vicarious or not) will lead to further aggression. There is no evidence that watching violent television reduces the occurrence of everyday violent behavior.

12. **Altruism** (also called **prosocial behavior**) refers to behaviors intended to benefit others without obvious return benefit to oneself.

13. **Bystander apathy** is the failure of people to help others in emergencies. Important variables are the **presence of others, costs and benefits of helping, characteristics of the helper and the victim,** and **situational factors.**

14. **Psychoanalytic theory** says that people internalize social values that influence helping. **Reinforcement theory** says that people are altruistic if they have been rewarded for prosocial behavior in the past.

15. Kohlberg's **theory of moral judgment** assumes that people pass through various stages of moral development in sequence: **preconventional, conventional,** and **postconventional.**

16. Latane and Darley's **cognitive analysis** proposes that a person must **perceive** and **interpret** a situation as requiring help, **decide** that it is one's responsibility to help, decide **what** to do, and then **do** it.

CHAPTER TWELVE

Personality and Individual Differences

———•———

Personality refers to those enduring characteristics by which we distinguish one person from another. It is thus the study of individual differences in people and largely reflects the psychometric approach to psychology that we discussed in Chapter One. Personality theories vary in what aspects of people to emphasize. Some theories emphasize what they consider to be the most salient human characteristics, not all of which are motivational. Other theories specifically emphasize differences in motivation. In this chapter we shall selectively look at a number of human motives that have particularly interested personality theorists.

THEORIES OF PERSONALITY

Trait Theories

Trait theories assume that every individual can be described in terms of some relatively small number of personal characteristics (such as friendliness, anxiousness, aggressiveness) and that every individual "possesses" these in some measurable degree. For example, George might be rated "7" on a ten-point scale of "aggressiveness," whereas Susan is only a "3." Susan might be an "8" on independence, however, whereas George is a "4." Most trait theorists think of traits as convenient ways of describing individuals without assuming that traits are "things." The number of traits in different well-known theories has varied from three (Eysenck, 1967) to sixteen (Cattell, 1965). Contemporary approaches to trait theory are generally dated to the work of Gordon Allport (1937) but the particular trait theory now in ascendance is Five Factor Theory, or just "The Big Five."

Five Factor Theory. Extensive research has consistently uncovered five personality traits that some researchers believe represent the basic "structure" of personality (Norman, 1963; Wiggins & Trapnell, 1997). The five basic traits are **extraversion, conscientiousness, agreeableness, emotional stability, and culture.** Traits are hierarchical, however, and a number of specific characteristics are subsumed under each of the five general traits (Table 12–1). Extraversion, for example, includes such more specific items as talkative versus silent, open versus secretive, adventurous versus cautious, and sociable versus reclusive. As the trait names suggest, not all traits are motivational. Thus extraversion and emotional stability (anxiousness) seem to have a more motivational quality than agreeableness, conscientiousness, and culture.

The primary criticisms of trait theories hinge on whether there are such permanent characteristics of people as traits or whether people just respond consistently to situations in which they repeatedly find themselves. The latter point of view is called **situationism** or **interactionism** (Endler, 1998; Mischel, 1973). For example, psychologists frequently distinguish between "perma-

TABLE 12-1.   Five-factor theory personality traits, with four scale items
used to measure each trait.

TRAIT FACTORS	SCALE ITEMS
Extraversion	Talkative versus silent
	Frank, open versus secretive
	Adventurous versus cautious
	Sociable versus reclusive
Agreeableness	Good-natured versus irritable
	Not jealous versus jealous
	Mild, gentle versus headstrong
	Cooperative versus negativistic
Conscientiousness	Fussy, tidy versus careless
	Responsible versus undependable
	Scrupulous versus unscrupulous
	Persevering versus quitting, fickle
Emotional stability	Nervous, tense versus poised
	Anxious versus calm
	Excitable versus composed
	Hypochondriacal versus not so
Culture	Artistically sensitive versus insensitive
	Intellectual versus unreflective, narrow
	Polished, refined versus crude, boorish
	Imaginative versus simple, direct

Source: Norman, 1963, pp. 574–583, Figure 1. Copyright 1963 by the American Psychological Association. Reprinted by permission.

nent" trait anxiety and "situational" state anxiety. We may then ask whether trait anxiety means that a person is always anxious or just tends to be anxious in many (but not all) situations. A person who is anxious in many harmless social situations, might nevertheless be fearless in the face of real danger. Similarly, we might ask whether an agreeable person is one who is always agreeable or who is agreeable in most situations but might be disagreeable in some. The trait versus situationism controversy seems likely to remain with us for a while.

Dynamic (Motivational) Theories

Nature of dynamic theories.   A dynamic theory of personality is specifically a motivational theory. Freud's psychoanalytic theory was a dynamic theory, abounding with unseen conflicting forces wreaking mental and behavioral havoc. Kurt Lewin's (1935) dynamic theory incorporated conflict but also had "tensions" produced by such events as uncompleted goal activities. Dollard and

Miller's (1941) behavioral approach to personality was based on drive theory. McAdams (1997) notes that the trend has been away from the tension reduction (regulatory) theories to more cognitive (purposive) theories. Emmons (1997) observed that there was something of a decline in interest in motivational concepts in personality theory as interest in drive theory declined, but that the "revitalization of the field of personality has been due in large part to a resurgence of interest in motivational concepts, especially goals. For example, we might describe one person as "power hungry" to mean that she consistently strives to put herself into a position of power, to control others, to promote herself, and so on. Another person might be described as a high achiever, to mean that he persistently and energetically strives to meet his goals. Such goals may be termed **needs,** like the need for power or need for achievement.

Goals.   What kinds of goals impel people to action? Emmons (1997) distinguishes two approaches to this question: **nomothetic** and **idiographic.** A nomothetic approach looks for general laws, and nomothetic goals are those that characterize "people in general." Idiographic goals are those that characterize a particular person. Which approach is more appropriate depends on what we want to do. For example, general scientific problems would take a more nomothetic approach, whereas clinical concerns about particular individuals would take a more ideographic approach.

Nomothetic goals.   People are asked to rate lists of goals on importance, relevance, and other dimensions. The goals are then grouped according to statistical analyses. Five general groupings have emerged from various studies (Emmons, 1997). These goal classifications constitute what look like chapter names for a text on human motivation:

1. **Enjoyment:** relaxation, fun, sensation-seeking, exploration, play
2. **Self-Assertion:** aggression, power, achievement, competition
3. **Esteem:** self-esteem, personal growth
4. **Interpersonal:** affection, support, affiliation, social relationships
5. **Avoidance of negative affect:** anxiety reduction, stress avoidance

Idiographic goals.   These have been characterized by various researchers as current concerns (Klinger, 1977), personal projects (Little, 1983), life tasks (Cantor & Langston, 1989), and personal striving (Emmons, 1986). Here are examples of these goals:

1. **Current concerns:** travel, family, job, religion, health
2. **Personal projects:** interpersonal, academic, recreational, family
3. **Personal striving:** interpersonal, achievement, affiliation, power, growth
4. **Personal goals:** work, school, social life, leisure

Thus, for example, enjoyment is a category of goals shared by many people, but travel, recreation, and social life are more specific goals by which people might obtain enjoyment.

Henry Murray.   Henry Murray (1938), one of the pioneers in personality research, distinguished between what he called **presses** and **needs.** A press is an environmental feature that is appraised as harmful or beneficial by a person, and hence it is avoided or approached. A need is a hypothetical internal state inferred from observation. Murray considered needs to represent states of disequilibrium in the organism, just as drive theorists did. These needs orient the organism toward certain ends (goals) that will reduce the needs.

Murray further distinguished between what he called **viscerogenic** and **psychogenic** needs. Viscerogenic, or primary, needs are due to periodic body changes and have readily identifiable localization in the body. These are needs for air, water, food, sex, lactation, urination, defecation, harm avoidance, nox avoidance (unpleasant stimuli), heat avoidance, cold avoidance, and sentience (pleasant stimulation). Some of these needs involve approach (e.g., sex), whereas others involve avoidance (e.g., heat). Psychogenic, or secondary, needs are not localized in any particular body place outside the brain, but Murray thought that they are derived from the primary needs. Among the many psychogenic needs he listed are needs for achievement, power, recognition, exhibition, dominance, aggression, and autonomy, and possibly play and curiosity. Murray proposed that hedonistic principles govern behavior. Because the need states are unpleasant, we try to rid ourselves of them, either by getting away from a noxious situation or approaching a pleasant one.

Three motives from Murray's list have received a great amount of attention from personality theorists: need for achievement, need for power, and need for affiliation. We look at achievement and power in this chapter, but defer affiliation to Chapter Fourteen.

ACHIEVEMENT MOTIVATION

McClelland's Theory

Definition of the need for achievement (n Ach).   Murray (1938, pp. 80–81) defined need for achievement as a desire or tendency "to overcome obstacles, to exercise power, to strive to do something difficult as well and as quickly as possible." Murray also devised the **Thematic Apperception Test** (TAT) as a means of studying personality and needs. This test consists of a series of pictures about which the individual tells a story to answer these questions: (1) What led up to the scene being depicted? (2) What is now happening in the scene? (3) How do the characters feel? (4) What will be the outcome? The relatively ambiguous pictures are supposed to evoke themes which will be characteristically different for different individuals.

Various scoring schemes for the stories are intended to detect themes indicative of the personality and needs of the individual telling the story. For example, one card shows a boy with a violin lying on a table in front of him while he looks into space. If the story is about a boy working hard to become a world-renowned violinist, the interpretation would be different from a story about a boy who is supposed to be practicing but who wants to be outside playing with his friends. The former story would indicate achievement, and the latter, affiliation. In the n Ach research, there are usually four pictures, with a time limit of five minutes for telling each story (Atkinson, 1958; McClelland et al., 1953). A more direct or objective test might seem better, but the fantasy measures have been successfully used for many years.

Need for achievement is said to be *aroused* by environmental cues but is not manipulated and controlled like hunger or thirst. People high in need for achievement are more persistent and work harder (McClelland, 1985). They also tend to be medium risk takers. This quality is often described as a balance between the likelihood of gaining the "pride of success" from doing a reasonably difficult task but still avoiding the "shame of failure" that would occur if a task were too difficult. The obvious questions are, What produces higher n Ach? And, Why does n Ach lead to better performance?

Development of achievement motivation.   David McClelland and his associates offered a hedonic interpretation of n Ach (McClelland, Atkinson, Clark & Lowell, 1953). Cues previously associated with hedonically positive events also arouse the previously experienced affect. When this positive affect has been aroused, a person is more likely to engage in achievement behaviors.[1] Thus a person who has found test-taking to be a rewarding experience is more likely to try hard on tests in the future. Conversely, if a person were punished for failing, a fear of failure could develop, and there would be a motive to avoid failure. If a competitive situation is a cue for rewarded achievement striving, then in competitive situations, the individual will work harder. In brief, this theory says that under appropriate conditions, people will do what they have been rewarded for doing. Men with high n Ach tend to come from families in which achievement striving is rewarded. Young adults with high n Ach often report that their parents were not particularly warm individuals, and that they emphasized achievement rather than affiliation.

Robert Eisenberger (1992) has proposed the concept of **learned industriousness** to account for some of the individual differences in work. Coming

---

[1]Note the similarity of this early statement and the more recent two-process learning theory discussed in Chapter Seven.

more from a tradition of animal learning research, Eisenberger argues that the sensory experience of effort (normally considered aversive) may be associated with rewards and thereby become a secondary reinforcer. According to the "law of least effort," organisms tend to take paths of least resistance to achieve goals. For example, most of us like to park as close as possible to the doors of our office buildings, and we cut across the grass rather than follow the longer paved path. The effect of associating perceived effort with reward is that the perception of effort becomes pleasant rather than aversive. Hence, rather than being punishing, increased effort becomes rewarding in itself. Research with both animals and humans lends strong support to the concept, and its relation to the development of achievement motivation seems clear.

The achieving society.   McClelland's interests broadened from laboratory tasks to social problems, and he tried to determine whether n Ach was related to the rise and fall of cultures (McClelland, 1961). This idea was related to Max Weber's thesis in *The Protestant Ethic and the Spirit of Capitalism* ([1904] 1930), that the Protestant Revolution had infused a more vigorous spirit into both workers and entrepreneurs. What a society teaches its children about being independent was related to Protestantism. The Protestant Reformation was a liberation movement, a break from the authoritarianism of the Catholic church that led to a greater social, as well as ecclesiastical, freedom. Freedom also carries with it, however, a greater stress on individual responsibility and independence. McClelland argued that Protestant individuals and countries should therefore show greater n Ach than Catholic individuals and countries. And, indeed, just as boys who are separated from their fathers and forced to be more independent evidenced higher n Ach, Protestant families stressed independence earlier than Irish or Italian Catholic families (McClelland, Rindlisbacher, & deCharms, 1955). Protestant children also scored higher on n Ach tests, and Protestant countries were more advanced economically. The latter was shown by comparing such measures of economic development as per capita use of electricity and amount of shipping. Children's books have also been scored for achievement themes and related to economic growth. For example, deCharms and Moeller (1962) found that between 1800 and 1850, there was first an increase and then a decrease in number of patents per 100,000 people in the United States. This was closely paralleled by a rise and fall in achievement imagery in the children's books in the preceding fifty years, with a correlation of .79 between the two measures. Although some other factor(s) might be affecting patents, the correlation is impressive.

Occupational preferences.   Individuals in "entrepreneurial" occupations should also have high n Ach scores. Occupation may have affected achievement scores rather than vice versa, but a longitudinal study avoids this ambiguity. McClelland (1965) found that 83 percent of Wesleyan graduates in entrepreneurial occupations fourteen years after graduation had scored high n Ach when they were students, whereas only 21 percent of those in nonentrepreneurial occupations had high n Ach scores. Individuals with high n Ach are also more independent and less concerned with the feelings of others. McClelland came to view the "managerial type" in business as being a medium risk taker, wanting immediate feedback for his or her behavior, and working harder under conditions of achievement arousal. This type of person is not happy unless continually rewarded with success.

Atkinson's Expectancy-Value Theory

John Atkinson (e.g., 1964) went a different direction with achievement motivation research. First, he put the theory into the framework of expectancy-value theory. Second, he emphasized the role of conflict, especially between need for achievement and fear of failure. Let us first look at expectancy value theory and then go on to Atkinson's variation.

Expectancy-value in classic economic theory. Expectancy-value theory is a theory of rational economic choice, and it dates back at least to the early-eighteenth-century mathematician Daniel Bernoulli. The basic idea is that people act in such a way as to "make the best deal" they can on the basis of what they consider *valuable* and *how likely* they are to get that valuable commodity. Often we must make a choice between a very valuable commodity with little chance of success and a less valuable commodity with a greater chance of success. For example, we might invest money in a very risky stock that has the potential to become very valuable. Or we could put our money into an interest-bearing account with no risk but relatively little payoff. To the extent that we can estimate probabilities and values, the theory is of considerable usefulness. There are certain formal situations in which this is feasible. The following concepts are basic to the theory.

The Expected Value (*EV*) of an Outcome = Outcome Probability × Outcome Value, or in abbreviated form: $EV = P \times V$. Suppose that we are manufacturing a product that has a demonstrated rate of 0.1 percent failure to pass inspection coming off the assembly line. It costs us $.50 to inspect each item to find the failure and remove it. Suppose that it costs us $50 if a faulty item is returned. Finally, suppose that we manufacture 10,000 items. Should we bother to inspect?

Cost of inspecting   = $ .50 × 10,000 = $5,000

Cost of not inspecting = (.001 × 10,000) × $50 = 10 × $50 = $500.

If these were the only considerations, the clear economic choice would be not to inspect. It often happens, of course, that we have no objective grounds for stating an objective probability for an event. What is the probability that one fighter will beat another if the two have never fought before? There is no history to give us a probability, such as "He has beaten him eight out of ten times," since two fighters are rarely matched often enough to do this. Nevertheless, odds makers do set probabilities for fights, for horse races, and so on. The only meaningful probability is subjective, our "feeling" that one is more likely to win than the other. This is called **subjective probability.**

In similar fashion, we may not have an objective measure of value. How valuable is winning a trophy or attracting a particular mate? We can seldom put a real number value to such events, but certainly some things are more valuable than others. The life of a pedestrian is certainly more valuable than the loss of a car wrecked when it hits a tree after swerving to avoid the pedestrian. In such cases, we use a **subjective measure of value,** called **utility.** This means that our choices are not as rational as the original theory had in mind. There are also other non-rational influences. For example, people are often risk-aversive, which is to say that they don't like to take very great risks even for great potential gains (such as putting all their money into a risky stock). Whether we use objective or subjective probabilities or values, we still use the same basic formula to arrive at a prediction of expected value, however.

Atkinson's achievement theory.   Atkinson's modification of achievement theory says that the tendency to engage in any particular achievement-oriented behavior depends on the probability of success and the incentive value of success, as well as need for achievement. The theory is distinguished from other incentive theories by the fact that it is concerned with the incentive value of *succeeding for success' sake,* however, not specifically with working for external rewards. The theory assumes that there is greater incentive value in achieving something difficult (where there is a low probability of success) than there is in achieving something easy (where there is a high probability of success). Therefore, the incentive value of success (Is) is defined as 1 − probability of success (1–Ps). Since probabilities range from zero to one, the lower the probability of success the greater the incentive value of success.

The tendency to success (T_s).   In Atkinson's theory the tendency to engage in achievement-oriented behaviors (tendency to success, or T_s) is a multiplicative function of

(1)   the **motivation** for success (M_s), which is the same as n Ach;
(2)   the **probability** of success (P_s); and
(3)   the **incentive value** of success ($I_s = 1–P_s$). The formula reads

$$T_s = M_s \times P_s \times I_s$$

If any of the components is zero, then there will be no tendency to strive for success in a particular situation. The formula is multiplicative like Hull's formula $(E = H \times D \times K)$, and there is an analogy between concepts. Thus M_s is an internal-state-like drive, P_s is a learning component corresponding roughly to habit, and I_s corresponds roughly to Hull's incentive, K.

There are obviously important differences from Hull, however, particularly with regard to P_s and I_s. To illustrate, as noted earlier, high n Ach people tend to be **medium risk takers**. Given a choice of activities with different chances of being successful (different values of P_s), they tend to choose activities with a medium level of P_s. The Atkinson model accounts for this as follows: Since P_s ranges from 0 to 1, and I_s ranges from 1 to 0, the maximum possible value of $P_s \times (1 - P_s)$ occurs when with $P_s = .50$. Plugging some numbers into the formula, if $Ms = 1$, $P_s = .50$, and $Is = .50$, then $T_s = 1.0 \times .50 \times .50 = .25$. Any other value of P_s will give a lower value of T_s. Table 12–2 illustrates some calculations, and the upper part of Figure 12–1 graphically illustrates the results for different values of P_s and I_s, which give us an inverted-U curve for values of T_s. If the task is too difficult, there is little chance of succeeding; and if it is too easy, there is no incentive for succeeding. Therefore, middle-level tasks are the most likely to be chosen. Consider how we divide up teams in pickup games of basketball. We elect two captains, who then proceed to choose players alternately. The whole idea is to get teams as evenly matched as possible so that the chances of winning (P_s) are as near .50 as possible for each team.

TABLE 12–2. Calculations of T_s and T_{af} for five different difficulty level tasks and different values of M_s and M_{af}.

			$T_s = M_s \times P_s \times I_s$ WHEN		
TASK	P_s	I_s	$M_s = 1$	$M_s = 3$	$M_s = 8$
A	.90	.10	.09	.27	.72
B	.70	.30	.21	.63	1.68
C	.50	.50	.25	.75	2.00
D	.30	.70	.21	.63	1.68
E	.10	.90	.09	.27	.72

			$T_{af} = M_{af} \times P_f \times I_{-f}$ WHEN		
	P_f	I_{-f}	$M_{af} = 1$	$M_{af} = 3$	$M_{af} = 8$
A	.10	−.90	−.09	−.27	− .72
B	.30	−.70	−.21	−.63	−1.68
C	.50	−.50	−.25	−.75	−2.00
D	.70	−.30	−.21	−.63	−1.68
E	.90	−.10	−.09	−.27	− .72

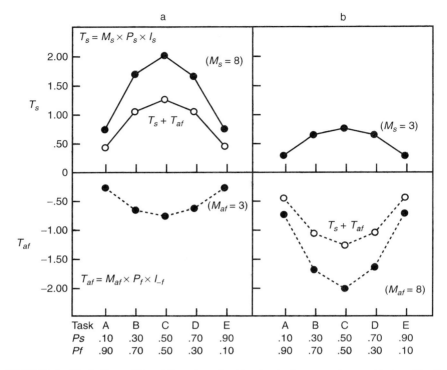

FIGURE 12–1. Illustrations of T_s and T_{af} and resultant tendencies to approach or avoid when $M_s = 3$ or 8 and when $M_{af} = 3$ or 8. In (a), the tendency to success is greater than the tendency to avoid failure; therefore, the resultant tendency, the algebraic summation of T_s and T_{af}, is positive. In (b) the situation is just reversed, with the resultant tendency being negative. Note also that T_s is a steeper function in (a) ($M_s = 8$) than in (b) ($M_s = 3$). This indicates why high n Ach individuals are medium-risk takers; medium probabilities of success produce much higher relative values of T_s when M_s is high.

As one test of the theory, Atkinson (1958) told female subjects that they were to compete for a prize of either $1.25 or $2.50, drawing X's inside small circles for twenty minutes. Four probabilities of winning were stated: .20, .33, .50, and .75. The high-reward group performed better than the low-reward group, as expected for the external reward. Performance declined for both groups, however, when P_s was said to be .75 rather than .50. This outcome confirmed the prediction of an inverted-U function for performance when one probability of success was greater than .50.

The tendency to avoid failure (T_{af}). Besides the "satisfaction" or "pride" that comes from success, there is "shame" from failure (tendency to avoid failure, or T_{af}). This negative affect presumably depends on one's previous experience with failure, for example, whether one was punished or ridiculed for failing. A multiplication formula is also used to determine the strength of the tendency to avoid failure. The components are

(1)   the **motive to avoid failure** (M_{af}), the fear of failure, commonly measured by a test anxiety questionnaire;

(2)   the **probability of failure** (P_f), which for any given task is $1 - P_s$; and

(3)   the **negative incentive value of failure** (I_{-f}) is $- (1 - P_f)$, which is the same as $- P_s$.

If the probability of failure is .90, then I_{-f} is $- (1 - .90) = -.10$. Since P_s for this example is $1 - .90 = .10$, then $I_{-f} = -P_s = -.10$. The tendency to avoid failure is thus given by the formula

$$T_{af} = M_{af} \times P_f \times I_{-f}$$

Table 12–2 and Figure 12–1 show more detailed illustrations. This formula says that if a person has motivation to avoid failure, there will be some tendency to avoid tasks that could potentially lead to failure. Furthermore, the maximum value of T_{af} will also occur with medium-probability tasks because the maximum value of $P_f \times I_{-f}$ occurs when $P_f = .50$. In this case, however, the product is a negative value. The tendency to avoid failure will be the strongest for tasks having a medium expectancy of failure, which is just the opposite of the prediction for individuals with high n Ach. In everyday language, the person afraid of failing may choose a task that is so easy that he or she almost cannot fail or one that is so difficult that there is no shame in failing. Since a task of medium difficulty is relatively easy to fail, it is avoided because the shame is great.

The combination of T_s and T_{af}.   The values of I_s, P_f, and I_{-f} are all determined once we know the value of P_s. What differentiates T_s and T_{af}, then, are the relative strengths of M_s and M_{af}. The resolution of the conflict between T_s and T_{af} is then represented as follows:

$$T_s + T_{af} = (M_s \times P_s \times I_s) + (M_{af} \times P_f \times I_{-f})$$

This says that we calculate the positive values of T_s and the negative values of T_{af}, using their respective formulae, and then add them together. If the $M_s > M_{af}$, the individual should *choose* medium-probability tasks, but if $M_{af} > M_s$, the person should tend to *avoid* medium-probability tasks. This guideline is illustrated in Figure 12–1. The theory, then, is like any other approach-avoidance conflict theory, where the resolution depends on the relative strengths of approach and avoidance tendencies. Atkinson's theory, with its special assumptions about positive and negative incentives for achievement, makes interesting and unique predictions, however. We shall illustrate these with task preference and level of aspiration.

Task preference.   McClelland (1958) showed that high n Ach children preferred to toss a ring at a peg (the ring toss game) from a medium distance, as compared with low n Ach children, who tended to choose either near or far distances. Atkinson and Litwin (1960) divided subjects into four groups of all combinations of high and low n Ach and of high and low anxiety. They predicted that high M_s, low M_{af} subjects would show the strongest tendency to choose medium distances in the ring toss game and that high M_{af}, low M_s subjects would avoid the middle range. The other two groups should fall between. The predictions were somewhat confirmed, as shown in Figure 12–2. The high M_{af}, low M_s group tended to choose a middle range, but their preferences were spread across a wider range of distances than for any other group. To obtain results exactly as predicted for the group where $M_{af} > M_s$ would depend on very exact measurements of M_{af} and M_s. It may not really be in the present situation that M_{af} was greater than M_s.

Level of aspiration.   Suppose a high M_s person chooses a task that he perceives to be of medium difficulty. By experimental prearrangement, he

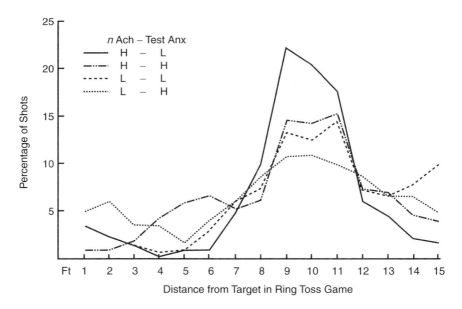

FIGURE 12–2. Percentage of shots taken from each distance by college men in a ring toss game. Graph is smoothed according to the method of running averages, for *Ss* classified as High or Low simultaneously in n Ach and test anxiety, H-L (N = 13), H-H (N = 10), L-L (N = 9), L-H (N = 13). (From Atkinson & Litwin, 1960, p. 55. Copyright © 1960 by the American Psychological Association. Used with permission.)

then either succeeds or fails. What difficulty level should he subsequently choose? One of the commonest results of such **level of aspiration** research is that people tend to change their goals realistically on the basis of experience (e.g., Lewin, Dembo, Festinger, & Sears, 1944). After failure, the goal is lowered; after success, it is raised. Atkinson's explanation is that after easy success, a person would perceive P_s as higher than previously expected. He therefore sets the next goal higher because that would bring P_s of this goal closer to his newly adjusted concept of a $p = .50$ goal. Conversely, if he failed, he would assume that P_s was lower than he had expected and hence would choose a simpler task to bring P_s up more nearly to .50. These are **typical shifts** in level-of-aspiration research.

There are sometimes peculiar **atypical shifts,** however. Some individuals *raise* their goals after failure and *lower* them after success. According to the theory, if $M_{af} > M_s$, then the individual should *avoid* medium-difficulty tasks. Now suppose that a high M_{af} subject is told she has a task where $P_s = .50$ and fails it. She may then believe that P_s was *lower* than she initially had thought, .35, for instance. An easier task would put her closer to $P_s = .50$, which should be aversive for her. She may therefore select a *more difficult task* (for example, where $P_s = .25$) than the one she failed at. Conversely, if successful at a task she believes to be $P_s = .50$, the subject may think that the task was easier than she had believed, such as $P_s = .65$. Therefore, she would next choose an even easier task because she wants to keep away from the $P_s = .50$ task. Moulton (1965) actually got such results, for high M_{af}, low M_s individuals, as well as showing that high M_s, low M_{af} subjects and $M_s = M_{af}$ subjects made typical shifts more frequently. This finding is rather remarkable support for the theory.

There have been many problems with both the McClelland and the Atkinson versions of achievement theory. First, there seem to be more dimensions of achievement motivation than just motivation for success and fear of failure. Second, much of the research with n Ach was restricted to males, raising the question whether men and women are different in achievement motivation. Research with different measures of achievement motivation than the TAT measures generally shows no sex differences. Third, many studies did not find differences between high and low n Ach people. See Beck (1990) for more detailed criticisms.

Spence and Helmreich's Achievement Theory

Spence & Helmreich (1983) established a theory of achievement motivation that has three achievement dimensions undoubtedly familiar to the typical student.

1. **Satisfaction in work itself,** in a job well done. When a student writes a term paper, she may well be concerned with the grade but also with the satisfaction of having turned out a good piece of work.

2. **A sense of completion,** of satisfaction with getting a job done. Sometimes we are pleased to get a job done at all. If we run the Boston Marathon, we are probably proud just to have completed the twenty-six-mile race even though coming in at Number 15,000.

3. **A sense of competitiveness,** as well as enjoyment of competition and winning that may come with schoolwork, job success, games, or any other competitive situation.

Spence and Helmreich devised an objectively scored test for these three aspects of achievement called the Work and Family Orientation Questionnaire (WOFO). Research in a rather impressive array of situations, ranging from grades in college to salaries in business organizations, regularly shows a consistent pattern of results illustrated in Figure 12–3. Grades and salaries are higher for people who have high levels of motivation for work and mastery if they are also low in competitiveness. If they are high in competitiveness, performance suffers. One explanation is that highly competitive people may focus so much on the competition rather than on doing a good job that they do less well than they would otherwise.

Attribution and Achievement

One of the puzzles for achievement theory to solve is that not all people respond the same way to success and failure. For example, some people respond to failure by trying harder, whereas others respond to initial failure by

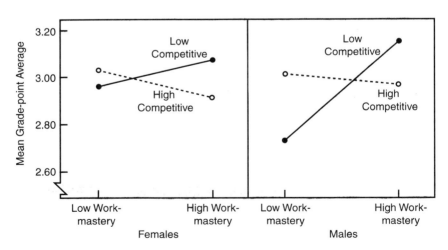

FIGURE 12–3.   Mean grade-point averages in Low Competitive and High Competitive male and female undergraduate students. Work and Mastery are put together on the same horizontal axis because the effect of competitiveness is the same whether Low or High Work or Low or High Mastery are compared. (From Spence & Helmreich, 1983. Copyright © 1983 by W. H. Freeman and Company. Used by permission.)

giving up. One reason for this variation in responding is that people may differ in what they see as the *causes* for success and failure. For example, people who attribute failure to bad luck may respond differently in the future than do people who attribute failure to their own stupidity. The attributional approach to achievement motivation deals with just such questions.

Nature of attribution.   Attribution theory is concerned with (1) the **causes** people find for their own behavior (or that of others) and (2) the **effects** of such attributions on emotion, motivation, and subsequent behaviors. Kelley (1967) suggested that people are motivated to obtain a **cognitive mastery** of the "causal structures" in their environment. They want to understand and make sense of how their environment works. The discovery of a correlation, or a cause, between two events is sought, and finding causes is rewarding. Once achieved, however, an attribution may serve only as knowledge by which we guide our behavior. The attribution by itself does not *necessarily* motivate us to do things (Bem, 1972). For example, if someone discovers that a sharp turn in a road has led to a number of accidents when people drive too fast (i.e., the accidents are attributed to the sharp turn), that person may use this information to adjust her driving speed at that point in the road.

Kinds of attributions.   One major dimension for distinguishing attributions is according to internal and external causes. Internal causes can be related to such concepts as *mastery, power,* and *competence.* We saw in the discussion of learned helplessness, however, that organisms without control over events may "give up" and not do anything in situations in which they could actually be effective. We would infer that attributions in such a case would be to external causes. DeCharms (1968) put the internal-external distinction in terms of **origins** and **pawns.** Some individuals feel that they originate their own activities and are responsible for their own rewards and punishments. Others feel that, like chess pawns, they have little freedom and that the freedom they do have is at the service of more powerful outside sources. Alfred Adler, once a follower of Freud, broke away from the master because he (Adler) believed that striving for personal control over one's own destiny was the most important form of motivation, not sex or aggression.

Weiner's Attributional Theory of Achievement.   Weiner (1985) has presented the most ambitious attributional theory of achievement motivation and emotion. This theory deals with the perceived causes of success and failure, the characteristics of causal thinking, and subsequent emotional experiences in relation to achievement behaviors. There is a large number of *possible* causes for any specific success or failure. A relatively small number of causes appear repeatedly in relation to many situations, however. These may be categorized as shown in the following sections.

Internal versus external attributions.   A person may attribute success to himself, such as "I have a lot of ability and work hard." There is a common bias to attribute success to oneself ("I am clever") but to attribute failure to outside factors ("The exam was too hard"). There is a phenomenon called the **fundamental attribution error,** which is the tendency to explain other people's actions in terms of internal causes and to explain one's own actions in terms of external causes. For example, "*He* fell down because he is clumsy," but "*I* fell down because the grass is slippery."

Stable versus unstable attributions.   A person might attribute success to ability (which is a relatively enduring characteristic) or to effort (which may be more fluctuating). Commonly ascribed stable and unstable external causes are **task difficulty** (stable) and **chance** (unstable); for example, "This is a very hard course" (task difficulty) or "I just didn't study the right things" (chance).

Controllable versus uncontrollable attributions.   Both lack of trying and being ill are internal and unstable causes for failure, but there is an obvious difference between them. The former is considered controllable, but the latter is not. I might decide to try harder and overcome failure, but I cannot as easily decide to overcome the flu. Effort is more controllable than illness.

More specific attributions can be found for particular situations, but the preceding dimensions cut across considerable research. In addition, detailed statistical analyses of the causes given by people to account for their actions have indicated that these categories are those used by real people and are not just figments of attribution theorists' imaginations. Table 12–3 summarizes these attributions, with examples.

Weiner argues that each causal attribution has a *specific emotional consequence.* Future behaviors are then determined by the expectancy of a certain outcome and the specific emotional consequence of that outcome. An expected outcome might be **good or bad,** in general terms, but involve **pride or shame** in more specific terms. For example, if a person does a job well, she should expect to feel pride (positive emotion). If she blunders and fails, she might expect to feel shame. The exact relationship between such specific emotions and future behavior remains to be determined.

Attributions for success and failure are of interest ultimately to the extent that they will predict future achievement behaviors. The evidence here is not compelling. Heckhausen (1975), for example, reported that even though subjects high in need for achievement attributed failure to their own lack of effort, they did *not* subsequently show increased effort in another task. The attribution was as expected, but it did not predict subsequent behavior. The most general conclusion that can be drawn about attributions and achievement, says McClelland (1985), is that subjects high in need for achievement tend to attribute success to ability and failure to lack of effort, whereas sub-

TABLE 12–3.   Summary of causal attribution categories, applied to tennis

	S = "I won because. . . ." STABLE	F = I lost because. . . ." UNSTABLE
	CONTROLLABLE	
Internal	Experience	Effort
	S: I'm well coached.	S: I tried very hard.
	F: I'm poorly coached.	F: I didn't concentrate.
External	Skill of Others	Effort of others
	S: My opponent did not have lessons.	S: My opponent didn't try.
	F: My opponent had good coaching.	F: My opponent really worked hard.
	UNCONTROLLABLE	
Internal	Ability	Fatigue, Mood, Illness
	S: I'm a natural athlete.	S: I really felt good.
	F: I'm uncoordinated.	F: I was too tired.
External	Task Difficulty	Luck
	S: My opponents are poor.	S: My serves went in.
	F: Tennis is too hard.	F: Line calls were bad.

jects low in need for achievement tend to attribute failure to lack of ability. McClelland does *not* consider it to be empirically demonstrated that attributions for past performance will predict future achievement behavior very well.

POWER AND CONTROL MOTIVES

Power

Measurement of power motivation.   Need for power is measured much as is the need for achievement. Winter (1973) developed a TAT scoring system for three categories of power imagery: (1) strong vigorous action that expresses power; (2) actions that arouse strong emotion in others; and (3) explicit concerns about reputation or position. Test-retest reliability is about the same as that obtained with scoring for achievement imagery ($r = .45$).

Energizing effects of power motivation.   It is assumed that like achievement, power is a dispositional motive that has to be "engaged" by circumstances. It is a latent (dormant) motive until aroused. Steele (1977) examined the arousal of power motivation by having subjects write TAT stories after listening to tape recordings of famous inspirational speeches. Power scores were significantly higher after the inspirational speeches than before, but they were unchanged by listening to travelogues (McClelland, 1985, p. 272.). Steele also obtained self-reports of perceived arousal as well as a physiological measure, the amount of adrenaline in the urine. Both measures were significantly higher after the inspirational speeches than after the travelogue, with power scores and adrenaline increase correlating +.71. The adrenaline change seems to rule out experimenter demand as an interpretation for the self-report changes. A person might report feeling more aroused after an inspirational speech because he thinks that he should be aroused under such circumstances, but it would seem more difficult to increase urinary adrenaline on demand. Furthermore, adrenaline increase was not correlated with achievement motivation scores obtained from the same subjects, meaning that the speeches selectively aroused power motivation, not all forms of motivation.

Selective effects of power motivation.   Power motivation may selectively tune us into power-related cues in the environment. McAdams and McClelland (1983) had subjects high and low in need for power listen to a tape recording of someone telling a story about a picture. The story had fifteen power-related facts, fifteen neutral facts, and fifteen facts related to intimacy. Subjects high in need for power recalled a significantly greater proportion of power-related facts than neutral facts. Similarly, subjects high in need for power learned power-related stimulus materials faster than subjects low in need for power (McClelland, Davidson, Saron, & Floor, 1980).

Power and behavior.   McClelland distinguished between **personal power** and **social power.** Personal power, which is considered to be more "primitive" than social power, is characterized by dominance over others. Social power is more subtle and has the aim of benefiting others. Persons high in either of these kinds of power might seek political office, but for the different reasons related to their kinds of power need—controlling or benefiting. Need for personal power is related to competitiveness and aggression. Men high in need for personal power have been found to do more fighting, drinking, gambling, and speeding than men low in need for personal power (McClelland, 1985). This finding is not true for women, however, possibly because women are taught to suppress aggressive tendencies more so than men. Such apparent socialization differences have also been found among men, however. Working-class men with high need for power have been found to be more aggressive than middle-class men with equivalent levels of power motivation. Middle-class men presumably have learned to suppress aggressive tendencies more than lower-class men.

People high in need for power act in many ways so as to appear powerful. For example, they collect such symbols of power as **prestige possessions,** including certain types of cars, wristwatches, jewelry, and so on (Winter, 1973).

They are more willing to take risks, drink more, and are more likely to surround themselves with lesser-known people who can be led. Power scores have actually been found to change with drinking, but the nature of the change depends on the type of power involved. Individuals high in personal power show progressively higher power scores with increased drinking. Individuals high in social power, on the other hand, show a decline in need-for-power scores when they drink heavily (Figure 12–4; McClelland, Davis, Kalin, & Wanner, 1972). Women appear to respond differently to alcohol, feeling more friendly after drinking rather than more powerful (McClelland, 1985, p. 299). The social implications of this difference are obvious and sometimes disastrous.

Need for power may express itself in what appear to be unusual occupational choices. For example, students with high need for power were most interested in teaching, psychology, ministry, business, and international diplomacy. Students low in need for power were more interested in government and politics, medicine, law, creative arts, and architecture. These seem like strange occupational preferences in relation to power, especially in relation to government. But when we think about it, there is a pattern. Teachers, psychologists, and ministers, for example, have occupations in which they normally exert considerable control over others in their day-to-day work. Politicians, on the other hand, spend a great deal of time bargaining and compromising in order to get things done.

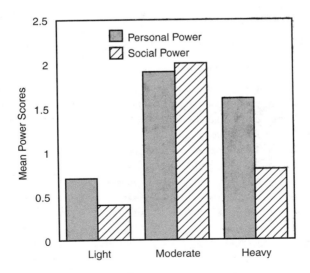

FIGURE 12–4. Mean social power and personal power scores with increasing consumption of 86 proof alcohol (light = 0.1 to 3.9 oz.; moderate = 4 to 6 oz.; heavy = 6.1 to 12 oz.). Social power scores show a sharp decline with heavy alcohol consumption. (From McClelland, Davis, Kalin, & Wanner, 1972. Copyright 1972 by David C. McClelland, William N. Davis, Rudolf Kalin, and Eric Wanner. Reprinted by permission of The Free Press, a Division of Macmillan, Inc.

Power and physical health.   Research by McClelland and his associates indicates that power motivation can have bad effects on health, depending on patterns of different motives. Two such patterns are the **inhibited power motive syndrome** and the **relaxed affiliative syndrome.** The inhibited power syndrome is characterized by the need for power being greater than the need for affiliation, coupled with inhibited expression of the need for power. It has been linked with high blood pressure, other physical illnesses, and increased stress responses (Jemmott, 1987). The relaxed affiliation syndrome is characterized by the need for affiliation being greater than the need for power, coupled with a low level of inhibition of the affiliation motive. The health effects are opposite to those related to inhibited power.

Competence and Effectance

Robert White (1950) argued that striving for **competence** is a major motive and that success produces feelings of **effectance.** Bandura (1977; 1982) proposed the concept of **self-efficacy,** which is the expectation that one can perform any particular action successfully. This is called an efficacy expectation. People with greater perceived self-efficacy actually do perform better on many kinds of tasks. Efficacy is not just a matter of "will power" or determination to try harder, however. Self-efficacy is established through actually having successes, just as in the development of an internal locus of control. Bandura (1977) lists the following principles.

1. **Self-efficacy increases with personal accomplishment.** Perceived efficacy is greater if we have more accomplishments, and efficacy expectations generalize across situations. This factor is important because it means that efficacy training is possible. We can, for example, set up situations that guarantee that children have some degree of success.
2. **Self-efficacy can increase or decrease if we see others similar to ourselves succeeding or failing at a task.** This principle is important with regard to modeling as a method of teaching, suggesting that a model similar to the subject be used, such as one child modeling for another. If a person does try to imitate a model, however, the degree of perceived success is determined by the actual degree of success. A person who tries to imitate the model and fails is *not* going to develop a sense of self-efficacy. The model simply provides a direction for behavior.
3. **We can be persuaded that we are capable of coping with a difficult situation,** but this process breaks down if we actually fail in such situations. Like modeling, persuasion may serve to get a person to try some activity, but the effort must be followed by perceived success at the actual task.
4. **Emotional arousal can affect our feeling of self-efficacy.** If we are upset, depressed, or overly anxious about some activity, such as giving a speech, we do not perceive our self-efficacy as high as when we are in a better

mood. We may learn to use our emotion as a cue for lower self-efficacy, as in "I just cannot cope today," as a result of some particular emotional experience.

Desire for Control

From the usual discussions of control, one might conclude that control is always desirable and sought, but this is not necessarily so. Indeed, if a person does not care about having control, then lack of control should pose no threat, and control might even be aversive and avoided. The first step in getting at such questions is to measure desire for control.

Burger and Cooper (1979) developed the **Desirability of Control (DC) Scale,** consisting of twenty items, such as "I try to avoid situations in which someone else tells me what to do." The scale does not correlate with Rotter's locus of control scale, so it is not just another measure of perceived locus of control. Males generally score higher than females, a finding that fits much data indicating that males are generally more assertive than females. Burger and Cooper (1979) also showed that people with high desire for control are also more likely in ambiguous situations to perceive that they do have control. In a gambling game, for example, subjects were given the **illusion of control** by letting them believe that their own actions determined the outcome of a random bet. The high DC subjects bet more than subjects not given the illusion of control, but low DC subjects were not affected by the illusion of control manipulation. A variety of predictions about differences between people who are high and low in desire for control have been supported by research (Burger, 1989).

SENSATION SEEKING

Are bungee jumping, skydiving, and riding on world-class roller coasters your idea of a good afternoon's fun? If so, you may wonder why other people fail to see the enjoyment in these activities. The individual differences in the extent to which people seek out and enjoy exciting experiences have been captured in the measurement of a personality trait called sensation seeking.

Description and Measurement of Sensation Seeking

Zuckerman (1994) states that "Sensation seeking represents the optimistic tendency to approach novel stimuli and explore the environment" (p. 385). Approach may be manifest in many different specific behaviors, and Zuckerman (1979) distinguishes four different kinds of sensation seeking, which are defined by his **Sensation Seeking Scale,** that is shown in Table 12–4.

TABLE 12–4. Items from the subscales of Zuckerman's Sensation Seeking Scale.

Thrill and Adventure Seeking

_____ I often wish I could be a mountain climber.
_____ I sometimes like to do things that are a little frightening.
_____ I would like to take up the sport of waterskiing.
_____ I would like to try surfboard riding.
_____ I would like to go scuba diving.
_____ I would like to learn to fly an airplane.
_____ I would like to try parachute jumping.
_____ I like to dive off the high board.
_____ I would like to sail a long distance in a small but seaworthy sailing craft.
_____ I think I would enjoy the sensations of skiing very fast down a high mountain slope.

Experience Seeking

_____ I like some of the earthy body smells.
_____ I like to explore a strange city or section of town myself, even if it means getting lost.
_____ I have tried marijuana or would like to.
_____ I would like to try some of the new drugs that produce hallucinations.
_____ I like to try new foods that I have never tasted before.
_____ I would like to take off on a trip with no preplanned or definite routes or timetables.
_____ I would like to make friends in some of the "far-out" groups like artists or "hippies."
_____ I would like to meet some people who are homosexual (men or women).
_____ I often find beauty in the "clashing" colors and irregular form of modern painting.
_____ People should dress in individual ways even if the effects are sometimes strange.

Disinhibition

_____ I like wild, "uninhibited" parties.
_____ I enjoy the company of real "swingers."
_____ I often like to get high (drinking liquor or smoking marijuana).
_____ I like to have new and exciting experiences and sensations, even if they are a little unconventional or illegal.
_____ I like to date members of the opposite sex who are physically exciting.
_____ Keeping the drinks full is the key to a good party.
_____ A person should have considerable sexual experience before marriage.
_____ I could conceive of myself seeking pleasures around the world with the "jet set."
_____ I enjoy watching many of the "sexy" scenes in movies.
_____ I feel best after taking a couple of drinks.

Boredom Susceptibility

_____ I can't stand watching a movie that I've seen before.
_____ I get bored seeing the same old faces.
_____ When you can predict almost everything a person will do and say, he or she must be a bore.
_____ I usually don't enjoy a movie or play where I can predict what will happen in advance.
_____ Looking at someone's home movies or travel slides bores me tremendously.
_____ I prefer friends who are excitingly unpredictable.
_____ I get very restless if I have to stay around home for any length of time.
_____ The worst social sin is to be a bore.
_____ I like people who are sharp and witty even if they do sometimes insult others.
_____ I have no patience with dull or boring parties.

Thrill and adventure seeking (TAS). Bungee jumpers and sky divers fit into this class of sensation seekers. Other activities might involve job choices, such as preferring to work high iron in construction or to be in law enforcement rather than an office job.

Experience seeking (ES). This is seeking sensation through the mind and the senses or through a nonconforming life style. Not all sensation seeking has to involve dangerous or exciting physical activity.

Disinhibition (Dis). Sensation may be sought through social stimulation in such a way that normal inhibitions are released, such as at wild parties. Social drinking may serve the same function, to "loosen up" oneself.

Boredom susceptibility (BS). This is characterized by an aversion to monotonous, unchanging situations and by restlessness while in such situations.

The Sensation Seeking Scales correlate with behaviors across many different domains of activity. These are just a few (Zuckerman, 1994):

- Males are higher SS than females, especially regarding physical risk and permissive attitudes toward sex.
- SS generally declines with age.
- High SS people engage in riskier behaviors but tend to take precautions to reduce the risk. For example, they may engage in sex with more partners but protect themselves against disease or unwanted pregnancy as much as low SS individuals do.
- High SS have a greater need for novelty and change, and they are more open to new experience.
- Anxiety is generally not correlated with sensation seeking. Thus sensation seeking does not occur just because some people are more fearless than others.
- High SS males and females tend to be more aggressive.
- High SS people are politically more liberal.

Theory of Sensation Seeking

Optimal level of arousal. The basic theory is the same as optimal level of arousal theory discussed in Chapter Six, which says that there is an optimal level of stimulation that is best for performance and that it is desirable. People seek out situations and activities that will lead to and maintain this optimal level. Level of arousal for most theorists was equated with activity of the brain stem reticular activating system (Lindsley, 1951; Hebb, 1955). One of the great perceived advantages of this line of theory was that it accounted for why people seek increases in stimulation as well as decreases. Tension reduction theories, including Hull's drive theory, seemed only to account for why organisms seek lower levels of drive or stimulation.

Individual differences in sensation seeking would be explained in terms of different people's needing different levels of stimulation to achieve an optimal level of arousal. For some people, the optimal level of arousal is achieved with relatively low levels of stimulation. It is easy for these people to be overstimulated, leading them to seek a less stimulating situation and to avoid highly stimulating situations. For other people, it takes a great deal of stimulation to reach the optimal level of arousal. Therefore, such people actively search out exciting situations that for them produce only a moderate level of arousal, and they avoid boring situations. Thus the same situation that is too exciting for one person may be too boring for another, and just right for a third. This range is illustrated in Figure 12–5, which shows how three different people might respond to the same levels of stimulation.

The problem with optimal level of arousal theory (Zuckerman, 1994) is that predicted differences in arousal between high and low sensation seekers are not always found. For example, measures of EEG or skin conductance have shown that high sensation seekers react *more strongly* to stimulation than do low sensation seekers, just the opposite of what the theory predicts. Also, high sensation seekers show greater use of stimulant drugs, as predicted, but they also show greater use of depressant drugs, a result that runs counter to the theory. This led Zuckerman to a new theory.

Monoamine oxidase theory. The monoamines are a class of neurotransmitters that include noradrenaline, dopamine, and serotonin. The first two of these are associated with pleasure and excitement, and serotonin is a neural inhibitor. Monoamine oxidase (MAO) breaks down the monoamines in the synapse or upon reuptake into the neuron from which the neurotransmitter was released. This process keeps the transmitter from cumulating in

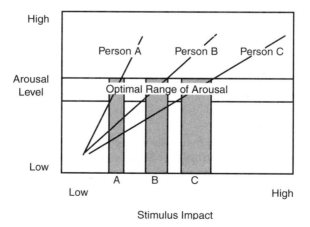

FIGURE 12–5.   Optimal levels (ranges) of arousal for three different people: A, B, and C. Person A is easily aroused by stimuli and reaches his optimal level with a low level of stimulus impact. Person C takes a higher level of stimulus impact to reach her optimal range of arousal. Person B falls in between. In this example the optimal ranges are nonoverlapping. The optimal range for Person B is too high for A and too low for C.

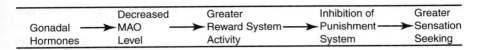

	Decreased	Greater	Inhibition of	Greater
Gonadal	⟶ MAO	⟶ Reward System ⟶	Punishment ⟶	Sensation
Hormones	Level	Activity	System	Seeking

FIGURE 12–6.   Zuckerman's monoamine oxidation level theory of sensation seeking.

the synapse and continuing to act after the neuron has stopped firing. How does this relate to sensation seeking?

Gonadal hormones in males are related to sensation seeking and would account for the sex differences in sensation seeking (males are higher SS). However, the gonadal hormones also reduce the level of MAO, which allows greater activity in the monamine systems regulated by MAO. Thus there would be greater activity in the dopamine reward systems (Zuckerman, 1994). The level of MAO is in large part genetically determined. So, says the theory, there are heritable individual differences in the degree to which our dopamine reward systems are aroused by stimulation. Activation of the reward system may also inhibit activity in the punishment system (Gray's behavioral inhibition system), suggesting that there is an interplay between relative levels of arousal in reward and punishment systems that is crucial for sensation seeking. This theory is summarized in Figure 12–6. We saw in Chapter Six how emotions that are related to reward and punishment can counteract each other. In any case, the reward system that we have seen to be so important in other aspects of motivation is also important for the pleasurable aspects of sensory experience.

As noted before, high SS people do not seek the pleasures of excitement at the expense of carelessness. Piet (1987), for example, found that dangerous thrill seeking was *not* the motivation of professional stunt performers, whose lives are regularly at stake. They displayed the same kind of strong motivation for achievement that characterizes leaders in any field, but they emphasized that because of their ability and training, the dangers they faced were relatively small. The hazards of stunting were perceived as *controllable* by skill and preparation. Hazards of everyday life, in contrast, are not controllable because they depend on other people. The stunt performers interviewed by Piet were in agreement that they could not afford to be afraid if they were to survive. In the overall context of hedonistic theory, stunt performers do not live for the thrill of the moment—they take the ultimate long term view of what is to their benefit (staying alive).

COGNITIVE MOTIVATION: MAKING SENSE OF THE WORLD

Loewenstein (1994, p. 94) described research on problem solving in the last quarter century thusly: "Virtually all of this research has examined the cognitive strategies that people use to solve problems. Amazingly there has been almost no research on why people are so powerfully driven to solve such problems. . . ." It would seem to be true that people or animals engage in activities that are driven neither by hunger nor pain, nor rewarded by food or solace. This view takes us back to the stimulus theories of reinforcement in Chapter Seven, where we saw that monkeys would work to see a toy electric train travel in circles, that rats would run mazes without reward, and that pigeons would choose to peck at a colored disk for apparently just the reward of getting information about when food might be coming. Humans work puzzles, read, and do research "for fun." It is this "motivation inherent in information processing" (Hunt, 1965) to which we turn now. The question is, Why should people be so attracted to situations that confer no other benefits than to help make sense of the world?

Curiosity has been characterized as an internally driven desire for information, as a passion for learning, and as a longing or appetite for knowledge (Loewenstein, 1994). It is clearly motivational in that it directs and energizes behavior and that people obtain pleasure from the activities involved. But what fundamental process is common to all the activities we include under curiosity? In order to understand the theories that follow, we should first know a little about control theory.

Control Theory

Control theory in engineering is concerned with machines that engage in "purposive" behaviors aimed at some precisely defined goal (Hyland, 1988). The idea is that *deviation from some norm* sets a system into action. For example, in order to control room temperature, we set the thermostat at a point called the **reference criterion,** such as 72°F. A sensor (called a **comparator**) detects a difference between the thermostat reference and the actual room temperature. When the difference (**detected error**) is large enough (e.g., 2 degrees), a heater is turned on. The rising temperature provides a negative feedback signal, and when the detected error is reduced to zero (room temperature = thermostat setting), the system turns off. The "purpose" of the system is to keep the room temperature at a certain level, but the "purposefulness" is entirely within the physical properties of the system. Figure 12–7 illustrates the system. In living organisms we speak of motivational systems that reduce discrepancies. Departure from an internal body temperature of 98.6°F stimulates homeostatic mechanisms to return temperature to "normal." Or, departure from an optimal level of arousal may instigate activities to restore arousal to the optimal level. In each of these instances, we can conceive of a thermostat-like mechanism that triggers appropriate activities to reduce the discrepancy between some reference condition and an actual condition.

Sokolov's model of attention.   E. N. Sokolov (1960) proposed a widely accepted control theory of attention. We have all experienced situations in which attention-getting stimuli go unnoticed after a while. For example, we notice

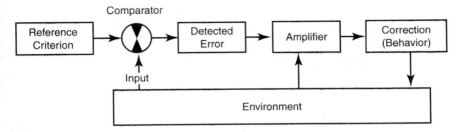

FIGURE 12–7. Basic control system. Using the system as a thermostat, a reference criterion of some temperature would be set, such as 72°. A comparator within the thermostat would detect any error between the reference criterion and the surrounding environment, such as when the temperature drops too low. The error signal would be amplified so that corrective action (turning on the furnace) would occur.

when an air conditioner turns on, but we stop noticing the sound after a while. This phenomenon is called **habituation** and is readily demonstrated in the laboratory. A simple *change* in sound, however, may immediately command our attention. Thus we also notice when the air conditioner goes off. Experimental subjects show an aroused EEG if just the pitch, but not the loudness, of a habituated tone is slightly changed. This response tells us that there must be processing of the habituated stimulus inputs somewhere in the brain or we could not be aroused by a change in the stimulus. Sokolov's theory says that repetitious inputs are stored in the nervous system as a reference against which new inputs are *compared*. If input and storage are the same, then attention is not aroused. If an input signal is different from those previously stored, there is arousal (see Figure 12–8). Pavlov called such behavioral arousal the **orienting reflex.** We "perk up" at a novel stimulus, and by paying attention, we are more prepared to cope with either beneficial or dangerous events.

The TOTE model. Miller, Galanter, and Pribram (1960) applied the control concept to events ranging from neurological to cognitive and social. Their basic unit for analysis was what they called the TOTE unit, an acronym for Test-Operate-Test-Exit. Suppose we want to hammer a nail into a board. We have a plan in our head of what we want. We look at the nail (test) and see that it is not in the board. There is an incongruity between our plan and our image of how things actually are. We hit the nail with a hammer (operate) and then look again (test) to see whether the nail and board are congruous with our plan. When our plan and the nail in the board coincide, the incongruity is gone, and we turn to something else (exit). Incongruity is thus a motivating force to keep us at the task until the incongruity is sufficiently diminished. The TOTE analysis is illustrated in Figure 12–9.

These applications of control theory tell us that across a wide spectrum of human events, we are aroused physiologically and behaviorally by incon-

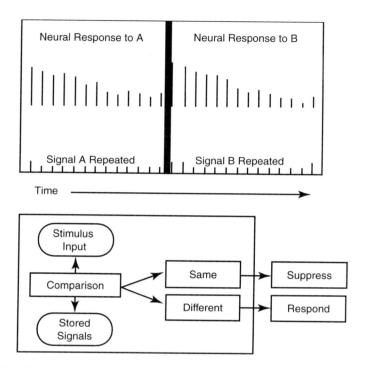

FIGURE 12–8. Sokolov model for habituation of orienting responses. The magnitude of neural responses to repetitious Signal A (such as a tone) gradually declines. If a new Signal, B, only slightly different from Signal A, is presented, there is once again a large response. According to Sokolov, stimulus inputs are compared with stored signals. If the stimuli are the same as the stored signals, there is suppression of responses to the stimuli. If the incoming stimulus is different from the stored signal, there is a neural response. The brain responds to changing stimulation.

gruous events and that our arousal is reduced when the incongruity is reduced (see also Chapter Six). We solve a puzzle, and we then understand something that we did not understand before; uncertainty is reduced. This is a tension and tension-reduction model that accounts for our staying with a problem until the incongruity or uncertainty disappears and the tension is reduced. But how would the theory account for our **seeking out** problems and puzzles in the first place? Is it not this feature of curiosity that sets it apart from other behaviors?

Hunt's Information Processing Model

J. McV. Hunt (1965) championed a discrepancy view of curiosity that leaned heavily on control theory concepts but that fell back on optimal level of arousal theory to explain why people put themselves into incongruous situations. He proposed that there is an optimal level of arousal, neither too high

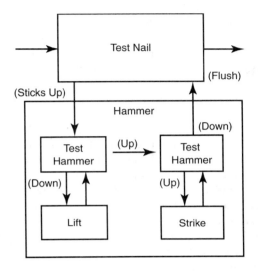

FIGURE 12–9. Test-Operate-Test-Exit (TOTE) model, illustrating a hierarchical plan for hammering a nail. The hammer and nail are both tested repeatedly until the nail is flush, at which time there is an exit to another nail or task. (From Miller, Galanter, & Pribram, 1960. Used with permission of Holt, Rinehart, and Winston, Pub.).

nor too low, that people seek. As a person deals intellectually with the environment, the person learns about it, and incongruities are reduced to such a low level that they are no longer arousing. However, if the environment becomes so predictable that there is no incongruity between expectation and occurrence, the person **seeks out** stimuli that produce incongruity. Hence, we seek out new situations, puzzles, games, problems, reading, and other sources of arousal. We may recall from Chapter Seven that Dember and Earl (1957) proposed that when we have learned to cope with a particular level of incongruity in the environment, we seek more complicated situations, so that we are always growing in our capacity to deal with events.

Loewenstein's Information-Gap Theory

Loewenstein (1994, p. 90) says that curiosity is aroused when one becomes attentive to a gap in one's knowledge. An information gap is the difference between what one knows and what one wants to know. What one *wants* to know is the reference point in a control system. We compare what we want to know with what we do know. This is the "test" in the TOTE model. If there is a discrepancy, we are aroused to do something to reduce the discrepancy ("operate" in TOTE), and then we compare again ("test"). When we have done enough to reduce the discrepancy, we "exit" and move on to something else. The same degree of knowledge may or may not evoke curiosity, depending on *how much* we want to know. For example, most people's curiosity about computers seems to be satisfied when they can run the specific programs they want. They are "driven" to learn what they need to know to run their software, but they don't really want to know any more about how computers work. Their "curiosity" about computers is satisfied relatively easily because their information gap is relatively small.

The theory makes a variety of predictions. For example, the degree of curiosity about a piece of information should be related to the capacity of the information to close a person's information gap. This theory was supported in an experiment by Loewenstein, Adler, Behrens, and Gillis (1992; described in Loewenstein, 1994). Subjects were shown two lists of states and asked to guess the rule by which each list was generated. One list had ten states, and one five states, but the actual rule was the same in both cases. After guessing a rule for each list, the subjects were asked to choose which rule they would like to learn. Seventy percent of the subjects chose the rule for the longer list. This result had been predicted on the grounds that the subjects would perceive that the rule for the long list would give them more information than would the rule for the short list.

The question of why people seek out discrepancies arises for Loewenstein's theory just as for Hunt's, however. Why do people voluntarily put themselves into information gaps, such as problem solving situations? Loewenstein states (1994, p. 90) that "the interpretation of curiosity proposed here assumes that curiosity is always aversive." He then argues that the process of satisfying curiosity is more pleasurable than the curiosity itself is aversive. A person who voluntarily puts herself into a puzzle situation must anticipate that the pleasure of solving the puzzle will be greater than the aversion of the puzzle itself. The theory postulates that curiosity satisfaction is pleasurable but offers no mechanism for the pleasure. Loewenstein rejected an optimal level of arousal explanation. It might be proposed that reduction of the information gap arouses the same dopamine/endorphin pleasure system that underlies other rewards. One speculative prediction from this hypothesis would therefore be that subjects given naloxone, which antagonizes endorphins, would find information less rewarding than subjects not given naloxone. To our knowledge, however, this prediction has not been tested.

Two other motivational concepts related to the preceding theories are the **need for closure** and the **need for cognition.**

The Need for Closure

Kruglanski and Webster (1996) propose a theory in which "need for cognitive closure" is the key construct. Need for closure is defined as a desire for an answer on a given topic, *any* answer, as compared with confusion and ambiguity. It is a "distinctly motivational concept." According to the theory, people who have a high need for such closure tend to quickly "seize" upon an answer to their question or problem and then to "freeze" on that answer, closing themselves to further information. Individual differences are measured by the **Need for Closure Scale** (Webster & Kruglanski, 1994). This scale has five dimensions, which are shown in Table 12–5 with a sample item for each subscale. The total scale correlates about −.28 with the **Need for Cognition Scale** (see later) and positively about .28 with scales of dogmatism, authoritarianism, and intolerance of ambiguity. Authoritarianism is related to prejudice, discrimination, desire for law and order, and unwillingness to entertain alternative views (Adorno, Frenkel-Brunswik, Levinson, & Sanford, 1950) .

Need for closure is a personality characteristic, like a trait, but it can also be demanded by particular situations. People with a high need for closure should respond more strongly to situations calling for closure than individuals with a weak need for closure. They should tend to base their final judgments of a problem on early cues that they are given. This inclination is indicated, for example, with the **primacy effect** in impression formation, which is the tendency to base impressions of people more on information presented early in a sequence rather than later (Asch, 1946). Webster and Kruglanski (1994) had subjects high or low in need for closure form impressions of a hypothetical candidate for the presidency of a company. Positive and negative information about the candidate was presented in opposite orders for two groups. The usual primacy effect is that the positive-then-negative group rates the candidate more favorably than the negative-then-positive, even though both groups get exactly the same information. Table 12–6, from Webster and Kruglanski, summarizes the results. The usual effect of order of information was found only for those subjects who were high in need for closure. Subjects low in need for closure did not show the primacy effect at all.

What are the origins of individual differences in need for closure? Kruglanski and Webster (1996) merely suggest that there may be differences in personal histories or social norms. The differences may run deeper than this, however. Recall that need for closure is correlated with, among other things, authoritarianism. Some aspects of authoritarianism, in turn, have

TABLE 12–5. Dimensions and sample items from the Need for Closure Scale.

DIMENSION	SAMPLE SCALE ITEM
1. Preference for order	"I enjoy having a clear and structured mode of life."
2. Preference for predictability	"I dislike unpredictable situations."
3. Decisiveness	"I usually make important decisions quickly and confidently."
4. Discomfort with ambiguity	"I dislike it when a person's statement could mean many different things."
5. Closed-mindedness	"I do not usually consult many different opinions before forming my own view."

Source: Kruglanski, Webster, & Klem (1993). © American Psychological Association, 1993. Used by permission.

TABLE 12–6. Mean ratings of job candidate's personality as a function of need for closure and information sequence. Higher numbers are more positive evaluations.

INFORMATION SEQUENCE	NEED FOR CLOSURE CLASSIFICATION	
	HIGH NEED FOR CLOSURE	LOW NEED FOR CLOSURE
Positive-Negative	112.2	88.5
Negative-Positive	61.1	90.2

Source: Webster & Kruglanski, 1994, pp. 1049–1062, Table 5. © American Psychological Association. Used by permission.

been found in twin studies to have estimated heritability coefficients in the 40 percent to 50 percent range (Tesser, 1993). Thus differences in need for closure may be partially inherited just as many other personality differences are.

The Need for Cognition

Possibly related to the need for closure is a "need for cognition," or for information. Cacioppo and Petty (1982) argued that there are such individual differences in this need and devised a "need for cognition" scale to measure them. They defined need for cognition as "the tendency for an individual to engage in and enjoy thinking." The scale has such items as "I really enjoy a task that involves coming up with new solutions to problems" and "When something I read confuses me, I just put it down and forget it" (scored negatively). They then had high- and low-scoring subjects do a simple or complex number-circling task for ten minutes. In the simple task, subjects were told to circle as many 1s, 5s, and 7s as they could from a list of 3,500 random digits. In the complex task, the subjects circled all 3s, any 6 that preceded a 7, and every other 4. Subjects reported enjoyment of the task on a seven-point scale. Nobody was terribly thrilled by such a boring task, but the subjects with a high need for cognition did enjoy the complex task more than the simple one, and the low-need subjects enjoyed the simple task more. It thus appears there are individual differences in the degree to which information processing activities are found pleasant and, presumably, reinforcing.

SUMMARY

1. **Personality** refers to those enduring characteristics by which we distinguish one person from another. **Trait theories** refer to permanent characteristics, some of which are nonmotivational. **Dynamic theories** are specifically motivational. One of the major distinctions among people is the **goals** that they consider important and strive to achieve.

2. Henry Murray distinguished between **presses** (environmental features appraised as harmful or beneficial) and **needs** (internal states). He further distinguished between **viscerogenic needs** due to periodic body changes (such as hunger or thirst) and **psychogenic needs** (which do not have a clear physiological basis outside the brain, such as achievement motivation).

3. **Need for achievement** (n Ach) is defined as a desire or tendency "to overcome obstacles, to exercise power, to strive to do something difficult as well and as quickly as possible." McClelland argued that achievement need develops out of previously rewarded achievement behavior and the positive affect associated with achievement.

4. A more mathematical theory developed by Atkinson says that the tendency to engage in achievement behaviors (T_s) is the product of the motive for success (M_s), the probability of success (P_s), and the incentive value of success (I_s). P_s and I_s are inversely related: $I_s = 1 - P_s$. There is also a tendency to avoid failure (T_{af}), based on a fear of failure. T_s and T_{af} are additive, with behavioral predictions based on which one is greater.

5. Spence and Helmreich developed an achievement theory with the dimensions of **mastery, completion,** and **competitiveness.** People high in competitiveness often do not perform as well as people who are less competitive.

6. **Attributional** approaches to achievement have tried to take individual differences in achievement motivation into account in terms of the attributions that people give for success or failure.

7. Weiner's attributional theory has three attributional dimensions: (1) **internal versus external locus of control,** (2) **stable versus unstable factors,** and (3) **controllable versus uncontrollable factors.** It is assumed that each specific causal attribution for success or failure has particular emotional consequences, which in turn influence future achievement-oriented behaviors.

8. People differ in their **desire for control** (DC). Low DC individuals with control are not as affected by perceived loss of control as are high DC individuals. Conversely, the "good effects" that accrue to people with control may not be so perceived by people with low desire for control.

10. **Power motivation** is defined as the desire to have control over others. It is measured by scoring imaginative stories for power imagery relating to strong, vigorous action, actions that arouse strong emotion in others and that demonstrate explicit concerns about reputation or position.

11. People high in need for power show increased internal arousal when power need is engaged. People with high need for power also tend to respond more selectively to environmental cues related to power, such as better remembering power-related stimuli.

12. **Personal power** is distinguished from **social power,** which is more altruistic. Men high in personal power tend to be aggressive and competitive, but women high in personal power are not. Socialization seems partly to determine such behaviors, since middle-class men are less aggressive than lower-class men with equal power scores.

13. Bandura's theory of **self-efficacy** says that people who believe that their behavior will be more effective also perform more effectively. There are several ways to enhance self-efficacy, but **personal accomplishment** is the most powerful and enduring.

14. People vary in how much they enjoy **sensation-seeking.** One theory to account for this variance says that there are individual differences in the circumstances

that produce an **optimal level of arousal;** some people are more easily aroused to their optimal level than others. Zuckerman has also proposed a **monoamine oxidase** theory, which says that people vary in the degree to which the neurotransmitter **dopamine** is released.

15. There are a number of different approaches to the question of how people are motivated by discrepancies or uncertainty. One general **control theory** idea is that discrepancies of various kinds motivate action to reduce the discrepancies. People often seek out mild discrepancies in the form of games and puzzles, possibly seeking a mild increase in arousal level.

16. People also vary in their **need for cognitive closure;** some people want an answer to a question immediately, and so thus quickly seize upon whatever answer they are given because that answer satisfies their need for closure. The need for closure is also influenced by particular situations.

17. **Need for cognition** refers to the fact that people differ in their tendencies to engage in and enjoy thinking. Differences here are relevant to the kinds of work and leisure activities that people choose.

CHAPTER THIRTEEN

Attitudes and Cognitive Consistency

———•———

DEFINITION OF ATTITUDE

In Chapter One we defined motivation in terms of the choices of anticipated behavioral outcomes. These choices, in turn, were defined in terms of hedonic preferences and the concepts of desire and aversion, of things that people like and want or dislike and avoid. We define attitudes in these same terms. Attitudes are positive or negative feelings about something. Attitude and attitude change are major topics in their own right, but in our view, they are also part of the fundamental motivational processes. Specifically, an attitude is a positive or negative affective response directed toward a specific person, object, situation, and so on. The object of the attitude lies on the hedonic continuum as illustrated in Figure 13–1. Below, there is a negative attitude (aversion) toward Person A and a mildly positive attitude toward Object X. We generally think of the attitudes as being relatively weak affective responses, but attitudes may erupt into strong emotional responses, as in the case of attitudes toward a politician, for example.

When the topic of attitudes first entered social psychology, attitudes were conceived as affective responses in the manner just described. The definition began to drift for some theorists who argued that attitudes have three distinct components, not just affect. These components were affect, cognition, and conation (action).

Affective response. This is the basic attitude, referring to a positive or negative feeling, a like or dislike, with regard to a particular person, object, or thing.

Cognition. This refers to ideas and perceptions about the attitude object (e.g., ideas about Republicans versus Democrats, Candidate A versus Candidate B). How does our knowledge of Bill Clinton, Bob Dole, Jesse Helms, or Newt Gingrich affect our attitudes toward them? How do our attitudes affect what we pay attention to about them or what we believe about them (e.g., Clinton's alleged philandering, Dole's age, Helms's radical right beliefs, Gingrich's taking a multimillion-dollar advance from a book publisher within months of becoming Speaker of the House)?

Conation (action). How does your attitude affect the way you behave? Are you more or less likely to vote or work for (or against) a candidate be-

Object:	Person A	Object X	
Attitude:	–5	0	+5
	Aversion	Neutrality	Desire

FIGURE 13–1. Objects of attitude (Person A, Object X) lying along the hedonic continuum.

cause of your attitude? John F. Kennedy had many young voters working hard for him just because they found him so appealing. If you are highly frustrated (aversive condition) with the economy, how does this condition affect your voting behavior? Whom do you most associate the problem with? Are you more likely to vote against whoever you think is responsible?

In effect, however, these three components fit just about any topic in psychology that we can imagine, and attitude theorists are now moving back to the affect concept of attitude. Baron and Byrne (1997), for example, accept the definition that "attitudes are associations between objects and evaluations of those objects." It is recognized, however, that the affective component (attitude) influences and is influenced by cognition and conation.

ATTITUDE MEASUREMENT

Attitudes have been measured in many different ways, varying in the degree of directness, but all these ways attempt to locate an attitude object on an hedonic scale. These different ways of operationalizing attitudes clarify what we mean by attitude. We discuss three of these. Two of these, the Likert Scale and the Semantic Differential, have had wide use. The third, "automatic activation of attitudes" is a laboratory procedure. In addition, in public polling procedures sometimes there is a simple "For"or "Against" choice, such as with regard to a public policy or referendum. For detailed discussion of attitude measures, see Eagly and Chaiken (1993).

Likert Scale

On a Likert scale you indicate the extent to which you agree or disagree with a strongly positive or negative statement about some thing or person. An example is illustrated in Figure 13–2.

Semantic Differential

An attitude object is located at one of seven locations between two polar adjectives, illustrated in Figure 13–3. In accord with the dimensional approaches to emotion (see Chapter Two), statistical analyses consistently show that there are three underlying dimensions accounting for the evaluative meaning of such polar opposite words: (1) **evaluation,** for example, good-

---

Newt Gingrich is a prince of a man.
Agree: 1   2   3   4   5:   Disagree

FIGURE 13–2. Example of a Likert scale, recording agreement or disagreement with extreme statements. If the statement were worded negatively, e.g., "Newt Gingrich is a rascal," strong disagreement would indicate a positive attitude toward Gingrich.

Hillary Clinton

Good ___:___:___:___:___:___:___ Bad
Active ___:___:___:___:___:___:___ Passive
Strong ___:___:___:___:___:___:___ Weak

FIGURE 13–3. Semantic differential. A check mark is made at some point between each pair of polar opposite adjectives.

bad, pleasant-unpleasant, foul-fragrant; (2) **activity,** for example, fast-slow, active-passive, sharp-dull; and (3) **potency,** for example, heavy-light, strong-weak (e.g., Osgood, Suci, & Tannebaum, 1957). We can then make a three-dimensional "attitude space" into which we can put various attitude objects and see their similarities and differences. For most purposes, a two-dimensional space works well, just using the evaluative and activity dimensions.

Automatic Activation of Evaluations by Attitude Objects

Sometimes researchers are concerned about the extent to which such direct methods of attitude measurement as Likert scales may be influenced by nonattitudinal factors. For example, it may be socially undesirable (or, politically incorrect) to express one's true attitude with regard to some issue. Therefore, researchers may attempt to assess attitudes by indirect measures, so that the subject does not know just what is being assessed. The automatic activation procedure is one of the most indirect methods, relying on the fact that we can evaluate stimuli without being conscious of them. In the **priming paradigm** that we saw earlier, stimuli that are presented too rapidly to be consciously perceived can influence judgments about subsequent stimuli. For example, if the priming word is SADDLE, a subject who is asked subsequently to fill a letter into HO_SE is more likely to enter an R (horse) rather than a U (house). The reverse holds true if the priming word is ROOM. In similar fashion, words with positive or negative meanings can serve as **evaluative primes,** coloring the meaning of subsequent stimuli. Consider the following example from Fazio, Sanbonmatsu, Powell, & Kardes (1986). Suppose that the attitude object is vodka, which an individual evaluates positively. If the word **vodka** is used as a prime, it *automatically activates* a positive evaluation. If a target adjective following the prime is also positive (e.g., **happy**), then the subject may indicate more quickly that the target has a positive connotation than if there was no prime or if the prime was just a meaningless string of letters (e.g., XXXX). Conversely, a negative prime will facilitate identification of a negative adjective.

Since this is a relatively complicated procedure, it is interesting only if it produces especially interesting results as compared with simpler measures. In fact, results by this method sometimes are different than are found with some of the more traditional measures. For example, a person may indicate on a

Likert scale that he or she favors something, such as a particular ethnic group, but under the automatic activation procedure, may show the opposite. Thus, hypothetically, a person might claim some positive affinity to Klingons on a Likert scale, but the word KLINGON might facilitate negative judgment of the word BAD. That is, the judgment is made faster when primed by KLINGON than when primed by XXX. One would therefore be led to believe that somewhere deep down, the subject really does **not** like Klingons.

We must be careful not to treat this procedure as if it were a method of lie detection or a royal road to the unconscious. It is not a magical method for detecting truth in our psyches. Its effectiveness in the laboratory depends on procedures that are difficult to imagine in large-scale attitude surveys. It is an intriguing method for helping us understand the nature of attitudes, however, and may help us to develop better measures. We might, for example, use this procedure to help us validate other methods of measurement that could be used in a more practical way.

When Do Attitudes Predict Behavior?

Attitudes are not, and cannot be, the sole predictors of behavior. Let us remind ourselves that **Behavior = f(person, environment)** and that there are multiple aspects of both the person and the environment that determine behavior. In order for attitudes to predict behavior, we must have an appropriate measure of attitudes and must know what other factors besides attitudes influence any particular behavior we are trying to predict. For example, how might a person vote. An example of how a nonattitudinal influence might affect behavior is a liberal politician elected from a conservative district. The politician may feel it necessary to express attitudes that do not completely reflect her or his own views simply because she or he must get elected in order to do anything. In such a case, the expressed attitude and subsequent behavior might not coincide very well.

If attitudes are measured properly, they can predict behavior rather well, as shown by the success of political pollsters in recent years. Election outcomes can be accurately predicted within two or three percentage points. In a carefully conducted research study, Bowman and Fishbein (1978) found a very high correlation ($r = .80$) between attitudes and subsequent voting on a referendum for a nuclear power plant.

A number of different factors determine the extent to which attitudes can predict behavior. These are as follows:

1. The attitude measure is specific to an object or issue (e.g., attitude toward a nuclear power plant).
2. The attitude measure is reliable.
3. Nonattitudinal considerations do not override accurate attitude statements.

4. Survey sampling is appropriate (e.g., random sampling from the relevant population).
5. The attitude does not change between the time the measure is collected and the time the to-be-predicted behavior occurs (e.g., voting). Intervening events may affect attitudes (e.g., a nuclear accident, war, change in economy, something about a candidate).

ATTITUDES AND LEARNING

Psychologists generally assume that attitudes are learned in a social context, and often not by direct experience. We have positive or negative attitudes toward people or events that we have never directly experienced. How do these develop?

Classical Conditioning

Classical conditioning (Chapter Four) plays an important role (Staats & Staats, 1958; Staats, 1983). If the economy shows a sharp decline and people lose their jobs, they are likely to associate these events with the most visible person in the government, the president. We would diagram this association in classical conditioning terms as shown in Figure 13–4.

The slander technique of guilt by association works in this manner. You associate someone's name with something bad, and by association that person becomes "guilty" and therefore also "bad." In the 1950s, the senator from Wisconsin, Joseph McCarthy, used this technique widely, associating the names of highly respectable citizens with communism, thereby causing them to lose jobs. This practice was particularly destructive in the Hollywood community of writers, directors, and actors. Richard Milhouse Nixon gained his California seat to the United States Senate in 1950 by accusing his opponent, Helen Gahagan Douglas, of being a communist sympathizer and thereby developed a negative attitude toward her. On the positive side, there is celebrity advertising, by which a product becomes "good" by being associated with a famous athlete or other personality. Paul Reiser and Candace Bergen have ad-

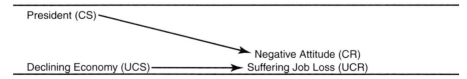

FIGURE 13–4. Classical conditioning of attitudes. If the president is associated with bad events, such as losing one's job, he is likely to be viewed negatively. Interestingly, in 1998 when President Clinton was in difficulty on account of his association with Monica Lewinsky, his popularity was reaching an all-time high. This trend was generally thought to be due in no small part to the fact that the economy had been doing exceptionally well for several years.

vertised long distance phone calls, Michael Jordan advertises shoes, and Joe Namath once upon a time advertised panty hose.

Evaluative conditioning. Evaluative conditioning refers to the transfer of affective responses from one stimulus to another, particularly important for attitude change (Razran, 1954; Martin & Levey, 1978; Levey & Martin, 1987; Baeyens, Eelen, & Van den Bergh, 1990). This process is distinguished from "signal conditioning," whereby the CS signals the impending UCS. Knowing that the UCS is coming is not the same as liking or disliking the UCS, however. And learning that the CS predicts the UCS is not the same as liking or disliking the CS. It is the transfer of liking or disliking from one stimulus to another that characterizes attitude change and evaluative conditioning. Evaluative conditioning is said to differ from signal conditioning in several ways. For example, evaluative conditioning is thought to be an unconscious process and does not depend on the subject's awareness of the CS-UCS relation. Also, evaluative conditioning has been thought to produce a long-lasting evaluative change that is highly resistant to extinction.

A commonly used paradigm to study evaluative conditioning was developed by Levey and Martin (1975). They paired neutral pictures with pictures rated as either liked or disliked. First, subjects sorted a set of fifty unfamiliar paintings into three piles labeled "liked," "neutral," and "disliked." On the basis of these sorts, the pictures were paired and presented in these sequences: neutral-liked, neutral-disliked, neutral-neutral, liked-neutral, and disliked-neutral. The pictures were rated for subsequent liking after the paired presentations. The evaluation of the liked and disliked pictures was transferred to the neutral pictures, as judged by the change in ratings of the neutral pictures after pairings. Other researchers have questioned whether evaluative conditioning is truly a different kind of conditioning from signal conditioning, or even whether it is conditioning at all (Öhman, 1983; Page, 1974; Shanks & Dickinson, 1990). Nevertheless, the experimental procedures do appear to produce a transfer of likes and dislikes that characterize attitude change and may be a useful procedure for studying the process of attitude learning.

Imitation and Reinforcement

Children tend to take on the attitudes of their parents. They hear parents say positive or negative things and imitate these statements or actions. In turn, they are reinforced by parents for the imitation. We talk about adolescent rebellion, but at the level of politics, there is a strong association between the way high school students vote in straw polls and the way elections actually come out. Since the students don't vote, they must be reflecting the way that their elders communicate to them. This possibility does not mean, of course, that high school students reflect their parents on all issues (e.g., music, sex, drinking, driving). Children may find more reinforcement (or punishment) from their peers than from their parents on many issues.

BIOLOGY OF ATTITUDES

Genetics

Psychologists have usually treated attitudes as if they are entirely learned, but there is good evidence for biological inheritance as well. Tesser (1993, p. 129) observed that "the list of behavioral domains that appear to have sizable heritabilities is both long and surprising" and cites attitude-related studies showing heritability coefficients in the range of 50 percent. These include studies of job satisfaction, attitudes toward God, attitudes toward drinking alcohol (but not drinking coffee or smoking cigarets), the political attitude of authoritarianism, and radical political views. Attitudes with high heritability are stronger than attitudes with low heritability, they are responded to more quickly, and they are harder to change. The larger question then is, What are the mechanisms by which the genetic effects are demonstrated? Tesser suggests that sensory structures, body chemistry, intelligence, temperament and activity level, and conditionability all play a role. In a more global way, genetic factors may affect general dispositions, such as mood or extraversion. A genetic tendency toward extraversion, for example, might generally affect the development of more positive attitudes.

Physiological Measurement

If attitudes are emotional responses, then we should expect some physiological responses to be correlated with attitude arousal. Cacioppo, Crites, and Gardner (1996) recorded event-related brain potentials (ERPs) from the scalp over the two hemispheres. As compared with cyclic EEG waves, ERPs are specific responses to stimuli. The results were that the ERPs were larger over the right hemisphere than the left when subjects were required to make evaluative (good-bad) judgments about stimuli. When subjects were asked to make nonevaluative judgments, the right and left hemisphere ERPs were equal. This finding matches part of a general pattern for emotional responsiveness by the brain discussed in Chapter Two. Specifically, there appears to be a greater right-brain participation in emotional acts. We may conclude that there is a partial genetic determination of attitudes, probably mediated by certain other heritable characteristics, such as temperament.

ATTITUDES AND COGNITIVE CONSISTENCY

Meaning of Cognitive Consistency

Cognitive consistency refers to the occurrence of events as we expect them to occur. We may say that inconsistency, or incongruity, exists when an event is perceived to be different from expectation. For example, a dog with wings would be incongruous only to a person who has already become familiar with dogs of the normal variety. In control theory terms, the familiar (expected) dog is a reference point, and a comparator detects an "error," the difference between the expected and the observed dog. This detection triggers an internal arousal, along with attempts to deal with the incongruity. It is the motivating effect of incongruity as it produces striving for consistency that concerns us. Consistency and inconsistency are often in the eye of the beholder, however. One person may detect in unfolding events a consistent pattern that completely eludes someone else. Our concern, then, is with **consistency as perceived by an individual.** This consistency involves beliefs and thoughts as well as perception.

Balance Theory

Suppose that I like you and you like me, but we are in strong disagreement about a political candidate. We are in what Heider (1958) called a **state of imbalance.** If we agreed on the merits of the candidate, we would be in a state of **balance.** Imbalance is considered aversive, and we would therefore do something to reduce the imbalance. When "equilibrium" is restored, we are "satisfied." Imbalance is therefore like drive: Its presence initiates action, and its reduction reinforces that action. There are a variety of cognitive or behavioral things one might do to reduce imbalance. For example, you might change your mind about the candidate, or about me, or about both of us. Or you might avoid me until after the election.

A simple state of perceived interpersonal imbalance can occur with just two people. If Frank likes Jane, and Jane likes Frank, they both have a positive relation toward each other. If the affective sign of the relation is the same for both individuals (either positive or negative), the situation is balanced, and there is no "strain" to change it. A particularly interesting two-person case is unrequited love: One person has a strong positive sentiment for the other, but the second person is neutral or negative toward the first. It is here that we may see rapidly changing love-hate relationships. The individual whose positive sentiment is not returned may quickly come to be negative toward the second party, thus bringing the relationship back into balance. Since the problem is perceptual, there may be interesting "distortions." For example, Frank may like Jane and perceive that she does *not* like him, when in fact she does. Frank's perception of the situation, not the "real" state of affairs, determines the imbalance.

The more general case, however, to which most researchers have directed their attention is like our initial illustration. It involves a person (*A*), another person (*B*), and an entity (*X*), which may, for example, be an object, a third person, an idea, or an event. Using the symbolism of Theodore Newcomb, there are three possible pairs of relationships within an **ABX triad:** (1) *AB*, where *A* holds some affect toward *B*; (2) *AX*, where *A* holds some affect toward X; and (3) BX, where B holds some affect toward X. A is the person with whom, by definition, we are concerned at a particular time: It is A's perception of the relationships that we are examining. Each of these three relationships can be positive or negative, and the general rule is that a triad is balanced if the algebraic product of the three is positive and imbalanced if the product is negative. This rule gives four balanced and four imbalanced triads, summarized in Table 13–1. Figure 13–5 illustrates two balanced and two imbalanced triads involving you (A), me (B), and the President of the United States (X).

Let us put Relationship 3 (balanced) and Relationship 6 (imbalanced) from Figure 13–5 into verbal form. In 3, you are A and have negative affect toward both me (B) and the President (X); since I like the President, the triad is balanced from the point of view of the focal person (A, who is you). If we were to shift the diagram so that I am the focal person, the situation might or might not remain balanced, depending on whether my attitude toward you were positive or negative. In Relationship 6, you have a negative attitude toward me, but we are both positive toward the President. By definition, this represents an imbalanced situation. In any real situation the valence sign (+ or −) and intensity of affect would be determined by many factors (you might like some of the President's policies, but not others), and the degree of imbalance would in turn depend on these intensities as well as on signs. A mild imbalance would not produce much effort toward reducing the imbalance. We also assume that X is of interest or relevance to both A and B before there could be any imbalance. If neither A nor B was concerned about X one way or another, there would be no triad.

Although imbalance is generally considered undesirable, we can readily see, from the point of view of activation theory, for example, that some imbalance (like some activation or some frustration) often may be sought. Up to a point, we may enjoy political arguments with our friends.

Newcomb (1968) proposes that balanced relations 1 and 2 in Table 13–1 are in fact different from 3 and 4. Considerable research cited by Newcomb indicates that although 1 and 2 are desirable, 3, 4, 5, and 6 are all mildly undesirable, and 7 and 8 are the most undesirable. Newcomb, there-

TABLE 13–1.   Balanced and imbalanced relationships with all combinations of positive and negative *AB, AX,* and *BX* relationships.

BALANCED				IMBALANCED		
AB	*AX*	*BX*		*AB*	*AX*	*BX*
1. +	+	+	5.	−	−	−
2. +	−	−	6.	−	+	+
3. −	−	+	7.	+	+	−
4. −	+	−	8.	+	−	+

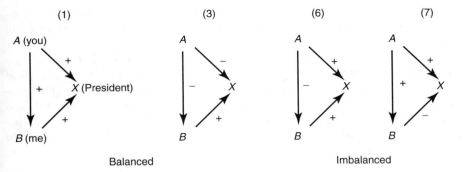

FIGURE 13–5.   Balanced triads (1 and 3) and imbalanced triads (6 and 7). See text and Table 13–1 for details.

fore, prefers to consider 1 and 2 balanced (pleasant), 3, 4, 5, and 6 nonbalanced (relatively neutral), and 7 and 8 imbalanced (unpleasant). The reason for this view may be that negative relations are unpleasant, even though they may be balanced. Two people who do not like each other form a balanced situation, but neither may enjoy the situation. The evidence cited by Newcomb is not always consistent, but it does point up the fact that the logical relations (algebraic products) defining balance and imbalance do not necessarily coincide with the individual's perception of the situation or the affect that he or she experiences.

ATTITUDES AND COGNITIVE DISSONANCE

When Prophecy Fails

For almost two millennia, there have been recurring predictions of the second coming of Christ, the impending end of the world, or other cataclysmic events. These have been accompanied by individuals who claim to have been given "divine warning," sometimes including very specific dates, of the time such events would occur. In the early 1950s in Minnesota, a Mrs. Kreech began to receive messages first from "Elder Brother" and then from a being named "Sananda" that a cataclysmic event was going to occur. The messages were received via "automatic writing" (not under the volition of the writer) and warned that the Earth was going to split from the northern polar region down to Mexico, with great flooding. As Mrs. Kreech told others of these spiritual messages, a small group of believers formed. Over about three months, the messages continued, including word that a spaceship from the planet Ceron would come to take away the faithful. This event was to happen on December 21, which the group believed was the actual birth date of Christ. The group prepared for the event and held vigil, waiting for the spaceship. Needless to say it did not arrive, nor did the Earth split. The members of the group, however, seemed not to lose faith. Indeed, some of them began to proselytize more strongly.

The preceding sequence of events was described at book length by Festinger, Riecken, & Schachter (1956) and is often taken to be the prototypical example of cognitive dissonance. When faced with a firm belief (the cataclysm and the spaceship) and its disconfirmation, at least some of the believers held their belief even more strongly. Cognitive dissonance theory is an account of why people sometimes respond to contradictory events in paradoxical ways.

Definition of Cognitive Dissonance

Cognitive dissonance is said to occur when two beliefs are incongruent or are logically contradictory. Thus the cult members' belief that a spaceship was coming was incongruent with the fact that it did not come. Such inconsistencies are considered aversive. Some of the members reduced this aversive state, not by surrendering their belief, but by rationalizing the failure of the spaceship to come. They became even stronger believers.

There are many possible ways of reducing dissonance, but those that have been researched the most involve a change in cognitions. A chain-smoker might add a new cognition ("the lung cancer research has produced ambiguous results") or might alter existing ones ("cancer really isn't all that dangerous"). Note that the cognitions (beliefs) are important, but not necessarily accurate. We might seek more information to try to reduce our dissonance, such as reading further on the problem of lung cancer. Doing this could lead to the apocryphal outcome that "I read so much about lung cancer and smoking that I gave up reading." Facetious, perhaps, but not an entirely unreal possibility. We might change our behavior, rather than our cognition, and give up cigarettes as a means of reducing dissonance.

Dissonance, however, would not be the only factor determining whether we stopped smoking. Dissonance theory is not all-encompassing and was never intended to be. Other desires and aversions might override dissonance, and we might even engage in *dissonance-producing* activities. Group pressure, for example, might push an adolescent into doing something that is at odds with her beliefs about herself.

Attitude Change and Forced Compliance

The most widely used approach to the study of cognitive dissonance employs a procedure involving **forced compliance** and **insufficient justification.** The situation is so structured that the subjects find it difficult not to do what the experimenter asked (forced compliance), but at the same time they have little **apparent** reason for doing so (insufficient justification). An experiment often used as the standard for explaining and describing dissonance is by Festinger and Carlsmith (1959). Their subjects were initially required to do the very tedious task of turning pegs in holes. When they were finished, the subjects were asked if they would help persuade other persons to be subjects. This persuasion would involve telling the potential subjects that the task was interesting. The only potential subject was a research assistant.

Half the real subjects were told they would receive a $20 retainer for their services, and the rest that they would receive $1. All subjects agreed to serve (indicating the power of the forced-compliance aspect). The critical measure of dissonance reduction was how the subjects evaluated the task after trying to persuade the assistant. It was independently ascertained that the task really was boring and that the main assumption of the experiment was that making positive statements about the task would be discrepant with one's private evaluation. Incentive theory might say that the subjects receiving $20 would view the task as more attractive, since it is associated with a large incentive. Receiving $20 should produce little dissonance, however, because $20 is "adequate justification" for making the discrepant statements. Therefore, according to dissonance theory, the subjects receiving $1 should show the most positive evaluation of the task. And that is how the experiment turned out. As Festinger has commonly described the situation, "You come to love what you suffer for." The experiment is diagrammed in Figure 13–6.

As another example of such a forced-compliance experiment, A. R. Cohen, Brehm, and Fleming (1958) asked college students to write an essay supporting a view opposite to their own opinion on a matter of current interest. Some students were given minimal reasons for engaging in the discrepant activity, but others were given many good reasons (such as helping the experimenter get his PhD). Again, subjects with minimal justification changed more favorably toward the view they had supported than did subjects with greater justification. This procedure has become one of the most common in dissonance research.

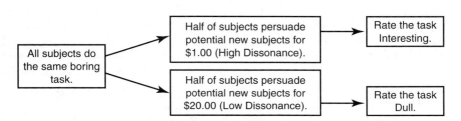

FIGURE 13–6. The experimental plan and results of the Festinger-Carlsmith cognitive dissonance experiment. The *High Dissonance* subjects seemed to convince themselves that the boring task was actually rather interesting.

Conditions Necessary to Produce Attitude Change

Research over the years has shown, however, that it takes more than just conflicting cognitions to produce attitude change in dissonance experiments. The following conditions are also necessary.

Belief in free choice.   Research has consistently shown that subjects must perceive that they *freely chose to engage in behavior that contradicts their attitudes.* The subject must believe that he or she actually freely chose to engage in the counterattitudinal behavior. In fact, the "forced compliance" paradigm is one in which virtually all subjects choose to engage in the behavior, so there is little real choice, except in the subjects' minds. In practice, subjects are placed into high choice versus low choice conditions. In the Festinger and Carlsmith experiment, subjects in the $20 condition had low choice, whereas those in the $1 condition had high choice. So, a basic condition for getting dissonance effects is that subjects be in a counterattitudinal, high choice condition. Proattitudinal essays, regardless of choice, are not expected to produce dissonance.

Intent to deceive.   The subject must believe that she or he is doing something (e.g., writing a counterattitudinal essay) that will be deceptive as far as her or his real attitude is concerned. Deception is intended if a person (a) perceives she or he has a choice between making or not making a statement against her or his own attitude, (b) knows that someone will or will not be deceived, and (c) chooses to make the counterattitudinal statement. If a person does not foresee the consequences of her or his possible actions, then intent is not present or can be denied. In this case, attitude change does not occur (Cooper & Fazio, 1984).

Belief that the action affects someone.   Nel, Helmreich, and Aronson (1969) found that subjects giving counterattitudinal speeches to an audience changed their own attitude only if the audience was perceived as noncommittal with regard to the topic (legalization of marijuana). If the audience was perceived as either firmly for or against legalization and hence would not change, the speaker (the experimental subject) showed no attitude change. The subject must believe that he or she has had an *effect* on someone and must find this belief annoying. The subject finds it unpleasant to believe that he or she has deceived someone and does what he or she can (attitude change) to reduce the unpleasantness.

Major Questions about Dissonance Theory

Are dissonant cognitions necessary for dissonance effects?   The heart of dissonance theory, of course, is that aversive dissonance produces attitude change. Unfortunately, direct tests of this presupposition have not always supported the theory. Scher and Cooper (1989) had different groups of subjects write essays either in favor of (proattitudinal) or against (counterattitudinal) increasing *student fees*. (This is one of two topics guaranteed to have all the subjects on the same side; the other involves *parking fees*.) Half of each group believed that their essays would have the intended effect on the school's Board of Trustees, but the other half were led to believe that their essays would have the opposite effect (a **boomerang effect**). The boomerang effect is that an essay favoring an increase would really have the opposite effect and be more persuasive for reducing fees. Conversely, an essay against raising fees would really be more persuasive for increasing fees. Since all the subjects are actually against raising fees, either the direct argument or the boomerang argument for raising fees would be aversive and lead to attitude change. Table 13–2 summarizes the predicted effects for various conditions.

The results were that conditions that were expected to have aversive consequences for the subjects, whether consistent or inconsistent with real attitude, were rated by the subjects as being aversive and produced attitude change. The conclusion is that it is the *expected aversive consequences* of writing the essay (probable increase in fees) that leads to attitude change, not inconsistency with one's own position. This outcome is not detected in the typical dissonance experiment.

Johnson, Kelly, and LeBlanc (1995) ran a somewhat different test of the hypothesis that inconsistency is not necessary for cognitive dissonance effects. They had subjects telephone a confederate and make arguments that were either consistent or inconsistent with their (the subjects') own attitudes. Feedback to the subjects indicated either aversive or nonaversive consequences, regardless of whether the subjects' behaviors were proattitudinal or counterattitudinal. Unlike the preceding Scher and Cooper results, attitude toward the topic changed only when behaviors were both inconsistent and counterattitudinal. That is, the results were as predicted by dissonance theory.

It is not clear why there should have been a difference in the results of these two experiments. We are left with the conclusion, however, that aversion is necessary. It is less sure that the aversion must be produced by dissonance.

TABLE 13–2. Summary of Scher and Cooper (1989) experiment. (See text for details).

	EXPERIMENTAL DESIGN	
ESSAY TYPE	NO-BOOMERANG	BOOMERANG
Pro-attitude (consistent) (against increase)	(1) Okay	(2) Aversive
Con-attitude (inconsistent) (for increase)	(3) Aversive	(4) Okay

Does dissonance produce physiological arousal?   If dissonance has drive-like arousal properties, then there should be evidence for such arousal besides just attitude change. There should be some *independent* measure of arousal. Three lines of evidence are taken to support the existence of such arousal (Cooper & Fazio, 1984): (1) drivelike effects on simple versus complex tasks, (2) attribution effects, based on predictions from cognitive-arousal theory, and (3) physiological measures.

Drivelike effects of dissonance on performance.   According to Hull's drive theory (see Chapter Six), high levels of drive should facilitate performance on simple, dominant responses but interfere with performance on more complex, nondominant responses. Several early studies indicated that high dissonance did have performance effects similar to those produced by high anxiety (e.g., Cottrell & Wack, 1967; Waterman, 1969). Unfortunately, attitude changes were not demonstrated in the same experiments. Pallak and Pittman (1972) did report attitude change along with the drivelike effects, but the amount of evidence for both of these occurring together is not great.

Attribution and dissonance.   Following the Schachter and Singer (1962) cognitive-arousal theory, it can be argued that dissonance-produced arousal should be subject to **cognitive labeling** the same as any other arousal. If the arousal is attributed to the dissonance, attitude change *should* occur. But if the attribution is directed to some other source, attitude change *should not* occur. In support of the attribution hypothesis, Zanna and Cooper (1974) found that subjects given a placebo pill with the supposed side effect of producing tension did not show as much attitude change as did subjects given the placebo without this supposed side effect. The arousal was presumably attributed to the pill rather than to dissonance, so the subjects did not engage in dissonance-reducing attitude change. Conversely, subjects under high dissonance conditions did not show attitude change if given phenobarbital, a central nervous system depressant (Cooper, Zanna, & Taves, 1978). Presumably, the drug reduced the dissonance-produced arousal, so that there was no need for further dissonance-reducing activity. It was also found that attitude change was heightened by *misattributing* external arousal to dissonance. Subjects given a pill containing amphetamine (which increases physiological arousal) showed greater attitude change than control subjects.

Physiological measures of dissonance arousal.   Although it is a basic tenet of the theory that dissonance produces aversive arousal, for reasons that are not clear, the theory was around for a quarter-century before anyone reported a direct measure of arousal. Croyle and Cooper (1983) attempted to measure arousal with the galvanic skin response (GSR). They used the standard procedure of having subjects write essays in opposition to their own attitudes. Supporting dissonance theory, only high-dissonance subjects (high-choice, counterattitudinal essay) showed elevated GSR levels immediately after writing their essays. Low-dissonance subjects (either low-choice and counterattitudinal essay, or high-choice and proattitudinal essay) showed lower increments in GSR level than the high-dissonance group. This experiment did not attempt to demonstrate a reduction of the GSR following attitude change, however.

In a later experiment, Elkin and Leippe (1986) had subjects write counterattitudinal essays in favor of a higher parking fee on campus. They also found that high-dissonance subjects showed larger GSR increments than low-dissonance subjects. However, contrary to theory, the GSR *did not go down* within even five minutes after the subjects had expressed their changed attitude. Elkin and Leippe argued that their data contradict dissonance theory because the theory says that dissonance arousal should be reduced by attitude change. Dissonance is supposedly an unpleasant state of tension (drive) that is reduced by bringing one's attitude into line with one's behavior. Thus in two experiments it appears that autonomic arousal (GSR) may be produced by dissonance, but there is no evidence that arousal reduction accounts for attitude change.

Although the GSR data are intriguing and a step in the right direction, we have also seen (in Chapter Six) that arousal cannot be equated with any single physiological measure. Arousal can be separated into behavioral arousal, EEG arousal, and autonomic arousal. There is no indication as to which of these would be relevant to dissonance. Elliot and Devine (1994) argued that GSR measures arousal but does not necessarily measure differences in **affect** (emotion). Therefore, they used a self-report measure of **psychological discomfort** collected at different times in the dissonance-producing experiment. They found that subjects had a higher level of discomfort after writing a counterattitudinal essay and that this discomfort decreased only after they reported their (changed) attitude toward the topic. This is the best support available for the hypothesis that attitude change produces dissonance reduction.

In summary, the evidence seems fairly convincing that experimental *procedures* for producing dissonance may also produce arousal of the GSR. But there is little compelling evidence that dissonance produces arousal and that attitude change is reinforced by dissonance reduction. The usual "dissonance" procedures may produce arousal, but for some reason other than dissonance per se. This process is illustrated in Figure 13–7.

Alternative Explanations

Aronson's expectancy interpretation. Aronson (1968) suggested that dissonance does not occur with just any contradiction but that it is specific to a violation of expectancies. Walking in the rain and not getting wet would create dissonance because walking in the rain arouses the expectancy of

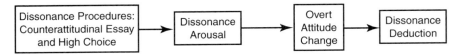

FIGURE 13–7(a). Illustration of Cognitive Dissonance Theory. (1) Freely writing an essay counter to one's own attitude produces (2) dissonance between one's attitude and one's behavior. This dissonance is a state of aversive arousal. (3) To get rid of this unpleasant arousal, a person expesses an attitude more in favor of the essay topic than previously expressed. (4) The attitude change reduces the dissonance, and arousal is therefore reduced.

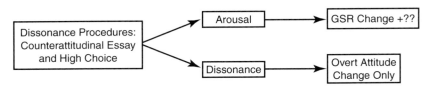

FIGURE 13–7(b). Alternatives to the Dissonance Theory. Dissonance procedures may produce arousal for some reason other than cognitive dissonance. The dissonance may lead to attitude change following self-perception, or as a means of better self-presentation, or for some other reason. Arousal may not be a link in the chain of events leading from dissonance procedures to overt attitude change.

getting wet. If we did not have this expectancy, there would be no dissonance. According to Aronson, dissonance is especially likely to occur in relation to one's self-concept. Aronson suggested that in the Festinger-Carlsmith experiment, for example, the dissonance was *not* just the result of telling someone that the task was interesting when in fact it was boring. Rather, the dissonance resulted from the subjects' violation of their self-concepts. The individual who lies for $1 is doing something out of line with her concept of how she normally behaves. Aronson concluded that the strongest dissonance effects have been obtained in experiments in which the self-concept was clearly involved.

Bem's self-perception theory. Bem (1967; 1970) proposed to account for all the cognitive dissonance research with an essentially nonmotivational, Skinnerian approach. Rather than argue that subjects perform as they do because inconsistent cognitions are aversive, Bem proposed that the individual views her or his *own* behavior and the situation *just as she or he would view the behavior of another person in the same situation.* In the Festinger-Carlsmith experiment, suppose we could invisibly observe a college student offered $20 to lie to someone and then see her do it. We also see another student tell the same lie for a mere $1. What might we conclude? One reasonable interpretation would be that "for $20 the subject doesn't *have* to believe in what she's doing, but if the other subject is doing it for a crummy dollar, maybe he does believe it." Bem's interpretation is that the subject may look at his own behavior and draw the same conclusion.

Bem (1967) had subjects simply listen to tape-recorded descriptions of the Festinger-Carlsmith experiment (without hearing the actual results). Bem's subjects then rated the experimental task as they thought that the Festinger-Carlsmith subjects would. There were three different conditions: the $1 inducement, the $20 inducement, and a control group with no inducement. Bem's subjects rated the task on a scale from − 5 (very dull) to + 5 (very interesting). Table 13–3 compares Bem's ratings with those from the original experiment. The absolute numerical values in the two experiments are different, but the trend of results is the same: The $1 group is more positive than either of the other groups in the experiment.

Bem (1970) argued with many experimental and "real-life" illustrations that our behavior often determines our attitudes, rather than the other way around. For example, factory workers who become shop stewards suddenly shift their attitudes to a more prolabor position, whereas workers who are promoted to foreman shift suddenly in a promanagement direction. The proposition that we come to like (or believe) what we see ourselves do, sounds intuitively backward, because we have all been brought up with the reverse notion, that our feelings determine our behavior. Note, however, that this belief is essentially the Cartesian dualistic interpretation of the mind-body relation discussed in Chapter One, that is, mind (attitudes, beliefs, etc.) causes behavior. Bem's position is that circumstances dictate behaviors and that we infer our mental state, at least in part, from these circumstances and behaviors. An especially pernicious consequence of this argument is that people who confess to a crime may come to believe that they *are* guilty, and the freer the confession, the firmer the guilt feeling (Bem, 1970).

Impression management. We can imagine that a subject in a dissonance experiment might not want to give the impression that he could be cheaply bought to engage in self-contradictory behavior, such as writing a counterattitudinal essay. To give the experimenter a more favorable impression, the subject might *report* a changed attitude more in line with his inconsistent behavior.

TABLE 13–3. Comparison of Bem's (1967) results with the Festinger-Carlsmith (1959) results (see text for details).

STUDY	CONTROL	$1 COMPENSATION	$20 COMPENSATION
		EXPERIMENTAL CONDITION	
Festinger-Carlsmith	−0.45	+1.35	−0.05
Bem	−1.56	+0.52	−1.96

From Bem, 1967. Copyright © 1967 by the American Psychological Association. Used by permission.

The subject fibs a little about his attitude so that the experimenter will believe that he has actually developed the attitude he is now expressing. By this interpretation, there is no great moral dilemma, no unpleasantly overpowering state of arousal, and no attempt to figure out the discrepant behavior. One prediction from the impression-management hypothesis would be that if subjects thought the experimenter did not *know* that they had changed their attitude or if they believed that the experimenter had a foolproof way to tell what their real attitude was, subjects should not show attitude change. Evidence for these hypotheses is ambiguous (Cooper & Fazio, 1984).

A potentially troublesome finding for the impression management interpretation is that subjects *do* appear to show increased arousal in the dissonance situation. If this arousal is actually related to their attitude change, then impression management theory would have to take this element into account. Schlenker (1982) has proposed that the activity of selling oneself cheaply produces arousal because the subject wants to protect his or her self-esteem. Attitude change is one way to do this. This interpretation runs into some of the same problems as the dissonance-reduction interpretation. That is, if the arousal (social anxiety? guilt?) does not decrease after the changed attitude is expressed, what does arousal do? It may be that arousal does nothing at all. Arousal and impression management may in fact be parallel events, neither one causing the other. This situation could also be true of arousal and dissonance; the two might occur in parallel, but without causal significance for each other.

Change in the motivational basis of dissonance.   Greenwald and Ronis (1978) pointed out that there has been a drift in the nature of the motivational principle supposedly underlying cognitive dissonance. Initially, it was said that any two contradictory actions or beliefs were a source of dissonance. Then, inconsistency was said to be a major force only if the individual was *committed to behaving* in an inconsistent manner (Brehm & Cohen, 1962). Aronson (1968) then suggested that the **self-concept** was importantly involved. Wicklund and Brehm (1976) argued that dissonance reduction occurs only when the dissonant elements have been brought together through the **personal responsibility** of the individual who feels the dissonance. Impression management theorists argue that social anxiety is the motivating force. Greenwald and Ronis suggest that the more recent approaches are more akin to **ego-defensive actions,** as proposed by many personality theorists, than to dissonance and its reduction, as proposed by Festinger.

The increasing emphasis on the self-concept, suggest Greenwald and Ronis, is not bad. But it may not really be dissonance, either. It is possible that the shift in focus has been due to a greater emphasis on those aspects of dissonance procedures that happen to overlap with ego-defensive activities. If the ego-defensive behaviors are particularly powerful (and the procedures for manipulating threat to the ego or self-esteem are strong), then these behavior would in the "natural course of things" lead to a greater concern with them. The net effect may then be that dissonance theory in its original formulation has not been fully tested, because the predictions made by subsequent revisions simply are not relevant to the original statement.

In summary, cognitive dissonance theory has been a highly *fruitful* theory, generating much new research, controversy, and theory. The attitude change data generated by tests of the theory are often interpreted in other ways, and the theory is much less influential than it once was.

CONFORMITY AND NONCONFORMITY

In a classic experiment, Solomon Asch (1951) had several subjects judge which of a set of lines matched the length of a standard line. All but one of the subjects were actually accomplices of the experimenter. The accomplices all made their judgments before the real subject made his, and on some occasions they made obviously incorrect judgments. Under these circumstances the real subjects frequently went along with what they thought were the judgments of the other subjects. In other words, they took what the other subjects said as a **norm** and conformed to that norm. In fact, the real subjects often did not privately believe that the false answer was actually correct, but they publicly went along with it. They were concerned about the effects of being different from the norm, and their "error correction" procedure was to "go along."

In general, research shows a strong tendency for individuals to conform to whatever standards are set by their group. A person is rewarded for conformity but sanctioned for nonconformity. A group, like an individual, has goals, such as to maintain production or win a game. The group pressure for cooperation helps attain these goals, and the group, or its leader, provides rewards and punishments for individuals who do or do not "go along." Schacter (1951) found that individuals who consistently differed from a group in their attitudes were rejected by other group members. This rejection can be severe punishment. The college freshman who dearly wants to become a member of a particular fraternity, for example, is not likely to deviate much from the norms of that group lest she not be invited. In terms of discrepancy, then, what we see are **group mechanisms** for keeping social behavior at an expected (reference) level. If individual behaviors depart from this, appropriate corrective actions are taken to bring the behavior back into line.

SUMMARY

1. An attitude is a **positive or negative affective response** directed toward a specific person, object, or situation. The attitude object falls somewhere on a hedonic continuum.

2. There are many ways of measuring attitudes. Two relatively direct techniques are **Likert scales** and the **semantic differential.** One indirect way is to measure reaction times in response to attitude-related words.

3. Attitudes are not the only determinants of behavior, and measures of attitude do not always predict behavior well. A number of different factors determine how well attitude measures will predict behavior. For example, attitudes toward more specific objects or events predict future behavior better.

4. Attitudes are **learned** through **classical conditioning, instrumental conditioning,** and **imitation of others.**

5. There is a **genetic** component to attitudes, although the mechanism by which this works is not clear. There is a greater **right hemisphere** involvement with attitudes, as with emotion in general.

6. **Cognitive inconsistency** occurs when an event is perceived to be different from expectation. Such inconsistencies may be arousing and may induce attitude change.

7. Heider's **balance theory** concerns the consistency of relations among different people, a social perception. If *A* likes *B*, and *B* likes *C*, but *A* strongly dislikes *C*, there is an **imbalance** for *A*. Balance theory has been particularly concerned with **attitude change** as a way to restore balance.

8. **Cognitive dissonance** is said to occur when the same individual holds **contradictory beliefs,** or acts contrary to his or her beliefs. Dissonance is said to be aversive, and dissonance reduction is reinforcing.

9. In a typical dissonance experiment, subjects are subtly coerced to write essays *against* their own attitude regarding some topic (such as parking on campus). Subjects show attitude changes away from their original attitude if they believe that their inconsistent behavior has actually affected someone and if they believe that they have chosen freely to engage in the counterattitudinal behavior.

10. There is some controversy over whether attitude change occurs because of incongruence between belief and behavior or whether one must **anticipate an aversive consequence** of the behavior, even though it might be consistent with one's beliefs.

11. **Evidence that dissonance is actually arousing is slight,** and mostly inferred from behavior. Dissonance-arousing conditions produce an increase in the galvanic skin response, but the arousal may not be causally related to reported attitude change. Self-reported change in affect does seem to be related to attitude change.

12. There are several alternative explanations for the results of dissonance experiments. Bem's **self-perception** theory says that people infer their own attitudes the same way that they infer the attitudes of other people, **by observing their own behavior.** According to **impression management theory,** subjects wish to maintain their self-esteem, therefore they report a changed attitude so that they will not appear to be easily swayed by the experimenter.

13. **Conformity** research shows the importance of dissonance reduction in social situations. When individuals fail to conform to group norms, they may be ostracized; therefore, they may conform to reduce the level of aversiveness of group reaction to their nonconformity.

CHAPTER FOURTEEN

Interpersonal Attraction

———•———

Across the spectrum of animal life, different species vary markedly in gregariousness. Ants and bees are almost invariably in large groups, but bears and tigers live an almost solitary existence. Some species of monkeys live in tribes, whereas individuals of other monkey species are all nearly isolates. Humans are variable but on the whole are relatively social. The question for this chapter is, What attracts humans to each other? However, we need to distinguish three different aspects of attraction—affiliating, liking, and loving.

People may affiliate for many reasons, but liking and loving are not defining characteristics of affiliation. As the saying goes, politics makes strange bedfellows. We may affiliate with others for **instrumental** reasons, because the affiliation is necessary to get something else we want. Any positive feelings are related to the goal we are trying to achieve; we may or may not have strongly positive feelings for the people we relate to in order to achieve the goal. Liking and loving involve relationships that in themselves have positive affect attached to another person. It is still necessary to distinguish between these, however. Such dictionary statements as "liking is a **fondness** for someone else" or "loving involves **affection or passion**" point up a difference, but there is still disagreement among psychologists about the similarities and differences between the two. Thus, is loving just a lot of liking, or are liking and loving two different processes? In this chapter we explore some of the **determinants** of affiliation, liking, and loving, and describe how some *theories* account for these.

AFFILIATION

Measurement of Need for Affiliation

Individual differences in the **need for affiliation** (n Aff) have been measured with the same approach used for measuring achievement or power. Subjects write fantasy stories about appropriate pictures, and the stories are scored in terms of affiliation themes (Boyatzis, 1973). Shipley and Veroff (1952) defined n Aff in terms of a need for security and tested whether it could be aroused in a group of fraternity members by having them rate each other on different personality characteristics, a procedure intended to make them think about interpersonal relations. A control group rated food preferences. Both groups then wrote their fantasy stories, in which statements indicating "concern about separation" were considered especially indicative of n Aff. As predicted, the experimental group wrote more such themes. Atkinson, Heyns, and Veroff (1954) used a similar arousal technique, but in their scoring they emphasized themes related to seeking social acceptance. Again, the aroused subjects showed more such themes than control subjects. This finding raises the question whether there are possibly two different kinds of n Aff, **hope of affiliation** and **fear of rejection,** corresponding to hope of success and fear of failure in achievement motivation. The TAT scoring procedures do not make the distinction well (Boyatzis, 1973), and the issue of two different kinds of affiliation is unsettled.

A number of studies provided evidence for the validity of n Aff scoring in relation to some of the characteristics that we might expect in people with high n Aff. In comparison with low n Aff subjects, high n Aff subjects (1) more accurately picked out faces from among briefly exposed stimuli (Atkinson & Walker, 1956); (2) more accurately described other people as those people described themselves, suggesting greater social sensitivity; (3) got better grades in courses taught by teachers judged to be warm and considerate (McKeachie, Lin, Milholland, & Issacson, 1966); and (4) got better grades in cooperatively structured groups than in competitively structured groups.

There seems to be a *curvilinear* relationship between n Aff and managerial performance, with most effective performance by managers with moderate levels. Those with low n Aff may be too little concerned with interpersonal relationships to be effective, and those with high n Aff may let their concern for others interfere with getting the job done (Boyatzis, 1973). Research on leadership generally indicates the importance of a balance between "concern for people" and "concern for production," which may be best achieved by a person with a medium level n Aff (Fiedler, 1971).

Determinants of Affiliation

Biological factors. In evolutionary terms, the role of any individual is to perpetuate himself or herself by contributing to the gene pool of the species. The individual thus becomes "immortal" by literally putting a part of his or her protoplasm into the gene pool. We are each the offspring of millions of years of "perfect parentage," the direct descendants of an unbroken line of parents who were attracted to each other at least long enough to mate.

Prolonged social isolation so frequently leads to loneliness and depression that these consequences often seem inevitable and therefore appear to have some degree of genetic determination. John Bowlby (1969) suggested that such **attachment behaviors** as clinging to the mother or acting distressed when the mother departs are biologically based. According to Cairns (1979), however, the degree of the child's attachment at one age is not a good predictor of degree of attachment for the same child just a few months later. This finding suggests that attachment behaviors have a strong learning component. Among monkeys, there are species differences in attachment behaviors. Such cross-species comparisons may not be relevant to individual differences *within the same species,* such as when we are looking at differences among humans.

McClelland, Patel, Stier, and Brown (1987) found experimental results implicating a role of hormonal arousal in affiliation. After looking at films with affiliation themes, subjects high in n Aff demonstrated higher levels of dopamine release than did Ss low in n Aff. Since they did not show changes in levels of cortisol, epinephrine, or norepinephrine, the effect was not just due to a general arousal. Given the great variety of situations in which arousal in the dopamine system is involved, it is easy to speculate that people are just one more form of incentive that arouses the dopamine/endorphin system.

Need to belong.   Baumeister and Leary (1995) argue that the "need to belong" is a fundamental human motivation to form and maintain some minimum amount of relatively enduring and pleasant interpersonal relationships. In evolutionary terms, such a motive should have both survival and reproductive benefits. Groups share resources and protect members from outside harm and make mates available. One prediction from this view is that if there is a basic biological need for belonging, then groups should form easily. Many studies confirm that it is easy to form groups in what is called the **minimal intergroup** situation. If a larger group of subjects is randomly divided into two smaller groups by some completely arbitrary and trivial criterion, the groups almost immediately show favoritism toward their group and some degree of antagonism toward the other. By the same token, people should be reluctant to break established group bonds, and this tendency turns out also to be true. There is a large literature on in-group versus out-group differences and the ease with which such groups are established, which is striking.

Fear and anxiety.   When we feel afraid, we often want to be with someone who might calm our fears. This reaction would be affiliation to reduce negative affect. Even among laboratory rats, the presence of another animal reduces the fearful behaviors of an animal that has been shocked in an experimental apparatus. One such fearful response is "crouching in the corner," becoming very inactive. A previously shocked animal is more active if another animal is present, and more active yet if the other animal has itself *not* been shocked (Davitz & Mason, 1955). We can think of several ways that the presence of another person might reduce our responsiveness to aversive situations. A companion might serve either as a "calm model" to be imitated or as a distraction. It is also possible that just the mere presence of another person might be fear-reducing, even if the other person does nothing (Epley, 1974). Schachter (1959) studied fear and affiliation by threatening subjects with either strong or weak electric shock, and then giving them the choice of waiting for their punishment alone or with someone else. The strong-shock subjects did prefer to be with someone else, and Wrightsman (1960) subsequently reported that subjects are less afraid when waiting with someone else in a threatening situation. It has also been predicted, according to Hull's theory (Chapter Six), that the presence of others should reduce **drive** (anxiety) and thereby facilitate performance on complex tasks and impair performance on simple tasks. The fact that the results have been ambiguous (Epley,

1974) is not really surprising, however, since we have also seen that the presence of others may *increase* drive, the **social facilitation** effect (Zajonc, 1965). Harrison (1976) concluded that people might not want to affiliate in anxiety-arousing situations if the presence of other people would lower their self-esteem. For example, an adult might not want others to watch him or her perform such an embarrassing act as drinking from a baby bottle. Affiliation and anxiety, then, may depend on the reasons for being anxious, not just the fact of being anxious.

Other people as resources. There is a variety of reasons why we may affiliate with others who may be of some service to us.

- **Assistance.** We often need assistance from other people to achieve our goals, and so we affiliate with others because of this need. The assistance that they give us may reinforce and maintain our affiliative behavior over long periods of time.
- **Stimulation.** Earlier we discussed the importance of *stimulus variation* as a source of arousal for optimal performance. What in fact is more variable, more full of surprises, or more stimulating than other people? Interesting people attract more friends or followers than boring people. There appears to be an optimal level of stimulation here also; a given person may be too stimulating for some people, too dull for others, and just right for somebody else.
- **Information.** We have also seen that behavior is reinforced by new information. We read newspapers to get information, but other people also provide information or reduce uncertainty for us, so we associate with them. Information may be important (world news) or trivial (gossip), but it is reinforcing and sought.
- **Self-evaluation.** We all need to evaluate ourselves, our opinions, our abilities, or our work from time to time. Lacking objective standards (such as for appearance), we often compare ourselves with other people. According to Festinger (1954), we make **social comparisons,** requiring affiliation, when we are uncertain about ourselves. We tend to seek normative information to judge ourselves from someone who is *similar* to us (in age, background, interest, experience, etc.) rather than from someone who is very dissimilar. We seek information about the social norms that apply to us. Mills and Mintz (1972) used an interesting extension of cognitive arousal theory in connection with this aspect of affiliation. Subjects who were given caffeine but were misinformed about its arousing effects chose more often to affiliate with other subjects than did subjects who were *not* given caffeine (not aroused) or subjects who were told about the caffeine effects (correctly understood what was happening to them). Presumably, the misinformed subjects were uncertain about the source of their arousal and searched for the cause of the arousal by associating with other subjects in the same situation, whom they thought could help them evaluate their own condition.
- **Freedom from internal constraint.** Groups frequently restrain their members from doing certain things but sometimes have just the opposite effect, reinforcing **uninhibited** behavior. If an individual at a particular time is seeking freedom from self-imposed or typical group-imposed constraints, she or he may choose to affiliate with others even in so innocuous a situation as a party where the restraints can temporarily be discarded. We may become relatively anony-

mous, free of responsibility, and "act crazy." Such **deindividuation** may temporarily be enjoyable, but Zimbardo (1969) suggests that after a while, **reindividuation** may become desirable; we want recognition from others.

ATTRACTION AND ITS DETERMINANTS

The importance of interpersonal attraction in everyday matters can hardly be overstated. Walster and Walster (1976) put the situation bluntly: "A person who is liked by his comrades will amass enormous benefits; a person who is hated is in trouble" (p. 279). It is only recently, however, that psychologists have done serious research on liking and loving, perhaps because the topic was previously considered too sensitive. A respectable body of research and theory on interpersonal attraction is now accumulating on a number of different aspects of the problem.

Physical Attractiveness

Advantages of physical attractiveness. Physical attractiveness draws preferential treatment from infancy through old age (Brehm, 1985). Attractive children are treated better in school; attractive adults receive more assistance and cooperation than their less-attractive counterparts and are reprimanded less severely for transgressions. There are several possible explanations for such preferential treatment of attractive persons.

- There is an **attractiveness stereotype,** an implicit personality theory that assumes that attractive people have other virtues in addition to their appearance. Preferential treatment is thus perceived as their due (Brehm, 1985). Many people seem to have this stereotype view of others (Baron & Byrne, 1997).
- Attractive people *are* in fact more self-confident and have better mental health These qualities may result from being treated better by others and having more opportunity to be reinforced for social skills, as if in a reverse "vicious cycle."
- Other people may wish to associate with attractive people because such an association *enhances one's own self-image.* Sigall and Landy (1973) found that a man seated with an attractive woman was rated positively but was rated negatively when seated with an unattractive woman. Attractiveness seems to be a relatively more important factor in dating than in marrying (Stroebe, Insko, Thompson & Layton, 1971), but Mathes (1975) found that over a series of five dates, physical attractiveness was considered increasingly important.
- An attractive person *produces more positive affect* in others and thus elicits preferential treatment in hope of maintaining or increasing that affect. Put more bluntly, being around an attractive person makes you feel good, and you want to maintain or increase the feeling.

In a classic study, a "computer dance" was arranged for University of Minnesota freshmen, who signed up and were paired randomly. At the original sign-up, the experimenters rated the subjects' attractiveness to provide more objective ratings of attractiveness than those given by the subjects. At the dance intermission, the subjects rated their partners on various characteristics, including attractiveness. Three times as many of the most attractive women were later asked for dates by their partners than were the unattractive women, about 33 percent versus 10 percent. The subjects' attractiveness ratings of their partners were the single best predictor of who would be asked out on a date, indicating both that attractiveness is important and that to some degree it was in the eye of the beholder (Walster, Aronson, Abrahams, & Rottman, 1966).

Standards of attractiveness.   Attractiveness has many dimensions, which may vary in importance to different people, e.g., facial features, body characteristics, movement, and so on. Men are often though to be taken more by attractiveness than women, but this seems not to be the case. The importance of attractiveness may just be expressed in a somewhat different manner by men and women. First, men may just be more open about the issue. Second, Coombs and Kenkel (1966) found that males rated attractiveness more important *before* having a date with a particular woman. Women, on the other hand, had more complaints about the attractiveness of a date *afterwards*. Third, it is definitely not true that the physically most attractive member of the opposite sex is the one who will necessarily be most sought after or who will provide the best relationship. The **matching principle** comes into play here.

The matching principle.   People tend to be attracted to others with similar physical characteristics, such as height and weight (Berscheid & Walster, 1969). The matching principle may work for reasons beyond attractiveness, however. A man might *prefer* an exceptionally attractive woman, but if he is of medium attractiveness himself, he might believe that she would not date him. He therefore seeks the most attractive woman who would date him. The optimal choice, then, might be to choose a woman of medium attractiveness so that there is a good probability of a successful relationship. This explanation is very similar to achievement theory, in which the tendency to choose a particular activity (in this case, asking for a date) depends on the probability of success (Ps) and the incentive value of success (Is). A very attractive date could have a high incentive value, but the probability of success in getting a date with her may be perceived to be very low. Conversely, an unattractive date has a very low incentive value even though the perceived probability of success in getting a date is high. A man should then approach the most attractive woman that *he* could reasonably expect to date *him*. On the other side, a woman of average attractiveness might accept a date from the most attractive man who asks her out.

In a study of the matching principle involving 120 couples with varying degrees of relationship (casual, serious, cohabiting, engaged/married),

White (1980) found that couples more similar in attractiveness did stay together longer. There was a greater similarity of attractiveness ($r = .63$) between the engaged/married pairs than for the casually dating pairs ($r = .18$). In the casual and serious groups, the greater the dissimilarity, the more likely the couple were to break up during the time of the research (a school year). Part of the breakup was related to the desire of the more attractive pair member to have a relationship with someone else.

Evolutionary approaches to attractiveness.   In Chapter Three we briefly discussed evolutionary psychology, the application of biological principles of survival and evolution to psychology. Since mating is essential for the normal transmission of genes from generation to generation among humans, it has been speculated that there are biologically determined aspects of beauty. Several studies show that males or females with highly exaggerated physical features are not generally considered the most attractive. For example, S. Beck Ward-Hull, and Mclear (1976) presented female subjects with silhouette drawings of male and female figures in which chest/breast, buttocks, and leg size were varied. They found that moderate-size male and female silhouettes with small buttocks were preferred for either male or female figures.

Waist-to-hip-ratio.   One hypothesis from evolutionary psychology (Singh, 1993) links signals of female attractiveness and reproductive potential (fertility). If men "wish" to pass on their genes to future generations, the most attractive females should be those with signs of good reproductive potential. It has been reported that a waist-to-hip-ratio of about 0.7 (e.g. $26''/36'' = .72$) and a moderate size are rated most attractive and most fecund (capable of childbirth). Tassinary and Hansen (1998) tested this hypothesis in the most thorough study to date, in which they independently varied weight, waist size, and hip size in schematic drawings. Figure 14–1 illustrates some of their stimuli. Male and female subjects ranked the stimuli for both attractiveness and fecundity. Light-weight and moderate-weight figures were judged more attractive, and moderate-weight and heavy-weight figures more fecund. There was almost no correlation between the two sets of judgments The authors conclude that although the waist-to-hip-ratio hypothesis may have some intuitive appeal, it has little predictive value.

Health.   It has also been hypothesized that visible signs of poor health should indicate a lower likelihood of offspring and therefore make a person a less attractive mate. Conversely, signs of good health should make a person a more attractive mate. Signs of health and attractiveness should therefore be correlated. Kalick et al. (1998) tested this hypothesis in a longitudinal study in which subjects rated facial photographs of adolescent males and females for attractiveness and health. They correlated these two ratings with each other, as well as with actual health records during adolescence, middle adult

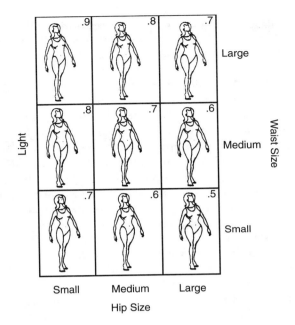

FIGURE 14–1. Schematic waist-to-hip ratios for light-weight women with different waist sizes. There are three different waist sizes (small, medium, large) and different hip sizes (small, medium, large) for each waist size. The number accompanying each figure is the ratio of waist-to-hip size. There were equivalent sets of nine drawings for moderate and heavy women used in the experiment. Overall, no specific waist-to-hip ratio was perceived as most attractive or fecund, contrary to evolutionary hypotheses that have been proposed. See text for details. From Tassinary & Hansen, 1998, pp. 150–155, Figure 2. Used by permission.

hood, and later adulthood. Subjects' ratings of attractiveness and perceived health correlated substantially (above .60), but attractiveness did not correlate with actual health at the time the photos were taken, nor did attractiveness predict future health (correlations approximately zero). The authors suggest that people may be "blinded by beauty" in their judgments of health. This finding seems to be another example of the beauty stereotype discussed before. Martin and Leary (1998) found that females who are thought to be exercising regularly, even though overweight, are considered more attractive than their non-exercising counterparts. This finding is at least congruent with the health hypothesis.

Facial averageness. When we see a person with a spectacularly beautiful face, are we looking at an extremely average face? Sir Francis Galton in 1878 used photographic techniques to average different portraits and found the composite faces to be more attractive than their components, "a result that frustrated his attempts to create the prototypical criminal face" (Rhodes & Tremewan, 1996, p. 105). Langlois and Roggman (1990) used a computer technique to separately average 32 male faces and 32 female faces to form composite male and female faces. The averages literally were the statistical averages of numerical gray-scale values for photographs scanned into a computer and digitized. They were *not* the averages of subjective judgments about the faces. The composite faces were rated significantly more attractive than the average ratings of the sets of faces from which they had been generated.

The facial-average results provide a parsimonious explanation for two facts: Infants prefer attractive to unattractive faces, and cross-cultural judgments of attractiveness are more similar than different. Both of these facts run contrary to the notion that what is attractive is learned within a specific cultural context. Rather, it is suggested that as a person views different faces, he or she develops a mental representation of the average of the faces, and this becomes the standard of attractiveness. This average face is more familiar even though it would be rare for any particular face to match this standard. Various criticisms have been leveled at the averaging procedure (Alley & Cunningham, 1991; Pittenger, 1991), but these seem to have been answered effectively (Langlois, Roggman, Musselman, & Acton, 1991). Rhodes and Tremewan (1996) also supported the averageness hypothesis, using a computerized caricature generator to vary averageness of line drawings of faces. They found that attractiveness was negatively correlated with distinctiveness. For reasons of their individual histories, we would expect that some persons will find particular deviations from the norm attractive, but that fact does not in itself negate the more general principle of attractiveness in the average.

Tactics of mate attraction.   Buss (1988) suggested that there are four components of competition for mates among humans that are more common than direct confrontations of competing individuals. These are (1) skill at locating mates, such as going to places where they "hang out"; (2) displaying mate-attracting behaviors (e.g., signaling interest or availability); (3) acquiring resources desired by members of the opposite sex; and (4) altering one's body shape or appearance to make it more attractive (dieting, surgery, cosmetics).

There was some support for these hypotheses. For example, men displayed and bragged about resources more than females did. Women, in turn, altered their appearance and wore jewelry more than men did. Many of the predicted sex differences in favor of females did not occur, including such behaviors as grooming, wearing sexy clothes, and flirting. Perhaps some of the differences that do occur (e.g., wearing jewelry) depend on what subculture you look at. Men's jewelry is becoming more popular and men more frequently adorn their bodies with tattoos, although women are now more commonly getting tattoos. Furthermore, given the importance of male mating displays in other species, it seems rather paradoxical that displays of strength, athleticism, and showing off were not predicted to be differentiated by sex. However, males engaged in these behaviors more than females. This whole approach to human mate selection is so new that it is difficult to evaluate, partly because it is difficult to know what predictions to make. After the fact, any behaviors differing between the sexes could be rationalized to have evolutionary value.

Proximity, Familiarity, Similarity, and Reciprocity

Proximity. As the song says, "How can I ignore / the boy next door?" We are more likely to become friends with people who are physically close to us. In dormitories, for example, people who are thrown together by the chance of alphabetical grouping are more likely to become friends with each other than with people who live farther away in the same dormitory (Newcomb, 1961; Priest & Sawyer, 1967; Segal, 1974). In the Segal study, there was a very high correlation (.90) between liking a person and how close in the alphabet that person's name was to the rater's name. In purely practical terms, it takes less effort to interact and become friendly with people close by.

Familiarity. The effects of proximity are partly explained by the fact that when individuals live or work close to each other, they can become more familiar with each other. As we have already seen with the mere exposure effect, we generally tend to like better the persons, objects, or even strange words in a foreign language the more that we have been exposed to them. The mere exposure effect seems to run contrary to the adage that "familiarity breeds contempt," but factors other than mere exposure are involved. For example, Burgess and Sales (1971) obtained the mere exposure effect with subjects who felt good about the overall experimental context, but not with subjects who disliked the experimental situation. Other factors, such as the behavior of the other person whom we are thrown together with, also affect liking. If another person's behavior were agreeable, we would expect increased liking with increased exposure, but we would expect disliking if the person were disagreeable.

Similarity. According to the **need complementary hypothesis** (Winch, 1958), people with opposite interests, characteristics, and so on should be attracted to each other because they fulfill the deficiencies of each other. There is little support for this theory. For example, both dominant and submissive people prefer more dominant individuals as friends (Palmer & Byrne, 1970), and introverts and extraverts both prefer extraverts (Hendrick & Brown, 1971). People who are *similar* are more likely to get together. People may be similar in many different ways, however, including attitudes, personality, physical characteristics, and reciprocity of behavior.

Research on **attitudinal similarity** indicates that the greater the percentage of topics on which two people have similar attitudes, the greater the liking (Byrne & Nelson, 1965). According to Schneider (1976), such attitudinal effects are not as strong in real-life situations as in research settings. The purpose of laboratory research, however, is precisely to separate out variables that are weaker in less controlled situations. There are several general qualifications regarding similarity and liking that are worth noting, however (Sherrod, 1982): (1) Physical attractiveness overrides attitudinal similarity, at least for a first date; (2) if the similar individual is unattractive in some way, such as being emotionally disturbed or obnoxious, liking is *decreased;* (3) a *fear of rejection* by similar individuals may direct a person to dissimilar individuals who might be more accepting; and (4) a too-similar person may be rejected because an individual wishes to appear unique.

Reciprocity.   We are more prone to like others if we think they like us, which is the reciprocity principle (Peplau, 1982). Salespeople use this principle in face-to-face contacts, immediately asking your first name and showing great interest in you. Large companies use it on a mass advertising basis ("Fly the friendly skies of United" or "Bank with the folks at your friendly multi-billion-dollar corporation"). In laboratory discussion groups, subjects with low self-esteem have been found more prone to like the group if they believe that the group likes them (Dittes, 1959). Subjects with high self-esteem, however, were less likely to be swayed by how they thought the group felt. A person can go too far in trying to attract others by expressing liking for them, however. Such **ingratiation** may work if it is perceived as sincere but have just the opposite effect, producing dislike, if perceived as a phony attempt to gain some advantage (Jones, 1964). What is perceived as "overdoing" praise or liking may depend very much on who is receiving the flattery, however. People starved for attention or praise may believe almost anything that will enhance their self-image, no matter how ingratiating or insincere.

THEORIES OF LIKING AND LOVING

There are several theories of liking and loving that attempt to account for interpersonal attraction. Sternberg (1987) divides these into theories that consider liking and loving are (1) on a **quantitative continuum,** with loving as the equivalent of a lot of liking, (2) **qualitatively** different, (3) **overlapping sets,** with some similarities and some differences, and (4) where liking is a **subset** of loving, having some but not all the features of loving.

Liking and Loving as Quantitative Differences in Level of Attraction

Reinforcement theory.   According to this theory, if John experiences reward in the presence of Mary, she becomes a **secondary reinforcer,** and he comes to like her (Lott & Lott, 1974). Attraction can develop even accidentally if a particular person just happens to be present when rewards are received. In one study, for example, children came to like their *classmates* more if they were systematically rewarded by their teacher for various activities not directly related to their classmates. Their classmates just happened to be there. The opposite also happens; the messenger who delivers the bad news is seldom popular. Clore and Byrne (1974) suggested that a rewarding experience produces a positive emotional response that becomes attached to someone present at the time. This theory was related to Byrne's research on attraction and attitudinal similarity. The more similar the attitudes of two people, the more they reinforce each other, hence the greater their attraction to each other. A wide range of things may be reinforcing, including *intrinsic characteristics* of the other person (such as attractiveness, sense of humor, or intelligence) and *behaviors* of the other person (such as giving attention or other favors).

Social exchange theory.   This uses terminology borrowed from the marketplace and deals with mutually rewarding behaviors between people (Rubin, 1973). Associating with another person involves **benefits** and **costs.** Positive attraction occurs when the anticipated benefits (rewards) are greater than the costs (punishers). Avoidance occurs when the costs exceed the benefits. A man and a woman may each have socially desirable qualities they can "trade off" to each other. A man gains more prestige by being seen with an attractive woman than with an unattractive one, and attractive women are more likely to date or marry men of higher social status than their own. A physically less-attractive man can bring money, prestige, and power to the interpersonal bargaining table, as well as intellect, wit, and charm. Political power seems to be a universal bargaining commodity, as is the prestige of rock stars and athletes that can be traded for sexual favors.

Equity theory.   This is a variation of social exchange theory. The distinguishing characteristic of equity theory is that a person in a relationship compares his or her **personal ratio** of costs to benefits with those of some **reference.** The standard terminology of equity theory is in term of inputs and outputs, where **input (I) = costs,** and **output (O) = benefits.** There are then three general possibilities for ratios:

1. $Ip/Op = Ir/Or$. In this case, the ratio of I/O for the person (p) in question is the same as that for the reference (r). Person p perceives that there is **equity** between his or her inputs and outputs and those of the reference. The reference used may specifically be the other person in the relationship, some past relationship, or some abstract standard. When there is equity, there is satisfaction with the relationship. The major problem that arises, of course, is when there is **inequity,** as in the second case.

2. $Ip/Op > Ir/Or$. If person p perceives that he or she puts more into the relationship than the reference but gets less out of it, there is a strain, and the person

will try to restore equity. Equity is a matter of perception, as well as reality, so it is important to change perceived equity. For example, if a woman feels that a man does not spend enough time with her, he may try to persuade her that his time is being used (such as working) to their mutual long-term benefit.

3. *Ip/Op < Ir/Or.* What happens in a relationship if a person feels that she or he is getting *more* than is equitable out of a relationship? Equity may be restored by putting more into the relationship or by getting the other person to put *less* into the relationship.

These are just a few of the many predictions of equity theory, and the theory has received rather good support in research (e.g., Walster, Walster, & Berscheid, 1978).

Investment theory.   Why does a person stay in a relationship or leave it? Rusbult (1983) has proposed an economic theory of interpersonal relations that is aimed at answering this question. Her model combines features of several of the models previously discussed and adds the additional component of **investment** to account for why people become committed to relationships. Stated briefly, investment theory says

Satisfaction with a relationship = (Rewards − Costs) − Comparison Level

A person will be satisfied with a relationship if there are many rewards and few costs and if the difference is greater than the person's expectations about what he or she should get out of a relationship (the comparison level). In addition, the net satisfaction from Relationship X should be greater than that of some alternative. If we can get the same rewards with fewer costs in a different relationship, then that alternative would be preferred. If one has **invested** a great deal of time, money, or emotional involvement in a relationship, it is more difficult to withdraw because one does not want to lose one's investment. It is rather like a poker game in which someone plays out a doubtful hand because the only possible way to recoup a large investment in the pot is to keep playing.

Commitment to a particular relationship depends on **satisfaction** with the relationship, **investment** in the relationship, and possible **alternatives.** Given that a person has a fixed comparison level for expectations about relationships generally, then

Commitment to X = (Rewards$_x$ − Costs$_x$) + Investment$_x$ − Alternatives

Thus, if rewards, costs, and alternatives were the same, there would be greater commitment to a relationship if there were a greater investment. The model says that satisfaction and commitment need not necessarily be highly correlated. Strong commitment to a relationship could result even with relatively few rewards if the costs were low, the investment high, and alternatives poor. Alternatively, a person might quit a relatively satisfactory relationship because there was little investment and a better alternative. Rusbult (1983) tested the model in a seven-month longitudinal study of dating college students. The data were gathered by periodic questionnaires. The results were as follows: (1) Increases in rewards led to greater satisfaction, but (2) variations in cost did not affect satisfaction. (3) Greater satisfaction and investment and poorer alternatives promoted a higher level of commitment. (4) For those individuals who stayed in relationships, rewards increased over time, costs rose slightly, satisfaction increased, investment increased, quality of alternatives declined, and commitment increased. For those who left relationships, the opposite changes occurred: Rewards, satisfaction, and investment decreased, whereas costs and quality of alternatives increased. The data thus provide reasonable support for the model.

Cognitive consistency theory.   This can be applied to interpersonal attraction just as it is applied to interpersonal relationships of other kinds, as we saw in our earlier discussion of cognitive consistency theories (e.g., Festinger, 1957; Heider, 1958; Newcomb, 1968). Dissonance theory, for example, predicts that how we treat someone should affect our liking of that person. If we treat an innocent person cruelly for no good reason, this treatment should produce some dissonance between our behavior and our concept of self as a kind and honorable person. Paradoxically, then, we can develop a negative attitude toward someone to whom we have "done wrong" because this change in attitude reduces the dissonance produced by the fact that we *have* done the person wrong. Davis and Jones (1960) found support for this theory experimentally but also found that the derogation of someone else did not occur if the subjects knew in advance that they could make amends to the other person (a laboratory assistant to whom they had read falsely negative evaluations). In this case, dissonance presumably did not develop. Even more paradoxically, the nicer we think we are, the more we must derogate someone else because of the greater dissonance. Conversely, we may come to have a more positive attitude toward a neutral person toward whom we have been unusually kind. We might also expect, however, that this positive effect would be less aversive, and hence less attitude change could occur. The evidence is in fact weak (e.g., Berscheid & Walster, 1969; Schopler & Compere, 1971).

Liking and Loving as Qualitatively Different

Clinical theory.   Some theories have always distinguished liking and loving as two different entities. Freud (1938) looked upon love as a modified (sublimated) form of sexuality. That is, love occurs because sex is repressed. Maslow (1970) distinguished two kinds of love, D-Love and B-Love. D-Love (**deficiency love**) arises from lack of feelings of security and belongingness. B-Love (**being love**) comes from the desire for self-actualization. Other clinical theories have proposed other kinds of love, but in none of them is love generally considered as just a strong form of liking (Sternberg, 1987).

Cognitive-arousal theory. In his *Ars Amatoria (The Art of Love)*, a first-century how-to manual for romantic conquest, the Roman poet Ovid provided many helpful hints for would-be lovers. These involved grooming and behavior, as well as the suggestion that a good time to arouse passion in a woman was while watching gladiators fight in the arena. In modern times a football game or hockey match might suffice. A nineteenth-century German psychologist named Adolph Horwicz similarly proposed that any strong emotional arousal could facilitate love. The Ovid-Horwicz effect, until recently, was limited to empirical observation; it seemed to work. We now have cognitive-arousal theory to account for the effect (Walster, 1971; Patterson, 1976; Rubin, 1973).

According to cognitive arousal theory, emotional arousal is diffuse until labeled by the person experiencing the arousal (Schachter & Singer, 1962) (see Chapter Two here). For example, White, Fishbein, and Rutstein (1981) found that an attractive person was rated as more attractive after two minutes of running in place than after fifteen seconds. Similar results were obtained in an experiment with both pleasant arousal (by a Steve Martin comedy clip) and unpleasant arousal (a grisly murder/mayhem clip). The authors conclude that type of arousal is irrelevant, again supporting cognitive arousal theory. Dutton and Aron (1974) conducted a field study in which a female gathered information from males just after they had crossed a high, swinging bridge. She was more likely to be contacted later than when she had been at the end of a low, stable bridge. The swinging bridge presumably produced greater arousal, which was attributed to the female experimenter. It is also possible that there was a subject selection factor, so in a laboratory experiment Aron and Dutton randomly assigned males to high and low arousal conditions (threat of shock or no threat). Again, a female experimenter was more likely to be contacted later by subjects in the high arousal condition, supporting the cognitive-arousal interpretation.

Applying the theory to passionate love, if a member of the opposite sex is present, arousal produced for any reason may be misinterpreted as love. Sexual arousal itself is readily interpreted as passionate because there are usually specific physiological and anatomical cues, but other sources of arousal (such as mild fear, frustration, excitement about an athletic contest, or exercise) may be labeled as love if a particular person happens along at the right time.

Recall from Chapter Two that there are problems with cognitive-arousal theory but that excitation transfer theory is better supported. This latter theory would say that if there is *already* some degree of sexual arousal, this may be *intensified* by additional arousal from an unrelated source. This effect explains a number of curious phenomena, for example, why a "hard-to-get" person may be more attractive. The apparently unobtainable person produces feelings of frustration, a form of arousal. This arousal may transfer to other feelings and be interpreted as heightened love. Even rejection or discovering that the object of one's romantic inclination has another partner may produce an emotional arousal that is interpreted as being even stronger love than existed before. Some people are also "turned on" by a certain amount of "danger" in lovemaking (for example, having sex in locations where they might be observed). All these situations make sense in terms of excitation-transfer theory.

Liking and Loving as Overlapping Sets

Rubin's theory of liking and loving. Rubin (1970) distinguished liking as being based on **affection** and **respect,** whereas loving was said to be based on **attachment, caring,** and **intimacy.** One of the major contributions to this area of research was Rubin's incorporation of these concepts into two scales for the measurement of liking and loving. On his scales, each of thirteen items is rated on a scale from "Not at all true" (1), to "Definitely true" (9). The "love scale" has such items as "If I were lonely, my first thought would be to seek (name) out." The "liking scale" has such items as "I have great confidence in (name)'s good judgment." The validity of the scales was shown in several ways. The correlation between love scale score and simply *saying* that you are in love with somebody is .61 for women and .50 for men. In addition, loving and liking for one's romantic partner were higher than for one's same-sex friends. Other scales have since been developed (e.g., Lee, 1977; Levinger, Rands, & Talober, 1977; Steffen, McLaney, & Hustedt, 1982; Swensen, 1972), but the most important aspect of them all is the attempt to measure what so often has been considered the unmeasurable.

Sternberg and Grajek's theory of overlaying bonds. Sternberg and Grajek (1984) used complex statistical procedures to examine measures of liking and loving for one's lover, mother, father, sibling closest in age, and best friend of the same sex. Subjects were thirty-five men and fifty women ranging in age from 18 to 70 years. The major findings were that (1) love seemed to consist of three major components, called **intimacy, passion,** and **decision/commitment** (described more fully later) and (2) intimacy was involved in all the kinds of love relationships studied, but passion and decision/commitment varied. The authors concluded that love has a common core of the preceding elements but that the *experience* of love may differ depending on what other elements, or **bonds,** occur. Thus the experience of love varies with the presence or absence of emotions other than passion, of other thought processes besides decision/commitment, and of motives other than love.

Liking as a Subset of Loving

Cluster theory. Davis (1985) proposed that liking (friendship) consists of **enjoyment, mutual assistance, spontaneity, acceptance, trust, understanding,** and **confidence.** **Loving** consists of all elements of liking **plus** the elements of **passion, sexual desire, exclusiveness,** and **caring.** Davis's research indicates that spouses, lovers, and close friends do not differ much with regard to the elements of friendship. Spouses and lovers do differ from close friends, however, on the elements of loving, especially passion and caring.

Triangular theory of liking and loving. Sternberg (1986; 1987) has proposed what he calls the triangular theory of love, based on the three dimensions given before: (1) intimacy, (2) passion, and (3) decision/commitment. **Intimacy** refers to feelings of **closeness** or **connectedness** between two people, including such factors as concern with the welfare of the loved one, mutual understanding, and sharing. **Passion** consists of the sources of arousal that we generally label as passion (emotional feelings and physical arousal). Sexual arousal is certainly a strong element, but such needs as for affiliation may also be involved. **Decision/commitment** refers to short-term and long-term elements. In the short term, one person makes the **decision** that he or she loves another person. In the long term, one makes a **commitment** to maintain that love. The two do not necessarily go together; one can decide that one is in love at the moment without making any long-term commitment. Likewise, one can make a long-term commitment (such as marriage) without necessarily deciding that one is in love at the moment.

In simple form, the presence or absence of each of the preceding three components of love can result in eight possible combinations, which comprise eight different kinds of liking or loving, as summarized in Table 14–1. Sternberg's names for each are also given. Figure 14–2 also illustrates the theory.

TABLE 14–1.   Sternberg's taxonomy of kinds of love based on his triangular theory of love.

KIND OF LOVE	COMPONENTS		
	INTIMACY	PASSION	DECISION/COMMITMENT
1. Nonlove	0	0	0
2. Liking	+	0	0
3. Infatuated love	0	+	0
4. Empty love	0	0	+
5. Romantic love	+	+	0
6. Companionate love	+	0	+
7. Fatuous love	0	+	+
8. Consummate love	+	+	+

Note: + = component present; 0 = component absent. Most loving relationships fall somewhere between these "pure" types because the various components are present in various degrees, not in all-or-none fashion as indicated in the table.

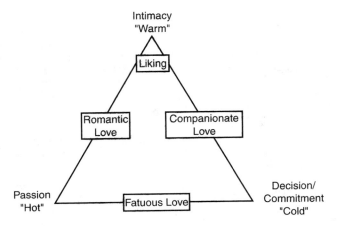

FIGURE 14–2. Sternberg's "triangular" theory of love. Different "types" of liking and loving relationships are defined by location with reference to the vertices of the triangle.

Some brief descriptions of the eight types are as follows: (1) **Nonlove** means what the name implies, the absence of love (it is always a good idea to keep in mind that **zero** is a perfectly good mathematical quantity when describing something). (2) **Liking** is intimacy, without passion or commitment. Friendships can endure for decades without friends' seeing each other for years at a time; love often is not so durable in this manner. (3) **Infatuated love** (infatuation) is a kind of love at first sight phenomenon, passion without intimacy or commitment (students always refer to this as the "one-night stand"). (4) **Empty love** seems as vacuous as nonlove but characterizes such social phenomena as arranged marriages, where there is commitment without intimacy or passion. It also characterizes a "burned-out marriage" or the end of some other long-term relation. (5) **Romantic love** has intimacy and passion, and is a kind of storybook love. There is stronger emotional bonding (intimacy) than with infatuated love, but not commitment. (6) **Companionate love** refers to a long-term, committed friendship. Such a friendship might characterize a marriage after the passion has died down. (7) **Fatuous love** is a combination of passion and decision/commitment, such as a whirlwind courtship and marriage. The commitment is based on passion rather than intimacy. (8) **Consummate love** represents a kind of ideal toward which we might strive, a kind of love to be found more in our dreams than in reality. And, if found, it may be very hard to maintain.

Styles of love. Hendrick and Hendrick (1986) distinguished six types or "styles" of love, and they developed six corresponding scales for measuring each type.

The six styles, along with a sample scale item for each, are as follows:

1. **Eros.** Erotic love with strong physical preferences and commitment to the lover. *Sample item:* "My lover and I have the right physical 'chemistry' between us."
2. **Ludus.** Love is a game to be played with many partners. There is no great depth of feeling, and there is a manipulative quality to it. Many love relationships have a gamelike quality but are not as extreme as Ludus. *Sample item:* "I try to keep my lover uncertain about my commitment to him/her."
3. **Storge.** This is merging of love and friendship. It lacks the fiery quality of Eros and is more like companionate love. *Sample item:* "The best kind of love grows out of a long friendship."
4. **Pragma.** This style is rational and pragmatic, searching for the potential benefits and losses from the relationship. Love is planned. *Sample item:* "I try to plan my life carefully before choosing a lover."
5. **Mania.** This style is based on uncertainty about oneself and one's lover and on greater concern with losing the lover than on positive aspects. *Sample item:* "I cannot relax if I suspect that my lover is with someone else."
6. **Agape.** A selfless, all-giving kind of love. *Sample item:* "I would rather suffer myself than let my lover suffer."

Research with the scales indicates that males tend to be more "ludic" (game-playing) than females but that females are somewhat more storgic, pragmatic, and manic than males. Males and females are about the same on Eros and Agape. Furthermore, individuals who score high on the Eros scale tend to have higher self-esteem, whereas those who score high on Mania tend to have lower self-esteem (Hendrick & Hendrick, 1986).

The range of theories and of types of love within a theory strongly indicates that love is not a single process that applies the same to all people in all situations. Love may mean different things to different people because **there are different kinds of love** masquerading under one name. As the different types or styles of love become more clearly distinguished by research, we should better be able to understand the development of love and the relationship of love (or lack thereof) to other behaviors.

SUMMARY

1. **Interpersonal attraction** can be divided into **affiliation, liking,** and **loving.** These may overlap but have different characteristics.
2. Affiliation does not necessarily involve liking another. Reasons for affiliation may include **biological attachment, need to belong, reduction of fear, assistance, stimulation, information, self-evaluation,** and occasional **freedom from internal constraint.**
3. Determinants of attraction include **physical attractiveness, proximity, familiarity, similarity,** and **reciprocity.**
4. Physical attractiveness is of major importance; attractive people are generally more liked and better treated. There is an **attractiveness stereotype,** an implicit personality theory that assumes that attractive people have other virtues in addi-

tion to their appearance. Associating with attractive people may enhance one's own image, as well as produce good feelings in oneself.

5. There are a number of theories about what makes one person more attractive than another. According to the **matching principle,** people are attracted to people of the same level of physical attractiveness as themselves. There is evidence that such couples stay together longer.

6. Buss has suggested that there are different biologically determined **tactics of mate attraction,** such as skill at locating mates and displaying mate-attracting behaviors.

7. According to some **evolutionary psychology** approaches, female attractiveness is linked to signals of reproductive potential, including body shape and general signs of health. Evidence for these is not strong.

8. According to the **facial averageness hypothesis,** the most attractive face is a composite of all the faces a person has seen. There is strong evidence for this hypothesis.

9. Considerable research shows that we are more likely to be attracted to people who are geographically **close** to us, who are **familiar** to us, who are **similar** to us, and whom we believe to **like** us.

10. Theories of liking and loving can be categorized as follows: (1) liking and loving vary only **quantitatively;** (2) liking and loving are **qualitatively different;** (3) liking and loving **share some common characteristics;** and (4) liking has **some of the features of loving,** but not all.

11. Views of loving as being a "lot of liking" include **reinforcement theory, social exchange theory, equity theory, investment theory,** and **cognitive arousal theory.**

12. According to reinforcement theory, if rewards are experienced while in the presence of someone, that person becomes a **secondary reinforcer.**

13. **Social exchange theory, equity theory,** and **investment theory** are "economic" approaches to attraction. Each deals with the **costs and benefits** of being in a relationship. According to investment theory, the more resources that people have in a relationship, the stronger the commitment to that relationship if the rewards are greater than the costs.

14. **Cognitive-arousal theory** says that if arousal occurs while in the presence of another person, the first person may misinterpret the arousal and label it as love. This phenomenon may also account for the attractiveness of the "hard to get" person, whereby frustration might be mislabeled as love.

15. Rubin (1970) distinguished liking as being based on **affection** and **respect,** whereas loving was said to be based on **attachment, caring,** and **intimacy.**

16. Davis's **cluster theory** says that liking consists of such elements as enjoyment and acceptance but that loving consists of those elements **plus** passion, sexual desire, exclusiveness, and caring.

17. Sternberg's **triangular theory** says that love is based on the three dimensions of **intimacy, passion,** and **decision/commitment.** The relative amounts of each of these define eight different types of love.

18. Hendrick and Hendrick distinguished six **"styles" of love** and developed corresponding scales for each type.

CHAPTER FIFTEEN

Applications of Motivation Theory

———●———

ᴠ

In this chapter we look at some applications of general principles of motivation to specific instances. There is no difference between so-called "pure" and "applied" research as far as the rules for conducting research are concerned. The two kinds of research differ only in that pure research may be done because a problem is interesting in its own right or it contributes to theory and applied research is done with a more immediate practical goal in mind. For example, one psychologist might be concerned with the general question of how people interact in groups, and another psychologist with specific interactions in sports teams. Or one researcher might be interested in the reason why people are attracted to a particular kind of stimulus, whereas another researcher might be interested in advertising. In previous chapters we have often looked at specific applications through the lens of general theories. In this chapter we just do this in more detail for some selected problems.

JOB MOTIVAT'ON AND SATISFACTION

Orientation to Job Motivation

A common question from managers is "How can I motivate people to work harder?" **Job motivation** theories in business and industry are not unlike the more general psychological theories of motivation discussed thus far. And the reason is simple: People are people whether at home or on the job. Quite separately from research or psychological theory, some philosophical views may affect how workers are treated by their superiors.

Philosophical views. Motivation "theory" in business used to be largely speculative, related to the perceived nature of humans. Such philosophical views as the following, accurate or not, have influenced managerial thinking about dealing with workers.

1. **Rational-economic person.** This view assumes that people are motivated solely by economic considerations and can make rational economic decisions. Workers are considered to be inherently lazy and will not work unless paid. Manipulation of wages and incentives should be sufficient to make them work. People are considered relatively interchangeable since they can be controlled by money.

2. **Social person.** The famous Hawthorne studies (Roethlisberger & Dickson, 1947) showed that such environmental conditions as lighting affected production far less than did such social factors as job satisfaction, social groupings, and conformity. The concept of the social person developed from these studies, suggesting that workers are primarily motivated by social needs that are not met just by work. Workers may be more responsive to their peers than to their company.

3. **Self-actualizing person.** "According to the self-actualizing conception, man is seen as intrinsically motivated. He takes pride in his work because it is **his** work"

(Wrightsman, 1972, p. 510). Pride and satisfaction are not always possible in large amounts (as in menial labor), but where there is possibility for personal growth and accomplishment for the worker, a good leader will provide the opportunity.

4. **Complex person.** This view recognizes the variation in motives, emotions, experiences, and abilities of different people and that these change over time. New motives and skills, as well as successes and failures, affect a worker's attitude about a job and how well the job can be handled. There is therefore no single strategy for dealing with all workers, and perhaps not even with the same worker at different times.

Theory X and Theory Y.   Douglas McGregor (1960) distinguished two approaches to management and the worker that he simply identified as Theory X and Theory Y, summarized by DuBrin (1980, p. 39) as follows:

- Theory X assumes that people dislike work and must be coerced, controlled, and directed toward organizational goals. Furthermore, most people prefer to be treated this way so that they can avoid responsibility.
- Theory Y emphasizes people's intrinsic interest in their work, their desire to be self-directing and to seek responsibility, and their capacity to be creative in solving business problems.

A marketing manager who believes in Theory X might try to motivate sales representatives as follows, again quoting DuBrin (p. 39):

We have established sales quotas for each of you. Each year that your quota is reached, the company will pay for a five-day trip for you and your spouse. This will be in addition to your normal vacation. . . . Sales representatives who are unable to meet their quotas for three consecutive quarters will probably not be invited back for a fourth quarter.

On the other hand, a Theory Y believer might say the following:

You and your sales managers will get together on establishing sales quotas for each year. If you achieve your quotas, you will receive extra money. High performance in sales is one important factor in being considered for a management assignment. Another important part of your job besides selling is to keep our product-planning group informed about changes in consumer demand. Many of our new products in the past stemmed directly from the suggestions of sales representatives.

The newer views, departing from the economic person approach, have developed in part because research has shown that workers are indeed more complex than Theory X supposes. Unfortunately, it is still true that many employers believe that simply paying a person is sufficient to get the most there is to be gotten from a worker.

Theories of Job Motivation

The previous philosophical approaches indicate different orientations to the questions of worker motivation but are not articulated theories in any specific sense. We now look at more detailed theories.

Herzberg's two-factor theory. Frederick Herzberg (1968) suggested that some aspects of a job allow people to satisfy "higher level" needs, which he called **satisfiers** or **motivators.** He argued that people want more from their jobs than pay, such as recognition, responsibility, feelings of achievement, prestige, pleasure from social interactions, stimulation, and challenge. Some job elements are noticeable in their *absence*, however, and produce **dissatisfaction.** Such **dissatisfiers** tend to relate to annoying external conditions, such as company policy and its administration, supervision, working conditions, relations with others, status, and job security. Satisfaction of these needs is called **hygiene.** The heart of Herzberg's approach is that dissatisfaction may lower performance but that hygienic measures will not markedly improve performance.

Herzberg repeatedly claimed that external incentives are *not* motivators. The distinction that Herzberg seemed to be trying to convey was between external rewards and intrinsic motivation. This distinction is certainly not unimportant, but since Herzberg did not make it clear, his resulting ideas were sometimes unusual. To argue that supervision is *not* motivating (whether by threat of firing or control of rewards) and that achievement, recognition, and responsibility *are* motivating simply flies in the face of any other major theoretical approach to motivation (e.g., see Locke, 1976). Achievement and recognition may be good motivators, but this observation is not equivalent to saying that supervisory practices or pay incentives have no role as motivators.

Maslow's need hierarchy. Maslow's need hierarchy theory (e.g., Maslow, 1970) stratifies needs from the most basic biological to the most ethereal psychological: (1) **physiological** (such as hunger-thirst), (2) **safety and security,** (3) **love and belongingness,** (4) **self-esteem** (achievement, recognition), and (5) **self-actualization** (reaching one's highest potential). The essence of the theory is that the needs lower in the hierarchy have to be at least partly fulfilled before the higher needs become active. As Maslow saw it, few individuals ever really reach the highest plateau, self-actualization, because of overconcern about lower-level needs, self-esteem, for example.

Maslow's theory sometimes seems to make sense in the industrial situation. For example, lower-level workers seem to be more motivated by money (needed for food and shelter) and are not much motivated to work creatively in their jobs. At higher levels, where income is sufficient to keep the wolf from the door, self-actualization seems more important. The theory is extremely difficult to falsify, however, because in lower-level jobs, there may be no **opportunity** for self-expression. Therefore, workers may seek other satisfactions **outside** the job. Research indicates that two "levels" of motivation are sufficient to account for work motivation. One level is the physiological-safety-belonging classification; the other is an esteem-achievement-actualization classification. This looks suspiciously like restatement of the external reward/intrinsic motivation distinction (e.g., see Steers & Porter, 1975; Landy & Trumbo, 1980).

Vroom's valence-instrumentality-expectancy (VIE) theory. According to Vroom's (1964) theory, **expectancy** is the perceived probability that a particular amount of effort will be **instrumental** in achieving a **valued** goal. A worker might consider, "What are the chances I will get promoted if I work hard?" Based upon knowledge of the situation, the probability might be low, medium, or high. For example, a female in a male-dominated organization might consider the probability of advancement to be much lower than would a man in the same position. The second component of the expectancy is the **valence** (value) that some outcome (such as promotion) has for the worker. If a person does not value a promotion, we would not expect her or him to work hard for it. Putting this formulation into Vroom's terms produces Figure 15–1, which is the expectancy that work will lead to a certain level of **performance** and that this performance will be instrumental in achieving the long-term goal (promotion). If a person expects that hard work will *not* produce a high level of performance or that high performance will *not* achieve the goal, the perceived instrumentality will be low, and the person is not likely to work very hard.

Equity theory. The author once listened to the complaint of a construction worker about having to do some welding one day when the regular welder was sick. His complaint was not that he disliked welding (he actually liked it) or that it was more difficult or harder work than his regular job (it was easier). Rather, he was dissatisfied because welders earn more than his own job paid, and he considered it unfair that he should be asked to weld but be paid at his own regular rate. This type of response is not readily explained

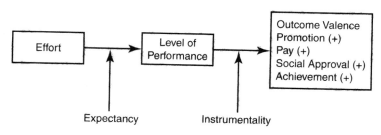

FIGURE 15–1. Vroom's VIE model of job motivation and performance.

by the previous theories but is exactly what equity theory was designed to explain.

Equity theory (Adams, 1975) is the idea that a person **compares** how hard he is working with what he is getting in return, and if he perceives a discrepancy, he is unhappy. The discrepancy may be between the person's **internal** standard for what is equitable return for a certain amount of effort, or it may be in comparison with some **external reference.** Our construction worker (let's call him Frank) used other welders as a reference. Welders get paid so much an hour for their work. Frank was getting paid less. Therefore, the ratio of his pay to his work was less than that of the regular welders. Thus

Frank's Pay for Welder's Work < Welder's Pay for Welder's Work

This discrepancy produced an aversive emotional state in Frank, a degree of tension. This is a frustrating situation for Frank because his goal is equity. How does Frank respond to this if he is forced to weld for the day? According to the theory, he would do something to make his ratio of pay to work more equal to the reference. He might reduce his own work until he perceives that his return is proportionally the same as that of a regular welder. Or he might try to get a raise. Or he might just complain and be rather unpleasant to be around (as he was).

Suppose that instead of Frank, there is Frieda, who is getting a perceived low return for effort compared with that of male workers. What might she do? She might accept one of the traditional excuses for paying women less, such as "a man has a family to support." She might quit her job. She might ask for a raise. She might reduce her work output. She might file a complaint with the government under the Equal Pay Act or the Fair Employment Practices Act. In any event, neither Frank nor Frieda is going to be a happy camper until there is some resolution to their perceived inequities.

What would happen if a person received *more* than he or she perceives to be deserved? There is some evidence that people will actually work harder, for a while at least, apparently in order to restore equity. It does seem, however, that people adapt to the new level of return for their work so that it is no longer perceived as high, and work may drop back to where it had been previously.

The problems of research with equity theory in the industrial setting are that (1) pay is not the only work outcome and (2) the appropriateness of the reference person that an individual compares himself or herself with is not always clear (Gibson, Ivancevich, & Donnelly, 1979, p. 117). There certainly is enough evidence from a variety of sources, however, to indicate that such discrepancies may indeed produce tension and disharmony (Landy & Trumbo, 1980). Equitable treatment is important in most situations, not just business.

Behavior theory and goal setting. Any method of rewarding work or punishing nonwork (such as by threat of firing a recalcitrant worker) is an application of instrumental (operant) conditioning to job motivation. The problem is that usually the people who use these applications are often not well versed in the details of this approach. A more sophisticated operant conditioning approach proceeds in three parts:

1. Setting up environmental conditions to make particular behaviors more or less likely to occur. For example, working without interruption is easier if one's desk is not in a place that many people go by each day;
2. Setting goals so that the individual knows what performance is expected; and
3. Reinforcing individuals for achieving those goals. Many questions still arise, however. Who will set the goals? How will reinforcement (feedback about success) be given?

Emery Air Freight. One of the best-documented cases of company-wide adoption of these principles is the experience at the Emery Air Freight Company (Feeney, 1972). The problem was simple: Employees were using the wrong size cardboard cartons for shipping. Because too-large cartons take up more space, there are fewer cartons per load and less profit. The "cure" for the problem was almost equally simple: Employees were *told* how to load cartons properly and were verbally reinforced for doing so. Improvement was immediate. Employees were also instructed to pay close attention to such details as the scheduling of pickups and deliveries, and goals were set for these. Again, performance improved markedly.

The "real" problem had been that the employees did not know either what they *were* doing or what they *should* have been doing. They estimated that they were about 90 percent efficient in their loading, whereas they were actually closer to 45 percent efficiency. Once it was determined where performance really was and careful records were being kept, it was possible to institute rapid change at little expense. An initial investment of $5,000 in the program brought about improved efficiency ultimately worth millions of dollars.

Locke's theory of goal setting. Edwin Locke (e.g., 1968; Locke & Latham, 1984) proposed two major principles of goal setting:

1. Hard goals produce higher performance than easy goals.
2. Specific goals produce higher performance than vague goals, such as "Do the best you can."

This proposal was illustrated in the Emery Air Freight case, but even better in a report by Latham and Baldes (1975). The problem was that logging trucks were not being loaded nearly to capacity, so that more runs than necessary were being made by each truck. The solution was to tell each driver specifically to load her or his truck to 94 percent of the truck's legal weight, as compared with the approximately 60 percent average that the drivers had been carrying. Figure 15–2 shows the result, a marked and sustained improvement. The drivers were given verbal praise for improving their load size, but they got no other reward, and there was no special training for either drivers or supervisors.

Two additional principles in the application of goal-setting techniques should be adhered to, however. First, goals should be **attainable.** Specific goals should be difficult, not impossible. Research on United Fund campaigns illustrates this principle. When a goal of 20 percent increase over the previous year was set, productivity went up 25 percent. But a goal of 80 percent increase resulted in only a 12 percent rise, and performance declined when the goal was doubled (Dessler, 1980). Second, goals should be **relevant**

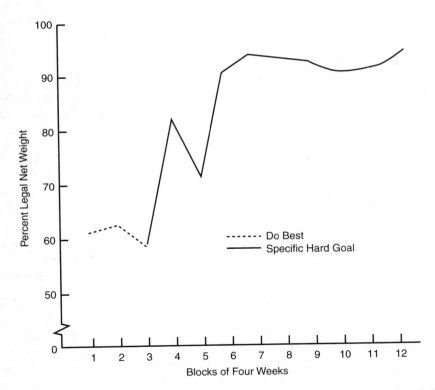

FIGURE 15–2. When drivers were told to "do their best" loading trucks (dotted portion of curve), they loaded them only to about 60 percent of legal capacity. When given the specific instructions to load them to 94 percent, however, there was an immediate and sustained increase in load size. (From Latham & Baldes, 1975. Used with permission. Copyright © 1975 by the American Psychological Association.)

to the job at hand. A production supervisor should set goals for production, not sales. The goals should also be measured in objective and relevant terms, such as amount produced per unit time. There is also considerable value in **employee participation** in goal setting. What a supervisor sees as an attainable goal may differ sharply from what an employee sees. Therefore, if supervisor and employee jointly set a goal that is satisfactory to both, there is a greater chance of success because the goal is realistic and the employee is committed to trying to achieve the goal. Participation also increases job satisfaction.

Job Satisfaction

Between 1935 and 1976, there were over 3,000 *published* studies of job satisfaction, an average of one every five days (Locke, 1976). Between 1989 and 1998, PsychINFO (a computerized abstracting service for psychology-related journals and books, operated by the American Psychological Association) showed 3,191 entries with the phrase "job satisfaction" in the abstract. Interest in the topic seems not to have dimmed in the last ten years. Job satisfaction is considered so important because of the costs of dissatisfaction in employee turnover, absenteeism, and work performance. Turnover is one of the most expensive of personnel problems because of time and money that are lost in training workers. The relationship between job satisfaction and absenteeism is somewhat difficult to document, but Smith (1977) cleverly did so. During a snowstorm in Chicago, job satisfaction predicted rather well among a large number of managers who would or would not show up for work. Given a good excuse not to come to work, the less satisfied managers in a large corporation did not come to work, but better satisfied managers did. On the same day in New York City, where the weather was nice, job satisfaction did not predict absenteeism among comparable managers. It took the combination of environmental factors (storm) and personal factors (job satisfaction) to tease out the effect of job satisfaction on absenteeism.

Meaning and measurement of job satisfaction. Job satisfaction may be defined as "the attitude one has toward his or her job" (McCormick & Ilgen, 1980, p. 303). An attitude, as we saw in Chapter Thirteen, is an emotional response toward something (in this case, a job), which can vary from positive to negative in any degree. Whatever might be said about attitudes in general applies to job satisfaction in particular. Thus the measurement of job satisfaction, the relation of job satisfaction to behavior, and methods of improving job satisfaction are all special cases of the same problems raised about attitudes. Furthermore, just as a job has many characteristics, so job satisfaction is necessarily a summation of worker attitudes about all these characteristics. Good and bad features of a job are balanced so that job satisfaction "on the whole" is relatively high or low. Table 15–1 shows a dozen dimensions of work that are related to job satisfaction.

TABLE 15–1.   Job dimensions typically relevant to job satisfaction.

GENERAL CATEGORIES	SPECIFIC DIMENSION	DIMENSION DESCRIPTIONS
I. Events or Conditions		
1. Work	Work itself	Includes intrinsic interest, variety, opportunity for learning, difficulty, amount, chances for success, control over work flow, etc.
2. Rewards	Pay	Amount of fairness or equity of, basis for pay, etc.
	Promotions	Opportunities for, basis of, fairness of, etc.
	Recognition	Praise, criticism, credit for work done, etc.
3. Context of work	Working conditions	Hours, rest pauses, equipment, quality of the workspace, temperature, ventilation, location of plant, etc.
	Benefits	Pensions, medical and life insurance plans, annual leave, vacations, etc.
II. Agents		
1. Self	Self	Values, skills and abilities, etc.
2. Others (in-company)	Supervision	Supervisory style and influence, technical adequacy, administrative skills, etc.
	Coworkers	Competence, friendliness, helpfulness, technical competence, etc.
3. Others (outside company)	Customers	Technical competence, friendliness, etc.
	Family members*	Supportiveness, knowledge of job, demands for time, etc.
	Others	Depending upon position, e.g., students, parents, voters

*Not included in Locke's discussion.
Adapted from Locke, 1976, 1302. Used by permission of Rand-McNally.

Job satisfaction and behavior.   It is only partly true that "happy workers are good workers." The relationship between job satisfaction and performance is considerably less than perfect, and where such a correlation does exist, the cause may not be the one implied. For example, good performance may lead to high job satisfaction rather than the other way around. Lawler and Porter (1967) proposed that performance that leads to rewards produces satisfaction with the work and also produces the expectation that future performance will also lead to rewards. This model is illustrated in Figure 15–3.

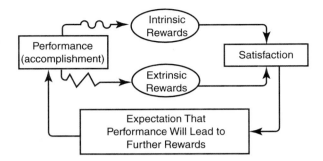

FIGURE 15–3. The Lawler-Porter model of job satisfaction, showing how performance leads to rewards and satisfaction and the expectation of future rewards. (From Lawler & Porter, 1967, Fig. 1. Figure slightly adapted by Dessler, 1980. Used with permission of Reston Publ. Co.)

Several studies testing Lawler and Porter's model have indicated that there is greater job satisfaction when rewards are specifically related to job performance than when equal rewards are given but not specifically related to job performance. This finding suggests that job satisfaction comes with perceived **control** over events that produce success. Organizational attempts to "increase morale" by contrived programs may have some positive effects but do not necessarily lead to better performance, since the "morale building events" are not related to performance.

Theories of Job Satisfaction

Theories of job satisfaction involve motivational, emotional, and informational components. The following three theories are illustrative.

Instrumentality theory. Job satisfaction is high to the extent that the job is instrumental in getting the worker what he or she values or wants from the job. This might be pleasure in the work, security, prestige, money, short hours, flex time, autonomy, convenient location, day care, or anything else the worker considers valuable.

Equity theory. As discussed earlier, people generally want to get what they consider a fair (equitable) return for their behavior, suggesting that there is greater job satisfaction if the worker perceives that the return for her or his work is equitable.

The job characteristics model. Hackman and Lawler (1971) defined six job attributes that might relate to job satisfaction: (1) **variety of work** on the job; (2) **autonomy** in doing work and making decisions; (3) **task identity,** doing a piece of work that can be clearly identified as the result of the worker's efforts; (4) receiving **performance feedback** about how well one is doing on the job; (5) **dealing with other people;** and (6) **friendship opportunities** on the job. Using a statistical procedure called **path analysis,** Hackman and Oldham (1976) found that the appropriate combinations of these factors did predict job satisfaction rather well.

Reith (1988) tested the generality of the Hackman-Oldham results by translating the model into academic terms. Her basic assumption was that going to school is a student's job and that all the elements that apply to satisfaction with other jobs would also apply to the classroom. Reith studied 180 students taking introductory psychology and found that measures of the combination of the various aspects of job satisfaction just described did correlate about +.60 with course satisfaction. Overall, Reith's results were very similar to those reported by Hackman and Oldham (1976), showing that job satisfaction can be fruitfully studied in academic settings. Although it would be unwise to study job satisfaction exclusively in academia, there is some value in being able to test theories in less formidable surroundings than unionized industries and in applying models that might suggest improvements in academia. Reith also found a significant relationship between degree of perceived equity in grading and course satisfaction.

MOTIVATION IN SPORTS

Orientation

Sports behavior is just as complex as any other form of behavior, involving many sets of skills, thoughts, motives, and environmental settings. We can take the formula

$$\text{Behavior} = f(\text{Person, Environment})$$

and just make it more specific.

$$\text{Sports Behavior} = f(\text{Person}_{\text{motives, skills, knowledge}} \text{ and Environment}_{\text{physical, social}})$$

which just indicates more specifically some aspects of the person and the environment that might concern us. "Person" could refer to players, coaches, or fans. The environment could be such physical surroundings as those around a playing field. It could also include social aspects of other people participating in an event (e.g., trash talking), as well as people viewing an event (fans cheering, booing, or remaining eerily silent).

The problems to be addressed by sports psychologists are tremendously varied, depending on (1) what person(s) we are interested in, (2) what behavior we are interested in, and (3) the environment in which we are working, including rules (and their interpretations). These elements are illustrated in Table 15–2.

Motivation Theories Commonly Applied to Sports

Success or failure in sports depends on factors in addition to motivation, such as athletic ability, training, practice, and coaching. All of these are relevant to skill levels. Motivational factors are relevant to many aspects of sports, however. These include the goals a person has for being involved in sport, willingness to overcome obstacles to participate (e.g., endure hardship of training, expense of participation, loss of time from other activities, and so on). Table 15–3, which refers to topics from previous chapters, shows theories of motivation that are obviously relevant to sports. We shall limit ourselves to a few selected topics here.

Why Do People Play Sports?

People engage in sports for many different reasons, just as they choose to participate in any other activity for different reasons. The following are some motivational factors.

Arousal.   The excitement produced by playing may make playful behavior rewarding for its own sake. In Chapter Six we discussed the fact that people and animals may engage in activities that serve to increase their arousal, bringing them more nearly to an optimum level. Sports may bring a degree of **variety,** or **stimulus change,** into one's life. Thus a person who

TABLE 15–2.   Some topics that might be of interest to a sports psychologist.

	YOUTH SPORTS	YOUNG ADULT	ADULT
Players	Recreational	Recreational	Recreational
or	Competitive	Competitive	Competitive
Coaches	Elite	High school varsity	Elite amateur, e.g., Olympic
		College varsity	Professional
		Elite amateur	
Behaviors	Skilled athletic performance (learning and maintenance)		
	Persistence in staying with sport (e.g., youth)		
	Violence or other rule-breaking (on field and in the stands)		
	Competitors only, no coaches or referees (e.g., pickup games)		
Environment	Parents and a few fans		
	Large audiences, many fans, television cameras		
	Home field versus away		

TABLE 15–3.   Some major theories of motivation relevant to sports.

Achievement Motivation (Hope of success and fear of failure)
Task persistence, performance intensity, choice of tasks

Activation (Arousal) Theory
Optimal level of arousal and performance

Aggression Theory
Frustration-aggression, stimulus-aroused aggression, instrumental aggression

Attribution Theory of Achievement (Weiner)
Effects of success/failure attributions (perceived causes) on subsequent performance

Drive Theory
Social facilitation effects and type of task

Expectancy-Value Theory
Effects of expected outcome and value of outcome on performance

Frustration Theory
Punishing effects of frustration, drive effects, frustration-aggression

Goal Setting Theory (Locke)
Types of goals (winning, mastery of task, social, money)
Determining what goal levels are most effective for performance

Reinforcement Theory
E.g., fans, other players, coaches selectively reinforcing certain behaviors
Schedules of reinforcement, choice of reinforcers

Self-Efficacy Theory ("Self-confidence")
How feelings of efficacy develop and what their effects are on performance

works at a routine job all day may enjoy the change of pace and challenge provided by recreational activities.

Achievement and competition. The pride of achievement may be sought in sports, as well as in work. Similarly, competitiveness may also be experienced in sports.

Self-expression. Sports can be a form of self-expression for some people in the same way that music, art, writing, or hobbies are vehicles for self-expression for other people (Weinberg, 1984). Self-expression could also be viewed in terms of intrinsic motivation.

Social rewards. Many people enjoy sports because sports satisfy an **affiliation** motive through opportunity for interaction with others. A friendly

414   *Applications of Motivation Theory*

softball game can be a family affair as much as a sports competition. A game of tennis may be played at a level below the capabilities of the players just in order to keep the game friendly and to have a pleasant outing.

Changes in motivation with aging. As children get older, interest in organized sports depends on the rewards gained from sports as compared with the rewarding aspects of other activities. After about age twelve, there is a marked decline in the numbers of boys and girls engaging in organized sport. One reason is that children perceive that they are *not mastering* their particular sport and therefore do not find it rewarding (Roberts, 1984). At the same time, the other rewards (e.g., opportunities to socialize) are not strong enough to hold them if those rewards can be gained more easily elsewhere. From a strictly sports point of view, this tendency is unfortunate because slower-maturing children who are not the best of athletes in early adolescence may subsequently surpass the abilities of many of their earlier-maturing age mates (Roberts, 1984) and could enjoy sports activities later. Children who are attracted to a sport as a social event persist longer in the sport than those who are attracted to it because they believe they can get recognition by being good performers.

The extent to which a sport is rewarding for an individual depends partly on the goals that he or she sets. A mediocre athlete may play tennis regularly if the goal is to get some exercise, have a good time, and make a good shot now and then. Achievement theory (Chapter Twelve) suggests that maximum enjoyment comes where there are about equal chances of winning or losing regardless of how well a person plays. In team or individual sports, we usually put ourselves into competitions where we can have some successes but also risk failing. Without that risk, the successes mean little.

Arousal and Performance

Optimal levels of arousal. It is a common observation that either an individual or a team can be "too psyched up" to perform well. According to the Yerkes-Dodson law, the more complex the behavior is, the lower the optimal level of motivation (Chapter Six). Different activities in different sports require different complexities of behavior and should therefore have different optimal levels of arousal. A football coach might try to work his team into a passionate frenzy for a big game ("Win this one for the Gipper!"), but a golf coach would hardly do so. Because golf requires delicately controlled movements, golfers have to keep themselves calm.

Oxendine (1970) examined the question of optimal levels for different sports activities. He ranked different sports in terms of the amount of fine muscular control and judgment involved. Bowling, field goal kicking, skating, and tournament-level golfing require very delicate control, whereas weight lifting, sprinting, and football blocking and tackling do not require as much control. Weinberg and Genuchi (1980) reported that golfers performed better with low levels of anxiety, as expected. For basketball, however, it has been reported that medium anxiety levels are more effective (Sonstroem & Bernardo, 1982). Klavora (1978) assessed the pregame anxiety levels of ninety-five boys during a high school basketball season. Performance level was determined by having coaches rate the players in terms of their customary levels of ability. Performance was again found to be better with medium levels of anxiety.

Sonstroem (1984) and Neiss (1988) have both made the point, however, that there are several problems in applying the optimal level notion. First, it is difficult to quantify arousal levels. Psychologists usually look at motivation levels in terms of groups that have more or less motivation than do other groups. This procedure does not allow discovery of an optimal level because it takes a number of well-defined motivational values to determine any inverted function, much less to compare different ones. Consequently, we may not be able to define arousal levels precisely enough to test the inverted-U hypothesis well. Second, even if we could define levels of arousal accurately, there are ethical sanctions against inducing extreme levels of arousal in experimental situations. Third, we must ask whether there is more than one kind of arousal.

In sports psychology, being "anxious" and being "psyched up" refer to two different kinds of arousal. These two kinds of arousal seem to be like Thayer's energetic-sleepy and tense-relaxed dimensions of arousal (see Chapter Two), and there is some physiological evidence for such a distinction. Exercise-induced arousal produces an increase in epinephrine output, but not cortisol (an adrenal cortex stress hormone). Exercise plus fear produces an increase in both (Neiss, 1988). This being the case, we would then have to ask in any particular situation *which* arousal dimension we are referring to if we say that arousal is low, medium, or high. Furthermore, suppose that an athlete also gets angry. Is anger a third type of arousal? And for each of these types of arousal, is the optimal level of arousal the same?

A final consideration in evaluating the inverted-U function hypothesis concerns the methods used to produce arousal. The operations for producing arousal may have both **arousal** effects and **stimulus** effects. Thus the crowd at an athletic event might be a "social facilitator," raising the level of **irrelevant drive,** but a screaming crowd might also be a **distracting stimulus** as well. If performance were worse with such a crowd, it would be difffficult to know whether the motivational element (irrelevant drive) or the stimulus element (distracting noise) were the important determinant of performance. Both might be important.

In the face of such difficulties, Neiss (1988) argues that the inverted-U hypothesis is given only weak support in the motor performance literature. High arousal on one dimension (such as energetic-sleepy, or psyched up) might facilitate performance, but on another dimension (such as tensed-relaxed, or anxious) it might inhibit performance. We need to specify which kind of arousal is related to performance and an inverted-U.

Ideally, we would try to help an athlete adjust his or her level of motivation to the optimal level for his or her sport at a given time. Part of the art of coaching is to recognize when individual performers are not aroused enough or are too highly aroused. At the beginning of an important game, for example, players may be too highly aroused (too tense) and make errors, and the coach may call time out to calm down the players. Or a team may be so confident of winning that the coach must work hard to get the team aroused to optimum performance. One of the most important motivational insights that we can have about motivation and athletics is that the *highest possible level of arousal is seldom the best level of arousal for best performance.*

Self-regulation of arousal. Athletes themselves engage in various strategies to raise or lower their own arousal levels, just as people try to control their own anxiety or stress levels in other situations. Some athletes relax themselves with meditation before a contest, and others engage in relaxation exercises. Some pray. During the 1988 World Series, Dodgers pitcher Orel Hershiser sang hymns to himself in the dugout. Good athletes commonly engage in **thought stopping,** tuning out thoughts that would be disruptive or anxiety arousing in relation to performance. For example, a golfer who just shot a double-bogey cannot afford to dwell on that thought as she or he continues to play, nor can a player who makes an error in the World Series dwell on the error. Among world-class athletes of similar ability in any sport, the small edge gained by psychological training may be the difference between an Olympic medal and oblivion.

Aggression in Sports

Player aggression. Violent behavior is inherent in such contact sports as hockey and football, but it is also frequent in such "noncontact" sports as basketball and soccer. It is important to distinguish between **assertiveness** and **aggressiveness,** however. In everyday conversation, people often **label** "trying hard" as being "aggressive," not using the term "aggressive" in the more precise sense of intending to harm someone. Two players diving to the floor for a loose basketball may be *called* aggressive when in fact they are being assertive. An injury resulting from the collision would be incidental to the assertiveness, an unintended harm. In contrast, intentional elbowing under the basket may be done to intimidate an opponent by hurting him or her. Such intimidation and other harmful activities become more acceptable if we blur the distinction between assertion and aggression. It is, of course, difficult for an observer to say when harmful behavior is in fact aggressive, so such behaviors are even more likely to pass unchallenged.

Why does truly aggressive behavior occur in sports? Some aggressive behavior may be stimulus-induced, following a painful encounter, for example. The frustration-aggression hypothesis also makes much sense here. When a player or team is frustrated in attempts to win, aggression may ensue. The story is made more complicated, however, by **instrumental aggression**. In many sports, a certain degree of departure from the rules is allowed in order to maintain the flow of play. It is up to the referee(s) to keep play from getting out of hand. In important games, such as the NBA finals, referees are reluctant to "take the game out of the hands of the players" by too-frequent whistles. Under such conditions it is not uncommon for fights to erupt because players become frustrated but also because aggressive behavior may lead to greater success. Furthermore, fans, coaches, and fellow players often reward individual violent behavior. It is often said that hockey fans go more to see the fights than to see hockey. A hockey player on the bench may be expected to leap into a fight on the ice or be considered a coward or not a true team member if she or he fails to do so.

Fan aggression and mob behavior.   Chapter Ten presented two opposing views of the effects of observing violence: (1) Viewing is **cathartic** and reduces violence, and (2) observed violence is a **model** that leads to more violence. Considerable evidence suggests that the latter view is more nearly correct. For example, fans were interviewed before and after both the 1969 Army-Navy football game and the Army-Temple gymnastics meet held in the same month. There was a significant increase in reported hostility after the football game but not after the gymnastics meet, regardless of which team was supported (Goldstein & Arma, 1971). Similar results were found in a study of ice hockey and professional wrestling in contrast to swimming (Arma, Russell, & Sandelands, 1979). Such studies, along with casual observation, suggest that fan hostility increases with contact sports more than with noncontact sports. Player violence and fan violence may fuel each other. Soccer crowds have become so unruly on the European continent, especially when English teams are involved, that in 1985 several countries joined in a pact to reduce the violence. The critical incident was a riot between British and Italian fans in Belgium in which forty-one people were killed.

How can we account for such violent behavior? One reason offered for the Belgian riot was that the English fans came from an economically depressed area. They had time on their hands, their lives were dull, and they were livening things up for themselves. It is generally conceded that the English fans went to Belgium "looking for trouble." We may, then, partly account for the riot in terms of the frustration-aggression hypothesis. Frustrated in their everyday lives, the fans became aggressive elsewhere.

Fan violence is so often reported in soccer that it is sometimes considered the norm. In fact, however, fan violence in England and Europe is more a political problem than a sports problem. It is brought about by organized groups (e.g., the skinheads in England, and radical right-wing, neo-Nazi groups in Germany). The violence does not just erupt among fans of opposing sides, it is planned in advance, with battle plans drawn. In contrast, at the World Cup match between Mexico and Italy in Washington, D.C., in 1994, opposing fans took pictures with each other. They were just happy to be there.

There are other factors as well. The fans of one team may form a highly cohesive in-group that rejects outsiders, producing an "us versus them" feeling that is frequently related to aggressive behavior (Sherif et al., 1961). Fans of one team reinforce each other for behavior that leads to trouble, such as shouting obscenities at opposing fans. It is also easier to be anonymous in a crowd, so that the chances of being identified and caught for illegal behavior is reduced.

Interestingly, there is little fan violence in the United States. We talk about the Cameron Crazies (the Duke University students at home basketball games in Cameron Indoor Stadium), but in fact they (and many other fans) only **act** that way. It is what they do, not who they are. They are not violent. There are several possible reasons why Americans may be somewhat "better socialized" (if we are):

- Our professional teams rarely cross national boundaries for regular competition (only to Canada for baseball and basketball), and there are no long-term national rivalries along political lines as there are in Europe.
- We diffuse our allegiances among many sports (football, basketball, baseball, hockey, and so on, whereas other countries around the world tend to be more limited, mostly to soccer).
- Many of our major allegiances are with college teams rather than professional teams, with a continually shifting audience and players.
- The density of professional teams is much greater in many other countries. For example, England, a country about the size of Oregon, has twenty-two professional soccer teams at the highest level. Imagine that we have twenty professional football teams in any U.S. state: Where would we put them? What rivalries would develop?

Motivation for Watching Sports

The 1982 World Cup soccer match final drew an estimated 1.4 *billion* television viewers. Television advertising time during recent Superbowl games has sold for about $1 million a minute. Several cable TV networks now devote twenty-four hours a day to sports, and the major networks carry almost every sporting event of national interest. What is so attractive to viewers about sports?

Basking in the reflected glory of the home team.   Many viewers have a favorite team with which they can identify. When the "home team" (which might be the Atlanta Braves, which calls itself "America's Team" wins, its fans feel proud and happy; when it loses, they are mightily unhappy. The depth of this feeling is shown by the harassment of coaches who lose too often, as if the fans themselves had been the losers. This possibility may be true. The fans may have their self-esteem lowered if their team performs badly because they feel that losing somehow reflects on them. At the very least, their team losing does reflect on their ability to choose a winning team to support. The "national pride" of "winning" the Olympics and the "shame" of not winning highlights this whole phenomenon.

Watching sports for arousal. Many people go to sporting events because of the excitement of the crowd, the thrill of "being there." Sporting events, like movies, are also a **stimulus change,** a variation in the everyday routine of life and an opportunity for **affiliation** with one's friends.

Sport as art. Such events as gymnastics, diving, and figure skating are judged by artistic standards as well as by athletic ones. In gymnastics there are required moves, demonstrating strength and balance, for example, but within these limits the ease and grace with which the moves are performed also determine the winner. Ballet movements and choreography have indeed become integral to gymnastics and figure skating. To a considerable extent, particular athletes gain a following because of the artistic manner in which they perform. A balletic action slam dunk by Michael Jordan is a work of art by any standard.

Environment and Performance

Social facilitation. If you have ever stood in front of an audience and been afraid or excited, you have an idea of the effect of an audience on athletic performance. An audience may be just another competitor, or it may be a stadium full of people. Attempts to break track records invariably involve competition because runners run faster with competition, and a loud supportive audience is also an asset.

Audience effects depend on the type of activity, however. For well-learned or simple skills, an audience should improve performance. For complex or not-well-learned skills, an audience may make performance worse (see Chapter Six). Most observers seem surprised when a very young competitor does well at a great sporting event, such as Wimbledon or the U.S. Open in tennis. We may equate the pressure with social facilitation. But these young players have been playing tournament tennis from very early ages, are used to large audiences, and therefore were probably not as aroused as some other players their age might have been.

Home-field advantage. It is widely held that there is a home-field advantage in sports, which might might be due to a supportive home crowd

("We've got to get the crowd into the game"), the disadvantages of traveling (especially in professional sports that have long road trips, such as baseball and basketball), or peculiarities of the field or court (e.g., a domed stadium). It was sometimes alleged that the Boston Celtics had a home-court advantage in the old Boston Garden because they knew the dead spots on the parquet floor! What do the data show about home-field advantage?

In general, the home-field advantage is relatively slight. Courneya and Carron (1991) examined 1,812 Double A baseball games and found that the home team won 55 percent of the games. However, this finding was unrelated to travel per se. The results were not predicted by such factors as length of home stand or visitor's road trip. Gayton and Coombs (1995) also concluded that the effects of travel on the home-court advantage was minimal in high school basketball games. Acker (1997) examined 1,568 professional football games between 1988 and 1994 and found that the home team outscored the opponent by 2.91 points. There was a slightly greater home-field advantage for teams with domed stadiums (3.22 points) as compared with open stadiums (3.01 points). There appears to be no single overwhelming factor determining home-field advantage.

Home field disadvantage? Baumeister and Steinhilber (1984) suggested that a supportive home crowd might actually be disadvantageous to a team because the players might be more self-conscious and distracted from what they are doing. They found that in baseball World Series, home teams tend to win early games but to lose the final games, especially when these games were decisive for winning the series. Benjafield, Liddell, and Benjafield (1989), however, disputed the generality of a home-field disadvantage and said that it was true only for championship series involving the New York Yankees, the Boston Celtics (so much for the parquet floor), and the Montreal Canadiens. They suggest that the home crowds of persistent champions (as these teams were) communicate a pressure to win that interferes with these teams. This pressure might lead to heightened self-awareness or could be due to overarousal.

MOTIVATION AND ADVERTISING

The Communication Model

One of the most frequently used psychological frameworks for advertising is the **communication model** of attitude change and persuasion (e.g., Faison, 1980; Petty & Cacioppo, 1984). Advertising, of course, is the attempt to persuade people to buy some product, commonly assuming that sales will be greater if attitudes toward the product are more positive. The model says, briefly, that the **source** of communication (sender) **encodes** an idea into a

message that is transmitted to an **audience** (receiver) that **decodes** the message. Researchers have systematically studied characteristics of the source, message, and audience to determine what makes persuasive messages effective. We briefly outline some of the main findings of such research and then turn to the relevant motivational/emotional factors related to advertising.

1. The two most important **source characteristics** are **credibility** (a combination of trustworthiness and expertise) and **likability**.

2. **Message** characteristics are very complex, depending on the nature of the medium (e.g., visual, written, or oral), the type of arguments presented (one-sided versus two-sided), the order of presentation of arguments, and logical versus emotional appeals.

3. **Audience** characteristics include interest in and knowledge of the topic, and mood (which we may take to include motivational/emotional states in general).

The Source

The primary purpose of appealing to motives in advertising is to attract **attention** to a product or to make a product **more favorable** (Petty & Cacioppo, 1984). Since the prospective audience is faced with literally hundreds of advertisements competing for attention, the advertiser's problem is to make its ad more attention-getting in some way. Other factors then determine whether a product will be purchased.

One method of increasing *apparent* source credibility is to have actors or actresses portray characters who symbolize credibility and honesty. The general assumption is that the *association* of the product with the credible or likable character will add credibility or likability to the product. This is classical conditioning at work. Thus, Robert Young, an actor well-known to TV audiences for his portrayal of a medical doctor, advertised Maxwell House coffee. Similarly, "Four out of five doctors prefer . . . (fill in the name of your favorite across-the-counter medical product)." Joe Namath, a football hero and all-around likable character, advertised popcorn poppers and panty hose (which he wore in TV commercials). General Mills puts famous athletes on the front of Wheaties packages. Perfumes (including men's), clothes, and other products have famous people associated with them, shoes are associated with athletes, and so on.

Such ads have been considered most effective in changing viewer attitudes, however, when the viewer is not greatly involved with the product (Petty, Cacioppo, & Schumann, 1983). Panty hose and popcorn poppers would seem to be in this category. Advertisements in recent years, however, have also used such celebrities to promote sales of automobiles, which are products that bear a hefty price tag and do have considerable consumer "involvement."

Research dating back to the 1950s (Hovland & Weiss, 1957) indicates that a source is more effective if he or she argues *against* his or her own self-interest and does not appear to be trying to influence us. If the source puts on a "hard sell" too strongly, the audience may react against the message. If people believe that they are being coerced or manipulated, they tend to react negatively. Obviously, a person in an ad *is* trying to sell the product, but this intention can be softened in various ways. For example, the ad may show apparently unsolicited testimonials for the product, the source of the message apparently not trying to sell. The viewer does not know how many people had to be filmed to get one unsolicited testimonial, and such "soft sells" may avoid reactance.

The Message

Approach arousal.   Sex in advertising is a time-honored way to attract attention to the ad. Semiclad buxom females are associated with everything from shoes to motorcycles. The "Maidenform woman" and her brassieres have been around for years, but more recently ads for blue jeans and undershorts have drawn attention to other parts of the anatomy. Sex does not necessarily have a favorable result in advertising, however. In a study in which different versions of the same ad showed different amounts of clothing on a female model, it was found that explicit nudity lowered the perceived quality of either body oil or ratchet sets (Peterson & Kerin, 1977). A more modest but still sexy model enhanced body oil but not ratchet sets. Thus moderately sexy advertisements may enhance products for which an attractive body is relevant to the ad (such as body oil) but not if it is irrelevant (such as with tool kits). The Maidenform woman, of course, wears the relevant product, and rounded derrieres are covered by the denim product advertised. Too-explicit sexual advertising may arouse negative responses from viewers, regardless of the product. Latour and Henthorne (1994) showed 199 adults in a shopping mall two different advertisements, one having a strong overt theme and the other a mild sexual theme. Regardless of their gender, respondents did not like the strongly sexual ads. What is considered *too* explicit by the viewing audience, however, does change with the times, and this factor has to be judged by continual research. Nudity is far more acceptable now than, say, twenty-five years ago.

Fear arousal.   Traders in persuasive messages have long debated the value of negative emotional appeals in advertising. It would appear, for example, that health products could be sold more effectively if a certain amount of fear were introduced into the product advertising. The difficulties in doing this, however, are made obvious by the relative ineffectiveness of the Surgeon General's warnings on cigarette packages to cut down on cigarette consumption. Fear of lung cancer seems not to deter a great percentage of smokers. To the extent that fear arousal is effective, two fairly simple rules may be followed (Secord & Backman, 1974):

1. **"Action instructions"** (what to do) are not very effective without any fear arousal at all, but a small amount of arousal is about as effective as a large

amount. Very strong fear arousal may, indeed, produce a defensive reaction such that the viewer puts the whole issue out of his or her mind. Faison (1980, p. 244) describes an audience reaction test to two different toothpaste commercials. One of them simply showed that a person using Brand X for a long time had few cavities. The other commercial showed acid dripping on a tooth, and the tooth disintegrating before the viewers' eyes. The product name associated with this fearsome scene was less well remembered than with the more mundane scene, apparently because the scene was so aversive that the viewers tuned out the name of the product.

2. **Fear arousal is more effective if the action proposed is something that will reduce the fear.** An effective tire advertisement showed a woman on a lonely road gazing at a flat tire on her car. The caption said, "When there's no man around, Goodyear should be" (Kleppner, 1977). Two aspects of this ad are important. First, there is a small amount of fear arousal about the consequences of not having good tires. Second, there is something suggested that the viewer can do, that is, buy Goodyear tires. Fear arousal without instructions on how to reduce fear is just fear arousal.

The Audience

The motivational state of the consumer audience may determine the effectiveness of an advertisement. For example, an ad for a cold remedy is much less likely to influence your purchase if you do not have a cold. But if you have a sniffly cold in the middle of winter, a TV commercial with a well-known actor extolling the virtues of a cold medicine may be very effective. In politics the audience for a political speech is often "warmed up" by food and drink to make it more receptive to the candidate's message.

Subliminal Advertising

Who believes in it?   Every few years the question arises whether persuasive techniques, including advertising, can be effective without people's being aware of them. This is known as **subliminal advertising,** using stimuli below the threshold for conscious awareness. Two different studies have looked at the extent to which people are familiar with it and believe that it is effective and/or being used. Zanot (1983) in a telephone survey found that 81 percent of 209 respondents had knowledge of subliminal advertising and believed that it was being used. Two-thirds thought that it was unethical. Well-educated individuals were more likely to have heard of it. Rogers and Smith (1993) interviewed 400 people by telephone and found that 74 percent had heard of subliminal advertising, 61 percent believed that it is used by advertisers, and 45 percent believed that it would affect whether they would buy the product. Again, respondents with more education believed more strongly that subliminal advertising works. The numbers vary in these two studies, but in both studies, the percentages of people who believe that subliminal advertising is effective are impressive. What, then, do the data show about effectiveness?

How effective is it? The most notorious claims came in 1957 when a theater manager said he had flashed slides saying BUY POPCORN on the screen during the showing of a film. Supposedly the slide presentations were so brief that the audience was not consciously aware of them. He claimed a dramatic increase in popcorn sales as a result. The spectre of such powerful mind control caused something of a furor, and bills making subliminal advertising illegal were even introduced into Congress. A number of good experimental psychologists also went to their laboratories to research the subject, with the result that no one could substantiate the original claims. For example, subjects "subliminally" subjected to the word "beef" did not subsequently choose beef in preference to other meat sandwiches (Byrne, 1959). In a field study, local TV stations participated by sending out messages in the manner described for the "buy popcorn" report. Telephone surveys taken immediately afterwards showed no effect of these messages on any kind of viewer behavior. Research on this topic so repeatedly came up dry that Dixon (1971) was prompted to say that he knew of no evidence to support the "buy popcorn" effect. There has been no evidence for the effect since then, either. Three different analyses of available research results concluded that any such effects are minimal, if present at all (Trappey, 1996; Theus, 1994; and Moore, 1983). The dates of these reviews indicate that the yield has not improved with time. Other research on subliminal stimulation generally supports the negative results with advertising research, including research on self-help tapes.

Self-Help Tapes

For a few dollars, you can buy audio tapes to play throughout the day and that supposedly carry subliminal messages to your brain. These messages range from telling you how to gain self-confidence, to being less anxious, to how to play better golf. Sometimes these messages are disguised by music that you can enjoy. Sometimes it is claimed that there are *only* subliminal messages and that these will help you. Do they work? In an extensive field experiment, the effectiveness of several such tapes was studied (Greenwald, Spangenberg, Pratkanis, & Eskenazi, 1991). Greenwald et al. used commercially available tapes sold with the claims of improving either memory or self-esteem. The experiment was done under realistic conditions, following manufacturers' instructions. The subjects used the tapes for a month and then were tested for both their **real effects** on the subjects and for **the effects that the subjects perceived to have happened.** What the subjects did not know was that the tapes were labeled in different ways and that the subjects had been randomly assigned to the different labeling conditions with a double-blind procedure. That is, neither the person giving out the tapes to the subjects nor the subjects knew what the real content of the tapes was. For some subjects, self-esteem tapes were labeled "self-esteem," but for others they were labeled "memory." Similarly, memory tapes were labeled either "memory" or "self-esteem." Following the month's use of a tape, each subject completed several tests of self-esteem and of memory.

The results were that the subjects showed significant effects of listening to the tapes but that these effects resulted from the **labels** on the tapes, not the **contents** of the tapes. They showed better memory if the tapes were labeled memory than if they were labeled self-esteem, but actual tape content made no difference. Presumably the same effects could have been obtained with any tape content as long as the buyer knew the tape label. Had the subjects actually purchased and used these tapes, they probably would have been pleased with what they thought were the results—even though those results did not actually occur.

Actually, psychologists had been researching the topics of perception and persuasion for many years prior to the popcorn claim, and there was no reason to believe that so-called subliminal (below-threshold) messages should have been effective. First, whether or not *consciously* perceived, a message would have to get through the eyes and into the nervous system in order to affect behavior. It is doubtful that such messages could be received with brief flashes of a slide mixed in with thousands of other unrelated movie frames. Second, even if the signal did reach the nervous system, there is no reason to expect that a viewer should perform like a robot to go out and buy anything. Although we may perceive some messages via stimuli of near-threshold intensity or duration, such effects are difficult-to-achieve laboratory phenomena obtained under very restricted conditions. The most recent claims of any *behavioral* effects of such messages (e.g., Silverman, 1982) have been severely challenged on grounds of weak methodology and the failure of other researchers to reproduce the phenomena (Balay & Shevrin, 1988). The general conclusion to be reached about subliminal advertising is that it is truly a subliminal phenomenon. This is not to say that subliminal stimuli have no effects on us. We have already seen that they do. The data do suggest, however, that such effects are relatively narrow. They do not seem to be strong enough to support the claims that subliminal advertisers have made. Given the apparent widespread belief in subliminal advertising, however, the topic calls for continued research.

Summary

1. **Job motivation** refers to those motivational variables that influence worker productivity. **Job satisfaction** refers to worker attitudes (positive or negative) toward the job.

2. Many "theories" of worker behavior have been more philosophical than scientific. McGregor distinguished two broadly different approaches to worker motivation. **Theory X,** representing traditional views, assumes that workers dislike work and have to be coerced to do it. **Theory Y,** a more modern view, empha-

sizes that workers want self-satisfaction from work, which includes responsibility and autonomy.

3. Maslow's **need hierarchy theory** distinguishes physiological, safety, belongingness, self-esteem, and self-actualization needs. The latter become more dominant when the former have been satisfied. Research evidence supports only a two-level approach, however (combining the first three and the last two needs into two separate groupings).

4. **Expectancy theories,** much like achievement theory, emphasize workers' perceptions of the probabilities and values of successfully completing some job. Vroom's **instrumentality theory** emphasizes the importance of workers' perceptions that a given behavior will be instrumental in obtaining a desired goal.

5. **Equity theory** emphasizes workers' desires to get an equitable return for work done. What is considered equitable may be based on some internal standard or on some external reference, such as what another worker gets for doing similar work. Perceived inequity produces tension, which a worker may try to reduce by working less hard, trying to get more money, and so on.

6. **Goal-setting theory** emphasizes setting **high** (but reachable) and **specific** goals, and giving feedback about whether these goals are being achieved.

7. Job **satisfaction** is only partly related to job **productivity.** Performance that leads to rewards produces satisfaction, which leads to the expectation that future performance will also lead to rewards. Job satisfaction alone does not greatly increase productivity.

8. Theories accounting for job satisfaction include **instrumentality theory, equity theory,** and **job characteristics** theory.

9. The motivation for engaging in sports activities is much the same as for other activities: to provide arousal, achievement and competition, self-expression, and social rewards such as affiliation. After about age twelve, there is a sharp decline in participation in organized sports as children see that they are not mastering their sport.

10. An important problem for competitors is to achieve the **optimal level of motivation** for a sport. The optimal level of arousal varies with the kind of sport (e.g., golf has a lower optimal level than football), and many athletes learn effectively to increase or decrease their own arousal levels to make them more optimal.

11. Player **aggression** in sports may occur as the result of **frustration** or **pain** that occur during the course of play (stimulus aroused aggression), and because players and fans **reinforce** aggressive behavior, which is instrumental to winning.

12. Some of the reasons why people watch sports are that they feel good if the team they identify with is successful, they enjoy the excitement of the contest, and the contest provides opportunity for affiliation with others. Fan aggression more severe than player aggression is sometimes stimulated by athletic contests.

13. The **environment,** including arena and fans, may influence athletes. Arousal level may be increased because of social facilitation effects of an audience, sometimes thought to be an actual disadvantage of playing at home. There seems to be relatively little home-field advantage.

14. A framework for encompassing many aspects of advertising is the **communication model,** which looks upon persuasive communications from the points of view of a **source,** a **message,** and an **audience.**

15. The two most important source characteristics are **credibility** and **likability.** Advertisers try to capitalize on these by using as sources people who give the ap-

pearance of credibility or who are popular celebrities. A source is also considered to be more effective if she or he does not appear to be trying to influence the audience too heavily.

16. A major emotional content of advertising messages is sexual, but research suggests that moderate sexuality that is relevant to the product advertised is most effective. Too-explicit nudity or sexual connotations for irrelevant products may backfire and engender negative attitudes toward an ad.

17. Some **fear arousal** in advertising may be effective if accompanied by instructions about what to do to reduce the threat that produces the fear. Overly strong fear arousal may simply cause the audience to tune out the message.

18. The **motivational state** or **mood** of an audience modifies the effect of an advertising message. A person with a cold is more likely to pay attention to cold remedy ads.

19. Claims have been made that **subliminal advertising** is a powerful tool for influencing consumers. There is virtually no evidence, however, that advertising messages below the level of conscious awareness have any unique influence on consumer behavior.

References

———●———

ABRAMSON, L. Y., SELIGMAN, M. E. P., & TEASDALE, J. (1978). Learned helplessness in humans: Critique and reformulation. *Journal of Abnormal Psychology, 87,* 49–74.

ACKER, J. C. (1997). Location variations in professional football. *Journal of Sport Behavior, 20,* 247–259.

ADAMETZ, J. H. (1959). Rate of recovery of functioning in cats with rostral reticular lesions. *Journal of Neurosurgery, 16,* 85–98.

ADAMS, J. S. (1975). Inequity in social exchange. In R. M. Steers & L. W. Porter (Eds.), *Motivation and work behavior.* New York: McGraw-Hill.

ADORNO, T. W., FRENKEL-BRUNSWIK, E., LEVINSON, D. J., & SANFORD, R. N. (1950). *The authoritarian personality.* New York: Harper & Brothers.

ALCOTT, J. (1979). *Animal behavior: An evolutionary approach* (2nd ed.). Sunderland, M.: Sinauer Associates, Inc.

ALLEY, T. R., & CUNNINGHAM, M. R. (1991). Averaged faces are attractive, but attractive faces are not average. *Psychological Science, 2,* 123–125.

ALLPORT, G. (1937). *Personality: A psychological interpretation.* New York: Holt.

AMSEL, A. (1958). The role of frustrative nonreward in noncontinuous reward situations. *Psychological Bulletin, 55,* 102–119.

AMSEL, A. (1962). Frustrative nonreward in partial reinforcement and discrimination learning: Some recent history and a theoretical extension. *Psychological Review, 69,* 306–328.

AMSEL, A. (1968). Secondary reinforcement and frustration. *Psychological Bulletin, 69,* 278.

AMSEL, A. (1992). *Frustration theory.* New York: Cambridge University Press.

AMSEL, A., & ROUSSEL, J. (1952). Motivational properties of frustration: I. Effect on running response of the addition of frustration to the motivational complex. *Journal of Experimental Psychology, 43,* 363–368.

ANDERSON, G., & ANDERSON, D. (1984). Ambient temperature and violent crimes: Tests of the linear and curvilinear hypotheses. *Journal of Personality and Social Psychology, 46,* 91–97.

ANDERSON, K. J. (1994). Impulsivity, caffeine, and task difficult: A within-subjects test of the Yerkes-Dodson Law. *Personality and Individual Differences*, 16, 813–829.

ANDERSON, R., MANOOGIAN, S., & REZNICK, S. (1976). The undermining and enhancing of intrinsic motivation in preschool children. *Journal of Personality and Social Psychology, 34*, 915–922.

ANDERSSON, B. (1952). Polydipsia caused by intrahypothalamic injections of hypertonic NaCl solutions. *Experientia, 8,* 157–158.

ANGER, D. (1963). The role of temporal discrimination in the reinforcement of Sidman avoidance behavior. *Journal of the Experimental Analysis of Behavior, 6,* 477–506.

ARDREY, R. *The territorial imperative.* New York: Dell, 1966.

ARMA, R., RUSSELL, G., & SANDELANDS, M. (1979). Effects of the hostility of spectators on viewing aggressive sports. *Social Psychology Quarterly, 42,* 274–279.

ARONOFF, J., BARCLAY, A. M., & STEVENSON, L. A. (1988). The recognition of threatening facial stimuli. *Journal of Personality and Social Psychology, 54,* 647–655.

Aronoff, J., Woike, B.A., & Hyman, L .M. (1992). Which are the stimuli in facial displays of anger and happiness? Configurational bases of emotion recognition. *Journal of Personality and Social Psychology, 62*(6), 1050–1066.

ARONSON, E. (1968). Dissonance theory: Progress and problems. In R. P. Abelson, E. Aronson, W. J. McGuire, T. M. Newcomb, M. J. Rosenberg, & P. H. Tannenbaum (Eds.), *Theories of cognitive consistency: A sourcebook.* Chicago: Rand McNally.

ARTHUR, A. Z. (1986). Stress of predictable and unpredictable shock. *Psychological Bulletin, 100,* 379–383.

ASCH, S. E. (1946). Forming impressions of personality. *Journal of Abnormal and Social Psychology, 41,* 258–290.

ASCH, S. (1951). Effects of group pressure upon the modification and distortion of judgment. In Z. H. Guetzkokw (Ed.), *Groups, leadership, and men.* Pittsburgh: Carnegie.

ASERINSKY, E., & KLEITMAN, N. (1953). Regularly occurring periods of eye motility and concomitant phenomena during sleep. *Science, 118,* 273.

ATKINSON, J. W. (1958). *Motives in fantasy, action, and society.* New York: D. Van Nostrand.

ATKINSON, J. W. (1964). *An introduction to motivation.* New York: D. Van Nostrand.

ATKINSON, J. W., & BIRCH, D. (1970). *The dynamics of action.* New York: Wiley.

ATKINSON, J. W., & BIRCH, D. (1978). *Introduction to motivation* (2nd ed.). New York: D. Van Nostrand.

ATKINSON, J. W., BONGORT, K., & PRICE, L. H. (1977). Explorations using computer simulation to comprehend TAT measurement of motivation. *Motivation and Emotion, 1,* 1–27.

ATKINSON, J. W., HEYNS, R. W., & VEROFF, J. (1954). The effect of experimental arousal of the affiliation motive on thematic apperception. *Journal of Abnormal and Social Psychology, 49,* 405–410.

ATKINSON, J. W., & LITWIN, G. H. (1960). Achievement motive and test anxiety conceived as motive to approach success and motive to avoid failure. *Journal of Abnormal and Social Psychology,* 60, 52–63.

ATKINSON, J. W., & WALKER, E. L. (1956). The affiliation motive and perceptual sensitivity to faces. *Journal of Abnormal and Social Psychology, 53,* 38–41.

AVERILL, J. (1978). Anger. In H. E. Howe & R. A. Dienstbier (Eds.), *Nebraska Symposium on Motivation: 1978.* Lincoln: University of Nebraska Press.

AVERILL, J. (1982). *Anger and aggression: An essay on emotion.* New York: Springer-Verlag.

AVERILL, J. (1983). Studies on anger and aggression: Implications for theories of emotion. *American Psychologist, 38,* 1145–1160.

AZRIN, N. H., & HOLZ, W. C. (1966). Punishment. In W. K. Honig (Ed.), *Operant behavior: Areas of research and application.* New York: Appleton-Century-Crofts.

BAEYENS, F., EELEN, P., & VAN DEN BERGH, O. (1990). Contingency awareness in evaluative conditioning: A case for unaware effective-evaluative learning. *Cognition and Emotion, 4,* 3–18.

BAILEY, C. J. (1955). The effectiveness of drives as cues. *Journal of Comparative and Physiological Psychology, 48,* 183–187.

BALAY, J., & SHEVRIN, H. (1988). The subliminal psychodynamic activation method: A critical review. *American Psychologist, 43,* 161–174.

BANDURA, A. (1973). *Aggression: A social learning analysis.* Englewood Cliffs, NJ: Prentice-Hall, Inc.

BANDURA, A. (1977). Self-efficacy: Toward a unifying theory of behavioral change. *Psychological Review, 84,* 191–215.

BANDURA, A. (1982). Self-efficacy mechanism in human agency. *American Psychologist, 37,* 122–147.

BANDURA, A., ROSS, D., & ROSS, S. A. (1963). Imitation of film-mediated aggressive models. *Journal of Abnormal and Social Psychology, 66,* 3–11.

BARASH, D. P. (1978). *Sociobiology and behavior.* New York: Elsevier.

BARON, R. A., BYRNE, D. (1977). *Social psychology: Understanding human interaction.* Boston: Allyn and Bacon.

BARON, R. A., & BYRNE, D. (1997). *Social psychology,* 8th ed. Boston: Allyn and Bacon.

BAUMEISTER, R. F., & LEARY, M. R. (1995). The need to belong: Desire for interpersonal attachments as a fundamental human motivation. *Psychological Bulletin, 117,* 497–529.

BAUMEISTER, R. F., & STEINHILBER, A. (1984). Paradoxical effects of supportive audiences on performance under pressure: The home field disadvantage in sports championships. *Journal of Personality and Social Psychology, 47,* 85–93.

BEACH, F. A. (1942). Analysis of factors involved in the arousal, maintenance, and manifestation of sexual excitement in male animals. *Psychosomatic Medicine, 4,* 173–179.

BEACH, F. A. (1955). The descent of instinct. *Psychological Review, 62,* 401–410.

BEACH, F. A. (1969). Locks and beagles. *American Psychologist, 24,* 971–989.

BEAMER, W., BERMONT, G., & CLEGG, M. (1969). Copulatory behavior of the ram, *Ovis aries.* II. Factors affecting copulatory satiety. *Animal Behavior, 17,* 706–711.

BECK, A. T. (1967). *Depression: Clinical, experimental and theoretical aspects.* New York: Harper and Row.

BECK, A. T. (1976). *Cognitive therapy and the emotional disorders.* New York: International Universities Press.

BECK, A. T., & RUSH, A. J. (1980). A cognitive model of anxiety formation and anxiety reduction. In C. D. Spielberger & I. W. Sarason (Eds.), *Stress and anxiety* (Vol 10, pp. 349–365).

BECK, R. C. (1961). On secondary reinforcement and shock termination. *Psychological Bulletin, 58,* 28–45.

BECK, R. C. (1978). *Motivation: Theories and principles* (first edition). Englewood Cliffs, NJ: Prentice Hall.

BECK, R. C. (1990). *Motivation: Theories and principles* (3rd ed.). Englewood Cliffs, NJ: Prentice-Hall.

BECK, R. C., & BIDWELL, L. D. (1974). Incentive properties of sucrose and saccharin under different deprivation conditions. *Learning and Motivation, 5,* 328–335.

BECK, R. C., GIBSON, C., ELLIOT, W., SIMMONS, C., MATTESON, N., & McDANIEL, L. (1988). False physiological feedback and emotion. *Motivation and Emotion, 12,* 217–256.

Beck, R. C., & Godfrey, E. (1998). Aversive conditioning with pleasant and unpleasant schematic facial configurations as conditioned stimuli. Unpublished research.

BECK, R. C., & MEINRATH, A. (1978). *Some physiological variables related to incentive motivation.* Paper presented at the 86th Annual Convention of the American Psychological Association, Toronto, Canada.

BECK, R. C., NASH, R., VIERNSTEIN, L., & GORDON, L. (1972). Sucrose preferences of hungry and thirsty rats as a function of duration of presentation of test solutions. *Journals of Comparative and Physiological Psychology, 78,* 40–50.

BECK, S. B., WARD-HULL, C., & McLEAR, P. M. (1976). Variables related to women's somatic preferences of the male and female body. *Journal of Personality and Social Psychology, 34,* 1200–1210.

BELL, P. A., FISHER, J. D., & LOOMIS, R. J. (1978). *Environmental psychology.* Philadelphia: W. B. Saunders.

BELL, R. W., NOAH, J. C., & DAVIS, J. R., JR. (1965). Interactive effects of shock intensity and delay of reinforcement on escape conditioning. *Psychonomic Science, 3,* 505–506.

BELLOWS, R. T. (1939). Time factors in water drinking in dogs. *American Journal of Physiology, 125,* 87–97.

BEM, D. J. (1967). Self-perception: An alternative interpretation of cognitive dissonance phenomena. *Psychological Review, 74,* 183–200.

BEM, D. J. (1970). *Beliefs, attitudes, and human affairs.* Monterey, CA: Brooks/Cole.

BEM, D. J. (1972). Self-perception theory. In L. Berkowitz (Ed.), *Advances in experimental social psychology* (Vol. 6). New York: Academic.

BENJAFIELD, J., LIDDELL, W. W., & BENJAFIELD, I. (1989). Is there a home field disadvantage in professional sports championships? *Social Behavior and Personality, 17,* 45–50.

BENTLEY, D. R. (1977) Control of cricket song patterns by descending interneurons. *Journal of Comparative Physiology,* 19–38.

BENTLEY, D. R., & HOY, R. R. (1972). Genetic control of the neuronal network generating cricket song patterns. *Animal Behavior, 20,* 478–492.

BERKELEY, G. (1939). Principles of human knowledge. In E. A. Burtt (Ed.), *The English philosophers from Bacon to Mill.* New York: Modern Library. (Original work published 1710)

BERKOWITZ, L. (1974). Some determinants of impulsive aggression: Role of mediated associations with reinforcements for aggression. *Psychological Review, 81,* 165–176.

BERKOWITZ, L. (1983). Aversively stimulated aggression: Some parallels and differences in research with animals and humans. *American Psychologist, 38,* 1135–1144.

BERKOWITZ, L. (1984). Some effects of thoughts on anti- and prosocial influences of media events: A cognitive-neoassociation analysis. *Psychological Bulletin, 95,* 410–427.

BERKOWITZ, L. (1988). Frustrations, appraisals, and aversively stimulated aggression. *Aggressive Behavior, 14*(1), 3–11.

BERKOWITZ, L., & LE PAGE, A. (1967). Weapons as aggression-eliciting stimuli. *Journal of Personality and Social Psychology, 7,* 202–207.

BERLYNE, D. E. (1958). The influence of complexity and novelty in visual figures as orienting responses. *Journal of Experimental Psychology, 55,* 289–296.

BERLYNE, D. E. (1960). *Conflict, arousal, and curiosity.* New York: McGraw-Hill.

BERLYNE, D. E. (1970). Novelty, complexity and hedonic value. *Perception and Psychophysics, 8,* 279–286.

BERLYNE, D. E. (1971). *Aesthetics and psychobiology.* New York: Appleton-Century-Crofts.

BERMAN, M. E., & COCCARO, E. F. (1998). Neurobiological correlates of violence: Relevance to criminal responsibility. *Behavioral Sciences & the Law, 16,* 303–318.

BERMOND, B., NIEUWENHUYSE, B., FASOTTI, L., & SCHUERMAN, J. (1991). Spinal cord lesions, peripheral feedback, and intensities of emotional feelings. *Cognition and Emotion, 5,* 201–220.

BERNARD, C. (1957). *An introduction to the study of experimental medicine* (H. C. Greene, Trans.). New York: Dover. (Original work published 1865)

BERNARDIS, L. L., & BELLINGER, L. L. (1996). The lateral hypothalamic area revisited: Ingestive behavior. *Neuroscience and Biobehavioral Reviews, 20,* 189–287.

BERRIDGE, K. C. (1991). Modulation of taste affect by hunger, caloric satiety, and sensory-specific satiety in the rat. *Appetite, 16,* 103–120.

BERRIDGE, K. C. (1996). Food reward: Brain substrates of wanting and liking. *Neuroscience & Biobehavioral Reviews, 20,* 1–25.

BERSCHEID, E., & WALSTER, E. H. (1969). *Interpersonal attraction.* Reading, MA: Addison-Wesley.

BETTLEHEIM, B. (1960). *The informed heart.* New York: The Free Press.

BEXTON, W. H., HERON, W., & SCOTT, T. H. (1954). Effects of decreased variation in the sensory environment. *Canadian Journal of Psychology, 8,* 70–76.

BINDRA, D. (1969). The interrelated mechanisms of reinforcement and motivation, and the nature of their influence on response. In W. J. Arnold & D. Levine (Eds.), *Nebraska symposium on motivation.* Lincoln: University of Nebraska Press.

BINDRA, D. (1978). How adaptive behavior is produced: A perceptual-motivational alternative to response-reinforcement. *The Behavioral and Brain Sciences, 1,* 41–91.

BINDRA, D., & PALFAI, T. (1967). Nature of positive and negative incentive-motivational effects on general activity. *Journal of Comparative and Physiological Psychology, 52,* 165–166.

BIRCH, L. L., & FISHER, J. A. (1996). The role of experience in the development of children's eating behavior. In E.D. Capaldi (Ed.), *Why we eat what we eat: The psychology of eating.* Washington, DC: American Psychological Association

BITTERMAN, M. E. (1967). Learning in animals. In H. Helson & W. Bevan (Eds.), *Contemporary approaches to psychology.* New York: Van Nostrand.

BLACK, A. H., CARLSON, N. J., & SOLOMON, R. L. (1962). Exploratory studies of the conditioning of autonomic responses on curarized dogs. *Psychological Monographs, 76,* (Whole No. 548).

BLACK, R. W. (1969). Incentive motivation and the parameters of reward in instrumental conditioning. In W. J. Arnold & D. Levine (Eds.), *Nebraska symposium on motivation.* Lincoln: University of Nebraska Press.

BLANEY, P. H. (1986). Affect and memory: A review. *Psychological Bulletin, 99,* 229–246.

BOLLES, R. C. (1967). *Theory of motivation.* New York: Harper & Row.

BOLLES, R. C. (1970). Species-specific defense reactions and avoidance learning. *Psychological Review, 71,* 32–48.

BOLLES, R. C. (1972). Reinforcement, expectancy, and learning. *Psychological Review, 79,* 394–409.

BOLLES, R. C. (1975). *Theory of motivation* (2nd ed.). New York: Harper & Row.

BOLLES, R. C. (Ed.) (1991). *The hedonics of taste.* Hillsdale, NJ: Lawrence Erlbaum Associates.

BOLLES, R. C., & MOOT, S. A. (1972). Derived motives. *Annual Review of Psychology, 23,* 51–72.

BOULZE, D., MONTRATRUC, P., & CABANAC, M. (1983). Water intake, pleasure and water intake in humans. *Physiology and Behavior, 30,* 97–102.

BOWER, G. H. (1981). Mood and memory. *American Psychologist, 36,* 129–148.

BOWER, G. H., FOWLER, H., & TRAPOLD, M. A. (1959). Escape learning as a function of amount of shock reduction. *Journal of Experimental Psychology, 58,* 482–484.

BOWER, G. H., MCLEAN, J., & MEACHAM, J. (1966). Value of knowing when reinforcement is due. *Journal of Comparative and Physiological Psychology, 62,* 183–192.

BOWLBY, J. (1969). *Attachment and loss* (Vol. 1. Attachment). London: Hogarth.

BOWMAN, C. H. & Fishbein, M. (1978). Understanding public reaction to energy proposals: An application of the Fishbein model. *Journal of Applied Social Psychology, 8,* 319–340.

BOYATZIS, R. E. (1973). Affiliation motivation, In D. C. McClelland & R. S. Steel (Eds.), *Human motivation: A book of readings.* Morristown, NJ: General Learning Press.

BRADY, J. V. (1958). Ulcers in "executive" monkeys. *Scientific American, 199,* 95–100.

BREHM, J. W. (1962). Motivational effects of cognitive dissonance. *Nebraska symposium on motivation.* Lincoln: University of Nebraska Press.

BREHM, J. W., & COHEN, A. R. (1962). *Explorations in cognitive dissonance.* New York: Wiley.

BREHM, S. S. (1985). *Intimate relationships.* New York: Random House.

BRELAND, K., & BRELAND, M. (1961). The misbehavior of organisms. *American Psychologist, 16,* 681–684.

BRIDGMAN, P. W. (1927). *The logic of modern physics.* New York: Macmillan.

BROADHURST, P. L. (1957). Emotionality and the Yerkes-Dodson Law. *Journal of Experimental Psychology, 54,* 345–352.

BROGDEN, W. J., LIPMAN, E. A., & CULLER, E. (1938). The role of incentive in conditioning and learning. *American Journal of Psychology, 51,* 109–117.

BROOKS, C. I. (1969). Frustration to nonreward following limited reward experience. *Journal of Experimental Psychology, 81,* 403–405.

BROWN, J. S. (1948). Gradients of approach and avoidance responses and their relation to level of motivation. *Journal of Comparative and Physiological Psychology, 41,* 451–465.

BROWN, J. S. (1961). *The motivation of behavior.* New York: McGraw-Hill.

BROWN, J. S., & FARBER, I. E. (1951). Emotions conceptualized as intervening variables—With suggestions toward a theory of frustration. *Psychological Bulletin, 48,* 465–495.

BROWN, J. S., KALISH, H. I., & FARBER, I. E. (1951). Conditioned fear as revealed by magnitude of startle response to an auditory stimulus. *Journal of Experimental Psychology, 41,* 317–328.

BRYAN, J. H., & TEST, M. A. (1967). Models and helping: Naturalistic studies in aiding behavior. *Journal of Personality and Social Psychology, 6,* 400–407.

BUGELSKI, B. R. (1956). *The psychology of learning.* New York: Holt, Rinehart, and Winston.

BURGER, J. (1989). Negative reactions to increases in perceived personal control. *Journal of Personality and Social Psychology, 56,* 246–256.

BURGER, J. M. (1980). *Effectance motivation and the overjustification effect.* Unpublished doctoral dissertation. University of Missouri-Columbia.

BURGER, J. M., & COOPER, H. M. (1979). The desirability of control. *Motivation and Emotion, 3,* 381–393.

BURGESS, T. D. G., & SALES, S. M. (1971). Attitudinal effects of "mere exposure": A reevaluation. *Journal of Experimental Social Psychology, 7,* 461–472.

BURNSTEIN, E., & WORCHEL, P. (1962). Arbitrariness of frustration and its consequences for aggression in a social situation. *Journal of Personality, 30,* 528–541.

BUSS, D. M. (1988). The evolution of human intrasexual competition: Tactics of mate attraction. *Journal of Personality and Social Psychology, 54,* 616–628.

BUSS, D. M. (1995). Evolutionary psychology: A new paradigm for psychological science. *Psychological Inquiry, 6,* 1–30.

BUSS, A. H., BOOKER, A., & BUSS, E. (1972). Firing a weapon and aggression. *Journal of Personality and Social Psychology, 22,* 296–302.

BUSS, D. M., HASELTON, M. G., SHACKELFORD, T. K., BLESKE, A. L., & WAKEFIELD, J. C. (1998). Adaptations, exaptations, and spandrels. *American Psychologist, 53,* 533–548.

BYKOV, K. M. (1957). *The cerebral cortex and the internal organs* (W. H. Gantt, Trans. and Ed.). New York: Chemical Publishing.

References   433

BYRNE, D. (1959). The effects of a subliminal food stimulus on verbal responses. *Journal of Applied Psychology, 43,* 249–252.

BYRNE, D. (1974). *An introduction to psychology* (2nd ed.). Englewood Cliffs, NJ: Prentice-Hall.

BYRNE, D., & NELSON, D. (1965). Attraction as a linear function of proportion of positive reinforcements. *Journal of Personality and Social Psychology, 1,* 659–663.

CABANAC, M. (1990). Taste: The maximization of multidimensional pleasure. In E. Capaldi & T. Powley (Eds). *Taste, experience, and feeding.* Washington, DC: American Psychological Association.

CACIOPPO, J. T., & BERNTSON, G. G. (1994). Relationship between attitudes and evaluative space: A critical review, with emphasis on the separability of positive and negative substrates. *Psychological Bulletin, 115,* 401–423.

CACIOPPO, J. T., CRITES, S. L., GARDNER, W. L. (1996). Attitudes to the right: Evaluative processing is associated with lateralized late positive event-related brain potentials. *Personality and Social Psychology Bulletin, 22,* 1205–1219.

CACIOPPO, J. T., GARDNER, W. L., & BERNTSON, G. G. (1997). Beyond bipolar conceptualizations and measures: The case of attitudes and evaluative space. *Personality and Social Psychology Review, 1,* 3–25.

CACIOPPO, J. T., & PETTY, R. E. (1982). The need for cognition. *Journal of Personality and Social Psychology, 42,* 116–131.

CACIOPPO, J., PETTY, R., LOSCH, M., & KIM, H. (1986). Electromyographic activity over facial muscle regions can differentiate the valence and intensity of affective reactions. *Journal of Personality and Social Psychology, 50*(2), 260–268.

CAIRNS, R. B. (1979). *Social development.* San Francisco: Freeman.

CALHOUN, J. B. (1962). Population density and social pathology. *Scientific American, 206,* 139–148.

CAMERON, J., & PIERCE, W. D. (1994). Reinforcement, reward and intrinsic motivation: A meta-analysis. *Review of Educational Research, 64,* 363.

CAMP, D. S., RAYMOND, G. A., & CHURCH, R. M. (1967). Temporal relationship between response and punishment. *Journal of Experimental Psychology, 74,* 114–123.

CAMPBELL, B. A. (1964). Theory and research on the effects of water deprivation on random activity in the rat. In M. J. Wayner (Ed.), *Thirst.* Oxford: Pergamon.

CAMPBELL, B. A., & CHURCH, R. M. (1969). *Punishment and aversive behavior.* New York: Appleton-Century-Crofts.

CAMPBELL, B. A., & CICALA, G. A. (1962). Studies of water deprivation in rats as a function of age. *Journal of Comparative and Physiological Psychology, 55,* 763–768.

CAMPBELL, B. A., & KRAELING, D. (1953). Response strengths as a function of drive level and amount of drive reduction. *Journal of Experimental Psychology, 45,* 97–101.

CAMPBELL, B. A., & MASTERSON, F. A. (1969). Psychophysics of punishment. In B. A. Campbell & R. M. Church (Eds.), *Punishment and aversive behavior.* New York: Appleton-Century- Crofts.

CAMPBELL, B. A., SMITH, N. F., MISANIN, J. R., & JAYNES, J. (1966). Species differences in activity during hunger and thirst. *Journal of Comparative and Physiological Psychology, 61,* 123–127.

CANNON, W. B. (1927). The James-Lange theory of emotions: A critical examination and an alternative theory. *American Journal of Psychology, 39,* 106–124.

CANNON, W. B. (1934). Hunger and thirst. In C. Murchison (Ed.), *Handbook of general experimental psychology.* Worcester, MA: Clark University Press.

CANNON, W. B. (1939a). *Bodily changes in pain, hunger, fear and rage: An account of recent researches into the function of emotional excitement* (2nd ed.). New York: Appleton- Century-Crofts.

CANNON, W. B. (1939b). *The wisdom of the body.* New York: Norton.

CANTOR, J. R., ZILLMAN, D., & BRYANT, J. (1975). Enhancement of experienced sexual arousal in response to erotic stimuli through misattribution of unrelated residual excitation. *Journal of Personality and Social Psychology, 32,* 69–75.

CANTOR, N., & LANGSTON, C. A. (1989). Ups and downs of life tasks in a life transition. In L. A. Pervin (Ed.), *Goal concepts in personality and social psychology* (pp. 87–126). Hillsdale, NJ: Erlbaum.

CAPALDI, E. D., & DAVIDSON, T. L. (1979). Control of instrumental behavior by deprivation stimuli. *Journal of Experimental Psychology: Animal Behavoir Processes, 5,* 355–367.

CAPALDI, E. D., & MYERS, D. E. (1982). Taste preferences as a function of food deprivation during original taste exposure. *Animal learning and behavior, 10,* 211–219.

CAPALDI, E. D., VIVIEROS, D. M., & DAVIDSON, T. L. (1981). Deprivation stimulus intensity and incentive factors in the control of instrumental responding. *Journal of Experimental Psychology: Animal Behavior Processes, 7,* 140–149.

CARLSMITH, J. M., & ANDERSON, C. A. (1979). Ambient temperature and the occurrence of collective violence: A new analysis. *Journal of Personality and Social Psychology, 37,* 337–344.

CARLSON, N. R. (1980). *Physiology of behavior* (2nd ed.). Boston: Allyn & Bacon.

CARLSON, N. R. (1987). *Physiology of behavior* (3rd ed.). Boston: Allyn & Bacon.

CARLSON, N. R. (1994). *Physiology of behavior* (5th ed.). Boston: Allyn & Bacon.

CARR, H. A. (1925). *Psychology, a study of mental activity.* New York: Longmans.

CARROLL, J. M., & RUSSELL, J. A. (1996). Do facial expressions signal specific emotions? Judging emotion from the face in context. *Journal of Personality and Social Psychology, 70,* 205–218.

CARROLL, J. M., & RUSSELL, J. A. (1997). Facial expressions in Hollywood's portrayal of emotion. *Journal of Personality and Social Psychology, 72,* 164–176.

CATTELL, R. B. (1965). *Scientific analysis of personality.* Baltimore: Penguin.

CATTELL, R. B., & SCHEIER, I. (1961). *The meaning and measurement of neuroticism and anxiety.* New York: Wiley.

CHURCH, R. M. (1969). Response suppression. In B. A. Campbell & R. M. Church (Eds.), *Punishment and aversive behavior.* New York: Appleton-Century-Crofts.

CHWALISZ, K., DIENER, E., & GALLAGHER, D. (1988). Autonomic arousal and emotional experience: Evidence from the spinal cord injured. *Journal of Personality and Social Psychology, 54,* 820–828.

CLARK, M. S., & ISEN, A. (1982). Toward understanding the relationship between feeling states and social behavior. In A. Hastorf & A. Isen (Eds.), *Cognitive social psychology* (pp. 73–108). Amsterdam: Elsevier North-Holland.

CLORE, G. L., & BYRNE, D. (1974). A reinforcement-affect model of attraction. In T. C. Houston (Ed.), *Foundations of interpersonal attraction,* New York: Academic Press.

COHEN, A. R., BREHM, J. W., & FLEMING, W. H. (1958). Attitude change and justification for compliance. *Journal of Abnormal and Social Psychology, 56,* 276–278.

COHEN, P. S., & TOKIEDA, F. (1972). Sucrose-water preference reversal in the water-deprived rat. *Journal of Comparative and Physiological Psychology, 79,* 254–258.

COHEN, S., KRANTZ, D. S., EVANS, G. W., & STOKOLS, D. (1982). Community noise, behavior, and health: The Los Angeles noise project. In A. Baum & J. Singer (Eds.), *Advances in environmental psychology* (Vol. 4: Environment and Health). Hillsdale, NJ: Lawrence Erlbaum Associates.

COHEN, S., & WEINSTEIN, N. (1981). Nonauditory effects of noise on behavior and health. *Journal of Social Issues, 37,* 36–70.

COLLET, L., & DUCLAUX, R. (1986). Hemispheric lateralizations of emotions: Absence of electrophysiological arguments. *Physiology and Behavior, 40,* 215–220.

COLLIER, G., HIRSCH, E., & HAMLIN, P. (1972). The ecological determinants of reinforcement. *Physiology and Behavior, 9,* 705–716.

COLLIER, G., KANAREK, R., HIRSCH, E., & MARWINE, A. (1976). Environmental determinants of feeding behavior or how to turn a rat into a tiger. In M. H. Siegel & H. P. Zeigler (Eds.), *Psychological research: The inside story.* New York: Harper & Row.

COLLIER, G., & MYERS, L. (1961). The loci of reinforcement. *Journal of Experimental Psychology, 61,* 57–66.

COMPTON-BURNETT, I. (1949). *Bullivant and the lambs.* New York: Knopf.

COOMBS, R. H., & KENKEL, W. F. (1966). Sex differences in dating aspirations and satisfaction with computer-selected partners. *Journal of Marriage, 28,* 62–66.

COOPER, J., & FAZIO, R. H. (1984). A new look at dissonance theory. In L. Berkowitz (Ed.), *Advances in experimental social psychology* (Vol. 17, pp. 229–266). New York: Academic Press.

COOPER, J., ZANNA, M. P., & TAVES, P. A. (1978). Arousal as a necessary condition for attitude change following induced compliance. *Journal of Personality and Social Psychology, 36,* 1101–1106.

CORBIT, J. D. (1969). Osmotic thirst: Theoretical and experimental analysis. *Journal of Comparative and Physiological Psychology, 67,* 3–14.

COTTRELL, N. B., & WACK, D. C. (1967). The energizing effect of cognitive dissonance on dominant and subordinate responses. *Journal of Personality and Social Psychology, 16,* 132–138.

COURNEYA, K. S., & CARRON, A. V. (1991). Effects of travel and length of home stand/road trip on the home advantage. *Journal of Sport and Exercise Psychology, 13,* 42–49.

COX, V. C., PAULUS, P. B., McCAIN, G., & KARLOVAC, M. (1982). The relationship between crowding and health. In A. Baum & J. E. Singer (Eds.), *Advances in environmental psychology* Vol. 4: Environment and health. Hillsdale, NJ: Lawrence Erlbaum Associates.

Coyne, J. C., & Gotlieb, I. H. (1983). The role of cognition in depression: A critical appraisal. *Psychological Bulletin, 94*, 472–505.

Crawford, M. (1977). Brief "response prevention" in a novel place can facilitate avoidance extinction. *Learning and Motivation, 8*, 39–53.

Crespi, L. P. (1942). Quantitative variation of incentive and performance in the white rat. *American Journal of Psychology, 55*, 457–517.

Crespi, L. P. (1944). Amount of reinforcement and level of performance. *Psychological Review, 51*, 341–357.

Cronbach, L. J. (1957). The two disciplines of scientific psychology. *American Psychologist, 12*, 671–684.

Croyle, R. T., & Cooper, J. (1983). Dissonance arousal: Physiological evidence. *Journal of Personality and Social Psychology, 45*, 782–791.

Csikszentmihalyi, M. (1978). Intrinsic rewards and emergent motivation. In M. Lepper & D. Greene (Eds.), *The hidden costs of reward.* New York: Lawrence Erlbaum Associates, Inc.

Dackis, C. A., & Gold, M. S. (1985). New concepts in cocaine addiction: The dopamine depletion hypothesis. *Neuroscience and Neurobehavioral Reviews, 9*, 469–477.

Daly, H. B. (1974). Reinforcing properties of escape from frustration aroused in various learning situations. In G. H. Bower (Ed.), *The psychology of learning and motivation* (Vol. 8). New York: Academic.

D'Amato, M. R., & Safarjan, W. R. (1979). Preference for information about shock duration in rats. *Animal Learning and Behavior, 7*, 89–94.

Darley, J. M., & Bateson, C. D. (1973). From Jerusalem to Jericho: A study of situational and dispositional variables in helping behavior. *Journal of Personality and Social Psychology, 27*, 100–108.

Darwin, C. R. (1936). *The origin of the species.* Modern Library, No. G 27. New York: Random House. (Original work published 1859)

Darwin, C. R. (1998). *The expression of the emotions in man and animals* (3rd ed.). Oxford: Oxford University Press. (Original work published 1872)

Dashiell, J. F. (1925). A quantitative demonstration of animal drive. *Journal of Comparative and Physiological Psychology, 5*, 205–208.

Davidson, R. (1994). Honoring biology in the study of affective style. In P. Ekman & R. Davidson (Eds.), *The nature of emotion: Fundamental questions.* New York: Oxford.

Davis, C. M. (1939). Results of the self-selection of diets by young children. *Canadian Medical Association Journal, 41*, 257–261.

Davis, J. D., & Miller, N. E. (1963). Fear and pain: Their effect on self-injection of amobarbital sodium by rats. *Science, 141*, 1286–1287.

Davis, K. E. (1985, February). Near and dear: Friendship and love compared. *Psychology Today*, pp. 23–30.

Davis, K. E., & Jones, E. E. (1960). Changes in interpersonal perception as a means of reducing cognitive dissonance. *Journal of Abnormal and Social Psychology, 61*, 402–410.

Davis, M. (1986). Pharmacological and anatomical analysis of fear conditioning using the fear-potentiated startle paradigm. *Behavioral Neuroscience, 100*(6), 814–824.

Davis, M., & Astrachan, D. I. (1978). Conditioned fear and startle magnitude. *Journal of Experimental Psychology: Animal Behavior Processes, 4*, 95–103.

Davitz, J. R. (1955). Reinforcement of fear at the beginning and end of shock. *Journal of Comparative and Physiological Psychology, 48*, 152–155.

Davitz, J. R. (1970). A dictionary and grammar of emotion. In M. L. Arnold (Ed.), *Feelings and emotions: The Loyola symposium.* New York: Academic Press.

Davitz, J. R., & Mason, D. J. (1955). Socially facilitated reduction of a fear response in rats. *Journal of Comparative and Physiological Psychology, 48*, 149–151.

De Castro, J. M. (1993). The effects of the spontaneous ingestion of particular foods or beverages on the meal pattern and overall nutrient intake of humans. *Physiology and Behavior, 53*, 1133–1144.

DeCastro, J. M., & Brewer, E. M. (1991). The amount eaten in meals by humans is a power function of the number of people present. *Physiology and Behavior, 51*, 121–125.

deCharms, R. (1968). *Personal causation: The internal affective determinants of behavior.* New York: Academic.

deCharms, R., & Moeller, G. H. (1962). Values expressed in children's readers: 1800–1950. *Journal of Abnormal and Social Psychology, 64*, 136–142.

DECI, E. L. (1975). *Intrinsic motivation.* New York: Plenum.

DECI, E. L. (1978). Applications of research on the effects of rewards. In M. Lepper & D. Greene (Eds.), *The hidden cost of reward.* New York: Lawrence Erlbaum Associates, Inc.

DECI, E. L. (1980). *The psychology of self-determination.* Lexington, MA: D. C. Heath and Company.

DECI, E. L., & RYAN, R. M. (1985). *Intrinsic motivation and self-determination in human behavior.* New York: Plenum Press.

DELGADO, J. M. R., ROBERTS, W. W., & MILLER, N. E. (1954). Learning motivated by electrical stimulation of the brain. *American Journal of Physiology, 179,* 587–593.

DELMONTE, M. M. (1984). Biochemical indices associated with meditation practice: A literature review. *Neuroscience and Biobehavioral Reviews, 9,* 557–561.

DEMBER, W. M. (1965). The new look in motivation. *American Scientist, 53,* 409–427.

DEMBER, W. M., & EARL, R. W. (1957). Analysis of exploratory, manipulatory, and curiosity behaviors. *Psychological Review, 64,* 91–96.

DEMBER, W., & RICHMAN, C. L. (1989). *Spontaneous alternation behavior.* New York: Springer-Verlag.

DEMENT, W., & KLEITMAN, N. (1957). Cyclic variations in EEG during sleep and their relation to eye movements, body motility, and dreaming. *Electroencephalography and Clinical Neurophysiology, 9,* 673–690.

DENENBERG, V. H. (1963). Early experience and emotional development. *Scientific American, 208,* 138–146.

DENNY, M. R. (1971). Relaxation theory and experiments. In F. R. Brush (Ed.), *Aversive conditioning and learning.* New York: Academic.

DENNY, M. R., & ADELMAN, H. M. (1955). Elicitation theory: I. An analysis of two typical learning situations. *Psychological Review, 62,* 290–296.

DESCARTES, R. (1892). Les passions l'âme. In H. A. P. Torrey (Trans.), *The philosophy of Descartes in extracts from his writings.* New York: Holt. (Original work published in 1650)

DESSLER, G. (1980). *Human behavior: Improving performance at work.* Reston, VA: Reston Publishing Company.

DIAMOND, E. (1982). The role of anger and hostility in essential hypertension and coronary heart disease. *Psychological Bulletin, 92*(2), 410–433.

DITTES, J. E. (1959). Attractiveness of a group as a function of self-esteem and acceptance by group. *Journal of Abnormal and Social Psychology, 59,* 77–82.

DIXON, N. F. (1971). *Subliminal perception: The nature of a controversy.* London: McGraw-Hill.

DOLLARD, J., DOOB, L., MILLER, N. E., MOWRER, O. H., & SEARS, R. (1939). *Frustration and aggression.* New Haven, CT: Yale University Press.

DOLLARD, J., & MILLER, N. E. (1941). *Social learning and imitation.* New Haven, CT: Yale University Press.

DREWNOWSKI, A. (1996). The behavioral phenotype in human obesity. In E. D. Capaldi (Ed.), *Why we eat what we eat: The psychology of eating.* Washington, D.C.: American Psychological Association.

DREWNOWSKI, A., KRAHN, D. D., DEMITRACK, M. A., NAIRN, K., & GOSNELL, B. A. (1992). Taste responses and preferences for sweet high-fat foods: Evidence for opioid involvement. *Physiology and Behavior, 51,* 371–379.

DUBRIN, A. J. (1980). *Effective business psychology.* Reston, VA: Reston Publishing Company.

DUFFY, E. (1934). Emotion: An example of the need for reorientation in psychology. *Psychological Review, 41,* 184–198.

DUFFY, E. (1962). *Activation and behavior.* New York: Wiley.

DUNCAN, G. M. (TR.). (1890). *The philosophical works of Leibnitz.* New Haven, CT: Yale.

DUNHAM, P. J. (1971). Punishment: Method and theory. *Psychological Review, 78,* 58–70.

DUNLAP, K. (1919). Are there any instincts? *Journal of Abnormal Psychology, 14,* 307–311.

DUTTON, D. G., & ARON, A. P. (1974). Some evidence for heightened sexual attraction under conditions of high anxiety. *Journal of Personality and Social Psychology, 30,* 570–577.

EAGLY, A., & CHAIKEN, S. (1993). *The psychology of attitudes.* Forth Worth: Harcourt Brace Jovanovich.

EASTERBROOK, J. A. (1959). The effect of emotion on cue utilization and the organization of behavior. *Psychological Review, 66,* 183–201.

EGGER, M. D., & MILLER, N. E. (1962). Secondary reinforcement in rats as a function of information value and reliability of the stimulus. *Journal of Experimental Psychology, 64,* 97–104.

EGGER, M. D., & MILLER, N. E. (1963). When is a reward reinforcing? An experimental study of the information hypothesis. *Journal of Comparative and Physiological Psychology, 56,* 132–137.

EIBL-EIBESFELDT, I. (1975). *Ethology: The biology of behavior* (2nd ed., E. Klinghammer, Trans.). New York: Holt, Rinehart and Winston.

EICH, E. (1995). Searching for mood dependent memory. *Psychological Science, 6,* 67–75.

EIFERT, G. H., CRAILL, L., CAREY, E., & O'CONNOR, C. (1988). Affect modification through evaluative conditioning with music. *Behavior Research and Therapy, 26,* 321–330.

EISENBERGER, R. (1992). Learned industriousness. *Psychological Review, 99,* 248–267.

EISENBERGER, R., & CAMERON, J. (1996). Detrimental effects of reward: Reality or myth? *American Psychologist, 51,* 1153–1166.

EKMAN, P. (1972). Universals and cultural differences in facial expressions of emotion. In J. Cole (Ed.). *Nebraska Symposium on motivation.* Lincoln, NE: University of Nebraska Press.

EKMAN, P. (1994). Strong evidence for universals in facial expressions: A reply to Russell's mistaken critique. *Psychological Bulletin, 115,* 268–287.

EKMAN, P., & FRIESEN, W. V. (1971). Constants across cultures in the face and emotion. *Journal of Personality and Social Psychology, 17,* 124–129.

EKMAN, P., & FRIESEN, W. V. (1975). *Unmasking the face.* Englewood Cliffs, NJ: Prentice-Hall, Inc.

EKMAN, P. H., & FRIESEN, W. V. (1978). *The facial action coding system (FACS): A technique for the measurement of facial action.* Palo Alto, CA: Consulting Psychologists Press.

EKMAN, P., & FRIESEN, W. V. (1986). A new pancultural facial expression of emotion. *Motivation and Emotion, 10,* 159–168.

EKMAN, P., & OSTER, H. (1979). Facial expressions of emotion. In M. R. Rosenzwerg and L. W. Porter (Eds.), *Annual review of psychology.* Palo Alto, CA: Annual Reviews, Inc.

ELKIN, R. A., & LEIPPE, M. R. (1986). Physiological arousal, dissonance, and attitude change: Evidence for a dissonance-arousal link and a "don't remind me effect." *Journal of Personality and Social Psychology, 51*(1), 55–65.

ELLIOTT, A. J., & Devine, P. G. (1994). On the motivational nature of cognitive dissonance: Dissonance as psychological discomfort. *Journal of Personality and Social Psychology, 67,* 382–394.

ELLIS, H. C., THOMAS, R. L., McFARLAND, D., & LANE, W. L. (1985). Emotional mood states and retrieval in episodic memory. *Journal of Experimental Psychology: Learning, Memory, and Cognition, 11,* 363–370.

ELLSWORTH, P. (1994). Levels of thought and levels of emotion. In P. Ekman & R. Davidson (Eds.), *The nature of emotion: Fundamental questions.* New York: Oxford.

EMMONS, R. A. (1986). Personal strivings: An approach to personality and subjective well-being. *Journal of Personality and Social Psychology, 51,* 1058–1068.

EMMONS, R. A. (1997). Motives and life goals. In R. Hogan, J. Johnson, & S. Briggs (Eds.), *Handbook of personality psychology.* New York: Academic Press.

ENDLER, N. S. (1998). Stress, anxiety and coping: The multidimensional interaction model. *Canadian Psychology, 38,* 136–150.

ENDLER, N. S., & HUNT, J. McV. (1966). Sources of behavioral variance as measured by the S-R inventory of anxiousness. *Psychological Bulletin, 65,* 336–346.

ENDLER, N. S., HUNT, J. McV., & ROSENSTEIN, A. J. (1962). An S-R inventory of anxiousness. *Psychological Monographs, 76* (Whole No. 536).

ENSWILLER, T., DEAUX, K., & WILLITS, J. E. (1971). Similarity, sex, and requests for small favors. *Journal of Applied Psychology, 1,* 284–291.

EPLEY, S. W. (1974). Reduction of the behavioral effects of aversive stimulation by the presence of companions. *Psychological Bulletin, 81,* 271–283.

EPSTEIN, A. N. (1967). Oropharyngeal factors in feeding and drinking. In C. F. Code (Ed.), *Handbook of physiology* (Section 6. Alimentary canal. Vol. 1). Washington, DC: American Physiological Society.

EPSTEIN, A. N. (1982). Instinct and motivation as explanations for complex behavior. In D. W. Pfaff (Ed.), *The physiological mechanisms of motivation.* New York: Springer-Verlag.

EPSTEIN, A. N., & TEITELBAUM, P. (1962). Regulation of food intake in the absence of taste, smell, and other oropharyngeal sensations. *Journal of Comparative and Physiological Psychology, 55,* 753–759.

EPSTEIN, L. H. (1990). Behavioral treatment of obesity. In E. M. Stricker (Ed.), *Handbook of behavioral neurobiology.* (Vol. 10: Neurobiology of food and fluid intake). New York: Plenum.

EPSTEIN, S. (1967). Toward a unified theory of anxiety. In B. Maher (Ed.), *Progress in experimental personality research.* New York: Academic.

438   *References*

EPSTEIN, S. (1986). Anxiety, arousal, and the self-concept. In C. Spielberger & I. G. Sarason (Eds.), *Stress and anxiety.* (Vol. 10: A sourcebook of theory and research). Washington: Hemisphere.

ERON, L. D. (1994). Theories of aggression: From drives to cognitions. In L. R. Huesman (Ed.), *Aggressive behavior: Current perspectives.* New York: Plenum.

ERON, L. D., LEFKOWITZ, M. M., HUESMANN, L. R., & WALDER, L. Q. (1972). Does television violence cause aggression? *American Psychologist, 27,* 253–263.

ESTES, W. K., & SKINNER, B. F. (1941). Some quantitative properties of anxiety. *Journal of Experimental Psychology, 29,* 390–400.

ESTEVES, F., PARRA, C., DIMBERG, U., & ÖHMAN A. (1994). Nonconscious associative learning: Pavlovian conditioning of skin conductances responses to masked fear-relevant facial stimuli. *Psychophysiology, 31,* 375–385.

ETTINGER, R. H., THOMPSON, S., & STADDON, J. E. R. (1986). Cholecystokinin, diet palatability, and feeding regulation in rats. *Physiology and Behavior, 36,* 801–809.

EVANS, G. W., HYGGE, S., & BULLINGER, M. (1995). Chronic noise and psychological stress. *Psychological Science, 6,* 333–338.

EYSENCK, H. J. (1967). *The biological basis of personality.* Springfield, IL: C. C. Thomas.

EYSENCK, M. W., MacLeod, C., & Mathews, A. (1987). Cognitive functioning and anxiety. *Psychological Research, 49,* 189–195.

EYSENCK, M. J. (1997). *Anxiety and cognition: A unified theory.* East Sussex, England: Psychology Press Limited.

FABRICIUS, E. (1951) Some experiments on imprinting phenomena in ducks. *Proceedings of the 10th International Ornithological Congress,* 375–379.

FAIRBURN, C. G., & WALSH, B. T. (1995). Atypical eating disorders. In K. D. Brownell & C. G. Fairburn (Eds), *Eating disorders and obesity.* New York: Guilford Press.

FAISON, E. W. (1980). *Advertising: A behavioral approach for managers.* New York: John Wiley & Sons.

FALK, J. L. (1961). The behavior regulation of water-electrolyte balance. In M. R. Jones (Ed.), *Nebraska symposium on motivation.* Lincoln: University of Nebraska Press.

FAZIO, R. H., SANBONMATSU, D. M., POWELL, M. C., & KARDES, F. F. (1986). On the automatic activation of attitudes. *Journal of Personality and Social Psychology, 50,* 229–238.

FEATHER, N. T., & BARBOR, J. G. (1983). Depressive reactions and unemployment. *Journal of Abnormal Psychology, 92,* 185–195.

FEENEY, E. J. (1972). Performance audit, feedback, and positive reinforcement. *Training and Development Journal, 26,* 8–13.

FERSTER, C. B., NURNBERGER, J. I., & LEVITT, E. B. (1962). The control of eating. *Journal of Mathematics, 1,* 87–109.

FESTINGER, L. (1954). A theory of social comparison processes. *Human Relations, 7,* 117–140.

FESTINGER, L. (1957). *A theory of cognitive dissonance.* Evanston, IL: Row, Peterson.

FESTINGER, L., & CARLSMITH, J. M. (1959). Cognitive consequences of forced compliance. *Journal of Abnormal and Social Psychology, 58,* 203–210.

FESTINGER, L., RIECKEN, H. W., & SCHACHTER, S. (1956). *When prophecy fails.* New York: Harper & Row.

FIEDLER, F. (1971). Validation and extension of the contingency model of leadership effectiveness: A review of empirical findings. *Psychological Bulletin, 76,* 128–148.

FINGER, F. L., REID, L. S., & WEASNER, M. H. (1957). The effect of reinforcement upon activity during cyclic food deprivation. *Journal of Comparative and Physiological Psychology, 50,* 495–498.

FINGER, F. W. (1965). Effect of food deprivation on running-wheel activity in naive rats. *Psychological Reports, 16,* 753–757.

FINN, P. R., YOUNG, S. N., PIHL, R. O., & ERVIN, F. R. (1998). The effects of acute plasma tryptophan manipulation on hostile mood: The influence of trait hostility. *Aggressive Behavior, 24,* 173–187.

FISHER, A. E. (1964). Chemical stimulation of the brain. *Scientific American, 210,* 60–68.

FISHER, S. (1984). *Stress and the perception of control.* Hillsdale, NJ: Lawrence Erlbaum Associates.

FITZSIMMONS, J. T. (1972). Thirst. *Psychological Review, 52,* 468–561.

FITZSIMMONS, J. T., & LeMAGNEN, J. (1969). Eating as a regulatory control of drinking in the rat. *Journal of Comparative and Physiological Psychology, 67,* 273–283.

FLAHERTY, C. F. (1982). Incentive contrast: A review of behavioral changes following shifts in reward. *Animal Learning and Behavior, 19,* 409–440.

FLYNN, J. P. (1972). Patterning mechanisms, patterned reflexes, and attack behavior in cats. J. Cole & D. Jensen (Eds). *Nebraska Symposium on Motivation.* Lincoln: University of Nebraska Press.

FOA, E. B., & KOZAK, M. J. (1986). Emotional processing of fear: Exposure to corrective information. *Psychological Bulletin, 99,* 20–35.

FOWLER, H., & MILLER, N. E. (1963). Facilitation and inhibition of runway performance by hind- and forepaw shock of various intensities. *Journal of Comparative and Physiological Psychology, 56,* 801–805.

FOWLER, H., & TRAPOLD, M. A. (1962). Escape performance as a function of delay of reinforcement. *Journal of Experimental Psychology, 63,* 464–467.

FREEDMAN, J. L. (1984). Effect of television violence on aggressiveness. *Psychological Bulletin, 96,* 227–246.

FREUD, S. (1935). *A general introduction to psycho-analysis.* New York: Liveright. (Original work published 1920)

FREUD, S. (1938). *The basic writings of Sigmund Freud.* (Ed. A. A. Brill). New York: Random House, Inc.

FREUD, S. ([1900] 1938). *The interpretation of dreams.* New York: The Modern Library.

FRIEDMAN, M., & ROSENMAN, R. H. (1974). *Type A behavior and your heart.* New York: Alfred A. Knopf.

FRIEDRICH-COFER, L., & HUSTON, A. C. (1986). Television violence and aggression: The debate continues. *Psychological Bulletin, 100,* 364–371.

FRIJDA, N. H. (1994). Emotions require cognitions, even if simple ones. In P. Ekman & R. Davidson (Eds.), *The nature of emotion: Fundamental questions.* New York: Oxford.

FUHRER, M., & BAER, P. E. (1965). Differential classical conditioning: Verbalization of stimulus contingencies. *Science, 150,* 1479–1481.

FUNK, S. C., & HOUSTON, B. K. (1987). A critical analysis of the Hardiness Scale's validity and utility. *Journal of Personality and Social Psychology, 53,* 572–578

GAINER, L., & BECK, R. C. (1987, March). *A look at hardiness and laboratory stress.* Paper presented at the meeting of the Southeastern Psychological Association, Atlanta.

GALEF, B. G., JR. (1971). Social effects in the weaning of the domestic rat pups. *Journal of Comparative and Physiological Psychology, 75,* 358–362.

GALEF, B. G., JR. (1991). A contrarian view of the wisdom of the body as it relates to food selection. *Psychological Review, 98,* 218–224.

GALEF, B. G., JR. (1996). Social influences on food preferences and feeding behaviors of vertebrates. In E. D. Capaldi (Ed.), *Why we eat what we eat: The psychology of eating.* Washington, DC: American Psychological Association.

GALEF, B. G., JR., & HENDERSON, P. W. (1972). Mother's milk: A determinant of the feeding preferences of weaning rat pups. *Journal of Comparative and Physiological Psychology, 78,* 213–219.

GALLAGHER, J. E., & ASH, M. (1978). Sexual imprinting: The stability of mate preference in Japanese quail (coturnix coturnix japonica). *Animal Learning and Behavior, 6,* 363–365.

GALLISTEL, C. R., SHIZGAL, P., & YEOMANS, J. S. (1981). A portrait of the substrate for self-stimulation. *Psychological Review, 88,* 228–273.

GARCIA, J., & ERVIN, R. R. (1968). Gustatory visceral and telereceptor cutaneous conditioning— Adaptation in external and internal milieus. *Communications in Behavioral Biology, 1* (Part A), 389–415.

GARCIA, J., & KOELLING, R. A. (1966) Relation of cue to consequence in avoidance learning. *Psychonomic Science, 4,* 123–124.

GARFINKEL, P. E. (1995). Classification and diagnosis of eating disorders. In K. D. Brownell & C. G. Fairburn (Eds), *Eating disorders and obesity.* New York: Guilford Press.

GARFINKEL, P., MOLODOFSKY, H., & GARNER, D. (1979). The stability of perceptual disturbances in anorexia nervosa. *Psychological Medicine, 9,* 703–708.

GARNER, W. R., HAKE, H. W., & ERIKSEN, C. W. (1956). Operationalism and the concept of perception. *Psychological Review, 63,* 149–159.

GAYTON, W. F., & COOMBS, R. (1995). The home advantage in high school basketball. *Perceptual and Motor Skills, 81,* 1344–1246.

GAZZANIGA, M. S. (1967). The split brain in man. *Scientific American, 217,* 24–29.

GEEN, R. G., & BERKOWITZ, L. (1967). Some conditions facilitating the occurrence of aggression after the observation of violence. *Journal of Personality, 35,* 666–667.

GEEN, R. G., & O'NEAL, E. C. (1969). Activation of cue-elicited aggression by general arousal. *Journal of Personality and Social Psychology, 11,* 289–292.

GIBSON, J. L., IVANCEVICH, J. M., & DONNELLY, J. H. (1979). *Organization: Behavior, structure, processes.* Dallas: Irwin-Dorsey.

GILMAN, A. (1937). The relation between blood osmotic pressure, fluid distribution, and voluntary water intake. *American Journal of Physiology, 120,* 323–328.

GLADUE, B. A., GREEN, R., HELLMAN, R. E. (1984). Neuroendocrine response to estrogen and sexual orientation. *Science, 225,* 1496–1499.

GLICKMAN, S. E., & SCHIFF, B. B. (1967). A biological theory of reinforcement. *Psychological Review, 74,* 81–109.

GOLDSMITH, H. H. (1993). Temperament: Variability in developing emotion systems. In M. Lewis & J. M. Haviland (Eds.), *Handbook of emotions.* New York: The Guilford Press.

GOLDSTEIN, J., & ARMA, R. (1971). Effect of observing athletic contests on hostility. *Sociometry, 54,* 83–91.

GORANSON, R., & BERKOWITZ, L. (1966). Reciprocity and responsibility reactions to prior help. *Journal of Personality and Social Psychology, 3,* 227–232.

GORDON, W. C. (1989). *Learning.* Belmont, CA: Wadsworth.

GOULD, S. J. (1991). Exaptation: A crucial tool for evolutionary psychology. *Journal of Social Issues, 47,* 43–65.

GRAY, J. (1971). *The psychology of fear and stress.* New York: McGraw-Hill.

GRAY, J. A. (1982a). *The neuropsychology of anxiety: An enquiry into the the functions of the septohippocampal system.* Oxford: Oxford University Press.

GRAY, J. A. (1982b). Precis of "The neuropsychology of anxiety: An enquiry into the functions of the septo-hippocampal system." *The Behavioral and Brain Sciences, 5,* 469–534.

GRAY, J. A. (1994). Three fundamental emotion systems. In P. Ekman & R. J. Davidson (Eds.), *The nature of emotion: Fundamental questions.* New York: Oxford University Press.

GREEN, D. P., GOLDMAN, S. L., & SALOVEY, P. (1993). Measurement error masks bipolarity in affect ratings. *Journal of Personality and Social Psychology, 64,* 1029–1041.

GREENWALD, A. G. (1992). New Look 3: Unconscious cognition reclaimed. *American Psychologist, 47,* 766–769.

GREENWALD, A. G., & RONIS, D. L. (1978). Twenty years of cognitive dissonance: Case study of the evolution of a theory. *Psychological Review, 85,* 53–57.

GREENWALD, A. G., SPANGENBERG, E. R., PRATKANIS, A. R., & ESKENAZI, J. (1991). Double-blind tests of subliminal self-help audiotapes. *Psychological Science, 2,* 119–122.

GREGORY, E., ENGLE, K., & PFAFF, D. (1975). Male hamster preference for odors of female hamster vaginal discharges: Studies of experiential and hormonal determinants. *Journal of Comparative and Physiological Psychology, 89,* 442–446.

GRILL, H. J., & KAPLAN, J. M. (1990). Caudal brainstem participates in the distributed neural control of feeding. In E. M. Stricker (Ed.), *Handbook of behavioral neurobiology* (Vol. 10: Neurobiology of food and fluid intake). New York: Plenum.

GUERIN, B., & INNES, J. M. (1984). Explanations of social facilitation: A review. *Current Psychological Research and Reviews, 3,* 32–52.

GUTTMAN, N. (1953). Operant conditioning, extinction, and periodic reinforcement in relation to concentration of sucrose used as reinforcing agent. *Journal of Experimental Psychology, 46,* 213–224.

GUTTMAN, N. (1954). Equal-reinforcement values for sucrose and glucose solutions compared with equal-sweetness values. *Journal of Comparative and Physiological Psychology, 47,* 358–361.

HACKMAN, J. R., & LAWLER, E. E. (1971). Employee reactions to job characteristics. *Journal of Applied Psychology, 55,* 259–286.

HACKMAN, J. R., & OLDHAM, G. R. (1976). Motivation through the design of work: Test of a theory. *Organizational Behavior and Human Performance, 16,* 250–279.

HALL, J. F. (1958). The influence of learning in activity wheel behavior. *Journal of Genetic Psychology, 92,* 121–125.

HAMER, D. (1997). The search for personality genes: Adventures of a molecular biologist. *Psychological Science, 6,* 111–114.

HAMILTON, W. D. (1964). The genetical theory of social behavior: I. and II. *Journal of Theoretical Biology.*

HAMMEN, C. L. (1985). Predicting depression: A cognitive-behavior perspective. In P. C. Kendall (Ed.), *Advances in cognitive-behavioral research and therapy* (Vol. 4, pp. 30–71). New York: Academic Press.

HARLOW, H. F. (1953). Mice, monkeys, men, and motives. *Psychological Review, 60,* 23–32.

HARLOW, H. F. (1958). The nature of love. *American Psychologist, 13,* 673–685.

HARMON-JONES, E., & ALLEN, J. B. (1998). Anger and frontal brain activity: EEG asymmetry consistent with approach motivation despite negative affective valence. *Journal of Personality and Social Psychology, 74,* 1310–1216.

HARMON-JONES, E., BREHM, J. W., GREENBERG, J., SIMON, L., & NELSON, D. E. (1996). Evidence that the production of aversive consequences is not necessary to create cognitive dissonance. *Journal of Personality and Social Psychology, 70,* 5–16.

HARRIS, L. J., CLAY, J., HARGREAVES, F. J., & WARD, A. (1933). Appetite and choice of diet: The ability of the vitamin B deficient rat to discriminate between diets containing and lacking the vitamin. *Proceedings of the Royal Society, London, 113*(Serial B), 161–190.

HARRISON, A. A. (1976). *Individuals and groups.* Monterey, CA: Brooks/Cole.

HEBB, D. O. (1946). On the nature of fear. *Psychological Review, 53,* 259–276.

HEBB, D. O. (1955). Drives and the CNS (conceptual nervous system). *Psychological Review, 62,* 243–254.

HECKER, M. H., CHESNEY, M. A., BLACK, G. W., & FRAUTSCHI, N. (1988). Coronary-prone behaviors in the Western Collaborative Group Study. *Psychosomatic Medicine, 50,* 153–164.

HECKHAUSEN, H. (1975). *Effort expenditure, aspiration level and self-evaluation before and after unexpected performance shifts.* Cited in McClelland (1985).

HEIDER, F. (1958). *The psychology of interpersonal relations.* New York: Wiley.

HENDRICK, C., & BROWN, S. R. (1971). Introversion, extroversion, and interpersonal attraction. *Journal of Personality and Social Psychology, 20,* 31–36.

HENDRICK, C., & HENDRICK, S. (1986). A theory and method of love. *Journal of Comparative and Physiological Psychology, 50,* 392–402.

HENDRY, D. P. (ED.). (1969). *Conditioned reinforcement.* Homewood, IL: Dorsey.

HERMAN, C. P. (1996). Human eating: Diagnosis and prognosis. *Neuroscience and Biobehavioral Reviews, 20,* 107–111.

HERRNSTEIN, R. J. (1969). Method and theory in the study of avoidance. *Psychological Review, 76,* 49–69.

HERZBERG, F. (1968). One more time: How do you motivate employees? *Harvard Business Review,* January-February.

HESS, E. H. (1962). Ethology: An approach toward the complete analysis of behavior. In R. Brown, E. Galanter, E. H. Hess, & G. Mandler (Eds.), *New directions in psychology.* New York: Holt, Rinehart and Winston.

HINDE, R. A., THORPE, W. H., & VINCE, M. A. (1956). The following response in young coots and moorhens. *Behaviour, 9,* 214–242.

HIROTO, D. S. (1974). Locus of control and learned helplessness. *Journal of Experimental Psychology, 102*(2), 187–193.

HIROTO, D. S., & SELIGMAN, M. E. P. (1975). Generality of learned helplessness in man. *Journal of Comparative and Physiological Psychology, 31,* 211–217.

HOBSON, J. A. (1988). *The dreaming brain.* New York: Basic Books.

HOEBEL, B. G. (1969). Feeding and self-stimulation. *Neural Regulation of Food and Water Intake. Annals of the New York Academy of Science, 157,* 758–778.

HOFFMAN, H. S., & FLESHLER, M. (1962). The course of emotionality in the development of avoidance. *Journal of Experimental Psychology, 64,* 288–294.

HOHMANN, G. W. (1966). Some effects on spinal cord lesions on experienced emotional feelings. *Psychophysiology, 3,* 143–156.

HOKANSON, J. E. (1970). Psychophysiological evaluation of the catharsis hypothesis. In E. I. Megargee & J. E. Hokanson (Eds.), *The dynamics of aggression.* New York: Harper & Row.

HOLMAN, G. L. (1969). Intragastric reinforcement effect. *Journal of Comparative and Physiological Psychology, 69,* 432–441.

HOLMES, D. S. (1984). Meditation and somatic arousal reduction: A review of the experimental evidence. *American Psychologist, 39,* 1–10.

HOLMES, T. H., & RAHE, R. H. (1967). The social readjustment rating scale. *Journal of Psychosomatic Research, 11,* 213–218.

HOVLAND, C., & WEISS, W. (1957). The influence of source credibility on communication effectiveness. *Public Opinion Quarterly, 15,* 635–650.

HOY, R. R., & CASADAY, G. B. (1979). Acoustic communication in crickets: Physiological analysis of auditory pathways. In G. Burghardt and M. Bekoff (Eds.) *The development of behavior: Comparative and evolutionary aspects.* New York: Garland.

HUESMANN, L. R., & ERON, L. D. (1984). Cognitive processes and the persistence of aggressive behavior. *Aggressive Behavior, 10,* 243–251.

HULL, C. L. (1931). Goal attraction and directing ideas conceived as habit phenomena. *Psychological Review, 38,* 487–506.

HULL, C. L. (1943). *Principles of behavior.* New York: Appleton-Century-Crofts.

HULL, C. L. (1952). *A behavior system.* New Haven, CT: Yale University Press.

HULL, C. L., HOVLAND, C. I., ROSS, R. T., HALL, M., PERKINS, D. T., & FITCH, F. B. (1940). *Mathematico-deductive theory of rote learning.* New Haven, CT: Yale University Press.

HUME, D. (1939). An enquiry concerning human understanding. In E. A. Burtt (Ed.), *The English philosophers from Bacon to Mill.* New York: Random House (Modern Library). (Original work published 1748)

HUNT, H. F., & BRADY, J. V. (1955). Some effects of punishment and intercurrent "anxiety" on a simple operant. *Journal of Comparative and Physiological Psychology, 48,* 305–310.

HUNT, J. McV. (1965). Intrinsic motivation and its role in psychological development. In D. Levine (Ed.), *Nebraska symposium on motivation.* Lincoln: University of Nebraska Press.

HUNT, J. McV. (1984). The role of early experience in the development of intelligence and personality. In N. Endler & J. M. Hunt (Eds.), *Personality and the behavior disorders* (2nd ed.). New York: John Wiley and Sons.

HURSH, S. R. (1984). Behavioral economics. *Journal of Experimental Analysis of Behavior, 42,* 435–452.

HUTCHINSON, B. R. (1972). The environmental causes of aggression. In J. K. Cole & D. D. Jensen (Eds), *Nebraska Symposium on Motivation.* Lincoln: University of Nebraska Press.

HYLAND, M. (1988). Motivational control theory: An integrated framework. *Journal of Personality and Social Psychology, 55,* 542–551.

IRWIN, F. W. (1971). *Intentional behavior and motivation: A cognitive theory.* Philadelphia: Lippincott.

ISEN, A. (1984). Toward understanding the role of affect in cognition. In R. S. Wyer & T. K. Srull (Eds.), *Handbook of social cognition* (Vol. 3, pp. 179–236). Hillsdale, NJ: Erlbaum.

IZARD, C. E. (1971). *The face of emotions.* New York: Appleton.

IZARD, C. E. (1977). *Human emotion.* New York: Plenum Press.

IZARD, C. E. (1991). *The psychology of emotions.* New York: Plenum.

JACKSON, D. N., AHMED, S. A., & HEAPY, N. A. (1976). Is achievement a unitary construct? *Journal of Research in Personality, 10,* 1–21.

JACOBS, G. D., & SNYDER, D. (1996). Frontal brain asymmetry predicts affective style in men. *Behavioral Neuroscience, 110,* 3–6.

JACOBS, H. L. (1964). Observations on the ontogeny of saccharin preference in the neonate rat. *Psychonomic Society, 1,* 105–106.

JAMES, W. (1884). What is an emotion? *Mind, 9,* 188–205.

JAMES, W. (1890). *Principles of psychology.* New York: Holt.

JANIS, I. L. (1972). *Victims of groupthink.* Boston: Houghton Mifflin.

JEMMOTT, J. B. (1987). Social motives and susceptibility to disease: Stalking individual differences in health risks. *Journal of Personality, 55,* 267–298.

JOHNSON, R. W., KELLY, R. J., & LEBLANC, B. A. (1995). Motivational basis of dissonance: Aversive consequences or inconsistency. *Personality and Social Psychology Bulletin, 8,* 850–855.

JONES, E. E. (1964). *Ingratiation.* New York: Appleton-Century-Crofts.

JONES, H. E., & JONES, M. C. (1928). A study of fear. *Childhood Education, 5,* 136–143.

JONES, M. C. (1924). The elimination of children's fears. *Journal of Experimental Psychology, 7,* 382–390.

JOUVET, M. (1967). The states of sleep. *Scientific American, 216,* 62–72.

KAGAN, J., REZNICK, J. S., & SNIDMAN, N. (1988). Biological bases of childhood shyness. *Science, 240,* 167–171.

KALAT, J. (1988). *Biological psychology* (3rd ed.). Belmont, CA: Wadsworth Publishing Company.

KALAT, J. W. (1995). *Biological psychology.* (5th ed.). Pacific Grove, CA: Brooks/Cole.

KALICK, S. M., ZEBROWITZ, L. A., LANGLOIS, J. H., & ROHNSON, R. M. (1998). Does human facial attractiveness honestly advertise health? Longitudinal data on an evolutionary question. *Psychological Science, 9,* 8–13.

KALISH, H. J. (1954). Strength of fear as a function of number of acquisition and extinction trials. *Journal of Experimental Psychology, 47,* 1–9.

KALLMAN, F. J. (1946). The genetic theory of schizophrenia. *American Journal of Psychiatry, 103,* 309–322.

KAMIN, L. J. (1956). The effects of termination of the CS and avoidance of the US on avoidance learning. *Journal of Comparative and Physiological Psychology, 49,* 420–424.

KAMIN, L. J., BRIMER, C. J., & BLACK, A. H. (1963). Conditioned suppression as a monitor of fear of the CS in the course of avoidance learning. *Journal of Comparative and Physiological Psychology, 56,* 497–501.

KANE, T. R., DOERGE, P., & TEDESCHI, J. T. (1973). When is intentional harm-doing perceived as aggressive? A naive reappraisal of the Berkowitz aggression paradigm. *Proceedings of the 81st*

Annual Convention of the American Psychological Association, Montreal, Canada, 8, 113–114. Washington, DC: American Psychological Association.

KAPPAUF, W. E., BURRIGHT, R. G., & DEMARCO, W. (1963). Sucrose-quinine mixtures which are isohedonic for the rat. *Journal of Comparative and Physiological Psychology, 56,* 138–143.

KAUFMAN, E. L., & MILLER, N. E. (1949). Effect of number of reinforcements on strength of approach in an approach-avoidance conflict. *Journal of Comparative and Physiological Psychology, 42,* 65–74.

KEESEY, R. E., & POWLEY, T. L. (1986). The regulation of body weight. *Annual Review of Psychology, 37,* 109–133.

KELLEY, H. H. (1967). Attribution theory in social psychology. In D. Levine (Ed.), *Nebraska symposium on motivation.* Lincoln: University of Nebraska Press.

KIMBLE, G. A. (1994a). A frame of reference for psychology. *American Psychologist, 49,* 510–519.

KIMBLE, G. A. (1994b). A new formula for behaviorism. *Psychological Review, 101,* 254–258.

KINSEY, A. C., POMEROY, W. B., & MARTIN, C. E. (1948). *Sexual behavior in the human male.* Philadelphia: Saunders.

KINSEY, A. C., POMEROY, W. B., MARTIN, C. E., & GEBHARD, P. (1953). *Sexual behavior in the human female.* Philadelphia: Saunders.

KIRSCH, I., & HENRY, D. (1979). Self-desensitization and meditation in the reduction of public speaking anxiety. *Journal of Consulting and Clinical Psychology, 47,* 536–541.

KIRSCH, P., & BOUCSEIN, W. (1997). Classical conditioning and information processing: Different mechanism for prepared and unprepared stimuli? *Integrative Physiological and Behavioral Science, 32,* 247–256.

KLAVORA, P. (1978). An attempt to derive inverted-U curves based on the relationship between anxiety and athletic performance. In D. M. Landers & R. W. Christina (Eds.), *Psychology of motor behavior and sport—1977.* Champaign, IL: Human Kinetics.

KLEPPNER, O. (1977). *Advertising procedure* (6th ed.). Englewood Cliffs, NJ: Prentice-Hall.

KLINGER, E. (1975). Consequences of commitment to and disengagement from incentives. *Psychological Review, 82,* 1–25.

KLINGER, E. (1977). *Meaning and void: Inner experience and the incentives in people's lives.* Minneapolis: University of Minnesota Press.

KLUGER, M. J., & ROTTENBERG, B. A. (1979). Fever and reduced iron: Their interaction as a host defense response to bacterial infection. *Science, 203,* 374–376.

KLUVER, H., & BUCY, P. C. (1937). Psychic blindness and other symptoms following bilateral temporal lobectomy in rhesus monkeys. *American Journal of Physiology, 119,* 352–353.

KOBASA, S. C. (1979). Stressful life events, personality and health: An inquiry into hardiness. *Journal of Personality and Social Psychology, 37,* 1–11.

KOHLBERG, L. (1964). Development of moral character and moral ideology. In M. L. Hoffman & L. W. Hoffman (Eds.), *Review of child development research* (Vol. 1). New York: Russell Sage Foundation.

KOHN, A. (1993a). *Punished by rewards.* Boston: Houghton Mifflin.

KOHN, A. (1993b, September-October). Why incentive plans cannot work. *Harvard Business Review, 71,* 54–63.

KRAELING, D. (1961). Analysis of amount of reward as a variable in learning. *Journal of Comparative and Physiological Psychology, 54,* 560–564.

KRALEY, F. S., SIMANSKY, K. J., COOGAN, L. A., & TRATTNER, M. S. (1985). Histamine and serotonin independently elicit drinking in the rat. *Physiology and Behavior, 34,* 963–967.

KRALY, S. F. (1984). Physiology of drinking elicited by eating. *Psychological Review, 91*(4), 478–490.

KRANTZ, D. S., & MANUCK, S. B. (1984). Acute psychophysiologic reactivity and risk of cardiovascular disease: A review and methodological critique. *Psychological Bulletin, 96,* 435–464.

KRAUT, R. E., & JOHNSTON, R. E. (1979). Social and emotional messages of smiling: An ethological approach. *Journal of Personality and Social Psychology, 37,* 1539–1553.

KRECH, D., CRUTCHFIELD, R., & LIVSON, N. (1970) *Elements of psychology.* New York: Alfred A. Knopf.

KRIECKHAUS, E. E., & WOLF, G. (1968). Acquisition of sodium by rats: Interaction of innate mechanisms and latent learning. *Journal of Comparative and Physiological Psychology, 65,* 197–201.

KRUGLANSKI, A. (1978). Endogenous attribution and intrinsic motivation. In M. R. Leppen & D. Greene (Eds.), *The hidden costs of reward.* Hillsdale, NJ: Erlbaum.

KRUGLANSKI, A. W., & Webster, D. M. (1996). Motivated closing of the mind: "Seizing" and "freezing." *Psychological Review, 103,* 263–283.

KRUGLANSKI, A. W., WEBSTER, D. M., & KLEM, A. (1993). Motivated resistance and openness to persuasion in the presence or absence of prior information. *Journal of Personality and Social Psychology, 65,* 861–876.

KUO, Z. Y. (1930). The genesis of the cat's response to the rat. *Journal of Comparative Psychology, 11,* 1–30.

KUO, Z. Y. (1932). Ontogeny of embryonic behavior in aves. *Journal of Experimental Biology, 61,* 395–430, 453–489.

KUO, Z. Y. (1922). How are instincts acquired: *Psychological Review, 29,* 244–265.

LACEY, J. I. (1962). Somatic response patterning and stress: Some revisions of activation theory. In M. H. Appley & R. Trumbull (Eds.), *Psychological stress: Issues in research.* Englewood Cliffs, NJ: Prentice-Hall.

LACEY, J. I., KAGAN, J., LACEY, B. C., & MOSS, H. A. (1963). The visceral level: Situational determinants and behavioral correlates of autonomic response. In P. Knapp (Ed.), *Expression of the emotions in man.* New York: International Universities Press.

LACEY, J. I., & LACEY, B. C. (1970). Some automatic-central nervous system interrelationships. In P. Black (Ed.), *Physiological correlates of emotion.* New York: Academic.

LAIRD, J. D. (1974). Self-attribution of emotion: The effects of expressive behavior on the quality of emotional experience. *Journal of Personality and Social Psychology, 29,* 475–486.

LANDY, F. J., & TRUMBO, D. H. (1980). *Psychology of work behavior.* Homewood, IL: The Dorsey Press.

LANG, P. J., BRADLEY, M. M., & CUTHBERT, B. N. (1989) Emotion, attention, and the startle reflex. *Psychological Review,* 97, 377–395.

LANGE, G. C. (1885). *Om sinds bivogelser.* Copenhagen.

LANGLOIS, J. H., & ROGGMAN, L. A. (1990). Attractive faces are only average. *Psychological Science, 1,* 115–121.

LANGLOIS, J. H., ROGGMAN, L. A., & MUSSELMAN, L. (1994). What is average and what is not average about attractive faces? *Psychological Science, 5,* 214–220.

LANGLOIS, J. H., ROGGMAN, L. A., MUSSELMAN, L., & ACTON, S. (1991). A picture is worth a thousand words: Reply to "On the difficulty of averaging faces." *Psychological Science, 5,* 354–357.

LASHLEY, K. S. (1938). Experimental analysis of instinctive behavior. *Psychological Review, 45,* 445–471.

LASHLEY, K. (1950). In search of the engram. *Symposium of the Society of Experimental Biology, 4,* 454–582.

LATANE, B. (1981). The psychology of social impact. *American Psychologist, 36,* 343–356.

LATANE, B., & DARLEY, J. M. (1970). *The unresponsive bystander: Why doesn't he help?* New York: Appleton-Century-Crofts.

LATHAM, G. P., & BALDES, J. J. (1975). The "practical significance" in Locke's theory of goal setting. *Journal of Applied Psychology, 60,* 122–124.

LATOUR, M. S., & HENTHORNE, T. L. (1994). Female nudity in advertisements, arousal and response: A parsimonious extension. *Psychological Reports, 75,* 1683–1690.

LAWLER, E. E., & PORTER, L. W. (1967). The effects of performance on job satisfaction. *Industrial Relations, 20,* 20–28.

LAWLESS, H. T. (1987). Gustatory psychophysics. In T. E. Finger & W. L. Silver (Eds.), *Neurobiology of taste and smell.* New York: Wiley Interscience.

LAWSON, R. (1965). *Frustration: The development of a scientific concept.* New York: Macmillan.

LAZARUS, R. S. (1968). Emotion and adaption: Conceptual and empirical relations In E. J. Arnold (Ed.), *Nebraska symposium on motivation.* Lincoln, NE: University of Nebraska Press.

LAZARUS, R. S. (1981). Little hassles can be dangerous to your health. *Psychology Today, 15,* 58–61.

LAZARUS, R. S. (1984). On the primacy of cognition. *American Psychologist, 39*(2), 124–129.

LAZARUS, R. S., & FOLKMAN, S. (1984). *Stress, appraisal, and coping.* New York: McGraw-Hill.

LEA, S. E. G. (1978). The psychology of economics of demand. *Psychological Bulletin, 85,* 441–466.

LEAF, R. C. (1964). Avoidance response evocation as a function of prior discriminative fear conditioning under curare. *Journal of Comparative and Physiological Psychology, 58,* 446–449.

LEATON, R. N., & BORSZCZ, B. (1985). Potentiated startle: Its relation to freezing and shock intensity in rats. *Journal of Experimental Psychology: Animal Behavior Processes, 11*(3), 421–428.

LEDOUX, J. E. (1993). Emotional networks in the brain. In M. Lewis & J. M. Haviland (Eds), *Handbook of emotions.* New York: The Guilford Press.

LeDoux, J. E. (1994). Cognitive-emotional interactions in the brain. In P. Ekman & R. Davidson (Eds.), *The nature of emotion: Fundamental questions.* New York: Oxford.

Lee, J. A. (1977). A typology of styles of loving. *Personality and Social Psychology Bulletin, 3,* 173–182.

Leeper, R. (1935). The role of motivation in learning: A study of the phenomenon of differential motivational control of the utilization of habits. *Journal of Genetic Psychology, 46,* 3–40.

Lepper, M., & Greene, D. (1978). *The hidden cost of reward.* New York: Lawrence Erlbaum Associates, Inc.

Leventhal, H., & Tomarken, A. (1986). Emotion: Today's problems. *Annual Review of Psychology, 37,* 565–610.

Levey, A. B., & Martin, I. (1987). Evaluative conditioning: A case for hedonic transfer. In H. J. Eysenck & I. Martin (Eds.). *Theoretical foundations of behaviour therapy* (pp. 113–132). London: Plenum.

Levey, A. B., & Martin, I. (1975). Classical conditioning of human "evaluative" responses. *Behaviour Research and Therapy, 13,* 221–116.

Levine, S. (1960). Stimulation in infancy. *Scientific American, 202,* 80–86.

Levinger, G., Rands, M., & Talober, R. (1977). *The assessment of involvement and rewardingness in close and casual pair relationships* (National Science Foundation Tech. Dept. DIC). Amherst: University of Massachusetts.

Lewin, K. (1935). *A dynamic theory of personality.* New York: McGraw-Hill.

Lewin, K., Dembo, T., Festinger, L., & Sears, P. S. (1944). Level of aspiration. In J. McV. Hunt (Ed.), *Personality and the behavior disorders.* New York: Ronald Press.

Lindsley, D. B. (1950). Emotions and the electroencephalogram. In M. Reymert (Ed.), The second international symposium in feelings and emotions. New York: McGraw-Hill.

Lindsley, D. B. (1951). Emotion. In S. S. Stevens (Ed.), *Handbook of experimental psychology.* New York: Wiley.

Lindsley, D. B., Schreiner, L. H., Knowles, W. B., & Magoun, H. W. (1950). Behavioral and EEG changes following chronic brain stem lesions in the cat. *Electroencephalography and Clinical Neurophysiology, 2,* 483–498.

Lippsitt, L., Reilly, B. M., Butcher, M. J., & Greenwood, M. M. (1976). The stability and interrelationships of newborn sucking and heart rate. *Developmental Psychobiology, 9,* 305–310.

Little, B. R. (1983). Personal projects: a rationale and method for investigation. *Environment and Behavior, 15,* 273–309.

Locke, E. A. (1968). Toward a theory of task motivation and incentives. *Organizational Behavior and Human Performance, 3,* 157–189.

Locke, E. A. (1976). Nature and causes of job satisfaction. In M. Dunnette (Ed.), *Handbook of industrial and organizational psychology.* New York: Rand-McNally.

Locke, E. A., & Latham, G. P. (1984). *Goal setting: A motivational technique that works!* Englewood Cliffs, NJ: Prentice-Hall, Inc.

Loewenstein, G. (1994). The psychology of curiosity: A review and reinterpretation. *Psychological Bulletin, 116,* 75–98.

Loewenstein, G., Adler, D., Behrens, D., & Gillis, J. (1992). *Why Pandora opened the box: Curiosity as a desire for missing information.* Working paper, Department of Social and Decision Sciences, Carnegie Mellon University, Pittsburgh, PA.

Loftus, E. F., & Klinger, M. R. (1992). Is the unconscious smart or dumb? *American Psychologist, 47,* 761–765.

Logan, F. A. (1960). *Incentive.* New Haven, CT: Yale University Press.

Logan, F. A. (1965). Decision making by rats: Delay versus amount of reward. *Journal of Comparative and Physiological Psychology, 59,* 1–12.

Logan, F. A. (1968). Incentive theory and changes in reward. In G. H. Bower (Ed.), *The psychology of learning and motivation* (Vol. 2). New York: Academic.

Lolordo, V. M. (1969). Positive conditioned reinforcement from aversive situations. *Psychological Bulletin, 72,* 193–203.

Lorenz, K. (1965). *On aggression.* New York: Harcourt Brace Jovanovich.

Lott, A. J., & Lott, B. E. (1974). The role of reward in the foundation of positive interpersonal attitudes. In T. C. Huston (Ed.), *Foundations of interpersonal attraction.* New York: Academic Press.

MacCorquodale, K., & Meehl, P. E. (1954). Edward C. Tolman. In W. Estes, S. Koch, K. MacCorquodale, P. E. Meehl, C. G. Mueller, W. N. Schoenfeld, & W. S. Verplanck (Eds.), *Modern learning theory.* New York: Appleton-Century-Crofts.

MAGOUN, H. W. (1954). The descending reticular system and wakefulness. In J. F. Delafresnaye (Ed.), *Brain mechanisms and consciousness*. Blackwell: Oxford.

MAIER, S. F., SELIGMAN, M. E. P., & Solomon, R. L. (1969). Pavlovian fear conditioning and learned helplessness: Effects on escape and avoidance behavior of (a) the CS-UCS contingency and (b) the independence of UCS and voluntary responding. In B. A. Campbell & R. M. Church (Eds.), *Punishment and aversive behavior*. New York: Appleton- Century-Crofts.

MAISTO, S. A., GALIZIO, M., & CONNORS, G. J. (1991). *Drug use and misuse*. Philadelphia: Holt, Rinehart & Winston.

MALMO, R. B. (1959). Activation: A neuropsychological dimension. *Psychological Review, 66,* 367–386.

MALMO, R. B. (1975). *Our emotions, needs, and our archaic brain*. New York: Holt, Rinehart and Winston.

MANDLER, G. (1962). Emotions. In T. M. Newcomb (Ed.), *New directions in psychology*. New York: Holt, Rinehart and Winston.

MANSSON, H. H. (1966). The cognitive control of thirst motivation: A dissonance approach. Unpublished doctoral dissertation, New York University. Cited in P. G. Zimbardo. The cognitive control of motivation. *Transactions of the New York Academy of Sciences*, Series II, *28,* 902–922.

MARLER, P. (1976). On animal aggression: The roles of strangeness and familiarity. *American Psychologist, 31,* 239–246.

MARSHALL, G. D., & ZIMBARDO, P. G. (1979). Affective consequences of inadequately explained physiological arousal. *Journal of Personality and Social Psychology, 37,* 970–988.

MARTIN, I., & LEVEY, A. B. (1978). Evaluative conditioning. *Advances in Behavioural Therapy,* 1, 57–102.

MARTIN, K. A., & LEARY, M. R. (1998). Single, female, physically active: Effects of exercise status and body weight on stereotyped perceptions of young women. Unpublished manuscript. Wake Forest University.

MASLACH, C. (1979). Negative emotional biasing of unexplained arousal. *Journal of Personality and Social Psychology, 37,* 953–969.

MASLOW, A. H. (1970). *Motivation and personality* (2nd ed.). New York: Harper & Row.

MASSERMAN, J. H. (1943). *Behavior and neurosis*. Chicago: University of Chicago Press.

MASTERS, W. H., & JOHNSON, V. (1966) *Human sexual response*. Boston: Little, Brown.

MATHES, E. W. (1975). The effects of physical attractiveness and anxiety on heterosexual attraction over a series of five encounters. *Journal of Marriage and the Family, 37,* 769–774.

MATSUMOTO, D. (1987). The role of facial response in the experience of emotion: More methodological problems and a meta-analysis. *Journal of Personality and Social Psychology, 52*(4), 769–774.

MCADAMS, D. P. (1997). A conceptual history of personality psychology. In R. Hogan, J. Johnson, & S. Briggs (Eds.), *Handbook of personality psychology*. New York: Academic Press.

MCADAMS, D. P., & McClelland, D. C. (1983). *Social motives and memory*. Unpublished manuscript, Harvard University, Department of Psychology and Social Relations. Cited in McClelland (1985, p. 279).

MCALLISTER, W. R., & MCALLISTER, D. E. (1971). Behavioral measurement of conditioned fear. In F. R. Brush (Ed.), *Aversive conditioning and learning*. New York: Academic.

MCALLISTER, W. R., MCALLISTER, D. E., SCOLES, M. T., & HAMPTON, S. R. (1986). Persistence of fear-reducing behavior: Relevance for the conditioning theory of neurosis. *Journal of Abnormal Psychology, 95,* 365–372.

MCCAIN, G. (1966). Partial reinforcement effects following a small number of acquisition trials. *Psychonomic Monograph Supplements, 1,* 251–270.

MCCLEARY, R. A., & LAZARUS, R. S. (1949). Autonomic discrimination without awareness: An interim report. *Journal of Personality, 18,* 171–179.

MCCLELLAND, D. C. (1985). *Human motivation*. New York: Scott-Freeman.

MCCLELLAND, D. C. (1958). Risk-taking in children with high and low need for achievement. In J. W. Atkinson (Ed.), *Motives in fantasy, action, and society*. Princeton: Van Nostrand.

MCCLELLAND, D. C. (1961). *The achieving society*. Princeton: Van Nostrand.

MCCLELLAND, D. C. (1965). N achievement and entrepreneurship: A longitudinal study. *Journal of Personality and Social Psychology, 1,* 389–392.

MCCLELLAND, D. C., ATKINSON, J. W., CLARK, R. A., & LOWELL, E. L. (1953). *The achievement motive.* New York: Appleton-Century-Crofts.

MCCLELLAND, D. C., DAVIDSON, R., SARON, C., & FLOOR, E. (1980). The need for power, brain norepinephrine turnover, and learning. *Biological Psychology, 10,* 93–102.

McClelland, D. C., Davis, W. W., Kalin, R., & Wanner, E. (1972). *The drinking man: Alcohol and human motivation.* New York: Free Press.

McClelland, D. C., Patel, V., Stier, D., & Brown, D. (1987). The relationship of affiliative arousal to dopamine release. *Motivation and emotion, 2,* 51–66.

McClelland, D. C., Rindlisbacher, A., & DeCharms, R. C. (1955). Religious and other sources of parental attitudes toward independence training. In D. C. McClelland (Ed.), *Studies in motivation.* New York: Appleton-Century-Crofts.

McCormick, E. J., & Ilgen, D. R. (1980). *Industrial psychology* (7th ed.). Englewood Cliffs, NJ: Prentice-Hall.

McDougall, W. (1923). *Outline of psychology.* New York: Charles Scribner's Sons.

McGinnies, E. (1949). Emotionality and perceptual defense. *Psychological Review, 56,* 244–251.

McGrath, J. E. (1970). *Social and psychological factors in stress.* New York: Holt, Rinehart and Winston.

McGregor, D. (1960). *The human side of enterprise.* New York: McGraw-Hill.

McKeachie, W. J., Lin, Y., Milholland, J., & Issacson, R. (1966). Student affiliation motives, teacher warmth, and academic achievement. *Journal of Personality and Social Psychology, 4,* 457–461.

McNally, R. J. (1987). Preparedness and phobias: A review. *Psychological Bulletin, 101,* 283–303.

Meehl, P. E. (1950). On the circularity of the law of effect. *Psychological Bulletin, 47,* 52–75.

Mehrabian, A. (1976). *Public spaces and private places.* New York: Basic Books.

Mendelson, J., & Chillag, D. (1970). Tongue cooling: A new reward for thirsty rodents. *Science, 170,* 1418–1421.

Meryman, J. J. (1961). *Magnitude of startle response as a function of hunger and fear.* Unpublished master's thesis, State University of Iowa. Cited by Brown, 1961.

Milgram, S. (1974). *Obedience to authority: An experimental view.* New York: Harper & Row.

Miller, G. A., Galanter, E., & Pribram, K. H. (1960). *Plans and the structure of behavior.* New York: Holt, Rinehart and Winston.

Miller, N. E. (1948). Studies of fear as an acquirable drive: I. Fear as motivation and fear- reduction as reinforcement in the learning of new responses. *Journal of Experimental Psychology, 38,* 89–101.

Miller, N. E. (1951a). Comments on multi-process conceptions of learning. *Psychological Review, 58,* 375–381.

Miller, N. E. (1951b). Learnable drives and rewards. In S. S. Stevens (Ed.), *Handbook of experimental psychology.* New York: Wiley.

Miller, N. E. (1959). Liberalization of basic S-R concepts: Extensions to conflict behavior, motivation and social learning. In S. Koch (Ed.), *Psychology: A study of a science* (Vol. 2). New York: McGraw-Hill.

Miller, N. E. (1960). Learning resistance to pain and fear: Effects of overlearning, exposure, and rewarded exposure in context. *Journal of Experimental Psychology, 60,* 137–145.

Miller, N. E., & Dollard, J. (1950). *Personality and psychotherapy.* New York: McGraw Hill.

Miller, N. E., & Kessen, M. L. (1952). Reward effects of food via stomach fistula compared with those of food via mouth. *Journal of Comparative and Physiological Psychology, 45,* 555–564.

Miller, R. R., Greco, C., Vigorito, M., & Marlin, N. A. (1983). Signaled tailshock is perceived as similar to a stronger unsignaled tailshock: Implications for a functional analysis of classical conditioning. *Journal of Experimental Psychology: Animal Behavior Processes, 9,* 105–131.

Miller, S. M., & Mangan, C. E. (1983). Interacting effects of information and coping style in adapting to gynecologic stress: Should the doctor tell all? *Journal of Personality and Social Psychology, 45,* 223–236.

Mills, J., & Mintz, P. M. (1972). Effect of unexplained arousal on affiliation. *Journal of Personality and Social Psychology, 24,* 11–13.

Mineka, S. (1979). The role of fear in theories of avoidance learning, flooding, and extinction. *Psychological Bulletin, 5,* 985–1010.

Mineka, S., & Henderson, R. W. (1985). Controllability and predictability in acquired motivation. *Annual Review of Psychology, 36,* 495–529.

Mischel, W. (1973). Toward a cognitive social learning reconceptualization of personality. *Psychological Review, 80,* 252–283.

Mitchell, J. E. (1986). Bulimia: Medical and physiological aspects. In K. D. Brownell & J. P. Foreyt (eds). Handbook of eating disorders. New York: Basic Books, Inc. Publishers.

Moltz, H. (1960). Imprinting: Empirical basis and theoretical significance. *Psychological Bulletin, 57,* 291–314.

MONAT, A., & LAZARUS, R. S. (1985). Stress and coping—some current issues and controversies. In A. Monat & R. Lazarus (Eds.), *Stress and coping* (2nd ed.). New York: Columbia University Press.

MONEY, J. (1987). Sin, sickness, or status: Homosexual gender identity and psychoneuroendocrinology. *American Psychologist, 42,* 284–299.

MONEY, J., & EHRHARDT, A. (1972). *Man & woman, boy & girl.* Baltimore: Johns Hopkins University Press.

MONTGOMERY, K. C. (1953). The effect of hunger and thirst drives upon exploratory behavior. *Journal of Comparative and Physiological Psychology, 46,* 315–319.

MOORE, T. E. (1982). Subliminal advertising: What you see is what you get. *Journal of Marketing, 46,* 38–47.

MORGAN, C. T. (1943). *Physiological psychology.* New York: McGraw-Hill.

MORGAN, C. T. (1959). Physiological theory of drive. In S. Koch (Ed.), *Psychology: A study of science* (Vol. 1). New York: McGraw-Hill.

MORRIS, C. W. (1938). Foundations of the theory of signs. In O. Neurath, R. Carnap, & C. Morris (Eds.), *International encyclopedia of unified science* (Vol. 1). Chicago: University of Chicago Press.

MORRIS, D. (1967). *The naked ape.* New York: Dell.

MORRIS, W. N. (1989). *Mood: The frame of mind.* New York: Springer-Verlag.

MORRISON, A. R. (1983). A window on the sleeping brain. *Scientific American, 248*(4), 94–102.

MORUZZI, G., & MAGOUN, H. W. (1949). Brain stem and reticular formation and activation of the EEG. *Electroencephalography and Clinical Neurophysiology, 1,* 455–473.

MOSCOVITCH, A., & LOLORDO, V. M. (1968). Role of safety in the Pavlovian backward fear conditioning procedure. *Journal of Comparative and Physiological Psychology, 66,* 673–678.

MOSS, M. K., & PAGE, R. A. (1972). Reinforcement and helping behavior. *Journal of Applied Social Psychology, 2,* 360–371.

MOULTON, R. W. (1965). Effects of success and failure on level of aspiration as related to achievement motives. *Journal of Personality and Social Psychology, 1,* 399–406.

MOWRER, O. H. (1939). A stimulus-response analysis of anxiety and its role as a reinforcing agent. *Psychological Review, 46,* 553–564.

MOWRER, O. H. (1960). *Learning theory and behavior.* New York: Wiley.

MOWRER, O. H., & AIKEN, E. G. (1954). Contiguity vs. drive-reduction in conditioned fear: Temporal variations in conditioned and unconditioned stimulus. *American Journal of Psychology, 67,* 26–38.

MOWRER, O. H., & LAMOREAUX, R. R. (1946). Fear as an intervening variable in avoidance conditioning. *Journal of Comparative Psychology, 39,* 29–50.

MOWRER, O. H., & VIEK, P. (1948). An experimental analogue of fear from a sense of helplessness. *Journal of Abnormal and Social Psychology, 83,* 193–200.

MOYER, K. E. (1971) The physiology of aggression and the implications of aggression control. In J. L. Singer (Ed.), *The control of aggression and violence: cognitive and physiological factors.* New York: Academic.

MUNTON, A. G. (1985–1986). Learned helplessness, attribution theory, and the nature of cognitions: A critical evaluation. *Current Psychological Research and Reviews,* Winter, 331–348.

MURPHY, S., & ZAJONC, R. B. (1993). Affect, cognition, and awareness: Affective priming with optimal and suboptimal stimulus exposures. *Journal of Personality and Social Psychology, 64,* 723–739.

MURRAY, H. A. (1938). *Explorations in personality.* New York: Oxford University Press.

NEISS, R. (1988). Reconceptualizing arousal: Psychobiological states in motor performance. *Psychological Bulletin, 103,* 345–366.

NEL, E., HELMREICH, R., & ARONSON, E. (1969). Opinion change in the advocate as a function of the persuasibility of the audience: A clarification of the meaning of dissonance. *Journal of Personality and Social Psychology, 12,* 117–124.

NEWCOMB, T. M. (1961). *The acquaintance process.* New York: Holt, Rinehart and Winston.

NEWCOMB, T. (1968). Interpersonal balance. In R. P. Abelson, E. Aronson, W. J. McGuire, T. M. Newcomb, M. J. Rosenberg, & P. H. Tannenbaum (Eds.), *Theories of cognitive consistency: A sourcebook.* Chicago: Rand McNally.

NICHOLAIDIS, S. (1968). Réponses des unites osmosensibles hypothalamiques aux stimulations saliens at aqueuses de la langue. *Competes rendus hebdomadaires des séances de l'académie des sciences,* Series C, *267,* 2352–2355.

Nisbett, R. E. (1972). Hunger, obesity, and the ventromedial hypothalamus. *Psychological Review, 79,* 433–453.

Norman, W. T. (1963) Toward an adequate taxonomy of personality attributes. *Journal of Abnormal and Social Psychology, 66,* 574–583.

Notz, W. W. (1975). Work motivation and the negative effects of extrinsic rewards: A review with implications for theory and practice. *American Psychologist, 9,* 844–891.

Novin, D. (1962). The relation between electrical conductivity of brain tissue and thirst in the rat. *Journal of Comparative and Physiological Psychology, 55,* 145–154.

Oatley, K., & Jenkins, J. M. (1996). *Understanding emotions.* Cambridge, MA: Blackwell Publishers.

Obrist, P. A. (1981). *Cardiovascular psychophysiology: A perspective.* New York: Plenum Press.

Öhman, A. (1983). Evaluating evaluative conditioning. Some comments on "Cognitions, Evaluations, and Conditioning: Rules of Sequence and Rules of Consequence" by Levey and Martin. *Advances in Behavior Research & Therapy, 4,* 213–218.

Öhman, A. (1985). Face the beast and fear the face: Animal and social fears as prototypes for evolutionary analyses of emotion. *Psychophysiology, 23,* 123–145.

Öhman, A. (1986). Face the beast and fear the face: Animal and social fears as prototypes for evolutionary analyses of emotion. *Psychophysiology, 23*(2), 123–145

O'Kelly, L. I., & Beck, R. C. (1960). Water regulation in the rat: III. The artificial control of thirst with stomach loads of water and sodium chloride. *Psychological Monographs, 74*(13, Whole No. 500).

O'Kelly, L. I., & Steckle, L. C. (1939). A note on long-enduring emotional responses in the rat. *Journal of Psychology, 8,* 125–131.

Olds, J. (1956). Pleasure centers in the brain. *Scientific American, 195,* 105–116.

Olds, J. (1958). Satiation effects in self-stimulation of the brain. *Journal of Comparative and Physiological Psychology, 51,* 675–678.

Olds, J., & Milner, P. (1954). Positive reinforcement produced by electrical stimulation of the septal area and other regions of the rat brain. *Journal of Comparative and Physiological Psychology, 47,* 419–427.

O'Leary, C. J., Willis, F. N., & Tomich, E. (1969). Conformity under deceptive and nondeceptive techniques. *Sociological Quarterly,* Winter, 87–93.

Ornstein, R. (1986). *The psychology of consciousness.* New York: Penguin.

Osgood, C. E. (1950). Can Tolman's theory of learning handle avoidance training? *Psychological Review, 57,* 133–137.

Osgood, C. E., Suci, G. J., & Tannenbaum, P. H. (1957). *The measurement of meaning.* Urbana: University of Illinois Press.

Overmier, J. B., & Seligman, M. E. P. (1967). Effects of inescapable shock upon subsequent escape and avoidance responding. *Journal of Comparative and Physiological Psychology, 63,* 28–33.

Oxendine, J. B. (1970). Emotional arousal and motor performance. *Quest, 13,* 23–32.

Page, H. A. (1955). The facilitation of experimental extinction by response prevention as a function of the acquisition of a new response. *Journal of Comparative and Physiological Psychology, 48,* 14–16.

Page, M. M., & Scheidt, R. J. (1971). The elusive weapons effect: Demand awareness, evaluation apprehension, and slightly sophisticated subjects. *Journal of Personality and Social Psychology, 20,* 304–318.

Page, M. M. (1974). Demand characteristics and the classical conditioning of attitudes experiment. *Journal of Personality and Social Psychology, 30,* 468–476.

Pallak, M. S., & Pittman, T. S. (1972). General motivational effects of dissonance arousal. *Journal of Personality and Social Psychology, 21,* 349–358.

Pallak, M. S., & Pittman, T. S. (1972). General motivational effects of dissonance arousal. *Journal of Personality and Social Psychology, 21,* 349–358.

Palmer, J., & Byrne, D. (1970). Attraction toward dominant and submissive strangers: Similarity versus complementarity. *Journal of Experimental Research in Psychology, 4,* 108–115.

Papez, J. W. (1937). A proposed mechanism of emotion. *Archives of Neurology and Psychiatry, 38,* 725–743.

Pastore, N. (1952). The role of arbitrariness in the frustration-aggression hypothesis. *Journal of Abnormal and Social Psychology, 57,* 728–731.

Patterson, M. L. (1976). An arousal model for interpersonal intimacy. *Psychological Review, 83,* 235–245.

Penfield, W., & Jasper, H. H. (1954). Epilepsy and the functional anatomy of the brain. Boston: Little Brown.

PEPLAU, L. A. (1982). Interpersonal attraction. In D. Sherrod (Ed.), *Social psychology*. New York: Random House.

PEPPER, S. (1959). A neural-identity theory of mind. In S. Hook (Ed.), *Dimensions of mind*. New York: Collier.

PERIN, C. T. (1942). Behavioral potentiality as a joint function of the amount of training and the degree of hunger at the time of extinction. *Journal of Experimental Psychology, 30,* 93–113.

PETERSON, R. A., & KERIN, R. A. (1977). The female role in advertising: Some experimental evidence. *Journal of Marketing, 41,* 59–63.

PETTY, R. E., & CACIOPPO, J. T. (1984). Motivational factors in consumer response to advertisements. In R. G. Geen, W. W. Beatty, & R. M. Arkin (Eds.), *Human motivation*. New York: Allyn and Bacon.

PETTY, R. E., CACIOPPO, J. T., & SCHUMANN, D. (1983). Central and peripheral routes to advertising effectiveness: The moderating role of involvement. *Journal of Consumer Research, 10,* 135–146.

PFAFFMANN, C., & BARE, J. K. (1950). Gustatory nerve discharges in normal and adrenalectomized rats. *Journal of Comparative and Physiological Psychology, 43,* 320–324.

PIET, S. (1987). What motivates stunt men? *Motivation and Emotion, 11*(2), 195–213.

PILLIAVIN, I., RODIN, J., & PILIAVIN, J. (1969). Good Samaritanism: An underground phenomenon? *Journal of Personality and Social Psychology, 13,* 289–299.

PITTENGER, J. B. (1991). On the difficulty of averaging faces: Comments on Langlois and Roggman. *Psychological Science, 5,* 351–353.

PLATT, J. R. (1961). Beauty: Pattern and change. In D. W. Fiske & S. R. Maddi (Eds.) Functions of varied experience. Homewood, IL: The Dorsey Press.

PLOMIN, R., FULKER, D. W., CORLEY, R., & DEFRIES, J. C. (1997). Nature, nurture, and cognitive development from 1 to 16 years: A parent-offspring adoption study. *Psychological Science, 6,* 442–447.

PLUTCHIK, R. (1980). *Emotion: A psychoevolutionary synthesis*. New York: Harper & Row.

POPPER, K. R. (1959). *The logic of scientific discovery*. New York: Harper & Row.

POSTMAN, L. (1947). The history and present status of the law of effect. *Psychological Bulletin, 44,* 489–563.

POSTMAN, L., BRONSON, W., & GROPPER, G. L. (1953). Is there a mechanism of perceptual defense? *Journal of Abnormal and Social Psychology, 48,* 215–224.

PREMACK, D. (1959). Toward empirical behavioral laws: I. Positive reinforcement. *Psychological Review, 66,* 219–233.

PREMACK, D. (1971). Catching up with common sense or two sides of a generalization: Reinforcement and punishment. In R. Glaser (Ed.), *The nature of reinforcement*. New York: Academic.

PRIEST, R. F., & SAWYER, J. (1967). Proximity and peership: Bases of balance in interpersonal attraction. *American Journal of Sociology, 7,* 21–27.

PRITCHARD, R. M. (1961). Stabilized images on the retina. *Scientific American, 204,* 72–78.

RAMIREZ, I., & FULLER, J. L. (1976). Genetic influence on water and sweetened water consumption in mice. *Physiology and Behavior, 16,* 163–168.

RAMSAY, D. S., SEELEY, R. J., BOLLES, R. C., & WOODS, S. C. (1996). Ingestive homeostasis: The primacy of learning. In E. D. Capaldi (Ed.), *Why we eat what we eat: The psychology of eating*. Washington, DC: American Psychological Association.

RANSON, S. W., FISCHER, C., & INGRAM, W. R. (1938). The hypothalamicohypophyseal mechanism in diabetes insipidus. Paper read before Association for Research in Nervous and Mental Diseases, December 1936. In *The pituitary gland*. Baltimore, MD: Williams and Wilkins.

RAY, O. (1963). The effects of tranquilizers on positively and negatively motivated bahavior in rats. *Psychopharmacologia, 4,* 326–342.

RAZRAN, G. H. (1938). Conditioning away social bias by the luncheon technique. *Psychological Bulletin, 35,* 693.

RAZRAN, G. (1954). The conditioned evocation of attitudes (cognitive conditioning?). *Journal of Experimental Psychology, 48,* 278–282.

RAZRAN, G. (1961). The observable unconscious and the inferable conscious in current Soviet psychophysiology: Interoceptive conditioning, semantic conditioning, and the orienting reflex. *Psychological Review, 68,* 81–147.

REISENZEIN, R. (1983). The Schachter theory of emotion: Two decades later. *Psychological Bulletin, 94,* 239–264.

REITH, J. (1988). *Job satisfaction parallels in higher education.* Unpublished master's thesis, Wake Forest University, Winston-Salem, NC.

RESCORLA, R. A. (1969). Establishment of a positive reinforcer through contrast with shock. *Journal of Comparative and Physiological Psychology, 67,* 260–263.

RESCORLA, R. A. (1987). A Pavlovian analysis of goal-directed behavior. *American Psychologist, 42,* 119–129.

RESCORLA, R. A., & LOLORDO, V. M. (1965). Inhibition of avoidance behavior. *Journal of Comparative and Physiological Psychology,* 59, 406–412.

RESCORLA, R. A., & SOLOMON, R. L. (1967). Two-process learning theory: Relationships between Pavlovian conditioning and instrumental learning. *Psychological Review, 74,* 151–182.

REVUSKY, S. H. (1967). Hunger level during food consumption: Effects on subsequent preferences. *Psychonomic Science, 7,* 109–110.

REVUSKY, S. H. (1968). Effects of thirst level during consumption of flavored water on subsequent preference. *Journal of Comparative and Physiological Psychology, 66,* 777–779.

REVUSKY, S. H., & GARCIA, J. (1970). Learned associations over long delays. In C. H. Bower & J. T. Spence (Eds.), *The psychology of learning and motivation: Advances in research and theory* (Vol. 4). New York: Academic.

RHODES, G., & TREMEWAN, T. (1996). Averageness, exaggeration, and facial attractiveness. *Psychological Science, 2,* 105–110.

RICHMAN, C. L., DEMBER, W., & KIM, P. (Winter 1986–87). Spontaneous alternation behavior in animals: A review. *Current Psychological Research and Reviews, 5,* 358–391.

RICHTER, C. P. (1936). Increased salt appetite in adrenalectomized rats. *American Journal of Physiology, 115,* 155–161.

RIMM, D. C., & MASTERS, J. C. (1979). *Behavior therapy: Techniques and empirical findings* (2nd ed.). New York: Academic Press.

RINN, W. (1984). The neuropsychology of facial expression: A review of the neurological and psychological mechanisms for producing facial expressions. *Psychological Bulletin, 95*(1), 52–77.

ROBBINS, D. (1969). Effect of duration of water reinforcement on running behavior and consummatory activity. *Journal of Comparative and Physiological Psychology, 69,* 311–316.

ROBERTS, G. C. (1984). Toward a new theory of motivation in sport: The role of perceived ability. In R. M. Silva & R. S. Weinberg (Eds.), Psychological foundations of sport. Champaign, IL: Human Kinetics Publishers, Inc.

ROBINS, C. J. (1988). Attributions and depression: Why is the literature so inconsistent? *Journal of Personality and Social Psychology, 54*(5), 880–889.

RODIN, J. (1981). Current status of the internal-external hypothesis for obesity: What went wrong? *American Psychologist, 36,* 361–372.

RODIN, J., BARTOSHUK, L., PETERSON, C., & SCHANK, D. (1990). Bulimia and taste: Possible interactions. *Journal of Abnormal Psychology, 99,* 32–39.

RODIN, J., & LANGER, E. J. (1977). Long-term effects of control-relevant intervention with the institutionalized aged. *Journal of Personality and Social Psychology, 35,* 897–902.

ROETHLISBERGER, F. J., & DICKSON, W. J. (1947)). *Management and the worker.* Cambridge, MA: Harvard University Press.

ROGERS, M., & SMITH, K. H. (1993). Public perceptions of subliminal advertising: Why practitioners shouldn't ignore this issue. *Journal-of-Advertising Research, 33,* 10–18.

ROTHBAUM, F., WEISZ, J. R., & SNYDER, S. S. (1982). Changing the world and changing the self: A two process model of perceived control. *Journal of Personality and Social Psychology, 42,* 5–37.

ROTTER, J. B. (1966). Generalized expectancies for internal versus external control of reinforcement. *Psychological Monographs, 80*(Whole No. 609).

ROUTTENBERG, A. (1968). The two-arousal hypothesis: Reticular formation and limbic system. *Psychological Review, 75,* 51–80.

ROZIN, P. (1996). Sociocultural influences on human food selection. In E.D. Capaldi (Ed.), *Why we eat what we eat: The psychology of eating.* Washington, DC: American Psychological Association.

ROZIN, P., & KALAT, J. W. (1971). Specific hungers and poison avoidance as adaptive specializations of learning. *Psychological Review, 78,* 459–486.

RUBIN, Z. (1970). Measurement of romantic love. *Journal of Personality and Social Psychology, 16,* 265–273.

RUBIN, Z. (1973). *Liking and loving.* New York: Holt, Rinehart and Winston.

RUSBULT, C. (1983). A longitudinal test of the investment model: The development (and deteric ration) of satisfaction and commitment in heterosexual involvements. *Journal of Personalit and Social Psychology, 45,* 101–117.

RUSSELL, J. A. (1979). Affective space is bipolar. *Journal of Personality and Social Psychology, 37* 345–356.

RUSSELL, J. A. (1980). A circumplex model of affect. *Journal of Personality and Social Psychology, 3* 1161–1178.

RUSSELL, J. A., & BULLOCK, M. (1985). Multidimensional scaling of emotional facial expressions: Sim ilarity from preschoolers to adults. *Journal of Personality and Social Psychology, 48,* 1290–1298.

RUSSELL, J. A., & MEHRABIAN, A. (1977). Evidence for a three-factor theory of emotions. *Journal o Research in Psychology, 11,* 273–294.

RYLE, G. (1949). *The concept of mind.* New York: Barnes & Noble.

SALOVEY, P., MAYER, J. D., & ROSENHAN, D. L. (1991). Mood and helping: Mood as a motivator o helping and helping as a regulator of mood. In M. S. Clark (Ed.), *Review of Personality an Social Psychology* (Vol. 12: Prosocial Behavior, pp. 295–237). Newbury Park, CA: Sage.

SATINOFF, E. (1983). A reevaluation of the concept of the homeostatic organization of tempera ture regulation. In E. Satinoff & P. Teitelbaum (Eds.), *Handbook of behavioral neurobiolog* (Vol. 6). New York: Plenum.

SCHACHTER, S. (1951). Deviation, rejection, and communication. *Journal of Abnormal and Socia Psychology, 46,* 190–207.

SCHACHTER, S. (1959). *The psychology of affiliation.* Palo Alto, CA: Stanford University Press.

SCHACHTER, S. (1971a). *Emotion, obesity, and crime.* New York: Academic.

SCHACHTER, S. (1971b). Some extraordinary facts about obese humans and rats. *American Psychol. gist, 26,* 129–144.

SCHACHTER, S., & SINGER, J. E. (1962). Cognitive, social, and physiological determinants of emc tional state. *Psychological Review, 69,* 379–399.

SCHAFE, G. E., & BERNSTEIN, I. L. (1996) Taste version learning. In E.D. Capaldi (Ed.), *Why we ec what we eat: The psychology of eating.* Washington, D.C.: American Psychological Associa tion.

SCHER, S. J., & COOPER, J. (1989). Motivation basis of dissonance: The singular role of behavior consequences. *Journal of Personality and Social Psychology, 56,* 899–906.

SCHLENKER, B. (1982). Translating actions into attitudes: An identity analytic approach to the e planation of social conduct. In L. Berkowitz (Ed.), *Advances in experimental social psycholog* (Vol. 15). New York: Academic Press.

SCHLOSBERG, H. (1954). Three dimensions of emotion. *Psychological Review, 61,* 81–88.

SCHMIDT, D. E., & KEATING, J. P. (1979). Human crowding and personal control: An integration o the research. *Psychological Bulletin, 86,* 680–700.

SCHNEIDER, A. M., & TARSHIS, B. (1975) *An introduction to physiological psychology.* New York: Ran dom House.

SCHNEIDER, D. J. (1976) *Social psychology.* Reading, MA: Addison-Wesley.

SCHOPLER, J., & COMPERE, J. S. (1971). Effects of being kind or harsh to another on liking. *Journc of Personality and Social Psychology, 20,* 155–159.

SCHWARTZ, S. (1968). Words, deeds, and the perception of consequences and responsibility in a tion situations. *Journal of Personality and Social Psychology, 10,* 232–242.

SCHWARTZ, S., & CLAUSEN, G. T. (1970). Responsibility, norms, and helping in an emergency. *Jou nal of Personality and Social Psychology, 16,* 299–310.

SCLAFANI, A. (1991). The hedonics of sugar and starch. In R. Bolles (Ed.), *The hedonics of tast* Hillsdale, NJ: Lawrence Erlbaum Associates.

SCLAFANI, A., & ACKROFF, K. (1993). Deprivation alters rats' flavor preferences for carbohydrat and fats. *Physiology and Behavior, 53,* 1091–1099.

SCLAFANI, A., & NISSENBAUM, J. W. (1987). Taste preference thresholds for polycose, maltose, an sucrose in rats. *Neuroscience and Biobehavioral Reviews, 11,* 181–185.

SCOTT, J. P. (1958). *Aggression.* Chicago: University of Chicago Press.

SCOTT, J. P. (1962). Critical periods in behavioral development. *Science, 138,* 949–958.

SCOTT, J. P. (1971). Theoretical issues concerning the origin and causes of fighting. In B. E. Elef heriou & J. P. Scott (Eds.), *The physiology of aggression and defeat.* New York: Plenum.

SCOTT, T. R. (1990). Gustatory control of food selection. In E. M. Stricker (Ed.), *Handbook of b havioral neurobiology* (Vol. 10: Neurobiology of food and fluid intake). New York: Plenum

SECORD, P. F., & BACKMAN, C. W. (1974). *Social psychology.* New York: McGraw-Hill.

SEGALL, M. H., Ember, C. R., & Ember, M. (1997). Aggression, crime, and warfare. In J. W. Berry, M. H. Segall, & C. Kagitcibasi (Eds.), *Handbook of cross-cultural psychology* (Vol 3. Social and behavioral applications). Boston: Allyn and Bacon.

SEGAL, M. W. (1974). Alphabet and attraction: An unobtrusive measure of the effect of propinquity in a field setting. *Journal of Personality and Social Psychology, 30,* 654–657.

SELIGMAN, M. E. P. (1970). On the generality of the laws of learning. *Psychological Review, 77,* 406–418.

SELIGMAN, M. E. P. (1971). Phobias and preparedness. *Behavior Therapy, 2,* 307–320.

SELIGMAN, M. E. P. (1975). *Helplessness: On depression, development and death.* San Francisco: W. H. Freeman.

SELIGMAN, M. E. P., ABRAMSON, L. Y., SEMMEL, A., & VON BAYER, C. (1979). Depressive attributional style. *Journal of Abnormal Psychology, 88,* 242–247.

SELIGMAN, M. E. P., & JOHNSTON, J. C. (1973). A cognitive theory of avoidance learning. In F. J. McGurgan & D. B. Lumsden (Eds.), *Contemporary approaches to conditioning and learning.* Washington, DC: Winston.

SELIGMAN, M. E. P., & MAIER, S. F. (1967). Failure to escape traumatic shock. *Journal of Experimental Psychology, 74,* 1–9.

SELYE, H. (1956). *The stress of life.* New York: McGraw-Hill.

SHANKS, D. R., & DICKINSON, A. (1990). Contingency awareness in evaluative conditioning: A comment on Baeyens, Eelen, and Van den Bergh. *Cognition and Emotion, 4,* 19–30.

SHEFFIELD, F. D. (1948). Avoidance training and the contiguity principle. *Journal of Comparative and Physiological Psychology, 41,* 165–177.

SHEFFIELD, F. D. (1966). New evidence on the drive-induction theory of reinforcement. In R. N. Haber (Ed.), *Current research in motivation.* New York: Holt, Rinehart and Winston.

SHEFFIELD, F. D., & ROBY, T. B. (1950). Reward value of a non-nutritive sweet taste. *Journal of Comparative and Physiological Psychology, 43,* 471–481.

SHEFFIELD, F. D., WULFF, J. J., & BACKER, R. (1951). Reward value of copulation without sex drive reduction. *Journal of Comparative and Physiological Psychology, 44,* 3–8.

SHERIDAN, C. L., & KING, R. G. (1972). Obedience to authority with an authentic victim. *Proceedings, Eightieth annual convention, American Psychological Association,* Honolulu, 165–166. Washington, DC: American Psychological Association.

SHERIF, M., HARVEY, O. J., WHITE, B., HOOD, W., & SHERIF, C. (1961). *Intergroup conflict and cooperation: The robber's cave experiment.* Norman, OK: Institute of Group Relations, University of Oklahoma.

SHERROD, D. (1982). *Social psychology.* New York: Random House.

SHERWOOD A., Allen, M. T., OBRIST, P. A., & LANGER, A. W. (1986). Evaluation of beta-adrenergic influences on cardiovascular and metabolic adjustments to physical and psychological stress. *Psychophysiology, 23*(1), 89–104.

SHIPLEY, T. E., & VEROFF, J. (1952). A projective measure of need for affiliation. *Journal of Experimental Psychology, 43,* 349–356.

SIDMAN, M. (1962). Reduction of shock frequency as reinforcement for avoidance behavior. *Journal of the Experimental Analysis of Behavior, 5,* 247–257.

SIDMAN, M. (1966). Avoidance behavior. In W. K. Honig (Ed.), *Operant behavior: Areas of research and application.* New York: Appleton-Century-Crofts.

SIEGMAN, A. W., DEMBROSKI, T. M., & RINGLE, N. (1987). Components of hostility and the severity of coronary artery disease. *Psychosomatic Medicine, 49,* 127–135.

SIEGEL, P. S., & MILBY, J. B. (1969). Secondary reinforcement in relation to shock termination. *Psychological Bulletin, 72,* 146–156.

SIGALL, H., & LANDY, D. (1973). Radiating beauty: Effects of having a physically attractive partner on person perception. *Journal of Personality and Social Psychology, 28,* 218–224.

SILVERMAN, L. (1982, May). Mommy and I are one. *Psychology Today,* 24–36.

SINGH, D. (1993). Adaptive significance of female physical attractiveness: Role of waist-to-hip ratio. *Journal of Personality and Social Psychology, 65,* 293–307.

SKINNER, B. F. (1938). *The behavior of organisms.* New York: Appleton-Century-Crofts.

SKINNER, B. F. (1948). *Walden II.* New York: Macmillan.

SKINNER, B. F. (1953). *Science and human behavior,* New York: The Macmillan Co.

SMITH, F. J. (1977). Work attitudes as predictors of attendance on a specific day. *Journal of Applied Psychology, 62,* 16–19.

SMITH, G. F., & DORFMAN, D. D. (1975). The effect of stimulus uncertainty on the relationship between frequency of exposure and liking. *Journal of Personality and Social Psychology, 31,* 150–155.

SMITH, G. P., & GIBBS, J. (1995). Peripheral physiological determinants of eating and body weight. In K. D. Brownell & C. G. Fairburn (Eds.) Eating disorders and obesity: A comprehensive handbook. New York: The Guilford Press.

SOKOLOV, E. N. (1960). Neuronal models of the orienting reflex. In M. A. B. Brazier (Ed.), *The central nervous system and behavior: Transaction of the third conference.* New York: Josiah Macy Jr., Foundation.

SOLOMON, R. L. (1980). The opponent-process theory of acquired motivation: The costs of pleasure and the benefits of pain. *American Psychologist, 35,* 691–712.

SOLOMON, R. L., & CORBIT, J. D. (1974). An opponent-process theory of motivation: I. Temporal dynamics of affect. *Psychological Review, 81,* 119–145.

SOLOMON, R. L., & TURNER, L. H. (1962). Discriminative classical conditioning in dogs paralyzed by curare can later control discriminative avoidance responses in the normal state. *Psychological Review, 69,* 202–219.

SOLOMON, R. L., & WYNNE, L. C. (1950). Avoidance conditioning in normal dogs and in dogs deprived of normal autonomic functioning. *American Psychologist, 5,* 264.

SOLOMON, R. L., & WYNNE, L. C. (1954). Traumatic avoidance learning: The principles of anxiety conservation and partial irreversibility. *Psychological Review, 61,* 353–385.

SONSTROEM, R. J. (1984). An overview of anxiety in sport. In J. M. Silva & R. S. Weinberg (Eds.) *Psychological foundations of sport.* Champaign, IL: Human Kinetics.

SONSTROEM, R. J., & BERNADO, P. B. (1982). Intraindividual pregame state anxiety and basketball performance: A re-examination of the inverted-U curve. *Journal of Sport Psychology, 4,* 235–245.

SPENCE, J., & HELMREICH, R. (1983). Types of achievement and achievement-related motives and rewards. In J. Spence (Ed.), *Achievement and achievement motives.* San Francisco: W. H. Freeman.

SPENCE, K. W. (1944). The nature of theory construction in contemporary psychology. *Psychological Review, 51,* 47–68.

SPENCE, K. W. (1956). *Behavior theory and conditioning.* New Haven, CT: Yale University Press.

SPENCE, K. W., & TAYLOR, J. (1951). Anxiety and strength of the U.S. as a determinant of eyelid conditioning. *Journal of Experimental Psychology, 42,* 183–188.

SPENCE, S., SHAPIRO, D., & ZAIDEL, E. (1996). The role of the right hemisphere in the physiological and cognitive components of emotional processing. *Psychophysiology, 33,* 112–122.

SPIELBERGER, C. D. (1966). Theory and research on anxiety. In C. D. Spielberger (Ed.), *Anxiety and behavior.* New York: Academic.

SPIELBERGER, C. D. (1976). The nature and measurement of anxiety. In C. D. Spielberger & R. Diaz-Guerrero (Eds.), *Cross-cultural anxiety.* Washington, DC: Hemisphere.

SPIELBERGER, C. D., GORSUCH, R. L., & LUSHENE, R. F. (1970). *Manual for the State-Trait Anxiety Inventory.* Palo Alto, CA: Consulting Psychologists Press.

SPRAGUE, J. M., CHAMBERS, W. W., & STELLAR, E. (1961). Attentive, affective, and adaptive behavior in the cat. *Science, 133,* 165–173.

STAATS, A. W. (1983). Paradigmatic behaviorism: Unified theory for social psychology. In L. Berkowit (Ed.), *Advances in experimental social psychology,* (Vol. 16). Orlando, FL: Academic Press.

STAATS, A. W., & STAATS, C. (1958). Attitudes established by classical conditioning. *Journal of Abnormal and Social Psychology, 57,* 35–40.

STAGNER, R. (1977). Homeostasis, discrepancy, and motivation. *Motivation and Emotion, 1,* 103–137.

STARR, M. D., & MINEKA, S. (1977). Determinants of fear over the course of avoidance learning. *Learning and Motivation, 8,* 332–350.

STAVELY, H. E., JR. (1966). Effect of escape duration and shock intensity on the acquisition and extinction of an escape response. *Journal of Experimental Psychology, 72,* 698–703.

STEELE, R. S. (1977). Power motivation, activation, and inspirational speeches. *Journal of Personality, 45,* 53–64.

STEERS, R. M., & PORTER, L. W. (1975). *Motivation and work behavior.* New York: McGraw-Hill.

STEFFEN, J. J., MCLANEY, M. A., & HUSTEDT, T. K. (1982). *The development of a scale of limerence.* Paper presented at the annual convention of the American Psychological Association, Washington, DC.

STEGGERDA, F. R. (1941). Observations on the water intake in an adult man with dysfunctioning salivary glands. *American Journal of Psychology, 132,* 517–521.

STELLAR, E. (1954). The physiology of motivation. *Psychological Review, 61,* 5–22.

STELLAR, J. R., & STELLAR, E. (1985). *The neurobiology of motivation and reward.* New York: Springer-Verlag.

STERNBERG, R. J. (1986). A triangular theory of love. *Psychological Review, 93,* 119–135.

STERNBERG, R. J. (1987). Liking versus loving: A comparative evaluation of theories. *Psychological Bulletin, 102,* 331–345.

STERNBERG, R. J., & GRAJEK, S. (1984). The nature of love. *Journal of Personality and Social Psychology, 47,* 312–329.

STORMS, M. D. (1983a). *Development of sexual orientation.* Washington, DC: Office of Social and Ethical Responsibility, American Psychological Association.

STORMS, M. D. (1983b). A theory of erotic orientation development. *Psychological Review, 88,* 340–353.

STROEBE, W. C., INSKO, A., THOMPSON, V. D., & LAYTON, B. D. (1971). Effects of physical attractiveness, attitude similarity, and sex on various aspects of interpersonal attraction. *Journal of Personality and Social Psychology, 18,* 79–91.

SUE, D. (1979). Erotic fantasies of college students during coitus. *Journal of Sex Research, 15,* 299–305.

SUEDFIELD, P. (1998). Homo invictus: The indomitable species. *Canadian Psychology, 38,* 164–173.

SULLIVAN, M., & BENDER, W. (1986). Facial electromyography: A measure of affective processes during sexual arousal. *Psychophysiology, 23*(2), 182–188.

SWEENEY, P. D., ANDERSON, K., & BAILEY, S. (1986). Attributional style in depression: A meta-analytic review. *Journal of Personality and Social Psychology, 50,* 947–991.

SWENSON, C. H. (1972). The behavior of love. In H. A. Otto (Ed.), *Love today.* New York: Associations Press.

TANNENBAUM, P. H., & ZILLMANN, D. (1975). Emotional arousal in the facilitation of aggression through communication. In L. Berkowitz (Ed.), *Advances in experimental social psychology* (Vol. 8). New York: Academic.

TASSINARY, L. G., & HANSEN, K. A. (1998). A critical test of the waist-to-hip-ratio hypothesis of female physical attractiveness. *Psychological Science, 9,* 150–155.

TAVRIS, C. (1983). *Anger: The misunderstood emotion.* New York: Simon & Schuster.

TAYLOR, J. A. (1953). A personality scale of manifest anxiety. *Journal of Abnormal and Social Psychology, 48,* 285–290.

TAYLOR, S. E. (1989). *Positive illusions: Creative self-deception and the healthy mind.* New York: Basic Books.

TEDESCHI, J. T., SMITH, R. B., III., & BROWN, R. C., JR. (1974). A reinterpretation of research on aggression. *Psychological Bulletin, 81,* 540–562.

TEITELBAUM, P., & EPSTEIN, A. N. (1962). The lateral hypothalamic syndrome: Recovery of feeding and drinking after lateral hypothalamic lesions. *Psychological Review, 69,* 74–90.

TESSER, A. (1993). The importance of heritability in psychological research: The case of attitudes. *Psychological Review, 100,* 129–142.

THAYER, R. C. (1978). Toward a psychological theory of multidimensional activation (arousal). *Motivation and Emotion, 2,* 1–34.

THEUS, K. T. (1994). Subliminal advertising and the psychology of processing unconscious stimuli: A review of research. *Psychology and Marketing, 11,* 271–290.

THISTLEWAITE, D. (1951). A critical review of latent learning and related experiments. *Psychological Bulletin, 48,* 97–129.

THOMPSON, S. C. (1981). Will it hurt less if I control it?: A complex answer to a simple question. *Psychological Bulletin, 90,* 89–101.

THOMPSON, T. I., & STURM, T. (1965). Visual reinforcer color and operant behavior in the Siamese fighting fish. *Journal of Experimental Analysis of Behavior, 8,* 341–344.

THORNDIKE, E. L. (1913). *The psychology of learning.* New York: Teachers College.

THORNDIKE, E. L. (1932). *The fundamentals of learning.* New York: Columbia University Press.

TINBERGEN, N. (1951). *The study of instinct.* Oxford: Clarendon.

TINKLEPAUGH, O.L. (1928). An experimental study of representative factors in monkeys. *Journal of Comparative Psychology, 8,* 197–236.

TOATES, F. M. (1979). Homeostasis and drinking. *The Behavioral and Brain Sciences, 2,* 95–139.

TOCH, H. (1970). The social psychology of violence. Division 8 invited address, American Psychological Association Meeting, New York, September, 1966. Reprinted in E. I. Megargee &

456   *References*

J. E. Hokanson (Eds.), *The dynamics of aggression: Individual, group and international analyses.* New York: Harper & Row.

TOLMAN, E. C. (1932). *Purposive behavior in animals and men.* New York: Appleton-Century-Crofts.

TOLMAN, E. C. (1938). The determiners of behavior at a choice point. *Psychological Review, 45,* 1–41.

TOLMAN, E. C. (1948). Cognitive maps in rats and men. *Psychological Review, 55,* 189–208.

TOLMAN, E. C. (1959). Principles of purposive behavior. In S. Koch (Ed.), *Psychology: A study of a science* (Vol. 2). New York: McGraw-Hill.

TOLMAN, E. C., & HONZIK, C. H. (1930). Degrees of hunger; reward and nonreward; and maze learning in rats. *University of California Publications in Psychology, 4,* 241–256.

TOMARKEN, A. J., DAVIDSON, R. J., WHEELER, R. E., & DOSS, R. C. (1992). Individual differences in anterior brain asymmetry and fundamental dimensions of emotion. *Journal of Personality and Social Psychology, 62,* 676–687.

TOMKINS, S. (1962). *Affect, imagery, and consciousness: The positive affects* (Vol. 1). New York: Springer.

TOMKINS, S. (1981). The quest for primary motives: Biography and autobiography of an idea. *Journal of Personality and Social Psychology, 41,* 306–329.

TOULMIN, S. (1953). *The philosophy of science—An introduction.* London: Hutchinson.

TOURANGEAU, R., & ELLSWORTH, P. (1979). The role of facial response in the experience of emotion. *Journal of Personality and Social Psychology, 37,* 1519–1531.

TOWBIN, E. J.(1949). Gastric distention as a factor in the satiation of thirst in esophagustomized dogs. *American Journal of Physiology, 159,* 533–541.

TRAPPEY, C. (1996). A meta-analysis of consumer choice and subliminal advertising. *Psychology and Marketing, 13,* 517–530.

TRIANDIS, H. C. (1994). *Culture and social behavior.* New York: McGraw-Hill.

TRIPPLET, N. (1897). The dynamogenic factors in pacemaking and competition. *American Journal of Psychology, 9,* 507–533.

TRYON, R. C. (1940). Genetic differences in maze learning in rats. In National Society for the Study of Education, the *Thirty-ninth Yearbook.* Bloomington, Ill.: Public School Publishing.

TUCKER, D. M. (1981). Lateral brain function, emotion, and conceptualization *Psychological Bulletin, 89,* 19–46.

TURNER, M. B. (1967). *Philosophy and the science of behavior.* New York: Appleton-Century-Crofts.

ULRICH, R. E., & AZRIN, N. H. (1962). Reflexive fighting in response to aversive stimulation. *Journal of the Experimental Analysis of Behavior, 5,* 511–520.

ULRICH, R. E., & CRAINE, W. H. (1964). Behavior: Persistence of shock-induced aggression. *Science, 143,* 971–973.

VALENSTEIN, E. S.(1973). *Brain control: A critical examination of brain stimulation and psychosurgery.* New York: Wiley.

VALENSTEIN, E. S., KAKOLEWSKI, J. W., & COX, V. C. (1967). Sex differences in taste preference for glucose and saccharine soutions. *Science,* 156, 942–943.

VALENTINE, C. W. (1930). The innate bases of fear. *Journal of Genetic Psychology, 37,* 394–419.

VALINS, S. (1966). Cognitive effects of false heart-rate feedback. *Journal of Personality and Social Psychology, 4,* 400–408.

VALINS, S. (1970). The perception and labeling of bodily changes as determinants of emotional behavior. In P. Black (Ed.), *Physiological correlates of emotion.* New York: Academic.

VANITALLIE, T. B., & KISSILEFF, H. R. (1990). Human obesity: A problem in body energy economics. In E. M. Stricker (Ed.), Handbook of behavioral Neurobiology, 10: Neurobiology of food and fluid intake.

VERNON, W. Animal aggression: Review of research. *Genetic Psychology Monographs,* 1969, *80,* 3–28.

VERNON, W., & ULRICH, R. E. (1966). Classical conditioning of pain-elicited aggression. *Science, 152,* 668–669.

VEROFF, J. (1957). Development and validation of projective measures of power motivation. *Journal of Abnormal and Social Psychology, 54,* 1–8.

VERTES, R. M. (1986). A life-sustaining function for REM sleep: A theory. *Neuroscience and Biobehavioral Reviews, 10,* 371–376.

VITZ, P. (1966). Affect as a function of stimulus variation. *Journal of Experimental Psychology, 71,* 74–79.

VON FRISCH, K. (1967). The dance language and orientation of bees. Cambridge, MA: Belknap Press of Harvard University Press.

VON HOLST, E., & VON ST. PAUL, U. (1962). Electrically controlled behavior. *Scientific American, 206,* 50–59.

VORSTEG, R. H. (1974). Operant reinforcement theory and determinism. *Behaviorism, 2*, 108–119.

VRANA, S. R., SPENCE, E. L., & LANG, P. J. (1988). The startle probe response: A new measure of emotion? *Journal of Abnormal Psychology, 97*, 487–491.

VROOM, V. H. (1964). *Work and motivation.* New York: Wiley.

WAGNER, A. R. (1963). Conditioned frustration as a learned drive. *Journal of Experimental Psychology, 66*, 142–148.

WALLACE, D. H., & WEHMER, G. (1972). Evaluation of visual erotica by sexual liberals and conservatives. *Journal of Sex Research, 8*, 147–153.

WALSTER, E. (1971). Passionate love. In B. Murstein (Ed.), *Theories of attraction and love.* New York: Springer.

WALSTER, E., ARONSON, E., ABRAHAMS, D., & ROTTMAN, L. (1966). Importance of physical attractiveness in dating behavior. *Journal of Personality and Social Psychology, 4*, 508–516.

WALSTER, E., & WALSTER, G. W. (1976). Interpersonal attraction. In B. Seidenberg & A. Snadowsky (Eds.), *Social psychology.* New York: The Free Press.

WALSTER, E., WALSTER, G. W., & BERSCHEID, E. (1978). *Equity: Theory and research.* Boston: Allyn & Bacon.

WARDEN, C. J. (1931). *Animal motivation: Experimental studies on the albino rat.* New York: Columbia University Press.

WARREN, R. M., & PFAFFMANN, C. (1958). Early experience and taste aversion. *Journal of Comparative and Physiological Psychology, 52*, 263–266.

WATERMAN, C. K. (1969). The facilitating and interfering effects of cognitive dissonance on simple and complex paired associates learning tasks. *Journal of Experimental Social Psychology, 5*, 31–42.

WATSON, J. B. (1924). *Psychology from the standpoint of a behaviorist.* Philadelphia: Lippincott.

WATSON, J. B., & RAYNER, R. (1920). Conditioned emotional reactions, *Journal of Experimental Psychology, 3*, 1–14.

WEBER, M. (1930). *The protestant ethic and the spirit of capitalism* (T. Parsons, Trans.). New York: Scribner. (Original work published 1904)

WEBSTER, D. M., & KRUGLANSKI, A. W. (1994). Individual differences in need for cognitive closure. *Journal of Personality and Social Psychology, 67*, 1049–1062. [contains the detailed development of the scale items, including five dimensions.]

WEINBERG, R. S., & GENUCHI, M. (1980). Relationship between competitive train anxiety, state anxiety, and golf performance: A field study. *Journal of Sport Psychology, 2*, 148–154.

WEINBERG, R. S. (1984). The relationship between extrinsic rewards and intrinsic motivation in sports. In R. M. Silva & R. S. Weinberg (Eds.), *Psychological foundations of sport.* Champaign, IL: Human Kinetics Publishers, Inc.

WEINER, B. (1985). An attributional theory of achievement motivation and emotion. *Psychological Review, 92*, 548–573.

WEISS, J. M. (1972). Psychological factors in stress and disease. *Scientific American, 226*, 104–113.

WEISS, J. M. (1977). Psychological and behavioral influences on gastrointestinal lesions in animal models. In J. Maser & M. E. P. Seligman (Eds.), *Psychopathology: Experimental models* (pp. 232–269). San Francisco: Freeman.

WEISS, R. F., & MILLER, F. G. (1971). The drive theory of social facilitation. *Psychological Review, 78*, 44–57.

WERBOFF, J., DUANE, D., & COHEN, B. D. (1964). Extinction of conditioned avoidance and heart rate responses in rats. *Journal of Psychosomatic Research, 8*, 29–33.

WEST, M. J., KING, A. P., & EASTZER, D. H. (1981). The cowbird: Reflections on development form an unlikely source. *American Scientist, 69*, 57–66.

WHALEN, R. E. (1966). Sexual motivation. *Psychological Review, 73*, 151–163.

WHITE, G. L. (1980). Physical attractiveness and courtship progress. *Journal of Personality and Social Psychology, 39*, 660–668.

WHITE, G. L., FISHBEIN, E., & RUTSTEIN, J. (1981). Passionate love: The misattribution of arousal. *Journal of Personality and Social Psychology, 41*, 56–62.

WHITE, R. W. (1959). Motivation reconsidered: The concept of competence. *Psychological Review, 66*, 297–333.

WHITE, T. H. (1954). *The bestiary: A book of beasts.* New York: Putnam.

WICKLUND, R. A., & BREHM, J. W. (1976). *Perspectives on cognitive dissonance.* Hillsdale, NJ: Erlbaum.

WIGGINS, J. S., & TRAPNELL, P. D. (1997). Personality structure: The return of the big five. In R. Hogan, J. Johnson, & S. Briggs (Eds). *Handbook of personality psychology.* New York: Academic Press.

WIKE, E. L. (1966). *Secondary reinforcement: Selected experiments.* New York: Harper & Row.

WILCOXIN, H. C., DRAGOIN, W. B., & KRAL, P. A. (1971). Illness-induced aversions in rat and quail: Relative salience of visual and gustatory cues. *Science, 171,* 826–828.

WILLIAMS, D. R., & TEITELBAUM, P. (1956). Control of drinking by means of an operant conditioning technique. *Science, 124,* 1294–1296.

WILLIAMS, J. J. G., WATTS, F. N., MACLEOD, C., & MATHEWS, A. (1997). Cognitive psychology and emotional disorders (2nd ed.). Chichester: Wiley.

WILLIAMS, R. B. (1994). *Anger kills: Seventeen strategies for controlling the hostility that can harm your health.* New York: HarperCollins Publishers.

WILSON, E. O. (1975). *Sociobiology, the new synthesis.* Cambridge, MA: Harvard University Press.

WINCH, R. F. (1958). *Mate selection: A study of complementary needs.* New York: Harper & Row.

WINTER, D. G. (1973). *The power motive.* New York: Free Press.

WINTER, D. G., JOHN, O. P., STEWARD, A. J., KLOHNEN, E. C., & DUNCAN, L. E. (1998). Traits and motives: Toward an integration of two traditions in personality research. *Psychological Review, 105,* 230–250.

WISE, R. A. (1989). Opiate reward: Sites and substrates. *Neuroscience & Biobehavioral Reviews, 13,* 129–133.

WOLF, A. V. (1958). *Thirst: Physiology of the urge to drink and problems of water lack.* Springfield, IL: Thomas.

WOLFE, J. (1933). Effectiveness of token rewards for chimpanzees. *Comparative Psychology Monographs,* 12, no. 60, 1–72.

WOLFGANG, M. E. (1957). Victim-precipitated criminal homicide. *Journal of Criminal Law, Criminology, and Police Science, 48,* 1–11.

WOLPE, J., & RACHMAN, S. (1960). Psychoanalytic "evidence": A critique based on Freud's case of Little Hans. *Journal of Nervous and Mental Disease, 131,* 135–148.

WOOD, W., WONG, F. Y., & CHACHERE, G. (1991). Effects of media violence on viewers' aggression in unconstrained social interaction. *Psychological Bulletin, 109,* 371–383.

WOODS, P. J. (1967). Performance changes in escape conditioning following shifts in the magnitude of reinforcement. *Journal of Experimental Psychology, 75,* 487–491.

WOODS, P. J., DAVIDSON, E. H., & PETERS, R. J., JR. (1964). Instrumental escape conditioning in water tank: Effects of variations in drive stimulus intensity and reinforcement magnitude. *Journal of Comparative and Physiological Psychology, 57,* 466–470.

WOODS, S. C. (1991). The eating paradox: How we tolerate food. *Psychological Review, 98,* 488–505.

WOODWORTH, R. S. (1938). *Experimental psychology.* New York: Holt.

WOODWORTH, R. S., & SCHLOSBERG, H. (1954). *Experimental psychology* (rev. ed.). New York: Holt, Rinehart and Winston.

WRIGHTSMAN, L. S. (1972). *Social psychology in the 70's.* Monterey, CA: Brooks/Cole.

WRIGHTSMAN, L. S., JR. (1960). Effects of waiting with others on changes in level of felt anxiety. *Journal of Abnormal and Social Psychology, 61,* 216–222.

WYER, R., & HARTWICK, J. (1980). The role of information retrieval and conditional inference processes in belief formation and change. In L. Berkowitz (Ed.), *Advances in experimental social psychology* (Vol. 13, pp. 243–284). New York: Academic Press.

YATES, A. J. (1962). *Frustration and conflict.* New York: Wiley.

YERKES, R. M., & DODSON, J. D. (1908). The relation of strength of stimulus to rapidity of habit-formation. *Journal of Comparative and Neurological Psychology, 18,* 459–482.

YOUNG, P. T. (1936). *Motivation of behavior: The fundamental determinants of human and animal activity.* New York: John Wiley & Sons.

YOUNG, P. T. (1959). The role of affective processes in learning and motivation. *Psychological Review, 66,* 104–125.

YOUNG, P. T. (1961). *Motivation and emotion: A survey of the determinants of human and animal activity.* New York: Wiley.

YOUNG, P. T. (1966). Hedonic organization and regulation of behavior. *Psychological Review, 73,* 59–86.

YOUNG, P. T. (1968). Evaluation and preferences in behavioral development. *Psychological Review, 75,* 222–241.

YOUNG, P. T., & CHAPLIN, J. P. (1945). Studies of food preference, appetite and dietary habit: III. Palatability and appetite in relation to bodily need. *Comparative Psychology Monographs,* 1945, *18,* No. 3, 1–45.

Young, P. T., & Christensen, K. R. (1962). Algebraic summation of hedonic processes. *Journal of Comparative and Physiological Psychology*, 55, 332–336.

ZAJONC, R. B. (1965). Social facilitation. *Science, 149,* 269–274.

ZAJONC, R. B. (1968). Attitudinal effects of mere exposure. *Journal of Personality and Social Psychology Monograph Supplements, 9* (2, Pt. 2), 1–27.

ZAJONC, R. B. (1984). On the primacy of affect. *American Psychologist, 39*(2), 117–123.

ZAJONC, R. B. (1985). Emotion and facial efference: A theory reclaimed. *Science, 228,* 15–21.

ZAJONC, R. B., MURPHY, S. T., & INGLEHART, M. (1989). Feeling and facial efference: Implications of the vascular theory of emotions. *Psychological Review, 96,* 395–416.

ZAJONC, R. B., & SALES, S. M. (1966). Social facilitation of dominant and subordinate responses. *Journal of Experimental and Social Psychology, 2,* 160–168.

ZANNA, M. P., & COOPER, J. (1974). Dissonance and the pill: An attribution approach to studying the arousal properties of dissonance. *Journal of Personality and Social Psychology, 29,* 703–709.

ZANOT, E. J., PINCUS, J. D., & LAMP, E. J. (1983). Public perceptions of subliminal advertising. *Journal of Advertising, 12,* 39–45.

ZEAMAN, D. (1949). Response latency as a function of the amount of reinforcement. *Journal of Experimental Psychology, 39,* 466–483.

ZEIGLER, H. P. (1964). Displacement activity and motivational theory: A case study in the history of ethology. *Psychological Bulletin, 61,* 362–376.

ZILLMAN, D. (1978). Attribution and misattribution of excitatory reactions. In J. H. Harvey, W. J. Ickes, & R. F. Kidd, (Eds.), *New directions in attribution research* (Vol. 2, pp. 355–368). Hillsdale, NJ: Erlbaum.

ZIMBARDO, P. G. (1966). The cognitive control of motivation. *Transactions of the New York Academy of Sciences,* Series II, 28, 902–922.

ZIMBARDO, P. G. (1969). The human choice: Individualization, reason, and order versus deindividuation, impulse, and chaos. In W. Arnold & M. Levine (Eds.), *Nebraska symposium on motivation.* Lincoln: University of Nebraska Press.

ZIMMERMAN, D. W. (1957). Durable secondary reinforcement: Method and theory. *Psychological Review, 64,* 373–383.

ZIMMERMAN, D. W. (1959). Sustained performance in rats based on secondary reinforcement. *Journal of Comparative and Physiological Psychology, 52,* 353–358.

ZUCKERMAN, M. (1979). *Sensation seeking: Beyond the optimal level of arousal.* Hillsdale, NJ: Lawrence Erlbaum Associates.

ZUCKERMAN, M. (1984). Sensation-seeking: A comparative approach to a human trait. *Behavioral and Brain Sciences, 7,* 413–434.

ZUCKERMAN, M. (1991). *Psychobiology of personality.* Cambridge: Cambridge University Press.

ZUCKERMAN, M. (1994). *Behavioral expressions and biosocial bases of sensation seeking.* Cambridge: Cambridge University Press.

ZUCKERMAN, M., EYSENCK, S., & EYSENCK, H. J. (1978). Sensation seeking in England and America: Cross-cultural, age, and sex comparisons. *Journal of Consulting and Clinical Psychology, 46,* 139–149.

ZUGER, D. (1976). Monozygotic twins discordant for homosexuality: Report of a pair and significance of the phenomenon. *Comprehensive Psychiatry, 17,* 661–669.

Author Index

Subject Index

Incentive theory, 231–232
Inclusive fitness theory, 84
Innate releasing mechanism, 74
Instinct. *See also* Species-specific behavior
  examples of, 66–68
  history of concept of, 70–72
  meanings of, 68–70
Interpersonal attraction, 379–399
  affiliation and, 380–384
  attraction and, 384–390
  liking/loving theories, 390–398
Intervening variables
  desire and aversion as, 27–31
  drive as, 149–151
  emotions as, 40–42
  fear as, 158–159
  motivational, 151–154
  motivational concepts as, 26–27

J
Job motivation, 401–408
  behavior theory and goal setting, 406
  equity theory, 404–405
  Herzberg's two-factor theory of, 403
  Locke's goal setting theory of, 406–408
  Maslow's need hierarchy of, 403–404
  McGregor's Theory X and Y of, 402
  philosophical views on, 401–402
  Vroom's valence-instrumentality-expectancy theory, 404
Job satisfaction, 408–411
  behavior and, 409–410
  equity theory of, 410
  instrumentality theory of, 410
  job characteristics model and, 410–411
  meaning/measurement of, 408–409

K
Kluver-Bucy Syndrome, 38–39

L
Lateral hypothalamic syndrome, 99–101
Law of Effect, 179–181
Learned helplessness, 278–281
Learned industriousness, 328–329
Learning
  addiction and, 125
  attitude and, 362–363
  avoidance, 239–247
  classical conditioning, 109–112
  drives, 158–161
  escape, 229–232
  feeding behavior and, 112–114
  latent, 209–210
  to prevent thirst, 134
  social, 314–315
  two-process theory of, 215–217
Leerlaufreaktion, 75–76

Liking. *See also* Affiliation; Attraction; Loving
  as overlapping set with loving, 395
  qualitative differences between loving and, 393–395
  as subset of loving, 395–398
  theories of, 390–393
Limbic system, 38–39
Little Albert experiment, 232
Locus of control, 278–280
Loving. *See also* Affiliation; Attraction; Liking
  clinical theory of, 393–394
  cluster theory of, 395–396
  cognitive-arousal theory of, 394–395
  cognitive consistency theory of, 392–393
  equity theory of, 391–392
  investment theory of, 392–393
  overlaying bonds theory of, 395
  reinforcement theory of, 390–391
  social exchange theory of, 391
  styles of, 397–398
  triangular theory of, 396–397

M
Mapping, 6–7
  cognitive, 212
Matching principle, 384–386
Measurement, 5. *See also* Psychometric psychology
  of attitude, 359–362
  of emotion, 42–43
  of job satisfaction/meaning, 408–409
  of power motivation, 339
  of sensation seeking, 343–345
Meditation, 286–287
Mere exposure effect, 56
Mind-body problem, 11–17
  dualisms in, 12–14
  monisms in, 14–17
Monisms
  materialistic, 15–17
  mentalistic, 14–15
Mood
  and altruism, 318
  two-process learning theory and, 216–217
Mood congruent memory, 268
Moral judgement theory, 319
Motivation
  defined, 3
  desire and aversion in, 27–31
  hierarchy of, 31
  intrinsic, and extrinsic rewards, 194–198
  motivational concepts in, 26–27
  regulatory *vs.* purposive approaches to, 24–26
  vs. instinct, 72